Granville Barker and His Correspondents

Harley Granville Barker. Drawing by W. Strang.
Photo courtesy Hoblitzelle Theatre Arts Collection.
The University of Texas at Austin.

GRANVILLE BARKER
and His Correspondents

A Selection of Letters by Him and to Him

Edited and annotated by Eric Salmon

Wayne State University Press, Detroit, 1986

Library of Congress Cataloging in Publication Data

Granville-Barker, Harley, 1877–1946.
  Granville Barker and his correspondents.

  Includes index.
    1. Granville-Barker, Harley, 1877–1946—Correspondence.
  2. Theatrical producers and directors—Great Britain—
  Correspondence.   3. Authors, English—20th century—
  Correspondence.   I. Salmon, Eric.   II. Title.
  PN2598.G655A4   1986   792′.0233′0924 [B]   84-27040
  ISBN 0-8143-1754-5

Other books by Eric Salmon
 Another Morning Coming (a collection of verse)
 The Dark Journey: John Whiting as Dramatist
 Granville Barker: A Secret Life
 Bernhardt and the Theatre of Her Time

To John Courtenay Trewin,
dramatic critic, doyen of British theater historians,
enthusiast, mentor, and friend,
this book is gratefully dedicated.

❧ Contents

Foreword *by Sir John Gielgud*   9
Illustrations   *11*
Prefatory Note   *13*
Acknowledgments   *19*
Chronology   *21*

Chapter I: Harley Granville Barker and His Times   *25*
Chapter II: William Archer, 1856–1924   *35*
Chapter III: Bernard Shaw, 1856–1950   *111*
Chapter IV: Lillah McCarthy, 1875–1960   *165*
Chapter V: Gilbert Murray, 1866–1957   *195*
Chapter VI: Helen Huntington, 1867–1950   *299*
Chapter VII: Thomas Hardy, 1840–1928   *367*
Chapter VIII: T. E. Lawrence, 1888–1935   *387*
Chapter IX: Sir John Gielgud, 1904–   *405*
Chapter X: Other Actors and Directors   *435*
Chapter XI: Various Playwrights   *489*
Chapter XII: Various Correspondents   *521*
Appendixes   *569*
Indexes   *587*

Foreword

T*he two most* brilliant theatre geniuses of the first years of this century were undoubtedly Edward Gordon Craig and Harley Granville Barker. Both men began pursuing fairly successful careers as young actors. But their ambitions and talents soon drove them to seek for wider ideals—never, alas, to be fully realised.

Sadly, they never worked together. Craig, when I spoke to him in his old age of Barker, dismissed him perfunctorily, but I never had an opportunity of talking to Barker about Craig, who was probably jealous of Barker's qualities and the esteem in which he was held in England.

The two men were utterly unlike in personality—Craig jolly, pig-headed, volatile and undependable; Barker prim and cold, autocratic, conscientious and in supreme control of himself and the work he was determined to carry through. Barker had no pictorial talent, but excellent taste in recognising it in others. Craig was an inspired designer, and an equally hard worker in his own individual way. Both men were gifted writers and fascinating correspondents, and both felt their careers completely shattered by the outbreak of the First World War.

Craig never admitted that he wanted to be a director in the theatre, though he did make many claims to demand absolute control if he was to accomplish the results he envisaged. He achieved several early experimental productions of opera with amateur casts (and one spectacular failure with Ibsen's *The Pretenders,* even though his mother appeared in it). But one can hardly imagine his succeeding in controlling all the details of an ambitious production with the conscientious concentration and patience with which Barker so brilliantly laboured in his great years. Craig's later productions—with Stanislavsky in Moscow and the Poulsen brothers in Copenhagen—must have been strictly limited in communication owing to language difficulties, and he

9

cannot in either case have succeeded in establishing much rapport with the players. (Like Barker, he had enthusiasm for Shakespeare, Greek tragedy and Ibsen, but none of Barker's interest in contemporary playwrights whose work would give little scope for his scenic gifts. But I fancy he was more interested in music than Barker ever was.) Barker, on the other hand, though he kept his distance with remarkable discretion and was determined not to become involved in personal intrigues, gossip, or the intrusion of the press, was adored by actors and actresses, many of whom I knew well and worked with myself in their later careers. The few rehearsals at which I had the privilege of actually working with him were unforgettable days of inspiration to me. He combined an authoritative assurance with a spontaneous flexibility, never wasted a moment, criticised endlessly, ruthlessly, but kindly, was endlessly patient and demanding, with a very occasional word of praise which would alleviate one's despair in living up to the all-round perfection which he sought. His energy must have been tremendous in the years from 1904 to 1914, trying to divide his attention between his directing, management and writing.

His Savoy actors would tell one of the slim, enthusiastic bohemian, chewing nuts and wearing sandals, pinning notes on their dressing-room mirrors on first nights—"Be Swift. Be Swift. Be not Poetical" (Cathleen Nesbitt). Never have I felt so proud as when I received at last a note from him myself: "Lear is within your grasp. Great things are possible." By the time I met him he was no longer slim. He had become a sober, burly businessman in a black Homburg hat and with a rolled umbrella, but when he began to take a rehearsal the actors settled to their task with a passionate desire to carry out his wishes. His eyes would flash from under his beetling red eyebrows as he stood on the stage, book in hand, inspiring confidence and certainty, his concentration never flagging as he allowed no single detail to escape his attention: phrasing, character, rhythm, pause and climax. The moment a passage would seem to begin to satisfy him he would add another dimension to the design he had already begun to fashion.

I am so glad to be asked to write this very inadequate tribute to the greatest man in the theatre I ever met, and delighted that this fascinating collection of his letters should now be published, to give the present generation some idea of the genius whose loss to our theatre must always be remembered with so much pride as well as such infinite sadness.

John Gielgud

🌸 Illustrations

Harley Granville Barker, 1912   *frontispiece*
William Archer, about 1890   *36*
Bernard Shaw, about 1890   *112*
Lillah McCarthy, 1914   *166*
Gilbert Murray, 1943   *196*
Helen Huntington, about 1910   *300*
Thomas Hardy, 1915   *368*
T. E. Lawrence, 1918   *388*
Sir John Gielgud, 1978   *406*
Elizabeth Robins, 1886   *436*
Dennis Eadie, 1910   *436*
Joyce Redman and Nicholas Hannen, 1947   *436*
John Galsworthy   *490*
John Masefield   *490*
Harley Granville Barker, about 1910   *522*
Harley Granville Barker, 1906   *522*
Harley Granville Barker, 1936   *567*

❧ Prefatory Note

The *objective in* putting together this selection of letters has been two-fold: first, to try to re-create something of Granville Barker's elusive, magnetic, and many-sided personality; second, to provide—even if only in part—actual evidence and documentation in at least a few areas where up to now matters have been left largely to guesswork and gossip. In both of these respects many of the letters written *to* Barker are as illuminating and significant as those written *by* him, and this fact has therefore been allowed to dictate the format of the book. Each of the first nine chapters is devoted to a single correspondent; Chapters X and XI represent several correspondents, but correspondents within particular spheres of activity, Chapter X being given over to actors and directors and Chapter XI to dramatists. Chapter XII deals with particular subjects in which Barker was, throughout his life, especially interested—the possibility of a national theater, the question of censorship, and the like.

It is, perhaps, important to emphasize that what is given here is a selection only, even of those letters—already selected by the accidents of time, chance, and circumstance—which are known to be extant and available for publication. The more conscious selecting done for this volume has been motivated by a desire to avoid a book of excessive length and excessive repetition. It is hoped that the choices have been made in such a way that a fair representation and a view of the subject both balanced and coherent has been achieved. Most of the letters included are published here for the first time; where a letter, or a part of it, has been published before, that fact is mentioned in the notes.

A special word needs to be said about the correspondence with Bernard Shaw. Chapter III contains many more communications from Barker to Shaw than from Shaw to Barker. This is because most of Shaw's letters to Barker are already published and are easily accessible, both in the magnificent edition of Shaw's letters by Dan H. Laurence and in C. B. Purdom's *The Shaw-Barker Letters.* Incidentally, Purdom in his book says, "Barker's letters to Shaw have disappeared, and I am satisfied that with the exception of a few late ones they were destroyed." He is, in fact, in error in this statement. The British Library and the Humanities Research Center of the University of Texas at Austin both have letters from Barker to Shaw in their collections, and I am fairly sure that there are still others elsewhere. Thirty-four letters from Barker to Shaw are published here, along with a few previously unpublished Shaw items and—for the sake of continuity—one short letter from Shaw to Barker which is included in Purdom's book.

An introductory note to each chapter gives some biographical details of Barker's relationship with his correspondent. The letters follow, in chronological order.

Nature and Ownership of the Letters

The code at the head of each letter indicates the present ownership:

Berg Collection, New York Public Library	BERG
Bodleian Library	BOD
British Library	BL
British Theatre Museum	BTM
Butler Library, Columbia University	COL
University of Calgary	CALG
Trustees of Mrs. J. H. T. Cassel's Estate	CAS
Cornell University Library	COR
Diana Devlin	DD
Dorset County Museum, Dorset, England	DOR
Robert Eddison	EDD
Sir John Gielgud	JG
Houghton Library, Harvard University	HAR
Huntington Library	HUNT
University of Iowa	IOWA
University of London Library	LON
Eric Salmon	SAL
Athene Seyler	SEY
Humanities Research Center, University of Texas at Austin	TEX
Robin Whitworth	WHIT

The second element of the code designates the form:

Manuscript letter	MS
Typescript letter	TS
Typed carbon copy	TCC
Telegram	W
Postcard (handwritten)	PC

A Note on the Texts

Nothing has been cut from the text of any of the letters and nothing added except addresses and dates where these were missing and could be established. Such additions are enclosed in square brackets. With Barker's own letters, however, it has been necessary to tidy up the punctuation. His use, misuse, and non-use of the ordinary marks of punctuation is so unmethodical and irregular as to be downright exhilarating—that is, if one has time to pause over each manuscript to decode it. In print, however, this idiosyncrasy would lose half its charm, would look terribly untidy, and would often obscure meanings. I have, therefore, "regularized" the Barker punctuation. The most common alterations have been adding periods at the ends of sentences and commas at the logical ends of phrases; the occasional insertion of colons and semicolons (Barker scorns both of these) to break up long, meandering compound sentences; and, most of all, the closing of parentheses: frequently he begins a parenthetical comment with a dash, a comma, or a bracket, but forgets that it *is* parenthetical and drops back into the main sentence without warning or rushes headlong into a set of ideas which really belong to a completely new sentence. His favorite mark of punctuation is the dash, which gives some of the letters a very attractive air of excitement and breathlessness. For the sake of retaining this quality in the writing, I have retained the dashes where possible, even though they look rather plentiful on the page. Where it was not possible, I have translated them into commas, colons, periods, or brackets—for all of which marks Barker's dashes have done duty from time to time.

Where Barker uses contractions, he sometimes imitates the Shavian form ("didnt," "wont," etc.) but sometimes not. I have standardized them in the usual style (if only to leave G. B. S.'s eccentricity inviolate to himself).

Archer often—though not invariably—adopts American spelling; Barker fluctuates, but mostly favors British spelling; Shaw (as one would expect) is consistent but eccentric and uses Shavian spellings. A few of Shaw's experiments in spelling appear to have had some influence on Barker, though, again, not consistently. All these variations have been included in the individual letters here reproduced: no attempt has been made to standardize spelling among different letters and different writers. Where a curious spelling, or misspelling, might appear to be a misprint, it is noted so as to identify it with the original writer.

Barker's handwriting was notoriously poor, and reading his letters, especially those which were obviously written either in a hurry or under the stress of strong emotion, is a special skill for which one needs training and practice. After five years of close study, I still am quite frequently defeated by it. The love letters to Helen Huntington, especially, are by now impenetrable in places (and how the dashes—the headlong dashes—proliferate in those letters!). In transcribing Barker's letters for this volume, I have permitted myself no guesses. If, after examination with a magnifying glass and photographic and microfilm enlargement, a particular word still refused to surrender its secret, I have so indicated in a footnote. I have omitted two letters entirely because most of the words seemed illegible. What those who received his letters at breakfast with the morning paper made of them, I cannot imagine, and there is some good-natured badinage about this in a few of the replies in this collection.

A word must be said about the form of Barker's name. He is usually known now, and especially in North America, as Harley Granville-Barker, as if his family name had been Granville-Barker (with the hyphen). In fact, his birth certificate gives his father's name as Albert James Barker and his mother's as Mary Elizabeth Barker, formerly Bozzi-Granville. His parents' marriage certificate gives the same information. The child's given names are recorded as Harley Granville. At the start of his career he was always known and referred to in theater programs and newspapers as "Granville Barker" (with no initial "H"). The typescripts of his early plays, now in the British Library, sometimes have "Granville Barker" on their title pages and sometimes "H. Granville Barker." The first published edition of *The Madras House* (1911), for example, reads, "The Madras House: a Comedy, in Four Acts, by Granville Barker." *His Majesty,* on the other hand, issued seventeen years later by the same publisher, says "by Harley Granville-Barker."

The "Harley" was added before the hyphen. Shaw complained comically about it in a letter to Lillah McCarthy on May 30, 1906: "I cannot reconcile myself to his new name, which sounds harley appropriate. I wish you would call him Barker, or even B. Vulgar, but graphic & familiar . . . I really cannot stand Harley. Let's call him

Granny—Annie's Granny.[1] If the Shulamite is a success, it may mean that Hainley—there! this comes of calling a man Harley when his real name is Barker—that Ainley may soar into impossible terms[2] . . . Tell Barley (this seems after all the best compromise) . . . ," and so on.

The hyphen did not appear until the early nineteen-twenties. Theater people in London who disliked the second Mrs. Barker (and *all* theater people seem to have disliked her) and thought that she had spirited Barker away from them by some kind of American witchcraft (called "money," said the cynical) held the view that it was Helen Huntington who also compelled him, out of pure snobbishness, to add the fancy hyphen, to go with the grand English country house she had bought for them. There is no evidence of this. The name is rendered in the letters here in whichever form it appears. In my commentary I omit the hyphen and regard his "real name" (as Shaw said) as Barker. My own view is that the modern practice of listing him as "Granville-Barker, H." is quite incorrect, though by now widespread.

It will be noted that some of the letters, especially those to and from Shaw, appear without formal salutation. This was often Shaw's practice in letters to friends, and it was one which Barker adopted and imitated. I have reproduced the letters here exactly as they appear in the original, with or without salutation, as the case may be, and with such variations of names, initials, or nicknames as were used by the writer himself in the original letter.

One other Shavian eccentricity might bear mention here, since it too was adopted by Barker. This was the habit, when on holiday, of writing a series of picture postcards instead of a letter. As many as ten such cards, with pictures of the place visited, were sometimes written on the same day and mailed separately, with a message that continues from one card to the next, often breaking off in mid-sentence and picking up again on the next card. I have reproduced them here, in pieces, as they were originally written.

---

1. A reference to, and quotation from, *Man and Superman*. Lillah had played Ann Whitefield to Barker's John Tanner.
2. Henry Ainley was playing at the time in *The Shulamite*, by Claude Askew and Edward Knoblock, at the Savoy Theatre.

A Note on Footnotes

Footnotes have been kept to a minimum. While Barker is by no means a minor figure, he is not a purely literary figure (perhaps not even primarily a literary figure), and too ponderous a use of academic apparatus would over-weight the letters and (to change metaphors) destroy their special flavor. I have provided notes wherever the letters—especially those of Barker and Gilbert Murray—contain purely local or topical references which would be unlikely to be understood now by anyone but a specialist; the same applies to references to theaters and performers of the period.

A balance has also been aimed at between what seemed sensible and necessary for British readers and what American readers might find helpful. Nothing is more irritating than to be provided with massive footnoting explaining dozens of things of which one is already perfectly well aware. But some little help along the way is often welcome. Whether the things that a British reader can reasonably be expected to know, or work out, or guess at are the same as those which an American reader can know or work out or guess at, I am not sure. I suspect not, especially when it comes to things like the initials of the names of politicians or the names of the old railway companies of southeast England. And the difficulty operates both ways, so to speak, since Barker lived and worked both in England and in the United States, and was married first to an Englishwoman and then to an American. So here again, while trying to maintain the right kind of balance between being obscure and being patronizing, I have chosen—in the interests of not insulting readers' intelligences and of keeping the pages as uncluttered as possible—to err on the side of too few notes rather than too many.

Punctuation

As explained above, I have tidied up some of Barker's punctuation in his handwritten letters, but have otherwise not interfered with the punctuation of any of the letter-writers. However, I cannot answer with equal confidence for the punctuation in other parts of the book. My own punctuation of the chapter introductions, footnotes, etc. has been altered by the publishers to conform with what they describe as their "house style" and I cannot be held accountable for the resulting eccentricities, illogicalities and errors of sense.

♨ Acknowledgments

For *permission to* reproduce the letters, my thanks are due to the owners of the various copyrights: to the late Mr. J. C. Medley and to the Society of Authors for letters written by Granville Barker and by Helen Huntington Granville-Barker; to Mrs. Elinor Finley for William Archer's letters; to the Public Trustees and the Society of Authors for Shaw's letters; to Mr. Alexander Murray for letters written by Gilbert Murray; to Jonathan Cape Ltd. and the Trustees of the Estate of T. E. Lawrence for the letters of T. E. Lawrence; to Miss Athene Seyler for letters written by Nicholas Hannen; to Dr. Diana Devlin for a letter of Sir Lewis Casson's; to the Trustees of the Estate of John Galsworthy for two of his letters; to the Trustees of the Estate of John Masefield for six of his letters; to the Trustees of the Estate of Laurence Housman for three of his letters; to the late Mr. J. C. Medley for letters written by C. D. Medley; and to Mr. Robin Whitworth for letters written by his father, Geoffrey Whitworth.

For access to the original letters (and in many cases the most generous loan of them for copying purposes) I gratefully thank all the following individuals: Mr. Charles Aukin, Mrs. Rose Banks, Mr. M. W. Carey of Kennedy, Ponsonby and Prideaux (London), Dr. Diana Devlin, Mr. Robert Eddison, Sir John Gielgud, Miss Athene Seyler, Dr. James Tyler (curator of the Shaw Collection, Cornell University Library), and Mr. Robin Whitworth.

The research librarians, keepers of manuscripts, and general staffs of the following institutions have assisted by placing documents at my disposal and by sending photocopies of relevant papers to me. These resources have provided the core of the materials which make up the book, and my most grateful thanks are due to them: the Berg Collection of the New York Public Library (Mrs. Lola Szladits); the Bodleian Library (Miss Helen Langley); the British Library (many people); the Theatre Museum, Victoria and Albert Museum (Mr.

19

Alexander Schouvaloff); Dorset County Museum, Dorchester (Mr. R. N. R. Peers); the Houghton Library, Harvard University; the Huntington Library (Mrs. Valerie Franco); the George Arents Research Library, University of Syracuse (Ms. Carolyn A. Davis); the University of Iowa Library (Mr. Frank Paluka); the University of London Library (Miss H. M. Young); and the Humanities Research Center of the University of Texas at Austin (Mrs. Ellen S. Dunlap, to whom I owe very special thanks, and her entire staff).

I am most grateful to Professor Dennis Kennedy for valuable advice about the texts of some of the letters.

To the Social Sciences and Humanities Research Council of Canada I am indebted for generous financial support for the costs of various research journeys and the cost of preparing a final typescript.

This book has been published with the help of a grant from the Canadian Federation for the Humanities, using funds provided by the Social Sciences and Humanities Research Council of Canada.

❦ Chronology

1877	Harley Granville Barker born in London on November 25.
1891	First recorded appearance in a play (Anstey's *Vice Versa* at the Spa Rooms, Harrogate).
1891	Enrolled as a trainee in Sarah Thorne's theatrical school at the Theatre Royal, Margate.
1892	First stage appearance in London, in Charles Brookfield's *The Poet and The Puppets* at the Comedy Theatre.
1894	Engaged as general understudy in Florence Farr's company at the Avenue Theatre, London.
1895	Member of Ben Greet's touring company, in which he played Paris to the Juliet of Lillah McCarthy.
1895	Collaborated with Berte Thomas in writing "A Comedy of Fools," a play in four acts, not produced and not published.
1895–96	Collaborated with Berte Thomas in writing "The Family of the Oldroyds," a play in four acts, not produced and not published.
1896	Played in Charles Hawtrey's company in *Under the Red Robe* at the Haymarket Theatre, London.
1897	With Berte Thomas wrote *The Weather-Hen; or Invertebrata,* a comedy in prologue, two acts and an epilogue, unpublished.
1898–99	With Berte Thomas wrote "Our Visitor to 'Work-a-Day' ", a play in five acts, not produced and not published.
1899	Member of Mrs. Patrick Campbell's company in London and on tour; played Gordon Jayne in *The Second Mrs. Tanqueray* and Antonio Poppi in *The Notorious Mrs. Ebbsmith.*
1899	In London, played Selim in *Carlyon Sahib* by Gilbert Murray.

1899	*The Weather-Hen; or Invertebrata* produced at Terry's Theatre, London, with Madge McIntosh in the leading part.
1899	Played the title role in Shakespeare's *Richard II,* directed by William Poel.
1899	Wrote *The Marrying of Ann Leete* (probably the first play written by Barker without a collaborator).
1900	Played Bratsberg in first production of Archer's translation of Ibsen's *The League of Youth* for the Stage Society (a single performance).
1900	Directed Maeterlinck's *The Death of Tintagiles* for the Stage Society, with two other one-act plays.
1900	Played Lieutenant Wendowski in Sudermann's *Magda* for Mrs. Patrick Campbell's company at the Royalty Theatre, London.
1900	Played Marchbanks in first production of Shaw's *Candida* for the Stage Society (one performance only).
1900	Played the Earl of Rochester in *English Nell* at the Prince of Wales Theatre, with Marie Tempest as Nell Gwynn.
1900	Played Captain Kearney in first production of Shaw's *Captain Brassbound's Conversation* for two performances at the Stage Society.
1900	Wrote one-act verse play, "A Miracle," unpublished.
1900–1901	Wrote "Agnes Colander," a play in three acts, not produced and not published.
1901	Directed and played the part of Napoleon in Shaw's *The Man of Destiny* for a single matinee at the Comedy Theatre, London, under J. T. Grein's management.
1901	Played in *The Case of Rebellious Susan* at Wyndham's Theatre and in *Becky Sharp* at the Prince of Wales Theatre.
1901	Joined the Fabian Society.
1902	Directed first production of his play *The Marrying of Ann Leete* at the Royalty Theatre.
1902	Played Frank in first production of Shaw's *Mrs. Warren's Profession* at the New Lyric Club.
1902	Played Osric in Johnston Forbes-Robertson's production of *Hamlet* at the Lyric Theatre.
1903	Played Basil Kent in the first production of Somerset Maugham's first play, *A Man of Honour,* at the Imperial Theatre.
1903	Played the title role in William Poel's production of Marlowe's *Edward II.*

1903	Directed S. M. Fox's *The Waters of Bitterness* and Shaw's *The Admirable Bashville* at the Imperial Theatre.
1903–5	Wrote *The Voysey Inheritance.*
1904	With William Archer, wrote *A National Theatre* (published in 1907).
1904–7	With J. E. Vedrenne, ran the famous "repertory" seasons at the Court Theatre, Sloane Square, directing and appearing in many plays.
1906	Married Lillah McCarthy.
1906–7	Wrote *Waste.*
1908	First visit to the United States.
1909	Wrote *The Madras House.*
1909–10	Directed a repertory season at the Duke of York's theatre, London, with Charles Frohman as producer.
1910	Began writing "The Village Carpenter," never finished.
1911	Directed first production of Masefield's *The Witch,* with Lillah McCarthy as Anna Pedersdotter, at the Court Theatre.
1911	Directed and appeared in his own version of Schnitzler's *Anatol* at the Palace Theatre.
1911–12	Wrote *Rococo,* a one-act play.
1912	Directed Eden Philpotts's censored play *The Secret Woman* for two private performances at the Kingsway Theatre.
1912	Directed *The Winter's Tale* at the Savoy Theatre.
1912	Directed *Twelfth Night* at the Savoy Theatre.
1913	Directed first production of Shaw's *Androcles and the Lion* at the St. James's Theatre.
1913	Produced and directed a season of repertory at the St. James's Theatre.
1914	Directed *A Midsummer Night's Dream* at the Savoy Theatre.
1914	Wrote *Vote by Ballot,* a one-act play.
1914	Revised and continued "The Village Carpenter" under new title of "The Wicked Man"; still did not complete it.
1914	Visited Stanislavsky in Moscow.
1914	Directed Hardy's *The Dynasts* at the Kingsway Theatre, in a stage version which he himself prepared.
1915	Produced and directed a season of repertory at Wallack's Theatre, New York City.
1915	At the request of the Red Cross wrote a book about Red Cross work with the British army in France.

1915	In the autumn returned to New York to lecture on British theater.
1916	Wrote *Farewell to the Theatre,* a one-act play.
1916	From New York wrote to Lillah breaking off their marriage.
1917	Accepted commission in British Intelligence.
1918	Divorced Lillah McCarthy and married Helen Huntington.
1919	Bought Netherton Hall in Farway, Devon.
1919	Became chairman of the newly founded British Drama League.
1920	Translated Sacha Guitry's *Deburau* from the French for production in New York.
1921	Directed Maeterlinck's *The Betrothal* at the Gaiety Theatre, London.
1922	Published *The Exemplary Theatre.*
1919–22	Wrote and published *The Secret Life.*
1923	Began the writing of *His Majesty.*
1923	Publication of the first three volumes of *The Players' Shakespeare,* with introduction by Barker.
1927	Published first collected volume of *Prefaces to Shakespeare.*
1928	Published *His Majesty.*
1929	President of the Royal Society of Literature.
1931	Settled in Paris.
1937	Became director of the British Institute in Paris.
1940	In April, spent two weeks in London advising on the Gielgud-Casson production of *King Lear.*
1940	Arrived in Lisbon, from Paris, in June.
1940	Arrived in New York on September 6 and settled there for the duration of the war.
1942	Lectured at the University of Toronto.
1944	Lectured at Princeton University.
1945	Lectured at Harvard University.
1945	In May, returned to England.
1946	In March, returned to live in Paris.
1946	Died in Paris, August 31.

 # Chapter I

Harley Granville Barker and His Times

By *the time* the First World War began, in 1914, Barker was almost thirty-seven years old. By then he had an international reputation as an actor and a director and was the author of four important full-length plays and two one-act plays as well as co-author of several other plays and (with William Archer) of a book called *A National Theatre: Scheme and Estimates,* which set out, nearly sixty years before the opening of the National Theatre of Great Britain, not only the arguments in favor of a national repertory theater but also, in considerable detail, the finances and economics of such a theater, together with descriptions of the organizational methods that would be needed to run it and the kinds of plays it ought to present.

Barker had begun his working life, at the age of seventeen, as an actor, not so much, it would seem, because of any irresistible conviction that it was the one profession for which he was suited, or as the result of any conscious decision-making on his own or anyone else's part, but as a matter of course. His mother earned a modest living as a solo entertainer of sorts, reciting verses (a popular concert item at the time) and even doing imitations of bird calls. Occasionally, too, she organized and appeared in productions of plays, though never—as far as we know—in London. She apparently assumed that her son would assist in these endeavors, and from an early age he did so. There is no record of whether he liked this situation or not. That the experience taught him much that proved valuable when he became an actor, and that he became an actor simply because, in the circumstances, it seemed the obvious thing to do, can scarcely be doubted. He was trained for no other profession or career and had, so far as we know, little formal education. The earliest of his letters we possess (it is owned now by the Humanities Research Center of the University of Texas) is concerned with one of his very early experiences as an actor and is addressed to his mother, of whom he was obviously very fond. It reads:

Channel Islands Hotel,
Guernsey.
August 1, 1895

My darling Mother,

We have settled here. Miss Paunceforth, two of the other ladies
and I. 5/- a day, the best we can; the rooms (lodgings) are both
bad and expensive and this is at least very comfortable. Irving[1] is
staying here too, I believe. We had an excellent passage, smooth
as a lake. A rehearsal this afternoon, then we play the "Two
Roses" tomorrow. Masks, then "Money."[2]

I think the money I have with me will be quite enough. All I
want now is to get unpacked. If you could have seen the breakfast
I ate this morning! I had had nothing since dinner last night except
a B. and S. on the boat and some dry biscuits—I thought that was
the safest thing I could take.

Keep care of yourself, Gracie and Dad.

Best love, from
Little Dog[3]

Give my love to Dad. How is he? Likewise to Gracie. Tell her not
to be anxious. I'll most probably write you tomorrow and tell you
how I get on if I find the letter will reach you; if not, later, to Post
Restante, Lucerne.

Having wandered into the acting profession by a sort of accident, however, he quickly demonstrated two things that seem at odds
with each other: first, that he was almost immediately noticed as being
a quite remarkably good actor, far above the ordinary; and second,
that he disliked the profession—or, at least, disliked the state it was in
and the trivial things it compelled him to waste his time on. By the age
of twenty-one he is writing to William Archer, the leading dramatic
critic of the day, asking him to read and comment upon the script of a
play he has written (albeit in collaboration with a man nine years his
senior) and also asking him whether it might be a good idea for Barker
himself to "try his hand" at theater criticism. Even at this early stage
there is every indication that Barker did not foresee for himself a

---

1. H. B. Irving (1870–1919) was the leading man of the company (the company being
Ben Greet's Shakespeare and Old English Comedy Company).
2. *Two Roses* (1870), by James Albery, was an early vehicle for Henry Irving; H. B.
Irving was playing his father's role of Digby Grant. *Masks and Faces* (1852), by Tom
Taylor and Charles Reade, was a dramatization of the latter's novel about Peg
Woffington; in the Ben Greet tour of 1895 the part of Peg was played by Lillah
McCarthy. *Money* (1839–40), by Bulwer Lytton, was still, in the eighteen-nineties,
regarded as a play of some substance.
3. A family joke, apparently: the idea of "Little Dog" being a young Barker is certainly
appealing.

whole life spent as an actor and that he was, in fact, already beginning to think of himself as a writer.

Although his career as an actor had begun in a kind of automatic way and at a depressingly ordinary and conventional level, his instinct and inclination moved him very soon and very quickly in the direction of a more serious-minded and intellectually stimulating theater. His first part in a West End production had been a small supporting role in Charles Hawtrey's production of *Under the Red Robe* at the Haymarket Theater in 1896, when he was nineteen. The play, which, both in its own day and since, was scarcely ever mentioned apart from *The Prisoner of Zenda,* was a simple-minded dramatization of a novel, a Ruritanian romance, quite devoid of subtlety and quality. Three years later, Barker played the title role in Shakespeare's *Richard II* for William Poel and was praised for his performance by A. B. Walkley of *The Times.* When the Stage Society was founded especially to produce "advanced" plays that could not command a place in the commercial theater, Barker was one of its earliest actors. He appeared as Erik Bratsberg in Ibsen's *The League of Youth,* produced by Charles Charrington for the Stage Society at the Vaudeville Theater in 1900; thereafter, he was seen fairly frequently in Stage Society productions. One of these productions was Hauptmann's *Das Friedensfest,* in June, 1900, and Shaw, writing after Barker's death forty-six years later, said: "I saw him in Hauptmann's *Friedensfest* and immediately jumped at him for the poet in *Candida.* His performance of this part—a very difficult one to cast—was, humanly speaking, perfect."[4]

The production of *Candida* was also one of those presented by the Stage Society. It took place at the Strand Theatre on July 1, 1900, and had Janet Achurch and her husband, Charles Charrington, as Candida and Morell. Miss Garnett was played by Ellen Terry's daughter, Edith Craig. Barker's performance in this production provoked from Desmond MacCarthy a commendation which has since become famous: "Mr. Granville Barker succeeded in playing Eugene Marchbanks where almost every other actor would have failed, because the representation of a lyrical mood is one within the peculiar range of his powers. His voice, too, can express a contemplative ecstasy. . . . It is in his representation of intellectual emotions that he excels, and so he excels in this part."[5]

In retrospect, one sees this performance as a nodal point in

4. "Granville-Barker: Some Particulars by Shaw," *Drama,* n.s., No. 3 (Winter, 1946), p. 8.
5. Desmond MacCarthy, *The Court Theatre, 1904–1907* (London, 1907), pp. 71–72.

Barker's career, not so much because it marks a great leap forward in both his craft and his reputation as an actor (though it was crucial in this respect also) but for two other reasons: it marks the beginning of his collaborative work with Shaw (and this, in turn, was partly responsible for the development four years later of the Court Theatre experiment); and it demonstrates the special qualities of the man which would show themselves not only in his acting but in all his other artistic activities—in his approach to directing, in his work as a dramatist, in his critical thinking about the theater. MacCarthy catches the exact nature of those qualities very accurately: lyricism, intellectuality, and absolute commitment combined with a certain aloofness. The phrase "contemplative ecstasy" is marvelously right and could be applied with equal accuracy not only to all Barker's best work for the theater, whether as an actor, playwright, or critic, but also to his whole approach to life and the arts. The obliqueness and allusiveness (not to say elusiveness) of his delicately moulded dialogue, which later critics have often reckoned a difficulty and a weakness, are accounted for, justified, and placed in their proper perspective by that one phrase "contemplative ecstasy"—the equivalent of Wordsworth's "emotion recollected in tranquillity," an accurate description of the proper relation between life and art and an explanation of the purpose and function of form in art. Barker, no great theoretician or academic aesthetician, instinctively knew what art must do with and to its raw material, and this knowledge guided him later in his writing as it had done earlier in his acting. That oblique and allusive quality is especially evident in the early play *The Marrying of Ann Leete* (1899), as it is in the much later *The Secret Life* (1919–22). These two, because of the circumstances in which they were written (different from each other, but equally sympathetic to untrammelled expressiveness), are the fullest and most uninhibited expressions of his spirit and may yet, in spite of the adverse critical climate which at present prefers *The Madras House* and *The Voysey Inheritance,* become accepted as his best plays. Desmond MacCarthy was not the only one who noticed the innately *poetic* quality of that performance as Marchbanks, which launched Barker on the first major stage of his career. W. Bridges Adams, the director of the Shakespeare Memorial Theatre at Stratford-upon-Avon from 1919 to 1934, said in a radio talk for the BBC in July, 1953:

> It was as Marchbanks in "Candida" that I first set eyes on
> him. . . . He was the best Marchbanks I have ever seen. He
> moved with the slightly dangerous grace of a very high-bred wild
> animal. You believed he had been sleeping on the Embankment.

What is more, you believed he was a real poet, capable of flights beyond anything the author had given him to say.[6]

There can be little question that he could have gone on, had he chosen to do so, to become one of London's leading actors. He did not choose to do so. As he says in several of his letters (to Archer, to Shaw, and to Gilbert Murray), he actually disliked acting and as soon as he got the chance to do so, he gave it up. This chance came gradually, over the years 1904 to 1914, because during that time Barker created, in effect, a new kind of theater artist—namely, the person whom we now call the director (though Barker and his contemporaries in England called him the producer). This was not just a new style or attitude: it was, quite literally, a new function, a new office. The position of "director" as a separate and distinct entity with a particular and unique function to perform developed directly both in England and the United States from Barker's working methods at the Court Theatre (1904–1907), at the Duke of York's Theatre during Charles Frohman's repertory season (1910), in the three famous Shakespeare productions at the Savoy Theatre (1912–1914), and in his repertory season at the St. James's Theatre (1913). Barker gave up acting not only because he did not much care for it and preferred directing to acting but also because he realized (as Irving, Tree, Alexander, and the other nineteenth-century actor-managers had not) that to obtain the subtle, complex effects which he believed the theater ought to deal in and which the new drama of the early twentieth century demanded one could not simultaneously be the shaper of the production and the chief player in it. Barker's methods, in fact, both consciously and unconsciously, instinctively as well as intellectually, were aimed at the demolition of the "grand style" in acting and in stage presentation, a style which by the end of the nineteenth century had become a showy, empty, mannered thing, at once trivial, bombastic, and meretricious.

By 1914 Barker's revolutionary methods as a director, especially as applied to Shakespeare, were known from New York to Moscow. Judged by the standards of the nineteen-eighties, the tenets of Barker's revolutionary faith seem simple and obvious enough, but that is because he was one of those who, in the first two decades of the century, insisted on establishing those standards in the theater which we now take for granted—even if we do not always practice them. The essence of the matter was artistic truth: the play had to be one that

---

6. The talk was published as a pamphlet in 1954 by Sidgwick and Jackson under the title *The Lost Leader* (the reference being to Browning's poem, which begins "Just for a handful of silver he left us, / Just for a riband to stick in his coat").

took itself seriously as a work of art, and the playing of it had to be worthy of the play and a true reflection of its sense and spirit. He was enormously painstaking with his actors, working with them in great detail and with great persistence. One result of this was, judging from all contemporary accounts, immediately obvious: his productions were distinguished not only by the integrity and the veracity of the plays he chose to produce but also by the force, clarity, and fidelity of the performances, especially when considered from the ensemble point of view.

The period 1914–1918 utterly changed the direction of Barker's life; but whether this change was due to the war itself, to the pressures of particular personal events, or to the fact that there was change implicit and inherent in the pattern of his life and the chemistry of his temperament is extremely difficult to determine. Bridges Adams, in the radio talk already quoted, leans to the first theory: "If that infernal war could have been held back only a few years he might have set up a firm new tradition to replace the old tradition he had demolished. He inspired devotion, and he was gathering about him a company that might have become the flesh and blood of the National Theatre he was striving for; even the bricks and mortar might have followed." Barker himself, writing on December 1, 1914, to subscribers to his new repertory theater scheme, says: "But once the war is over I shall be more confident, not less, of the chance of bringing into being a serious theatre in London. No use of course has been made of the money. It is on deposit in a Repertory account at the London County and Westminster Bank. I shall be glad of your consent to leave it there until the moment comes when we can make a move: we shall choose the very earliest." But only a year later his mood has changed and his resolution gone. On February 4, 1916, he writes to William Archer: "Meanwhile, £25—the first subscription to that scheme. Well, that has gone by the board with many other things and someone else will now do the job."

The war years also brought another drastic change in Barker's life, for during that time he divorced his first wife, Lillah MacCarthy (the actress who had been in the Court Theatre company and whom he had married in 1906), and married Helen Huntington, niece and daughter-in-law of Collis Potter Huntington, the hardware store owner from Oneonta, New York, who made himself into a multi-millionaire by prospecting in railroads (he was the prime mover in the building of the Central Pacific, the first railroad to link the east and west coasts of the United States) and generally behaving as a nineteenth-century American robber baron was expected to behave. Barker met Helen in 1915 (by which time C. P. Huntington had been dead for fifteen years), when he was in New York to direct a repertory of plays at Wallack's Theatre. She had already been married twice.[7] She and Barker both spent the two years from 1916 to 1918 obtaining divorces. They were married in London in July, 1918, and in 1920 they went to live in Netherton Hall, a Jacobean mansion in Devon which Helen had bought. At that time, she had published four novels and two collections of verse in New York. She went on, during their married life, to publish a good deal more (see Appendix C) and also to collaborate with Barker in the translating and publishing of a number of plays from the Spanish and two or three from the French. Barker himself, after he married Helen, gave up active theater work (except for one or two special occasions) and devoted himself entirely to writing. His output was considerable and none of it negligible, but much the most important of the things he wrote between 1919 and his death in 1946 were the two plays *The Secret Life* (1922) and *His Majesty* (1928) and the *Prefaces to Shakespeare* (1927–1946). His other work included various pieces of theater history and theater criticism, some short stories, and a book of essays, which he edited for the Royal Society of Literature, of which he was president for a year.[8]

A major revolution in the English-speaking theater took place in Barker's lifetime, a revolution of which he himself had been one of the major instruments. The diversity of his contribution was truly astonishing: he functioned with distinction as an actor, a director, a manager-producer, a dramatist, a literary-dramatic critic, and a lecturer. His work was almost as well known in America as it was in England. Wilson Knight, following Purdom to some extent, suggested that Barker's work as actor and director was of greater value and significance than his critical writings; Bernard Shaw, in his obituary, says that Barker's work as a playwright has been unjustly neglected.[9] The truth, I think, is that he was equally important and significant in all these fields.

Opinions about him as a person were equally varied: Geoffrey Whitworth, in a radio talk broadcast by the B.B.C. in March, 1948,

---

7. In December, 1889, at the age of twenty-two, she married Thomas Ball Criss. There was one child, Mildred, from this marriage, which lasted only five years. In August, 1895, she married Archer Milton Huntington, the adopted son of her uncle, C. P. Huntington (he was the son of her uncle's second wife, Arabella Worsham).
8. A bibliography of Barker's written work—too long to be included in this volume—is found in Appendix III of C. B. Purdom's *Harley Granville Barker: Man of the Theatre, Dramatist and Scholar* (London, 1955), compiled by Frederick May and Margery M. Morgan. See also Margery Morgan's *A Drama of Political Man* (London, 1961), which is primarily a study of Barker's plays but also touches upon his other writings.
9. See Wilson Knight, *Shakespeare's Dramatic Challenge* (London, 1977); and Shaw, in *Drama* (Winter, 1946).

said, "Few could resist that charm and intelligence which he radiated";
however, Athene Seyler, the actress, said to me, in a conversation in
December, 1977: "He was a very cold man. My husband [the actor
Nicholas Hannen] always adored him—I could never understand quite
why, in a way, because they were very different kinds of people. I
myself was rather afraid of him. I once sat next to him at dinner and
couldn't think what on earth to say to him all through the meal. When
he came into a room, one felt rather as though God had suddenly
entered." John Gielgud made a similar remark to me: "He was a very
cold man—seemed terrified of familiarity of any kind." Lillah Mc-
Carthy, Barker's first wife, is reported to have said once: "Harley is not
afraid of poverty; but he's terrified of not having a butler" and Sybil
Thorndike, talking about Barker in a radio program in the early nine-
teen-seventies, said that he always seemed to have a yearning for and a
leaning toward luxury. Yet from 1907 to 1912 he was a member of the
executive committee of the Fabian Society and is reported to have been
very active and assiduous in his duties.[10] In 1908, moreover, although he
had recently pawned some of his clothes (according to Shaw) in order to
pay off his debts at the end of the Court Theatre venture, he turned
down—on purely artistic grounds—the proffered position of director of
the New Theatre (the "Millionaires' Theatre") in New York at an annual salary of twenty thousand dollars (an enormous sum for such a job
in those days). Not even the large salary, his own indigence, or his
alleged love of luxury would persuade him to associate himself with a
venture that seemed to him artistically unsound.

A brief biographical sketch such as this must necessarily omit
much; indeed, with the letters that follow telling their own story and
filling in many gaps (especially as to nuance and the tenor of the
times), it would be inappropriate here to go into much detail. But one
further aspect of Barker's work, to which I have referred only in
passing, should be emphasized: his life-long belief in and advocacy of
the repertory system. His influence in this area has been very considerable in the English-speaking theater. Continental European theaters
have, of course, practiced the repertory method for three centuries,
but at the time of Barker's active involvement in theater work at the
beginning of the century, such a system was unknown in Britain and
America. In curtain speeches after performances (one particularly famous one was after a performance of Galsworthy's *The Silver Box* at
the St. James's Theatre in 1913), in his book *A National Theatre,*
written in collaboration with William Archer and published in 1907, in

---

10. Edward R. Pease, *The History of the Fabian Society* (London, 1916).

his later book, *The Exemplary Theatre,* published in 1922, and most of all in his own managerial practice (when he got the chance), Barker proclaimed the merits of that form of theater which organizes itself around a standing, permanent company of actors with a repertory of several plays at its command at any one time, the plays being presented in rotation, several different ones in each week. There can be no question that the present practice of the National Theatre of Great Britain and of the Royal Shakespeare Company is founded directly upon the schemes which Barker drew up in the first two decades of the century and that they have been enormously influenced by the suggestions which he, personally, made. These two great companies, in many ways the most important theatrical organizations ever to appear in the English-speaking theater, in a very real sense owe their actual existence, as well as their methods, principles, and ideals, to the pioneering work, the thoughtful and thought-provoking utterances, and the blazing idealism of this one man. That idealism and its worth were recognized, at the time of his own work in the theater, not only in London but throughout England. In 1913 the *Yorkshire Evening Post,* a famous regional paper based in Leeds, had this to say:

> Mr. John Palmer, the brilliant dramatic critic of the "Saturday Review", writing of the repertory movement, asks whether it has dawned upon our playgoers that Mr. Granville Barker has kept open the St. James's Theatre for nearly four months without yielding an inch to the speculative manager's view of what the public is supposed to want?
>
> Towards the end of this adventurous period, when most experts of twenty years' experience expected Mr. Barker to retire into bankruptcy, he calmly announced that he would move into another theatre, and that he would there continue his novel policy of drawing to himself the English public by paying no attention whatever to their reputed taste and intelligence.
>
> If Mr. Barker continues long enough in the vein, it may yet be realised that the best way of pleasing your contemporaries is to please yourself. But it will take time to drive the point home. Nothing in the world is so amazing as the way in which beliefs continue to be held in the face of fact and experience.
>
> Speculative managers go on calmly rejecting plays as too good for the public, and calmly staging expensive absurdities on the strength of a twenty years' conviction that these absurdities are what the public wants. The absurdities fail; but the managers build upon their failure an even deeper faith in the assumption that they ought to have succeeded.[11]

---

11. December 20, 1913, p. 5.

The *Western Morning News,* of Plymouth, echoed these sentiments: "The Elizabethan Stage Society and the noble efforts of its founder [William Poel], followed by the disinterestedness, pluck, and rare ability of Mr. Granville Barker and Miss Lillah McCarthy, have started a Shakespeare renaissance which will prepare the country for such performances as it is hoped will be seen at the Shakespeare Theatre."[12]

Barker himself grew tired and disillusioned waiting for his dreamed-of National Theatre or Shakespeare Theatre to arrive, and who can blame him? But eventually, nearly twenty years after his death, *both* arrived: in effect, *two* national theaters, whose work has revolutionized British theater and has exercised vast influence throughout the world. Frances Briggs, who was the secretary of the British Drama League when Barker was its chairman, described to me a massively complicated scheme which he had worked out for establishing a working liaison with various continental repertory theaters—a kind of theater grid system for the exchange of information and of productions. It came to nothing in his own day, but it bore fruit later in the work of organizations such as the Edinburgh International Festival and Sir Peter Daubeny's World Theatre seasons at the Aldwych Theatre in the nineteen-sixties.

---

12. December 20, 1913, p. 7.

 # Chapter II

William Archer, 1856–1924

W_hen Barker began_ his correspondence with William Archer, in 1898, Archer was recognized not only as one of the principal dramatic critics of his day but also as a distinguished man of letters in several other literary fields connected with the theater. He had edited and published the dramatic criticism of Hazlitt and Leigh Hunt; his _English Dramatists of Today_ had been published in 1882; six of his translations of Ibsen had been produced in London (a few years later he would go on to publish a twelve-volume collection of Ibsen's works containing his own translations of most of the Ibsen plays from _Love's Comedy_ onward); and he had, of course, been a dramatic critic for various newspapers for many years—_London Figaro_ from 1878 to 1881, the _World_ from 1884 to 1906, the _Tribune_ from 1906 to 1908, and the _Nation_ from 1908 to 1910. Relatively late in his career he tried his hand at play-writing: what he produced was rather naïve—simple melodramas with stock situations—but with one of them he had a quite considerable commercial success both in London and in New York. The play was _The Green Goddess,_ first produced at the Walnut Street Theatre, Philadelphia, in 1921, then at the Booth Theatre in New York, and finally at the St. James's Theatre, London, in 1923; its success was, perhaps, mainly attributable to the performance of George Arliss as the Rajah. One or two of Archer's other efforts at play-writing are mentioned in his letters to Barker, though none of them repeated the success of _The Green Goddess._

Archer was twenty-two years older than Barker, having been born in 1856. He was the same age as Shaw, with whom Archer was also on very friendly terms for years. When Barker broke with Lillah McCarthy and married Helen Huntington, Archer was one of the few people who continued his friendship with Barker while maintaining his friendship with Lillah. He was a Scot, born in Perth; his paternal grandparents had emigrated from Scotland to Norway, and as a boy

William Archer, about 1890.
Photo J. Russell & Sons, London.

Archer spent a good deal of his time with his grandparents in Larvik, Norway. He was at school in Edinburgh and graduated from Edinburgh University. Actively engaged in journalism while still at the university, he reported the Vienna Exhibition of 1874 for the *Alloa Advertiser* and wrote a daily editorial for the *Edinburgh Evening News.* When he completed his university career, his parents persuaded him to take up law, and, after extending his travels to Australia and the United States, he returned to London with that intention. His first stint as a theater critic was undertaken while still studying for his law examination, which he passed in 1883. By then he had decided not to pursue a career in law, and in 1884 he obtained his first post as a regular, full-time critic with Edmund Yates's *World.* When he became acquainted with Granville Barker, he was one of the two most influential theater critics in London, the other being Clement Scott of the *Daily Telegraph,* Archer's great opponent in the debate over the importance of Ibsen.

Archer died in December, 1924, after an operation to remove a tumor from one of his kidneys, at the age of sixty-eight. Nine days earlier, from a nursing home, he wrote to Shaw and Granville Barker to say goodbye, just in case.

The quality of the man comes through very clearly in his letters to Barker. In the early correspondence Barker is very much the suppliant; by the time the world war engulfed them, this position is reversed, and after the war it is Archer who sues for his friend's good offices. The comments in which he compares their plays are a tribute not only to Archer's good sense and critical perceptiveness but also to his natural humility. Both men owed a good deal to the bond of friendship which gradually developed between them and which endured for over twenty years, and both freely and gladly acknowledged this indebtedness. But for that bond, there would surely have been much graver artistic disputes between them, for their views were really very different, as were their personalities. Barker was much the more austere and idealistic of the two; Archer's gifts were those of liberal-mindedness and sturdy common sense. In the final phase of their correspondence (1922–1924), these contrasts are particularly clear, as is the strong sense of affection between them which enabled them to overcome such differences of opinion.

BL/MS[1]
To Archer

8, York Buildings,
Adelphi
April 7, 1898

Dear Sir,

Miss Elizabeth Robins[2]—immediately before she left for America—wrote to me saying that the MS of a play she had (The Weather-Hen, written by Berte Thomas and myself) she had sent to you. She also said that I should hear from you about it.

I am not aware whether Miss Robins is returned but I should be grateful to know in the first place whether you have the M.S.

I am,

Faithfully yours,
H. Granville Barker

P.S. I write to you c/o The Editor of the "World" as I know of no other address.

---

1. All the letters in this chapter except the last one are deposited in the William Archer Archive at the British Library (Manuscripts Dept., Add. 45290). The last letter was sent to the *Times Literary Supplement* and published there.
2. An American actress, she spent most of her professional life in England; she was one of the first players of Ibsen in London.

BL/MS
To Archer

8, York Buildings,
Adelphi
April 12, 1898

Dear Sir,

Will you allow me to thank you very much for your letter (the MS has also arrived safely) and as your kindly criticism appears mainly to me in the light of a question will you forgive me if I answer it, more I fear for my own satisfaction than expecting you to take this further interest. I so far bow to your decision as to the play's unsuitability to the public that I may say that my friend Thomas and myself have been quite of that mind ever since the play was in embryo. I fear that with its refusal by the "New Century"[1] our last definite hope of production vanishes. Therefore should you, with the "longer record behind you", ever think fit to change that decision the "Weather

Hen" would—as matters now stand—be very much at your service. I need hardly say this.

As to your objection that the relationship between Eve and Jimmy (the obstacles to a relationship) was insufficient, also to the lack of "healthy human nature" in Eve, I can quite understand that through inexperience we have failed to give definite expression to what was in our minds. The crucial point of the play—that Eve who has sacrificed womanhood, real life and Jimmy for position, "Art" and her husband, should be rescued from this diseased life by Jimmy and placed on the road to healthy humanity by the man whom she has by her wanton misdoing caused to walk that road lonely and so placed him beyond the need of her, she herself acknowledging too late her need of him—at the end of the play—to do penance, alone in his steps.

I hope you will not regard the reading of this lengthy epistle as your penance for writing me a kind letter. If you do, please forgive my egoism in so pursuing the subject.

I am,

Faithfully yours,
H. Granville Barker

---

1. A theater society founded in 1897 by Archer for the production of plays of artistic significance but little commercial appeal, similar in intent—though not in importance—to J. T. Grein's Independent Theatre and the Stage Society.

BL/MS
To Archer

8, York Buildings,
Adelphi
June 11 [1899]

Dear Sir,

You may remember, some time ago, reading a play of ours "The Weather-Hen" and saying that you would be glad to see more of our work. "Weather-Hen" is to be played and we are greatly hoping that in the course of events you will be at the matinée.

I now send you what we have written since.

May I only ask you—if you read it—not to approach it from the point of view of what is commonly called an "actable" play.

This is perhaps a poor apology for what we have tried to do.

I am

Very faithfully yours
H. Granville Barker

BL/MS
To Archer

8, York Buildings,
Adelphi
April 9, [1900?]

Dear Mr. Archer,

I am sending you another play to see, though this time only a very little one—the result of two days' work about a month ago.[1]

Perhaps I can best apologise for and explain its form by saying that I've always laid it down a rule to myself—never attempt poetry until prose is too poor to express you. This was almost if not quite an "unpremeditated act" and took what form it would.

I am thinking of sending it to a magazine and I should be glad to know what you think of its reading qualities, if you will tell me.

I hope all you said to me the other day has not been wasted. I think it has not for I do quite recognise how one must avoid being a crank if one is to be listened to at all. My ideal is simplicity <u>and</u> strength, if I can have them both.

I wonder if I may ask your advice about something else? Do you think it would be good for me—should the opportunity occur—to try my hand at criticism? I've already done a certain—a very small—amount and naturally there was pleasure in seeing one's ideas in print but I look upon everything at present as to how it will influence my play writing. I know how my acting has helped me and how to a large extent it hinders me and now I'm wondering about this other—at present quite from a theoretical point of view—and I should be very grateful for your opinion. I think I should always take everything I did more or less seriously and you'll know what sort of habit of brain serious criticism breeds in one—I don't.

I am

Very faithfully yours
H. Granville Barker

---

1. The play must have been "A Miracle," since—so far as we know—it is the only original piece in which Barker attempted to write in verse (his translation of Guitry's *Deburau* is in a kind of loose, free verse). Margery M. Morgan and Frederick May, in their excellent Barker bibliography included in C. B. Purdom's *Harley Granville Barker,* conjecture that "A Miracle" was written in 1902, but there would appear to be, on the strength of this present letter to Archer, good reason for postulating an earlier date. The letter appears in the Archer papers between a letter of June 11, 1899, and one of January 26, 1901. The dates of both of these letters are fixed by external evidence: the performance of *The Weather-Hen* to which Barker refers is known to have been on June 29, 1899 (at Terry's Theatre), and the typescript of "Agnes Colander," to which he refers in the second letter, is dated January 10, 1901, in Barker's hand. The rest of the letters in this archive are all in strict chronological

order, so it is reasonable to suppose that the letter about "A Miracle" is also in its correct place. Barker dates it April, so the year must have been 1900, which, on this evidence, must have been the year in which "A Miracle" was written.

BL/MS
To Archer

> 8, York Buildings,
> Adelphi
> Jan. 26 [1901]

Dear Mr. Archer,

Is the New Century Theatre still alive and if it is will you consider if this, my latest play,[1] is producible [*sic*]? If it is not will you yet be good enough to read the play. I apologise for troubling you but your kind criticism of all my work brings a M.S. upon you about once a year. You'll see the M.S. is roughly typed and the play itself is somewhat unfinished, especially in the scenes between Agnes and Alec Flint but I had to round it off. I was getting distressed with it. I mention this so that you may know I am dissatisfied and feel there is more to be done.

Would it be incorrect for me to thank you for your very kind notice of me in "The World" some weeks ago?

I am,

> Very faithfully yours,
> H. Granville Barker

---

1. The play was called "Agnes Colander": the typescript is now in the British Library (C 116 g9).

BL/MS[1]
To Archer

> 8, York Buildings,
> Adelphi
> April 21, 1903

Dear Mr. Archer,

I want to trouble you with rather a long letter. Do you think there is anything in this idea? To take the Court Theatre for six months or a year and to run there a stock season of the uncommercial Drama: Hauptmann—Sudermann—Ibsen—Maeterlinck—Schnitzler—Shaw—Brieux, etc.

Not necessarily plays untried in England.

A fresh production every fortnight.

Not necessarily a stock company.

The highest price five or six shillings.

To be worked <u>mainly</u> as a subscription theatre.

One would require a guarantee of £5000—if possible 50 people putting down £100 each.

I think the working expenses could be kept to £250 a week. I would stake everything upon plays and acting—not attempt "productions".

It seems to me that we may wait a very long time for our National Theatre, and that when it comes we may have no modern National Drama to put in it. We must get vital drama from somewhere, and if we can't create it we must import it first.

I think there is a class of intellectual would-be playgoers who are profoundly bored by the theatre as it is. Matinée productions don't touch these people (who are all workers) and Sunday evening is expensive and incapable of expansion.

Our actors—and worse still our actresses—are becoming demoralised by lack of intellectual work—the continual demand for nothing but smartness and prettiness.

I think the Independent Theatre—the New Century—The Stage Society—have prepared the ground, and the time is ripe for starting a theatre upon these lines, upon a regular—however unpretending—basis.

And above all unless some effective pioneer work is done very soon, some play will be produced with twopenn'orth of idea and three penn'orth of technique, will be acclaimed as a masterpiece and all real progress will be set back for another ten or fifteen years.

As far as I can judge there are a greater number of people interested in the pioneer drama than ever there were and it seems to me that the regular managers are more timid and conservative than ever.

There'll be nothing new to you in all this—but this idea has been with me very strongly lately. If I am right and the time is ripe and passes unnoticed it will be a thousand pities.

Without doubt the National Theatre will come, but as Ibsen has leavened the whole English Theatre during the past fifteen years, so we ought to be getting some more leaven ready for the National Theatre when it does come.

I have the scheme in rather more detail than I have put it here. Of course the guarantee of £5000 is the practically insurmountable obstacle.

Please forgive this "epistle".

Very sincerely yours,
H. Granville-Barker

1. This letter, with one paragraph omitted, is reproduced in Charles Archer's *William Archer: Life, Work and Friendships* (London, 1931), p. 272.

BL/MS
To Archer

8, York Buildings,
Adelphi
April 28 [1903]

Dear Mr. Archer:

I have been meaning to write and thank you for coming and having that long talk with me. It is helpful to me in my impatience to get under the wing of your knowledge and experience sometimes. I don't think my "Court Theatre" scheme will come to anything and it is perhaps better that it should not.

But I do hope the National Theatre will hurry up and that it will fall into Liberal or even Radical hands and deliver us to some extent from the manager with the wooden head and the stage manager with the iron hand before another generation of actors (mine in this case) has gone to the devil artistically.

You were well out of the Clifford's Inn meeting the other day[1]—a very dull affair which may give birth to a tiny clique, but no more, I should think.

Very sincerely yours
H. Granville Barker

1. Clifford's Inn was the building in which the Fabian Society had its office and headquarters. At this time Barker was an active member of the Fabian Society, and the society as a whole (not only Barker and Shaw) was very interested in the promoting of a more responsible and serious-minded approach to the theater. The meeting to which Barker refers was one of many convened by the society to consider this question.

BL/MS
To Archer

8, York Buildings,
Adelphi
Sept. 9 [1903]

Dr Sr

Yr favor of yesterday's date rec'd. Yr proposal is quite agreeable to me. If I did not think you would take a mean advantage

of such a statement on my part I should say it was d—d generous.
Now you watch me keep the exes down!

I leave my present situation on Friday next.

Various ideas about Peer Gynt begin to float in my brain.
These I shall be happy to communicate to you at a shilling a time. 75%
of money returned if goods not suitable. By this means I hope to satisfy
my needs during the long* interregnum now to be anticipated.

I'm not sure about Wilde.

I am Sr

Yrs to Comnd
H. G. Barker

*I mean vacation or some other word of that ilk.

BL/MS
To Archer

8, York Buildings,
Adelphi
March 16, [1904?]

My dear Archer,

If you think well of my remarks on Hankin's play and think
well too to write anyone about me I shall be very grateful. For honestly, the stage seems to be slipping from me and what is worse I
have no great desire to cling to it. Writing is my bent I am sure and
acting takes the best of everything, which I grudge, and its uncertainty is very trying. My great dread of course is that I shall be forced
back on tour—the most horrible and useless vagabond life that I
know. Therefore if I could do anything at criticism, and I feel I
could, I think my energies would be spending themselves all in the
right direction.

That's my present outlook on things.

Till tomorrow.

Yours,
H. G. Barker

P.S. The Hankin notice was written under quite proper conditions—it
took an hour—someone else in the room all the while—and perhaps
another half-hour to correct.

BL/MS
To Archer

Royal Court Theatre
Sloane Square, S.W.
[Undated[1]]

Dear W. A.

Here is a typewritten letter for Scott's benefit.[2]

My feeling against Rosmersholm is that it must be almost too gloomy for us unless played by a company of geniuses. The Wild Duck is a bit blown on but not too much, I think. I suppose the Doll's House is. But what do you think? I would have a feeling for Hedda or the M.B.,[3] but I fear neither of these is quite practical politics.

By the way, can you give us the refusal of the W.D., for I suspect the Stage Society will have its eye on it—and that effete institution must not be allowed to interfere with us.

Glad about Gosse[4]—nothing from Meredith?[5]

I shall be visible quite late tomorrow afternoon—say 6 or after—I am rehearsing here till 4 or 5. Then I have to go through music somewhere in West End. Then I'm free.

Yours,
H. G. B.

---

1. Judging by the mention of *The Wild Duck,* Barker is discussing plays for the Court repertoire, so the letter must have been written after October, 1904, when the Barker-Vedrenne season at the Court Theatre began. *The Wild Duck* was produced on October 17, 1905, so this letter was probably written late in 1904 or some time in 1905—probably after his return from his holiday with Murray (see pp. 210–22).
2. Walter Scott was the London publisher who brought out Archer's five-volume edition of Ibsen in 1890-91, which contained all the modern prose plays from *The League of Youth* to *Hedda Gabler*. Most of the translations in this edition were by Archer himself. *The Wild Duck* was one of the exceptions; it was translated by Frances Archer, William Archer's wife, though Archer, as editor, had some hand in it and, judging from his introduction to the volume, went over it pretty carefully.
3. Ibsen's *The Master Builder.*
4. Barker is here inquiring about possible plays for the Court repertoire. Sir Edmund Gosse was the other principal Ibsen editor and translator of the time. Archer had had a very serious difference of opinion with him over *Hedda Gabler* in 1890. It was greatly to the credit of both men that they overcame this disagreement and that their friendship continued.
5. Barker, as well as others (notably Alfred Sutro), was trying to persuade Meredith to permit some of his novels to be turned into stage plays. Archer, who knew Meredith personally, was acting as intermediary. No Meredith play was, in fact, done at the Court, but Barker did a version of *The Sentimentalists* (a fragment found in Meredith's papers after his death) at the Duke of York's Theatre in 1910.

BL/MS
To Archer

Shipham Winscombe
Wed.[1]

Dear W. A.

I am now beginning to study the Duck. I miss "waddling", but "Don't sit there cricketizing me"[2] is a delight. I cannot yet make out your enthusiasm for France as Gregers.[3] Surely Relling's should be the public view of Gregers? "Don't you see the fellow's cracked—mad—demented?" However, I'll study on. What do you think of Esmond[4] as a possibility for Hialmar. Think what our possibilities are reducing themselves to and remember Esmond is a man who can always hold the stage—and is at his best in character parts—real "character" parts.

Yrs.
H. G. B.

---

1. See note 1 to the previous letter. On the basis of Barker's usual work methods, I would date this in August or September, 1905.
2. Gina, the down-to-earth wife of Hjalmar Ekdal in *The Wild Duck,* is characterized as a person who occasionally, because of her rudimentary education, uses an incorrect word. The example Barker quotes here, however, though it clearly refers to one of Gina's lines in Act 3 of the play, does not appear in Frances Archer's translation (or any other published translation). Barker must have been reading either a new translation that William Archer had prepared for him or some notes made by Archer about the play. There is no record of a complete translation of this play by Archer.
3. C. V. France played a number of parts in the Court repertory, but the part of Gregers was eventually played by Scott Buist.
4. H. V. Esmond (1870–1922) was an actor and playwright. His wife was the actress Eva Moore. Both were well-known in the London theater of the Edwardian period. Perhaps his best-known play was *Eliza Comes to Stay* (1914). He did not play Hjalmar in *The Wild Duck;* the part was played for the first three performances by Barker himself, then by Trevor Lowe.

BL/TS
To Archer

Court Theatre
November 8th 1905

My dear W. A.

I am so very glad you think well of the play, but I won't, won't, won't bring the curtain down on the handclasp at the end. The scene seems long because I cannot knock the point of it into Thalberg yet[1] and therefore he does it wrong, but the last bit is a necessary finish to the play which has been about Edward's Inheritance and not about his love for the girl. If you could read the thing I am sure you would see this in a moment. Of course they play the last scene six times too slow.

Yours always,
H. G. B.

P.S. I cannot get rid of the superstition that a good man on the stage must always be a strong one, and that a sensitively weak character cannot be interesting. The fluffing yesterday was fearful. They cut several important points.

---

1. In the first production of Barker's *The Voysey Inheritance,* Thalberg Corbett was playing the central role of Edward Voysey, a part which Barker himself played when the play was revived in the following February.

BL/TS
To Archer

Verdrenne-Barker Performances,
Royal Court Theatre,
Sloane Square, S.W.
June 27th, 1906

My dear W. A.

I had thought of asking Miss Robins to play "Hedda Gabler" but the conclusion I came to at the time was this—to put it bluntly—she might by now have become rather stale in her acting. She has I think only appeared once on stage within the last six or seven years and of course all her thoughts must have been given to her writing. If Hedda were a new part to her this might or might not be apparent, but as she has played it before any falling off would certainly be noticed. Also I have a certain feeling that it is better to find a "live" actress than a "dead" one, (you will see what I mean of course by these adjectives).

Now there is another thing. We can I think secure Lena Ashwell for our first series of Matinées and as she is, all things considered, a fairly interesting personality it might be worth while if we could pick on a play that she could appear in. Would it be good to put her in the part in "Little Eyolf" do you think? (I suppose she could not play Hedda.) If we want her we shall have to decide within a day or two in fact within the next 48 hours. Really I wish I could have talked the matter over with you to-day. Perhaps I will try and find you at the Club tomorrow about five or a little later. If I shall not find you, you might send me a line. The truth is of course that I must take another dive into these Ibsen plays myself.

Yours always,

H. G. B.

BL/TS
To Archer

Court Theatre

July 5, 1906

My dear Archer,

The "Hedda Gabler" row proceeds apace. I am forcing Heinemann into a very unpleasant position quite with his knowledge and consent, but I do not think that the power behind the throne realizes what that position will be. I don't want to go on being unpleasant and I very much wish that something could be done to obviate all the difficulty. I told Heinemann this morning that I had told you the facts by accident, thinking you would naturally know them. He was not pleased, but I quite gave him to understand that it was as if it had never been said. So I know nothing and you know nothing of the real facts of the case. The position is that Heinemann gives me the rights of the play subject to his approval of the cast, that he refuses to approve of Mrs. Campbell[1] and yet will give me no reason for disapproving; that he does not allege incompetency or unsuitability which are the only objections that I can see that he has a right to make. You can see how unpleasant this is all becoming and I wish you could impress upon the real subject that private feelings may be carried too far in dealing with matters of public interest. For of course I have no intention of keeping quiet about the matter.

Yours always,

H. G. B.

---

1. Mrs. Pat Campbell did, in fact, play the part.

BL/TS
To Archer

Court Theatre

Aug. 31st, 1906

Dear Archer,

If I am to take the copy of your letter to Dr. Ibsen as the reply to mine I had better reply again to you direct and send a copy to him.

You say that we ought to have offered the part of Hedda Gabler to Miss Elizabeth Robins.[1] I cannot see why. In the first place Mr. Heinemann incidentally informed me in one of our conversations that Miss Robins' reason for surrendering him her rights in the play was that she did not intend to appear in any of them again. In the second, I have never heard of this custom, which you imply, that the actor or actress creating a part becomes morally its proprietor. Where would such a custom end? We revived "The Wild Duck" lately without the original Hedvig, who had made as great a success as it was possible to make in the part. Is "The Doll's House" never to be played again with a new Nora? Is Mr. Tree to remain the sole English representative of Dr. Stockman? I need not point out to you that it would be absolutely impossible to conduct a Theatre intelligently if one made such a general rule; and in what way is this a special case? I know of no little feud. There is none I hope as yet between Ibsen's representatives and my partner and myself and I cannot see who else is concerned in the matter. Besides this is surely something more than a personal question? How is Ibsen's cause to be fought—for it still needs fighting—and how are Ibsen's plays to keep their hardly won place on the English stage if they are to be used as weapons in personal quarrels. I think I need not assure you that I have no personal feeling or interest in this matter beyond what I hope is the play's interest too.

Very sincerely yours,
H. Granville Barker

---

1. See note appended to Barker's letter of January 5, 1907, to Archer.

BL/handwritten by a secretary but initialed by Barker
To Archer

Court Theatre
October 30, 1906

Dear W. A.

For the man who prefers "The Fascinating Mr. Vanderveldt"[1] to "Man & Superman" there is nothing to be said, though had he worshipped at this temple of the Drama last night, he would have discovered that, by a slight alteration in the text, his low rag was being gratuitously advertised. But for the Sub-editor who places on p. 4, and halfway down the column at that, a notice of the revival, and at the bottom of p. 2 an announcement that the revival will take place this evening, there is much to be said! Was your desertion because you didn't have a dress-circle seat sent to you, for that can be remedied!

Fascinating Mr. Vanderveldt indeed!

Yrs,
H. G. B.

P.S. My wife wants to meet Mrs. Archer <u>professionally</u>. G. B. S. prescribes as Saturday the day she's in town?

---

1. By Alfred Sutro, produced at the Garrick Theatre, April 26, 1906.

BL/handwritten by a secretary but initialed by Barker
To Archer

Court Theatre
14 Nov. 1906

Dear W. A.

As we've an understanding with Shaw that nobody connected with the Press shall come to a dress-rehearsal, I had to mention to him that you said you would like to come, & he said he'd much rather you didn't, if you don't mind. There are two of the actors in particular that he's rather afraid your presence would fluster. Wherefore the theatre employees have orders to pull the beard of anybody trying to force an entrance into the theatre, in case it should be you in a false one! I believe that is the right way to deal with critics?

Thanks for the copy of your letter to George Alexander;[1] I'll return it tomorrow—I've left it at home, & am writing this from the theatre. It seems to me to be all that I can desire or deserve. My feeling is that I would very much like to make "Peer Gynt" the first Vedrenne-Barker matinee at the new theatre, if & when we go to one—and it's really only a question of when, for we obviously can't go on here much longer.

I am sorry you are so dead against omitting the fourth act, because, though I haven't studied it closely lately, my recollection is that it is so bound up with satire of Norwegian politics that it would be difficult to make a lot of it comprehensible. Would you propose, anyhow, to omit the mad house scene?—And yet I don't like making a petty cut like that. I'd sooner omit a whole act, and so own to doing it incompletely, so to speak. It seems to me that that is a better policy in dealing with a classic.

Yours,
H. G. B.

1. Alexander (1858–1918) was an actor-manager who was for twenty-seven years the tenant and controller of the St. James's Theatre.

BL/handwritten by a secretary but initialed by Barker
To Archer

Court Theatre
21 Nov. 1906

Dear W. A.

After the kind letter of last night, I expected a much worse slating in the Tribune this morning. I thought Louis Dubedat was a bad performance, & told Shaw so three days ago;[1] but I'm afraid I don't agree with you as to the reason, or as to what I gather is your reason. That is how people die when they are weak & short of breath. The scene does seem to me rather long, but Shaw wouldn't cut it. At least this is if you refer only to my voice. If you mean my conduct in that scene generally, I gather that Shaw meant the young gentleman to be piling it on, & thoroughly enjoying himself. Vide "Would you deprive the dying actor of his audience?" No, really I don't quite know what you do mean, though I daresay you are quite right, & as I said, I don't feel very right and good in it.

I looked for you in the Club today, but you were not; I'll look again tomorrow or Friday if I can get in.

Yours
H. G. B.

1. Barker played Dubedat in the first production of Shaw's *The Doctor's Dilemma* on November 20.

BL/handwritten by a secretary but initialed by Barker
To Archer

5 Jan. 1907

Dear W. A.

As to some of your suggestions for the cast,[1] I scorn them and spit upon them! They may be suitable enough, but they are bad actresses.

Can you tell me how to get a bust of Ibsen? If you are tactful, you will not ask for what. By the way, I think Mary Rorke is a good idea if she's obtainable, except that she will be lady-like at any cost, which is a pity.

I'll look you up with counter-suggestions soon.

Yrs.

H. G. B.

---

1. The play was Archer's translation of Ibsen's *Hedda Gabler,* which Barker was planning for production in March. The final cast included Mrs. Patrick Campbell as Hedda, Evelyn Weeden as Mrs. Elvsted, Adela Measor as Aunt Juliana, and Mary Raby as Berta.

BL/handwritten by a secretary but initialed by Barker
To Archer

Court Theatre
9 Jan. 1907

In the first place, Archer, I blush for you! In the second place I shall see that you are instantly removed from your post of great responsibility on the Tribune; if a bomb is necessary I will not shrink. I don't of course mind your praising The Reformer,[1] but as far as it concerns the English Drama, such a play doesn't matter a damn. But for the man who can jump on the Campden Wonder[2] which has in it the beginnings & more than the beginnings of good English drama of the soil, & can blame it & me (God help him) for its tautology, which is quite the most characteristic thing in West Country speech, for the man who can listen to such a speech as this:—

> I be a poor old widow woman, I be. I an't got no man, I an't, not since my poor man were took. Seventy year have I lived in Campden, & some time it have been hard, & some time it have been not so hard; & us have had our little home, us have, though us were poor. I have brought my sons up in the fear of the Lord. I wasn't never questioned like this afore. Us have borne a good name, us have, though us were poor. I be innocent, Sir, God forgive my poor lying boy.

& not know that he is in the presence of the real thing, for that man—well I have just sent my dresser out for three penny-worth of nitro-glycerine! You are a twelve shilling sneck-up of a Temple Barrister.

H. G. B.

---

1. A play by Cyril Harcourt, described as "a very light comedy," produced by Barker, which opened on January 8, 1907.
2. John Masefield's first play, included by Barker as an after-piece for *The Reformer.*

BL/TS
To Archer

3, Clement's Inn
W. C.
Thursday night [1907?]

Dear W. A.

My feeling would be—not to publish the letter[1] but to make use of it under the form of "A correspondent has sent us the following suggestions for . . . etc." Then you could give vent to its cry, and it's a just one and there is a crying need for some sort of organisation of the young actor of ten years' experience. If he isn't organised the present touring system, which really seems to be at its nadir (I've been seeing some of it tonight), will reduce him to a marionette altogether. But TWO stage managers are wanted—London is no use and I'm not sure about the old plays. Of course Repertory in the big towns and a revival of the circuit system in the smaller is the only thing. Of course you know all this, but everybody doesn't and if you make use of the letter to say this or something like it I think it will be good. I'd try to give vent to any cry, however crude; it is so discouraging not to, and apart from that I do seriously believe, seize every chance of a whack at the old nailhead. The subject is still fresh, though Heaven knows it don't seem so to us.

Yours
H. G. B.

No—you know I think—no ventilation does <u>harm</u>.

---

1. This is a letter which Archer had received from an actor, making suggestions for the improvement of theater conditions and the protection of the profession of acting. I have been unable to identify the actor.

BL/part TS, part MS
To Archer

Vann Cottage,
Fernhurst
Surrey.
Sunday [May, 1907]

Dear W. A.

I now feel like Tree—do you remember? This is a long letter. . . . ? I cannot deal with long letters. Margery Ventura etc.? I think I must wait until I see you and can talk. Can't you come down for a Sunday—or I shall be up for a day or two about June 1—dammit! As to Vedrenne there are points both ways, but I don't think his going is quite practical.[1] As to you—I have never deserved such a kind letter as you write to me and thinking of you as if you were Snooks[2] I have no strong instinct one way or the other; my judgement says Come—if we agree as to what this theatre is to do, for I think it will differ a bit from the blue book design.[3] But there again I'm a little vague and must think and would like to talk. The truth is that for the moment I'm giving my best energies to the play that I'm a-chewing of, which Redford will never pass[4]—therefore I'll have to go to America. I'm sending a letter to Otto Kahn[5] telling him the theatre is too big and the proscenium too wide. But I feel foolish. America looks rather real at moments and it would be the correct sequel to the blue book if we went together. Yes I think "Drama-turg" and "The authority on the drama on this Continent, Sir"—with a professorship at Harvard or Columbia is the thing. You have had enough of criticism. As I say, no man can act after thirty and not become less than a man—so no man can criticise after—? I have de-manded the head of Gosse on a charger (though Hedda should hang him!) that you might have his berth—but that doesn't come.

All right about Peer—I'll talk to Vedrenne in a week.[6] For-give this rubbish.

Yours,

H. G. B.

---

1. Barker had been invited to New York to consider the position of director of the New Theatre, then in the course of construction. He wanted somebody to go with him to give advice. Archer eventually went.
2. I.e., considering you quite impartially, as though you were unknown to me.
3. The reference is to *A National Theatre: Scheme and Estimates*, a book which Barker and Archer wrote and had privately printed in 1904. When the book was eventually published, in 1907, Barker wrote a new preface for it in which he referred to it as "this unofficial blue book."
4. The play was *Waste:* Barker had left London for the country to finish writing it, giving up three roles at the Court Theatre to do so. George Redford, examiner of plays in the office of the Lord Chamberlain, was the official responsible for the granting or withholding of a new play's license to be performed. Barker was right: *Waste* was banned by Redford and was not licensed until 1920.
5. A member of the group of wealthy men in New York which was building the New Theatre on Central Park West, between 62d and 63d streets, specifically to house repertory, to be subsidized and run on the lines Barker was advocating in London. The theater opened on November 8, 1909, with *Anthony and Cleopatra*, but the repertory scheme failed, and three years later the building's name was changed to the Century Theatre. It was demolished in 1930.
6. Barker and Vedrenne were planning to move their operation from the Court to the Savoy Theatre in the autumn of 1907. Barker was seriously considering *Peer Gynt* as the opening production of the new season. (In the event, the opening production was a revival of Shaw's *You Never Can Tell,* and Barker never directed or played in *Peer Gynt.*)

BL/TS
To Archer

Vann Cottage,
Fernhurst,
Surrey.
Tuesday [May or June, 1907]

Dear W. A.

I sent one or two comments on your business proposals to
Vedrenne and he says he is sending them on to you. I mayn't have
expressed them well for—to quote against you—I am a child in these
matters. One of my points was your own—that we do put in rather
unpriceable work and prestige (thanks to the people who give us dinners). But another was that your risk is limited while ours is not; for
instance an accident on the eve of production would certainly land us
into much greater losses than are provideable for on an ordinary estimate—and there are other chances. But a third point and one that
most concerned me is that I wished to use the N. C. T. money,[1] to a
large extent, in a way that I can't consistently tell my business partner
is profit making. I wanted to open it [the new season] on better music, better designs for the scenery and, for instance in the Dovre
scene [in *Peer Gynt*], perhaps on designs for the dresses. In fact I
wanted to behave for that production as if I were for once working
under an endowment. Were I a Tree I should be ashamed to tell you
this, but I do not think I should be merely extravagant. As a rule of
course we limit our expense to what I assure Vedrenne is absolutely
necessary and we especially pare away at any sort of decoration or
accessory and this involves much extra sweat too. And now if this
principle of sharing profits is to be admitted to any full extent, I shall
feel bound to do the same. I wondered if any bonus scheme were
practicable—or could so much be considered as a donation towards
the greater effectiveness and beauty of the production. Tell me if you
think I'm a Jew. Not that I mind jewing the N. C. T. in the least.
But I do want the best production I can get—I have staked my reputation with Vedrenne on it.

Yours,
H. G. B.

Regard the enclosed! Good, oh good, about the dinner.[2] What
is to be its programme, by the way? But I want to <u>invite</u> my father and
mother (I think they'll be in town). Shall I get the tickets bought or
apply for them myself—or what—do you think?

H. G. B.

1. New Century Theatre; Archer had offered N. C. T. funds to help start Barker's new season at the Savoy Theatre.
2. A special dinner, arranged under the chairmanship of Lord Lytton to honor Barker and Vedrenne, took place at the Criterion Restaurant on July 7.

BL/handwritten by a secretary but initialed by Barker
To Archer

Vedrenne-Barker Performances
London address: 52, Shaftesbury Ave, W
This week: Theatre Royal, Manchester
Next week: New Theatre, Cardiff.
23 Sept. 1908

Dear W. A.

I've just had a very nice letter from Pinero. He rubs in the "breach of etiquette", but of course it's no use taking that line. Shaw is tactless with Pinero, but nothing would ever put those two in double harness. I must say I think G. B. S. has been really trying, over this Authors' Society business. I'm glad we got the manifesto amended as much as we did.

It may seem as if I had left Pinero alone in his Chairmanship so to speak, but it isn't really so. He was strongly for amalgamation in the beginning, and he's got himself jumped out of it by Sutro, Carr & Co. The thing is that he got up on the fence and now he finds it uncomfortable. However, do let him know if you like, and if an opportunity occurs, that I, among the others, am very grateful to him for the way he responded to our call to arms. And—also if you like— that I was not responsible for the actual drawing up of that manifesto, but that I ameliorated it as much as I could. The person you ought to talk to like a father is Sutro, who has done his best to make Pinero cantankerous.

I beg to say that Garnett is none of mine: I disown him. And I put in Pollock and afterwards Cannan as two young Cambridge sparks that should appeal to Pinero. The thing is of course one must have some juniors who will do work, because none of your big pots will or did.

When is the first meeting of the National Theatre Committee to be, and when should our preliminary caucus meet? I would run up from Bournemouth the week after next on either Tuesday, Friday, or at a very severe pinch, Monday, but Heaven knows I don't want to. Then I have a fortnight in London, during which let us squeeze in anything we can. After that we're back here, and a day's journey impossible. Then at Birmingham, and I take it a day's journey just possible there. After that I'm unobtainable until the end of the tour, except for a possible Monday morning.

Very interesting about the New York people. £250 a year I should say, and cheap at the price.

I sent the tag of your letter on to Lillah, so look out for squalls if you don't re-insert that eulogy.

I have got a copy of the Blue Book with me, so any suggestions you make for the six sheets of foolscap I can look into.

Yours,
H. G. B.

BL/handwritten by a secretary but initialed by Barker
To Archer

Vedrenne-Barker Performances,
London address: 52, Shaftesbury Ave, W.
This week: Theatre Royal, Manchester
Next week: Prince of Wales Theatre,
Birmingham
Oct. 27, 1908

Dear W. A.

I return this document with some rather useless notes, but I really can't make up my mind that it will be of much use to the Committee.[1] It will of course be quite impossible for any chairman to confine our discussion to this, in fact I take it you don't expect to; and if you start elaborating it you enter upon a most troublesome, indeed an impossible task.

My suggestion for procedure is this, that first of all the Committee should agree upon one or two main principles; that each one of the Committee should read the book, and that each expert who is asked to give evidence should read the book too, especially those sections of it which he or she is principally supposed to be expert about;[2] that then we should have in the experts one by one and get them to make any definite tangible criticisms that they will. (They must of course be told beforehand that expressions of opinion are not so much needed as facts.) Then anybody should be at liberty of course to cross-examine them. That over, members of the Committee should bring up any definite points that they want to, in the light of the evidence, that these should be discussed and in this case voted upon. The Chairman should then draft the report.

I know that this may seem as if it would be a long and

cumbrous proceeding but in practice I feel pretty sure that it wouldn't be so. The book is exceedingly difficult to criticise and with a Chairman like Esher you may be sure that only relevant and definite criticisms would be admitted. They will practically amount to discussion on one or two vital points which would come up, book or no book, and the pulling about of the three principal sets of figures. If upon the figures the criticisms become finicking, the simple plan is to yield to them. By what other plan can you limit discussion, without stifling it as I feel sure no such Committee will consent to have it stifled, seeing that the Committee's report may involve considerable responsibility?

Unless you can quite convince me that I'm wrong, won't you send this to Lord Esher when you send your document?

Yours,

H. G. B.

---

1. The committee is the joint executive committee established by the amalgamation, earlier in the year, of the Shakespeare Memorial Committee and the National Theatre Committee.
2. The book which Barker recommends is *The National Theatre: Scheme and Estimates,* which he and Archer published the year before.

BL/TS
To Archer

Kingsway Theatre[1]
Great Queen Street, W.C.
[London]
November 1st, 1913

Master Absolon,[2]

You are right in every word you say, but that single minute more rightly employed—any employment of it that I can discover—is bound to take the attention off Anne. You have certainly come to the end of all <u>she</u> can do. I even feel that the new business that I have put in for Merete[3] and the Canon is wrong. We might get a transparency of her being burnt at the stake in the approved mid-Victorian style—I mean the transparency not the burning—I am dashed if I can think of anything else. Very interesting those two points about Lillah. The first partly my fault, I meant something of the sort to lead up to wishing him dead, but perhaps she has not quite got it, or perhaps it is not right. As to the second point, it is curious. I will watch it next time I go.

Murray is a perfect young dog. I cannot get hold of him. He

dashes up to town to take Chairs apparently in his aeroplane,[4] and dashes back again.

Yours,

H. G. B.

---

1. The Barker-McCarthy management moved to the Kingsway from the Little Theatre in 1912.
2. Absolon is one of the chief characters in *The Witch,* a play adapted by John Masefield from the Norwegian original by Wiers-Jenssen. Archer first discovered the play in Norway, and it was at his suggestion that Barker asked Masefield to do an English adaptation for Lillah McCarthy, who played Anne Pedersdotter, Absolon's wife. It was produced in 1910 (directed by Barker) and revived in their repertory from time to time.
3. Absolon's mother in *The Witch.*
4. A reference to Gilbert Murray's chairmanship of various societies and committees; the "aeroplane" is a joke.

BL/TCC
To Barker

27, Fitzroy Square,
London, WI
[11 Feb. 1914]

My dear H. G. B.

I daresay you could dispense with them, but I want to give you my impressions hot & hot.

On the whole I was charmed: the spirit is right, the decoration right, 99 details out of 100 absolutely right.[1] The treatment of the fairies is ingenious & excellent, the music & the dances admirable. I do not think there is a single positive lapse of taste in the whole show. I am very sorry I wasn't there on Friday, for I would certainly have written a very different notice from Anno Domini's.

There would only have been two serious limitations to my praise: the Puck is not quite right & the Bottom is not quite right. Both are good in their way, but their way is not the best way. Even if you are right in casting Calthrop for Puck (& I cannot see but what a boy would have been better) his get-up is surely not happy. What is the point of that mop of tow at the back of his head? As I write it occurs to me that perhaps it symbolizes the flame of the ignis fatuus; but I am quite uncertain, & even if I have guessed right, I wonder how many people in the audience rose to it? Then I don't see that he should be so absolutely marked off from the fairy folk. Granted that he is of a different order of spirits, still he is nearer to fairies than to mortals; whereas Calthrop is simply a human eccentric. Remember I think he does it quite cleverly—it is you, not him, I am criticizing.

Bottom, I am <u>sure</u>, is a miscasting. Playfair is bright, mercurial, intelligent; Bottom should be a monument of heavy stolid egoism. A much worse actor would have done it much better.

It's a pity your Theseus has such an untuned voice—you want a noble suavity for the part. I wonder if he shouldn't change parts with Philostrate—who, by the way, is quite excellent. And, by the bye, your costumer (Wilkinson?) has played Theseus a nasty trick in the hunting scene, where his dress, ugly in itself, accents the ungainliness of his attitudes. Couldn't he be restrained from sprawling about the stage as he does?

It is a great pleasure to hear scores of lines restored that Daly & Co. used to cut; but I think you go to the opposite extreme. There are a few lines—perhaps not fifty in all—that have "gone dead" & would be better away.

Marry, I bethink me, when I said there was no error in taste, I forgot the soliloquies spoken at the audience. This may be excusable in Bottom—but I can't agree with it in Helena.

My private criticism to you, which I wouldn't put in print, as it is only a vague impression, is that in attaining distinction you miss something of <u>delightfulness</u>. That was what I felt about TWELFTH NIGHT —there wasn't a thing in it that was wrong, & yet I had seen infinitely more faulty performances that gave me acuter pleasure. Here I have in a less degree the same feeling; there is much that is extremely delightful; but the comparative weakness of the Bottom & (I think) the retention of a few inert lines that don't get over the footlights, tended—or so I thought—to diminish the sheer enjoyment of the audience. You will probably disbelieve this; but remember I have seen a great many audiences, & ought to be able to take their temperature. The audience was pleased, undoubtedly; but I didn't feel that they would go away and say to their friends "Oh you must go & see that delightful production." I take it TWELFTH NIGHT didn't do much more than pay its way; if this should work out similarly, ask yourself if there mayn't be something in this feeling of mine. I don't for a moment believe that distinction & delightfulness are incompatible.

A man named Henry Stace[2] is going to send you a play which I promised to ask you to read. I see in it a sort of drab originality which is perhaps worth encouraging. I don't remember the title, but he will no doubt mention my name in sending it in.

I think you ought to hand the enclosed letter to your courteous & indefatigable acting-manager, whom I don't know—but do as you like about that.

Yours,
W. A.

1. He is discussing Barker's celebrated production of *A Midsummer Night's Dream,* which opened at the Savoy Theatre on February 6, 1914, with Lillah McCarthy playing Helena. Barker repeated the production in substantially the same form at Wallack's Theatre, New York, in the following year.
2. Stace eventually did have a play performed in London, *The Member for Turrington,* opening at the Players Theatre on February 21, 1930.

BL/TS
To Archer

Kingsway Theatre,
Great Queen Street, W.C.
February 14th, 1914

My dear W. A.,

I could not at all dispense with them and I wish I could have written hot and hot too, but I have had rather a job getting off. I do get off tomorrow. DV and WP.[1]

Yes, I do think that A. D.'s notice was rather stupid; it was not even intelligent blame.

Puck: I have improved a bit and he has improved himself a great deal. He has got younger and merrier. His red dress I know is not quite right but I still think the idea is right, and the yellow wig too which is only meant to look like tangled hair. It had got dressed wrong when you saw it. I do not think a boy would have the technical accomplishment to put it through. At least no boy that I could think of. I think I am right as to the difference between Puck and the fairies. The Fairies are undoubtedly foreign (surely it is quite a modern idea to think of them as English? It seemed so evident that Shakespeare didn't). Puck on the other hand is as English as he can be, and though sometimes he is invisible, sometimes he goes and lives among the village folk, as a grown up person at that. Still perhaps in trying to get the point we exaggerated it.

Yes, I see what you mean about Playfair, but he is comic by nature, he is egotistical, he is a bad actor—which I think Bottom ought to be. I cannot bear anybody to be slow in dealing with W. S., but Heaven knows Playfair doesn't bring it all off.

Then again, I do agree with what you say about the dead lines, and if I had felt that the non-cut, play-straight-through battle was really won I should have been tempted to take out a few; but it is not and we have nailed Shakespeare un-cut to the mast. Also it is a tricky business to cut. One is so apt to take things out because they don't suit you, because you don't understand them. But there are about 20 lines that I feel hang heavy. I do not think that they will make the real difference to the play though. What does is that the character drawing is very poor, very, and if the actors (Demetrius and Lysander especially) are not all the time better than their parts it is dull, dull, dull. It is a poor play from this point of view and there is an end of it, and I cannot afford young Gods at fifty pounds a week apiece, even if I could get them. That is the real difficulty.

I will write to you from Moscow and burn a candle for you to St. Isaac.[2]

Yours,
H. G. B.

P.S. Thanks too for the letter to the business manager and the affair with Parke, to whom I have written direct. They really did behave in a scandalous way, those papers. We only did what we and every other theatre has been doing for some years and they gave us absolutely no warning of their sudden retort to it. I don't mind much. They would have run down the production anyhow. Baughan I am sure would have disliked it, but can't you for this once now put a weekly article in the Daily News. I do think it is a pity we have not had your word even though now I know it is going to be more or less favourable!

---

1. *Deo Volente* and Weather Permitting (a common joke at the time).
2. He was going to visit Stanislavski and to see some of the work of the Moscow Art Theatre.

BL/MS
To Archer

Wingstone,
Manaton,
Devon
Friday [July, 1914]

Dear W. A.,

This is really to forward you the enclosed Ds about the BB.[1]

But also to say I hear you Queensberry'd at the Haymarket yesterday—stood up in the stalls and implored F. B. with tears in your voice to sign the pledge.[2] I say, was it very disgraceful? One is quite helpless except for the extreme course of

Yours,

H. G. B.

---

1. The Blue Book, or Barker and Archer's *A National Theatre.* "Ds" are documents; the use of initial letters in this way was a favorite device of Barker's. The "Ds" in question concerned the relationship between the plans described in the Blue Book and the plans being discussed in 1914 for Barker's proposed repertory theater (see Appendix B).
2. The play that night was *Within the Law,* and it is tempting to believe that "F. B." was one of the actors: the picture of Archer standing up in the stalls or dress circle to reprove an actor for drunkenness is an appealing one. However, there is no "F. B." in the cast list of *Within the Law.* J. C. Trewin has ingeniously suggested to me that the guilty party may have been Frank M. Boyd (1883–1954), dramatic critic and journalist.

BL/TS
To Archer

Wingstone,

Manaton,

Devon

Friday [July, 1914]

Dear W. A.,

No—I am not sure that I do. I dread big committees—they never do anything. I think they should have the power to fill vacancies by co-option. And I think a strong chairman must just force the resignations of those who won't attend. But I think that is all an elected body can ask—and on the whole, all that it is wise for it to ask. I am open to conviction but it is in this strain I am writing to Lytton. Shall I send you the letter to post to him so that if you very much object you need not? But I do not think that unchecked power to add to the number will work.

Do I know Whelan's scheme?[1] Was I not up to my neck in it just before I left England? Did I not insist on a second theatre being brought in to afford an escape from Tree? Was not that second theatre the Haymarket? Have we not now sickened Harrison[2] of matinées and me? Is not Whelan now in for the most terrific orgy of muddles? Lord! Lord! Such a pity, but however do they expect to get

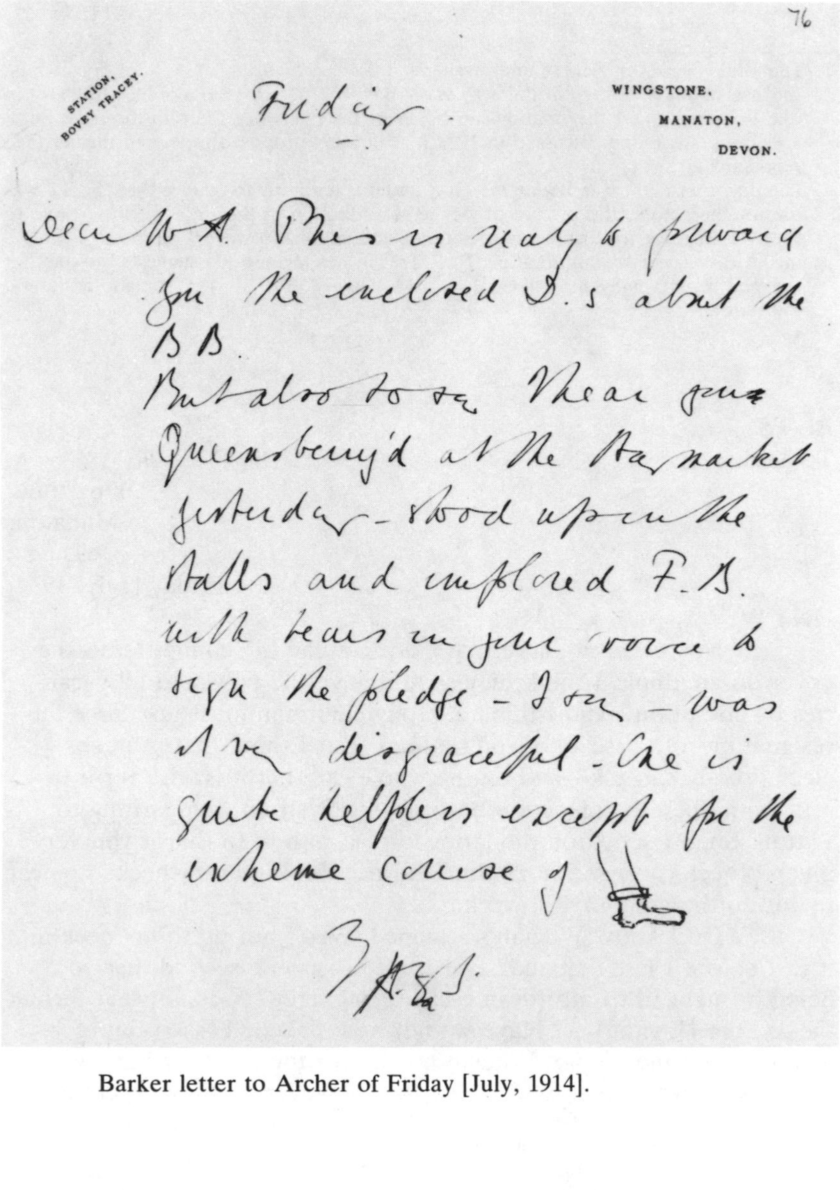

76

STATION, BOVEY TRACEY.

Friday.

WINGSTONE, MANATON, DEVON.

Dear W.A. This is really to forward you the enclosed D.'s about the B.B.

But also to say I hear you Queensberry'd at the Haymarket yesterday — stood up in the stalls and implored F.B. with tears in your voice to sign the pledge — Jon — was it very disgraceful — One is quite helpless except for the extreme course of

Y H.G.B.

Barker letter to Archer of Friday [July, 1914].

anything rehearsed with H. B. T. spreading himself over his beautiful theatre.[3]

Till we meet

Yours,
H. G. B.

---

1. Frederick Whelan was Beerbohm Tree's reader of plays: the "scheme" (of which the details remain obscure) was part of the plan for starting a repertory theater in London (see Appendix B).
2. Frederick Harrison, owner and manager of the Haymarket Theatre from 1896 to 1927.
3. Herbert Beerbohm Tree (1853–1917), the actor-manager, was the manager of the Haymarket Theatre from 1887 to 1896, when he moved across the street to Her Majesty's, which he built for his own use.

BL/TS (postscript MS)
To Archer

Kingsway Theatre
Great Queen Street, W.C.
December 1st, 1914

Dear Archer,

In December last when we made our appeal for a London Repertory Theatre you were good enough not only to give us your support but to send in earnest of it the first cheque for £25. Many excellent suggestions and some guarantee of substantial help brought about modifications of the original scheme. These were still proceeding when the outbreak of war stopped everything. At present there is very little to be done. But once the war is over I shall be more confident, not less, of the chances of bringing into being a serious theatre in London. No use of course has been made of the money. It is on deposit in a Repertory account at the London County and Westminster Bank. I shall be glad of your consent to leave it there until the moment comes when we can make a move; we shall choose the very earliest.

Yours sincerely,
H. Granville Barker

P.S. This is the formal letter I'm sending round. And if you want the cash (and who doesn't!) of course claim it at once. I'm off to New York tomorrow morning to get through, if possible, some business there.

I *was* proud of your notice of the Dynasts[1]—you were converted, were you?

1. A stage version of Hardy's *The Dynasts*, prepared by Barker and directed by him at the Kingsway Theatre, ran from November 25, 1914, to January 7, 1915.

BL/MS
To Archer

H.Q. British Red Cross
K.P.O.
B.E.F.[1]
February 4 [1916[2]]

My dear W. A.

Someday we "a-meet" and I'll tell you whys and wherefores.

Meanwhile, £25—the first subscription to that scheme. Well, that has gone by the board with many other things and someone else will now do the job.

Do you know W. A. if the millionaires had taken up that Blue Book of ours when it was written I'm not sure we shouldn't have found it a little easier (we, the B. P.[3]) to win this war.

I was so glad of your message the other day.

Yours,
H. G. B.

1. British Expeditionary Force (in France and Belgium). Barker had been commissioned by the Red Cross to write a book describing their work on the battlefields.
2. In my earlier book (*Granville Barker: A Secret Life*) I quoted this letter and conjectured its date as 1915. This was an error. Barker was in New York in February 1915, as his letters to Shaw show (see Chapter III).
3. British Public.

BL/MS
To Archer

Williams Inn,
Williamstown,
Massachusetts[1]
April 4 [1916]

My dear W. A.

I feel a pig for never having written you a real letter, for the little that you said in yours came warmly home to me. But I didn't want to write you without being quite open and telling you straight out of my separation from Lillah. To those who impute faults over such things let it appear—and quite justly—as my "fault". There is no use discussing it however and there is no "scandal" for mere busy-bodies to discuss. The thing is done—or rather it is only half done as yet. I wish it were quite done, for then it could be spoken out about and the busybodies would have no chance at all. That does not rest with me.

I shall be lecturing a little here on The Staging of Shakespeare, <u>talking</u> about it—and for various other reasons this is my abode at present, but not permanently of necessity. Though I have acquired your liking for America, especially when I get away from the cities. This place you probably know—Williams College—up in the Berkshires—not unlike Scotland and Switzerland mixed and then reduced in scale. The place itself with all the simplicity and friendliness of a small university.

I am settling down to write at last—doing my best to—and I will try and be a credit to you. It was in '99 (Lord help us) you told me I could do something if I tried. I remember vividly a talk in that Southampton Row room of yours, you tugging a watch chain and speaking with great deliberation, and I very shy (though you mayn't have known it). There's not been much done since then—three plays!—and it's now or never—so I hope it may be now. I haven't been to the theatre over here. Tree is booming away in Henry VIII and acting better outside the theatre than in—but I believe people go in. Otherwise there's a lot of struggle against worsening commercial conditions—healthier movements as to pageants and local playhouses and amateurs than anywhere else, I think. In England no struggle, though we must be patient there and content to wait some new birth, I suppose. And you are <u>a</u> Censer![2]

My love to you,
H. G. B.

---

1. Barker was staying in Williamstown to be as close as possible to Helen Huntington. This letter is written on notepaper with the printed letterhead of the Williams Inn, but underneath Barker has written: "Address: Algonquin Hotel, West 44th Street, New York City." However, the letter was mailed in Williamstown on April 4 (in this case the envelope has been preserved with the postmark and is also stamped "OPENED BY CENSOR").
2. Archer had recently joined the staff of the government department set up to examine captured German letters and documents and to censor out-going British mail, but Barker writes "Censer" (with capital letter), not "censor," as might be supposed. I do not think it is a mistake. A censer is the special, consecrated vessel in which incense is burned. I think that Barker means to say that, though the situation is gloomy, there is at least some hopefulness in the fact that Archer is one small vessel in which the true spirit of theater still remains and whose influence is spread like the fragrance from a censer. In other words, Barker intends the pun, I think.

BL/TS (Postscript in MS)
To Archer

Garrick Club,
Garrick Street, W.C.
June 28th, 1918

My dear W. A.

Forgive me for the interval of silence. Now this is what I think, put down rather confusedly I am afraid. The strength of the play[1] is that it is a document. Its weakness is that while the characters "constater" themselves clearly and well, they do not develop, unless Kessler's suicide is a development. That indicates to me that it should not be a three act but a three <u>scene</u> play.

This would let you cut out the additions—which I guess had not been to your own taste—cut out all the repetitions which weaken the thing and are occasionally dangerous—(For instance, the Colonel may protest against the heroics once, but if he does it twice, considering that he is giving vent to more heroics than anyone else in the play, it may strike an undesirable note of humour.)—Cut the talk in fact to the bare bones. I realise the difficulty of the change of scene, but I think with a little ingenuity the action might all take place on one spot, and the soldiers could well be breakfasting on the remains, so to speak, of the officers' dinner—something of that sort, if only the church and school difficulty could be got over. By some such means, I believe you would make it an <u>absolutely</u> sound thing of its sort.

Then, as to practical theatre politics, I still say that it is the business of the Ministry of Information to father it. Some time ago, I should have thought that it would be quite a Coliseum possibility. It might be, even now, if Stoll, a public spirited person, saw any public service in doing it. But of course English audiences altogether have rather supped full of horrors. America is indicated, and here again the Ministry of Information ought to be of most use.

I do not write casual compliments as you see, but what, even though you may well feel it is rather drastic, seems to me the most practically helpful and professional thing to say.

Yours,
H. G. B.

It does all ring true—and would play "true" I feel—but I am sure best keep it "stark"; that is the right artistic fitness.

---

1. Archer had sent Barker a play he had written, *War Is War, or The Germans in Belgium.* It was published in 1919 by Duckworth but was never produced. It was Archer's first attempt at an original play and was based, according to Charles Archer, on German documents which had come into Archer's hands while he was working for

the newly formed Bureau of War Intelligence. Needless to say, the play did not take the German point of view: it was a simple propaganda melodrama.

BL/TCC
To Barker

[27, Fitzroy Square, W.1]
28 June 1918

My dear H. G. B.

Of course your criticism of the great propagandist drama is perfectly sound from the artistic point of view. The piece is more of a picture-poster than a play—a historic picture-poster. The characters do not develop; but I do not imagine that much development of character took place in a Belgian Village in the 24 hours between the arrival of the Germans & the massacre. Not at any rate, in the average good sort of people whom I have assumed. Of course it would be possible to select a character or characters who would develop under the stress of a crushing calamity, & to study that development. But that would be "another story"—it is not what I wanted to do, nor do I think that it would be particularly useful at the present juncture. Perhaps I take this view because I haven't it in me to do it—but I don't think it is entirely that.

I may have recourse to your prescription as a last resource.[1] I may give the thing to someone and say "Take this and make a sketch of it". But that's not what I want.

What I wanted was to bring home to people what had come home so forcibly to me in studying the German evidence—namely the horrible experience of a little community living an absolutely peaceful and innocent life, devoid of any ambitions or rancours, either personal or political, on whom there descends out of the blue a horde of malevolent maniacs, self-worshipping, swaggering, pedantic, murderous.[2] Now to get that effect a certain amount of time is necessary. My own feeling about it is that it is too hurried as it stands. It is too schematic, if you know what I mean—too much of a diagram. The people say nothing and have no character that is not obviously conditioned by political purpose. If I knew how to humanize it by making it half an hour longer I would—but I don't know how.

You will probably say that that is just your point—it ought either to be humanized or cut to the bone—as it is it falls between two stools. Very likely you are right. But I must try whether there isn't something in my conception of an animated picture-poster.

I don't quite know what you take to be "additions". If you

have actually spotted the additions I made after seeing Courtneidge,[3] it is a fine piece of criticism. But any way, in my own view, the additions, with one doubtful exception, greatly improve the thing— were in fact indispensable.

Of course the repetition of "heroics" is a verbal oversight. But when you object on the ground that the Colonel is always using heroics himself, you remind me of an anecdote. On the first night of SWEET LAVENDER[4] I went, for some obscure reason, to the author's box & sat with the author's wife. When Pinero came in at the end of one of the acts, Mrs. Pin said to him "Oh do you know, Miss Victor is so nervous that she keeps on calling Dick Pheryl Mr. Funnel." "That, my dear" replied Pinero "is the author's humor." I leave you to make the application. Of course a laugh in a quite wrong place would be bad—but I humbly designed the Colonel for a tragi-comic character.

Forgive me for standing up for my one ewe lamb which you want to reduce to a skeleton. I am sincerely grateful none the less. But I needn't ask you to keep mum about your prescription until I have consulted other physicians.

Yours ever,
W. A.

---

1. He probably means "resort."
2. The comparison which springs to mind is with Maeterlinck's *The Burgomaster of Stilemonde,* written in 1917 and published in English (in the translation of Alexander Teixeira de Mattos) by Methuen in 1918, a year before it was published in the original French. Like the Archer play, it was simply a piece of patriotic propaganda, though there is no reason to suppose that Archer had read the Maeterlinck play before writing his own: the point of view expressed was a common enough one at the time.
3. Robert Courtneidge (1860–1939), a theater manager, actor, and minor playwright, who had, in the past, given Barker and Archer some advice upon the writing of the Blue Book. He was also, incidentally, the father of Cecily Courtneidge, the famous comedienne and musical comedy star.
4. Pinero's play, first published in 1888.

BL/TCC
To Barker

[27, Fitzroy Square, W1]
27 Decr. 1919

My dear H. G. B.

Many thanks for your P.P.C. note,[1] which has my best attention. I am going to repay it with a long letter entirely about myself; but you will be able to read it in less time than it took me to decipher yours, so honours are easy.

Of course a "visiting professorship" would amuse me a good deal; but the trouble is, as I see it, that if I am to pull up my roots here, I should have to have something that would keep me going for some time over there, else I should fall between two stools—into the Atlantic? (Never mind the mixture of metaphors.) The younger generation is knocking at the door here,[2] rather peremptorily, & it is a clever younger generation, confound it. So if once one drops out of the running, it's not so easy to find a place again. I discovered that even after my Indian year. I should naturally be delighted to consider a "visiting professorship", & would try to make it possible. But you might keep your eyes open for something more permanent—one never knows what may turn up in that amazing country.

It's not that I want to get away from London as it is; but circumstances might easily arise that would make it very dismal for me, & I want to secure a possible line of retreat.

And that brings me to the second head of this discourse. If I could make a little money—even two or three thousand pounds—out of this blessed play, it would ease the situation enormously. In that case I shouldn't trouble America, but go to Rome & write one or two books I have in mind, & return for the opening of the National Theatre in 1925, & then die happy. Therefore I bespeak your benevolence for THE RAJA OF RUKH.[3] In ten days or a fortnight I shall probably send you an MS of it, & leave it entirely in your hands to do what you think fit with—either place it in the hands of a more or less honest agent, or send it to Winthrop Ames, or to any one else you like. Of course if you see possibilities in it, but think it should be altered before it goes to a manager, I would take it kind if you would say so & point out what you think wrong. I have no amour propre in the matter, & have, indeed, only written the main scenes myself because I couldn't find a collaborator. Even now I would accept a collaborator to touch up the dialogue & put character into the people (the Raja excepted—he is pretty much what I want him to be)—but I don't think the said collaborator should go off with half the fees, unless a total reconstruction were necessary, & in that case I should rather incline to sell the thing outright & wash my hands of it.

When you've read it, I wish you would advise me about England. You know I wrote it for H. B., & I CANNOT see any one else in the part.[4] Ainley's too fat, & is much more of a tabby-cat than a tiger. Wontner is a splendid High Church curate, but hasn't an ounce of the barbarian in him. McKinnel—no, I won't have a Scotch Raja. Is there any one over there that could play the part?

I hope you are having a good time. Love to Helen & best wishes for 1920.

Yours ever

W. A.

---

1. Picture postcard; Barker and Helen, now married, were in America visiting Helen's mother while waiting for Netherton Hall to be ready for them to live in.
2. He is quoting from Act I of his translation of Ibsen's *The Master Builder*.
3. A play which was subsequently re-titled *The Green Goddess*.
4. H. B. Irving had died during the year. The part was eventually played by George Arliss, first in New York in 1921 and then in London.

BL/MS
To Archer

R.M.S. "Aquitania"

23.10.20

My dear W. H.

I thought I'd just send you another line to tell you that just before we sailed came another cable—Helen's mother died last night.

A bad smash for her. That life kept much of her heart in America and it is not good to be quite de-nationalised however much we may love our adopted country.

This means that we shall not stay long I think—but we should get just a glimpse of you when you come. I'll see that Ames knows where I am.

Our love to you,

H. G. B.

BL/MS
To Archer

Netherton Hall,

Honiton,

S. Devon

10.6.21

My dear W. A.

No, I fear we can't get up. I wish we were closer and that you could bring Massey down to call—I'd "certainly" (as they say in the land of The Great Stupidity[1]—useful article) like to meet him. But we must stick to work. Helen is now at a second long poem—the first really very good, but long for a magazine and very "New York" for an English one. I wish I could get her to believe how good much of her stuff is. But oh, she is diffident.

That is the best possible about the G. G.[2] I am sure—Archer, Ames and Arliss.

Now, not so much of your "intellectuals" on me. Tell them I am a popular writer. What I want is a few productions.

Come down again soon. When will you be free?

Yours,

H. G. B.

---

1. Archer had just published an article called "The Great Stupidity" in the *Atlantic Monthy*.
2. Archer's play, now re-titled *The Green Goddess*.

BL/MS
To Archer

Netherton Hall,
Honiton,
S. Devon
22.6.21

My dear W. A.

Helen gave me the lecture. It is indeed good to have you think that and say it about me—makes it worth while to go on trying and trying to get the job right. I have tried at least and I do try and almost all your criticisms I admit at once and the praise makes me, well, more grateful than I can say, for—I'll admit—it is depressing sometimes both to have the things lie there on the shelf and to find it so difficult to do more and to do them a little better, not worse. But you make it <u>well</u> worth while.

I think you said you meant to print the lectures. In case the quotations go in I must send you the "2nd version" of the V. I.[1] It's odd you chose to quote the scene I had re-written most!

This letter is dreadfully "ego".

So glad you are going to Norway—that will be a good holiday—and taking Murray, who'll make it a better one—and you for him. My Mediterranean voyage with him is red-lettered.[2] Come and see us as soon as you come back. I doubt if we shall stir before September. My teeth are in a play (more ego) and Helen's in another long poem.

Bless you,

H. G. B.

1. *The Voysey Inheritance,* originally written in 1903–5; published by Sidgwick and Jackson, 1909; revised, 1913; final version written in 1934.
2. A holiday taken in 1905; see Chapter V below, pp. 210-22.

BL/TS
To Archer

Netherton Hall,
Honiton,
S. Devon
Dec. 13th [1921]

Dictated
My dear W. A.

I must dictate this, but you'll be glad to be spared my hand-writing. I don't place The Magician[1] among your masterpieces, for the reason, I think, that when I get to the end of it I find that the people haven't really interested me very much, and I suppose that's what finally counts. Of course it stands up straight and square and would act and all the rest of it, but my belief is that the dialogue ought to develop the people a little more, and develop them more unexpectedly, if the comedy note is to be kept. And then I feel that you miss a chance in Act II, when Lancelot is brought up against his moral dilemma. To solve that problem over the telephone—no, no, W. A., no, no! It ought I believe to be the material for the play's c'est a faire—oh, comic material if you like, and, most importantly, I believe everybody ought to be brought into it, and something more ought to be left over for Act III, for really there's nothing very much in this but the comic torch business and the disclosure (and inciden-tally, I can't make out why MacNabb didn't know Van Tromp when he saw him). I haven't, I fear, time to read the play through again to discover. I can't write more now, and I fear this is a useless grum-bling sort of letter, anyway. If you'll come to Paris (Elysee-Bellevue Hotel, Rond Point des Champs Elysees) any time before Dec. 28th, or to Hotel Guglielmina, Santa Margherita Ligure, Italy, any time after, I will dispute the matter with you at any length you like. And that it never may be said I forget my promises, here is Drinkwater's Oliver Cromwell.

Yours,
H. Granville-Barker
pp L-K[2]

---

1. A play of Archer's which has not survived; it was neither produced nor published.
2. The letter is signed by Mr. Lister-Kaye, Barker's newly appointed secretary. The

famous hyphen here makes one of its early appearances. There is no way of knowing whether the idea originated with Barker himself, or his wife—or even with his already hyphenated secretary!

BL/TCC
To Barker

[London]
14 December 1921

My dear H. G. B.

My telegram didn't mean that I was impatient, but that I was doubtful of the efficiency of the post war express service. I imagined the MS kicking about among Christmas parcels at the Regent Street P.O.; & as I knew you were off to sunny climes & hadn't your address, the only way of putting salt on your tail was to telegraph.

You don't make the criticism I feared, though I daresay those you do make come to very much the same thing. I feared you would say "Too thin—the public will feel that it is all a much-ado-about nothing, & that they have been unjustifiably spoofed". You apparently don't object on principle to the element of spoof, but want more psychology & ethics & all the rest of it. My reply is that the foundation is too frail to bear any serious super-structure. I have tried to show three or four agreeable ordinary people engaged in an Arabian Night adventure, which is rendered possible through the fact that one of them has made a lot of money (which is the enchanter's wand of modern life), & likes to play with his power. The psychology is as obvious as that of "Aladdin", of which the play is a modern version; the psychology of the average human being is obvious. The demands of this sort of story play are met if the psychology is not obviously wrong. You don't seem to imply that it is, but only that it is shallow—which is God's truth.

As for the two individual points you mention: (a) the telephone incident in Act II is not in my conception to be regarded as by any means the crisis of the play. It merely enables Lancelot to clear away (as he inevitably must) one of the possibilities of the situation— namely that the Visitor is merely bluffing him & has no influence with Macnab & Mendoza. (An appreciative critic would have noted with admiration the name of that firm.) The Visitor has asked him in the first act not to mention him to Macnab, so it is perfectly possible that he is only a crook who has stumbled on the knowledge of Lancelot's appointment, & wants to make capital out of pretending to have influenced it. The telephone incident, in short, is only a mechanical detail of no importance—not in any sense a "solving of the moral problem". There is no moral problem. I don't want anyone to think that Lancelot is for one second tempted to let the Visitor have his way: not that he is quixotically virtuous, but because ordinary conventional honesty is in this case re-inforced by an instinctive resolve not to get on the wrong side of the law. And here, if you like, is profound psychology—to a man of Lancelot's temperament & traditions the vision of the Old Bailey lends an irresistable [*sic*] emphasis to the Ten Commandments.

(b) Macnab did know Van Tromp when he saw him—his whole function in the play is to identify Van Tromp. I think you must mean "Why did not Macnab know & at once declare, that Van Tromp & Percival Pentreath were one & the same person?" The answer is that he did know it, but had been instructed not to let on. Even so, he is on the point of letting the cat out of the bag. When the Visitor says "passed myself off as your uncle", Macnab ejaculates in surprise "Passed yourself off!" & the Visitor shuts him up by saying with emphasis, "Yes, passed myself off."

Your misunderstanding, however, points to what is very probably a technical weakness in the play—a question which, I think, can only be decided by experiment. There are several points in it which are left unexplained. I have what I think a good explanation for all of them, & could give it at the end in half a dozen repliques, only people wouldn't listen. For instance "Why does the Visitor, in the first act, put his foot in it about the family place & the portrait?" My answer is that he deliberately wishes to leave it in doubt whether he is the real uncle or not. If Lancelot had not the slightest reason to doubt his genuineness, then the temptation-scene of the second act would involve a serious conflict, which is what you apparently want, & I don't. The Visitor's deliberate purpose is to see how Lancelot would react to temptation on the part of a crook or a monomaniac, not to put him to the serious test of dealing with a strain of moral obliquity in an undoubted relative and benefactor. The whole fun of the thing seems to me to lie in the doubt. If there were no doubt, the play would be a sentimental comedy in one act. There would be no sense in the fantastic element in the Visitor's conduct. He might just as well introduce himself in the ordinary way, produce absolute proof of his identity (which he could of course do with the utmost ease) &, having failed to make Lancelot his accomplice, say there & then "I was only assaying your mettle—come to my arms my beamish boy!" If the audience can't be got to accept the Visitor as a humorist who delights in playing the star part in a plot of his own inventing then the play undoubtedly falls to the ground. On the other hand, I think he has a quite rational motive for wanting to put to some test this unknown nephew whom he is entrusting with a very valuable collection.

Summa summarum—your impression is discouraging inasmuch as the story in itself doesn't seem to have amused you as much as I hoped it might; but in regard to your actual criticisms, I take comfort in the idea that you apply more exacting standards than the B.P. or the A.P.[1] is likely to apply—that you want the play to stand on a higher level than it aspires to. What I myself feel discouraged about is the realization that it is too English for America. If the scene could be transplanted to the U.S.A. I think it might go down; but you can't import an "oncle d'Amerique" into America.

Love to Helen, who I hope is not overdoing it in the whirl of Gay Paree. (By the way, did she read the play? If she endorses your strictures I am indeed desolate.)

Yours,
[W. A.]

---

1. British Public; American Public.

BL/MS
To Archer

L'Elysee-Bellevue Hotel
Rond Point des Champs Elysees,
Paris
17.12.21

My dear W. A.

Ah no—I wrote in that jargon as an engineer talks in engineering terms of theology and a parson thinks in theological terms of engineering. But what I mean was—and this I think is true—that a play of that calibre must still have, in its own sort, all the qualities and complexities of—let us not say "Waste", but "King Lear". Yes, I do believe that is true. Comic psychology, development of character, unexpected turns of plot: it may all seem simple, it may all be simple, but the comic play must be just as full—though of quite other and lighter matter—as the "serious" one. And my complaint was that your Arabian Night peters out rather, instead of gathering strength as it goes along. But I grant you my opinion is—well, what's anyone's opinion? There's this other aspect too. Have you provided effective spaces for the actors to fill in—if you haven't filled them—as I hold you should have done. If you have (this seems an insult!) then all may be well. But emptiness in a play—no, that won't do. And—bar some such or other elaborations—I think you <u>could</u> have got your story told in 15 minutes. This in a great hurry.

I have seen one quite interesting play here. You will note my opinion of it in the Observer some weeks hence.

Helen <u>did</u> read the Arabian Night—she peruses your work with diligence. <u>Her</u> opinion? Let me tell you she does not always agree with me.

Yours,
H. G. B.[1]

---

1. This handwritten letter is initialed personally by Barker, without hyphens.

BL/MS
To Archer

Netherton Hall,
Honiton,
S. Devon
27.4.22

My dear W. A.

Many thanks for the two tomes, which I now return. I have ploughed steadily through them, from Betterton to ME! And a duller work—!

What is the origin of the division into 5 acts? Who is the best authority on the point? Are you? I have always believed Rare Ben J.[1] to be the culprit, but where I got the idea I don't know.

We saw All's Well at Stratford. My hat!—but William at his worst (though I don't own that is) is an angel compared to the others—to Swinburne's darlings! In fact William had a soul. I do think that company ought to be kept in being. It may not measure up to a high standard but it is the best there is—and could be much better with every chance given it. Any company <u>kept</u> <u>in</u> <u>being</u> will double its value in a year or two, don't you think?

We have both been laid low with colds: Helen hardly recovered. I come to town for a couple of days at the end of this week, but back on Sunday. Then we don't mean to stir for a month. When shall we see you? Let us know when you're free.

Our love,
H. G-B

---

1. Jonson's tomb in Westminster Abbey bears the now-famous epitaph, "O rare Ben Jonson," about which Aubrey, in his *Brief Lives,* has this to say: "Which was done at

the charge of Jack Young [i.e., Sir John Young] who, walking there when the grave was covering, gave the fellow 18 pence to cut it."

BL/TS
To Archer

Netherton Hall,
Honiton,
S. Devon
June 24th 1922

Dear W. A.

I've been meaning to write to you about Gertude, but till yesterday I hadn't had time to look her up. As usual no doubt I go too far, but still I think there's something in it.

Allow all you will for Hamlet's unfairness, for his obsession about his mother's sensual appetites, for his general unhealthy revulsion against the normal world—still I think there is something in it. Gertrude <u>was</u> in a bit of a hurry over Claudius. I read practically the whole of the Closet Scene as an exercise in irony—the reference to the blood being cold and waiting upon the judgement etc.—and I read a great deal into that outburst "assume a virtue if you have it not." What I think master Hamlet means to imply is "Here have I grown up thinking you a model of all the proprieties and virtues, and even now you take care to appear to be so (as all you "good" women do, so that even if you are as chaste as ice, like that child Ophelia, it's really safer to calumniate you), and now I discover what your inner life really is." Well, for all his obsessions Hamlet is no fool, and in Gertrude's make-up (take that in either sense you will) there must be at least this potentiality. Personally, I think that Hamlet's right, and that her conduct shows it, shows that there is that element of a wanton in her. One may make excuses. She has evidently no brains; notice the way she echoes Claudius right up to the Closet Scene, and even takes old Polonius' advice—I expect it was he made her summon Hamlet, and got a rapier in his guts for his trouble—and how feebly she blusters at the beginning of the scene.

When Hamlet has cleft her heart in twain—for the rest of the play—she does improve and acquire a little more personality; but it's easy, I think, to see the sort of lady she is, and it isn't the sort of respectable deep-voiced matron that we're accustomed to.

However, thanks to you I'm modifying my remarks when publishing the paper—though not, you'll be glad to hear, at this inordinate length.

Do come and see us when you can.

Over the Shakespeare Prefaces, they are returning to their muttons—the 3 guinea limited edition. But I am to get complete releases for any I have written, or even shall be writing, after two years, and I am as keen on a cheap edition with notes, as ever. It may take more doing than I think, but I am positive it is a thing to be done.

Yours,

H. G. B.

BL/MS
To Barker

R.M.S.P. Orca
In Havana harbour
30 Jan. 1923

My dear H. G-B

I must tell you of a remarkable letter I received from you last night—in a dream. Perhaps the most remarkable thing about it was that I could read it quite easily; but in dreams one accepts without question marvels of that sort. Anyway, I had no doubts of the authenticity of the missive. You had been reading something of mine, & wrote to warn me, seriously & even sternly, of the philistinism of my critical methods. Lest I should under-estimate the gravity of the situation, you drew a black line down the margin of the page to emphasize your sentiments. The only individual remark I remember was to this effect: "It is absurd to pretend that racy Lacy was prevented by Government from studying life more deeply." I understand this to mean that you understood me to mean that a certain Lacy had been gagged by the Censorship; & I could not imagine what gnat had stung you, for it had never entered my head that the Censorship had meddled with Lacy. Now, in my waking moments, I imagine that there was some despicable scribbler called Lacy in Restoration times (wasn't he an actor-playwright?)[1] but I never read a line of him or concerned myself in any way about him. "Racy Lacy" was entirely an inspiration of the moment.

I wonder what "Freudian wish" the psycho-analysts would discover in this dream?[2] My own interpretation is that it arises from a sub-conscious or semi-conscious realization that the criticism in my forthcoming book "The Old Drama & the New", is sure to be attacked by the younger generation as aridly technical, nationalistic, devoid of depth and spirituality. But it seems odd that this notion should crop up in a dream, for it certainly neither haunts nor perturbs me. Rather, one might say that

> He was more than usual ca'm,
> He did not give a single damn.

If climate is going to cure my ailments (which it isn't) I have certainly come to the right shop. I sit all day on deck under an awning & watch the brilliant sunshine on the pink walls of Morro Castle, & over this gay busy amusing harbour. There is a breeze all day long, & the shade temperature is ideal though the sun is hotter than in an English July. To add to the amenities of the scene, I look along the deck and descry the aristocratically aquiline features of Lord Burnham, slumbering in his deck-chair. I think he must know me, but he doesn't let on, & I am in no haste to claim his acquaintance. I have been very little ashore. The place has sad memories for me & is moreover Americanized out of all knowledge. The streets swarm with Ford "flivvers" to such a degree that they are almost as dangerous as Times Square, and the southern delight in noise leads to a tempestuous use of the motor-horn that is simply intolerable.

As I was coming off in the launch last night, I heard a lady say a nice thing: "They tell me" she said "that this is just about where Hobson sank the 'Maine'." N.B. She was an American. Lord Burnham and I are the only British Anglo-Saxons on board.

My dramatic affairs in New York do not greatly prosper. Ames's failure to rise to "Martha Washington" is a disaster.[3] I can't conceive that it will altogether fail to find a manager, but there aren't two Ameses. He certainly shows a disinterested love of art in spending thousands on "Will Shakespeare"[4] & turning down "Martha Washington". As for "Beatrice Joanna", Miss Marbury says Sam Harris would produce it if I would have Margaret Lawrence for Beatrice but I flatly decline; just as my eminent colleague Shakespeare would have declined Mary Jerrold if she had been proposed for Lady Macbeth.[5] Then there is Miss Blanche Yurka who is "crazy" about the part, but bears a discouraging resemblance to Miss Madge MacKintosh, not in her first youth. Providence doesn't seem to have provided in the matter of actresses for my appearance in the character of the William de Morgan of the drama.

Oh, I must tell you—a few days before I left New York, I lunched with Tancred & Lillebil Ibsen—the queerest experience. Imagine the grandson of those two giants Bjørnson and Ibsen as the prettiest little man you ever saw out of a fashion-plate,[6] with a correspondingly and exquisitely pretty little wife. They are really like Dresden china figurines, to be put under glass shades for mantelpiece ornaments. I like the little lady very much—she is to do Anitra in the Theatre Guild "Peer Gynt". Tancred is evidently no fool, but quite innocent of literary or dramatic interests.

Thank Helen, with my love, for her very welcome letter. I hope you are both prospering physically & spiritually. Love to the Maxes.[7]

W. A.

---

1. John Lacy (?–1681) was the original Bayes in Buckingham's *The Rehearsal* and author of three or four plays which were no more scurrilous than other plays of the period. But Barker was surprisingly puritanical about Restoration comedy (see, for example, chap. 4 of his *On Dramatic Method,* published in 1931), and Archer tends to follow him in this.
2. Archer had become very interested, in his later years, in the meaning of dreams. He had begun systematically to record his own dreams immediately upon waking, and he was working on a book on the subject when he died in 1924. It was published posthumously in 1935, edited by Theodore Bestermann; its title was *On Dreams.*
3. Archer had written a play called *Martha Washington* and had offered it to Winthrop Ames, who had produced and directed *The Green Goddess* in 1921 in New York.
4. A play by Clemence Dane, first produced at the Shaftesbury Theatre, London, on November 17, 1921. Ames's production opened at the National Theatre, New York, on January 1, 1923.
5. This play of Archer's was never produced; it was published in the 1927 posthumous collection called *Three Plays.* Elizabeth Marbury (1857–1933) was a New York literary agent specializing in plays.
6. Ibsen's son, Sigurd, married Bergliot Bjørnson, daughter of the other principal Norwegian dramatist of the period, in 1892. Their son, Tancred, was born on July 11, 1893.
7. Max Beerbohm and his wife.

BL/MS
To Barker

Grove Park Inn,
Asheville, N.C.
12 April, 1923

My dear H. G-B

I suppose you & Helen are back in England long ago—as I shall be myself in about a month from now—I sail on May 5th. It seems to me I wrote you from somewhere in the Gulf of Mexico, though what I said I have no idea. Probably I broke to you the sad news that America regards "Martha Washington" with chilling aloofness. The only chance for her, it appears, is to get her translated into Czecho-Slovak & re-translated into American, when the Theatre Guild will produce her expressionistically, or Arthur Hopkins will commission Robert Edmond Jones to design one scene (principally consisting of stairs) to serve for all the seven tableaux. Well well—I daresay poor Martha's turn will come some day—if only my exit doesn't precede her entrance.

I had a very amusing run round the West Indies & saw a good deal that I hadn't seen before. Then I spent three weeks in the Bermoothes which, though certainly "still-vext" (W. S. had a wonderful knack of getting the right epithet)[1] are extremely delightful and attractive. I think I shall go & lay my bones there—they have delightful, cool, clean, white, coral graves, which they dig by the dozen in advance, the rock being so hard that there is no time for ex post facto grave-making. Furthermore there is an admirable British military band there, in which I revelled after the truly infernal jazz stuff that makes life intolerable at sea now—even on the Majestic. Really and truly jazz is a national disease, a national vice, of the American people. It is a very serious symptom.

Returning from Bermuda, I was a week in New York, where I took Ames to see "Peer Gynt". He thought it the silliest play he had ever seen, & really I couldn't blame him. The Theatre Guild made a truly awful hash of it—in many ways worse than the Old Vic. Yet Schildkraut might have been good if he'd had a little sane guidance. It is really your bounden duty to do a decent production of "Peer Gynt" some day.

From New York I went to Florida, where I spent a delightful week with some very nice Scotch people. The son of the house was married to an ex-actress in a small way—name, Grace Croft—do you remember her at all? She says she was in Chesterton's "Magic" & other things. Thence I was so misguided as to come to this ghastly, pretentious, idiotic place—I wonder if Helen knows it—where America turns her very worst side to you. Praise the Lord, I leave for Boston the day after tomorrow. However, this place is almost as good for work as shipboard—there is no other escape from suicidal boredom. The result is that I have finished a play I began in Bermuda—at least I have done a full draft of it. Now I have to revise & touch up & translate one part into American & another into pidgin-English, in neither of which tongues am I proficient. I try to get my American out of "Babbitt", but he is not a safe guide—he is an independent "realtor" and can say "gosh" & "gee" and "rats" at his ease, which I take it a bank manager can't do with equal fluency. I think the play, in itself, is not without interest, but it has the terrible disadvantage of having no star part. Hitherto I, like Shakespeare, have always looked after my star. Talking of that, I believe I shall have to go next week & see "The Green Goddess" in Providence—

an ordeal from which I shrink. The very thought of that masterpiece bores me. Well, a rivederci fra poco.

Yours
W. A.

---

1. See *The Tempest,* Act I, sc. 2, l. 229.

BL/MS
To Archer

Netherton Hall,
Honiton,
S. Devon.
19.5.23

My dear W. A.

Have you had mumps? If you have you need not fear me. If you haven't you need not fear me greatly. But still consult your safety. I am in bed with a mild one-sided (thank Heaven) attack. Hence my rather more than usually illegible writing. But I'll be up tomorrow—up, but not guaranteed for three weeks. This considered, you have but to say the word. Come and bring your sheaves—of MS!—with you.

Old Drama and New[1] is here and thank you. I am reading it with the greatest interest. It's an irrefragable case, even if it omits—but we'll talk.

As to your sayings about me: I like to think you don't grossly over-praise me—you <u>underrate</u> all the early encouragement you <u>did</u> give to plays that weren't any use, except in intention. The odd thing is that my latest, which you shall read but which I won't read you (no soporifics are needed in Devon), is, so to speak, the "Ann Leete" of my second period.[2] You won't approve it. But from managing to get through writing it (I am Ambitioso, but perhaps—horrible thought!—too Supervacuo as well) I wish I'd read the 1st chapter of O.D. and N. before I finished and corrected an article for the July Quarterly[3]—into which, by the way, I have lifted one of your Ibsen stories. If you regard this as sheer theft I must discover one to exchange—I could have profited by it there.[4]

Our love to you,
H. G-B

---

1. Archer's most recent book was *The Old Drama and the New.*
2. *The Marrying of Ann Leete* was the first play Barker wrote without a collaborator: it

was given its first production (directed by Barker himself) in 1902, when he was twenty-five. The new play which he compares with it is *The Secret Life*.
3. The article was called "The Heritage of the Actor" and appeared in the *Quarterly Review* for July, 1923 (vol. 240, no. 476). It had originally been intended as a preface to *The Secret Life* but was finally deemed to be too long for that purpose and so was published separately.
4. The syntax here is decidedly shaky, though the general import is clear.

BL/MS
To Archer

Netherton Hall,
Honiton,
S. Devon.
29.5.23

Well, I'm damned, dear W. A. Couldn't you have combined business with pleasure? We're all disappointed, including the Maxes, to whom we promised you yesterday. Still, come when you will. A welcome always.

Greet Ames from me and let me know, will you, where to write to him, for I want to get him down here just for a Sunday if I can. I'm officially out of quarantine tomorrow week and I've been up and about these five days, within the garden limits. Our love to you. Don't leave coming too long.

H. G-B

I'll have some sort of a copy of the Secret Life for you soon.

BL/MS
To Archer

Netherton Hall,
Honiton,
S. Devon.
8.6.23

My dear W. A.

The letter, excellent, I think. And it is a matter—and an important matter—of controversy, so I feel you should not let a mis-statement of your position go.

The Maxes don't leave us till Monday and the weekend will be rather crowded. But between this (next) Monday and the next, nobody comes, unless it be Ames for the weekend. He hasn't answered me. I suppose he got my letter. So do come.

Here is The Secret Life for you. Now Sir! Let me have it back sometime soon.

Our love to you

H. G-B

BL/TCC
To Barker[1]

[London]

11 June 1923

My dear H. G.-B.

I spent a whole Sabbath day over THE SECRET LIFE; a very exciting day; & at the end I felt like Napoleon after the Sabbath of Waterloo—defeated in spite of numerous close calls upon victory. I read with constant admiration for the abounding originality, wit & even profundity of the thing, but with despair at the pervading sense that I am at least three generations removed from it. It is written for the next generation, if not for the next again: while I belong to the last generation, & cannot hope to overtake it. I thought again & again in the brilliant second act that I was really getting the hang of the thing & saw the drama crystallizing; but in the third act the crystals seemed to dissolve again, leaving behind them a sort of shimmering opalescence from which I could extract nothing solid. This means that I was looking for something that you didn't want to give, & could not find the thing you did want to give. In very great measure my fault, but also, I think, partly yours—for it is possible to be "though deep, yet clear". The greatest people have done it. In fact I'm not sure that any of the really great—except perhaps Aeschylus, whose obscurity is in part mere remoteness—have failed to do it.

I think I realize (though even in this I may be mistaken) that I am in part quarrelling with the very task you set yourself. Putting the title & the play together, I take it your theme is the importance of the undercurrents of life that never come to the surface. Therefore, if I am right, the absence of outward & visible drama is the very thing you set out to portray. But will you get even an audience of élite to see & accept this? Yes, one audience, two, three— but scarcely more. Perhaps thirty years hence audiences may be purged of all lust for the event, & may have their faculties sharpened & speeded-up to the sort of salmon-spearing by torchlight which the apprehension of your dialogue demands. But the theatre of thirty years hence leaves, & will leave, me strangely cold. I want another VOYSEY INHERITANCE & WASTE; & in this play you seem to be drifting away from, not towards, the theatre that is understood [*sic*] by the people—even the fairly intelligent people.

Of course I must allow for the fact that I saw both the VOYSEY and WASTE on the stage before I read them. Perhaps if I saw this play staged as you would stage it, I should feel differently about it. But the one speech in the play that I can entirely make my own is Susan's at the foot of p. 157—down to the !.[2] Of course a great deal of the dialogue is quite clear, & brilliant, & now & then deep. But it's especially at the crucial points that your people's minds take to working in a way that I never observed in real life—least of all, perhaps, in yourself.

The same post that brought me your proofs brought a long epistle from G. B. S. He agrees with the TIMES reviewer in thinking me an old dodderer talking in my sleep about some obsolete fetish called "construction". But it's nonsense to say, like the TIMES, that construction is as exploded as the unities. The unities never had any common-sense behind them, whereas construction is as common-sensible as the human skeleton—mankind, without it, would have only the intelligence of the oyster, or at best the bee. ALL THE PLAYS THAT HAVE HAD MORE THAN AN EPHEMERAL LIFE IN THIS WORLD ARE MORE OR LESS WELL-CONSTRUCTED PLAYS. I rack my brains to think of an exception to this rule. Of course I don't mean to say that THE SECRET LIFE is an unconstructed play, like HEARTBREAK HOUSE, which lives from moment to moment by the mere shillelagh-whirling of its dialogue. The trouble is, I fancy, that its construction is too subtle, too carefully dissembled. The mind gropes for it, &, not finding it, is desorienté.

Believe me, I'm not trying to make my own dramatic diversions a law for you. In my theatre the bones show through everywhere because I have mighty little flesh & blood to put on them. But if you could strike an average between my obviousness & your elusiveness, posterity might think less of you, but the contemporary theatre would profit more.

After each act I jotted down some interact notes, some of which, at all events, I shall copy out. You will see that I clamor for more information as to the bygone relations between Strowde & Joan & between Strowde & Lady Peckham. But now with the whole play in my eye, I feel inclined to withdraw that demand—I feel that these things don't matter—that nothing depends on them—that we should not understand the present any better for understanding the past. AND THIS, TOO, IS A CRITICISM.

I am perfectly certain, in all sincerity, that I shall see much deeper & more clearly into the play when I have time to read it again. But I read it yesterday with all deliberation, & a play ought to get home the first time, however much further it may get home the second & subsequent times. It is true I thought comparatively little of Ibsen's greatest play—THE WILD DUCK—the first time I read it. That ought to make one humble.

Let us talk these things out when I come down. I don't offer you your revenge upon my improvisations, for no one realises more clearly than I that there is no common measure between such plays as yours & my little melodramas.[3]

Yours in affection & admiration

W. A.

The notes enclosed with this letter follow.

After Act I

It would help if one knew earlier whose the house was; & there seems to be no reason of principle against this; for I note that the stage description of Act II opens "Braxted Abbey, Stephen Serocold's home".

p. 8: I observed the deletion with a glimmer of hope. It seemed as if conviction of sin were coming over you. But I was too sanguine.

p. 14: Why this "but"? Your ligatures of thought often trip me up.

p. 19: "Own". Do you mean that Bellingham is a lawyer? If so, Lloyd George will have you up for libel: if not, the "own" is superfluous.

p. 21: Awkward that Joan should use the same word in two different senses so close together.

p. 24: "Its revenges are simple". One of those speeches (rare so far) which make me feel like a blithering idiot, their application so entirely eludes me.

p. 30: "My marriage!" derailed me. "Hallo!" quoth I, "isn't she his sister?" Having assured myself that she is, I now see the meaning. But I think you'll have to lavish three more words on making it clear.

GENERAL REMARKS: I should be immensely grateful for a little more light on the previous relations of Mr. Strowde & Lady Westbury. What was the barrier between them? Was it objective, in the shape of a husband? or subjective, in the shape of "fine feelings & nice thoughts"?

After Act II

p. 42: A very trifling thing, but would there be any harm in letting us know who "these two" are? Of course one catches on in two seconds; but why keep an audience, or reader, groping for two unnecessary seconds?

p. 44: Three full pages of dialogue, & this is the first hint that Lady Peckham is Serocold's sister.

p. 47: Do you mean a mine that's only on a map, & cotton-field only on & c? If so, why not say so? If not, what do you mean?

p. 48: "Gets that genial" OH No No No—this isn't English. I'm not sure that Dickens doesn't use the locution; but he's the last educated man that did; & he wasn't educated.

p. 53: See post, GENERAL REMARKS

p. 55: I believe you originally wrote "What else is the present?" & then thought: "Good God! Three unnecessary, banal, commonplace words! Out with them!" If it weren't for the stage directions, one would imagine that you proposed cabling the text to America & knew that you saved a shilling for every word you struck out. But the stage directions negative that theory.

p. 60: Note the query.

p. 63: The "and" spoils the rhythm. Save a shilling!

p. 68: Baffling.

p. 71: Note query.

p. 84: If you would let her say "I live among echoes of other boys' voices, my dear", & then let him go on, after a pause "What am I to do please" & c.—it would be one of the most beautiful things in drama. But it would be sentimental, obvious—so the idea must be hidden away in a stage direction where it escapes being obvious by being invisible. The pity of it!

p. 86: £2 squandered.

p. 93: What does "flavourishly" mean?

p. 95: Don't understand "sine qua non me". Could see a glimmer of light in the subsequent "We" were "we" & the "sine qua non me" a mere parenthesis in the sentence.

GENERAL REMARKS: As after Act I, I should be grateful for some light on the external circumstances surrounding the genesis of Oliver. Was Lady Peckham at the time of his birth Mrs. Gauntlett? Did Mr. Gauntlett go to the Upper House as Earl of Peckham? Or did Mr. G. die, & his widow marry Lord Peckham? Was Oliver older or younger than Dolly? And what was the relation in time between this affair & the Lady Westbury idyll? I quite realize that it is an idle & perhaps vulgar curiosity that worries about these details; but one is human. . . .

---

1. This letter is quoted in part in Charles Archer's biography of W. A., pp. 393–94.
2. The speech reads: "It's wrong of me to be impatient just because I don't understand

you . . . or any of you. But this talk about everything, and nothing said about anything!"
3. For further remarks on the play see Archer's letter of September 28, 1923, and Barker's reply of October 1; also T. E. Lawrence's letter, in Chapter VIII, of February 7, 1924.

BL/TS
To Archer

Netherton Hall
Colyton,[1]
S. Devon.
June 22nd 1923

My dear W. A.

You are a brick. I haven't had time yet to go thoroughly into your notes,[2] and to tackle the Brodmeir book will take me weeks. How long may I keep this?

Generally speaking, I expect I merit your stern criticism about the rear stage. The worst of it is I've exposed myself to it unnecessarily, for I do not really mean to concern myself in these Prefaces with how the thing was done, except in so far as the text lays one under obligation to do it that way. What I'm always after is a stage that will enshrine the principles, as far as there are any, according to which W. S. worked. In Macbeth the only things of the sort that are dramatically important to my mind are the scene of the discovery and the last scene.

I dare say (to hark back) they did use the rear stage less than I allow for, but I feel that their playing was probably so elastic and so little stage-managed, in our present sense of meticulous arrangement, that they easily adapted themselves to whatever stage they found themselves on. And of course they did shift the plays about from theatre to Court and private to public theatre (didn't they?) a good deal. I have, by the way, and I expect you have, seen a performance of Götz von Berlichingen given with a rear stage constantly re-set with scenery, the characters beginning the scenes there, coming out of it when need be and the curtains closing on them while the scene was carried on to its end and the next scene set meanwhile.

There is one point about the Elisabethan [*sic*] stage which I fancy we're apt to forget. Our demand to be able to see the entire action of the play and see it all the time is a very modern one. In hardly any old theatre is it possible for the people at the sides to see more than half the stage. When I took the Savoy I found that from a large number of places in the gallery it was practically impossible to see the stage at all.

I don't know what the next plays in the edition are to be, if any, but I shall be thankful to consult you about what I write.

As to those diagrams of Rutherston's,[3] they puzzle me and I've had nothing to do with them. They represent some notion of his own that I expect his illustrations explain, but I haven't seen even these.

Yours,

H. G-B

All I could do was to mildly praise Roughwood,[4] and confess that I didn't know—had forgotten, rather—the other man.

---

1. The post office had just attached the village of Farway to Colyton instead of Honiton (it is a little closer to the former). Barker's letterhead still has the printed "Honiton"; he has crossed it out and typed in "Colyton."
2. These are not the notes which Archer made on *The Secret Life* (see previous letter) but are Archer's comments on Barker's preface to "The Players' Shakespeare" edition of *Macbeth*.
3. Albert Rutherston (formerly Rothenstein) was the general art editor in charge of the illustrations for the Players' Shakespeare, the series of texts of Shakespeare's plays for which Barker was writing the prefaces. These were published by Ernest Benn, Ltd. The plays were published separately, and the intention was to work through the entire canon, but only seven of the plays were actually published. These appeared between 1923 and 1927.
4. He is referring to Archer's concern as to who should play the part of Crespin in *The Green Goddess*. It was, in fact, played by Owen Roughwood, the actor mentioned here.

BL/MS
To Barker

Reform Club
Pall Mall, S.W.1
12 July 1923

My dear H. G-B

I have just read your <u>Quarterly</u> article[1] with high approval. I think it is the best of your prose works to date. It might start a "re-nascence" of English drama (the fourth or fifth within my memory) if playwrights would or could take its doctrines to heart. But that is as much to say if playwrights would or could be men of genius. However, if there <u>should</u> be a genius knocking around at a loose end, & if he <u>should</u> read your article, it might just give him the jolt that would set <u>him</u> going in the right direction.

I find the trouble with St. John Ervine is that I went to America and said that <u>Beyond the Horizon</u> was a much better play than <u>John</u> <u>Ferguson</u>.[2] Now I don't believe I ever said anything of the kind, either in America or any other continent. It never occurred to me to compare the two plays. But if I <u>did</u> think of comparing O'Neill & Ervine—oh Lord! He says you say O'Neill knows all about a play except how to write it, which is a pretty epigram on somewhat familiar lines, but not more than epigramatically true. I don't <u>like</u> O'Neill's work a bit, but he has power, & I don't think St. J. <u>E</u>. is wise to court comparison with him.

There is a ready-made play in today's papers—the Bowes-Lyon case.[3] Title: Harakiri. Young lady turns down young gentleman's advances: young gentleman shoots himself: young lady much cut-up, but young gentleman's father calls upon her & says: "My dear you mustn't let this weigh upon your mind & spoil your life. Adolphus was a selfish young hound & had no right to strike at you in this base fashion—to stab you in the back & run away".[4] Young lady dries her eyes & goes out to tea with Alexander.

Curtain.

Yours,

W. A.

---

1. "The Heritage of the Actors," mentioned above (see footnote 3 on p. 85).
2. *John Ferguson* is by St. John Ervine; *Beyond the Horizon* is by Eugene O'Neill.
3. Angus Patrick Bowes-Lyon, son of the Hon. Patrick Bowes-Lyon and nephew of Lord Strathmore (and first cousin of Elizabeth Bowes-Lyon, who had just married Prince Albert, the Duke of York, the future King George VI), committed suicide upon receiving a letter from his fiancée, Miss Freda Parsons, breaking off her engagement to marry him.
4. Archer's characterization of the father does not correspond with that of the suicide's father as described in newspaper accounts of the inquest that day.

BL/MS
To Archer

Netherton Hall,
Colyton,
Devon.
14.7.23

My dear W. A.

Damn it, I am the genuis!! The Q.R. article (which I rejoice indeed you approve of) was begun as a preface to The Secret Life. Now please say you knew this all the time.

The enclosed was sent me. Will you look through it and let

me have it back. W. de B. (who is an ass anyhow) has got his figures all wrong.[1] Do you think that you ought to indite a letter to the Times correcting them on the ground—and I think it is a good one—that Hansard stands as a record and that, uncorrected, this must stand to the prejudice of the N.T. in the eyes of possible advocates and benefactors.

In haste,
H. G-B

Our love to you.
Really I am glad you approve of the Q.R. But I've a muddled head—that's the truth. I didn't say quite that, or—rather—only that, about O'Neill. But he reflects the N. Y. theatre and the praise lavished on him reflects the N. Y. critical standard. He has guts though.

---

1. Barker had received a copy of the Hansard report of the debate of July 4, 1923, in the House of Lords on the subject of the Shakespeare Memorial Theatre in which Lord Willoughby de Broke had referred to the Barker-Archer book of 1907, *A National Theatre,* and said it asserted that "you could not sustain a national theatre in this country unless you were prepared to spend at least £70,000 or £80,000 a year."

BL/MS
To Archer

Hotel Lotti,
7 et 9, Rue de Castiglione,
Paris.
5.9.23

My dear W. A.

A triumph for your Green one[1] and to you. And may she resound and redound and abound to your credit and your cash balance for many months to come. Such is the wish, Sir, of your obliged and affectionate friends, Helen and Harley G-B.

We are on our way home from the Pyrenees, via Albi we came: did you never see Albi? Arriving at Netherton on Sunday. And we hope to see you soon.

Bless you.
H. G-B

---

1. *The Green Goddess* was due to open at the St. James's Theatre the next day.

BL/MS
To Archer

Netherton Hall,
Colyton,
Devon.
15.9.23

My dear W. A.

My thoughts did turn to you and yours when the news came from Japan.[1] But then I said—oh, no, all your people were back. I never thought of a younger generation. A ghastly business. And I suppose we can't appreciate the extreme confusion—of mind as of all else—that results. People going anywhere, saying anything, believing anything. This to account perhaps for the strange cablegram. And now we hear the reports have been "exaggerated": "only 200,000 or so" killed. You don't happen, do you, to have heard anything of Robert Nichols and his wife—the only people we knew out there. I fancy he was holidaying in California.

We shall be in town from the 8th to the 18th and hope to see you—and the G. G.

You had my letter from Paris and Helen's telegram?

Lord, but this world's mad enough. Earthquakes aren't needed.

Our love to you,
H. G-B

---

1. News had just reached England of a severe earthquake in Japan. Archer's nephew was killed in it.

BL/MS
To Archer[1]

Netherton Hall,
Colyton,
Devon.
19.9.23

My dear W. A.

Well, of course, the double theatre makes for actual economy in running a repertory—say 1½ times the receipts at 1¼–1⅓ times the costs. This is the only important discovery I've made since we wrote the book. My idea is that this competition[2] may "document" designs as the book has to a large extent "documented" the rest of the scheme. Hence the importance of this.

I should have thought that in drawing up the specification for the competition the smaller auditorium etc. might be provided for but not demanded in any detail, i.e. a plan for the whole building, an elevation, details of the larger auditorium and larger stage, etc., etc. I fancy the more unusual task might make it more interesting to the architect.

As to the public—well, it is our business to educate them. And they are so little inclined to the project anyhow at the moment that an extra auditorium will hardly be noticed as a "damper": it might even serve to make them sit up and take notice if it seems unusual.

Blessings on you.

About the Secret Goddess—I mean the Green Life—I met a politician here the other day—or a "statesman", may be, as he has been in the government; and he had got the hang of it all at one go. Never asked whether it would "act" or anything: which pleased me.

H. G-B

---

1. Short extracts from this letter and Archer's complete reply are quoted in Charles Archer's biography of W. A., p. 395.
2. A proposed competition for a design for a national theater.

BL/MS
To Barker

Reform Club,
Pall Mall, S.W.1
20 Sept., 1923

My dear H. G-B.,

There's a lot in your views on the duplex theatre question. They shall be duly submitted to the Committee. I fancy it is really a matter for architectural opinion—will the architects come forward? As you say, they might be tempted by the larger problem.

But what is this about the alleged "statesman"—a d—d diehard I hope—who showed his intelligence by never asking whether "The Secret Life" would act? If you are going to ignore that question, why do you write plays at all? Why subject yourself to the manifest and manifold drawbacks and trammels of the dramatic form, if you are writing for "the study"? That slip-shod, go-as-you-please thing, the novel, is the thing for the study, and all Downing Street shall not persuade me that it is a matter of indifference whether a play "would act". I daresay "The Secret Life" would act very well. I daresay that is just what it wants to clear up what I find cloudy in it. Of course your statesman might feel a delicacy in putting the question to <u>you</u>; but if he did not ask <u>himself</u> whether it would act, he was one of those drama-blind numskulls [*sic*] who are the curse of the British nation, and the real obstruction to the National Theatre. So there!

I attended last night a Green Room Club supper to Arliss—du Maurier in the chair—quite good fun.

Love to Helen from

Yours,
W.A.

BL/MS
To Archer[1]

Netherton Hall,
Colyton,
Devon.
22.9.23

No, no, no, no, no, no, no, no! What I meant to imply was that the statesman (none of your diehards; vice-chairman of the L. of N. [League of Nations] Union) had found the S. L. simple enough, possibly because his understanding of it was not balked by the recurrent question, "Will this act?" When I told him he need not expect to see it on the stage he said, indeed, "Why not? Couldn't you get it acted?" I answered, too optimistically: "Yes. I could get the actors, but not the audience that would listen."

I protest I never have—I <u>cannot</u>—write an unactable play; it would be against nature, against second nature anyhow: I act it as I write it. But there is no English company of actors so trained to interpret thought and the less crude emotions, nor, as a consequence, any selected audience interested in watching and listening to such things. But that, believe me, human fallibility apart—mine, to begin with—is the extent of the difficulty.

So blessings on thy still unfrosted pow[2]
John Anderson, my Jo.

H. G-B.

---

1. This letter is quoted in full in Charles Archer's biography of W. A., p. 396.
2. "Pow" is a Scottish dialect word meaning "head" (i.e., "pate"). The reference is to a Robert Burns poem; the first verse is as follows ("jo" means "sweetheart"):

John Anderson, my jo, John,
When we were first acquent,

Your locks were like the raven,
Your bonnie brow was brent;
But now your brow is beld, John,
Your locks are like the snow;
But blessings on your frosty pow,
John Anderson, my jo!

BL/TCC
To Barker

[London]
28 Septr. 1923

My dear H. G-B.

As I promised, or threatened, I have re-read THE SECRET
LIFE, very slowly & attentively, stopping to worry out knotty points,
& not easily letting them beat me. I want to try to clear my own
mind about it, & I know of no better way than to put my thoughts
about it on paper in a letter to you. But don't read it unless you
really want to. It is I myself (if anybody) that I hope may profit by it.

First, then, I lay the book down with an even higher admiration than before for the intellectual effort it represents. It is often
very witty, & it abounds in fine & suggestive & memorable things.
As a piece of literature, in short, apart from its specific merits as
drama, I rank it very high indeed.

Now to regard it as drama. In that aspect I enjoyed it much
more than I did before. I read the first act with keen interest, because I now knew who the people were, & was not always going off
on false scents. In the second act my interest rose to enthusiasm. It is
a quite brilliant piece of work, & I would give a lot to see it, & the
first act, played. In the third act I confess I cooled off a good deal. In
the other two I had a comfortable sense of being, as a rule, quite
within my depth: here I had the opposite sense, of being, as a rule,
out of my depth—diving into deep waters & only occasionally bringing up a pearl.

The great question is, as I see it: will this new technique
with which you are experimenting justify itself? (I rather fancy it is a
reversion to the technique of your very earliest plays, but there's no
importance in the word "new"—let us say this different technique.) I
have seen too much of the misadventures of critics who scoffed at a
new technique simply because of its unfamiliarity to want to imitate
them—but I have grave misgivings. I suspect this technique is too
personal, too negative, too irreducible to common-sense principles, to
have much chance of establishing itself. It is a technique for genius

only, & another genius will evolve his own technique. Of course you may say that is all right—you don't want to <u>faire</u> école, but only to express yourself in your own way. But my point is that a technique which is a real advance, which is in the true line of evolution, will "make a school", will, so to speak, meet a felt want, & will thereby impose itself on the public. I don't believe that the highest forms of drama ever have been, or ever will be, caviare to the general, though no doubt they have been fully appreciated only by the few. I am in mortal fear of seeing you become the eponymous hero of a Barker Society, meeting monthly at University College to read papers on your philosophy, & giving a Barker Festival every three years at the Lyric, Hammersmith.

What is the substance, the nucleus so to speak, of THE SECRET LIFE? Act I: A man & woman who have loved each other but shrunk from kicking over the traces, meet in middle life & indulge in a pensive retrospect. At the end of the act the woman learns (off stage) that her husband is dead: CURTAIN. Act II: They meet again after nine or ten months, & decide not to marry: CURTAIN. Act III: News arrives that the lady is dying of tumor on the brain. The man drops the threads of a political situation & sets off to America to see her, but is (if I understand rightly) recalled by a wireless message that she is dead. I have no doubt stated things crudely, but correct the language as you like—that is, so to speak, the backbone of the play. It is true that in Act II a second motive announces itself: the man has had an illegitimate son, now one of his entourage, who ultimately becomes his secretary. But of this nothing comes except an exchange of sentiments. It has (so far as I can discover) no influence whatever on the main theme. It is a pure side-show. Thus the essential personages of the play are two: Evan & Joan. Of the side-show the essential personages are two: the same Evan & Oliver. At a pinch we might add a third: Lady Peckham. Thus at the outside four persons are organically concerned in the two actions. The other eight characters form a brilliant portrait-gallery, but are there, so to speak, fortuitously—they might be replaced by any other six or eight or twelve or fifteen portraits without making any essential difference to the story. That word slipped out unintentionally—but after all, we must use the old nomenclature until a new is invented.

Now consider a few of the things that the vulgar playwright would have done with this theme. He would almost certainly (it would have been quite easy) have let the audience know or suspect before the scenes between Joan & Evan that her husband was dead. He would certainly have conveyed the news to Joan on the open stage, possibly in the presence of Evan, though better, perhaps, leav-

ing her to pass on the news to him. The conjuncture offers a larger
choice of possible scenes of open, as distinct from suppressed, drama.
So does the Evan-Oliver-Lady Peckham conjuncture. Oliver might
have learnt the secret of his birth suddenly & by some accident in the
presence of both his father & his mother. Or he might have stood in
some relation to his father—might have been pursuing some course of
action to him—which might have impelled his mother to reveal the
secret to him, only to find that he had known it all the time, & that
this knowledge was precisely the motive of his action. These are only
two out of many possibilities of vulgar drama. Then, again, the commonplace playwright would certainly have tried to interweave the
Joan motive with the Oliver motive—the possibilities are so numerous I need not speculate upon them. I think, too (though this is not
so clear) that our conventional friend would not have killed Joan with
a tumor—apparently as fortuitous as a flash of lightning or an earthquake—but would have made her death in some way traceable to, or
associated with, her refusal of life. I needn't go on—the possibilities
of vulgar drama are infinite, & I know that you have deliberately
renounced them all. But isn't the renunciation a bit too austere? Isn't
your ideal of suppression, retrospection, quietism au delà des forces
humaines?

You understand, of course, that I am not, for the moment
at any rate, claiming any superiority for the common or garden methods. I am only confronting the two ways of doing the thing in order
the better to understand yours. You have of course chosen it with
open eyes & quite realize what you are about. But I wonder if you
quite realize what a preponderantly reflective, gnomic tone (a word
used in the best Balliol circles) this method gives to your dialogue.
Your people are too busy philosophising—generalizing—about life,
ever to think about doing anything. From this one play I could select
a complete Granville-Barker Birthday Book with a sententious, often
a profound, reflection for each day in the year, each reflection complete in itself, without any reference to the character uttering it or to
the dramatic context. Of course I don't mean by this that the reflections are out of character. On the contrary, each character consists
in the general tone of his or her reflections. I don't say that they
wouldn't lose something by being snipped out of their context. But
they would be self-explanatory, & no one, picking up the birthday-
book, would feel them to be incomplete. This reflective method is
not for a moment to be confounded with Ibsen's retrospective
method. Ibsen withdrew veil after veil from the happenings of the
past. They might be external happenings or happenings in the soul,
but they were events, not mere ideas. In brief, your dialogue seems

to me too highly intellectualized for "human nature's daily food". It makes me think of the lines of Wordsworth which he himself rather tactlessly quoted in Macready's presence a day or two after Macready's assault upon Bunn:

> Action is transitory—a step, a blow,
> A motion of a muscle—this way or that—
> 'Tis done; & in the after vacancy
> We wonder at ourselves like men betrayed.

Your people never move a muscle, & I confess I sometimes wish they would—would give their grey matter a rest, & hit somebody.

This play entirely explains to me the slowness of its production. There are only a limited number of ways of doing the positive thing, but a quite unlimited number of ways of doing the negative thing, & I quite understand the embarrassment of choice. In the mind of a dramatic story-teller, a play grows from its germ with a sort of necessity, &, sometimes at any rate, he has to make haste in order to keep pace with its growth. But you, with an irreducible minimum of story to tell, & having renounced the scene à faire, the effet à chercher—setting out rather in quest of the effet à manquer (no, I mean the effet à eviter)—have the whole universe from which to select the cubes for your mosaic. I feel that you might go on all your life writing different versions of the same play—keeping what I have called your organic characters the same, but selecting a different set of reflections from the illimitable number possible, & surrounding them with a different set of inorganic personages, selected at random from WHO'S WHO.

Perhaps—indeed most probably—I am only an old fogey falling behind the march of progress. I always was an intellectual without much intellect. I never cared a cuss for Ibsen's ideas, but only for the stark drama of his work. Reduced to its basic elements, my aesthetic creed is "Cut the cackle & come to the 'osses".[1] But the point about Ibsen's cackle was that you couldn't cut a line of it without leaving a palpable gap in a closely-woven fabric of which the warp was character & the woof event. And my old-fogeydom only began at the fourth act of THE MADRAS HOUSE. Up to the end of the third act, I was in the foremost files of time. But now I confess my slogan (as Mr. Kittredge[2] would say) is BACK TO THE VOYSEY! I regard that as the perfect balance of character & action, & a masterpiece of effect without banality. You will say that an artist can't mark time—but can't he? I don't think Shakespeare was doing much more than marking time in the sequence HAMLET, OTHELLO, LEAR and MACBETH. Perhaps you may say that he presently progressed to TROILUS

and CORIOLANUS. I don't myself regard it as progress; but even supposing it was, you have plenty of time to give us your TROILUS when I
shan't be there to cavil at it.

I am in two minds about sending this letter at all. I feel that
I am playing with clumsy fingers upon a delicate instrument, & may
simply put it out of tune. But whatever you may think of my taste or
tact, I am sure you can't doubt my good-will, & will let that cover a
multitude of sins.

Yours ever affectionately,
W. A.

---

1. A popular saying, meaning, "Get down to the real business": it comes from the
   British theater of the early nineteenth century, when popular plays often included
   daring displays of equestrian skill.
2. A character in *The Secret Life*.

BL/MS
To Archer[1]

Netherton
1.10.23

My dear W. A.

You are a brick—you are a whole edifice of bricks. Sir, you
are a moral cathedral of Albi (q.v.).[2] But seriously—good to have
such a letter—and such a friend.

For besides it being so cheering to have you look this far
into the thing, to have you care to, it is tremendously useful as a
test—which I can make it—of how far I'm on the right road and
where I stray. I know I haven't arrived. But—as a first response—the
part of the technique that most worries you I mean to belong only to
this particular play, as germane to its particular subject. God do so to
me and more also if I intend to continue in it arbitrarily.

Now all that follows will be scrappy, but I have rather—to
save time—to take your letter as it comes and my thoughts on it as
they come.

The only technical axiom—I think the only one—which the
modern development of drama seems to have brought us—brought
me—to is "illusion of Life". To gain that I am inclined to sacrifice
thesis and story (in a story's sense of beginning, middle and end). I'm
prepared for material and external conventions. A theatre's a theatre.
I don't want unity of time or place and I admit—one must—convention of dialogue. I don't want untidy "natural" talk: it dissipates
strength and one has no time for it. So that accounts both for my

present notions of mechanism and of construction i.e. the slicing out
(apparently) of a protagonist's life of a simple sequence of events. I
would sacrifice much else to gain this illusion.

The later Ibsen is my master. And, by the way, what you
say about his "revealing" technique is most pertinent and convicts me
of betraying him. I don't name Tchekov. But (or "for" or "though")
it was when I saw the Moscow people interpreting Tchekov that I
fully realised what I had been struggling towards—and that I saw how
much actors could add to a play.

And now for the S. L. I am very rejoiced that on a third
reading (poor patient W. A.!) first and second acts became clear
(enough) to you. For I am convinced that actors can convey that
clarity by impersonation at a first sight and hearing—even if not exactly in those terms. An audience, that is, would get at the play's
meaning as one gets at a situation in the lives of real people near to
one, by a mixture of explanation, apprehension, observation. Nor am
I disappointed that Act 3 leaves you hanging loose; for it is the weak
act and it hangs loose. I'll own why later.

Of course, it all depends—I admit—on how much actors can
do. I bank on that but I think I know—given (Oh Lord!) the right
actors.

And—now to controvert you a little—I do deny that the
dialogue is too intellectualised. I have tried and tried to make it
simple. Of course there are spots where I'll have failed. But I don't
believe there are ten sentences the meaning of which cannot be made
clear in the instant. And—except for a little information, sheer character building and a conversational effect or so—I don't believe there
is one line that is not charged with emotion. But—and this I think to
be one of the modern dramatist's hardest problems, not to have only
"plot" in one speech and "passion" in another—the emotion often,
of necessity, underlies the argument. But it is there for the actor to
express.

And I protest that Evan-Oliver-Lady P. is not a side show
and that my other characters are not fortuitously out of "Who's
Who". No, here I am a little surprised at you.

It would be instructive, by the way—but long and very very
boring—to tell you the history of the play's development. How story
begat characters and then characters took on life and not so much
altered the story as reversed its emphasis; and, their tragedy being a
tragedy of negation, created round themselves (with my connivance)
what you justly call a negative technique as being the most fitted to
express them.

The tragedy of Evan and Joan is, if you like, the tragedy of

the barrenness of idealism. And the larger question involved in the
play is, I suppose, the very dreadful one, "How to propagate spiritual
goodness?" Not that I've any answer, of course. The nearest I can
come to it is Mr. Kittredge's "What I've learnt is how to sit here and
hold your hand" and "The generation of the spirit is not as the generation of the flesh, etc."

(Letter resumed a day later and thread somewhat lost) Joan
encounters on the one hand a "love she cannot live"; on the other
she accepts the "Devil's own second best"—though I don't quarrel
with her for that: the second best may be the best possible. Anyhow
the war and its consequences rob her of the emblems of it—her husband and sons. The war does for Evan's political idealism, too. I
couldn't enlarge on this for fear of making it too topical. In contrast
to this is set (beside the practical unemotional domestic life with Eleanor) the entirely un-ideal Lady Peckham and the consequences of
his un-spiritual liaison with her. She loses her son—in an entirely opposite sense to that in which Joan loses hers—for she can no longer
be of use to him, can give him nothing more that he wants. But
neither can Evan take him; he was begotten only of the flesh and not
of the spirit. Though, as Lady P. says, "If you can't take what's your
own I don't know what's to do you good". That is the play's main
"opposition". Then you have Dolly—the healthy young animal who
has been through nothing; Mr. Kittredge, who has been through
everything and says—laughingly (and this contrast is not important)—
that he now feels in his spirit the stirrings of a reckless youth. You
have Oliver, with all his idealism turned inside out, as it were, having
"given himself away" completely at the call of the war and feeling
that he ought to be—and is—dead. And Susan, silent all through the
second act, with her belief that life is a thing to be used wisely and
(bless her New England morality) that everything is quite simple if
people will only do their work and be good. Then there are the three
pointers: the Jew, the wordly-wise "superior" cynical intellectual; Sir
Leslie Heriot, the "practical" politician for whom ethical problems
don't exist except to supply him with platitudes; and Lord Leverhulme—or whatever I call him[3]—to whom, for the sake of the young
people and the future (not an ideal future in any sense, but one in
which "for comfort's sake they'll lead their busy lives", Oliver being
raised from the dead), to whom is given the last word, "Righteous-
ness is profit" etc. I had forgotten Serocold, but he is an allowable (I
think) solvent.

No, really, they are not fortuitously out of Who's Who.

Act III is weak, because I had speculated on the Oliver-
Evan theme fructifying and it doesn't. You can discover just where it

fails to; their scene is abruptly cut off. I tried and tried to complete it, but couldn't. Of course, in a sense, it is the right tragedy of the situation that they can't get into any fruitful touch with each other. But it is a dramatic misfortune. I ought not to have run that risk.

If I wanted to condemn the play—and I have condemned it, damned it, many a time—I should say that the subject is not really suitable for dramatic treatment. But as I have told you, it grew. The characters grew that way and the technique adhered to them. And I thought I would push through with it.

I hope all this won't bore you; you've been so good. And I do rejoice in the trouble you take with me.

What you say about the retrospective as against the reflective method shall go upon the tablets of my memory.

Our love to you.

We are to be in town from the 8th to the 18th. Mind we see you.

H. G-B

---

1. This letter is written on plain paper rather than Barker's usual letterhead. Above the salutation Barker wrote, "Not read over, but I trust legible."
2. See Barker's letter to Archer of September 5, 1923.
3. He means that Lord Clumbermere, the character in *The Secret Life,* somewhat resembles William Hesketh Lever, first Viscount Leverhulme (1851–1925), well-known industrialist, philanthropist, and politician, who made his money from the manufacture of soap.

BL/TCC
To Barker

[London]
5 October, 1923

My dear H. G-B.

As chance (or possibly Satan) will have it, I have read your letter on a morning when I am actually at a loss for something to do: therefore I put on paper some vague speculations which might otherwise have kept till we meet. Your handwriting has this advantage, that it necessitates slow & careful reading—no galloping, no skipping. The following are some of the notions engendered by a very deliberate perusal of your holograph.

I wonder whether you are not too much under the dominion of General Ideas?—such, for instance, as "Illusion of Life". I don't think the two dramatists with whom I am most familiar, William Shakespeare & William Archer, ever bothered about such things. They wrote the masterpieces that came to them, following the lines of least resistance, & then (if they had nothing better to do) invented their aesthetic principles afterwards, in a concatenation according. As Shaw used to say, "A man commits a crime because he wants to, & the police assign a motive afterwards." What I say is "Write your plays & let the critics discover your principles." I know this isn't very helpful advice if you have once contracted the habit of "thinking too precisely on the event". But think over this point of view.

"Illusion", anyway, is a desperately elusive idea. Does it exist at all? & if so in what sense? Of course you know that the young lions of today have altogether thrown it overboard, regarding it as an invention of the devil. I am far from agreeing with them: I think it is something real & something desirable. But the deuce of the thing is that it is a subjective condition which is identical in no two individuals. The sailor in the gallery who cries out "Don't you believe him Miss! He's married already!" is under an illusion which you & I could never attain: & the thing that illudes him seems to us childish. Then, again, we have the frame of mind which finds that a recall[1] at the end of an act "destroys all illusion". It doesn't for me: I don't attempt to carry illusion forward through the interacts: but the Italian practice of taking a recall in the middle of an act, after an effective exit, does destroy something which I call illusion. Talking of that, my wife tells me that Arliss said something to her which interests me: he said that he finds that he can keep "in the part" through an interact of about 8 minutes, but not longer. I should take this more seriously if Arliss did not yield upon the very gentlest compulsion to the American craze for demanding a speech from a star between the last two acts of a play. In sum, the mental state which we describe as illusion is one of enormous complexity, differs with each individual, & seldom or never amounts to the only condition which really deserves the name of illusion—the condition, namely, which would lead us to act as though the illusive presentation were real.

I fancy, then, that when you talk of the illusion of life you take as a standard whatever state of your own mind you are in the habit of calling illusion. I am far from saying or thinking that this is a false principle: it is probably the only one on which a sincere artist can proceed. But the state of your own mind is not an instinctive, inborn thing, a ready-made gift of God, so to speak. It is a product of an incalculable complex of experiences & influences; & unless your experiences & influences have induced in you a state of mind which roughly resembles the state of mind of some thousands of your contemporaries, it can afford no guide towards acceptance in the theatre. And one thing seems to me plain: in the theatre, interest must precede illusion, not vice-versa. That is where the necessity for story

comes in, & for a certain continuity & clarity of story. Any reasonably skilful producer could put on the stage a hundred scenes of modern life which could create absolute visual illusion, & any Anstey, or
E. V. Lucas, or Pett Ridge could supply the figures with chatter
which would at least not mar the visual illusion—it might even be
quite clever dialogue. But the illusion produced would not begin to
be <u>dramatic</u>, until some thread of <u>interest</u> had been introduced &
developed. Then—to take a second step in the argument—you of all
people don't need to be told that the art of creating & maintaining
interest in the theatre is a thing by itself, dependent on the most
complex & elusive conditions of mass-psychology. Whence it would
seem to ensue that, for the dramatist, the principle of illusion doesn't
fill the bill. It is, & ought to be, one principle in his Decalogue; but
there are at least nine other Commandments, all of which must be
observed on pain of a much more swift & certain damnation than the
theological one.

All this is quite elementary; but it sometimes helps to go
back to the rudiments & make sure that you haven't forgotten your
A B C. I have written quite without thought of THE SECRET LIFE.
Probably something of what I have said would be found to apply to
it, but I have not attempted to make the application.

Now to go to another matter. I think the reason that I am,
however unwillingly, an unsympathetic critic of a good deal in THE
SECRET LIFE, & of <u>something</u> even in your other plays, is that I am
congenitally obtuse to General Ideas in relation to the conduct of life.
I am only stating this limitation, not for a moment defending it. If I
were called upon to account for it, ex post facto, I think I should say
that men seem to me to be very slightly influenced by general ideas.
They have played no part in my own life, & I think the people who
really shape their course in accordance with them are very few, & are
apt to be what the eighteenth century called enthusiasts & we call
cranks. Whatever badges we may wear & catchwords we may adopt,
we are all abject utilitarians, & follow through life the line of least
resistance. When we think we are not doing so, we are under an
illusion. Our principles are only our fundamental prejudices. Of
course it is of great consequence that our prejudices should not be
too stupid or too blindly egoistic; & as what we vaguely call idealism
means a set of prejudices opposed to individual greed, stupidity &
cynicism, I have a general sympathy with idealism. But I think the
area of conduct in which we can even imagine our actions to be determined by free-will is very small, & consequently man as a "free
moral agent", guiding his conduct by large or subtle philosophic
views, does not greatly interest me. I feel that I am fumbling around

after a thought here, & not quite finding it—like Beerbohm Tree as described by Stevenson, "fishing for an idea in the bottomless pit he calls his mind". Perhaps the best way to put it would be to say that when we talk about principles & "isms" & such-like things we are not getting down to fundamental motives. Our unconscious or semi-conscious biases are so much more important than our conscious principles. Perhaps you may say that this is a horrible pessimistic necessitarianism, & that free-will is the essence of drama. But I am not a pessimist as regards the race, whatever I may be as regards the individual life. On the contrary, I am a long-distance optimist, for I am convinced that the fundamental prejudice or bias in human nature is a bias towards the Good, that being definable as something not at all unlike our old friend "the greatest happiness of the greatest number". I think that bias is bound ultimately—in centuries or millenniums—to make the world a reasonably habitable place; & then will be the time to decide whether life is worth living. The practical point is perhaps this: that I find your people too much disposed to explain themselves in general terms, without "getting down to cases." . . . I had to break off a little way back, & have rather lost the thread of my discourse—for which you may be devoutly thankful.

I was at Grove Lodge yesterday afternoon, & was rather shocked by J. G.'s[2] appearance. He looked, somehow, ghostly & fragile. He talked quite cheerfully, but has evidently had a serious set-back.

Of course we must meet when you are in town, but please let us seize the first opportunity, for I am likely to be a great deal away between this & the end of the month. And, by the way, we will NOT meet at Poel's lecture. I have a high ideal of the duties of friendship, but they do not include the obligation of listening to that old bletherer.

Love to Helen from

Yours long-windedly
W. A.

---

1. I.e., the actors coming forward at the end of each act to receive applause, which used to be the practice in the presentation of plays and still is, usually, in the presentation of opera.
2. John Galsworthy lived at Grove Lodge, Hampstead, when in London. He at this time was greatly worried over family matters, especially his wife's health and the break-up of his sister's marriage.

BL/TCC
To Barker

[London]
17 Decr. 1924

My dear H. G-B.

I have learnt today, to my great disgust, that I shall have to undergo an operation—the removal of a cyst or tumor somewhere in the region of the kidneys. I go into a nursing home tomorrow. I don't know that it is a very serious affair, & in fact I feel as fit as possible—I have had no pain or even uneasiness from the beastly thing. However, accidents will happen, & if they should happen I want to ask you to give my executors the benefit of your advice regarding the disposal of my dramatic works. The said exors. are my brothers Charles & James, who of course don't know very much about the theatre. I have instructed them, unless they see good reason to the contrary, to leave my affairs in the hands of Curtis Brown, but, when in doubt about anything, to ask you for your opinion. I hope all this is needless "proticipating", but there's no harm in being prepared.

You may of course take no news for good news; but as soon as I am fit for anything I shall let you have de mes nouvelles.

If I do go out, it will be in a blaze of social glory—I lunched today with the King of Norway & Prince Olaf, & actually exchanged about five & twenty words with his Majesty, who, by the way, seems a very nice fellow.

I went yesterday to a performance of FRATRICIDE PUNISHED, prefaced by an address by that arch impostor Poel.[1] I came away convinced that the thing is worthless as evidence as to Kyd's play, for it is manifestly post-Shakespearean. A lot of the stuff in it is Shakespeare, though terribly misremembered & murdered.

G. B. S. has taken like an angel my article on him in the BOOKMAN. I am especially glad in view of this operation business.

I hope you are all right & are settling down comfortably in Paris. Love to Helen from

Yours ever affectionately,
W. A.[2]

---

1. For another reference to Poel and *Fratricide Punished,* see n. 3 to the letter of March 7, 1937, to Bridges Adams in Chapter X below.
2. This was the last letter that passed between them. Archer died ten days later from the after-effects of the operation to which he refers in this letter.

Published letter
To the *Times Literary Supplement*[1]

Netherton Hall,
Colyton,
Devon.

Sir,

Will you allow me to ask the sympathetic reviewer of William Archer's "Life" to explain what he means by saying in conclusion that the writing of *The Green Goddess* "contradicted his life-long principles"? I should have thought that the peculiar strength of Archer's position as a dramatic critic lay in his patient willingness to appreciate any play of any kind if he could only discover it to be good of its kind. This certainly was one of the chief grounds of his influence in the theatre. While other literary men were apt to be off-hand with whatever they did not choose to call literature, he was always ready to apply the more purely dramatic, even the purely theatrical, test. Too ready, was the accusation that some of us were inclined to bring against him! It was an ill-considered one. For, coming into the inheritance, which he had done so much to prepare, of a drama and literature made, approximately at any rate (I quote your review), "one flesh", we too readily forgot the novelty and jeopardy of the union. His complaisances towards the more skittish partner to it were politic. Later there were those who, like your reviewer, would insist on identifying him solely with the sterner side. Again, he refused to be. To quote from the biography and a letter about *The Green Goddess* and its success: "I was amused by a remark of Desmond MacCarthy's in the *New Statesman*. He said he was glad I was no longer a critic, for this was not the sort of play I would have approved. But I don't know. I always had a weak spot for melodrama."

That is the Archer of 1923 looking back down the long hill (the road, he feared, now beginning to dip again) which he has climbed together with his beloved English drama, and the "weak spot" is fatherly affection for the honest simpleton of the family. But, during those fifty years—or nearly—of critical authority, to not the crudest melodrama set before him had he done other than painstaking justice. In one of his earliest books, moreover, we find him urging upon Sims and Pettitt and the "Adelphi" playwrights of the day the rich opportunities of the melodramatic convention, let but a little more care and common sense be brought to bear upon it. Long after, he successfully translates these precepts into practice. Here, he held, was the sort of play which need not wait for its writing upon inspiration—to which he made no pretence. But he had always extolled good craftsmanship. And he put forward *The Green Goddess* as an example of it; making no higher claim, thinking this, though, by no means a negligible one.

An essential thing to be said about Archer, it seems to me, is that, as single adventurer or pilot, in dramatic matters or in the wider interests of which his life was full (and which helped to keep him so salutary an influence in those dramatic matters), he could hold a course once he had laid it down, even though it seemed a commonplace course, and be turned from it neither by momentary failure nor by distracted enthusiasms. As to the theatre, he thought that it must always be primarily a popular entertainment. But, as a good Liberal, he would never admit that because of this it could not be, in its every aspect, a reasonably intelligent entertainment too. And I really cannot imagine upon what "principle" your reviewer supposes that he would have struck good melodrama from its canon.

Faithfully yours,
Harley Granville-Barker

---

1. In 1931 Barker wrote to the *Times Literary Supplement* in response to a review of Charles Archer's *William Archer: Life, Work and Friendships* which appeared in the *T.L.S.* on June 4, 1931. The letter, in the *T.L.S.* files, is undated.

 # Chapter III

Bernard Shaw, 1856–1950

Long *after their* estrangement, when Barker died, Shaw said of him in a letter to the *Times Literary Supplement,* "We clicked so well together that I regarded him as my contemporary until one day at rehearsal, when someone remarked that I was fifty, he said: 'You are the same age as my father.' After that it seemed impossible that he should die before me. The shock the news gave me made me realize how I had still cherished a hope that our old intimate relation might revive"[1] The intimacy to which Shaw refers sprang chiefly from their work together at the Court Theatre between 1904 and 1907, but, as pointed out in Chapter I, it spread to their private and family lives. During the first half of the 1914–18 war, after Barker had separated from Lillah McCarthy and before he married Helen Huntington, he treated the Shaw home in Ayot St. Lawrence as *his* home. He was living very much *pied-à-terre* at that time, moving frequently between London, New York, and France, but when he was in England his base was at the home of Bernard and Charlotte Shaw. Unlike the friendship with Archer, however, that with Shaw did not survive the incursion of Helen Huntington into Barker's life, and Shaw—again, unlike Archer—was never invited to Netherton Hall. St. John Ervine, in his *Bernard Shaw: His Life, Work and Friends,* has this comment:

> Once, while staying with G. B. S. in Torquay, we took him to lunch with Miss Clemence Dane at Axminster. On the way, we passed the entrance to a road which led to Granville-Barker's superbly appointed house at Farway, a house that was more like a museum than a home, one, too, in which the chief piece was Granville-Barker, and as we passed, I said to G. B. S.: "Harley Granville-Barker lives up that road." He looked at it in the odd way he

---

1. September 12, 1946. The complete text appears as the last letter in this chapter.

Bernard Shaw, about 1890.

had when he was moved, and, almost as if he were indifferent, said, "Oh, Harley!" But when G. B. S. was as terse as that, he was under deep emotion.

This was some time in the nineteen-thirties: Shaw's active, day-by-day contact with Barker had ended in 1918. On August 26 of that year, Shaw wrote to Barker:

It would be convenient occasionally to know something about you. I surmise that you are married; but it is only a surmise. It is desirable that your friends should be in a position to make a positive affirmation on the subject. An affectation of ecstasy so continuous as to make you forget all worldly considerations is ridiculous at your age. So just send me along any information that ought to be public, however briefly.[2]

Barker's reply (if there was one) has not been preserved, as far as can be determined.

C.B. Purdom's edition of the Shaw-Barker letters contains upwards of a hundred and fifty letters and postcards from Shaw to Barker, written between 1900 and 1918. There are also fifteen letters—mostly duplicating the Purdom collection—in the second volume of *Bernard Shaw: The Collected Letters,* edited by Dan H. Laurence (London, 1972). These two collections give a full and fascinating account of the theater productions which the two men did together. Shaw usually directed the first productions of his own plays, and those done at the Court Theatre in the 1904–1907 season usually had Barker in a leading role. Shaw's letters to Barker are full of details of staging, casting, theater policy, finances, and so on. The work of Purdom and Laurence has been thorough and comprehensive, and I imagine that there are very few of Shaw's letters of that period which have escaped their notice. I did come across one or two scraps, however, and these—for the sake of completeness—I include in this present chapter, which otherwise consists exclusively of Barker's letters to Shaw. These come from two phases of his life—the 1915–16 productions in New York and the period (1918–24) immediately following his second marriage. And, after that, a short, sad, frozen exchange in 1943.

When Barker first got to know Shaw and began to work with him on his plays, the older man was already quite well known in London. For three brilliant years he had been dramatic critic for the *Saturday Review* and had had several plays produced, both at home and abroad, but, though known as a dramatist, he was known as a

---

2. C. B. Purdom, *The Shaw-Barker Letters* (London, 1936), p. 197.

coterie dramatist. Barker's seasons at the Court Theatre established Shaw not only as a popular dramatist but as the leading playwright of the day. The debt, however, was by no means one-sided. Without any doubt, it was Shaw's plays which sustained the Court venture financially as well as artistically, and, quite apart from the financing of the plays themselves, both Shaw and his wife loaned quite large sums to Barker for investment in his various theatrical ventures at the Court and elsewhere—loans that were not infrequently converted into gifts when things went badly.[3] Almost all Shaw's biographers (and there are by now a good many) have emphasized the elements of contradiction in his personality: the public assertiveness and the private doubts; the paranoia about poverty and the personal generosity; the enormous energy and the constant complaints of ill-health; the instinct for survival and the hypochondria. Often these dichotomies are reflected in his letters, but the dominant tone in all his letters to Barker is a compound of affection and gaiety. Barker replied in kind, and it is not too far-fetched to suggest that much of Barker's letter-writing style was unconsciously founded upon Shaw's. That said, it must also be noted that their temperaments were very different. Many of the contradictions in Shaw's personality were present in Barker's as well, but in him they were under a much less certain control, subject to a much less authoritative personality; in a word, Barker had a great deal less toughness of mind and spirit than Shaw.

It needs to be remembered that Barker, Archer, Shaw, and Murray formed a close-knit and sympathetic group in the first two decades of the century. All were dedicated to, and were part of, the "new theater"; all made brilliant contributions to it, in various ways; and there were strong ties of a personal sort between them. There were also multiple connections of a practical kind. Shaw's very first attempt at play-writing *(Widowers' Houses)* began as a collaboration with Archer, who supplied the plot and worked out the construction but repudiated the play when he saw what Shaw had done with the dialogue in the first two acts. Gilbert Murray, as all the world now knows, was the model for Cusins in *Major Barbara*. Barker mounted and presented the first productions of several major Shaw plays (including *Major Barbara,* in which he himself played the Murray part) and also of Murray's vastly important translations of Euripides. Archer made the first English translations of many of Ibsen's plays and Shaw was one of Ibsen's stoutest early defenders in England, at a time when

---

3. See, for example, the letter of March 1, 1911, in which Shaw in effect writes off a debt of £5,250; the letter is reproduced on p. 171 of Purdom's collection.

defense was, artistically as well as socially speaking, urgently necessary. Barker, coming on the scene only slightly later, directed several distinguished Ibsen productions and was involved in some of the "second wave" controversies about the Norwegian dramatist. The community of interest between these four—critic, playwright, scholar, and *homme de théâtre*—was a vivid and powerful force. It would, indeed, be difficult to cite, in the history of British theater since that time, so impressive and forceful a combination of individual contributions.

COR/MS
To Shaw

8, York Buildings
Friday, 11.20 p.m.
December 8 [1900][1]

Dear Mr. Shaw,

No—Kismet be blowed![2] Why couldn't the Cadi double the
Captain? You may be surprised to hear that you've put me off the
part very much. I don't think I shall ever be in the least like what
you want—I doubt even if I'd better try too hard: such an extraordinary hybrid would be the result. If you can find anyone else to play it
I think you'd better. (There's a man called Fred W. Sidney, if C. C.[3]
could get hold of him: excellent—I saw him Americanise.) And I
can't rehearse tomorrow and I doubt if I can on Monday and all next
week. I've another part as long as my arm to study and rehearse (that
was the great objection to Redbrook,[4] who runs through two acts).
So for many reasons you'll be well rid of me, if you can manage it,
and honestly I shall be frightened as well as not a bit like it now. You
lifted the weight of a battle off my shoulders last night and now you
want to put it on again. However, if you still call on me I'll play it
because I hate being beaten. Tomorrow I meet the U.S. Naval
Attaché, a captain from Illinois. I shall expect him to answer to your
description.

Seriously, I think you'd be wise to get some one else if you
possibly can for you have made me feel that you're right and I'm
wrong which is not only almost unforgivable but generally fatal to any
decent work being done in a week.

Let me hear as soon as you can.[5]

Yours,
H. G. Barker

---

1. This letter is part of an exchange between Barker and Shaw during rehearsals for the
   first production of *Captain Brassbound's Conversion* by the Stage Society at the
   Strand Theatre on December 16, 1900. The director was Charles Charrington; Lady
   Cicely Waynflete was played by Janet Achurch (Charrington's wife). Three of Shaw's
   letters on the subject are included in Purdom's *The Shaw-Barker Letters* (pp. 6–8),
   this present letter from Barker being a direct reply to the second of these. The bone
   of contention was the role of Captain Kearney, the American naval officer, which
   Barker was playing. Shaw disliked his performance and said so.
2. Shaw's letter of December 7, 1900, began: "9.10 be blowed! I was not down to my
   own porridge until 9.20," and ended: "No: youve got to play the captain, spite of
   dead cats, bottles, turnips, putrid eggs, and authors. Kismet!"
3. Charles Charrington.
4. Charrington had originally offered Barker the part of Redbrook, and Shaw had also
   suggested this. Barker had expressed a strong preference for the role of Kearney (see
   letter to Charrington, Chapter X, p. 447).

5. In fact, Barker did play Captain Kearney. Shaw approved of the performance finally and, in a letter of January 2, 1901, said: "My only misgiving with regard to you is as to whether the stage, in its present miserable condition, is good enough for you."

TEX/TS
To Shaw

78, East Parade,
Harrogate.
Wednesday [September, 1908]

Churton Collins[1] being dead of midnight oil and the strong tea he took to help him burn it, I consider it absolutely necessary that W. A. should have his place as Professor of English Literature at Birmingham. Cannot your well-known tactlessness achieve this?

I have a theory. There are a certain number of people who come to every performance of every play of yours. They travel round with the company. I daresay I am paying their fares, for I don't look very carefully into the accounts: only the prices of the seats differ and this accounts for the very slight variation in the returns. We carry our own critics too and they say Schopenhauer and Nietzsche every Tuesday morning without fail. It bores me. I can't think why I engaged them.

The company is conscientious but a little lacking in moral force: any that I had has been prostituted to vanishing point. But the plays go wonderfully well most times. They sometimes laugh twice at one joke . . . a sure sign. Unless it is that the old hands see it quick and laugh at once and then have to explain it to the others. I wait politely for them to do so. Can't say yet how the tour will do financially. The advertising has been quite insufficient so far: I know—as usual. But that has been taken in hand and we shall see, if not at Manchester, at Cardiff.

I have written a long letter to Vedrenne telling him that this week by week business is no good, that what he must do is to start at once pencilling a tour for next year which will take in only a few of the best towns and stay there five or six weeks with four or five plays. In the provinces as in London we have to make an audience and that cannot be done in a week. So no more at present. Why am I spending a morning writing to you—I only meant to about W. A.

My best respects to Madam Charlotte,

H. G. B.

1. See footnote 1 to Barker's letter to Murray, September, 1908.

TEX/handwritten by a secretary but initialed by Barker
To Shaw

Vedrenne-Barker Performances,
London address: 52, Shaftesbury Ave.,
This week: Grand Theatre, Leeds
Next week: Theatre Royal, Manchester
16 Sept. 1908

Talking over the Censor with W. A. some weeks ago, I suggested what a lark it would be, when we were in Dublin and outside his jurisdiction, to give a public performance of "Waste". However we can't cast it among the company of course, but that suggestion led naturally to one that we should give some matinées of "Ghosts". I thought no more of it, principally because I have said to myself I'll be damned if I go on the stage one time more than is necessary. But now W. A. sends me a line urging me on and—well, what do you think? Would it be anything of a blow to Redford?[1] If so, I'd be tempted to do it. Would it prejudice our business in Dublin? You know with how much safety the bourgeois can be épaté there, and I don't. Poor Vd [J. E. Vedrenne]—I have not breathed a word to him. He'll faint at the very thought. I don't in the least want to do it, but to contribute to Redford's undoing—after all, if you come to that, why not import the necessary company and give performances of "Waste", "Oedipus Rex" and "Mrs. Warren", and advertise them as being done without Vd's consent?

H. G. B.

P.S. I discover I <u>could</u> cast "Waste" with the exception of about two men—Wot larx!

---

1. Examiner of plays for the Lord Chamberlain (in other words, the censor).

TEX/PC
To Barker

Bayreuth
[1908]

On a picture postcard showing a portrait of Wagner, Shaw writes:

Consciousness of genius extinguished by consciousness of a new coat of extra-special design.

G. B. S.

TEX/PC
To Barker

Bayreuth
[1908]

On a picture postcard of the Opera House at Bayreuth, Shaw writes:

This is what I call a Court Theatre.

G. B. S.

SAL/TS
To Barker

10, Adelphi Terrace,
London, W.C.
12th April, 1911

I do not think it is the least use your coming up until Saturday. In fact, I doubt if it is any use your coming at all: we shall only
get it tumbled through anyhow.[1] With luck, some of them will do
fairly. Juggins has worked the part out for himself uncommonly well:
I have said so little to him that he is getting scared lest I should have
given him up as hopeless.[2] Dorothy Minto has really worked intelligently at her part, and will pull it through if she is let have a 23/-pair
of boots which she is now yearning for. Harcourt Williams's success
(if he succeeds) will be the most striking thing since the success of
Irving in The Bells. Not until the day before yesterday did I discover
that Ricketts was back in England. He has sternly refused the rest of
the world to design any more dresses on the ground that in future he
is going to devote himself to painting; but he plunged head over heels
into our job, and the only question now is whether Symmons can
knock the dresses together before Tuesday.[3] Miss Hamilton is beyond
words. Poel's first efforts as Keegan were masterly and popular in
comparison: she is a nervous wreck and is worse even than you are in
point of dropping your speeches and playing the part in a whisper;
but she will get through somehow when she must, though poor Tapping is in despair about her. Lauzert plays Mephistopheles, and wants
to be cool and cynical: it would take another month to work him up
to the long speech; but the reality of his foreignness will pull him
through.[4] As to Lillah, I suppose she will get through somehow; but
your blasted producing has utterly destroyed her power of thinking

about anything else but the producer. When I conduct the scene like old Ardini trying to pull an Italian orchestra through Wagner, making faces at her and suggesting tones and interrupting and so on, she jumps at it and gets it all right so that you would suppose that she could never go wrong in it. Next time I retire to let them have a straight run at the words; and she instantly relapses into a maddening gabble that would drive you out of your senses. Sometimes the effect of this exhilarates her, whereupon she gabbles faster than ever. Sometimes she feels it is wrong, and then she gabbles harder than ever. The most interesting thing about it on such occasions is to watch her face while the others are speaking and try to conjecture the remote trains of fanciful speculation which are passing through her mind at that moment, pending the arrival of her cue. This part is really not in her nature: she is too Irish, too West Country, she has no idea of a chump like Margaret Knox.[5]

However, the mere terror of the approaching production will compel her to tackle the part for herself. I told her today that I was not going to produce her; that she was paid to act and she must act and I was not <u>going</u> to do her business. She said she would be all right when she knew what I wanted. You should not destroy people's minds in this fashion. You are like all theatrical producers—worse than Loraine himself[6]—you think that nothing matters except the play and the performance, forgetting that there are higher human considerations to which such trifles must give way. The consequence is that you get an unnecessarily good performance, much less effective than a reasonably bad one, and leave all your people dead for ever. I shall have not only to coach Lillah, but to raise her from the dead.

Daly says that the production of The Master Builder[7] is a triumph of mediocrity, by which he means that it is a triumph <u>with</u> mediocrity. He also means that he should have played Solness. He quite appreciates all your games, and put his finger on one spot worth noting. He says that at the end of the play Hilda should not come out of her trance—that the final waving of the scarf and cry of "My Master Builder" spoils the whole end unless one feels that she still sees him up there and hears the harps in the air. In this I am inclined to think Master Arnold is right; for I have seen it half come off with Miss Robins on occasions when she half did it in Daly's way. The importance of this is that we are both at a frightful loss for a producer in America; and Daly may be our man. I am half sorry that we did not prolong The Master Builder for another week and run him on as Solness. He would have done it sooner than not appear; and if we could hold him on to see a production of the Voysey (which he does not see a bit) he might save you the trouble of crossing to New York to produce it, as you will certainly have to do if the alternative is an ordinary commercial producer.

Vedrenne is to do matinées of John Bull with Eadie as Keegan, and the rest of the cast old hands from the Court including (Vd suggests) Sherbrooke as Tim Haffigan!

The Albert Hall having finally decided that Oedipus would bring it under the ban of the County Council, Whelen is negotiating for Earl's Court or Olympia.

There is the devil of a row on at the Stage Society. The Producing Committee with Hertz in the Chair ignored a quite decent cast proposed by Fernald[,] the author of the next play, and proposed a cast of their own with Margaret Halstan as the leading lady. You can imagine

(G. B. S. got called away when he got as far as this, and as I do not know when he will be back and it is now time for post, I am sending this in its unfinished condition.)

Judy Gillmore

---

1. Shaw was directing the first production of *Fanny's First Play* as the third offering in a season of plays presented by Barker in partnership with his wife, Lillah McCarthy. The Shaw piece opened on April 19, 1911, after barely two weeks of rehearsal, and proved to be the longest-running original production (622 performances) of any play in Shaw's career. It transferred from the Little to the Kingsway on January 1, 1912.
2. The actor playing the part of Juggins was H. K. Ayliff.
3. Ricketts is Charles Ricketts (1866–1931), who designed a number of Barker's productions.
4. Miss Hamilton is Cecily Hamilton, an actress and playwright (1872–1952); "Lauzert" is Raymond Lauzette, who played the part of Lieutenant Duvallet.
5. "Margaret Knox" is one of the characters in the play.
6. Robert Loraine (1876–1935) was a famous actor-manager.
7. The production immediately preceding *Fanny's First Play* was Ibsen's *The Master Builder,* which Barker had directed.

TEX/MS
To Barker[1]

10, Adelphi Terrace,   Ayot St. Lawrence,
W.C.   Welwyn, Herts.
                                                                16th Nov. 1911

Why in thunder should we resign?[2] You must be stark raving mad. Mrs. West and D. D. are working the business for all they are worth (Mrs. W's Earl's Court scheme is big enough to terrify T into asking for a sideshow in it); and they have about as much intention of letting that £100,000 get into T's pocket as of presenting it to the Labor Party.[3] Of course the men are doing nothing (especially you), except Bourchier, who at the last Executive—but I told you that story. Tomorrow I shall have some fun over that: never shall it be said that I sat calmly in the chair & saw honest Arthur Bourchier insulted by T.

I cannot advise you as to the best method of protesting and leaving the Executive. It won't make much difference as things go at present, will it? Now if you were to ask me as to the best method of attending the meetings, I might be disposed to give my mind to it.

Let me tell you one secret of public life. It is never worth while attending a committee meeting. There is always something better to do; and one is never in town. Therefore, unless you make up your mind doggedly that the acceptance of membership of a committee imposes a cast iron obligation on you to attend without arguing, no matter how much better use you could make of your time, you never will attend.

Here endeth etc., etc., etc.

G. B. S.

---

1. Not included in Purdom's collection of Shaw-Barker letters.
2. Barker had suggested that they both resign from the Executive Committee of the Shakespeare Memorial National Theatre as a protest against its inactivity and fumbling. There were many cross-currents in the matter of the proposed National Theatre, both inside and outside the official committee.
3. Mrs. West is Mrs. George Cornwallis West, who in 1911 raised £100,000 for the mounting of a Shakespeare Ball at the Royal Albert Hall and a Shakespeare exhibition—complete with performances of some of the plays on a replica of the Globe stage—at Earl's Court. "T" is Sir Herbert Beerbohm Tree, the actor-manager. I have not identified "D. D."

TEX/MS
To Barker
10, Adelphi Terrace,   Ayot St. Lawrence,
W.C.   Welwyn, Herts.
                                                       27th Nov. 1911

The advent of Nathan the Wise or Otherwise does not alter the situation except as far as it accentuates the utter hollowness of the proposal except as a means of nobbling Fanny.[1] You had better stick to it that the thing is off, as you cannot now come over, and that the subject can be taken up again next summer if necessary. You may also mention that I am not sanguine about Fanny as an American success, and that I thought all through that Getting Married would be the catch-on if there was a catch-on at all. Convey also that we are accustomed to proceed in a large way, as a Movement, and that these little flutters after separate shop successes do not attract us.

I repeat, by the way, that there is not the smallest reason why you and Galsworthy should take less than a straight ten per cent. If I got it 17 years ago, with not half your present reputation, why should you take less today?

I approve highly of the Savoy proceedings and of the Times today generally.[2] I do not at present intend to go up for the Dram. Club Lunch; but possibly Pinero might alter the situation. I wrote to him on Saturday to ask how he felt about it; but he has not yet replied. Massingham writes spiritedly demanding an article & offering to back us if we will strike against submitting plays to Dear Old Charlie. I cannot possibly interrupt my training for the Chesterton mill to write the article. Suppose you do it. (The Nation, 14, Henrietta St., Covent Garden; H. W. Massingham.)

Miss Marbury[3] wants Devil's Disc. for William Courtney, & Major Barbara & the Doctor for "young William Harris", son of one Harris of the Klaus & Erlanger-cum-Frohman syndicate. Says that if you are coming out, young William will wait for you to produce, select cast, etc. In short, will do anything we wish. Know you aught of this youth?

G. B. S.

---

1. *Nathan the Wise* is the title of a play by Gotthold Ephraim Lessing (1729–1781): Shaw here ironically refers to George Jean Nathan, the American theater critic whose powerful advocacy of the "new drama" was one of the chief factors in the introduction of Ibsen, Strindberg, Shaw, Hauptmann, and many other new writers to America. The reference here is to the fact that Nathan had just written an article in the *New York Herald* urging Barker to go to New York and launch a repertory theater. (Barker received several such invitations between 1908 and 1915.) In this instance Shaw regarded the idea merely as a ruse to enable New York to cash in on the success of *Fanny's First Play,* then running in London; in any case, Barker did not go to New York until December, 1914.
2. *The Times* that day announced the appointment of Charles Brookfield (1857–1913) as Joint Examiner of Plays (with G. A. Redford) in the Lord Chamberlain's office. There was also a report of a demonstration, organized by Barker at the Savoy Theatre, against this appointment (see Appendix A for full text of these newspaper announcements.)
3. Elizabeth Marbury, the New York literary agent.

BL/TS
To Shaw

Kingsway Theatre,
Great Queen Street, W. C.
November 29th 1912

I will see you Sunday, sir.

The Galsworthy does fairly well, is paying its way, and may, I think, continue to do so for a bit—that is until the Christmas slump, which I fancy will kill it unless it takes firmer hold before then.

I still think that CANDIDA without an attractive 45 minuter or a very startling cast might be flat. It is up to you to say.

JOHN BULL is the easiest substitute. No difficulty in casting that I can see except the Larry. Would you like Boucicault one end of the scale (he'd be darned unattractive and efficient) or McKinnel at the other?[1] I suggest McKinnel mainly as a man necessary to get in touch with in time, and, supposing that one changed one's mind to THE DOCTOR'S DILEMMA or supposing Calvert went off to Australia (or Timbuctoo), a conceivable Broadbent.

I have found a love to wipe your eye with, namely Maria Carmi!! She turned up at the Theatre on Wednesday, and comes a-visiting us next Sunday.

Yours,
H. G. B.

---

1. He refers to Dion Boucicault the younger (1859–1929) and the actor Norman McKinnel (1870–1932).

BL/TS
To Shaw

Kingsway Theatre,
Great Queen Street, W.C.
November 21st, 1913

Sir,

It is apparently useless my telling stage managers to send you calls for rehearsals. They regard the author as a mere worm and will not do it. For them I apologise. I had no idea you could get up in time to rehearse this morning, and do not remember making any D. D.[1] call. But here I was pegging away at The Philanderer[2] and hoping you might turn up. They have been right through the Dilemma now and I have dismissed them to learn their words for three or four days. I lost my voice yesterday afternoon showing Miss Mary Lawton how to play Julia! Leave her to me and I think I will shake her into something. Incidentally I can broaden Maude into something but really it means my teaching them both a lot of tricks and ways which they ought to know already and I foresee a pleasant time. You had much better rehearse in the foyer because the Little Theatre stage is considerably larger than our Kingsway stage and you are cramping yourself unnecessarily there, but have the stage if you like. Ring up this afternoon or tonight to say if you want it. Otherwise the foyer is fixed at 10.30 tomorrow and I hope you will give them the business for Acts three and four. From six to seven this evening I shall be endeavoring to secure you a better Paramore.[3] If I cannot do that I shall have Besant here tomorrow morning. If you ask me, the whole cast is pretty adjectived but we must do our best now.

You are expected to come down with me to Stansted on Saturday without fail. Except the signing and sealing Curzon[4] is settled, and God help me I have underwritten three thousand pounds. But [he] is doing the Pantomine Rehearsal at Christmas.

Yours,

H. G. B.

---

1. Barker was directing *The Doctor's Dilemma* as part of a repertory season at the St. James's Theatre.
2. The Shaw play; the production referred to here was abandoned before it got to the stage.
3. A character in *The Philanderer.*
4. Frank Curzon (1868–1927) was a theater manager (formerly an actor) with whom Barker was negotiating.

BL/W
To Shaw[1]

Fairseat.[2]   29 July 1914.   7.13 P.M.

To: Socialist, Strand, London.

Wheelers[3] staying bungalow Poldhu, Mullion, Cornwall. Would I am sure get you good rooms Poldhu, Mullion Cove or Housel Bay Hotels. Beautiful coast, good bathing. Lillah and I must remain here till August ninth then she rehearses and I would much like join you anywhere for a week. Might possibly be in town tomorrow or you might run down here for night and consult.

Barker

---

1. Punctuation added to this telegram.
2. The Barkers' home at this time was an Elizabethan farmhouse called Court Lodge, at Stansted, Kent. The nearest post office was in Fairseat, some two miles away.
3. C. E. Wheeler and his wife, Penelope, were old friends of Barker's. Wheeler had assisted him with the translations from Schnitzler.

BL/W
To Shaw[1]

New York.[2]   18 December 1914   11.56 A.M.

Propose doing repertory January. Androcles, with France's Dumb wife,[3] Midsummer Dream, Doctor's Dilemma, Madras House. Prospects good. Hope you approve. Why not come over also? Request for Barbara, Getting Married. Will report further. Our love.

Barker

14, East 60th Street, New York.

---

1. Punctuation added to this telegram.
2. Barker had been invited to direct a repertory season in New York, backed by a group of wealthy businessmen.
3. Anatole France's two-act farce *The Man Who Married a Dumb Wife.*

BL/W
To Shaw[1]

New York.   22 December 1914   3.37 P.M.

To: Socialist, Strand, London.

Do write analytical programmes Androcles, Dilemma, Getting Married, Misalliance and, if you please, Madras House.

Barker

Replied 23/12/14.[2]

Granville Barker, 14 East 60, New York.

Walking tour Webbs until second. Dead beat just now. Cannot guarantee programs [*sic*] in time. Cable date opening & order of production. Why Dream instead of Twelfth Night? Lillah's Viola most important.

Shaw

---

1. Punctuation added to this telegram.
2. The telegraph form on which Shaw received the previous communication from Barker is in the Shaw archive of the Department of Manuscripts, British Library, shelfmark ADD 50534. At the bottom of the form, in Shaw's hand, this reply is written.

BL/W
To Shaw[1]

New York.   25 Dec. 1914   10.05 A.M.

To: Socialist, London

Androcles January eighteen. Dilemma, Madras House at least fortnight later. Our love to all.

Barker

---

1. Punctuation added to this telegram.

BL/MS
To Shaw

~~Piping Rock Club,~~
~~Locust Valley~~
~~Long Island.~~
Wallack's Theatre,[1]
New York.
Jan. 3 [1915]

This is a sort of glorified golf club plus a private hotel of which they've made me a sort of member—to which anyhow Lillah and I fly for weekends—in glorious country, in reach of the sca.

I've taken Wallack's for six weeks, various people over here having guaranteed $15,000 to cover possible loss. I thought I'd go straight away for repertory instead of getting into the usual tangle of N.Y. commercial methods, which seem not only bad but worse than they have ever been!—as far as reckless gambling in any and every sort of play go.

I'll start with Androcles, with The Dumb Wife[2] (fits very well: I was an ass not to have discovered it before), then The Doctor's Dilemma, then The Madras House.

Heggie is here.[3] I've got Ian McLaren as the Captain and for Ridgeon and Constantine.[4] B. B.[5] is a difficulty. Do you think Heggie could play Dubedat?[6] I'm going to make him up and rehearse him privately. There are one or two innocent-looking young blackguards about to choose from but they won't know what it's about. However, I'll report further on that. On the main question, if this season goes well it will be possible to organise permanently a ten or twelve weeks season in N.Y. producing four or five plays with a very first-rate company. Then to split it up and send the essentials of each cast on the road with their particular play, if it has justified itself. That is my solution of the N.Y. difficulty of heavy rents and salaries

and expenses generally. You can afford your productions if they are
to earn back their cost on tour—the actors will cut their salaries down
for the surety of the N.Y. production and the chance of their full
money when they travel. (What usually happens here is the reverse—
any sort of production on the road, with the chance of New York.)
And under conditions of that sort I could give the time, thus limited,
to the productions.

However, of that in another few weeks.

I sent you my last cable because Elizabeth Marbury is on
the prowl seeking whom she may get 10% out of. I have just said
"Bring along your proposition", but first it meant a little theatre
called the Princess[7]—no use—then it meant the Shuberts. If it is a
little theatre game better stick to Ames, the one person here who
manages to maintain some sort of character and good standard in his
work. If it means the Shuberts—I can deal with them myself.

A quite good youngish American actress came along asking
after Major Barbara, demanding a production by me (referred to me
by a cable from you). She seemed quite possible so I said "Produce
your Undershaft and the rest can probably be managed". She hasn't
so far produced her Undershaft—and I rather doubt the finding him.
I've since discovered that she has to go to the Shuberts to run her, so
there again one may as well keep a free hand. But indeed I should
recommend now giving a trial to this plan of mine, holding up the
plays that matter till we see if anything of a permanent producing
institution with what we should call a good company can be established. Haphazard engaging here is hopeless. There has a sort of legend preceded me[8] that I make acting successes for people, so I find
them more or less anxious to join me. Otherwise some walk in—
they'd be dear in London at £10 a week—and tell me calmly that
$200 is their salary.

I've not seen Gertrude K.[9] nor indeed have I tried to. She
made a mess apparently of her N.Y. "Society" game—did something
to put their backs up. No reason she shouldn't get Great Catherine[10]
done, more likely in "Vaudeville" it seems, though it's less easy for a
woman to get in here at that game than a man—they have actresses
of their own—popular—it is actors they lack—very few young men
about. But she and I do not mix.

Nor did I see Pygmalion—it came off the very night we arrived. Tyler—besides going bankrupt—played the fool with it a great
deal, moving it from one theatre to another. I have had no trustwor-
thy account of the performance. Shubert complained to me bitterly of
Tyler taking over the contract upon any terms he was asked, knowing
perfectly well that he was going to smash. I don't know what it is

doing on the road but Mrs. P. C.[11] is angling for a New York production either of the Hichens play[12] (which might go—they fall to the sham-society business rather) or Tanqueray!! (God help us!)

You're a prominent person here, at the moment more because of <u>Common</u> <u>Sense</u> <u>about</u> <u>the</u> <u>War</u> than anything. I can't discover that comment on it is much different from or more intelligent than it was in England but it has been much more widely read. The Times circulation of it must be enormous.

I'd like you to see the place—it is the "biggest thing going"—that's true—and the river front at sunset one of the loveliest. And in spite of all their nonsense democracy does mean something—as you meet it in the streets—the bad manners are genuinely bad but the good manners are genuinely good. If you could limit a visit to ten days I'd say come, for you ought to see it some time. More might kill you. I don't know, though: there's a quality about the atmosphere. For the first week it tonics you to exhaustion, but after that it's like the alps in winter—your resistance gets adjusted and you feel inches taller and three more around the chest.

Our love to Charlotte—and to you.

H. G. B.

---

1. There have been three New York theaters of this name. Barker was using the middle one (chronologically speaking). It stood on the northeast corner of Broadway and 30th Street and was sold for demolition later in the year that Barker was there (1915).
2. France's farce was written in 1912; though not originally intended for the professional stage, it was produced with great success at the Théâtre du Porte Saint-Martin, Paris, that year. Barker had it translated by Curtis Hidden Page especially for this New York production, which also marked the beginning of the career of Robert Edmond Jones as a stage designer. His very striking setting for the France play was greatly admired, and his drawing of it is the first plate in his book *Drawings for the Theatre* (New York, 1925).
3. O. P. Heggie (1880–1936) played Androcles in the original production at the St. James's Theatre, London, in 1913.
4. The Captain is a character in *Androcles and the Lion*, Ridgeon in *The Doctor's Dilemma*, and Constantine in *The Madras House*.
5. A character in *The Doctor's Dilemma*.
6. Thus releasing Barker himself, who originally played Dubedat, to play B. B.
7. This was at 104 West 39th Street; it was demolished in 1955.
8. This curious syntactical structure is there in the original.
9. Gertrude Kingston (1866-1937), a British actress and (later) manageress.
10. This short play of Shaw's (it is in four scenes, amounting to one act of normal length) was first produced at the Vaudeville Theatre, London, in 1913 with Gertrude Kingston as Catherine; It was published in German (1914), then in English in *Everybody's Magazine* (New York) in 1915.
11. Mrs. Patrick Campbell was the first Eliza Doolittle in English (the first production of the play was in German), at His Majesty's Theatre, London, in 1914.
12. *The Law of the Sands*, by Robert Smythe Hichens: Mrs. Patrick Campbell, as it turned out, did not play it in New York, but played it in London the following year.

BL/W
To Shaw[1]

New York: 17 Jan. 1915   10.49 P.M.
To: Sokialist [*sic*], Strand, London.

Best thanks excellent analytical. Send others. Opening real repertory, Androcles, Friday, with Dumb Wife. Rehearsals promising. Dream, February first. Dilemma, week later, then Madras.

Barker

---

1. Punctuation added to this telegram.

BL/TS
To Shaw

Wallack's,
Broadway & 30th Street,
New York.

———

Lillah McCarthy
Granville Barker

———

January 22, 1915

My dear Bernard Shaw,

"Madras House" analytical arrived. Thank you again. As you sent nothing for the "Dilemma", and one ought to keep one in for all, I think I will stick in a bit out of the preface, what?

I am doing real repertory, but difficult to get under way at once with a scratch company, but starting with ANDROCLES, and then with THE DREAM only ten days later, is not bad. THE DUMB WIFE is rather jolly. I have got a very amusing way of producing it, and it fits in with ANDROCLES quite well. The cast for ANDROCLES is, in some ways, better than we had it in London. Lillah and Heggie, with Lucy for Spintho, Ian Maclaren as The Captain (great improvement on Webster) a man called Lionel Braham for Ferrovius—6½ feet tall and broad in proportion, and method like an overgrown good-natured bull; really rather magnificent, lacking, of course, a little finesse. A good Lentulus; Miss Carlyon as Magaera; a most admirable lion, far better than Sillwood. For The Emperor I just missed Quartermaine.[1] Oh Irony! He has been recalled to London for the part I got Barrie to cast him in the play that you upset. And thus the whirligig of time, etc., etc. There aren't any Emperors in America, and that is the truth. I have fallen back on Walter Creighton. 80% of what he is and

50% of what he does is very good. If I can only fake the remaining 50% all will be well. Anyhow, you will get a show.

I am worried about The Dilemma. I can't find either a good B. B. or a good Sir Patrick, nor a very good Dubedat, though that is a little easier. But I think I can manage, by going a little outside our original methods, with Sir P. and B. B.

I strongly expect I shall have to play in THE MADRAS HOUSE myself, but it probably won't get very many performances. It is all touch and go of course, and the expenses are rather terrifying, because I know it has been worth doing, and because it means, as I told you, we shall be able to establish some sort of a permanency here—to get over and have any play produced that we think fit to do.

You shall hear more by the next mail. Our dear love to you both.

H. G. B.

---

1. Leon Quartermaine (1876–1967) played the Emperor in the original production of *Androcles and the Lion* in London.

BL/TS
To Shaw

Wallack's,
Broadway & 30th Street,
New York.

———

Lillah McCarthy
Granville Barker

———

Jan'y 29, 1915

My dear Bernard Shaw,

ANDROCLES seems quite a go. I send you a lot of notices. More importantly, we had $1300 the first night, a little over $1000 the second night. and I expect more this evening. The performance was not at all bad. The Lion was a huge success—1600 times as good as Sillwood was. Ferrovius was slow—but all right. The Emperor pulled it nearly all off, and Maclaren a bit dull, but real. Lillah and Heggie as good as ever. The smaller parts, on the whole, were better played than in London.

I hope to get THE DREAM out in a week—after that the first modern one as soon as possible. I am not at all sure, if we are safe in a money way, that I shan't put THE MADRAS HOUSE on next, and if I find the DILEMMA impossible to cast, will put on MISALLIANCE. I suppose you won't object.

I am cabling you tonight about FANNY,[1] when I can collect my thoughts (I have been rehearsing hard since 10.30 this morning). But I don't think that you can be sure of more than £40 a performance, therefore why budget for £45? As to your cast, you really are getting fogeyish. This idea of sticking a leading lady in, whatever her age, seems to me mad. Lillah was really too old for "Margaret", and Lena[2] is, I think, nearly fifteen years her senior. You knocked the stuffing out of PYGMALION in the same way;[3] and having done that I suppose you felt FANNY doesn't matter. From the perfectly sordid point of view, I don't believe, either, that Lena will draw in a penny. Ainley, having been working with us for two or three years there, will, on the other hand. I want to keep people in work if I can, but it is no good hanging on doing the weak thing in this way. It is much better to shut up. However, you will get my cable long before you get this.

Yours,
H. G. B.

---

1. Shaw was directing a revival of *Fanny's First Play* at the Kingsway Theatre, where it opened on February 13, 1915.
2. Lena Ashwell (1872–1957), who played Margaret, was, in fact, only three years older than Lillah McCarthy (though nevertheless old for Margaret).
3. By casting Mrs. Patrick Campbell, who was forty-nine at the time, as Eliza Doolittle.

BL/TS
To Shaw

Wallack's
Broadway & 30th Street,
New York.

———

Lillah McCarthy
Granville Barker

———

February 2, 1915

Arrived today your DOCTOR'S DILEMMA programme. Many thanks. By the way, don't you wish it to appear that it is written by you? (I have only glanced through it, but see no references to Mr. Shaw.)

ANDROCLES is doing very well—no house under £200. Saturday's was well over three. I sneeze at your PYGMALION with its £1,500 a week. N.Y. under snow tonight so we may be a little down. I am saving up your fees for a week or two in case you should be tempted to spend them in running FANNY at the Kingsway. But you shall have a cheque on account by next Saturday. (Naturally, of course, the capital expenses have been rather heavy, and I have to pay Drinkwater back fourteen hundred which he is hungering for—that's the reason.)

I really do not see what there is to do but give up the Kingsway.[1] Look at what we have been losing ever since the war started. It is all very well doing that for Drinkwater's sake and Lena's and the staff. We have done our best, but we cannot have the Joffre of their personal circumstances nibble away every penny we possess.[2] It isn't sense. Nor do we need a permanent home so badly. The one advantage we have is that we can fly our banner anywhere. If we had any really likely plays to go on with, it would be another matter. But what is the real sense of reviving FANNY? You will see, I fear, that I am right in my £40 a performance estimate. You didn't understand my sporting cable, because you couldn't see the fellow one to Drinkwater, in which I raised his estimate £20 a week. I put it in the form of a bet, for out of my pocket it will come.

ANDROCLES is very well received here. I mean the audiences really listen to it more or less intelligently. We are pushing our way into repertory as quickly as possible. We produce THE DREAM on Sunday, and after that the others as quickly as I can, but of course with these heavy productions, eight performances a week, and the theatre with no equipment whatsoever, it is not a very easy job.

All for the moment,

Yours,
H. G. B.

---

1. The lessee of the Kingsway Theatre was Lena Ashwell. She had sublet it to the Barkers in 1912 on a long lease, and it was still in their hands, though they were away in New York. Their affairs at the Kingsway were being managed by A. E. Drinkwater (John Drinkwater's father). The production of *Fanny's First Play* which Shaw was directing was technically under Barker's management.
2. Marshal Joffre was notorious for his acceptance of policies of attrition and for his order to the French army early in World War I: "Stand and die, but do not retreat." Some may think this metaphor of Barker's rather highly colored.

BL/TS
To Shaw

Wallack's,
Broadway & 30th Street,
New York.

———

Lillah McCarthy
Granville Barker
Feb'y 5, 1915

ANDROCLES still goes along, and will get another week all to itself, as the DREAM—when I came to the first dress rehearsal—was not nearly ready. It will take me another three weeks to get out the third play I fear, although I could follow that with a fourth more quickly. But the company are very tired. Washington and Lincoln both saw fit to have birthdays at this time of year, which means two extra performances, and we have to give The Stage Society a Sunday night, which means a third.

How late in the season do you think we should do THE DOCTOR'S DILEMMA? My present inclination is to do THE MADRAS HOUSE third, and about the same time either a definitely "unpopular" triple bill—the Molière, PHILIP and TINTAGILES, or IPHIGENIA (if I could get the chorus tackled).[1] Lillah has been very good about Helenas and Lavinias and things of that sort, and has been an enormous strength to the cast, but she does feel a little bit that she ought to have one big acting chance during her first season here. Then I should quite deliberately do THE DOCTOR'S DILEMMA as late as possible, announcing at once that it would be performed again in the autumn. I have an idea that it might be rather good to (a) disappoint a large number of people of seeing it, and (b) give a sense of continuity to the seasons. Nor do I feel that this would be a bad business move from the play's point of view, but perhaps you may; if you do, you must cable me the latest date which you will allow it to be produced. THE MADRAS HOUSE I want to get done, but I don't suppose it will appeal to more than a limited number of people. Then next season if we could only get a good Undershaft (query Ainley—or would he be too stolid?) we ought to have a go at Major Barbara. It is good, in a sense, don't you think, to work through the later plays chronologically? Also, if one can get a company playing together, and, by elimination, really good, GETTING MARRIED and MISALLIANCE will have an infinitely better show than they would with a more scratchy performance.

I suppose you will be agreeable to ANDROCLES being sent on the road in the autumn. I should propose to send Heggie with it as the principal person, incidentally to look after the company, and to give him a slight interest in its proceeds as well as his salary. He does deserve very well of us, as he has been a perfect brick over the way he has worked at starting this season. I don't think I could have pulled it through without him, and he does deserve particularly well of us in this play.

Yours,

H. G. B.

---

1. These short plays, all of which he had directed in London, were Molière's *Le Mariage Forcé,* Masefield's *Philip The King,* Maeterlinck's *The Death of Tintagiles,* and Gilbert Murray's translation of the *Iphigenia* of Euripides.

BL/TS
To Shaw

Wallack's,
Broadway & 30th Street,
New York.

Lillah McCarthy
Granville Barker
February 19, 1915

You're a nice one. I sent Drinkwater the most definite instructions by letter and by cable, to give notice at the Kingsway, and he calmly writes—writes, mind you; doesn't even cable—to say that after consultation with you he has decided not to do it. Well, I hope you and he are prepared to pay the rent, that's all. Take notice, that I intend to deduct it from your ANDROCLES royalties. Seriously, though, what do you expect us to do with the Kingsway? Once before, by going on too long with a scheme after that scheme had served its purpose, I lost every penny I had made, and ran into debt to you besides. (I am very glad to say you have never had it all back.) It seems to me criminal lunacy to repeat the process with the Kingsway. I have done nothing for the last year but warn Drinkwater and Lillah that I intended to walk out. Neither of them would listen to me, nor even discuss the process of my doing so. So this is what happens. I wanted to make an arrangement by which somebody, or bodies, took over the greater part of the responsibility, leaving Lillah and me some interest in thc thing, which we would account for by leaving our good will, and doing what work for it we could. That's an arrangement, though, which cannot be made in a second, nor in the middle of the war can it probably be made at all. But I really cannot sit in England and watch theatrical London crumble around me, so the only thing left for us to do is to make a clean cut of our losses, which, since the war broke out, have been pretty severe. I come to America to keep the flag flying, and, incidentally, to make large royalties for you, and I am damned if you then don't go, according to the worthy A. E. D. [A. E. Drinkwater], and spur him to sink in the blessed Kingsway every penny we may make in New York. What do you think of yourself?

As to the contention that you cannot put up FANNY when the theatre is only yours on a three months notice, well—do you really think that as Lena is in the play and if it is still a success at the end of the three months she is going to take it off because the theatre has passed into her hands? I despair.

We produced The Dream on Tuesday, and it seems, for the moment, quite as much a success as ANDROCLES, which, again, I don't think it will in any way spoil. Its announcements and notices and the beginning of Lent, of course, knocked the business down a little, but for this, I suppose, you were prepared. But we did $800 on the first night of The Dream, over $1000 the second night, and ANDROCLES in between (and Ash Wednesday evening too) was over $1100. The Dream may not last like ANDROCLES. I don't myself think it will, but the policy is justified. I wish I could get the third play on at once, but the strain of the work has been rather severe. I am dog tired, and if I were to rush another one out in another ten days or so, the company would either strike or die. So I must go more leisurely, and we shan't get another production ready in much under four weeks from the time I write. I have taken the theatre though, until the end of April now, so that before the season finishes I think we really shall have had repertory in New York. There are various rumors around of wonderful offers to be made me, and theatres to be built me. They don't come to anything so far, nor do I really think they will. But what I do think is that we can organise a theatre of our own over here, for, at any rate, some months every year, possibly transporting the whole repertory to such places as Chicago and Boston—certainly sending the more popular pieces on the road by themselves.

I send you a notice or two of The Dream, also two pages from the Literary Digest, chiefly because I think the first sentence is worth reading. Actually, the France thing is rather jolly, and I am awfully glad to have had you two in a bill together. I forgive you much for standing pat on the repertory business. As it happens, I have had no one to consult except Lillah on the point, but needless to say, every one, or nearly every one, was on their knees to me to let ANDROCLES alone, and be content with that for the whole season, and had we been on shares with the management they would have brought considerable pressure to bear, then I should have been thankful to get behind you for the fight. Surely the New York problem isn't an easy one. I don't trust the public here; I think they are most alarmingly fickle, and if we were not in the old Court Theatre position (considerably improved), that is, if we had not a considerable stock of things on which to draw, I should doubt my ability to do the job. And I call heaven to witness that I will not do it for more than two or three years. Still, in two or three years in this country one can break down a prejudice and establish a custom. I think by the time I stop, we can have other people playing the game.

Find time to dictate me a letter, saying how you think things in England are. I don't mean theatrically, but generally. Newspaper news is no use to me. What is going to happen after the war? Can you prophesy at all? Is there going to be a fearful reaction against all the things we want socially, politically and dramatically? What is a worry to me is to be away. It would be a great mental relief to me to be in the trenches (and I suppose that's what it is to a great many people to go there). I notice that the 75% that have not been either killed or wounded seem to be having a blazing good time. If there was anything I could do—(I mean not by going "to the front"—for heaven knows I should be no use there—but at home) I should be delighted to drop all plans here—for after all, ultimately, this isn't my job—and to come back to England: but to find one had been out of everything and therefore must forever remain so—for that there could be no compensation. You're Irish—you don't really understand. I am mongrel enough for the feeling not to be at all unconscious. Still, I have the feeling!

You are not so loved here as you were. The "Common Sense about the War" raised you up many enemies, and turned some of your friends very sour. Dear Eleanor Robson,[1] now gone quite grey and become Mrs. Belmont, but still as beautiful and pleasant as ever, turned a very hard face on me over it. Other people did. The pro-allies as a rule are far more virulent than the jingoest Englishman. Still, I fancy that the people who really have the government difficulties to contend with, and the younger school of men, the set answering to our Fabians, understood and appreciated.

Yours,
H. G. B.

---

1. See Chapter XII, p. 561.

BL/TS
To Shaw

Wallack's,
Broadway & 30th Street,
New York.
February 26, 1915

Well, you see, according to cables up to the moment of writing, FANNY is doing just what I prophesied; forty odd pounds a performance. And on that, I suppose, we are losing a comfortable one hundred and fifty a week. Very pleasant! Its awfully good of you to have gone through with the fag of the production, since there seemed nothing else to be done. It is a shock to me to see here that inanely caddish attack on you in the Times and Westminster—a shock because it looks as if people were losing their nerve; you are case-hardened to these things. But to the theatre—what else is there to be done now but keep on reviving? What other results can we expect than the present? How long do you expect us to smile and smile and be a loser? What else can we do but give Lena notice?

The ways of the righteous over here are not entirely smooth. To begin with, the atmosphere inside and out of New York leaves me like a piece of chewed string. I am the victim of re-action at any time, and here the stimulus is so great (and one can get through a devil of a lot of work when one is doing it) that the re-action is the more appalling. And it seems so with business too. Listen to this: Saturday matinee of the Dream—$1680. Monday matinee of ANDROCLES (Washington's Birthday) $1700 something. Tuesday and Wednesday nights The Dream down to the four hundreds. Last night ANDROCLES made a sharp recovery to $1200 odd—and the Dream will improve again, by all the signs. But evidently one may be the victim of things of this sort. So it wants watching. And I am determined not to call upon the backers here for a farthing if I can avoid it this season (so I may fleece with the better conscience later on). I hardly dare follow with MADRAS HOUSE and THE WITCH. If The Dream was steady, I could. But as it is, I think THE DOCTOR'S DILEMMA will have to go in, and then THE WITCH, if possible. (Lillah owed her one big acting part, or what she considers so.)

The Founders of The New Theatre[1] give me a public dinner Sunday night, and I have to make a speech. I keep on making speeches and I shall become a good speaker if I don't die of it, and the signs are that we can establish a repertory here, or we can go around the country making money.

Don't you exasperate me by boasting of your PYGMALION returns. Have you so soon forgotten all you said about the performances at His Majesty's? You think you are going to tempt me to report to you on the performances here. You're not. But there's your choice.

I think I can get a pretty good DILEMMA performance. I very, very much want to do MAJOR BARBARA next year. Also there are plans on in order to fill up time and stamp ourselves as really high-class, to do two or three Greek plays in May in the Stadium at Harvard, which holds about 7000, the Bowl at Yale, which holds 71,000! (that I think we shall really have to cut in half) and the Greek Theatre at Berkeley, California, which holds a mere five or six thousand. Altogether, there is fun ahead, though in my mind's eye England still appears a very pleasant place.

As to MISALLIANCE, the difficulty is "Tarleton". I haven't got one here that I could rely on, though I should think one might be provided for next season. One admirable American actor—Thomas Wise—could do it, but he is not getable at the moment.

Advise Drinkwater any how you can, about the fate of the Kingsway, but on one point I am firm, and he must be absolutely forced to do something to save the situation for himself, if there is anything to be done.

I am planning to send ANDROCLES on the road in the Autumn, starting at Boston; Heggie to go with the company, and more or less in charge of it after I have done the production, and some of the present company. After Boston—Chicago, Philadelphia and that sort of thing. I conclude you approve.

Yours,

H. G. B.

---

1. See notes 1 and 5 on p. 54.

BL/TS
To Shaw

Wallack's Theatre,

New York.

April 16, 1915.

Things are very parlous here from a business point of view, as you may judge from the returns you receive. THE DOCTOR'S DILEMMA has never done any good after its first two or three performances; that is to say, it isn't getting down to the general New York public at all. In Holy Week, curiously enough, the business went up all round, and Easter and now, when it ought to be doing better, the bottom dropped out of it.

The financial position is rather serious, but can be weathered. I begin to wish, though, that the Kingsway had not absorbed so many pennies lately. I asked for $20,000 to run the season here, and got $10,000. with some difficulty. Had I been strictly businesslike, I suppose I should have done ANDROCLES alone as cheaply as might have been, and probably we should have pulled through quite satisfactorily. But I thought it better to go up or down with the repertory flag flying, so I added THE DREAM and then when things seemed to be turning badly, THE DILEMMA as a popular card. The $10,000 has gone, and I shall now have to find another $10,000 myself to go after it. I have held up all your cheques rather shamelessly, because if money ultimately had to be found in England to pay you (as it has), there was no object in transferring and re-transferring. I have cabled Drinkwater now to settle up with you and himself from English resources. I never know what I possess or what I don't, but at a rough guess he will be able to pay THE DUMB WIFE fees and the Kingsway expenses out of the money on deposit, but he will have to hand over to you some securities, which, if you will you might take at their face value for the moment. They are probably pretty good things, but it would obviously be madness to sell them now. Beyond this, there is little doubt (as theatrical doubt goes) that ANDROCLES will do something pretty good on the road, so I am booking it for the autumn, though not of course quite on the advantageous terms we would have if things had gone well here and we had enough capital ourselves. Still it seems probable that it will get back some of the New York losses. The $10,000 capital found by these people over here was simply to be paid back to them if it was there to pay back after the New York season was over, so I shall have no responsibility for that.

As to the future, I gave these New Theatre Founders up to yesterday to decide as to whether they would run for us or have us run for them a repertory theatre in New York twenty weeks in the year. As they have not decided I conclude they cannot raise the wretched $300,000. which it requires. Something may happen within the next week or ten days, but one should not count on it. Beyond that, I have had one or two suggestions as to running on in America on a strictly commercial basis. But though they sound very good, I have been thinking things over well, and have come now to a decision—either repertory or nothing. By nothing I mean that I will go through with the ANDROCLES and DOCTOR'S DILEMMA commitments, and after that no more management; no more producing. Somebody else must do the job. It will be an enormous relief: for American conditions, though better in some ways, make me chafe under the yoke even more than English ones do.

My one real success over here has been as an after dinner speaker, and it is characteristic too that I believe I can make quite a tidy sum of money out of a lecturing tour in the Autumn. They love being told what to do and then not doing it. However, <u>we</u> don't even like being told what to do.

I may be able to work THE DOCTOR'S DILEMMA into Boston and Chicago in the Autumn. But there are many objections made to its length. In New York the American public walks in at 8.30, no matter what the time announced is. I am told that outside of New York they always walk out at eleven. I have had many frantic demands to cut, but I have resisted them. In the first place one shouldn't; in the second place it wouldn't make more than seven or eight minutes difference. It is very curious here that they do not in the slightest appreciate the first act. You should hear the silence when Heggie says on the first entrance, "You removed her nuciform sac". We should, however, finish up with a fine flourish. We do both IPHIGENIA and THE TROJAN WOMEN in New York at a new Stadium they are building here; also in the Stadium at Harvard, the Yale Bowl and at Princeton. I think we ought to draw large crowds, though Heaven knows; but we are doing it on a whacking big scale, and really, as it ought to be done, and I think THE TROJAN WOMEN at least will be rather a glorious flare-up.

If I ask you to regard this letter as private, you will probably publish it in The Daily Mail. But you might show it to Drinkwater.

Yours,

H. G. B.

BL/MS
To Shaw

c/o F. C. Mathews & Co.,
110, Cannon Street,
London, E.C.
[undated]

This is Mathews' draft[1] and to save time would you send your answer direct to him here.

I shall be up from Stansted on Tuesday. Will you be visible then? I'm at Stansted till then.

H. G. B.

---

1. See next letter, below.

BL/TS
To Shaw[1]

c/o F. C. Mathews & Co.,
110, Cannon Street, E.C.
14/7/15

Dear Shaw,

As I have already explained to you the Trustees of my Marriage Settlement are applying to the Court for leave to raise upon the securities which I settled last October a sufficient sum to pay off my liabilities. My total liabilities are about £5,000 including the £2,000 I owe you. My Trustees are asking leave to raise £3,000 but I am advised that the Court will not grant them this leave unless they are satisfied that the sum raised will be sufficient to avoid any Bankruptcy proceedings being taken against me by any of my Creditors.

You have very kindly said that you are prepared to allow the repayment of the £2,000 I owe to you to stand over until I am in a position to meet it and that you will not require repayment out of the money the Trustees are asking leave to raise upon my Marriage Settlement funds. For the purpose of satisfying the Court will you please let me have a line confirming this arrangement.

Yours,
H. G. Barker

---

1. This letter was enclosed with the previous note.

BL/MS
To Shaw

H.Q. British Red Cross,
Army Post Office 3,
British Expeditionary Force.[1]
Aug. 16, 1915

I plan to sail on the Rotterdam from Falmouth on Sept. 10.[2] The intention of the H. A. [Holland-America] line in choosing that port is evidently that I should spend a day with you at Torquay, if that's where you'll be, on the way down. Meanwhile I stay here in Boulogne—or hereabouts—till the end of the month, seeing things and writing about them: some interesting; mostly dull.

That trustee business is nearly through—my God, the law's delays. A magnificent letter you wrote me: I only saw it in an exhibit to an affidavit the other day. The whole affair is rather sickening as I

look back on it. Burton continues to plague rather[3] and on one point
I think you'd better express an opinion.

The capital for the Androcles tour is £1,500 (I am finding
£1,000 and Burton £500). Burton, having pressed me for that, presses
me to say I'll find more if need be. But if need is I certainly can't
find it and you had better say before I leave for America what you
want done. I can

(a) tell Burton to go on with the thing at his own risk;

(b) ask the two honest theatre-men I know over there—
Winthrop Ames and John B. Williams—if either of them care to take
over my share;

(c) compel the tour to shut down;

(d) or of course it is up to you to find more money and send
the thing along if you wish.

Burton declares his willingness to find any sum in reason (as
long, of course, as I am finding double!) but whether it will be worth
while to do anything but (c) will depend I suppose on where the
"need be" finds us. I haven't a tour list with me. We open at Washington on Oct. 11. It is true that Lillah's salary and one thing and
another have lifted the expenses considerably and they were high
enough anyhow. So it is possible that we might have done badly before we reached Boston or Chicago or places where there would be
money to be made. You had better know how matters stand and
advise on them if you want to. And as to (a) and (b)—if it is to be
done it would perhaps be wiser to do it now, for if one waits till the
money is gone I should have to let them save the ship on their own
terms.

Of course I am not keen on giving up my control and unless
things go quite badly £1,500 ought to be enough. This said rather
confusedly for my mind is full of other things. It is clear to me that
my financial morale is completely destroyed—if, indeed, it ever stood
up very strong. It is as well that there is a certain share of crude
rectitude in me somewhere. To set out on a job knowing that £1,500
is not sufficient to carry it through, but knowing that if £1,500 isn't,
£15,000 very likely isn't either and that therefore £1,500 will probably
do—who can stand up against that sort of thing? Yet that is theatre
finance and I wish I had never put my finger to it.

What are you up to? When is the new war screed coming
out? I have been near up to things a little and—I tell you—it's the
stupidest business. But dreadful, too; really dreadful. Though it's like
naughty, vicious children playing, yet there's a deadliness about the
power they have and a devilishness about what happens that makes
one hopeless of ever being able to do the real fighting with the finer

weapons again. The fools—they don't know what <u>that</u> is or they wouldn't waste time and themselves like this.

Love to Charlotte, please.

H. G. B.

---

1. As mentioned above (see note to letter to Archer of February 4, 1916), Barker was writing a book for the Red Cross about that organization's work on the battlefields of France.
2. He was returning to the United States partly to supervise the tour of *Androcles and the Lion,* which had already been arranged, and partly to fulfill lecture engagements.
3. Percy Burton (1878–1948) worked both in England and in the United States. He was at various times theatrical manager for Beerbohm Tree, William Gillette, Sarah Bernhardt, and Edward Sothern, among others.

BL/MS
To Shaw

Stansted,

Wrotham,

Kent.

Wed. 18/8/15

I am back here for a few days at least looking after Lillah who has had, I am sorry to say, a sort of echo of the trouble of five years back.[1] Not dangerous, the doctor assures me, but serious enough to be very worrying. <u>And</u> he now positively forbids her to go to America in September. Whether he'll let her go a month later it is too soon yet to ask. I must break this at once to the wretched Burton. Is there anything <u>you</u> want to say about it meanwhile?

I'll send you further news of her.

Yours,

H. G. B.

---

1. Lillah had been ill in 1909 and again the following year with some kind of nervous disorder, the details of which are not known. In a letter to Gilbert Murray in September, 1909 (not included in this volume), Barker says that she has been ordered to bed for two months, seeing no one but a doctor and her nurse. In September, 1910 (not included in this volume), he writes Murray: "I may be bringing Lillah down here about that moment now. Which she is ill—not very—but two nasty chills (insiders) have made the doctor say that she must rest for a couple of months. . . . Sir, don't say Lillah is ill—it makes her wild to have people think or know it: and she isn't really; it's only she must rest."

BL/MS
To Shaw

Court Lodge,
Stansted,
Wrotham,
Kent.
[August, 1915?]

I've been staying a weekend with the Wheelers and saw about rooms in these hotels, hoping to go back with Lillah who now can't leave here for more than a day.[1]

---

1. This text fills the first page of this letter; the remaining pages are missing.

BL/PC
To Shaw[1]

Chicago.
Oct. 18, 1915

They've got a lot of this chap's stuff here—better a lot than this which is all they make a 1 cent p.c. of.

H. G. B.

---

1. This postcard shows Anders Zorn's painting "The Two Cousins," from the collection of the Art Institute of Chicago.

BL/MS
To Shaw

Algonquin Hotel,
New York.
Nov. 19 [1915]

I owe you several letters, but I have been galumphing round the country lecturing.

Androcles goes its way—up and down—not fatally down, not definitely up. We keep on. I have undertaken to see it through to Chicago but the company have accepted 25% reduction of salaries to get us there and devil a cent have I or Burton taken in salary at all. I am satisfied now, I think, that though Lillah would have made a difference she would not have made all the difference—and her salary would have been in great jeopardy. I can so far find no one who will put their pennies into G. M. [*Getting Married*] or Misalliance. Ames has another theatre—the Booth: quite a good size, but the Little is his ewe lamb and the Little has a clientèle of its own:[1] it plays to an average of receipts <u>whatever</u> it does—the only other house in N.Y. bar the opera that can boast this (except perhaps Frohman's Empire). I have seen William Harris, Jnr. He was polite about G. M. and M [*Misalliance*] and wondered if you couldn't be persuaded to bring Major Barbara up to date!—and since then he doesn't answer letters. No doubt he is one of the best—unfortunately among managers here that is not saying much. Calvert—fatter than ever!—told me that he was going on with M. B. whether you liked it or not—and so he apparently is.[2] They are making quite an earnest effort there: no quality in it, I fear, but that you can't look for—Grace George, you know. She is a most competent, in many ways a most attractive, actress but the Salvation Army would scarcely own her.[3] I daren't prophesy results to you but I daresay it won't be worse than Pygmalion.

I am trying to work the Pinero play for Lillah, but that isn't over-easy.

Souls on Fifth is a moral tale of 10,000 words.[4] It should be published by the S. P. P. G. (Society for the Prevention of the Propagation of the Gospel); as it is, Scribner's won't look at it. But remember that now I must pot-boil for my living as well as write decent plays. And don't you boast to me. Since August, though my mind hasn't been quite free from distraction, I have done 30,000 words for the Red Cross, Souls, adapted a three-scene play from Meredith, done two scenarios, an article, two more short stories and got 12,000 words along with a book on the theatre. I don't say it's all first-rate, but still.

I have taken the utmost pleasure in sending my resignation to the Dramatists.[5] I see the blundering paw of H. A. Jones in it. I nearly tweaked his nose last winter in a New York theatre for the same sort of thing: coram publico.

I give my last lecture on November 30 and mean to sail as soon after that as may be. Your lecture was reported a little in the New York Times. Well, the damned public threw over the prophets at the beginning of the war. Let them rot. Those who are fighting are sane and free. I met no other, at least—anywhere. They are sweet tempered about it. As for us, we must go on till we drop.

My love to Charlotte.

H. G. B.

---

1. The New York theater, of course, not the London Little. The New York house, at 238 West 44th Street, was built by Winthrop Ames especially to present plays which could not be expected to survive commercially on Broadway. Its capacity was originally only 299 but was later increased to about double that figure.
2. Louis Calvert (1859–1923) acted regularly in the Barker-Vedrenne 1904–7 season at

the Court Theatre. He was the original Undershaft in the 1905–6 production of *Major Barbara.*
3. Grace George (1879–1961), the wife of the theatrical manager William A. Brady, was a leading lady and a manager in her own right. She produced *Major Barbara* in New York in 1915 at the Playhouse, playing the title role. She also played Lady Ciccly in *Captain Brassbound's Conversion* in March of 1916, both plays being part of a repertory season which she and her husband put on at the Playhouse, a theater which he had built in 1911.
4. This short story was published by Little, Brown in 1916 and appeared in two parts in *The Fortnightly Review* in London the following year.
5. The Dramatists' Club had passed a resolution expelling Shaw from its membership because of his outspoken and highly unpopular views on the war. Barker was joined in his protest resignation by a number of others.

On January 5, 1916, Barker left New York for France in order to complete his work on the book he was writing for the Red Cross. Just before leaving, he had written to Lillah, his wife, telling her that he wanted to end their marriage (see Chapter IV, letter of January 3, 1916).

BL/W
To Shaw[1]
    Boulogne   20 Jan. 1916   9.30 A.M.
    Bernard Shaw, 10 Adelphi Terrace, Strand, London.
        Remerciements adresser Croix Rouge Britannique, Hotel Christol, Boulogne. Prier prendre action aussitot vous trouvez possible et bonne[2] car je veux bien telegraphier Amerique vendredi ou samedi si possible. Aussi Lillah ne sait pas ou je suis et deviendra inquiete.

                              Granville Barker

1. Punctuation added to this telegram.
2. According to Shaw long afterwards, Barker at this time was urging Shaw to persuade Lillah to agree to an immediate divorce. Shaw was, in fact, in constant touch with Lillah, and some of his letters to her throw further light on Barker's position; see *Bernard Shaw: Collected Letters,* ed. Dan H. Laurence, vol. 3 (London, 1982). For Shaw's account of the affair years later, see *Drama,* n.s., no. 3 (Winter, 1946):12.

On January 31 Barker's passport was stamped "via Boulogne à Londres." He was in England only briefly; his passport shows a Boulogne stamp on February 17. A week later he was back in England

(Folkstone, February 24). On February 29 he obtained a visa in Folk-stone giving him permission to cross the war zone by train. This stay in France was again short, and on March 11, at Bordeaux, his pass-port shows that he embarked for New York.

BL/MS
To Shaw

Williamstown,
Mass.
(address for safety—
Algonquin, New York City)
April 4 [1916]

Is Myles Mathews[1] a bloody fool or is he not? I do wish you could discover, for his letters to me certainly do not dispel that fear. (I'm sorry if all this that follows is repetition, but the mails take such ages and I can't remember just what I have written.) I found here a letter from Lillah saying practically that her chief concern was as to her financial future and that she had been told nothing about my proposals for that whatever. I cabled at once to Mathews to tell him to repeat them as distinctly as possible; also to consult you and Wheeler as to whether he should add as a condition that unreason-able delay or something we may call "misbehaviour" (as to which possibility I have no reason to be easy in my mind—apart from its inherent difficulties) might cause their reconsideration. The proposals were that I should, when the divorce was satisfactorily through, make up Lillah's income to half my own over an average of three years with a maximum payment by me of £1,000 a year (this so that I might not have to pay away too great a proportion of a windfall which ought to be capitalised). My legal obligations are apparently a fifth of my income <u>pendente lite</u> and one third as permanent alimony. Now he writes repeating all this clearly to <u>me</u> and saying he will consult Wheeler[2] as I suggest. Therefore is he a bloody fool or not?

I added Wheeler to you for purposes of consultation be-cause he is—or was—in friendly touch with her and you may not be except for the specific purpose of hearing things that will annoy me.

I have had no letter from you since the one of March 4.

Can we reach no milestone in this business?

First of all I wanted the finance proposals put as definitely as they legally may be to some representative of Lillah's, so that she may have no excuse for saying that she does not understand them. This postulates a lawyer for her (someone other than [A. E.] Drinkwater—to whom you may as well talk as to a batter pudding). I told Mathews to insist as far as possible on meeting a lawyer. I get no evidence that he has done so.

Further than this I suppose we cannot "officially" go—but it would give me great relief of mind if you would tackle Mathews and satisfy yourself and me that as far as this we have quite clearly gone.

Unofficially—well, you can judge if there is anything to be done better than I. What in heaven's name she is waiting for I don't know. I really believe she has some idea in her head that no divorce is complete without a scandal. But if she thinks that I am going to stir a finger to risk precipitating one she is vastly mistaken. For myself— what do I care?—pen, ink and paper, please God, will always be the only necessity of life for me; but I have—if nothing else—a certain British pride in caring to show American gentle-people that in England we are not all either barbarians or cads in such matters—and I wish I could get a little assistance in the effort.

Or perhaps she thinks that she can bluff or weary the third party[3] out of the business, not stopping to consider that, even if she could, it would then in a little be she that would want the divorce and I that should snap my fingers.

But of course she isn't thinking at all—merely making her own life more miserable, with the able assistance of Maggie.[4] If anger at the futility of it all left one any room for sorrow I could and would be sorry.

Well, do what you can and send me what news you have.

It's good news there's a play on hand[5]—and I hope you will have time to make it shorter! You put me to shame. I work my four hours here in the mornings, but slowly, for during my ten mile walk in the afternoon, when I ought to be thinking of what's to be done next day, I am worrying—that's the truth. No MS available of the new masterpiece—yours? I should not keep it to myself—for the proof sheets were much appreciated and as to the message about her book![6] (It was a message.)

Oh, this waste of time and life. And one has so little of either to spare.

H. G. B.

---

1. Barker's accountant in London.
2. Charles Edwin Wheeler (usually known as Christopher) was an old friend of Barker's. His wife, Penelope, an actress, was a member of Barker's company at the Court Theatre from time to time.
3. Helen Huntington.
4. Margot Asquith, wife of H. H. Asquith, leader of the Liberal Party and British prime minister at this time. Both Granville Barker and Lillah McCarthy were on very friendly terms with the Asquiths in the years immediately preceding the war.

5. Shaw was working on *Heartbreak House,* which he began on March 4, 1916 (see Bernard Shaw, *The Collected Plays with Their Prefaces,* ed. Dan H. Laurence [London, 1972], vol. 5).
6. I take this to be a reference to Helen Huntington, though I am not entirely sure. By this time she had published four novels and three collections of verse. She may have been working on *Eastern Red,* a novel published by Putnam's in 1918. Barker would almost certainly have told Shaw about Helen's literary aspirations and achievements.

BL/MS
To Shaw

New York
May 6 [1916]

 I am in here for a day doing some business and your letter from Weymouth finds me on the way back to Williamstown—just time to send you this. So glad to hear from you. I hope my last letter was not impossibly priggish and peevish but of course this strain does pull me a bit too hard sometimes. It should not, for I am being set an example of much goodness and patience and in a way things are easier for me than for her.[1] But it is all damnable, damnable—the waiting. Conscription now: I shall be called back, I suppose.

 No time for more now—my train waits; or, rather, <u>won't</u>.
 My love and homage to Charlotte.

H. G. B.

1. He refers, I think, to Helen Huntington, not to Lillah McCarthy.

BL/MS
To Shaw

Williamstown,
Mass.
May 26 [1916]

 A somewhat garbled version of Cave's warning to report for military service appeared in the papers here [1] and I cabled at once to Mathews to report on my behalf and cable me when I was personally wanted. Today's news says that the act has just been signed, so I suppose that means in thirty days from now. Anyway, I await his cable. What the results of the Act will be I don't know—to begin with I should think a large crop of bankruptcies. Unless I can be here in January to earn my next £1,000 lecturing I really do not know what is going to happen to my affairs. But if the British Empire thinks I can do it more service guarding a bridge with a gun—so be

it! I shall certainly ask no favours either of Asquith or anyone else. I
cannot. I don't object to conscription in theory—what socialist
would? I only object to these conscriptioners—and that is not a valid
reason.

　　　So, you see me when you see me, and—

My love to you both.

H. G. B.

---

1. George Cave (1856–1928), later Viscount Cave of Richmond, a Conservative Union-
   ist M.P. from 1906 to 1918, suceeded F. E. Smith as solicitor-general in 1915 in the
   coalition government of Asquith. In this capacity he was responsible for the enforce-
   ment of the Compulsory Service Act, which conscripted to the military forces all men
   between the ages of eighteen and forty-one. Barker was now thirty-eight.

*Barker left New York on July 6, 1916, for England. He enlisted as a
cadet gunner but was soon granted a commission in the Intelligence
Corps. During this period he saw Shaw and his wife fairly often, but
he also wrote to Shaw on occasion.*

BL/MS
To Shaw

Garrick Club
[London]
Sep. 19 [1917]

　　　Yes, these occasional incursions of yours into the "affaire"
are brilliant perhaps, but my fear is that as in between times you
forget the facts you may do some harm to the case while you are
picking them up again: the "brilliant" lawyer's weakness.

　　　Why I say "Let it alone" is that, arrangements being made
and the case down to be heard in a month, if everybody concerned
only sticks to the arrangements then "let alone" it should go quietly
through.

　　　Again, if there is to be any "jibbing", Lewis is the person
who must deal with it.[1] So it hardly seems wise to embroil her with
Lewis, who I am sure has done well for her over money matters.

　　　Again, you may remember that a lot of loose and inaccurate
talk about "millions" brought on me last year a set of impossible
demands and it was months before they were convinced of this impossibility. The thing is now settled—Lewis, at least, can hardly re-
open it. But one does not want that agitation repeated.

As to the money, I think I will send you accurate figures, but you may take it that these don't err much:

Allowance—I pay £250 a year for three years from Jan. 1, 1917 (but the money has been paid from June 24, 1916). After that I pay £650 a year.

She had between £100 and £200 in cash—the surrender value of my life insurance.

She has <u>now</u> paid into her bank (I enquired again yesterday) the interest on <u>all</u> the marriage settlement, which I think is £5,500.

She certainly did earn money during the first four or five months of this year—how much, I don't know, but it must have been some hundreds. She is now rehearsing for something, I think at the Kingsway.

To live in a flat with a rent of about £220 and to pay the rent of it two years in advance is all right if you can do it. But it isn't wartime economy (after all, jointly and severally the war has cut our sort of incomes to pieces) or even wartime finance. And you should not do it if you have to complain of being in desperate straits. At a pinch that flat can be let furnished for £350 or so. I don't say she should: but she should if her income was really £250.

There is no real danger that I shall not be able to make and pay the allowance and it is not right—or, I think, wise—of you to say there is. If I needed to go to America now, I almost certainly could, but I see a prospect of the money here before Xmas and I don't want to squander my requests for favours. After Xmas—we must see. The difficulties for me are, under present circumstances, to pay off Galsworthy's debt and release your securities. And till I do, the interest to the bank and the insurance are a heavy burden. But her allowance is not likely to be in danger.

I know the morals you draw, but they are not always the conclusions she comes to. You don't want to start an assumption that Lewis has not done his best for her, is even cheating her and that with "millions" in the offing[2] she may as well try for some more of them—do you?

Yes, do please send me the masterly document.

H. G. B.

P.S. I shan't need to worry you for the £25. I have arranged to nobble that and £10 more which will tide over the quarter.

P.P.S. I asked Medley about the money and this is his reply.[3] I think he overrates her present income a little—and mistakes what was meant by "delay". But these are the facts. And I am finding the

money, though you may wonder how. But I manage to earn something. And books now bring in steadily a small sum.

---

1. Sir George Lewis (1868–1927) was the London solicitor who was acting for Lillah in
   the divorce proceedings.
2. Rumors of the expected settlement in Helen Huntington's divorce suit must have
   leaked out. Archer M. Huntingon did in fact prove to be very generous in the
   settlement he made when Helen's divorce was finally settled.
3. C. D. Medley, of Field, Roscoe & Co., was Barker's solicitor for many years. A
   typed letter from him to Barker was enclosed with this; for the text, see Chapter IV,
   letter of September 19, 1917.

BL/MS
To Shaw

Connaught Hotel,
Mayfair, W.1
[London]
27.12.20

Yes, I can "thole"[1] with this! I'm not equipped to argue the
point of the preface with you anyway. I don't mean in specialist
knowledge (which it doesn't need!) but in the power of mental under-
cutting. But I have the will to believe that, or something very like it.
How many disappointments to that will is the average weak brother
capable of sustaining though? "If thy <u>faith</u> sin against thee seventy
and seven times—"? And I don't say I am not often on the edge of
following up your admission (p. xl) about the blind will to live by
asking if that is not all (with its further implications of enjoying life)
which you can expect in aspiration from the "lower" animals; and, as
to how much higher <u>man</u> is—circumspice. Consciousness of purpose—yes; but at what point need the purpose to live, to enjoy, to
better oneself, cease to be blind and become a spiritual purpose? In
my depressed moments it is as easy to find spirituality in the giraffe
as in man. In optimistic ones I do find spirituality in giraffes—I find it
in hippopotami—I even find it in Winston Churchill. But is it only my
general happy benevolence getting ready for the next shock?

I have now a reflex that my bath is ready so I must fall in with
my—no, it is not a habit (as I found out in the army)—of starting the
day clean; and I must take up the load of my Maeterlinck again.[2]

Thursday morning.

. . . And then comes in the difference between "public" and
"private" man. "Mankind in a loomp is bad" as the poet says. Cer-

tainly if you take away from him individually the terror of fear he becomes an amicable being and a comparatively reasonable being. But fears and shames and "negatives" of all sorts get hold upon a crowd very easily. And how many hundred thousand years does not mankind as a crowd fly back behind man as an individual? And the materialists, I believe, always think of him in the crowd and so betray the nascent honour of the individual. The idealists argue from the individual to the mass and then are crushed with shame and disappointment when it turns into a collective wild beast with—at the highest—a <u>blind</u> will to live as its directing virtue. Now you—I hazard this—who for some obscure reason (which the Freudians might discover for you) have directed individual affections to mankind as crowd, well, you cannot, not being a myopic idealist, endow the crowd with the individual standards of virtue—though I don't say one isn't right to preach them and demand them—so you toss and gore and kick and _____.[3] But then—per contra (and I think it is very contra)—you assess the individual by the crowd standard. Hence the entire beastliness of certain of your characters—that I inveigh against. The finest things in the later plays are always, I think, the saving of souls, the saving them from the hell of humanity—and at the same time the acceptance of the hell. The first and last steps are recognition and acceptance.

This seems a wandering from the point. I think it isn't. But I only meant to note one or two things in the preface:

1. (p. xiii[4]) ". . . according to the prosecuting lawyers!" Well, the drafting lawyers, if you like. But it is the twisted interpretation of the arts that always gets me.

2. (p. xxvii) I believe that a reliance on the actuality (wrong word) of time is another scientific superstition, <u>i.e.</u> if you tell me that you want 4,000 years to arrive at a particular perfection, I should reply "Nonsense, a thousand years are but as a day". I make this obvious remark because of the Methuselah subject itself. To have spiritual perfectibility depending on physical time is to be out of one prison and in at another. (But that is the play, probably.)

3. (p. lxix) Why trail your coat? In any case, as you prove in the next sentence, they're not even good commercial principles. But the one thing for which the fighting man does <u>not</u> fight is anything to do with commerce. The "crowd directors", Kaisers and demagogues may whip him up for that purpose, but not in its name.

4. (p. lxxv) This is the only sentence I had to read twice to get its meaning clear.

The bath reflex acts upon me again and I can't leave this for another morning.

Can I see the rest of the play?

H. G. B.

---

1. Tolerate; put up with: "thole" is now archaic, though still a local dialect word in some parts of England. What Barker is called upon to "thole" with in the present instance is the Preface, some eighty pages in length, to *Back to Methuselah,* the page proofs of which Shaw sent him to read.
2. Rehearsals were in progress for Maeterlinck's *The Betrothal,* which Barker was directing. The play is a sequel to *The Blue Bird.* The production opened at the Gaiety Theatre on January 8, 1921.
3. Word illegible.
4. Page references are to the first edition, published by Constable in 1921. Barker was adding marginal notes to the proof pages before returning them to Shaw.

BL/MS
To Shaw

Netherton Hall,
Honiton,
Devon.
9.2.21

After cogitation—I had better have been able to read it more carefully—I don't find I've anything very notable to say about the new Gulliver.[1]

I am very interested in the Swift parallel. If Swift had had your diet—or you his! If he had had Dickens, Blake and Mozart behind instead of before him—

Part I: I'll confess, leaves me cold.

Part II: Exhilarates me.

Part III: I hate. You seem to me to be kicking the wretched Asquith-George[2] long after he is spiritually dead, but rather, it is true, as if you were a fellow-soul in torment, trying to escape and kicking viciously because you can't. But it is all rather a vacuum to me, an empty space (philosophically) between the before and after.

Part IV: I like best of all. Perhaps because I am an elderly gentleman—was born one. But besides that, the ingredients— the satire, the fantasy and the rest—seem to me better mixed. The whole thing balances better dramatically.

Part V: is Gulliver in excelsis. But it raises one question: how far can one use pure satire in the theatre? For satire scarifies hu-

manity. The theatre uses it as a medium and must therefore be
tender to it. Now in Part V it is quite possible that the automata
would be the most moving and appealing figures, leaving the
others—what? How do you practically proceed to adjust your
scale when you are using living actors—i.e. automata, all of
them? If you degrade the _____[3] end you falsify your case. If
you don't—! One other point: why do I so loathe the "newly
born"?[4] Why does she strike on me like a bit of <u>bad</u> Stravinsky
in the midst of a Mozart symphony? Is it because, far from being
an "all Shaw" writer as the common cant goes, you are a conscientious observer of men's insides—so that when you do observe
wrong, or merely, rather, observe the outside, the result is appalling. You must so loathe the newly born (your tradition of
manners not being hers—I did not know your mother for nothing—though you may have debauched them truckling insults to
your English tyrants) that you just write down the common Stravinsky scream you hear. You don't look inside her, knowing perhaps it would be a waste of time. But neither do you pass her
through your consciousness. That would make her "all of a
piece" artistically. I can't surely suggest the right solution but I
know there is something wrong. And I believe Part V should be
"all of a piece". As it has to be "de-humanised" and yet is to be
played by human beings, it perhaps had better be de-character-
ised. Perfect formality may be dramatically (interpretively) speaking what it will need.

I am ploughing slowly through my theatre book,[5] which I
wish I had never touched—I am unskilful in such matters.

Whether we shall drive the workmen out[6] before they drive
us crazy is still a question.

H. G. B.

---

1. He is still talking about *Back to Methuselah,* having now read the play as well as the
   Preface.
2. In Parts II and III of *Back to Methuselah,* Shaw parodies the political struggle between Asquith and David Lloyd-George, which had culminated in December, 1916,
   with Lloyd-George's replacing Asquith as prime minister and leader of the Liberal
   Party.
3. Word illegible.
4. A character in Part V of *Back to Methuselah.*
5. He was at work on *The Exemplary Theatre.*
6. Of Netherton Hall, that is.

BL/MS
To Shaw

Netherton Hall,
Honiton,
S. Devon.
25.6.21

Methuselah arrived this morning with my early tea. Thanks much. I have been dipping into it at intervals since—stolen from legitimate grind. And think—for the next week or so I shall have to ward off, from my miniaturing, dashes of your fresco style!

The "Elderly Gentleman" for me, I'm sure. As I open at random that "sings out" to me in a way the others don't—that and the preface. But Lord! I couldn't criticize it. I have the sensation of the judge in a horse show if someone came into the ring leading a Megatherium (No, no: that is <u>not</u> meant to imply pre-historic. Of a future breed, if you like.) He might say feebly "Something queer about its hocks isn't there?" But the proper thing would only be "Who wants a ride?" But it makes me feel youthful no longer to have you say "Spurgeon—a once-famous preacher".[1] By the way, the last act seems—at a glance—to be rather different.[2] Is it?

You had my note that the back debt was paid off? As the simplest plan, the bank was told to communicate direct with you. I hope they haven't given as much trouble handing back the securities as they did taking them over. I've not heard from them since. They are tiresome and incompetent—and the biggest bank in England. But if they are being a nuisance please do let me know and I'll nullify that somehow.

Love to Charlotte, please.

H. G. B.

---

1. The fame of the Reverend Charles Haddon Spurgeon (1834–1892) was at its height when Barker was a young man. As Shaw's comment indicates, by now he was almost forgotten, reminding Barker of the passage of time in his own case as well.
2. I.e., different from the first version Barker had read in proof.

TEX/MS
To Shaw

Hotel Victoria,
Lausanne.
8.4.22

Though my constitution is not what it was (and never has been!) I can still take a tonic—so your letter about the E. T.[1] was very welcome. But why in the name of 20,000 devils did you tear up the corrected proof sheets?

> The E. T. by H. G. B. made readable
> by G. B. S. illustrated by Max [Beerbohm]
> (he has done five beauties and
> written a prefatory poem besides!)
> Technical notes by W. A. (author of
> the works of Ibsen, the Norwegian
> Ossian)

—why it would have sold in thousands!

Yes, I know the form is damnable. The cause of that is mainly that I began the thing in 1914 (!) as a short pot-boiler, wrote it once on those lines and then discovered that the theatre I had nicely outlined would be no sort of use. It was, in fact, a simple set of directions to people asking the way to Putney as to how to get there. But now what I want to impress upon them is just that it is no good going to Putney or even to Wimbledon—they had better first stop and look about them.

And some of the sentences are damnable, though—oddly enough—one of those that rouses your ire doesn't—still doesn't—seem so to me. And as to it not being right to speak of a life "complete in falsity"—! I am writing of psychological things which are only to be expressed in terms of paradox—Damn it, Sir, have you never heard of a paradox?

I could have got the whole thing clearer and simpler by writing it a third time, no doubt. But it was ever thus with me—I discover what I'm writing about in the process of writing it only. You have the pull in knowing before you start. You are positive to begin with and no doubt superlative to end with!! I am comparative ever. So the argumentum ad Shaw is always hard for me to apply. What you say about clarity, though, is of course the soundest sense—a pale echo, as it happens, of Helen's wingèd words on the subject. She was not brought up intellectually on French literature for nothing. I may yet arrive at clarity but I must work through my Ann Leete vein to do it,[2] for that prevails in me. The devil of it is that I am interested in things which can never, in the nature of them, be made materially clear. In the fog of the E. T. there is more to be found than your impatience admits. If you have a fault it may be impatience (with things: too much patience with people) and that disables you a bit aesthetically!

Confound you, Benjamin, your Heartbreak House. In matter for the theatre it may be 50 years before its time. But the actors of 50 years hence may equally find its _manner_ abhorrent to them. It sets them no artistic problem. What you have always wanted for a leading man is a Barry Sullivan with your brains. But do the two things ever go together?

The argument that most impresses me is that plays create their actors. I wonder ? Shakespeare ? Ibsen ? It leaves out of account the influence of organisation on the theatre (c.f. the Théâtre Français and the German State Theatres) and on the other hand the tendency of the actor to suit himself only to the mode of the minute, whatever that may be. No, I think I could counter that.

We are on our way home, as this address will suggest. It was not, I think, the Lausanne weather which first caused Gibbon to deny the existence of a God—but it might have been.

Rapallo has on the whole been equally beastly in that respect, the Max Beerbohms supplying most of the sunshine themselves. We stay for a bit in London seeing dentists and such, then home when they have released us.

I have just done the first draft of an outrageously Ann Leetish play.[3] I shall spend the summer translating it into English.

Our love to Charlotte.

H. G-B.

---

1 *The Exemplary Theatre* had just been published.
2. Barker's early play *The Marrying of Ann Leete* was written (perhaps consciously and deliberately) in an allusive, oblique, impressionistic style.
3. *The Secret Life.*

BL/MS
To Shaw

Netherton Hall,
Colyton,[1]
Devon.
12.4.24

Well, we burned a candle to St. Joan as we passed by. For me, she covers a multitude of Heartbreak Houses and Methuselahs, Parts II and III. I believe it might be tagged "A Ratiocinative Mystery" play. The century of its subject is the century of its act—not in the Wardour Street sense! As _theatre_-act just as—well, I _could_ say, crude; but let's say, simple. The only difference is between God and a comic devil, cheek by jowl, and the divine and the comic all rolled into one. But the approach to it is, I believe, just the approach of the authors of the Chester Plays. Though in addition, of course, the ratiocination—the Platonic dialogue touch. And personally I like that scene better than any—the "Protestantism" scene between the three men. Matter and method seem to me to come together there to give the actors their best chance. All three good and Swete excellent there[2]—and no use at all in the later scene. So ask yourself why.

That would be my complaint, if I weren't too grateful for the whole to press it. Monotony of method in the acting and I think the method of the parts' writing is to blame. They all, so to say, begin at A and speak straight on to Z. And all so steadily occupied doing and saying, that what they <u>are</u>—!? Oddly enough this is hardest, to my mind, on Joan. Because it must have been what she quite silently <u>was</u> which impressed people—oh, far more than anything she said. I don't believe she was as glib as that—peasant girls (even saints) aren't glib. And when she suddenly turned Candida (with the Bastard)! Her last speech, though, in that church scene is magnificent—and Miss T [Sybil Thorndike] did it magnificently. Oh, if that had been the first time she really found her tongue! Otherwise, as far as Joan is concerned, the trial scene for me.

I am all for the epilogue, of course—though, there again, I could wish it had been done differently. It would have been mere tactics to make the actors play a new tune to refresh the ears of an audience that could not but be tired. Casson had to[3]—and what a difference that made. Thesiger half tried to:[4] but it needed co-operation. Though I see you did not want the usual "dream stunt".

And that division in the trial scene to mark the turning <u>did</u> need someone to do what you'll never bother to. As long as your meaning gets over, what do you care? A composer conducting!

But the acting very sound on the whole. And Lord! The sheep that had <u>style</u> and the goats that hadn't.

Are <u>you</u> well—and Charlotte? We are, and glad to be back—though Algiers was a success. I did a preface and nearly all the first draft of a play.[5] Then called away suddenly with the news my mother was dying. But she didn't: made an amazing recovery. So having watched it we came on back with some lost time to make up for.

H. G. B.

Have you read Shane Leslie's "Doomsland"? If not, do.

---

1. Farway's post office was now Colyton, as noted earlier.
2. E. Lyall Swete played the Earl of Warwick in the first British production of *St. Joan* at the New Theatre, London; the production opened on March 26, 1924. The play had already been presented in New York, opening there on December 28, 1923.
3. Lewis Casson played the Chaplain, John de Stogumber.
4. Ernest Thesiger played the Dauphin.
5. *His Majesty,* which was Barker's last play, took four years to write and was published by Sidgwick and Jackson in 1928. It has never had a major professional production.

Barker's letter about St. Joan *produced an unexpected result, which Shaw describes in a letter of June 15, 1924, to Florence Hardy (Thomas Hardy's second wife). He begins by saying that he has heard that "Mrs. Granville-Barker had been asking you whether you or your great husband had really been saying the dreadful things imputed to you by me in a terrible letter exploded by me on that peacefully luxurious household." He goes on to admit: "It was a most frightful letter, calculated to make him [i.e., Barker] either go out into the well kept garden and hang himself, or else write a thundering good play to refute me and prove that his Helen had been only nursing his wits for a masterpiece that would leave him first and the rest of us nowhere. He gave me the opportunity by writing to me about Saint Joan, which I told him was only a dare to him to produce something better or be for ever silent." Then later in the letter Shaw explains: "I cannot believe that he is an extinct volcano; but it is clear that Helen is sitting on the crater; and I want to provoke a vigorous eruption to dislodge her for her own sake as well as his; for if she succeeds in extinguishing him he will never forgive her: these grudges are deadly in marriage." Whether his own explanation of his motives is accurate or whether Shaw was simply furiously jealous of Helen (and either is possible) must remain an open question. The fact is that there is now a long gap in the known correspondence between Barker and Shaw. Whether this should be taken as indicating that there was literally no correspondence between the two, or that such letters as were written were not preserved by either party, or that some letters were written but have not yet come to light, it is impossible to say. There is still a mystery to be solved about what happened to his books and papers when Barker died in 1946 and, again, what happened to Helen's papers (and any of Barker's she may have retained) when she died in 1950. Specific bequests of books, set out in Barker's will, were never put into effect; and whoever kept the books may well have kept letters and papers also. On the other hand, the letters in this present chapter written by Barker to Shaw are now mostly in the possession of the British Library (Department of Manuscripts; shelfmark ADD 50534). They came directly from Shaw's papers after his death and it is reasonable to suppose that if there had been others Shaw would have kept them in the same way as he kept these and that they would, therefore, have turned up in the Shaw Archive in the same way. The probability is that during the period 1925–1942 there was little or no interchange of letters between Shaw and Barker and that they had drifted far from their former intimacy. In 1943, however, Shaw did write to Barker. The communication was brief, contained on a postcard, as follows:*

TEX/PC
To Barker[1]

4, Whitehall Court,
London, S.W.1
14/9/43

Charlotte died last Sunday, the 12th September, at half past two in the morning. She had not forgotten you.

Since 1939 she has suffered much pain and lately some distress from hallucinations of crowds of people in her room; and the disease, a horror called osteitis deformans which bent and furrowed her into a Macbeth witch (an amiable one), was progressing steadily and incurably. But last Friday a miracle occurred. She suddenly threw off her years, her visions, her furrows, her distresses, and had thirty hours of youth and happiness before the little breath she could draw failed. By morning she looked twenty years younger than you or I ever knew her.

It was a blessedly happy ending; but you could not have believed that I should be as deeply moved. You will not, I know, mind my writing this to you. She was 86. I am 87.

G. B. S.

---

1. This postcard is included in *The Shaw-Barker Letters,* p. 199.

"To this postcard," says C. B. Purdom in The Shaw-Barker Letters, *"Barker replied but the letter has not survived." In fact, it has survived and is now in the Shaw Archive at the British Library. It reads as follows:*

BL/MS
To Shaw

Mayfair House,
Park Avenue at Sixty-fifth Street,
New York.
Oct. 10, 1943[1]

I have in my memory many pictures of Charlotte, and since her death they have been exceptionally vivid to me; recollections too of her never-failing kindness and affection. But thankyou indeed for sending me this last picture of the thirty miraculous hours of youth and peace and happiness. They must have meant much to her and to you. And I think I do understand what her loss has meant, and will mean, to you. Yes, thank you for writing.

H. G-B.

---

1. Immediately under the date written by Barker, Shaw has added—in a now-shaky hand—"received Dec. 9, 1943 (air mail!)."

*That, so far as is known, was the end of the correspondence between
them, but when—less than three years later, on August 31, 1946—
Barker himself died at the age of sixty-eight, Shaw wrote to the* Times
Literary Supplement *the letter that has already been quoted in part
(see p. 111). Its full text reads as follows:*

Sir,

The enclosed photograph of Harley Granville-Barker, taken
by me at The Old House, Harmer Green, when our collaboration,
now historic, was at its inception, may interest your readers.

We clicked so well together that I regarded him as my contemporary until one day at rehearsal, when someone remarked that I
was fifty, he said, "You are the same age as my father." After that it
seemed impossible that he should die before me. The shock the news
gave me made me realize how I had still cherished a hope that our
old intimate relation might revive.

But

Marriage and death and division
Make barren our lives
                              and the elderly Professor could have
                              little use for the nonagenarian ex-playwright.

G. Bernard Shaw

Shaw died four years after Barker, on November 2, 1950.

Chapter IV

Lillah McCarthy, 1875–1960

Lila Emma McCarthy (Lillah was a stage name), the daughter of Jonadab McCarthy, was born in Cheltenham in 1875, the seventh of eight children. She claims in her autobiography that she was destined for the stage from the time she was a small child. Whether this is really true scarcely matters now; certainly she began her stage career very early, and by the time she was in her middle twenties she was already established in London as a leading player, having toured Australia and South Africa with Wilson Barrett and America with Ben Greet before that. It was her association with Shaw and Granville Barker, which began in 1905, that lifted her out of the standard repertoire of the day and made her into the best-known actress of the "new" theater. All the contemporary reports speak of the great beauty and flexibility of her voice, her commanding stage presence, and the beauty of her face and figure. Photographs—and there are scores of them—do not always entirely bear out that last point, but the camera can lie. The *Daily Telegraph* on December 3, 1913, carried a short item on this point:

A Fortune for an Actress
To judge from the numerous paragraphs in the papers about Miss Lillah McCarthy having been left a substantial fortune by her father, great interest is being shown by the public in the private concerns of this handsome and very popular actress. Portraits are given of her, all unflattering. The truth is, she does not photograph well, and her beautiful figure suffers from the camera even more that her bright, intellectual face. She is an ornament of the modern stage and has as part of her equipment a clear, melodious voice and perfect elocution, by no means common gifts.

Nobody, I think, disputed the point about Lillah's photographs, but there was some disagreement about the "fortune," as witness the fol-

Lillah McCarthy as Helena in *A Midsummer Night's Dream*,
1914. Photo courtesy Hoblitzelle Theatre Arts Collection,
The University of Texas at Austin.

lowing, from the *Daily Mirror* of the same date: "I have seen it stated in various places that Lillah McCarthy has been left £ 50,000—that is, that she divides her late father's estate of £100,000 with her brother Dan. But the fortune was to be equally divided among all the children, and 'Old Mac,' as he was called in Cheltenham, had three daughters and five sons."

Lillah and Barker were married in 1906. Shaw claimed, years afterward, that he knew from the start that the marriage was doomed to failure, and Barker himself maintained, in his letter to Lillah of January 3, 1916, that the marriage was a mistake and never should have happened, but these comments may simply reflect the wisdom of hindsight. When Barker raised the issue of divorce, Lillah at first fiercely resisted it. She was persuaded to it only by dint of considerable pressure from Shaw, Barrie, and other friends. She tried to continue her career as actress and producer after the divorce in 1918, but was unsuccessful. Without Barker, she lacked the capacity for choosing the right parts and the right plays, and her touch as a manager-producer was leaden compared with the quicksilver dash of his. The years from 1918 to 1921 were occupied with a series of disappointing failures, both artistically and financially.

In 1920 she married Professor (later Sir) F. W. Keeble, the holder of the Sherardian Chair in the University of Oxford. Though on her second marriage she abandoned her stage career to be the chatelaine of Keeble's beautiful country house in Oxfordshire, her letters to Shaw show that even as late as 1934 she still had thoughts of returning to the theater. These letters also show, rather pathetically, that her idea of returning to the theater was rooted in the notion of reviving her former triumphs. In 1930, when she was fifty-five, she tried to get Shaw to persuade Barry Jackson, the director of the Birmingham Repertory Theatre, to revive Masefield's *The Tragedy of Nan,* in which she had played the lead, a girl of twenty or so, in the first production in 1908. In 1932 she was pressing Shaw for a revival of either *Man and Superman,* in which she had played Ann Whitefield in 1905, or *Androcles and the Lion,* in which she played Lavinia in 1913. Shaw, in reply, admonished her in these terms: "You must begin a new career as a new woman, as Mrs. Charles Calvert did. I am sure that this is sound policy."[1] In a way, Lillah took Shaw's advice, abandoning the idea of reviving her old roles and looking round for new ones. But by the thirties it was not only her

---

1. Letter of August 21, 1932, Humanities Research Center collection, University of Texas at Austin.

ideas of the theater that were old-fashioned: her contacts with the profession were so as well.

In 1933 she turned to Shaw again, this time petitioning for the part of the mysterious Lady at the end of Act I of *On the Rocks,* the first production of which was being planned for later that year. Shaw wrote to her on August 26 saying:

> Are you really in earnest about this? If Van Druten's play [*The Distaff Side*] proves a success Sybil [Thorndike] may not be available; and you could make the big effect (such as it is: it's only a trifle) as well as she. . . . But would you really go through with it? The part has only 48 speeches, mostly two or three words to feed the leading man (nobody else on the stage), at the end of the first act; and she does not reappear. . . . Can you stand going back from being comfortable Lady Keeble at Hammels[2] or exploring the Andes[3] to the old professional drudgery of London lodgings and eight shows a week and Freddy deserted and in great danger of being rescued by some Brazilian beauty who has lost her heart to him on the ship or elsewhere?[4]

Shaw turned out to be right: Lillah was only *dreaming* of a return to the theater. She did not play the Lady, and the following year she turned down—as being beneath her dignity—the part of Queen Philippa in Shaw's *The Six of Calais,* the first production of which was presented at the Open Air Theatre, Regent's Park, on July 17, 1934, along with a revival of *Androcles and the Lion.* One reason why Lillah refused the part of Queen Philippa was that Shaw would not consider her for the part of Lavinia in *Androcles.* She would play the Queen if he would persuade the producer to give her Lavinia as well, she said. Shaw pointed out, quite reasonably, that Lavinia was meant to be a young woman and that the Open Air Theatre Company had two or three quite eligible young women who could play the part. This rather sad incident shows how out of touch with theatrical reality she had become. Lavinia was eventually played by Margaretta Scott, who was twenty-two at the time—thirty-seven years younger than Lillah. Even the Queen Philippa, Phyllis Neilson-Terry, was seventeen years younger than Lillah McCarthy. Lillah finally contented herself by setting up as *une grande dame du théâtre,* giving occasional recitals of verse, and so on. Shaw once wrote to her about one of these, to which she had invited him: "What a frightful swindle! I would not pay more

---

2. Sir Frederick Keeble's country house.
3. One of the things Sir Frederick had done, accompanied by Lillah.
4. Letter in the Humanities Research Center collection, University of Texas at Austin.

than five shilliings to hear Jesus recite the Sermon on the Mount. However, I will pay a guinea for the pleasure of seeing you. One for Charlotte also, please."[5]

Similarly revealing was Lillah's venture into authorship. In 1930 she began to write her memoirs, again leaning on Shaw for advice and support. Apparently, she wanted to include some of Shaw's letters to Barker which she still had in her possession. On September 4, 1930, Shaw wrote to her from Malvern: "The letters to Harley cannot be published without his permission, as they belong to him (as material objects) and I cannot authorize their publication decently unless he consents, which we cannot very well ask him to do. Besides, they are not of any particular interest in *your* life." The memoirs were first published in serialized form in the *Strand Magazine* in 1931. Edited by Lady Vaughan, they have a rather nauseating socialite tone, filled with mindless genuflections to famous names in all directions and on the slightest pretexts. Lillah was particularly proud of her friendship with Shaw and made great play with it in her book, presumably because this gave her some intellectual as well as social standing.

Immediately after the publication of the magazine articles, Lillah set about turning them into book form, under the title *Myself and My Friends*. She added some material, but the cloying tone remains the same. Moreover, at book length the repetitive patterns become more obvious. The one that deals with her actual work on the stage is particularly rigid and goes something like this:

a) We next produced _____ in which I played _____ [leading role];

b) This was a particularly striking part in a particularly striking play;

c) I wore the loveliest dress I've ever worn on stage;

d) X [famous name] said it was the best play he had ever seen;

e) Afterwards we gave a party and X, Y, and Z [famous names] were there.

Before publication, she sent copies of the book to various people for comment, notably to Shaw and to Desmond MacCarthy, the theater critic (who, despite the similarity of names, was no relation to her). To Shaw she actually sent the page proofs, which he filled with marginal notes—advice, suggested changes of text, and so on. Alongside a rather naive and jejune passage which Lillah had written about socialism and the Fabian Society, in which she had ventured some

---

5. Letter of November 5, 1930, Humanities Research Center collection, University of Texas at Austin.

opinions about the relationship between political systems and individual liberties, Shaw scribbled: "Out of your depth and out of date. Russia has made an end of all that poppycock." And he suggested an amendment to a passage in which Lillah had unctuously compared his methods as a director of plays with those of Beerbohm Tree: "Shaw, serious, painstaking, concentrated, relentless in pursuit of perfection: Tree, using the broader brush of the impressionist; casual but full of inventiveness." Shaw's suggestion was that she should cut "using the broader brush," etc., and replace it by "scatterbrained beyond description, making one wonder how any play could ever be produced at his theatre. But he was full of inventions, some of them very effective, however irrelevant. It is impossible to classify him: he was like nothing on earth: an interesting and successful Monster." On both Tree and the Fabian Society, Lillah stuck to her own versions of matters. Here and there she did accept Shaw's amendments, but never when he was being forthright or trenchant, especially about famous people. Lillah's style and strategy with the famous was ingratiation.

The Humanities Research Center at the University of Texas now has in its possession the page proofs which Shaw annotated for Lillah and also a set of the second page proofs. (Lillah had had these two sets of proofs bound together in hard covers.) The proofs differ in many details from each other, and both are different from the finally published version. An interesting, if minor, exercise is the page-by-page comparison of these three versions.

Desmond MacCarthy's comments on the early version of the book which Lillah sent to him are contained in a letter which he wrote to Lillah on July 11, 1931.[6] He begins by saying: "I have read your reminiscences and I enjoyed the early part. I had no idea that you made your way so quickly: a Leading Lady at sixteen! I found all the chapters about your career interesting, but not the social and travel chapters. I know that the public like reading about 'good times' and 'good friends,' but those subjects bore me in memoirs." A little further on, he elaborates:

> What I should like to read would be an account of what your parts meant to you and *how* you interpreted them; what you found difficult either in itself or owing to the acting of others. . . . Your idea of having a chapter on each of the producers you have worked for, comparing Powell,[7] Barrett, Tree, Granville Barker, Shaw is a

---

6. Letter in the collection of Humanities Research Center, University of Texas at Austin.
7. He means William Poel.

splendid idea.[8] But I want to read, too, your recollections of your difficulties and triumphs in your parts—*how* you managed to get an effect which satisfied you, why you had to be satisfied with this or that compromise in other places. Actors and actresses do not tell us nearly enough about such things. . . . The book would no longer be "My memoirs" by Lillah McCarthy but "*My parts.*" The only way to write it would be to study your old parts again. . . . But this is not a book which anyone could, with your help, write for you. You would have to write it yourself. . . . If at any time I could be of use to you, I should be very glad, but I know I could not *write* such a book.

The fact that Lillah had asked MacCarthy to do so was characteristic and, in a way, rather sad: it indicates that her motive for writing at all, like her motive for wanting to return to the stage, was related more to her need to establish new relationships with the social milieu which she remembered as important to her than to any intrinsic importance of writing or acting.

She made one other, similar, request for help which had unforeseen and startling results. The request was, again, to Shaw—that he should provide a foreword for the book. He agreed to do so and chose, in it, to tell in some detail the story of Lillah's marriage to Granville Barker, with full details of the divorce. The publisher of the book, Thornton Butterworth, took fright when he read it and, before committing it to print, consulted C. D. Medley, Barker's long-time legal adviser. Medley, of course, referred the matter to Barker and sent him a copy of Shaw's foreword. Barker was—predictably—furious, though with Shaw rather than Lillah. C. B. Purdom's account of the matter, which I think needs some modifying, reads as follows:

In the end, a new Foreword entitled "An Aside" was substituted. Barker had made it clear that there should be no reference whatever to himself anywhere in the book. With every mention of Barker, direct or indirect, eliminated, Lillah thought the book should not be published, and would have no more to do with it; but her husband did not agree and took over the book to re-write it, which he did thoroughly. Thus it came about that nothing at all was said in it of Barker's connection with the Court Theatre, or with the Shakespeare productions at the Savoy; even the fact that he and Lillah were married was omitted. In the revised version there was this reference to him: When I was touring with Ben Greet in 1895 there was a young man who played Paris to my

---

8. Lillah did not, in fact, pursue the idea in the final version of the book.

Juliet. I met him again at the Court Theatre in 1905. In April we were married. But even that was cut out, for Barker finally demanded that nothing should be said of him at all.[9]

J. C. Trewin, in the *Dictionary of National Biography,* acknowledging Purdom as one of his sources, follows Purdom's lead, saying: "Her autobiography, *Myself and My Friends* (in which Granville-Barker forbade any mention of his name), published in 1933, is the record of a warm-hearted woman and potentially fine actress."

Some letters which have come to light since both these accounts were written give a rather different perspective to the matter, however. The first of these is a brief note from Barker to St. John Ervine, the playwright and theater critic who died in 1971 at the age of eighty-eight: it appears along with other letters to Ervine in Chapter XI of this volume, but since it is short and very much to our present point, I will quote it here as well:

I see you are to review "Myself and My Friends" by Lillah McCarthy. I would just like to say this to you, if I may. It is by my own desire that my name is given no prominence in the book. I gather that it does not appear at all; but to this I make no objection. I feel sure that in your review you also will respect both the desire and the lack of objection. That would be friendly.[10]

One judges from that "I gather that it does not appear at all" that the decision to excise Barker's name completely from the book was Lillah's, not Barker's. All he had requested was that his name be "given no prominence"—and this request was evidently made after he had seen the kind of prominence Shaw had proposed to give it.

The other letters which shed further light on Purdom's account of Lillah's book, and which have fairly recently become available, were written by Purdom himself to Lady Keeble (Lillah) in 1952. There are some half a dozen of them, and they, too, are now at the University of Texas, Purdom having died in 1965. The correspondence began when Purdom, who was the secretary of an organization called the Shakespeare Stage Society, wrote to ask Lillah to take the chair at one of the society's meetings. It continued with a request from him for permission to edit certain letters—presumably Shaw's letters to Barker, which Purdom published in 1956 and which we know, from Purdom's acknowledgment in his *Harley Granville Barker* (1955), had remained in Lillah's possession. He actually says, in that acknowledg-

---

9. *Harley Granville Barker,* p. 191.
10. Letter of July 16, 1933, Humanities Research Center collection, University of Texas at Austin.

ment, "Without the letters of Bernard Shaw to Granville Barker this book would hardly have been written and I owe great thanks to Lady Keeble (Miss Lillah McCarthy) for letting me use them, and for her papers and recollections, which she has made fully available to me." Among the letters at the University of Texas are one or two in which Purdom, in 1952, seeks appointments to interview Lady Keeble. The tone of these letters and the fact that his book was published while Lady Keeble was still alive suggest very strongly that Lillah's "recollections" were accepted rather uncritically by Purdom and that, by the time they came to be written down, they had acquired in his mind something of the status of Holy Writ. He had been to Delphi, had heard the pronouncements of the Sibyl, and, like a humble scribe or amanuensis, had transcribed her words. We need to remind ourselves, I think, that in 1952, when Purdom talked to her, Lillah was seventy-seven, and the events connected with the writing of her book had occurred twenty years earlier. It is little wonder that the story Purdom received was a bit hazy, a bit inaccurate, and a bit prejudiced. Purdom says: "With every mention of Barker, direct or indirect, eliminated, Lillah thought the book should not be published." I have no doubt that this is what Lillah told him in 1952, but I doubt very much whether that is what she thought in 1932. For example, in the bound volume of page proofs at the University of Texas, there is a single large sheet of notepaper in Lillah's hand, headed "NOTES FOR SIR FREDDIE." The notes are all concerned with the deletion of Barker's name from *Myself and My Friends* ("p. 70—Should Barker's play be omitted?" "p. 74—Is G. B.'s name mentioned in collaboration with the play 'Prunella'?"[11] etc., etc.). It may be true (though I regard it as doubtful) that her husband urged the continuation of the plan to publish the book, but the guiding hand was still Lillah's and she certainly did not disown the book. My own copy of it, a reissue in 1934 (for Butterworth's Keystone Library) of the text of 1933, is inscribed by Lillah in her own hand, as follows: "To Sir Lewis Casson & Sybil with great love from the Old Pal, & not so much older than 'Rickie Tickie Tavy' of 1906. Bless you, dears—Old Lillah, April 1951."[12]

This copy, too, in spite of Purdom's statement to the con-

---

11. *Prunella,* produced at the Court Theatre in 1904, was written by Barker in collaboration with Laurence Housman.
12. Lewis Casson played Octavius in the original production, in 1905–6, of *Man and Superman,* in which Lillah created the part of Ann Whitefield. Octavius' nickname in the play is Ricky Ticky Tavy, after Kipling's mongoose, Rikki-Tikki-Tavi, in *The Second Jungle Book.* Kipling, Shaw, and Lillah all had their own ways of spelling the mongoose's name. Casson was only one month younger than Lillah, having been born in October, 1875.

trary, *does* contain the reference to Lillah's first marriage, without mentioning Barker by name: "When I was touring with Ben Greet in 1895 there was a young man who played Paris to my Juliet." The first set of page proofs of *Myself and My Friends* contains, in fact, a good many references to Barker, not all of them slighting or ungenerous. "Then came a Shakespeare season at the Savoy Theatre," she says on page 158, "under the joint management of Granville Barker and myself. The company seconded him magnificently and the tributes to all he did with them and for the cause of Shakespeare were—from those who knew and cared about such things—great and deserved."

In the second set of page proofs, this passage was printed in the same form as before, but in the margin a penciled note in Lillah's handwriting gives a slightly different version, in which Barker still gets a mention but loses most of the credit, which is transferred to Lillah: "Then came a Shakespeare season at the Savoy Theatre under the joint management of Granville Barker and myself which brought me the happiest experience an actress can have: the playing in company with a splendid cast and the enthusiasm of those whose judgement is as sure as it is generous." The version which finally got into the published volume omits Barker altogether: "Then came a Shakespeare season at the Savoy Theatre which brought me the happiest experience . . . etc." And so on, throughout the book.

What probably happened, I think (C. B. Purdom and J. C. Trewin notwithstanding), was this: (a) in the original version of the book, Lillah mentioned Barker as little as possible but as much as truth demanded; (b) she was inordinately proud of her connection with Shaw (who by 1931 was quite the most famous man in England), and so she asked him to write the foreword; (c) Shaw, who could be as tactless and cruel on some occasions as he could be gentle and generous on others, wrote a piece which clearly showed whose side he was on in the McCarthy-Barker-Huntington affair; (d) Barker leapt to Helen's defense and demanded of Shaw that he withdraw the mischievous foreword; (e) this made Lillah furious in turn, and so, when Barker—now in very much more restrained fashion (he must have known, in any case, that he could not *demand* or insist that she leave out his name if she chose not to)—requested that he not be given a very prominent place in the book, she childishly went through it line by line and took out *every* mention of his name, getting Sir Frederick to help her (her own English style being none too secure) to paper over the resultant cracks. (One almost hears her muttering wrathfully, "*I'll* show him!")

Some of the cracks never really did get papered over, however. Chapters Fourteen, Fifteen, and Sixteen still read very disjointedly and really make little sense unless one happens to know that, although she never mentions it, she is really talking about the break-up of her marriage with Barker.

Myself and My Friends, with its Shavian-and-water prologue, was published in London by Thornton Butterworth in 1933. It remains a theatrical curio: unpleasant, snobbish, full of stock responses and received opinion, all dished up in an embarrassingly gushing style which is made all the more objectionable by the insensitivity that shows through at every turn. Great play is made, for instance, with the author's passion for poetry, and, to demonstrate this, Chapter Three ends thus:

> Yet of the poetry I have heard spoken the most beautiful was that of a—to me—unknown voice which I heard over the wireless on the night when the General Strike came to an end. After announcing the news, the voice spoke with beauty surpassing any that I have heard Blake's lines on Jerusalem. The emotion with which I listened to the concluding lines is evoked every time they recur to my memory:
>
> > I will not cease from mortal strife
> > Nor shall the sword sleep in my hand
> > Till we have built Jerusalem
> > In England's green and pleasant land.

Unfortunately, whenever the lines recurred to Lillah's memory, they apparently recurred wrongly.

The four dedicatory quatrains from the preface to Blake's *Milton,* set to music by Sir Hubert Parry and popularly known as "Blake's Jerusalem" (which, of course, they aren't), were practically a national anthem in England in the nineteen-thirties, sung with crusading zeal and religious-patriotic fervor on occasions as various as the annual meeting of the Trades Union Congress, the Football Association Cup Final every May at Wembley Stadium, and the monthly meetings of the village Women's Institutes. A memory that could translate Blake's "I will not cease from Mental Fight" (the capital letters are Blake's) into "I will not cease from mortal strife" must have been insensitive indeed not only to the fine precision of poetry as such and to Blake, whose point in his preface to *Milton* is that mental struggle should replace physical warfare,[13] but also to the popular subculture of the day and what passed for poetry among "serious" people. The truth is that Lillah, despite all her protestations in this book, had

---

13. "For we have Hirelings in the Camp, the Court & the University: who would if they could, for ever depress Mental & prolong Corporeal War," says Blake in the Preface.

very little feeling for poetry: what she was fascinated by was spoken verse, especially verse spoken by herself. She was a performer first and last. That she was, in the years of her ascendency on the stage, a fine actress there can be no doubt: there is ample and reliable testimony to this effect. That she was also a jealous, possessive, over-ambitious and rather silly woman seems also to be demonstrable in the light of the evidence. Sir John Gielgud told me that she became, in her later years, very solemn and pompous, very much La Grande Dame,[14] but in her days as an actress she had been lively, vivacious, warm-hearted, and very well liked. Cathleen Nesbitt,[15] who played Perdita to Lillah's Hermione in 1912, told me at Chichester in 1978 that she remembered very clearly the esteem in which the rest of the cast held Lillah. She also said that she considered Lillah a very good actress, "though not always very intelligent." Barker, Miss Nesbitt thought, knew exactly how to direct her in order to get the best performance out of her, and it was, in Miss Nesbitt's opinion, probably the absence of Barker professionally rather than personally that "finished Lillah's career." T. Sturge Moore, the poet and playwright, expressed a similar view, ahead of the event, when he wrote to Lillah in January, 1917:

> I thought as we were interrupted when I had said so little that I should like to drop you a line to assure you of my whole-hearted sympathy and also to say that the only person who had previously spoken to me about the estrangement of your husband was Ricketts[16] and he was regretting it very sincerely as he said that united you were a considerable force for art in regard to the stage but that separated it was very doubtful if either of you could produce any kind of equivalent for the loss of that force.[17]

The truth probably lies somewhere in the region of Moore's view, so far as their practical work in the theater is concerned. This work frustrated, Barker still had other fruitful resources where Lillah had not. The story of her later years, in spite of the comfortable

---

14. "How could Barker come to marry *two* such awful women?" was Sir John's summing-up of the situation.
15. This remarkable British actress, who was born in 1889, made her first stage appearance at the Court Theatre in 1910 and in 1978 was still pursuing an active professional career—being in that latter year a member of the Chichester Festival company. In the intervening sixty-eight years she was constantly at work in the theater, playing every sort of part from the title role in *The Duchess of Malfi* to Mrs. Hardcastle in *Love on the Dole.* She twice played under Granville Barker's direction, in *The Winter's Tale* in 1912 and in *The Madras House* in 1925.
16. Charles Ricketts (1866–1931), the artist and stage designer.
17. Letter in the collection of Humanities Research Center, University of Texas at Austin.

surroundings and the prestige, is a rather sad one. Her attempts to reestablish herself in the theater, her magazine articles, her poetry recitals, her book, were all—though unconsciously—part of a rehabilitation exercise, designed to reassert and reestablish herself both in the eyes of that over-heated little circle which she regarded as the world and in her own eyes. She died in 1960, fourteen years after Barker and ten years after both Helen and Shaw, at the age of eighty-five. She and Barker had not met since 1917, when, in a stormy interview at Shaw's London flat, she had unsuccessfully tried to persuade him to leave Helen and return to his first marriage.

TEX/MS
To Lillah McCarthy

3, Clement's Inn,
Strand,
London, W.C.
[undated]
6.30 P.M.

My dear,

I am making for the 7 o'clock down[1] in hope to get those two pages done tomorrow and I think I may be able to. It is important that I come up on Monday and have the week in town.[2]

I would like to stay, dear—and I am in a slightly better temper. You are nice to me, if you please. Sorry I was a grumpy idiot. Au 'voir. Bless you.

Love,
H.

If I don't do I shall feel a fool.

---

1. In England, all trains are "up" or "down" trains: "up" means going to London, from whatever direction; "down" means going away from London.
2. The Barkers had a small London flat in the same building as the office of the Fabian Society. They had a succession of country cottages where they spent weekends and holidays.

TEX/PC
To Lillah McCarthy

[Paris]
April 10, 1907

1st postcard—a beautiful crossing, a fairly good sleep, a shave, a walk down the Boulevard du Strassbourg, postcards, coffee while I write on the pavement near the station. 8.40 to Bâle in a few minutes.

H.

TEX/PC
To Lillah McCarthy

[France]
April 10, 1907

2nd postcard
How are you?

TEX/PC
To Lillah McCarthy

[France]
April 10, 1907

<u>4th</u> <u>postcard</u>

I am wondering if I should tuck my napkin under my chin like a true Frenchman. Not one good face has passed me while I've sat here. The women are all like the posters. Paris isn't France—that's the thing. My love to you. More from Bâle.

H.

TEX/PC
To Lillah McCarthy

Siena,
Italy.
April 16, 1907

Monday.

It didn't matter so much your not being at Florence, since you know it; but you musn't miss this place some time or other. It is quite gorgeous—not pictures but just the town itself <u>and</u> the country round.

H.

TEX/MS
To Lillah McCarthy

[Court Lodge, Stansted, Kent.]
April 16, 1909

I'll come up and see the Vic. Sq. house whenever you like (Maggie's letter), but £450 premium! I've not heard from the Heath place yet—you shall hear when I do!

Oh, I can't <u>think</u>. In the depths of depression and temper. No work.[1] Damn L——[2] and damn all houses, country and town and damn furniture and damn Barrie and Frohman and Trench[3] and me.

I thought really of coming up this afternoon but I may do something tomorrow. If I don't make a start really I think I shall dash up from pure fidgets. Curse—blow—hang—devil—blast! Oh!

Love to you, my dear. See you tomorrow some time anyhow.

H.

1. He was staying away from London specifically to continue the writing of *The Madras House,* which he had started some months before.
2. The remainder of the name is illegible.
3. J. M. Barrie had persuaded Charles Frohman, the American theater manager, to plan a repertory season at the Duke of York's theater in London, with Barker as the artistic director. Herbert Trench (1866–1923), the poet-dramatist, was peripherally involved in that *he* had also been asked (by Lord Howard de Walden) to manage a repertory season at the Haymarket Theatre and had come to Barker for advice.

TEX/MS
To Lillah McCarthy

Court Lodge,
Stansted,
Kent.
[June 22, 1909]

My dear,

I went to Ash[1] and telephoned to Matthews and he said he had heard all about it from you, so now it is doubly sure. They object to the new sink, so I am writing again to press it. The furniture-patterns will be sent to you. I hope Macbeth goes well.[2] I get ahead, if a little slowly. I shall not come up tomorrow: am writing to make peace with Barrie. As to Friday, write if you'd like me to see Lady M. again—anything new in her. There's a Fabian,[3] too, and Colonial Press at Sidney Low's[4]—but if I could have Act III done by Sunday— though I fear it's hopeless to expect that.

Oh I am behind-hand with letters.

I could not have got to Hankin's funeral[5] after getting the letter this morning anyhow. I am sorry in a way not to have been there. We must see her sometime.

Well, I think you had certainly better come for your rest here and not go to the Massinghams,[6] don't you? That amount of county[7] after your week's work won't be any good. Pray for a hot day and the Tokah[8] on the verandah here.

Love,
H.

1. A village in Kent, about three miles from Stansted.
2. Lillah was playing Lady Sybil in the first production of Barrie's *What Every Woman Knows,* which had been running at the Duke of York's Theatre, where it was presented by Charles Frohman, since September, 1908. She was also playing Lady Macbeth, directed by William Poel, at matinee performances for the Elizabethan Stage Society, at Fulham Theatre. She shared the part of Lady Macbeth with Evelyn Weeden, the Macbeth being Hubert Carter. Six performances in all were given, of which Lillah played three. There is a fascinating account of this production in Robert Speaight's *William Poel and the Elizabethan Revival* (London, 1954).

3. A meeting of the executive committee of the Fabian Society, of which Barker was a member, having been elected to the committee in 1907.
4. Sir Sidney Low (1857–1932), an author and journalist, was knighted in 1918. His best-known work is *The Governance of England* (1904).
5. St. John Hankin, the brilliant young dramatist whose *The Return of the Prodigal* Barker had included in the Court Theatre repertory in 1905, committed suicide by drowning on June 15, 1909, believing that he had inherited syphilis from his father. His funeral was held in London on June 22.
6. H. W. Massingham (1860–1924), journalist, was editor of *The Nation* from 1907 to 1923.
7. By "county" Barker means aristocratic society with country houses as well as London homes.
8. Not a reference which I can recognize or place.

TEX/PC
To Lillah McCarthy

Dusseldorf
Germany.
October 21, 1910

A jolly town, you know! This is the principal street. I'm just off to the Harz—have wired you all the address I can; so much depends on weather. Shall send more cards en route. Love to you, dear. So glad of Burford hens!!!!

H.

TEX/PC
To Lillah McCarthy

Oker,
Germany.
October 22, 1910
Sat. 12.30

[1]

From Goslar this morning—the most fascinating place—see the various postcards I send you. Into the Harz which are—well, there.

I lost

TEX/PC
To Lillah McCarthy

Oker,
Germany.
October 22, 1910

(2)

my way for half an hour and wandered, but I'm so far right. Having mittagessen in front of this,[1] which is really high. 150 ft. I should say.

---

1. The picture on the card is of the Romkerwasserfall at Okertal, in the Harz Mountains.

TEX/PC
To Lillah McCarthy

Oker,
Germany.
October 22, 1910

(3)

I feel much a pig being here without you. Do you have moments of being cross with me? This Harz really is gorgeous—we

TEX/PC
To Lillah McCarthy

Oker,
Germany.
October 22, 1910

(4)

must come. They say it's wonderful in the snow. Good now—for you meet nobody. Finding the way not over-easy. Thus it is Maudirections[1] until you get on a

---

1. This appears to be a rather ponderous Anglo-French pun on the French verb *maudire* (which means both "to curse" and "to rue" or "censure").

TEX/PC
To Lillah McCarthy

Oker,
Germany.
October 22, 1910

(5)
Gross-weg. Having lured you there—they stop—mysterious numbers—then nothing. If I hadn't had the sun to steer by—. I shall
reach the Brocken tonight, I think. More from there. Love to you,
my dear. I wish you were here.

H.

TEX/PC
To Lillah McCarthy

Oker,
Germany.
October 22, 1910

I must send one more card to tell you that I lunch outside
off a fat blue forelle (D'you remember them at Hoch Finstermunz?[1])
and there's a black large dog to lunch with.

H.

---

1. A place in Austria where they had been on holiday together in 1906, just after their
   marriage.

TEX/PC
To Lillah McCarthy

Halberstadt,
Germany.
October 24, 1910

[1]
I shall just have had one hour here for tea—look around—letters—
then shall get to Berlin at 7. Just eating a most unsatisfactory thing
called a Nieuburger Bisquit.

TEX/PC
To Lillah McCarthy

Halberstadt,
Germany.
October 24, 1910

(2)

Got your letters. Thankyou dear. Murray's is to say that Trench will do Oedipus after Xmas.[1] More of that when I get home. I want news of the flat! And of the bitch![2] More from Berlin. Meanwhile, love to you, dear.

H.

---

1. Barker for some time had been discussing with Gilbert Murray the possibility of his directing a production of Murray's new translation of Sophocles' *Oedipus Rex* for Herbert Trench's new repertory company at the Haymarket Theatre (see letter of April 16, 1909, above, and the correspondence with Murray in Chapter V). The production failed to materialize, and Barker never did, in fact, direct *Oedipus Rex*. Murray's translation of the play was finally produced at Covent Garden in 1912, directed by Max Reinhardt, with Lillah McCarthy as Jocasta.
2. Whether "bitch" is meant literally or metaphorically, I do not know. If the latter, the reference would be to Gertrude Kingston, whom Barker heartily disliked (see letter of January 3, 1915, to Shaw), and who was the owner of the Little Theatre in John Street; the flat which Barker and Lillah were negotiating for was a part of the Little Theatre building.

TEX/PC
To Lillah McCarthy

Schierke,
Germany.
October 25, 1910

It'll be like this pretty soon, I should think.[1] The question is shall I wait for the sun to come out? No, I think not.

---

1. The picture on the postcard bears the caption "Brocken im Winter" and looks correspondingly bleak.

TEX/PC
To Lillah McCarthy

Dusseldorf,
Germany.
[date illegible]

This is the back of it.[1] Don't forget to go see Hayward and hold up the John Street flat by some means, will you?

---

1. The picture on the card is of the Schauspielhaus in Dusseldorf.

TEX/PC
To Lillah McCarthy

Coin,
Germany.
November 3, 1910

Last p.c. to you dear. It will probably arrive after I do. This is the beautiful church in Coin. I write waiting for Othello to start at the Schauspielhaus.

TEX/PC
To Lillah McCarthy

Nemours,
France.
[April, 1911]

Monday—at dejeuner
A pretty little place. I've spent an idle morning here—Now to walk back. I came by train. Bless you.

H.

TEX/PC
To Lillah McCarthy

Fontainebleau,
France.
April 21, 1911

Have written you to John Street.[1]

Love,
H.

1. When they took a lease of the Little Theatre in John Street for their joint management venture, they also rented, as their London home, a flat in the same building.
   The building was a converted eighteenth-century bank.

TEX/PC
To Lillah McCarthy

Leipzig,
Germany.
[1911]

9—10, Sunday morning
Ich habe wohl Gesellschaft,
Hier Kommt das Speisewagen
Wir mussen das Fruhstich haben
Au revoir, miene liebling!

H.

TEX/PC
To Barker

Norway
August 2, 1911

Tomorrow we go back to Bergen: I wonder shall we see
you, dear heart.

Your Wife

TEX/PC
To Lillah McCarthy

Weymouth
1912

A jolly walk. Very little rain. Wonderful sea and sky.
Neither of us overdone. Love to you, my dear.

H.

TEX/PC
To Lillah McCarthy

York.

April 25, 1912

10.45

Just off in N.W. direction. Shall wire you address later.
Love to you, my dear.

H.

SAL/PC
To Lillah McCarthy

Harrogate.

April 26, 1912

Lunch here. Saxon crypt.[1] Barker barked his elbow. Car
started!

---

1. The picture is of Ripon cathedral, which has one of the very few remaining pre-Norman crypts in Europe.

TEX/PC
To Lillah McCarthy

Verona,

Italy.

December 25, 1912[1]

(2)

of that tomorrow. I stopped a couple of hours in Verona—oh, a jolly
place, built by people who just couldn't help it being beautiful. North
Italy when it likes does knock everything into 3 cocked hats and
that's all about it. You are just on your way

---

1. This postcard, numbered 2, is one of a series all written at the same time, but the rest of them have disappeared.

TEX/PC
To Lillah McCarthy

Rouen,
France.[1]
July 29, 1915

[1]

   This—to speak the blank truth—is very boring. Stores, a
hospital barge on the river (jolly enough) but this afternoon

---

1. Barker, as mentioned earlier, was in France on behalf of the Red Cross, writing a
 book for that organization about its work with the British war-wounded.

TEX/PC
To Lillah McCarthy

Rouen,
France.
July 29, 1915

(2)

the regulation Officers' Hospital of which the R. C. are so proud—
and there the regulation silliness and snobbery which makes the British army

TEX/PC
To Lillah McCarthy

Rouen,
France.
July 29, 1915

(3)

a laughing-stock through which many men's good nature and a few
men's brains manage to shine. Yesterday was better. We motored all
day looking at little "detention"

TEX/PC
To Lillah McCarthy

Rouen,
France.
July 29, 1915

(4)
hospitals on the way, containing 9 or 10 beds each (local cases are
sent to them) run by women and very well run. Not that women run
the things better than men but they seem to run them better by themselves and as small affairs. I go back to Boulogne tomorrow and then
I must try to see

TEX/PC
To Lillah McCarthy

Rouen,
France.
July 29, 1915

(5)
some jobs being done. They do them well, but the moment things
slacken their minds revert to trifles and they become petty and foolish. You cannot get English people to use their brains for the sake of
using them. Perhaps they're right.

TEX/PC
To Lillah McCarthy

Rouen,
France.
July 29, 1915

(6)
Otherwise, if nothing's going forward, I shall take a day or so trying
to write and then, I think, seize the time to go down to Monte Carlo
to see mother.[1] I look for news of you when I get back to Boulogne.
I'll try to see Knight Bruce here, but he's outside the town, I gather.

H.

---

1. Barker's mother had settled in Monte Carlo some years before the war started.

LON/MS
To Lillah McCarthy

On board S.S. "Celtic"[1]
[September, 1915]

(2)

. . . work—and am not months behindhand and irritable to get back
to it—and when will that be?

Meanwhile I'd go to the country and breathe air and cogitate.

You're with Charlotte at the Albert Hall tonight—that's an
interesting show I expect. I perceive this voyage is going to make me
double-chinned and liverish—there's too much to eat and a beastly
orchestra. However, I've a table in my cabin and I'll get through
some work if I can.

Bless you, dear Lillah—my dear wife—I love you very much
if you please and I'm not far from you. Distance doesn't mainly
count.

Get a healthy time; breathe air—and I'll be back soon.

Bless you—I love you, my dearest.

H.

Oh, letters—well I don't suppose many will come. Any marked private must just wait. The others you might open but I don't expect
you'll be able to do anything with them. Use your judgement, dear, if
you will, please.

---

1. Barker interrupted his work on the Red Cross book in order to return to the United
   States to fulfill lecture engagements which he had arranged when in America at the
   beginning of the year. Lillah was to have accompanied him on this journey but at the
   last moment was taken ill and was unable to travel (see Chapter III, letter to Shaw of
   August 18, 1915). On the voyage from England to America, Barker wrote to Lillah:
   only part of the letter survives.

Stanley Weintraub begins Chapter 6 of his Journey to Heartbreak
*(New York, 1971) with these words: "On January 3, 1916, early in the
evening, Lillah McCarthy received a long letter from New York."
Weintraub has his information from Purdom, who says, "On January
3, 1916, before the performance of* Judith, *Lillah received . . . ," etc.
In fact, the letter was* written *on January 3 and is clearly so dated. The
following is the text of it.*

TEX/MS
To Lillah McCarthy

New York.
Jan. 3, 1916

My dear Lillah,

I have made up my mind that I cannot return to you and I want you to set me free. This is the whole situation. When Helen Huntington and I came to care for each other in the Spring it did not begin as a flirtation nor did it develop then nor has it since into a "criminal" intrigue. But instead we both recognized what a very serious matter it was and we agreed in justice to ourselves and the other people concerned we must put it to the test of time and absence. The position was very difficult. Loving her, I felt I could not go on living with you as your husband, but as my feelings <u>might</u> have changed I did not want to upset you unnecessarily especially as things were strained between us then in any case. However, you suspected something. I could not lie to you about it, but as you would not believe what I did tell you it became difficult to tell you any more. I should have done so. I would have done so—but you must remember certain things you did and threats you made. In the face of these it seemed to me wiser to let matters rest where they were and, as I had all along intended, to let the thing itself have its test. I am very sorry for any blunders I made in June. Suffering there must always be over a matter of this sort to everyone concerned, but it should not have to be suffering at such cross purposes as that. I did not see her nor hear from her (except for a couple of lines) for some time after I got back here. I tell you this so that you may know that while I have suppressed things about myself in my letters to you I have written you nothing untrue. During this past two months we have met fairly often and corresponded a great deal. We have, I think, considered every possibility—saying goodbye (we have tested that and found that we felt we could not)—planning to remain just friends. But in the end we are convinced that what we both want more than anything else in the world is to be able to spend the rest of our lives together. And in this I know we shall not now change. I don't wish to speak of anything we have "gone through" during this time. For myself I had not believed I was capable of feeling things so deeply. But it has at least proved to me beyond a doubt that much more than any passing happiness is concerned. This does in a very real sense mean my future life to me.

Huntington has of course been told everything from the beginning as I am telling you. He recognises the present situation and accepts it. But the divorce law here is simpler and swifter than it is with us and, naturally, before he takes any steps in that direction or helps his wife to, he wishes to be reassured about my situation in that respect.

Now even if she had decided that she wishes to make no change in her life I should have to tell you the rest of this. As a husband of course I could not come back to you. I do not think you would long have tolerated living in the house with me knowing not only that I did not love you but that I did love another woman. That would not be fair to you. I had thought at first, while things were still uncertain here, of coming back to tell you personally and asking you what you wanted to do. But with my own mind so absolutely made up it seemed that this could only cause useless pain to us both. I therefore decided during this last fortnight that whatever happened here I would not return.

I did you a very great wrong in asking you to marry me at all. Though I explained at the time how mixed my feelings were and you said you understood nevertheless I should not have let you accept the risk that someday there might happen what has happened now. Though I was willing to accept such a risk as far as you were concerned that does not much affect the matter. For I never loved you as I know—and did know—that I ought to love a woman to want to be married to her. I thought I might learn to. I have tried to. There have been times when I thought I had learnt to, but that—I even knew it at the time—was only self deception. And though I have tried (not <u>always</u> successfully I am afraid) to behave well and make you happy I think you have always known in your heart what the truth of the matter was. I am and have been all the time deeply regretful about this. How much longer our life together could have lasted in any case it is of course difficult now to say. Though I have had to suppress one important fact, what I have been writing to you during these past months has been as true as I could make it. I was perhaps not outspoken enough, but that is sometimes a fault of mine. Partly I did not want to say <u>more</u> than the truth—and one always tends to make things sound as pleasant as one can. I am more than willing to take the blame. But for the past four or five years I have been growing unhappy because I was slipping into habits of deception and cowardice with you, in everyday things. It was deteriorating [*sic*] me—and I knew it—to such an extent that there was manifest danger of our ending in quarrels and perhaps a sordid sort of infidelity. I did not want a break to occur that way. And I was getting to feel—as I told you—that I must go away. And I know now that being away I should have felt also in any case that I could not come back.

So I must write this. I am sending it you through G. B. S. partly because I do not want it to come to you when you may be alone, partly because he is the best friend we have and the wisest. The one we always go to for help and advice.

I am not going to protest my sorrow about all this. You must believe that I have looked at it and felt about it from every point of view and in every way of which I am capable. That is, I have questioned myself day by day as to whether my convictions about our life together were genuine and inevitable and I know they are. And also as to whether this other thing I have come to want was right to me and vital to me or not. And I know it is. I have tried to be as straight and as honest about the whole thing as circumstances would let me and I do ask you to think generously of it all. What else I want you to do is obvious without my asking.

This letter will perhaps seem to you purely selfish. It would be hypocrisy to try and <u>make</u> it seem otherwise. I can only tell you that—in other circumstances—it is how I should wish you to write to me. For look at things how one will, there is only one <u>real</u> alternative now and that would be our trying to start our married life over again. Now, quite apart from all you must feel after what I have told you, that is for me—as I have said—in any case impossible and it will remain so. I know this and any attempt to prove it would mean added and useless misery to us both, nothing more.

Do not think either that I am under the influence of "excitement". I had meant to keep my counsel about the whole matter for a year. And there has naturally had to be over here such ample discussion of the practical side of things that "excitement" would hardly have survived it.

I hope you will not still disbelieve, as you did, what I told you of my actual relations so far to Helen Huntington. We have never met except quite openly in perfectly public places—picture galleries, theatres, the tea rooms of hotels or shops. There has been no "criminal" intrigue and nothing has taken place that could even remotely point to one.

I have gone on trying to settle business for you here—for work is always the best thing. If I had not been able to work these last six months I don't know what I should have done.

I am going now direct to France to finish my Red Cross job. When that is done—and if they have no more for me to do—I shall probably go to some village beyond Paris or in Normandy and write. If you wish to see me and think it well I will of course come over from Boulogne. I meant not to because it seemed to me it would cause needless pain to us both and that there was no possible good end to be served.

H.

BL/TCC
From Medley[1] to Barker

36, Lincoln's Inn Fields,
London, W.C. 2
19th Sept. 1917

Dear Barker,

The financial position is that you have made, or are making at the present time, the following allowance to Mrs. Barker: you are paying £250 a year free of tax. Upon your instructions the whole of the income from the Settlement by you and Mrs. Barker is being paid to her. That this is being paid I myself know, as I arranged for payment with the Solicitors for the Trustees, and those instructions have been carried out. This is a further sum of about £250 a year. It was, as you know, to enable this income to be set free that the arrangements were made under which the loan raised by the Trustees was, with the assistance of Mr. Galsworthy and Mr. Shaw, discharged. You have also given up the Policy on your life, and I understood from Lewis[2] that this had since been surrendered, and the money from the Insurance Office received by Mrs. Barker. You have also given up any interest in the furniture and such like matters. As nearly as I can calculate these various arrangements involve you in finding between £800 to £1000 a year at the present time, and with the increased annual payment to Mrs. Barker which you intend to make in the future, a larger sum will be needed. At the present time I should think Mrs. Barker's income, apart from anything she may earn, and apart from money received from the Insurance Company and the sale of Stansted, amounts to about £700 a year, and this will increase in the future to £1,000.

I should just like to say a word about the "delay" which has been referred to, in the proceedings. Of course Mrs. Barker must ask Lewis about this, but in fact it is quite certain that Lewis has lost no time whatever. He has taken every step at the earliest time that the rules allow. The reason why the business is dragging on into the late autumn is simply that the Judges having made no serious attempt to cope with the undefended Divorce list, the result was that several hundred cases which had been set down for trial last term, and which ought to have been, and according to the usual practice of the Court, would have been disposed of last term, were never reached at all, but were thrown over the Long Vacation, that is to say from July until October or November. This, so far as I know, is the sole cause of any delay.

Yours sincerely,
C. D. Medley

---

1. C. D. Medley, Barker's lawyer.
2. Sir George Lewis was the lawyer acting for Lillah McCarthy.

# Chapter V

Gilbert Murray, 1866–1957

It *is evident* from the letters gathered in this chapter that Barker was probably more at ease with Gilbert Murray than with anyone else in his life. There is a sustained tone of gaiety, warmth, and confidence in Barker's letters to Murray, especially in the decade immediately preceding the 1914–1918 war, which does not appear in his letters to any of his other friends, close though some of those other friendships were. And the same sense of rapport is there in Murray's early letters to Barker. One gets the very strong impression of two men whose minds chimed easily together and who each responded spontaneously to the sense of high seriousness which he found in the other. Each greatly admired, moreover, the particular skills of the other, and this admiration is obvious in their correspondence. More even, in some ways, than in the case of Barker and Shaw, Murray and Barker were, in their theater work, perfect foils and perfect complements for each other.

Another striking quality of the letters written by Barker to Murray during the period 1904 to 1907 is that they give us by far the best account of Barker's way of approaching a play-in-production and of the day-to-day life of that extraordinary venture at the Court Theatre. The letters at the beginning of this present chapter rather suggest that it was Barker's connection with Murray, via the production of the *Hippolytus,* that provided one of the main motives for launching the repertory season at the Court. It is usual to regard Barker's friendship and collaboration with Shaw as the sole inspiration for Barker's move to the Court (Purdom, for instance, very clearly implies this); indeed, Shaw's influence was important and, later in the venture, paramount. But it would appear that in the initial stages—and especially in the formative stages—Murray's influence and help was probably more important than Shaw's. Murray, for example, put money into the venture before Shaw did, though in the long run he did not contribute nearly as

Gilbert Murray in 1943, aged seventy-seven.
Photo © Karsh, Ottawa.

often or as substantially as did Shaw. Though the production, at the Court itself, of *Candida* in April of 1904 is usually cited as the real beginning of the Vedrenne-Barker-Court idea, it appears to have been Barker's production of (and playing in) Murray's translation of the *Hippolytus* of Euripides in the following month which really triggered off the scheme. Notice, for example, the postscript to his letter to Murray of June 5, 1904: "J. H. Leigh [the lessee of the Court Theatre] has expressed himself bitten with the idea of doing Greek plays. Not a word—but let us talk anon." *Candida* had been a way of getting an example of the "new drama" into the Court, but *Hippolytus* inspired the idea of using the Court for a whole series of plays—standard works as well as new works—presented in repertory. In a very real sense, Barker's connection with Murray led to the single most important development of his career, and the forming and moulding of that development was the result of the creative impact of their two minds.

Barker first knew Murray not as a translator and classical scholar but as an author of original plays. Murray had written a play called *Carlyon Sahib,* which Mrs. Patrick Campbell produced in 1899. Barker, as a young actor of twenty-one, was in her company and played the part of Selim. Murray had not at that time any thought of trying to secure professional performances of his translations of Greek plays. According to the *Dictionary of National Biography,* he undertook the translations for purely pedagogical reasons: "His versions of Greek drama began as lecturing devices," writes M. I. Henderson in the *D. N. B.* But Murray, nevertheless, was vitally and passionately interested in the theater, and in 1901, two years after *Carlyon Sahib,* another of his plays was produced in London; it was, this time, on a Greek subject, though an original work, not a translation; its title was *Andromache.* A year later, on a suggestion from Shaw, Murray published his translation of Euripides' *Hippolytus,* and this led directly to Barker's production at the Lyric Theatre in May, 1904.

Murray, who was just over ten years older than Barker (and about ten years younger than Shaw), was born in Sydney, Australia, on January 2, 1866. His father was Sir Terence Murray and his mother was a cousin of Sir W. S. Gilbert, after whom Gilbert Murray was named. When Sir Terence died, in 1877, his widow left Australia for London, taking her son with her. He was educated at Merchant Taylors' School and St. John's College, Oxford. By the age of twenty-two he was a Fellow of New College; a year later Sir Richard Jebb called him "the most accomplished Greek scholar of the day." In 1889 he accepted the Chair of Greek at the University of Glasgow, and in the same year he married Lady Mary Howard, the eldest daughter of the ninth Earl of Carlisle. Lady Mary's background, as well as her own personal inclinations, made her a ready sympathizer with Murray's interest in the arts, in literature, and in the causes of liberalism and humanitarianism. Her father was an amateur painter of some distinction, and her mother was an ardent feminist and radical reformer. Murray, then, well-connected through both his own and his wife's family, was in an ideal position to exert considerable influence on the social, political, and cultural life of his time, and this he did most effectively, sparing himself nothing in the process.

In 1899 he was compelled, through overwork, to resign his chair at Glasgow and to retire for a time to a quiet country life at Churt, in Surrey. In 1905 he returned to Oxford, again as a Fellow of New College, his chief work at that time being the editing of Euripides texts. In 1908 he was appointed Regius Professor of Greek at Oxford, a position he held until 1936.

Murray was anything but an ivory tower academic. Though a fine scholar and a first-rate lecturer, he also pursued many other serious interests. He was one of the founders of the League of Nations Union and chairman of its executive council from 1923 to 1938. After World War II, he was joint president and then sole president of the United Nations Association, a post which he held for twelve years. This proclivity for seeing affinities between the academic, cultural life and political affairs is of special significance to his connection with and possible influence upon Granville Barker, for this same sense of art as both a yeast working within the mix of everyday matters and a treasury of what is best and most permanent saved from the diurnal flux, is very strongly felt not only in Barker's own attitudes to the world (many of the letters in this present volume are vivid evidence of it) but also in the best of his plays (even as early as *The Marrying of Ann Leete* it is there, and it receives its fullest and most poignant expression in *The Secret Life* and *His Majesty*).

Murray's own most lasting memorial remains his translations of Greek plays, especially, perhaps, those of Euripides. Looked at askance by some today because of their sometimes self-conscious lushness and sweetness, their faintly Swinburnian, Pre-Raphaelite air, they nevertheless still have enormous authority. They are also, in spite of the rougher and more austere translations which have succeeded them, still among the most *theatrical* renderings we have of the Greek plays in English. It was, of course, this theatrical quality which attracted Barker to them. As can be gathered from his letters about these plays, Barker saw them as being at once both ancient and modern, timeless yet timely, universal yet particular, perfect works for the serious theater of his own day. It is my personal view not only that he was right but also that these translations would still play triumphantly, if any theatrical management could be found with courage enough to give them the chance.

BOD/MS
To Murray

8, York Buildings,
Adelphi,
London.
June 2, 1904

Dear Murray,

Thank you for the little bill. Tomorrow, Sir, your account shall be settled. Can you add to your esteemed favours by bringing the rest of the Cambridge clothes to the Lyric tomorrow[1] (I think you said there were a few still at Palace Green). As you allowed me discretion I concluded <u>not</u> to send that letter on to Mr. Tapping. Beyond a point, fussing over these actors makes them too self-conscious. Now if the National Theatre were built, tomorrow would not be the last performance. (Where are those proofs![2]) Oh, but I have been sent to about producing the plays abroad! I'll tell you.

Yours,
H. G. B.

---

1. Murray had arranged for Barker to borrow some costumes from Cambridge University for the first production of his translation of the *Hippolytus*, which Barker had directed at the Lyric Theatre the previous month.
2. Of Murray's translation of the *Bacchae*, which he was preparing for publication (it was published in November).

BOD/MS
From William Poel to Barker

5, Amersham Road,
Putney
[London]
June 4th, 1904

Dear Mr. Barker,

Thank you for your letter. Is nothing more being done about <u>Hippolytus</u>? I was very struck with its dramatic construction. Like <u>Everyman</u> its interest is so well maintained and the story so well unfolded. The piece never loses grip over one's attention—I believe that the play taken round the country in the same way that <u>Everyman</u> was and acted chiefly in the Town Halls would make money. The English tours of <u>Everyman</u> under my direction have returned a profit so far of £800.

<u>Everyman</u> has still drawing power but I feel that if it went out again it would want other pieces to go with it. Now <u>Hippolytus</u>,

Everyman and Samson Agonistes (Milton's)—for which I have all the costumes, since it was given by the Society a few years since—could all three pieces be acted by the same cast as is needed for Hippolytus, and the same scene, with only slight modifications, could be used for all three. If then anything more is proposed to be done with Hippolytus and any capital is required for financing a tour, I would be willing to put money into the undertaking provided I might book a tour on the same lines as Everyman and do the two other plays mentioned with Hippolytus, which would allow of filling out a week in a town, giving Hippolytus three days out of the six, Everyman two days and Samson, one day. If my suggestion comes within the scope of practical politics, can I have a talk to you about it?

    With regard to Richard II, it is difficult to give the piece before the end of October[1] as the schools have not settled down and of course this is just the busy time with everyone.

Yours truly,
W. Poel

---

1. There seems to have been a suggestion that Poel's production of 1899, in which Barker had played Richard, might be repeated. Nothing came of this, doubtless because, by the October which Poel mentions, Barker had embarked upon the Court Theatre venture that would occupy him fully for the next three years.

BOD/MS
To Murray

8, York Buildings,
Adelphi,
London.
June 5, 1904

Dear Murray,

    We are in doubts as to where to address the costumes to— The Fitzwilliam or the Theatre. Could you send me a wire tomorrow? Also, what about accounts for them—and Chapman's fee and exes. For on Tuesday everything must be settled and the fount of cash will dry up.

Yours,
H. G. B.

J. H. Leigh has expressed himself bitten with the idea of doing Greek plays. Not a word—but let us talk anon.

Sunday night
    I did not post this yesterday as I should have done for I

didn't get the list: I'll post that on. From memory it is 3 straps, 1 armlet, 1 brooch.

But now I've had the letter from Poel which I enclose (and I hope you can read it). I've told him that I see no reason Hippolytus shouldn't be toured so and that he'd better communicate with you direct. If I may advise, I wouldn't let him do it in London, for he may produce it in a rather cracked though clever way, not that that is so much a business reason as that there may well be a London revival in it as done just now. Also, I'd be very sharp over your contract with him, for Poel is one of those limpid-eyed enthusiasts who sacrifices himself body, soul and pocket to his cause, and expects and is absolutely unscrupulous in making everyone else do the same thing.

As a matter of fact, a joint Earldom has been offered, the title to be worn year and year about. But W. A. and I shall probably conclude to take cash.[1]

Well, might I perhaps come down to you next weekend? But I seem all over work—mostly other people's.

Yours,
H. G. B.

---

1. This is obviously a reply to some joke in Murray's last letter, but Murray's letter is no longer extant, and it seems impossible to guess what the mythical award was supposed to be for.

BOD/MS
To Murray

8, York Buildings,
Adelphi,
London.
Wednesday night [June, 1904]

Dear Murray,

I have sent Chapman his cheque and expect to hear tomorrow that the dresses have arrived safely. I had forgotten all about a fee for them, to tell the truth. But anyhow £10 is absurd (I don't think Nathan's bill was much more), as I remember now gently hinting at the Verrall's table and from whatever we pay I think we should deduct the cost of cleaning the things (£1-1-0) and the carriage, which will be nearly as much. We must of course get their opinions on the subject but I should then propose paying £5, with one or both of the deductions I mentioned.

I do see a distinct possibility of reviving Hippolytus in London and possibly of doing performances at Oxford and Cambridge. This I'd like to talk over with you.

I'd like much to come down on Saturday if no earthquake occurs (I am doing an S.S. production remember[1]) but hasn't Lady Mary her hands full and her house overrun with half-term holiday-makers and wouldn't she rather be without me? I could come some other time—well, Sunday fortnight, perhaps (but don't settle anything with Poel till we've talked).

Yours,
H. G. B.

---

1. Barker was directing Yeats' play *Where There Is Nothing* at the Court Theatre for the Stage Society.

BOD/MS
To Murray

8, York Buildings,
Adelphi,
London.
Tuesday morning [June, 1904]

Dear Murray,

Are you returning to Churt without seeing me? This is not tolerable and not to be endured. Though as a matter of fact all I want to know for the moment is about Poel and Bourchier—if we're safe in arranging for Hippolytus at the Court and if not whether you could undertake to let us have Electra in its place? Come and see the "Pout's"[1] play.

Yours,
H. G. Barker

I shall be at the Court of course this afternoon.

---

1. Some sort of pun on "poet." A joke at Yeats' expense, I take it: his Irish accent, perhaps? (Though this was not very pronounced.)

BOD/MS
To Murray

> 8, York Buildings.
> Adelphi,
> London.
> July 9, 1904

Dear Murray,

The only adequate reply to Poel is "Skittles". His system of payment may be Elizabethan but it won't do. It reminds one of "Toe Master Murry for writting ye plaie VIII pence". The guarantee of 18 performances in 6 weeks seems reasonable. But clearly, if he expects his exes to be £1,000 and he is attempting to treat you on a 5% basis, the sum paid down should be £50, not £18. £50 is what I would ask on account of fees. But Poel's system is no use anyhow—it's too complicated, for one thing; for the other, quite to his advantage. What you should have is the £50 down <u>on account of fees</u>, 5% on the gross receipts of each performance up to £100; when the receipts exceed £100, 10%. Being pressed—but only being pressed—you might alter that to go to 7½%, but it must be on the entire receipts, not on the amount <u>above</u> £100 (I can't express this clearly—you'll understand).

You must give him discretion as to cast. All you can ask for is a veto, with the understanding that you won't exercise it except in a flagrant instance. In view of this, I don't think the first paragraph of your letter to him is much to the point.

I re-enclose you—or as I write, I mean to—Poel's letter and your own.

We mean at the Court to do Hippolytus second, that's to say early in November; and we'd like an option to do it again in the Spring, either for six more matinées or for some weeks in the evening.

And can we have another play for the Spring? Spring dates will be definitely arranged by November 15. I incline to the Troades, with Genevieve Ward as Hecuba. I believe she's finer than ever. If only I knew how to burn Troy! I have definitely come to the conclusion that the Bacchae <u>won't</u> do. By the way, will you have all the same people in November for Hippolytus, if we can get them? For I must be writing to them now. But Rosina Filippi <u>wants</u> to play the Nurse and I don't want Aphrodite again.

Now, another matter of which I'd meant to write to you today: do you still care to find me £200 for the production of the Housman-Barker play at the Court? It is to be done about December 22 for 3 weeks certain—2 performances a day. Its gross cost will be, I think, £1,400–1,500 and £1,000 capital is being found. Leigh, £600; Vedrenne, £200; myself, £200. A quarter of this is to be called up at once (next week) to commission the music and pay an advance on the play—and, I suppose, partly to book the theatre with.

The terms I'd propose for the money are—a first charge of 10% on the profits, to you; after that 4/5ths to me and 1/5th to you until you have received 25%. This is the arrangement I have with my backer for the matinées and it seems to be equitable. However, I should tell you that a city man who was very willing to find the money kicked at the limit of 25% and offered simply to go halves with me right through. But I stuck out about the 25%: it seems to me all a capitalist should get, even on a great risk. The chances of this play doing well seem to me quite good, as such things go; but of course it is a risk. I am told that the Xmas play at the Court last year did quite well and paid, though it was an inferior sort of thing. This year, too, we shall have the advantage of any reputation the matinées will bring us.

You ought to see the play, or what there is of it so far. That I could send you. Better still, I could read it you. But by Monday week (when I purpose paying an afternoon call on my way bicycling from Bexhill to Bristol) it all ought to be settled. Indeed, I can't well leave town till it is. Will you think it over and let me know as soon as you can, just what you feel inclined to do about it?

This is a mightily long letter but I had no time to make it shorter (that is a good saying).

Yours,
H. G. B.

BOD/MS
To Murray

8, York Buildings,
Adelphi,
London.
July 12, 1904.

Dear Murray,

You are shockingly ignorant of the ways of theatrical finance. You should have hummed and ha'ed and consulted your aunts and first cousins and second cousins and my second cousins and your conscience and the fortune teller and then have said you'd think about it. However, thank you for the cheque (which won't be passed through for a few days yet) and I'll write you further when things are quite complete. Also, about plays—I incline towards the Troades, though perhaps the Electra is safer. On Monday week (now) I shall be in Blackpool, Heaven help me. I have to go and play Cayley Drummle with Mrs. P. C.[1] there and next week at the Vaudeville. Money, money, money, though not much and I am weary. No matter.

Yours,

H. G. B.

---

1. Mrs. Patrick Campbell was doing one of her many revivals of Pinero's *The Second Mrs. Tanqueray* (she played Paula Tanqueray for the first time in 1893).

BOD/MS
To Murray

8, York Buildings,
Adelphi,
London.
July 22, 1904

Dear Murray,

This is written in the theatre during a rehearsal, so excuse any resulting vagueness. I chased you round to the N. L. C.[1] the other day but you were not. I drummle here till the end of the week and then at Blackpool! for a week. I shall be in town just for Monday, August 3, so we might meet then. I've not heard from Bright: ought I to write to him? —for I am regarding Hippolytus as a settled thing, so the sooner it actually is the better perhaps.

I am also anxious to hear about the Troades and the Electra—you preserve a discreet silence. But by November 15 we have to decide whether we will or will not do <u>six</u> more plays in the Spring and why not the Troades <u>and</u> the Electra?

By the bye, how would you like Mrs. P. C. for Electra? She offered—and sincerely, I think—to play Aglavaine for me when she gets back from America and if she could then. But I don't think we can keep Aglavaine waiting till then on that chance.[2]

About Prunella—the other parties have been playing the "theatre-backer" game properly as I described it to you, so actual papers aren't signed yet. But it is all settled and satisfactorily, I think. Will you have a formal letter or a contract or anything from me about your £200? I am quite content with my letter and yours, which have already passed, but of course it is for you to say. Please remember me to Lady Mary <u>and</u> to St. John.

Yours,

H. G. B.

P.S. You blossom out into two initials new to me.[3]

1. National Liberal Club.
2. Barker was planning to include Maeterlinck's *Aglavaine and Selysette* in his forthcoming season at the Court Theatre. It was actually produced on November 15, 1904, with Edyth Olive as Aglavaine.
3. Murray's full name was, in fact, George Gilbert Aimé Murray. Barker had begun, about this time, to use his own and Murray's initials in his letters, this being—in the fashion of the time—the next stage of intimacy after "Dear Mr. Murray," "Dear Murray," and "My dear Murray." I suspect that, in one of his replies, Murray had deliberately put in *all* his own initials as a joke, gently mocking the fashion. Barker, once he got to the initials stage, always addressed Murray as "G. M." (not G. G. A. M.!). Murray himself rarely resorted to the initials device at all.

BOD/MS
To Murray

29, Peter Street,
Blackpool
Friday [July or August?, 1904]

Dear Murray,

Does the fact that you sleep at Palace Green on Tuesday night imply that you won't be in town on Monday, when I had rather counted on seeing you? Not that I have much to say, though. I am anxious to hear the Troades. My disposition is to believe in it dramatically. Certainly it has no action but the situation is tremendous and played without any (appreciable) interval this could sustain even a Gothic interest. I mean a Goth's interest. I will write to Bright. I shall propose just what I said Poel ought to give you: 5% up to a hundred a performance; 7½% beyond. Will that do? Oh, but it is for him to say. Ye Gods (Thou, Poseidon!) have you ever been to Blackpool? Have you any conception how hideous humanity festers here? I leave at nine fifty on Sunday morning and count the minutes till then.

Yours,
H. G. B.

P.S. I know—I had meant to show you or read you "Prunella", but later I can read it you.

BOD/MS
To Murray

> Royal Court Theatre,
> Sloane Square, S.W.
> December 29, 1904

Dear Murray,

Thank you for the £50. And while we're on this unpleasant subject—prepare for the worst over Prunella. The business is <u>awful</u>: so bad that we seriously discussed today whether or not to close on Saturday and cut all the loss we could. But it will cost so little more to keep open another week that we shall do that. I cannot understand it—the people who come seem most enthusiastic, but so few of them come. One can only conclude that it's a real failure. I saw the first part of Act I from the front this afternoon and it is quite good—I enjoyed it. We've done our best and there it is. Of course, your loss is at the worst limited to £200—but oh my dear Murray: £200! I shall never forgive myself—I thought that £50 was the most you might drop. Vedrenne will go delicately—like Agag—over the finance and by compromising the rent and so on, we may save something. But really, things are very bad. I won't go on to express my feelings about this and you—you must imagine them.

I'll write to Miss Brayton[1] and ask her to see me next week. I'm not fit for much this, with two performances a day.

Marie Brema[2] seems willing. Vedrenne lunches with her on Monday, takes—with your permission—a copy of the Troades (mine!) for her to read. I, though invited, remain in the background. She has of course asked for parts for Tita—but I think the "You Never Can Tell" bait played properly will suffice that hungry pike.[3]

Why have you sent money to Harvey? He tells me he has a place in a bookseller's shop. I gave him a reference and was thankful it was off the stage. Please thank Lady Mary for sending my pen.

My mind reverts to Prunella—so I close this letter hastily.

> Yours,
> H. G. B.

Come up and see the blessed thing. Its last night will—if things continue thus—be Friday 6th.

---

1. Lily Brayton (1876–1953) began her career with Benson and in 1901 became a major London actress on the strength of her Viola in Tree's revival of *Twelfth Night*, which ran for three months at His Majesty's Theatre. She never appeared at the Court Theatre or in any subsequent Barker production.
2. Marie Brema (1866–1925), a famous mezzosoprano, specialized in Wagnerian roles; she sang Ortrud, Fricka, and Kundry at Bayreuth in 1894. Barker had conceived the idea of having her play Hecuba in *The Trojan Women*. She did so, apparently with disastrous results.

3. Tita Brand, Marie Brema's daughter, started her acting career with Ben Greet in 1901; in 1902 she played in William Poel's famous production of *Everyman* at St. George's Hall; her mother's intercession with Barker was evidently successful, since she played Leader of the Chorus in *Hippolytus* in October, 1904, and Gloria in Shaw's *You Never Can Tell* in May and June of 1905. Her career as an actress did not develop however, and she dropped out of the profession early.

BOD/MS
To Murray

[no address]
Monday   January, 1905

My dear Murray,

I'm glad you liked Act III. 17 in the house this afternoon and 3 calls at the end of the play. I cannot make this blessed public out. However, Bright may induce Seymour Hicks and his wife to do it—and then you'll see! What it wants is a few coon songs.

Shaw has not only written to you but to Miss Kingston[1] (he is a beast and a divel when he likes). Miss K. writes me tonight, wanting to play and saying that her first appearances as an amateur were as Clytemnestra and as Penelope. Now my position is this: I was the original person, I believe, to think of her as Helen, then you told me Helen was something like Mrs. Bishop, only more so, and I cooled off. But now I am drawn towards Miss K. for various reasons. For one—we're in, I think, for Marie Brema; therefore we may as well have a really sporting cast while we're about it. For another— Gertrude Kingston can't but be interesting and she would be very keen to do it.

But my real concern is this: it seems to me that Euripides first does the pity and terror business (Cassandra), then the simple and pathetic (Andromache) and then—knowing that the real business of the play, Hecuba and Troy, is to come—proceeds to brace up the minds of the audience to appreciate this by means of a little intellectual exercise and so writes the Helen scene. I felt and found this in reading the play to Marie Brema. That scene is intellectual exercise and I think must be recognized as such and treated accordingly. Now G. K. would get the meaning of the speech and the scene into the heads of the audience. She is quite beautiful to look at—in rather a serpent-of-old-Nile-brought-up-to-date way. But she is clever; she will be sure and polished, very sweet—sweetness suggesting hardness, certainly. Mondaine describes her in modern things. But the woman has appreciation, principally of cleverness, no religion except the Roman Catholic (which doesn't count) and great intention. Just for her cleverness I'd have her.

Now about Miss Farr,[2] whom we shall settle with of course. I dread that she may be writing tin-pot choruses—the former ones I'm not so afraid of, but those bits with Hecuba at the last. What is to be done? Miss Farr is taken to discover in the psaltery all sorts of progressions and phrases which to her simple ear are quite effective and might be to ours if the composer of the Belle of New York, not to mention Verdi and Wagner, had not accustomed us to them for other purposes. Now this is torture to a musical ear (so I'm told). You see, she really has a big subject to deal with this time—far bigger than Hippolytus—one that mustn't be wobbled or patheticised about. Would it be possible to drop a little sound musical advice on her head? I am really worried.

Please thank Lady Mary for her letter, which I'll answer. I'm very sorry she'll miss Prunella.

Yours,

H. G. B.

---

1. Gertrude Kingston did, in fact, play the part of Helen when *The Trojan Women* was produced on April 11, 1905 (see also Chapter III for letter to Shaw of January 3, 1915, and Chapter IV for postcard to Lillah McCarthy, October 24, 1910).
2. Florence Farr had played Leader of the Chorus in the *Hippolytus* and had also devised the accompanying music and trained the Chorus speakers.

BOD/MS
To Murray

[no address]
[London]
January 27 [1905]

Dear G. M.,

I always like to impress upon authors that they are a confounded nuisance and far better in Crete. I could here make an awful pun about concrete and abstract but, refraining, I pass on to say that I shall miss you from the Troades rehearsal if you go and indeed, if it were not that having aborted some of your ideas over Hippolytus I think I can't utterly neglect them, I would urge you to stay. But as it is, though, I shall miss you. I think you'll be safe in leaving it, if no more. At the end of which wonderful sentence I add—Coward, Coward: you are flying before the face of Brema and Kingston and you know it: Coward!

O dear, you <u>must</u> not ask Miss Kingston to read a part on approval. Did I fearfully tell you that I meant to? I think she is settled as Helen.

My mind inclines to Irene Rooke for Andromache, a sweet, rather pale-voiced thing with a good deal of not very apparent character. I grow more and more to think it a rather good piece of casting. Pallas a little forbidding, eh? Poseidon very noble—I would like both the Gods intellectual, not like the Venus de Medici and Father Thames. I know it will end in Goodhart as Menelaus: he is so like it.

Yours,
H. G. B.

BOD/MS
To Murray

The Court
Tuesday [June?, 1905]

Dear Murray,

I hope there was more than fun in your plans for a Papa Yanni steamboat or a mountain or a plain or summat. Do come away with me on July 2. I'll go where you will and stay how long you will. I don't know what sort of a companion I'll be but you, Murray, will come as a boon and a blessing.

Also there's this—I am now carrying on a sort of semi-business flirtation with Mrs. Campbell. Now would you like her for Electra? If not, who is your alternative? Shall I mention its existence to her at all? (By the way, I am going to dine with her on Thursday.) And how is it getting on? When will it suit you for us to do it—early spring: February or so—or what? I also want to discuss an evening bill—Hippolytus and Troades or Electra. I want it to be two plays. When are you in town? I hope you're not getting to <u>like</u> Oxford. To be a mere number in a mere sheet!

My best regards,
Yours,
H. G. B.

I send this to New College for I don't know the mere number in the mere sheet. I suppose there's no one else who professes and calls himself a Murray.

EDD/TS
To Barker

131, Banbury Road,
Oxford.
June 11, 1905

My dear Barker,

Your letter was forwarded to a wrong address by the New College porter, who must have gone temporarily mad. Hence it did not reach me for six days, and my other letters[1] were not answers to it.

Pleasure first. If you don't trust Father John or fear quarantine, why not come straight to Chamonix, or Murren or Bel Alp or the Rifi or Riffel Haus? It is very simple; get into a train on July 2, and there you are. Places will not be crowded so early. Or again, why not go to some almost uninhabited sea side, the Lizard or Macrihanish. Though perhaps Switzerland is more amusing. A holiday is always an awful thing. Or you might call at Cook's and ask about short voyages. to the fjords &c. I want some day to go on a wherry on the Norfolk Broads. Unless anything really good turns up, I recommend Switzerland. If you had more time, and I also, I would say Dalmatia.

Business second. February will suit me as well as any time; and I think on the whole the Electra will shape into a goodish play. It is both exciting and psychologically interesting, though it never sweeps you away. I am now about half through, and hope I may finish it before I have to begin preparing lectures for next term.

As to Mrs. Campbell, I think on the whole she is the best person we can get. But: (1) Will she do what we want? (2) If willing, can she speak a long continuous speech? The main effects, as usual, depend on long speeches, and I have just a fear that she may be too restless and scrappy in her methods. She could not face the long speech of Phaedra at all. Still she would be splendid in some ways; and on the whole, if we can get her, we ought to be thankful.

Bradley was lecturing on Antony & Cleopatra yesterday; and his account of the latter—highly appreciative—reminded me of Mrs. Campbell at every turn.

I don't think Miss Olive would be very safe for Electra; and another point is that, if Mrs. Campbell did Electra and liked it, she might afterwards do Medea for us—a part that no one else whom I can think of could touch! But of course Medea is not ready, and she ought to act some other Greek part first, to get comfortable in the convention.

I dreamed last night that I was being tried for some offence or other which was entirely due to Hay Fever. The magistrate said he

had never come across a genuine case of hay fever, though it was
always being offered as an excuse in that court; but he knew all about
Drink, and so saying gave me six months! It was horrible.

Yours ever,

G. M.

---

1. That is, those of June 8 and 10, which follow.

EDD/TS
To Barker

131, Banbury Road,
Oxford.
June 8, 1905

My dear Barker,

    I have twice been in town for a night, being Wanted at Bow
St., but have never been free at times when you were likely to be
free, so I could not lay before you any proposals for July.

    1. The Papayanni SS Austrian, 4500 tons burden, generally
second-rate, leaves on July 5 for Gibraltar, Corfu, Patras, Syra,
Smyrna, Constantinople and Odessa. Fare to Constantinople £13,
time 17 days. Return to Cple (excuse increasing brevity) is cheaper,
but you have to wait for the steamer to go round by Odessa, so that
the whole voyage takes about 7 to 8 weeks; which is too long.

    Suppose you go straight to Cple, starting on the 5th, you
arrive on the 22nd; catch a Messagerie to Marseilles on the 25th,
arrive Marseilles 30th; back in London the 2nd or 3rd of August.
This is the quickest I can find out. Total expenses might come to £30.

    Also, it must be admitted that there will probably be sick-
ness in some of the ports, and there is very often quarantine on ships
returning from Cple. Also, if you are run down to start with, the
sea-sickness may be troublesome. Otherwise, with a biggish ship and
summer weather, you would not have more than a day or two of it.

    This seems to me the best ship for our purpose, if we try
the Mediterranean.

    2. There is an Orient Pleasure steamer going—in search of
pleasure—to Spitzbergen; a 15 days cruise for varying fares from £15
upwards. Some large fjords on the way; it cannot get into the smaller
fjords. This leaves me cold; but not hostile. It starts July 8.

    3. If you like Switzerland, I do not mind seeing the squalid
place and sitting through the funereal table d'hôtes for a week or
two; but then I should have to join Rosalind and Miss Blimfield, for

at least some part of the time. R is not well yet, and will go to a mountain instead of returning to school at half-term.

4. But, as far as terra firma is concerned, I slightly prefer an English sea-coast; the Lizard, say, or Holy Island or any other quiet and sandy place. And this fits in with another consideration, that is rather upsetting: viz. that I may be called as a witness in a further adjournment of Brailsford's trial.[1] It is now adjourned to the 26th, at the Old Bailey; but the Law Officers want to have a Trial at Bar, before three Judges of the King's Bench, like the Jameson Raiders and suchlike distinguished persons. Our counsel hopes to get them to forgo this. If they insist, it may come before the King's Bench early in August, and interfere with distant excursions. I can get off appearing, as I am only wanted for evidence to character. But: (1) I am rather a dab at evidence to character (and quite at your service, if ever you are under a cloud), and have known Brailsford since he was a boy; (2) Though my help will be very slight, I should hate to refuse it on any ground of my own convenience, as B is rather miserable. (If in your own case you would prefer an alibi, I think I could bring that off all right, with a little practice, and it is far more convincing.)

If you have a spare night, you might come down and talk it over. This house is like Barford through the wrong end of a telescope.

Archer tells me you are more and more overworked.

Yours ever,

G. M.

---

1. H. N. Brailsford (1873–1958) was a distinguished journalist and one of the best and best-known of the early British Socialists, a man of brilliant mind, unimpeachable character, and high principle. He had been one of the best of Murray's pupils in Greek at the University of Glasgow. The trial to which this letter refers was for civil disobedience offenses in connection with his active support of the Suffragist movement.

EDD/MS
To Murray

National Liberal Club,
Whitehall Place,
[London], S.W.
Friday [June, 1905]

Dear Murray,

What I can get abroad is a fortnight or three weeks—though if I found a place where I could finish my poor play, then a little longer.

I have just been at an atlas and there seems lots of places in the world. My heart goes out to Papayanni a little but—should I be ill all the time? I have had a great shock at hearing that Rodjeshevski's men, after going all that way, were mostly seasick during the battle (of course it may have been funk—however!) also, would it be very hot and would there be flies of Egypt? But my real fear on board any boat is that the moment we are out of sight of land someone will come up to me and say "Surely you acted in <u>John</u> <u>Bull's</u> <u>Other</u> <u>Island</u> at the Court Theatre—what a <u>nice</u> play—how funny Mr. Bernard Shaw is—was it your own hair you wore or a wig?" I should have to go overboard.

But now—shall we try the mild Mediterranean?

For mountains—their great advantage being that they don't rock much and that you can step off them—my soul certainly goes out to a mountain. I had not thought of Switzerland and table d'hôtes—no—no. I had had the Austrian tyrol in mind. There's Venice and Trieste and a funny part of the Adriatic to the south and there are more mountains and Bohemia and Vienna to the north and just beyond Vienna, the Carpathians.

I suppose Pau and the Pyrenees would be too hot? What about the Basques?

Then Desmond MacCarthy tells me of the pine forests of the Jura looking towards Strasbourg on one side and France on the other. Shall we walk—shall we bicycle to or through or to without through or through without to the Pine Forests of the Jura!

Near home there is Brittany, but that's only a foreign Cornwall. Oh, not England—Murray, not England an you love me. No, of course, you must give evidence about Brailsford's character. But surely the 26th will see it through. If it doesn't, one can but say—plans are upset—Kismet—and any worse language one knows.

We might go to Troy and see how it looks without Marie Brema—or to Tauris. But is the risk of Papayanni turning out a failure too great? I can't decide this in my own mind. Do you say what you think. Patras and Corfu sound awfully fine. I can't help thinking that the Tyrol has points.

One should, in a way, go to a place where the people are nice, where they rob you politely and only murder you in your sleep. Then again, these Pyrenees loom large. By all of this—done on slippy paper with a slippy pen—otherwise not done at all—you'll gather that as long as on SUNDAY, JULY 2 I shake the dust of Sloane Square, London and England off my poor tired feet, I'll go quiet anywheres.

The last phrase used in recognition of your exploits at Bow Street.
Now I must go and "candid".

Yours,
H. G. B.

EDD/TS
To Barker

131, Banbury Road,
Oxford.
June 10, 1905

O Man,

It is dawning upon me, after painful reflection, that perhaps
we want rather different things. You see, my first object is to avoid
Hay Fever: which implies either (1) a sea voyage; (2) a sandy and
barren sea-side, not very far away, because of the railway journey;
(3) a very high mountain, or a glacier. And 3 is further complicated
by the conditions that the railway journey will start my disease, and
secondly that I can't make ordinary genteel expeditions or walk in
meadows or bicycle about. I could, for instance, take a railway
journey straight to the Rhone Glacier and there sit admiring the
works of the Creator until they bored me, but I could not play about
in the Jura or the Vosges. Nor could I go as far as Trieste.

Now an English or Breton sea-side is rather boring to the
young and adventurous, though they might do well enough for me
and my falling leaves. (I am doing a lyric passage to-day, in the Electra.) A sea voyage seems the possible meeting place. On it I would
offer the following remarks:

1. It is very concentrated holiday, very restful, very full of
change, and you come out fat at the end of it.

2. Sickness will pass after about a day, but you will never
feel absolutely free from a suspicion of biliousness. You will dislike
the food, were it the food of angels. (Angels, by the way, were believed by Liebig to live on Chocolate until he invented his patent
food: then they took to that.)

3. Your opinion of me will sink very, very low.

4. The weather will probably be something heavenly and
rapturous, though dashed slightly by smells of oil or cooking. It will
not be too hot at sea, though it will be in the ports. But you will be
too lazy to mind.

5. You will try to work, but will be too stupid.

6. When you get home again you will give thanks in a loud voice and leap like a young lamb just discharged from penal servitude.

7. On board the fashionable passenger steamers there will be people who have seen John Bull and Candida—duchesses, in fact; but on Papa-Yanni there will only be about six passengers altogether and none of them will ever have heard of Shaw or seen any play but musical comedies in Liverpool and Benson's Shakespeare. There will be a man travelling in rope; a married couple going as missionaries or perhaps consuls to Beyrout, and a young Scotchwoman going to be governess in a Russian family in Odessa. There will be a lady secluded in her cabin, and an elderly person who clamours intempestively for sheep's head . . . Here my vision fails me.

8. There is of course a bare possibility that you may be one of the few people who remain sea-sick a long time. Then it would be hellish. But this is very unlikely. I am one of the worst sailors in the world.

9. For "pure gaiety and diversion" I do not recommend it; far from it. But it is a wonderful rest and change, and the new strange places are interesting to see and to remember.

I have been looking up other possible voyages, but the dates are very bad. P & 0 yacht to Spitzbergen July 7; to Naples July 8; nothing else till the 12 and 14. Unless you could catch a North German Lloyd from Southampton on July 1? Of course time is getting on, and we might not find a berth in the Papa.

My wife advises you to go your own ways to the Jura, without me. She thinks the Papa would be too risky for you and the Jura bad for me. I, if left alone, shall probably go quietly to Holy Island and live in a cell, thinking of my friends' sins.

Besides which, there called here yesterday the owner—yes, the owner—of one of the Lofoten Islands, who raised my opinion of Norway and the Arctic circle. (You can get a Lofoten Island for £50 a year.) The great point is that after crossing the North Sea to Bergen, you are in smooth water practically the whole time; also, you are in very big and comfortable ships if you go by P & 0 or Orient.

Let us now take Fate by the hand! I send you books showing:

1. Father John; SS Austrian, July 5. At a pinch we need only to go Corfu or Patras, and then run across to Athens, or take a Thessalian coasting steamer. The difficulty is getting back if you are pressed for time. I have never been in Thessaly.

2. Two days later, P & 0 to Spitzbergen: very comfortable; rather too fashionable and populous; dearish; takes a month. Cheapest tickets £30, but if there are only dearer places going owing to our delay, I will (if you will allow me) stand the excesses. If only the very

dear places are going, they are not for the likes of us; say, not over
£45.

This is July 7 to Aug. 4. I am told, it is not really cold; a
little less warm, but finer, than an English summer. You want water-
proofs and heavy boots for glaciers.

3. July 8, one day later, the Orient cruise of a fortnight,
returning to Grimsby July 21. Fares £12.12 and upwards. This has
merits. It would give you your clear fortnight of compulsory rest, and
then leave you free to do some work in England or elsewhere.

I think 2 and 3 are <u>safer</u> for you than Father John is: though
of course you might meet your duchesses. There is no risk of extreme
discomfort, nor yet of quarantine. Father John however seems to
have improved since I travelled with him. He treated passengers as
vermin then; now he caters for them. Of course the one way you will
have great heat (with sea-breezes) and gorgeous weather, the other
way refreshing cold.

In any case, you might come here on July 2 to discuss the
last details and browse in College Gardens at the beginning of the
Vac. A slight rest, even as little as five days, will be very useful in
meeting your sea-sickness. If you are tired it is worse!

Now, here it comes! <u>Will</u> <u>you</u> <u>go</u> to <u>Cook's</u> and <u>engage</u>
<u>berths</u> on one or another of these ships. I enclose a cheque for instal-
ment of passage money; they mostly want it. I send £20.

If it is the Papa, we want PASSPORTS. Will you try to get
them at Cook's mentioning that I am a friend of Brailsford's. But
there is plenty of time for that.

By the way, will you, in engaging berths, mention that you
are a vegetarian and that you expect to be properly fed, on milk,
eggs, cheese, macaroni, porridge, fruit, and not fish or flesh? If you
are particular, you can say it is me, and not you. That is less simple;
but perhaps more effective . . . a vegetarian friend, deeply diseased
and with a devil of a temper. If one warns them beforehand, I think
it is all right.

My wife says emphatically Norway; but she has always been
unjust to the Papa.

Yours ever,
G. M.

BOD/MS
To Murray

Gilmuire,
Ascot.
Sunday June, 1905

Micawber, have I deserved this? I who never have deserted you, who never will desert you, Micawber!

Let us risk Pappayanni. At the worst—if I live—I can but get off at Gibralter and make my way back through Spain a broken man, while you hold your Ulyssean course for the East. Shall I see about berths, or will you?

Should this fail—yes, a seaside place in Brittany will do me quite well. But if your heart really draws you towards Holy Island there I will not come for there I can—and shall—get newspapers and telegrams—then I would mount my arab bicycle and set forth alone.

But I will risk all and Papyan Eastwoods—Syracuse— C'ple—yes, I want to see them.

Yours,
H. G. B.

BOD/MS
To Murray

[no address]
Monday, [June, 1905]

Oh, Murray—when I have worked myself up into a state of bravery about Pere Jean, reminding myself that no one has really ever died of seasickness, that quarantine never lasts more than 21 days. Then you descend on me with suggestions of cowardly mountains. Well, I put it on you—I have never done more than cross a channel and I have prayed fervently for a channel tunnel—if I die you must play Keegan and Tanner in the autumn and otherwise help to run the orphaned Court. But I will spend a morning with Cook[1] tomorrow.

About Mrs. P. C.—I will talk to her seriously about Electra—as to whether or no she can do it simply and without mannerisms and reminiscences of the attitudes she thought Burne Jones liked.

I should have made it 12 months hard for hayfever.[2]
Will you be in town soon?

Yours,
H. G. B.

P.S. Are there cockroaches on Pa Jack's?

1. Thomas Cook and Sons Ltd., the British firm which "invented" the idea of travel agencies.
2. This refers to the last sentence of Murray's letter of June 11, which Barker had evidently just received; "12 months hard" means twelve months' imprisonment at hard labor.

BOD/MS
To Murray

National Liberal Club,
Whitehall Place, S.W.
Tuesday [June, 1905]

Dear G. M.,

There is no electric light but nevertheless I have inquired what cabin is to be got and shall know on Thursday. Where shall we book to?*

Archer says why don't we go to Norway—they'd very probably make you King: he thinks you'd do it very well. Certainly you would. Yes, there's Norway—is it hay feverish? I have been told Finland is the place to go to. I send you the information I got about Brittany (Britanny). The seasick weary Barker (Romeo and Juliet, Act IV) will probably spread his bones there when Padre Giovanni has racked them his worst. I also send a bit about the Marseilles boats but I don't think there's anything much to that.

Let me tell you, Sir, that your method of drawing a cheque and leaving me to divide it is a coward's method—and it shall not avail you. You'll receive dozens of letters yet.

Yours,
H.G.B.

*If we book to Smyrna and then go on they'll charge us local rates but I don't think that matters much. I felt much better after talking to Cook about it this morning. He praised the boats.

BOD/MS
To Murray

8, York Buildings,
Adelphi.
Thursday [June, 1905]

I see what it is, Murray: you wish to blow up Abdul the Damned and I'm to get your passport—but you're foiled: fill the form up yourself. The Lily of Cambridge goes instead of the Austrian (much more appropriate). She is a hundred tons bigger. The pencilled cabins were free. I have applied for the inked one as being furthest forward. I have said it must be reserved for us two and that they must feed us semi-vegetarianly. I put semi- because I thought otherwise they'd give us only French beans and bread—you take eggs and fish, don't you?

I have also inquired as to the points of booking to Syria, Smyrna or C'ple.

This will all be settled tomorrow, so wire me here first thing any remarks you have to make and may the Lord have mercy on your—Little Mary.[1]

Yours,

H. G. B.

---

1. "Little Mary" was polite British slang for stomach or belly. There was at the time a Music Hall song which contained the line (referring to seasickness), "Little Mary keeps troubling me."

BOD/MS
To Murray

Royal Court Theatre,
Sloane Square, S.W.
Tuesday night [June, 1905]

Dear Murray,

How are you? Shall I find a letter from you at home? I have not been there for a day—I am staying out of town now all I can, so this address is best for me.

The Papayanni deal is complete, I believe, though I've not yet had a receipt for my cheque. Have you sent your passport form back to them direct?

I am going to see Mrs. Campbell tomorrow to talk about Electra. When will it be actually ready for? If she's inclined to do it, it'll mean a certain fitting of dates. By the way, we have one lot of matinées still unsettled for October—I suppose it won't be done by then? If it <u>will</u> be, you might wire me when you get this tomorrow.

Oh, I want my holiday and I'm acting so badly.

Yours,

H. G. B.

BOD/MS
To Murray

Shipham,
Wenscombe,
Somerset.
Saturday [August, 1905]

My dear Murray,

My old friend Baksheesh Pasha—he was Baksheesh Bey in those days—used to remark to me that a sign of high civilization both in men and states was the non-payment of debts. Ah, many is the argument we have had round the campfire in the summer of '78 with Hornbeam Bey snoring in the shadow of the tent, Ah, well, I shall see neither of them again. But the point of this little anecdote is, my dear Murray, that I find myself in your debt to the extent of to wit i.e. viz. q.v. (sic) passim:

1 Hairless Author
1 Hairless shaving brush
2 bottles of Pope Roach (these will be kept, for if Shaw worries me much more I must cross to Ireland and beard him in his Derry).
1 Constantinople bag—or 17 francs (Take my advice and the 17 francs)
a demi-portion of sundry monies expended by you upon creature comforts and discomforts in the latter part of our Rush across Europe (see the Star for Aug. 3). Kindly furnish an abstract of these same and oblige.

Yours faithfully,
BARKER AND BOUNCER
per H. G. B.

I next must call your attention to the fact that

There was a young man of Geneva
Who suffered a deal from hayfever
He sneezed and he snoze
Till he bust all his clothes
So his wife says. But you can't believe her.

I should also add that

The Haig-ite[1] is an awful brute
It feeds on milk and nuts and fruit
It never smokes, it seldom steals
It never drinks between its meals.
I wouldn't be a nasty Haig-it
No, not for all the wealth I may git

> By writing verses like this 'ere.
> Gimme a steak and a bottle of beer.

Rather wanklin.[2] You were quite right: I don't quite know the meaning of what I've been saying. And then there's the drive wanted behind the whole thing, which comes but by prayer and fasting. I don't know how to pray and I can't fast for it gives me pains. Shaw writes me that Adolphus Cusins[3] "Quotes screeds of the Bacchae". (I knew it'd be the Bacchae—Blow the Bacchae!)

What are you doing—the Electra? When am I going to see that? Have you any further ideas about the music? Who is to break the matter to Miss Farr? Someone must steal her psalteries first for we shall want them. Of course, I'll ask her to come and play and chant someone else's music. She won't even answer that. Oh Lor!

Please give my tenderest regards to Lady Mary. I only saw her for that flash. It's a naice place, Shipham. I laike a naice place—can ye' get poastcaards thear?[4] I will conclude by observing

> A baldheaded buffer of Bristol
> Assaulted his Aunt with a pistol;
> But the gallant old lady
> Said "one maravedi
> To sixpence it doesn't go off".

As she pointed out to me—no one could rhyme at such a moment—the great thing was to say something. Her name was Mrs. O'Driscoll. He was a rather charming man who travelled in tallow and collected butterflies in his spare moments. But a sunstroke brought on religious mania—he said his aunt was the seven deadly sins.

Yours,

H. G. B.

---

1. A reference, I think, to Arthur Elam Haigh (1855–1905), classical scholar, editor of classical texts, and author of *The Attic Theatre* (1899), etc. Murray is comically pictured in Barker's verse as a follower of Haigh.
2. For a comment on this dialect word see footnote in letter to Murray, February 23, 1912. Incidentally, it here refers not to what has gone immediately before in the letter but to Barker's play *The Voysey Inheritance,* which he had just completed and read to Murray prior to producing it. (Its first performance was in November, 1905.)
3. Adolphus Cusins, the character in *Major Barbara* whom Shaw modeled on Murray. Shaw was working on the play at the time, and it had already been agreed that the first production of it would be at the Court Theatre under the Barker-Vedrenne management.
4. Of all the affectations which have been imposed on the English language, perhaps the silliest—including the sub-technology and would-be smartness of the North American advertising man and computerized man—is the politely distorted vowel sounds of the British upper middle classes, especially in the smaller country towns of southern England. It is amusing to find Barker parodying this in the first decade of the century because it is still there today, as fantastically fatuous as ever.

EDD/TS
To Barker

Naworth Castle,
Carlisle.
August 11, 1905

My dear B:

This is mere business, though I should like to indulge in memories of Baksheesh Bey and the young men of Bohemia.

1. As to Miss Farr, she writes to me the enclosed, to which I have returned an evasive answer. Would it be a possible thing to soften the change of Chorus-leadership by letting her work her will on the Bacchae? And if so, should I say it must not be at the Court? I should on the whole slightly prefer not having the Bacchae done by her; but I care very little one way or the other. Have you any feeling?

2. Your debts to me on arrival in London amounted—you will be dismayed to hear—to either 20 or 23 shillings, I can't be sure which. You then no sooner saw my wife than you borrowed 5s of her—which sum she has made me pay back once and is still trying to make me pay back twice.

3. I am sure that the root situation of the Voyseys is very good indeed, and the main characters and construction good. So I think it will come out good if you just get it clear and true. I see what you mean about a lack of driving power, at least, as I heard it. But I think that came from the uncertainty which you had left about the main problem. If you get that clear—to speak roughly, that the old man is wrong and a failure and Edward right—I think you will find that the driving power is mostly achieved. Do you see that Giacosa's last play is about a dishonest father and an honest son? But not in the least like your treatment. The son simply finds the old man out and leaves him, in spite of his amiability and private virtues.

I have done a lot of Electra, and ought to finish in a few days. It is rather bad, and so am I. I mean, in health. My character is as beautiful as ever.

Yours ever,
G. M.

Tell GBS that I try to be a Christian and can stand a good deal, as such. But if people call me Adolphus,[1] they do so at their peril. Moses, if you like, or even Ferdinand. But not Adolphus.

---

1. *Major Barbara*'s Adolphus Cusins.

BOD/MS
To Murray

Shipham,
Wenscombe.
Sunday morning [September, 1905]

Dear G. M.

I always knew I was a thief—hence my sympathy with
Voysey Senior.[1] I had completely forgotten the 5/- incident: do apologise for me to Lady Mary—oh, and pay her twice; Murray, pay her
twice—that is the least you can do under the circumstances. Here's a
cheque for £1.10.0 which if a Sunday morning calculation is
accurate—and of course it shouldn't be—is 23/- and 5/- and 17f. Now
once more I can look my fellow man in the face.

As to Miss Farr, the question is a little serious. From my
point of view there is the free-trade or Protection question complicated by the further question—what good or harm will a production—an archaic, an archaotic, production by Miss Farr do to the
Greek play cause as a whole? I think she may well get a more
"beautiful" production than we do at the Court because Beauty is her
sole idea. But I fear that it would be quite outside the Theatre Scale
(so to speak), while I want to make the plays come as naturally to
the theatre as possible; and also I have an uneasy feeling that all
through, to get good results, Miss Farr lowers the standard. This is a
device that is least easily seen through and it is most dangerous, I'm
sure.

For Heaven's sake, she musn't play about with Maskelyne
and Cook[2] transparencies. Then there's the question how time and
space will cohere and jump. I want the Electra in the Spring at
matinées and thereabouts if possible an evening bill of Hippolytus,
Troades (?) and the Electra—following up its matinée success which
it has got to have. Now I don't really want to get rid of Miss Farr at
all; at the very least I want her psalteries. But I want someone to
replace her jejune harmonics with something better and her muddling
with a little real training of the chorus: Miss Farr's music for the
Hippolytus and a chorus properly trained. Which music for the
Troades? And a chorus properly trained (? with or without Miss
Farr). With Miss Farr's psalteries? But not with Miss Farr as leader
in either of the three plays (but that doesn't involve Tita!).

This wants much discussion—the Peace negotiations at Portsmouth aren't in it.[3] It seems to me that at the slightest of these proposed changes—even the Electra one—Miss Farr will throw us over: I
wonder! But we must make our plans very soon for there's work in

this. Let me know about what time would suit you best to have Electra done—between January and Easter.

Yours,
H. G. B.

---

1. Edward Voysey, Senior, a character in Barker's *The Voysey Inheritance,* was a lawyer
   who made a fat living for years by cheating his clients.
2. Maskelyne and Cook were famous "illusionists," giving performances, in various
   halls and theaters, in which spectacular "magic" events and occurrences were represented. Maskelyne also had another partner—Devant—and Maskelyne and Devant
   were even better known than Maskelyne and Cook.
3. Not Portsmouth, England, but Portsmouth, New Hampshire, where President Roosevelt had convened a conference between Russian and Japanese representatives to try
   to bring an end to the Russo-Japanese War.

EDD/TS
To Barker

Naworth Castle,
Carlisle.
August 19, 1905

My dear Barker,

Primo, I have finished the Electra, though there are still
some bad bits, and there are no stage directions yet. I shall do it over
in the next few days.

Secundo, as to Miss Farr, I do not see our way clearly. (As
to the Bacchae, I think we should only give her permission to perform as a last resort, in case we get into difficulties with her about
e.g. the music of the Hippolytus.) I agree with all your letter, subject
to the following remarks: (1) Is it wise to be off with the old Chorus-
Leader before you have at least some idea of a new one with whom
you wish to be "on"? I agree in being dissatisfied with Miss Farr, but
I have no person or system in my mind who would be better . . . nor,
as far as I can see, as good. (2) On thinking things over, I am clearly
against making the choruses more <u>musical</u> . . . I mean, against sacrificing the words to the music. I would sooner get the words clear
than have even a very good unintelligible song. I think you agree.
This is a serious consideration in approaching any musician. (3) As to
the leading of the Chorus, the actual leading, on the stage, I think
there is rather a disadvantage in the second Hippolytus arrangement—I mean in having Miss Farr, who has composed the music, in
the ordinary chorus, and someone else leading and directing her. But
really everything depends on your substitute for Miss F.

How are the Voyseys? I have just been hearing of a similar case in Carlisle. Only there the thing was found out at the father's death, and the honest son, who knew nothing about it, was taken as partner in the house that had wound up the father's affairs and exposed him. That is more in the style of the old-fashioned drama. The post blares at me!

Yours ever,
G. M.

BOD/MS
To Murray

Court Theatre
Saturday [September?, 1905]

My dear G. M.,
   This is too belated to be called an answer to your letter. I've heard nothing more from Mrs. Campbell—and I haven't yet got Electra. But I will tell her that she should let you read it to her—but she refused to let me!!!
   I think I have discovered a way out of the chorus difficulty—Percy Pitt to arrange matters. But also I want to try how simple speaking together would sound. I could get Miss Lamborn, Miss Thompson and another to try it. Will you be in town anytime— you ought, in fact you must, hear it?

Yours,
H. G. B.

Also, I want to "study" you.[1]

---

1. Barker was preparing to play the "Murray" character, Adolphus Cusins, in *Major Barbara*.

BOD/TS
To Murray

Royal Court Theatre,
Sloane Square, S.W.
Sept 27th, 1905

My dear Murray,
   I also saw Mrs. Campbell the day after you read the play to her and she is I think really anxious to do "Electra". We are now going to make a proposal to her of the 6 matinées in January and of

18 more matinées right through the London Season. This we think would be financially sound and probably an arrangement she would be able to accept at once as it would not interfere with any evening engagement she may have.

She told me in her childish way that you were quite willing that we should hand the rights of the play over to her; I replied in my childish way that however willing you might be I had no intention of doing so.

Now I would be very careful about giving her any American rights. It seems to me the important thing is that the first time the plays are done in America (and indeed every time) they should be done according to our design and your approval. It would be quite easy for us to arrange with Frohman or with Mrs. Campbell or as it would probably turn out in practice with both to send a production to America, that is, the scenery, the chorus, the costumes the cast and the business arranged as you and I have done it, with Mrs. Campbell as "Electra"—and why not as "Phaedra"—and could she play "Hecuba"? I think this would be a better game than letting Mrs. Campbell loose to do what she liked with the play; for one thing my experience of her as a leading woman producing plays is that she sends all the other actors into a Lunatic Asylum before the curtain ever rises. It would certainly be more satisfactory to us. Of course we must take care that no deadlock results from trying to make this arrangement, but I think that could be managed.

Could you by chance have me down on Sunday? I am not sure at the moment that I can come, but could you have me if I could? I may want to see you rather.

Yours always,
H. G. B.

BOD/MS
To Murray

Court Theatre
Wednesday night [October, 1905]

Dear G. M.,

Only a line—for I'm wild-quacked to death.[1] I hope I'm doing right in this matter—here is our today's letter to Hawksley.[2] You'll see by it just what my point is with Mrs. P. C. I want her either to go to some trouble over the play—which she'll do if she makes a success here, or to leave it alone—which she'll do if she doesn't. But I think to let her have it carelessly to use or let alone as she likes would be bad policy.

But I take it that you are in agreement with me that she ought to re-produce the Court production as we arrange it—otherwise, of course, the position we take up on the matter is not sound from your point of view—but this is so isn't it?

And if she makes a decent offer (for the Electra only!) and it comes to our practically acting only as your agent in the matter—I think we'll get more satisfactory terms out of her than you would. But do let me know candidly what you think of all this.

Yours,

H. G. B.

---

1. He refers to his intensive preparations for a production of Ibsen's *The Wild Duck,* which was due to open on October 17 (see his correspondence with Archer in Chapter II).
2. Bourchier F. Hawksley, solicitor, acted for Mrs. Patrick Campbell in the negotiations concerning the possibility of her playing Electra under Barker's direction at the Court Theatre. There was an acid correspondence between Vedrenne and Hawksley on the subject (the letters are in the Murray archive at the Bodleian Library).

BOD/MS
To Murray

Court Theatre

Monday [October, 1905]

Dear Murray,

The point of all this is, of course, that these Greek plays must not be put into a repertory. It means in the case of the Electra—Mrs. P. C. as a star, the rest of the cast as it happens and the chorus anyhow (for a repertory company cannot carry a Greek Chorus). Now you cannot book the Electra alone for an American tour and therefore if Mrs. P. C. gets this one piece to play about with, part of a repertory is its only fate. So I want to arrange matters that the 3 plays we've done so far may be tied together (with Mrs. P. C. in the centre by all means if she'll do it). That will make it worth while to send out a special company to play them—you can afford for 3 plays what you can't afford for one. Or if we can't bring this off, I want to let her have the Electra only on such conditions— as to chorus, scenery, cast—as will ensure a proper start for Euripides-Murray in America.

I hope you think I'm right in this and will back me up.

I think she means to play the part here and I very much

hope she will—but I shouldn't <u>break</u> my heart if she didn't. And anyhow she's not a lady to give way to. I saw her yesterday: she's intelligent about it, of course—but too precious: she doesn't yet see, I'm sure, where the point of the thing lies—but she'll get to it.

Yours,
H. G. B.

BOD/TS
To Murray

Royal Court Theatre
Sloane Square, S.W.
Nov. 4, 1905

My dear Murray,

Mrs. Campbell is off. I am not altogether sorry and now I am going to try this girl Miss Crawford of whom I have great hopes. Also we must try the chorus. Also I must see you some time to have a talk about things especially about America. We have had no line from Frohman yet, but there is a distinct opening with Ben Greet if that is worth taking but there are objections. I think you will be condemned to another talk on the telephone. By the way I am at 3 Clements Inn now and my number is 2382 Holborn. My regret for Mrs. Campbell is lessened by the news that she intended to have the chorus moving rythmatically [*sic*]. Are you coming up to see "Voysey"?[1]

Yours sincerely,
H. G. B.

P.S. I have more to say to you but I'm dashed if I can remember what. I must have you read me those two Bacchae choruses.

---

1. The first production of Barker's *The Voysey Inheritance* opened on November 7, 1905, with Barker as director.

BOD/TS
To Murray

Royal Court Theatre,
Sloane Square, S.W.
Nov. 21, 1905

My dear Murray,

I have given a preliminary trial to Miss Alice Crawford and I am very doubtful as to what she can do. She has every personal advantage for the part but she would need so much teaching that I fear she could not disguise the fact that she had been taught. I should myself regard Miss Edith Wynne-Matthison as safer; would you be content with her if we could get her? If you won't, we must certainly still consider Miss Crawford and I think you ought to come up and hear her for I have talked to her about the meaning of the part and that may have some good effect. My personal inclination is to settle with Miss Matthison at once if we can get her and to bother no further, but let me know what you think of this.

Also how about Ainley for Orestes? I do not think I ought to play in the piece. My acting is getting worse every day and the production is so important and my mind will be upon that and not upon a part.

Yours always,
H. G. B.

Since writing, it has become more important to settle with Miss Matthison and I think it'd be the safe plan—or have you any better suggestion? We can't have Ainley. Miss M. is very keen on the Electra and anyhow she has the method all there, good and clean. We should only have to give her the meanings. True, she can't transcend above a certain point—but then Electra doesn't as Andromache does, does she? And Miss M would be willing—is anxious—to go to America with all three plays and she's a great draw there.

BOD/MS
To Murray

Royal Court Theatre,
Sloane Square, S.W.
Dec. 5th, 1905

My dear Murray,

Surely Miss Olive is too young for Clytemnestra. I fear you are cultivating a conscience about Miss Olive. This is wrong; however, I will dispute that matter further in a moment. I had thought of Miss Frances Ivor who is the rather battered woman of 45 that I suppose Clytemnestra should be. That or something like that will, it seems to me, be a professional and businesslike piece of casting. The Miss Olive idea strikes me as a little amateurish.[1] Orestes is most difficult. I never for a moment thought of anybody like Hearn and I think the rejected Hippolytus has not anything like enough experience. I am inclining towards Harcourt Williams who can speak verse and although he is rather inclined to strain after his effects he is

about the right weak-strong personality. I can make any appointment
you like on Friday the 9th before 12-30 in the morning or will you
dine with me at 6 o'clock either at the Club or Clements Inn? I
would like you to see my Clements Inn rooms. I shall be coming up
to town from Cambridge on Monday and could see you that afternoon if that would do for you, or I could manage this Saturday and
then I am freerer* than on Friday. Suggest the arrangement that suits
you best, but I do not think we ought to postpone it until the 17th.
As to the music, one of Pitt's choruses was quite good in method, the
other quite bad. However, we have settled to go on with him for he
is a competent man and will be amenable to do what we want.

Yours,
H. G. B.

*a good word; I won't alter it.

---

1. Nevertheless, Edyth Olive did play Clytemnestra when Barker finally produced the
   play on January 16, 1906.

BOD/TS
To Murray

Royal Court Theatre,
Sloane Square, S.W.
Dec. 14th, 1905

My dear Murray,
        You will have my wire and I will have your answer before
this reaches you. I have done my best to see Miss Olive as Clytemnestra and I cannot. It seems to me essential to have a woman who
has lost all her ideals and illusions. Miss Olive is morally hoydenish,
full of ideals and illusions and she cannot prevent this coming out.
However much she might disguise herself she would still appear
younger than Miss Matthison for she is essentially girlish in her
movements and in the particular abandon which characterizes her
methods. You see I know her work very well and just what I can
get out of her and what I cannot and I do hope you will agree with
me that she had better not have a try at Clytemnestra for I am very
strongly persuaded of it. This may land me in a difficulty but it is
one that must be faced. Miss Marion Terry, if we could get her,
would of course be exactly right, I feel, and would lend great
strength to the cast; if we could get her. The only other two names
that occur to me for the moment are Miss Cecil Cromwell—the
right age but perhaps rather too mondaine; and Miss Madge McIn-

tosh—the wrong age but clever and able to give me the tired note which I feel is wanted.

Now about the old man: I cannot get Swete[1] and I cannot get George. I think J. H. Barnes would be a safe and a good cast if we could afford him. I cannot get Arthur Whitby for the peasant without sacrificing him when the play is done in the evening and I don't want to alter the cast if I can possibly avoid it; so, I am trying for Stratton Rodney who is a very good man. We have settled with Harcourt Williams for Orestes. He is a bit romantic but I think can be shaped.

I propose to work Castor and Polydeuces through a transparency above the roof of the hut. I hope this will be effective. They will appear in the tree which is above the hut; that I suppose don't matter.

So far as I know rehearsals will start on Monday. Yes, I think I shall anyway do this if it is only to rehearse Electra, Orestes and the old man and possibly the peasant, for I cannot tell if the chorus music will be ready before Tuesday, although I shall prefer to start with the chorus first. However, you shall hear about this. Let me have an answer upon all these matters by return.

Yours,
H. G. B.

---

1. E. Lyall Swete (1866–1930).

BOD/TS
To Murray

Royal Court Theatre,
Sloane Square, S.W.
Jan. 31st, 1906.

My dear G. M.,

I have talked to Vedrenne about the Miss Farr question but we both think it would be better to leave matters as they are at the present arranged. In the first place there is the objection to upsetting any arrangement which is comfortably made. In the second the particular objection to this upsetting is, first, that another leader is already engaged. Second, that it will be perfectly impossible with the extra rehearsals for "Electra" to give Miss Farr the time she would require to go about things in her own way again. Third, that we now have the chorus rather full of the professional persons whose work Miss Farr dislikes, whom she cannot get on with and consequently makes very uncomfortable, and fourth, that I went in front for the last chorus of "Electra" the other day and they were doing it so well and I could hear the words so distinctly that I could not feel this to be anything but an advantage we have gained by not having Miss Farr training the chorus.

I think in this instance that you may be right and I am very probably wrong, but just for practical politics I think it is better to leave things as they are. I am really a little frightened at the rush of work that is just coming on and perhaps another straw might break this camel's back.

Yours always,

H. G. B.

BOD/MS
To Murray

Hoch Ginstermunz,

Tirol.

May 10 [1906]

Dear G. M.,

I'd like to write you a really proper and well-spelt letter saying all or most of what I think and feel towards you—3 vols Qto it would be. But I will now content myself with hoping that you've escaped the witch doctors at last—that your operation for hayfever (apply ice to the feet for a cold in the head) has been entirely successful—by stating that this is the most beautiful place I have ever seen, that I have just begun to tackle seriously my play,[1] that I have not yet beaten my wife with a red hot poker (there are none in the Tirol) but otherwise am only an average husband—and by inquiring after Medea's health.

Let me have word of you. Truly I received the Times every day—but what is that: mere Education Bill.

Yours,

H. G. B.

---

1. He was beginning to write *Waste*. He and Lillah were on their first holiday together, having been married in London in April, 1906.

BOD/MS
To Murray

Hoch Ginstermunz,
Tirol.
May 19 [1906]

Dear G. M.,

I have just written a perfect pamphlet to Lord Lytton on the 'orrible economic conditions of the theatrical profession—therefore I am dashed if I write a long letter to you in my orrible condition (when I've worked for two days and done precious little, I get a headache).

But I will simply inquire, will Medea be ready by the New Year? We are talking out arrangements now, Vedrenne and I. I am nearly through the Life of Gladstone[1]. I haven't been so fascinated with a book for years. It is cheering to discover (1) how consistently unpopular he was because (2) no-one ever understood him. And very interesting to see, not what he got to, but what he came from. I wish Morley wouldn't talk about his "fourscore years" quite so much. My homage to you all.

H. G. B.

P.S. A cloud has just walked in at my window and wetted me all over. We are on such terms of familiarity with the climate here as never was.

---

1. Morley's *Life of Gladstone* was first published in 1903. Barker's reason for reading it now was, at least in part, because his own play, *Waste,* has as its central character a liberal politician—not that Henry Trebell, in *Waste,* is in the least like Gladstone, but Barker wanted all the background he could get on how politics actually worked. He sought Shaw's advice on the same question (see Shaw's letter to Lillah McCarthy of May 30, 1906, in *Bernard Shaw: Collected Letters,* ed. Dan H. Laurence. [London, 1972], 2:264).

BOD/TS
To Murray

Royal Court Theatre,
Sloane Square, S.W.
Oct. 11th, 1906

My dear G. M.,

1. Eating and drinking for five hours, Oh!

2. Walford Davies is of course an excellent known composer; he did "Everyman".[1]

3. I have read a lyric or two to Mrs. Lee Mathews and she is going to have a try at them and you shall hear.

4. It goes very much against the grain with me to postpone indefinitely any play because it seems impossible to cast it. On that ground, half the plays would never get done at all. And of course abandoning it is out of the question. You don't mean that do you? But I think it will be wise to make up our minds to do it at the most convenient date in 1907 that is compatible with a good Medea.[2] Certainly Constance Collier is in it. She is tiring for two hours but she has a certain amount of devilry. Mrs. Campbell definitely says she is going to America in the Spring so we are now tackling her about the Autumn.

Yours,

H. G. B.

1. This *Everyman* was an oratorio by Walford Davies first performed in 1904, three years after William Poel's rediscovery and production of the play (Poel took his text for his production from a manuscript in the library of Lincoln Cathedral). It was Poel's production of *Everyman* in 1901 which gave Davies the initial idea for his oratorio.
2. The production of *Medea* was finally presented on October 22, 1907, with Edyth Olive as Medea, but it was at the Savoy Theatre, to which the Barker-Vedrenne management moved from the Court during 1907.

BOD/TS
To Murray

London.

Monday [1906]

Dear G. M.

One thing I must know before I see Mrs. Campbell . . . do you stick to your decision about the American conditions . . . are the plays to be performed there as here or not? I of course feel I must advise you to stick to the condition, your financial tenure in America is already precarious . . . your artistic tenure may become more precarious still. But on the other hand we can apparently offer you no immediate alternative. If you decide to make no effective restrictions as to her method of performing them, I very much wish that you need not hand her over unrestricted powers until you have at least seen what her own performance is like; and do in any case insist on a strict time-limit . . . entire surrender of rights if she doesn't perform within a year or something.

Yours,

H. G. B.

BOD/TS
To Murray

Royal Court Theatre,
Sloane Square, S.W.
Oct. 13th, 1906

My dear G. M.,
   The other day I saw Mrs. Campbell. She asked me if we would give up the "Medea" in order to let her produce it in London for some matinées in November and take it to America in the Spring. She asked me if I would attend five or six rehearsals and apparently help her produce it, but I said at once this was out of the question for I cannot produce Greek plays in five or six rehearsals, as you know, and also I am nothing like ready with it.
   On the main question of letting the play go I have spoken to Vedrenne and our position is this—we should very much regret losing the play and breaking the continuity of your association with us. But at the same time we feel that we ought not to stand in the way of what you may consider a more advantageous chance. What we can guarantee you is this—a production for eight matinées sometime during 1907, and a Medea of whom you approve: Mrs. Patrick Campbell as well as another if she would come on reasonable terms and make her arrangements a reasonable way ahead, but as it seems impossible to induce her to be at all businesslike I should say this practically means not Mrs. Campbell. Now you must consider if she can go one better.
   Vedrenne & Barker being now in competition cannot offer you any advice on the subject, but Barker can and does. It is only this—that you should consider very carefully the sort of production you will get from Mrs. Campbell at short notice, with no idea as to the chorus, and with a fair percentage of her American Modern Comedy Company playing the parts. Against this danger there is the great asset of her personality and her obvious liking for the play. I am not sure myself which way the scale dips, but that is what you have to consider.

Yours,
H. G. B.

I hope I've made all this quite clear—we <u>shall</u> regret losing the play if you take it from us—<u>very</u> <u>much</u> <u>indeed</u>—but we do feel you ought to be free.

BOD/TS
To Murray

Royal Court Theatre,
Sloane Square, S.W.
Oct. 15th, 1906.

My dear G. M.,

I am very glad indeed at your letter and so is Vedrenne. I rang him up to tell him this morning. But I still don't quite feel with you as to the comparative easiness of casting "Medea". However, now I shall start to study it more or less and I may see whose failings in the part will matter least.

Now will you please write yourself to Mrs. Campbell and inform her that we have played the game by putting the matter before you and we will in turn make her a final offer of the part if she will give us any idea as to when she will be in London. This if you think wise.

Yours faithfully,
H. G. Barker

BOD/handwritten by a secretary but initialed by Barker
To Murray

Court Theatre
2 Nov. 1906.

Dear G. M.,

The trial of the new chorus takes place here at 5.15 p.m. on Tuesday afternoon. Will you attend if you feel so disposed.

As to the "Trojan Women", I am at the moment more annoyed than I can say, for after all the trouble we have taken, Genevieve Ward at the last moment lets us through, and for some reason, I suspect quite a silly one, will not do it.

This brings us again to the "Medea" for the Spring, & if that reduces us to Constance Collier, which Vedrenne & I for the moment feel that it does, then, if she is still with Tree, he may not let her play for us, & that postpones any classic till the autumn which is a nuisance. Or is there an alternative Medea in Edyth Olive? My thoughts have been towards her a little bit, but of course I want to read the play again more carefully.

Yours,
H. G. B.

BOD/handwritten by a secretary but initialed by Barker
To Murray

Court Theatre
7 Nov. 1906.

Dear G. M.,

I heard the new idea for the Chorus last night, & I think that we are on the right track at last, or as near as we can get to it. It is very simple & dignified, you can hear the rhythm, & you get something of a choric effect, & rather more dramatic effect at the same time. All its sins are sins of omission & not sins of commission.

Yours,
H. G. B.

P.S. Would you like to come & play Tanner till Xmas, for I am getting very tired of him, & he is getting very tired of me. You really might return Shaw & me the Major Barbara compliment.

BOD/TS
To Murray

Vann Cottage,
Fernhurst,
Surrey.
Sunday [May or June, 1907]

Dear G. M.,

I wait to hear how the Greek Medea struck you. I will get at the play myself as soon as I can for casting and I am setting Mrs. Lee Mathews on to the Choruses . . . if she definitely will; and I am discussing with Vedrenne its place in the Autumn bill. Meanwhile will you send him direct your suggestions for a Medea for that is the crux of the matter and the sooner it is settled the better . . . send them to me too, but to him direct. My Statesman[1] progresses slowly . . . I am not really good at drafting disestablishment bills. You must give advice.

Yours . . . H. G. B.

---

1. In Barker's play, *Waste,* the politician-statesman Trebell seeks to launch a bill for the disestablishment of the Church of England.

BOD/TS
To Murray

> Vann Cottage,
> Fernhurst,
> Surrey.
> Sunday [May or June, 1907[1]]

Dear G. M.,

It is good to hear you are back. When do we meet? . . . you are tied at Oxford I suppose . . . I am busy here. There are all sorts of pros and cons about Medea, which I must write to you; they concern the wisdom of opening with it and the safeness of Miss Olive. I want if possible to open[2] with something which could not have been so well done at the Court, something sensational if may be and something the success of which hangs rather on the ensemble than on one person. I had hoped for Peer Gynt but there are difficulties. I wish the Trojan Women were still to do with a good Hecuba!

> Yours,
> H. G. B.

How are you and Lady Mary, to whom salutations.

---

1. Purdom dates this letter October, 1906, but clearly this is a mistake: these four letters from Vann Cottage to Murray exactly parallel (in subjects discussed, type of notepaper, and typewriter) four letters from Vann Cottage to Archer (see pp. 53–55), and, in one of the letters to Archer, Barker says, "or I shall be up for a day or two about June 1." Moreover, in October, 1906, Barker was very heavily engaged at the Court: he directed the first productions of Galsworthy's *The Silver Box* and St. John Hankin's *The Charity That Began at Home,* both for several matinée performances; he played Tanner in evening performances of *Man and Superman,* and he rehearsed for the original production of *The Doctor's Dilemma,* in which he played Dubedat. That would hardly be the month for retiring to the country to work on the writing of *Waste.* It is also very unlikely that the move to the Savoy, to which Barker refers in two of these letters to Murray written from Vann Cottage, had been thought of, let alone planned, as early as October, 1906.
2. To open the new season at the Savoy Theatre, which began in October.

BOD/TS
To Murray

> Vann Cottage,
> Fernhurst,
> Haslemere.
> Sunday [May or June, 1907]

Dear G. M.,

I am choked with work and bloodless with inability to do it. But I must see you about Medea; in fact, that is part of the work. I can

do nothing tomorrow except my play and an overdue preface to that
Blue Book[1] which now has to come out suddenly . . . Heaven's malison
on it! Toosday . . . ? Yep, it might be. What I am taking to now is . . .
play all morning then letters for an hour or more and a rest and a short
ride and tea . . . then play again till dinner. I can't come over to lunch
unless my brain stops, when I will go anywhere, anywhen, to forget it. I
might get in all my work before tea and then come over to you or I might
come really for the evening . . . it isn't such a long ride back. Lillah is
here for next week anyhow I think. Thus it is!

Yours,

H. G. B.

---

1. *A National Theatre: Scheme and Estimates,* by Archer and Barker.

BOD/TS
To Murray

Vedrenne-Barker Performances,
[offices during July and August, 1907:
37, King Street, Covent Garden, W.C.]
Wednesday morning
[July or August, 1907]

Dear G. M.,
        There is this about Miss Olive I have just thought of and
perhaps it is important. A day or two ago I heard from her asking for
a part in my new play and for a certain part in the Voysey . . .
AND . . . offering to read it to me on approbation. Now is this accounted for only by her knowing me somewhat better than she knows
you? . . . I don't think so. Does it mean that she is keen on modern
work and is thinking that her connection with Greek tragedy has
landed her in the professional hole that I'm sure she thinks she is in?
If so this is not quite the spirit in which to approach Medea. Looking
back on the fact that she has played in every one of the plays so far
and thinking of the sort of success she has made in them . . . has she
ever mastered her opportunity . . . and will she master this opportunity which is so much more important? One cannot teach a really
leading part. I doubt her being able to control the play and keep its
meaning clear. A few purple passages will not do this time and that is
all about it. Miss Matthison is barred by circumstances as well as by
our judgment . . . she is playing two leading parts with us quite con-
tiguous. <u>How seriously can we take Miss Achurch</u>? For if Lillah is
also barred either by circumstances or Vedrenne,[1] are we approaching

an impasse? I don't think Tita is possible; I really don't. Troades revival is a weak move. Is the Bacchae possible anyway with the Chorus we have as yet . . . have you a copy of it with you? We cannot do a POTTY performance of anything. The outlook is not what it might be and I should not be writing letters at this time in the morning.

Yours,

H. G. B.

---

1. Vedrenne had made a rule that while Barker was the director and part manager in the venture, his wife was not to be given all the leading parts.

BOD/MS
To Murray

3, Clement's Inn,

W.C.

Sunday night [October, 1907]

Dear G. M.,

Of course I don't want the book to read—but it does look well to have a little Greek literature on one's shelves.[1] Still, starting from last night I'm well into chapter II and, I say G. M., it is good— not at all the sort of book I ought to have around when I'm studying Waste and Dick Dudgeon.[2] The bit about Classics— and I chortled over the sentence about the Oedipus family. I think you might have mentioned that we saw the ships waiting to get up the Hellespont.

Yes, I am on to the gospel according to Murray—it makes good, as I suppose they told you at Harvard.

Yours,

H. G. B.

---

1. Murray had sent him a copy of his *The Rise of the Greek Epic,* just published.
2. *The Devil's Disciple* was in the new season at the Savoy Theatre. Barker was not playing Dick Dudgeon, however, but General Burgoyne.

BOD/handwritten by a secretary but initialed by Barker
To Murray

Savoy Theatre.

25 Oct. 1907

Dear G. M.,

His wife probably plays Phaedra![1] Penelope to lead & train the Chorus might be a good move.[2] As to the scenery, he could have ours at a great reduction if there is anything left of it, which I doubt but can discover. Do you remember in Nicholas Nickleby how when Mrs. Grudden opened the door three men and a boy tumbled excitedly into the pit? Yes, you should have been at "Medea" this afternoon.

Yours,

H. G. B.

Sunday week it is I come to Oxford to talk to the Fabians. Would you like to see me?

---

1. "He" is B. Iden Payne, the director of Miss Horniman's new repertory company at the Gaiety Theatre, Manchester, who was seeking Murray's permission to include *Hippolytus* in his 1908 season (see also Barker's letter of December 2, 1907, to Murray).
2. "Penelope" is Penelope Wheeler, an actress who played frequently with the Gaiety company. Both she and her husband were old friends of Barker's. The *Hippolytus* was produced in Manchester in October, 1908: Penelope Wheeler played Phaedra, and Lewis Casson (who had been in Barker's production of the play at the Court in 1904) directed it and played the Henchman, as Barker had done.

BOD/handwritten by a secretary but initialed by Barker
To Murray

Savoy Theatre.
30 Oct. 1907

Dear G. M.,

Barrie has suggested a committee meeting on the Censorship—has written to you about it I think. Couldn't you manage this Saturday & travel up with me on the Sunday perhaps? It's my last fairly free day, and also I think the sooner arrangements are put in hand for the deputation, the better. W. A. is full of ideas & has been imparting them to me, so I am fairly posted.

Yours,

H. G. B.

BOD/handwritten by a secretary but initialed by Barker
To Murray

Savoy Theatre.
2 Dec. 1907

Dear G. M.,

Mine is the hand concealed behind the Iden Payne proposal.[1] They have also engaged Casson and I put him on to making them do Greek Tragedy, and if possible letting him produce them as well as play

Messengers. Their enterprise is of course much better than Neilson's,[2] though it won't remain so if Iden Payne insists on managing, producing and playing every leading part himself. Actors will be fairly keen to go to the Gaiety Theatre, Manchester; their tours from there are, so far, rubbish.

We start rehearsing "Arms and the Man" this week. I wish I were away, writing another play. (This is poetry.)

Glad to see you to any and every meal about the 10th. Let us know. I suggest dinner at 6.0 the night you go to "Irene Wycherly".[3]

Yours always,
H. G. B.

Or to a Wednesday matinée of "Irene Wycherly"; I might then go with you.

---

1. See letter to Murray of October 25, 1907.
2. Harold V. Neilson (1874–1956), an actor and manager, was also trying to get permission to produce Murray's translations in Manchester. He had strong connections with Manchester, having been born there and educated at Manchester Grammar School. He began his acting career in Benson's company and in 1901 went into management on his own account, touring several productions of Shaw, Ibsen, Maeterlinck, etc. He had presented some of these in Manchester, which is what gave him the idea of returning to that city with a production of Euripides-Murray.
3. The first play of "Antony P. Wharton" (the pseudonym of Alister McAllister) and the first play to be presented by Lena Ashwell when she took over the Kingsway Theatre in October, 1907. She herself played the title role.

BOD/handwritten by a secretary but initialed by Barker
To Murray

Savoy Theatre.
28 Dec. 1907

Dear G. M.,

Neilson saw Vedrenne today before I had had time to retail your letter to him, so all Vedrenne did was to let him talk and demand copies of the correspondence before he gave any opinion as to whether you had entered into a contract or not. If you've got a copy of your letter to Neilson let us have it, indeed copies of any letters you've written to him.

From the last I hear, and indeed in fairness to Neilson, I should be equally careful about Payne. Encourage these good people to do the things, but force up their standard to such a pitch that they will think and say is impossible. It is kindness to them in the end, and to yourself anyhow. Manchester is not going to be put off with any second-rate production of Greek tragedy, if I know anything about it.

It's awfully difficult to know when to hold out for the right man, and when to take what you can get, isn't it?

Yours,

H. G. B.

P.S. Payne just been here, talking with good intentions but rather vaguely. He is to see Vedrenne on Monday. I didn't gather anything at all definite from him, but I impressed him with the difficulty of Hippolytus & the necessity for doing it well.

EDD/MS
To Murray

Savoy Theatre,
[London]
Thursday night [December, 1907]

My very dear Friend,

I won't sit down to tell you—describe to you—the joy that your Xmas letter gives me, nor will I go putting on paper the love I have for you—it's a particular sort and kind that I haven't for anyone else in the world—though this is a time when one is allowed to come nearest to saying these things. I'm sure you know; you know so many things that can't just be learnt by rote. But just this: it is very much that you have a corner in your heart for me.

I like much the bookcase—I wish it meant I was to travel for a whole year. There is to be a photograph of me for you; it hasn't come in time for Xmas, though. Lillah asked today if I hadn't written you a love-letter in its place. I can now reply that I have.

I have been owing you a letter about "Waste" for more than a month: it has not been the letter that was difficult but the subject. I've not been able to look at it since it was done. With the new year, though, I must get at it. I hope now for a talk with you instead of a letter. May I come down to Gilmuire just for lunch one Sunday? If the roads would behave I'd bicycle over from Windsor. My love, till then, and a good new year.

Yours,

H. G. B.

EDD/TS
To Barker

131, Banbury Road,
Oxford.
Feb. 5, 1908

My dear B,

I have been lecturing away in Manchester and talking to Payne and the Helen-like Mona Limerick. The upshot is that Payne is quite ready to start with Electra, and I have consequently written a very civil letter to Neilson saying that I still hope for a friendly settlement and proposing two courses, either of which will satisfy me:

"1. Will you consent to give up the claim which you believe you possess upon the Hippolytus, if I undertake that no one else shall produce it this spring in Manchester? If you like, you can add certain other towns to be excluded and I will consider them.

2. Failing this, will you lay before me within a week from now your definite proposals for the production, recognising fully my right as author to veto any castings or arrangements which I think seriously objectionable or inadequate. I will undertake to consider your proposals with bona fides. If you think my demands unreasonable on any point, I do not mind having an arbitrator to settle the point, provided that he is a person in whose knowledge of Greek plays I have confidence."

Supposing Payne does Electra, I think it will be a question of Penelope for Electra. She has gained so much in confidence and power that I think she can do it. She will look well, speak well, and do the intellectual things right—which are very hard in the Electra. Also I can teach her some things, and Casson others. Also she watched Miss W-M[1] very closely and knows the piece well. So I am content to have her, and cannot think of anyone available whom I should prefer. I think Payne's idea is to keep Phaedra and Medea waiting till Mona Limerick is well enough to take them. She is a beautiful and uncanny creature; they say she won't learn from any one and she does not seem to me to possess much understanding. But if you don't know her, you might as well see her.

By the way, I meant to tell you that I was more than ever struck by the goodness of the writing of Waste, when we read it on Tuesday.[2] It impressed me greatly. Perhaps that is one of the reasons why we made so comparatively few mistakes in emphasis.

Yours ever,
G. M.

1. Edith Wynne-Matthison (1876–1955) played the part of Electra under Barker's direction at the Court Theatre in January, 1906.
2. He refers to a public reading of the play, given in order to establish copyright. Murray, Archer, Shaw, Galsworthy, and other notable figures had all taken part in the reading.

BOD/TS
To Murray

> 78, East Parade,
> Harrogate.
> Wednesday [September, 1908]

Dear G. M.,

Churton Collins used to do all his work at night, I hear, and drink strong tea to keep him awake for it. Then he got so that he couldn't sleep I suppose and then . . .[1] But I don't really write to tell you that, but to say—cannot W. A. have that Professorship of English Literature? Can't it be worked somehow?

I don't know yet where I stay in Manchester next week but wherever it is will you come and stay with me for the day or two that we are there together? . . . Do. My exile . . . oh, my exile.[2] Casson gives me quite exciting accounts of the Hippolytus. I hope to see something of a rehearsal of it while I am there.

How are you all? My love and homage.

> Yours,
> H. G. B.

---

1. John Churton Collins (1848–1908), a lecturer and writer, died, while on holiday, by drowning in a shallow ditch into which he fell, it was thought, while under the influence of sleep-inducing drugs (though the incident took place in the middle of the day). His death was publicly regarded as something of a mystery, and there was inevitably some suspicion of suicide, though this was later dismissed as improbable. Collins was the author of a few books of literary commentary, among them *Studies in Shakespeare* (1904) and *Voltaire, Montesquieu and Rousseau in England* (1905). He was also well known as a lecturer on literary subjects in London. His professorship at the University of Birmingham came relatively late in his career. He had, indeed, a feeling that he was unjustly neglected by the literary and academic world and was somewhat embittered on that account. (See another reference to him in Barker's letter to Shaw of September, 1908.)
2. Barker was on tour, playing Bluntschli in *Arms and the Man*.

BOD/handwritten by a secretary but initialed by Barker
To Murray

Prince of Wales Theatre,
Birmingham.
November 4, 1908

Dear G. M.,

I saw the Bacchaes Bacchaeing on Monday and should have written to you before if Wade[1] had not had his hands quite full of writing reams to Poel on the subject. Now I hear you are going up tomorrow. The sight may offend and upset you, for of course it is no more Greek than I am—(well, I don't know, by the way.)

However, if you can, conceal any horror you feel, for Poel and Lillah are in the depths of despair and terror, it will be of great use I think to explain to them a lot of the meanings which they seem to me to miss. I go up on Friday, I think, to have another look at it. My impression is that he is getting some very striking effects and that plastically it may be very beautiful indeed.

Yours,
H. G. B.

---

1. Alan Wade, an actor, became Barker's secretary and was with him from 1907 to 1914. By special arrangement, which Barker and Murray had discussed earlier at some length, the *Bacchae* was being produced for two special matinees at the Court Theatre by William Poel and Lillah McCarthy. In addition, Poel directed the play and Lillah played Dionysus.

BOD/W
To Murray

Dublin:[1]   Nov. 14, 1908   1.49 p.m.
To: Murray, 131, Banbury Road, Oxford.

Suggest your seeing Poel, insisting that chorus must be audible[2] and intelligible which means that Fates must speak either a whole line each or some lines all together, that singer must sing or, better, chant articulately to some proper music. Suggest Mrs. Lee Mathews could find enough Mozart for strings without piano in ten minutes. As to end of play, explain precisely to him what it means and give him 24 hours to present you with his own modified or new interpretation of that meaning. Accept or reject this. Sorry there's this bother but think if you were Shakespeare.

Barker

---

1. Punctuation added to this telegram. Barker was still on tour with *Arms and the Man* (see also Chapter III: letter to Shaw of September 16, 1908).

2. The underlining is there on the telegram (which argues either very great persistence on Barker's part or a very superior telegraph service!).

BOD/handwritten by a secretary
To Murray

3, Clement's Inn,
W.C.
2 Mar. 1909

Sir,

I seem to remember you vaguely. You represent Oxford in the Liberal interest I think. Howsumdever, "Strife" is struggling to its birth amid bursts of incompetence and despair. I'm getting on all right.

No reason at all that Payne shouldn't do the Voysey and many reasons that he should. I told him he might a year or two ago, but wanted to be satisfied as to the cast. But now Galsworthy reports a very good company of men for The Silver Box, and that's the important thing for the Voysey. I don't think I need produce it entirely. To begin with, it's very difficult to get the time, but I could see two or three rehearsals and put a polish on. That would be enough I think.

You're coming up to see 'Strife', aren't you? Can we meet then?

Yours,
H. G. B.
PP aw[1]

---

1. Per pro Alan Wade.

EDD/TS
To Murray

Little Franklyn,
Hook Heath,
Woking
Sunday [March, 1909]

Sir . . . Come right along. Favor the official—Box-Office Manager Cyrus P. Skute, who so urbanely presides over the Thespian Temple on Martin's Lane[1]—favor him, I say Sir, with a copy of your birth certificate on Toosday next and if he does not immediately fork out a brace of fauteuils for you and the honourable Lady Murray, draw a bead on the skulking coyote: hold him up, Sir, in the sacred name of Liberty.

I shall be down here, I expect, so shan't see you. But do you and Lady Mary look round to Lillah's dressing room after the performance: she will be so disappointed, she says, if you don't.

I have been conversing in the utmost secrecy with a certain Tr-nch, at his request giving him advice—which he probably won't take. But I feel that we all ought to combine to push him on to the repertory game. Nothing else matters now, I feel. Everybody wants to do something good: Tree would swear to that for himself. But it is the system, the system, the system in a thousand ways that will continue to handicap us. All our lot of dramatists are slacking off in production because they can't be sure of anything but matinée audiences—lucky if they get that. It is hard work to push push push at the blessed Old English—and repertory is our salvation. I don't want the final advance to be over the corpses of most of us: therefore, repertory as speedily as possible.

Yours,
H. G. B.

When do I <u>see</u> you?

---

1. The "Thespian Temple" is the Duke of York's Theatre, where Barker had just produced and directed Galsworthy's *Strife,* in which Lillah McCarthy was playing the part of Madge Thomas.

EDD/MS
To Murray

Court Lodge,
Stansted,
Kent.
Sat. night [July, 1909]

Dear G. M.,

I have this day done the last bit of the first draft of a new play[1]—and there's lots wrong with it: principally I know that its philosophic flats are not joined. I seem to have said something quite different from what I had set out to say. And I'd rather like to inflict it on you—if you'd bear it and that were possible—and get your sentiments. I'm free-ish now for a week or two until Lillah gets off, then I hope to dash away with her abroad somewhere. Oh, by Jove, no. I have to give evidence on August 5 or summat—and of course now

I'm going to spend time in preparing censorship ammunition. But I think I could make a dash down to Aldeburgh for a night—and the rest of this letter is, therefore, to Lady Mary to ask if she'd like to see me on such an errand.

I think I'll be going to London on Monday: 20 Alexandra Court (sounds like Redford's address).[2] And by the way, I don't know how much this censorship business may keep me by the leg next week.

By the way, I don't think this new play is quite Redfordilus puerisque.[3] Oh me! I've never been depressed at finishing a play before.

Yours,

H. G. B.

---

1. *The Madras House.*
2. Redford was the Lord Chamberlain's Examiner of Plays—the censor, in other words, and as such a Court official. Alexandra was the wife of King Edward VII.
3. Translates as "Redford and the boys" and is, I think, a reference to R. L. Stevenson's *Virginibus puerisque,* published in 1881.

BOD/MS
To Murray

20, Alexandra Court,
Queen's Gate, S.W.
Friday [1909]

Dear G. M.

No, I suppose we can't tackle Barrie just for the moment[1]— though the sooner we can the better, for him (don't you think?). But I am writing to Frohman by tomorrow's mail asking him to send a formal confirmation of the arrangement Barrie made with you. Will this do or do you want something more definite? We none of us (Shaw, Galsworthy and I) have anything more definite about our plays[2]—nothing on paper that is. In case he makes no answer—or too vague a one—he'll be over in November. But if that delay will be too long, then I shall certainly take it on myself to make a definite arrangement with you sooner than let nibbles (the impudence of these other people) become bites.

Yes, I know all that is wrong with the play (mine). I'm battling with it.

Yours,

H. G. B.

---

1. Barrie's wife, Mary, early in August, 1909, asked him to divorce her in order that she might marry Gilbert Cannan.

2. He is referring to the arrangements which were then being made for the repertory season at the Duke of York's Theatre in 1910 to be financed by Charles Frohman and directed by Barker. Barrie, who was a great friend of Frohman's, had been instrumental in persuading Frohman to undertake this venture. The three plays with which the repertory season opened were *Justice* (Galsworthy), *Misalliance* (Shaw), and *The Madras House* (Barker). There was a suggestion that Murray's translation of *Iphigenia in Tauris* be included later in the season, but because of financial losses, Frohman closed the season down early.

EDD/TS
To Barker

82, Woodstock Road,
Oxford.
March 11 [1910]

My dear Barker,

I do not think there would be any difficulty in having one scene for Hip. Med. and at a pinch Iph. and Tro. and El.[1] But the three last would want modifications, obviously. On the whole I do not much like the idea, as there is after all only one scene wanted for each play as it is. And the one scene would have to be rather colourless.

One set of dresses would do all right, with slight variations. Chorus dressed like the Medea Chorus. Also we could use one method for all choruses.

As to the oleograph, I think I agree, but am not quite sure of your meaning. I think our performances should be more straightforward and passionate.

What are the difficulties about Iphigenia? I understand about Lillah perhaps not being able to play for a certain time. (What time?) Of course I do not think her indispensable for the part, but I am quite willing to wait a reasonable time if you will mention a time and consider it fixed. I rather dislike the idea of doing a revival instead, unless some reason is definitely stated. It unduly crabs Iphigenia and so far injures the Greek play movement, by leaving the impression that only two or three plays are possible on the stage and that the limit has been reached. I return from Castle Howard on the 18th—here, but could come to town some day then.

Yours ever,
G. M.

P.S. Hope I don't sound cross. I am rather seedy and full of toothache.

---

1. Barker had suggested the possibility of including in the repertory program not only *Iphigenia* but also two or three other Greek plays, all to be presented in a common

style, on a common set. It was an experiment which he never got the chance to try, either in the Frohman repertory season or later. He himself has some comments on it in his reply to Murray (see the next letter).

EDD/handwritten by a secretary but initialed by Barker
To Murray

Duke of York's Theatre
St. Martin's Lane
[London], W.C.
March 12, 1910

Dear G. M.,

I go back, I think, on my idea of one scene—well, I go back I think to this extent: could we have one platform and one set of seats for the chorus and then vary the background? This is not so much for the sake of cheapness as in order to standardize the arrangements, for I am convinced that there is only <u>one</u> best way, and I am trying to wipe my mind clear of what we've done before in order to discover that one. At present I incline to setting them up and down stage on each side, like the stalls in the choir of a cathedral.

Then ought there to be an altar in the middle of the stage? This seems more or less indicated in Iphigenia; it could be used in Hippolytus with effect I suppose, but there is nothing to it in Electra or the The Trojan Women, is there? I do believe it would be a magnificent effect to have a life-size bit of the Temple of Paestum as a scene? I shall part from this idea with great reluctance.

Yes, I rather think with you, I'm afraid, that the revival before Iphigenia is bad. The notion sprang from several rather confusing currents of events; one thing that was in my mind was, as we had Casson in the Company, to let him repeat for a few performances his production of Hippolytus. I very much want to get in some other producers than myself. But there's the casting difficulty again and the powers that be didn't jump at it. I also thought we might try some of the people we have got upon a thing that after all had had its show and was known more or less at its best; for the real Iphigenia difficulty is the cast, and Lillah's health is by no means the only point in it.

But to take her position first, it will be a great disappointment to me if she doesn't play it, and more than disappointment, indeed a bitter grief, to her, for she has been studying it and knows it already, she is that keen. Putting that aside as the personal aspect of the matter, she may be able to do it by the end of May. She is sure she could, and I think she could. The doctors won't say yet, indeed Christopher[1] shakes his head. But she picks up quite marvellously. We shall know in another fortnight. By the autumn of course she would have fifty percent more strength to give to it. I see I harp on the personal question, but you'll understand and forgive that.

But supposing it is done without her, who is the substitute? Frankly I practically know that they won't consent to Penelope doing it—they don't consider that she has weight or authority enough for it. My half-formed plan for Hippolytus has included her as Phaedra and there was immediate doubt about that. I fear I don't think that she could carry off Iphigenia either, though of course there will be an awkwardness in expressing my opinion, and I only do so now to you.

Then what are the other alternatives? There's Lena Ashwell who seems, to judge by one performance she gives for us, hopeless in anything of the sort; there's Violet Vanburgh, wandering about in music halls, but really I don't advise her. Still, somebody might be found. But, for the rest of the cast: I have no Orestes, Bryant would be hopeless in it—he is rather a disappointment to us so far; Valentine could play Thoas, and Casson one of the Messengers, but—here is the real point—if it were to mean special engagements outside the Company for Iphigenia, Orestes, one Messenger, perhaps Athena, and at least two thirds of the Chorus, it makes it very expensive at two performances a week, which is what it might average.

A little shifting is going on in the Company which might make matters easier, but it hasn't so far. My hope is in the autumn when we shall have one or two robuster plays to do that we may have collected more likely people; the only way of forming this Company (it isn't really formed yet) not quite ruinously, is to engage people for two or three plays.

I write this at great length and rather confusedly. I wish I could talk to you, for there are many complications and I am not, of course, in any absolute authority. But what principally ties me up over an immediate production is an Iphigenia—bar Lillah—and an Orestes. (I want Forbes Robertson; a pleasant sort of want—none of these young men do; they are all either too thin or too fat—none of them fate-haunted.)

Well, write and let me know what you think. I must stop now or Wade will strike.[2]

Yours,
H. G. B.

1. Charles Edwin Wheeler, known to his friends as Christopher, a medical doctor and long-time friend of Barker's. His wife, Penelope, was an actress who frequently played in Barker's plays.
2. It was Barker's practice to dictate letters directly to Alan Wade, who took them down then and there in longhand.

EDD/MS
To Murray

> Court Lodge,
> Stansted,
> Kent.
> Wed. [March, 1910]

Dear G. M.,

First—personally—thank you ever so much about Lillah: it would have been a bad smash to her to have missed it. Impersonally, I hope you won't regret the wait and I don't think you will.

But shall we wait if we need not, or produce in June if we can? I'd a littler rather wait for October. You can certainly have an approximate date—I will speak to Frohman and I don't see why we shouldn't do one more during next season—say Troades—but that I must discuss with them, I suppose. We have none of us had any agreements, by the way. I do not even know yet what royalties I have for the M. H., such is the adventurous way we have done it all. (I have much to tell you.) And when can I see you, by the way, for I cannot write about the scene and chorus question.

A possible Orestes looms in A. E. Anson—do you remember him: a part in a Sutro play, Dick Gurvil in "Nan"?[1]

I must stop now for the post. I hope you will see the M. H. I did not think a play could have been so misunderstood even by "mean sensual men".[2]

> Yours,
> H. G. B.

---

1. "Nan" refers to *The Tragedy of Nan,* by John Masefield, of which Barker directed the first production in 1908.
2. "Mean sensual men" is an ironic quotation from Act III of *The Madras House.*

EDD/handwritten by a secretary but initialed by Barker
To Murray

Duke of York's Theatre,
The Repertory Theatre,
[London]
Mar. 22, 1910

Dear G. M.,

Following up my last letter: you need not think that anyone whose judgment matters has abated a bit of their interest in Euripides. But we are still only just shaking down, and there are difficulties.

What about the Chorus? I'm inclined to think that our Medea was the best we've had so far. Do you think we should try and repeat this? Whether Mrs. L. M. could and would I don't know. Should we ask Penelope, do you think?

I am down at Stansted as much as I can now, though up day by day to rehearse. I suppose you couldn't come down there for a day and a night—that would be very jolly. I expect I shall be there from tomorrow to Monday clear, possibly up on Saturday; but anyhow we ought to meet.

Yours always,
H. G. B.

BOD/MS
To Murray

Court Lodge,
Stansted,
Wrotham,
Kent.
Sunday [April, 1910]

Dear G. M.

These letters roughly explain themselves!

The effect of the shock has now rather worn off with me.[1] You will imagine the particular feeling with which I hand it on to you.

But now, before you decide anything, I wish we could have had a talk about this as to what is the way round it that best suits you and about the whole situation, rendered a little critical by this action of Frohman's, I think. Is it possible—when and where? The Barkers, by the way—Lillah and H. G. B.—have developed a sudden desire to hear Roosevelt's Romanes lecture. Is <u>that</u> possible or not?

I shall be in town Tuesday, otherwise I'm here trying to get

Madras House ready for printing—awaiting Frohman's decision about my last—<u>his</u> next production.

Yours,

H. G. B.

---

1. The "shock" was Frohman's decision to bring the repertory season at the Duke of York's Theatre to a close, which made it impossible to produce the *Iphigenia* there.

EDD/TS
To Barker

Mill House,
Wobbleswick-on-the-Putrid-Marsh[1]
Suffolk.
July 8, 1910

My dear B.

I have at last got off here, after an increasing whirl of work which has left me dull and sodden, and just fit for this health resort.

Frohman sent me two beautiful contracts, bound in blue borders. He signed them "Lestocq", which I understand is one of his aliases.[2] It is to be matinées in the autumn, produced by you (or Lestocq is to commit hari-kari) or else evening performances in the spring. This I take it, means the autumn. Anyhow, that is what Bantock ought to be ready for.[3] It is not likely he will risk evening performances if he can help it.*

I have hay fever and a game eye. Otherwise I am doing Oedipus lazily, and having my portrait re-painted by One who before made me look like the Corpse of Aegisthus. We live in daily fear of Rosalind's book coming out, and have a paragraph ready to send to the Central News to say it is not by her but by her Australian cousin of the same name.[4]

Yours ever,
G. M.

*If not produced by the Spring, in the evening, by you, Frohman undertakes to scalp Lestocq, subscribe £10,000 for the maintenance of compulsory Greek, and pass Smalls.

---

1. He was, in fact, taking a holiday at Walberswack, on the Suffolk coast between Dunwich and Southwold.
2. William Lestocq (1851–1920) was for many years Charles Frohman's London manager.
3. Barker and Murray had decided to ask Granville Bantock (1868–1946), a well-known and prolific composer, to compose incidental music for *Iphigenia,* but this project came to nothing.
4. Rosalind was Murray's daughter (see also footnote to letter of January, 1914, towards the end of this chapter, p. 283).

BOD/MS
To Murray

Court Lodge,
Stansted,
Wrotham,
Kent.
Monday [1910]

Dear G. M.,
Well—about Iph.: so far so—as good as maybe. But now about Bantock. He said he could do the music for the autumn. I asked him about business arrangements. He asked me to propose them. Then came the standstill. If I write to America and ask for authority to go on with the matter, I shall either get the vaguest of answers or none. On the other hand, it is no use trying to get that music done at a month's notice—which is what Frohman will give— and the same remark applies to Miss Morris, whom I wanted (who I wanted) to arrange the chorus movements. What am I to do? To Bantock I suppose either I or you could say that you would consider his music a necessary part of the production as long as his business proposals were reasonable. With Miss Morris it is more difficult. But to get that chorus right we ought to have at least 10 weeks' notice of the production. How to get it?

Yours,
H. G. B.

P.S. Do you know the charming Anglo-Australian authoress of The Leading Note? (Order the book at once.) She is staying with us.

EDD/TS
To Barker

Brackland,
Hindhead,
Surrey.
July 19, 1910

My dear Barker,
Evidently Bantock must be put to work at once. I should think it was quite safe. Frohman must know—or can be shown—that it is necessary to have the music and the movements for the Chorus carefully settled.

Can't you (1) agree with Bantock and set him going; (2) write to Frohman and tell him you have done so and assume that he approves unless he cables to say that he does not; (3) explain this to Bantock, promising to let him know instantly if F does object?

I think you might do just the same with Miss Morris. But anyhow they ought to be set going at once. Is the fee a difficulty?

Yes: I have met that Australian authoress and liked her. Only she was staying about with theatrical people and the Asquith family and suchlike.

Oedipus's eyes are just rolling on to his beard. There will be an awful mess if I don't attend to them.

Yours ever,

G. M.

BOD/MS
To Murray

Court Lodge,
Stansted,
Wrotham,
Kent.
Wednesday [1910]

Dear G. M.,

Well, I'll write to Bantock and Frohman, but I doubt if F will authorize me to make a business arrangement with B. However B will most likely go ahead without.

The difficulty with Miss Morris is that she must have the people engaged to train 8 weeks ahead and I know F won't give us that notice. ? How to make him.

I see your Academy is announced. I have a perverse desire to throw a stone at its study window.

Oh, by the way, Lillah has perhaps written to you today.

I want to work it that Ames does one of the Euripides at the New Theatre this autumn:[1]

(a) I think he ought;

(b) I'd like Lillah (if you approve) to get a smack at it;

(c) I want to go over and produce. I find I can't produce rot; I ruin it—show it up—even if I get that to do in the autumn, and I must earn some money some how.

Have you any views? Have you had any passages with Ames?

Yours,

H. G. B.

---

1. Winthrop Ames, director of the New Theatre, New York, which opened in 1909. (See Chapter II, letter to Archer of May, 1907.)

EDD/TS
To Barker

Brackland,
Hindhead,
Surrey.
July 20 [1910]

My dear Barker,

I have not heard from Lillah, but, on the face of it, I should very greatly like to have any Euripides plays produced by you at the New Theatre. I suppose it is the Noo Theatre, Noo York, that you mean? As for Ames—the only Ames I know is the Secretary of an institution whose windows you (in company with all my family) wish to break. Would the Noo York plan interfere with Iphigenia here? If it does, I do not much care, if you have a preference for Noo York. But perhaps I shall hear from Lillah.

As for Iphigenia, I enclose you a letter of the old-gent-inside-swearin-awful type to use on Frohman. The Novelist[1] says that Miss Morris is a Chit; that she was at school with her herself and knows it; and that you ought to entrust the Chorus to some one of experience, like Miss Elizabeth Asquith. But, Lord, these young novelists would say anything.

Oh, that Academic Committee! I did not go to the meeting of it, chiefly from laziness, partly because my wife's language about it and all its members, including me, was so extreme; so I don't know what they contemplate doing. Nor do I know who have refused to join; probably Barrie and Kipling. What of Shaw and Wells? Obviously, if the thing is not to be absurd, they ought to be on. And I should have thought Galsworthy, and, as a pendant to Pinero, you. On the whole I think they were right to start the society with a nucleus of stodgy, old and academic people: people of judgement rather than genius, who could then proceed to choose the rest. Much better than to start with F. M. Hueffer and Emil Reich and Christabel Pankhurst. I heartily wish the thing did not exist; as it does, I hope it will be as free as possible from the grosser and more loathsome vices.

A jolly old mess with Oedipus's eyes. But they are well out now, and everyone contented again.

Yours ever,
G. M.

---

1. "The Novelist" is Murray's daughter, Rosalind.

BOD/MS
To Murray

> Court Lodge,
> Stansted,
> Wrotham,
> Kent.
> August 2, 1910

Dear G. M.,

Bantock wrote saying he must give up doing the music. I wrote dissuading him and committed myself to the statement I underline in his letter because I thought that if I were wrong, we'd be no worse off than with him refusing altogether—for who else is there to trust to do music knowing, having experience that is, of the sort of thing wanted. But say if I have done wrong.

No word from Frohman. I committed him (F) to a guinea a performance in fees for the music. I thought that couldn't hurt.

> Yours,
> H. G. B.

EDD/TS
To Barker

> Brackland,
> Hindhead,
> Surrey.
> Aug. 6, 1910

My dear B,

All right about Iphigenia. The spring is as good as another time. Only that will involve Frohman putting it on in the evening, and then no one will come: though perhaps he would also come in the afternoon. I have just finished a rough first draft of Oedipus and may at any moment send you a copy to read. But this is not imminent, as I have not got a copy made. I do not really in my heart believe in the music for choruses, but we had better try it again. The O.T.[1] chorus consists of old men like me, with lumbago and several false teeth. Such persons are considered very attractive.

Do you really think of America? I have had a lot of photographs and a few royalties from the Coburn company who are doing

Electra. One photograph, Electra and Old Peasant is very good in conception; others baddish.

Yours ever,

G. M.

---

1. *Oedipus Tyrannus.*

EDD/MS
To Barker

[no address]

Sept. 2, 1910

My dear B,

How blessed it is to be without a family! Mine have gone off gradually, multitude by multitude: first all their young friends, undergraduates, etc. Then we had at last enough beds to go round. Then the four elder children with their belongings and spiritual advisers and directresses. Then the Sun came out and my wife and I walked and sat in the heather and there was peace among the meadows like a tree. Today, Baby and Nurse are gone. My mind has become clear and I have thought out clearly what Religion is,[1] and I want to sit down and do some honest work. I could write poetry or anything if only I were left alone. And my affection for my fellow-creatures grows. A familiar stomach-ache which I have had for six weeks seems like a quaint old friend. I can even write with a pen.

However, this was not specially what I was going to say. I wish I had been over to see you, but I have had such a beast of a summer that I never had the time or spirit. I will get O. T. copied when I get to Castle Howard[2] (Monday night or after) and will send you a copy. My version is not satisfactory: I can make it better. As to Iffige, I seem to have lost heart about it. But £200 would always be a pleasure to receive. I get pleasing little cheques from America for the Electra performances; and as for the performance, "I have been spared the worst: I could not see", as the Messenger in O.T. says.

How are you? How is the play?[3] Why don't you come up to Castle Howard some time, to pretend to talk business with me? I am going today to rehearse (or lecture on) Hippolytus at East Grinstead, then tomorrow evening to town to make Wheeler jolly well cure my stomach-ache or not pretend to be a doctor any more. My folly is so great that I am probably about to plunge into a great big publisher's undertaking, but my good angel may deliver me yet. <u>Private at present</u>.

I met Margaret Davis and Janet Case the other day and they talked with enthusiasm about the Madras House for a good hour. Nice people they are. They were also full of The Leading Note.

Well, our blessings on you.

G. M.

---

1. He was beginning to write *Four Stages of Greek Religion,* which was first published in 1912 (a revised version, called *Five Stages of Greek Religion,* was published in 1925).
2. Castle Howard, the magnificent Vanbrugh house in Yorkshire, was one of the great estates belonging to the Earl of Carlisle, Murray's father-in-law.
3. The new play on which Barker was working was at that time called "The Village Carpenter." Some time later (probably about 1914), Barker changed its title to "The Wicked Man." It was never completed, but the typescript of the first two acts is in the possession of the Enthoven Collection, British Theatre Museum. See also Chapter XI, letters from Masefield, of August 26, 1914, and September 19, 1914.

BOD/MS
To Murray

Garrick Club,
W.C.
Thursday Sept. 1910

Dear G. M.,

I go up to Glasgow tonight: Royalty Theatre until Monday fortnight.

Tree, I hear, wants to do an Oedipus. Shall I tell him you have translated it or would you sooner I killed you at once?

Don't you feel that on Oct. 11 or 12 it will really be necessary for you to go to Berlin for a week to talk things over with [Wil?[1]] and see the German drammer? I have a reason for asking.

No good sending <u>you</u> polite telegrams.

You know, I suppose, that the Little Theatre opens with the Lysistrata—blessed by Redford.[2]

I don't get that copy of Oedipus: but there.

Yours,
H. G. B.

---

1. The name is illegible, but it is obviously someone connected with Max Reinhardt's recent production of an Oedipus. The illegible name appears to begin with the letters WIL—.
2. The censor, or Examiner of Plays for the Lord Chamberlain.

BOD/MS
To Murray

St. Enoch Station Hotel,
Glasgow.

Dear G. M.,

Just finished Oedipus—a <u>whacking</u> fine play. Doesn't it work up? Can't quite fathom the end—what Creon means? Why doesn't Oedip. go wandering after all? Do they mean to have another go at Loxias? Of course I can't help feeling that those daughters are dragged on—at least I feel it until the scene is well under weigh and its horror has got you—then it justifies itself: until then, I feel—ah, Euripides didn't work things this way in the Troades.

And, oh, I say—Enter a Stranger! Enter Sardou with a telegram!!

Let us write a Greek play with the aid of the telegram. One character, or at most two, and four telegraph boys—or gradually-swelling chorus of telegraph boys (I say—how fine the scene with the old shepherd is, though). There's nothing in the choruses to touch the other gents to my mind though "The white brides of Helicon laughed for delight" is a gem of a line. (Dashed if I don't think that's your best line to date!)

I don't think that Redford will pass it—though Lord knows he may. Meanwhile let us proceed with a burlesque which Redford would love to pass:

<u>Adipose—King of Greece</u>
(Grease)

Refrain for 1st chorus:

. . .But my spirit turns to the Ga—
-iety and unto the strain
of Yip-i-adi-I.e., I.e.

Then we will write on the top of our notepaper—say it in any theatre almost you go into—

If honour for such things be
Why should I dance <u>my</u> dance?

That's a great comfort.

Oh, it's a big play. I think you were right at first—McKinnel and Trench should be the combination.[1]

I stay here till the 10th producing Anne Pedersdotter, which we call The Witch[2]—and playing (Heaven help me) Man and Superman for the fortnight's rehearsal: this to raise a little money, <u>not</u> for love of it. Do I dance that dance though after what you can see in London at the moment—well, it's Homer to Alfred Austin. This was to have been for Lillah, but as she has to play at the Duke of York's she'll only be here this next week for Maud S.

On the 12th I hope to go to Berlin for a week. When do you get back to O?[3]

Years hence you'll find (or remember) the polite telegram— Ah!

Yours,

H. G. B.

---

1. The suggestion at that stage of negotiations was that Herbert Trench should produce the play with Norman McKinnel as Oedipus.
2. This was an adaptation from the Norwegian, made at Barker's request by John Masefield. The suggestion had originally come from William Archer; see also Chapter XI, letter of August 26, 1909, to Masefield.
3. Oedipus.

BOD/MS
To Murray

St. Enoch Hotel,

Glasgow.

Monday [Oct. 1910]

Yesterday, being the Sabbath, we went to Greenock and fed the gulls and Lillah read Adipose—renewed enthusiasm, coupled with vitriolic abuse of the modern drama: <u>me</u> for congregation and text.

But the thing that came up was—Forbes Robertson—he wouldn't do it here—he's passé—of all enthusiasm, but might he at the New Theatre, New York—but then Ames is a fool over these particular things. But it remains, I think, that Forbes is the best possible. Oh for the blessed National Theatre! What a place England is!

Yours,

H. G. B.

EDD/MS
To Murray

Hotel Frederich,
Eichhornstrasse, 3,
Berlin, W.
Thursday, [October, 1910]

Dear G. M.,

I am at this moment just off to see a rehearsal of Oedipus (Reinhardt's production) in the Schumann theatre here.

It is now the afternoon and I have been and come back.

Going to be quite interesting and for the direct dramatic—almost violence—of the Oedipus, suitable. And the Germans make it more violent again—though they make it big. I feel I shouldn't quite like it for Euripides: I want more philosophy.

Nothing now against having Oedipus sent to the L. C.[1] at once is there? Indeed, a measure of precaution before one begins to give thought to it.

I leave here Tuesday or Wednesday and as soon after as may be I'll try to see you.

Theatre here so alive and interesting it makes me ashamed. But we have the potentialities I am sure—and of something even better than the Germans, something on a higher, serener plane. But it's their vitality we want first. D'you think it comes from so much food and drink? The less good part of it, yes; but the better from their thoroughness. I do admire the brutes!

Yours,
H. G. B.

---

1. Lord Chamberlain.

BOD/MS
To Murray

Court Lodge,
Stansted,
Wrotham,
Kent.
Sunday [November 1910]

Dear G. M.,

What if the L. C. and his committee do refuse Oedipus? I suggest to you a public reading at the Queen's Hall, the play cast as it would have been, chorus and all—in fact, a performance minus costume and movement. It would be most effective. I also should be rejoiced at a public declaration (at the same time) from you that you would <u>not</u> re-submit the play for licence. My fear is that the L. C. means to scotch opposition by making as many concessions as he can. We—the general body of opposers—are so rottenly divided on the question of principle that it would be an easy job if he had the wisdom to set about it. Personally, one will be glad to see the Oedipus through but at once everyone will bless the name of the committee and say that nothing more need be done.

How are you?

Me as the Bard![1] It was dignified foolery!

Yours,

H. G. B.

---

1. Barker had just played the part of Shakespeare in the first production, on November 24, 1910, of Shaw's *The Dark Lady of the Sonnets*.

EDD/TS
To Barker

82, Woodstock Road,
Oxford.
Dec. 9, 1910

My dear B,

The exact Oedipus situation is as follows:

Trench has got the Lord C's licence and writes to me that he cannot think of producing it "for months yet". To this I have replied by asking for a definite date before which. To this he makes the natural retort of not answering my letter.

Meantime Tree writes asking my terms and saying that he has a plan in his mind which he is sure I shall like. It evidently is the Berlin plan of a performance in a Circus with vast crowds and performing elephants. Whelen says it was very effective indeed in Berlin. But then it was Hofmannsthal's version: sure to be coarse and strong, suitable for laying on thick. Still, I am unprejudiced. Have you any view, and could you produce it in that style?

I have told Tree that I have asked Trench for a date and will write to him when I hear.

Of course I will urge Trench to have you. And also Tree, if it comes to that. I have taken that rather for granted with him so far, and have said that I want the same sort of production—with al-

lowance for the large stage and different style of play—as we have
had before. But I don't think there is much chance for Feb.

Yours ever,
G. M.

Court Lodge,
Stansted,
Wrotham,
Kent.
Tuesday [December, 1910]

Dear G. M.,

Well, that's like Tree's d—d impertinence and as to
Trench—oh, but we are beginning to know our Trench.

However, now that you've so charmingly insulted Tree by
suggesting that he—he—He—may be "taking over" Reinhardt's production, we may have some pretty developments. Anyhow, several
things are coming on to the tablecloth and somewhen soon we ought
to meet and talk. Is there any chance? Don't you go a-tempting me
with your furrin health-resort. I took my busman's holiday in Berlin.
The temptation is, though, that Lillah ought to have one and I wish I
could get her abroad for a week or two. But I fear it can't be done.
Will you be alone there, then; or with whom?

Damn it, Sir, what's the fare and do a young married couple
travel as one? I understood the French nation wished to encourage
matrimony.

Yours,
H. G. B.

Court Lodge,
Stansted,
Wrotham,
Kent.
Tuesday [December, 1910, or January, 1911]

Sir,

My own belief has always been that Frohman won't do

"Iphy" or indeed touch anything "repertory" again with a pair of tongs—but I have absolutely no evidence to bring on the subject.

If Payne writes to him personally, he probably won't answer. If Payne goes to Lestocq, he might get provincial rights or a consideration, if there were any to give. But you've no detailed contract with Frohman, have you?

Frohman might well consider that a previous country production absolved him from a London one: he is funny—a little—about these things and probably would.

On the other hand he'd probably act quite squarely over the £200—though if it got left with Lestocq he (L.) would save him (F.) every penny of money he decently could. My opinion is—on the whole—that as Payne has many "undone" Euripideses to choose from, as far as Manchester is concerned, it would be safer to let him do one of those and not disturb the Frohman arrangement in any way, as it matures at Easter. Also, a Payne "2 nights" at the Coronet would wreck its chances for the time with any London management whatever. Whereas, things being as they are, you are quite sure of £200 or its equivalent and reasonably sure (I think) of the £200 and then of a series of matinées in London.

Bless you, I can't get to no John the Looses.[1]

W. A. has been here—says you were lunching with Tree on Monday: not where you eat, Sir, but where you were eaten. What result?

You are a milder man than I (being Greek) but I would have had a 2 in. strip of skin off Trench's back for that paragraph in Monday's Times.

Yours,
H. G. B.

---

1. This pun eludes me. I cannot connect it with either the title or the author of any play in London at that time, nor to any concert or lecture.

BOD/part TS, part MS
To Murray

17, John Street,
Adelphi.
January 4 [1911]

Dear G. M.,

Having lunched with a real Theatrical Knight you are evidently too proud to write to me at all. What is now the Tree and OEDIPUS position?

I go on the Music Halls, as I explained, and shall be in London all February and half March.

I produce The Witch for Lillah at the Court on Jan. 31.

If by chance the Capital for this <u>increases</u> in the process—not decreases—and if the perfide Frohman fails—what about Iphi? Though hardly at the Court. These be some of my lightest thoughts. Join them with yours and so farewell.

Yours,

H. G. B.

Did you see this of W. A.'s?

BOD/MS
To Murray

Court Lodge,

Stansted,

Wrotham,

Kent.

Saturday [1911]

Dear G. M.,

There ain't a circus left in London that I can think of. Perhaps it's the Albert Hall. Yes, I think there are possibilities in a production like that. Reinhardt's—as far as I could judge from the two rehearsals I saw—promised to be unnecessarily violent. But I don't see H. B. T.[1] wanting me to interfere—though Heaven knows, for his own sake he'd better have <u>somebody</u> or he'll never learn Oedipus.

Well, let me hear more; it would be larks.

Yours,

H. G. B.

---

1. Sir Herbert Beerbohm Tree.

EDD/TS
To Barker

82, Woodstock Road,

Oxford.

Feb. 10 [1911]

My dear B,

Anatol[1] seems to have been a success. Best congratulations, though in my heart I feel "Not here, O Apollo, are haunts meet for thee."

Now about witch-burning:[2] I had arranged to come up to-day, when suddenly I find there is a meeting of the Extension Delegacy with a lot of important business about the Working Men Centres which I cannot with decency cut. On all Tuesdays I am lecturing and making jokes while Lillah is burning—or nearly up to the time; on next Friday I can cut an English Board at a pinch and come up for the afternoon, if you will be so kind as to give a poor man a ticket. I am very anxious not to miss the Witch altogether, as I missed the Madras House.

By the way, Term is over on March 17. The best date for our Drama Society meeting is March 4, but we will re-arrange it to suit you, if you can come and read Act III of Madras, or anything else you like, to us. Do come if you can.

Bourchier's lecture: I don't know how bad it may have been, but to have the University turning out in robes to the Sheldonian to hear Bourchier, and thinking they were learning the highest truth about Drama . . . My God, what a world!

Yours ever,
G. M.

---

1. Barker was playing in his own translation and adaptation of Schnitzler's *Anatol*.
2. Barker had invited him to the production of Masefield's *The Witch*.

BOD/MS
To Murray

Court Lodge,
Stansted,
Wrotham,
Kent.
Sunday [February, 1911]

Dear G. M.,

No—Anatol is pot-boiling.[1] I've taken the trouble to devise a new sauce to boil that's all (metaphor gone wrong!).

Friday: why, yes—there'll be a seat kept for you. If you find you can't come (Heaven forfend) send a wire to Drinkwater (business manager) at the Court.

March 4: I can't—I shall still be at the Palace. It may be my last night there; if so, I could come any night immediately after. It may not (I shall know by the end of this week), in which case I could only come a Sunday—impossible for you? I should really have more news tomorrow. I have been writing out casts for them rather at random. Reinhardt is undoubtedly keen and the Albert Hall miscarriage is a scandal.

As to the Drama Society, I could come either <u>May 23</u> or May 25 if I didn't have to leave town before about O.[2] I've got to lecture to the Fabian in June and might have it ready by then. Otherwise, I suggested—didn't I?—to read Act III of the M. H. and be fired at about it—if you think that'd be sporting.

Yours,

H. G. B.

---

1. Barker had translated, with Dr. Charles Wheeler, Schnitzler's cycle of seven one-act plays, collectively called *Anatol,* which had been produced in Vienna the year before. He and Lillah and Nigel Playfair were presenting one of these—the one called *Ask No Questions and You'll Hear No Stories*—as a "turn" in a variety program at the Palace Theatre. It was then repeated, along with the one called *A Farewell Supper,* at the Little Theatre in March, 1911.
2. Oedipus: Barker means unless he has to visit Murray at an earlier date to discuss the proposed production of *Oedipus.*

BOD/TCC
To Barker

82, Woodstock Road,
Oxford.
February 20, 1911

My dear Barker,

I enjoyed The Witch very much. A good, tight, well-made foreign melodrama, with some really fine scenes. I thought Lillah exceedingly good, better than in anything I have seen except possibly Nan. The long scene where she wishes Absolon dead seemed to me really fine tragic acting of the sort one hardly ever sees.

Now as to Oedipus. I trust you are in the inmost counsels of Ordinski and Whelen[1] and will be in those of Reinhardt. You are the only person on whom I can really lean this professorial head.

Ordinski writes to me as if all were practically settled. I have sent a book to Reinhardt at his request and Stoll has gone to Berlin and "after his coming back will go in a hurry for prepare the work". So Ordinski puts it. He also says R. will give me full authority over the words. As to this, I suggest that in the Albert Hall we shall have to cut largely. Speech there has to be very slow, has it not? Anyhow I am ready to consider cutting.

We must clearly have an English producer to act with Reinhardt, who cannot produce the speaking, etc. This should be you, if you can manage it. And of course me with you. We must alter the old method into something more formal, large and spectacular—eh?

Further, I have had a cable from Coburn, "retain rights Oedipus" (he has done the Electra quite a lot of times, about 24, sometimes with big houses. Casson says he was not so bad.) But if the Reinhardt business comes off and is a success, R. might like to do the same thing in America. What do you think? And we might even do the Troades in the same sort of way, with an immense stage, and have a perfectly gorgeous time over it. So I am not closing with Coburn till I hear something definite from Reinhardt.

At any moment the Devil might suggest to him to cut Sophocles and just get a translation of Hofmannsthal, or a new play of the sort composed by Sir Herbert's secretaries.

Yours,
Gilbert Murray

---

1. Ordinski was one of Reinhardt's assistants; Frederick Whelen was Beerbohm Tree's reader of plays, among many other things.

BOD/MS
To Murray

Court Lodge,
Stansted,
Wrotham,
Kent.
Sunday [April 25, 1911]

Dear G. M.,

Well, I've been reading the H. U. L. books[1] and it occurred to me that I <u>might</u> be able to do "Modern English Drama", beginning at the abolition of the monopoly—1846 (I think). I'm not at all sure—for I've never tackled such a job before—and it had to be done at once: no, for I mustn't think of anything till I've done this play—I hope by the end of the summer (July). But if the publishers have nothing else in view but dropping it, could I leave it till then and then write to you again. And this further struck me—did W. A. <u>refuse</u> to do it? For if I got the plan and the material in my head and yet found I couldn't write it—I am so slow and stupid at these things—he might collaborate when he came back from Mexico (a p.c. to say he has gone there) and that would ensure it, so to speak.

I think those terms quite right for Oedipus if it's to be a circus production. Say 10 performances a year and if he wants it for five years, let him average over the middle years. But is it really coming off?

They think of "flying" The Master Builder and "Fanny" to Oxford. Is it too late now?

Yours,

H. G. B.

---

1. The Home University Library was founded in 1911 by Williams and Norgate, taken over in 1928 by Thornton Butterworth, and bought by Oxford University Press in 1941. Murray was one of its original editors, the others being Julian Huxley and H. A. L. Fisher.

BOD/MS
To Murray

Court Lodge,
Stansted,
Wrotham,
Kent.
Wednesday [1911]

Dear G. M.,

To resume: I continue to be deeply moved at the prospect of "The Drammer", muchly I think because it would mean seeing something of you, sometime.

But first I'm not at all clear as to its scope (the book's). You'd do a chapter or two on the Past—Greece? Yes. Rome? I suppose so. Mystery plays—Elizabethan—Molière—Lope da Vega—the Italian Jossers[1] (don't know many of their names)—the Immortal Kotzebue, etc. How wide a net can you and should you throw and where will your past end? If you could tackle it up to—say—1889 and work in besides the modern Spaniards, America (that doesn't publish), Italy and the Germans and Scandinavians and Russians that I can't read (Japan and China might go in a footnote), then I would go at what was left and help you out with Ibsen.

Or perhaps it shouldn't be historical and concrete at all but abstract and critical. Can it be done that way?

You remember I suggested "Modern English Drama" for I saw my way to that. But even if it comes—without much reason—to "Drama: Ancient Greek and Modern English" by "two as has done it" you won't be able to help referring to Euripides by name. Shall I be able to avoid the words Jones, Henry Arthur? I don't think I'm capable of writing critically on any foreign drama (bar Ibsen), though French I could read up. And everything interesting in England has come since 1880 and mostly from living men. Could one avoid mentioning names? I thought at first one couldn't. But seeing the smallness of the book, one might do a good deal about technique and organization. But I fear it'd be deadly dull without pointing morals and adorning tails (even by treading on 'em). I foresaw that my Modern English Drama (squashed!) would be frankly partisan and so at first put away the idea of it. Then discovered that I really didn't feel so narrow-minded, prepared to treat Tree on the assumption that he was a good actor of his sort (but a word about the sort) and that his productions were good—of their sort (but a word about the staging of S.[2]) and that on the whole I'd only be partisan for the future as against the past, which wouldn't get past.

See how I respond to your breezy encouraging tone—the moment I return to your letter.

No: there's no reason of course to criticize actors or managers (they don't much matter) but I do think it'll be difficult to mention "a few large tendencies" and avoid the names of the "tendent" (?) ones except when their principal tendency is to be dead.

To resume peroration: I do think the book must be done. If it comes from America—my God—it will be awful unless it's by Brander Matthews and then it'll be so dull that the book won't open.

No, Sir: we must get a cinch on the subject right here. And me, coupled with a real professor (with a wooden leg). My next play will be in blank verse.

I'd like you to revolve and resolve some of these doubts.

Curiously enough I go to Liverpool on Friday. I generally call in at Oxford on the way—though it isn't.

Yours,
H. G. B.

Come to Portugal by the Booth line—and bathe.

---

1. "Josser" was a slang word for "chap" or "fellow," always used jocularly, never with pejorative intent. It stayed in British slang until about 1940, then gradually died out.
2. Shakespeare.

EDD/TS
To Barker

82, Woodstock Road,
Oxford.
July 8 [1911]

My dear B.

The drama is very tempting, but the real objection to it

from my side is that I shall not have any time this year to write a word. And next year I go to America to lecture in the spring.

I have (1) to prepare lectures for next term; (2) to write my book on Greece for the H U L; (3) to do an Oxford Book of Gk. Verse. 4 & 5 are complicated.

4 is that the other day at Overstrand I was poking the wall of a house with my stick in an absentminded way, when the owner asked me what the Dickens I meant. I said, like Artemus Ward: "I am poking it to see if I like it, because if I like it I'll buy it." And in a few minutes I found I had bought it. So now it has got to be furnished and there is generally the devil to pay (besides the lawyers). It may be described as a Nobleman's Cottage Residence with Pigstye, and we shall use it instead of lodgings.

5 is that my dentist has fallen into low spirits and says that nothing will cheer him except being allowed to take out all my top teeth at one sitting. I offered him two or three, but he says there is no fun unless it is ten at least. It will incapacitate me for lecturing for ever so long, so I have urged him to try someone else. I am not the only possessor of teeth. You, for instance, have dozens of excellent ones—just the sort he likes.

So on the whole I do not see that I can promise to help in the drama book just now, nor let them advertise it. But we might keep the idea before us. It would be great fun to collaborate with you. By the way, Margoliouth[1] has made out that Aristotle did really define Tragedy as "a representation of Felicity". By Felicity—not a satisfactory translation—he means High Life, the sort of life one desires or considers good. Very interesting; and shows what an imagination the old fellow really had. E.g. the death of Crippen is not tragic,[2] but that of a martyr is.

When we do write the book, we will write only what interests us and seems to matter. No history, no information: only we must pay great attention to the Irishy and Brieux and all that seems to affect the future.

Did I tell you Rosalind's new book is coming out directly? Called "Moonseed". Some will call it morbid, but I think it is good.

Yours ever,

G. M.

---

1. David Margoliouth (1858–1940) was the author of—among many other things—*The Early Development of Mohammedanism* (London, 1913).
2. Hawley Harvey Crippen (1862–1910), who poisoned his wife and then dismembered her body, was hanged at Pentonville prison on November 23, 1910, following one of the most sensational trials of the era.

BOD/TS
To Murray

17, John Street,
Adelphi, W.S.
September 5th, 1911

My dear G. M.,

I have been meaning to write to you for ever so long. First it was to say that I have been reading the "Rise of the Greek Epic" for, I think, the third time; and by Jove, it would be such an education to me to do anything with you, that you must not let the book on the Drama go right out of your mind. You really must not. I want to do it.

The second thing is, that Lillah has her eye on the Iphigenia for matinées, about November I should say. At least this is the position. They want to stay on at the Little Theatre after Christmas, but they don't know yet if they can. If they have to move to another, it might be a more suitable one for Iphigenia and in that case better postpone until the Spring—otherwise about November.

Granville Bantock now says definitely that he can't do the music. I have got S. P. Waddington to have a try at it. He is very interested, and if it comes off, it should be very right, because he is very anxious to put the verse and the meaning of the choruses first, and the music second. I hope you approve, but you are not committed. I am trying to cultivate a lieutenant for productions—at the present moment in the person of Harcourt Williams (he did Pompey)[1] so the production might be by me and by him so to speak. Again do you approve? What about Oedipus? What is the meaning of your version and Courtney's?

How are you?

Yours,
H. G. B.

---

1. *The Tragedy of Pompey the Great,* by John Masefield. Williams mounted the first production of it on December 4, 1910, for the Stage Society at the Aldwych Theatre. Barker had had no hand in that production but had greatly admired it: "it gains on the stage and is biggish, I think," he said about the play. Barker's mention of Harcourt Williams in this letter is an example of his constant endeavor to train a group of younger directors in his methods with the express purpose of carrying on his work (Iden Payne and Lewis Casson provide further examples of this).

EDD/TS
To Murray

> The Little Theatre,
> John Street,
> Adelphi,
> [London]
> November 29, 1911

Dear G. M.,

We had a heated time at the Dramatists' Club to-day. Hawkins put a resolution protesting against the Brookfield appointment[1] and out of about 18 present, only 8 voted for it. It was carried, because only 6 or 7 voted against.

Pinero sat in the chair and was dignified. But that of course puts an end to the Dramatists' Club as being of any use but for a luncheon club which—Heaven help us!—nobody wants to attend. It seems unlikely that the Dramatists who do object will publish a protest over their signatures because the Dramatists who affectionately call Brookfield "Charlie" would probably reply with a manifestation in his favour. Individually I fancy we may do something, and do you, please, do <u>anything</u>, and I should suggest writing to any Members of the Government that you felt you could. I think the row will go on, though there may be no practical result, and the Dramatists—to their shame—will have no official part in it.

> Yours,
> H. G. B.

---

1. The appointment was as Joint Examiner of Plays (with Redford). See Appendix A to this volume.

BOD/TS
To Murray

> The Little Theatre,
> John Street,
> Adelphi.
> December 2nd, 1911

My dear G. M.,

About the Brookfield business—you will have seen about McKenna in the House yesterday, and look at the "Morning Leader" of this morning. The only practical thing there seems left to do for the moment is to get a discussion in the House of Lords where Spencer is bound to answer for himself. Most unfortunately I must go away on Monday morning. However, I will do what I can. Do you think that Gore would do anything?—A Bishop is the proper person on this occasion!—if he would, it would be a great score.

I have had a talk to McKenna, who practically admitted that the appointment was scandalous, and that the situation—if it had not to do with an Officer of the King's Household—would be impossible of defence. But he won't promise legislation unless he is actually forced into it. and I think what we have to do is to get enough fuss made to force him. Do devise anything you can.

Yours always,
H. G. B.

P.S. This message from Lillah—she'd much like to talk with you over Jocasta. Could you possibly come to us a weekend? Very jolly if you could. Or could we or she come to you—and when, which, where or why?

BOD/MS
To Murray

Stansted.
Sunday [January, 1912]

Dear G. M.,

I do very much wish (1) that for your own satisfaction you had seen Waddington and Miss Morris first—I'm sorry I didn't arrange it, and (2) that otherwise you had neither seen nor heard anything about the chorus till I was in a position to report to you or show it to you myself. I start working at it tomorrow. I think I know the rhythm you want—at least I thought I did, but my mind isn't as balanced on the whole matter now. You puzzle me, though, when you say you don't expect to hear the words, since it is to that that in theory everything has been sacrificed until now and now the only point of having this peculiar sort of chant-music written has been that the words may be heard and the rhythm kept. However—

I think I am through with the cast: Orestes is the bother—there's no one at all right for it. It has seemed to lie between Wontner and Tearle and I mean to choose Tearle because he is less modern, more robust and "heroic". He won't look as if he'd been haunted by the Furies but he'll take command of the second half of the play better. I hope I'm doing right—it's a choice of evils. But I am casting all the play on the "robust" side. I feel somehow it wants that, being an "adventure" and cast in a savage place. Pylades—Bridges-Adams; Herdsman—Jules Shaw; Messenger—Rathbone (?); Thoas—Hewetson (not beef enough in him but the best I can do, I

think). I'll keep Wednesday afternoon for you. Will you wire me
when you've arrived so that I may fix other things—or rather see
they don't get in the way. I've much I want to ask you—besides your
reading me the choruses—about the libations, the <u>sex</u> of the Temple
attendants (important) and the Goddess question.

But I'm coming to the conclusion that the Duncans are
right—Greek plays want such special treatment that they must be
left outside the scope of the commonplace theatre. The standard of
production has gone up much (and very rightly) since we did Hippolytus and were pleased with ourselves; and what with playwriting
and censorship and the ordinary worries of management, I can't
really come to terms with it. But I want these matinées to be as good
as I can get them, for I mean them to be my last. It's nine years since
I started with the Hipp. and it's good and appropriate to be finishing
with Iph. After this—whatever evening bills I must; one snap at William S.; but for the rest—other people must get on with it.

See you Wed.

Yours,
H. G. B.

BOD/TS
To Murray

Kingsway Theatre,
Great Queen Street, W.C.
Feb. 23rd, 1912

My dear G. M.,

I doubt if you will ever like either the sound or the sight of
the Chorus, but I am quite sure that if you saw them now you would
have six fits; therefore, by Apollo, you shall not see them!!

When I have worked at them a week or so you may then
get through the sight of it with only a fit and a half. When I have
done with them I think on the whole that I shall like them very
much, and anyhow I feel that we are committed to the experiment. I
promise you that, like or dislike, it shan't be a disgrace. The only real
fault in the music is that he has pitched it rather tryingly high, but for
the rest, it is designedly stuff that can be worked on, malleable stuff,
conceived in the loosest form possible.

I hope to get the play cast and to start work on it about the
middle of next week. For the next two or three days I shall be trying to
find out what it means, and if in any important parts I fail, may I drop
down on you sudden for a couple of hours' talk? Will you say if there is
any time that you <u>can't</u> have me between now and say Wednesday.

Will you trust the casting to me? It will have to be experimental—that is to say there is no Orestes that is thoroughly good. At present I think it rests between Godfrey Tearle, Guy Rathbone (both too stockish and fat but of the right weight and intensity) and Arthur Wontner (he played the young man in The Witch, if you remember). He has good points and looks all right but is rather "wankling",[1] won't stay "put". The rest of the cast is of course not over-difficult. Must stop now.

Yours,

H. G. B.

---

1. "Wanklin" and "wankling" are local dialect variants of "wankle," a word at one time standard English but now obsolete. It is still preserved, however, in some of the dialects of northern England and in Scotland. The *O. E. D.* gives its meaning as "unsteady, insecure, changeable, unsettled, inconstant, wavering." Partridge, in his *Dictionary of Slang and Unconventional English,* does not list "wankle," "wanklin," or "wankling" but *does* list "wanky": "c. 1890: unsteady, precarious, delicate in health." Barker uses several variants of the word in his letters from time to time; see, for example, letter to Murray of Saturday, August, 1905, above.

BOD/TS
To Murray

Kingsway Theatre,
Great Queen Street, W.C.
Feb. 29th, 1912

My dear G. M.

I stupidly did not say to you all I meant to about Dean[1] and the IPHIGENIA production.

I have devised a plan over our productions here, that we should always, if possible, acquire the country rights of the play we do, that I should have somebody by my side at rehearsals (as for IPHIGENIA I have Harold Chapin, who has been producing up in Glasgow) and that then when the Repertory Theatres want to do the play, we should send them our production, our scenery or its designs, our costumes—and my production—in this sense: that my assistant should go down and rehearse the company from the prompt book he will have made under me, and that then I should attend the last two or three rehearsals and polish it up. This plan over the matinées was to make it more worth our while to spend all we reasonably wanted to on the production here in the hope that handing it on to the other theatres would help to re-pay us. We have not any country rights in the IPHIGENIA that I know, and you may not like the plan—and then there'd be no more to be said. But if you do, and could arrange for Dean (and later, perhaps, Casson or Wareing) to fall in with it, I should be, for various reasons, very glad. Chapin is quite good enough a man to exercise a lot of individual discretion in rehearsing other companies, but the thing that would remain would be the general scheme which I had worked out, one hopes more or less with your approval—but that's to show. I had thought too that it would be better for the author to have <u>one</u> work at his play when it first came out instead of perhaps two or three scrappy goes at it when it was done in various places.

There is to be a Debate in the House of Lords on the Censorship on March 13th, to be opened by Lord Newton, who, I presume, is still pro-censor (he certainly was, on the committee). It is vitally important—don't you think?—that we should be strongly and well represented. <u>Do</u> bring any influence you can to bear on possible peers to speak on our side. I suppose Gore is still unattainable? Has Curzon any opinions, did you gather? Anyway, do consider what is best to be done. Do you see, also, that the Managers are getting up a counter-petition to retain the censorship? This means that the thing Whelen is in charge of[2] will need all the influential people it can get at the back of it. Altogether, though we may be in for another defeat, it seems that we are in for another battle!

I will let you know about next Friday.

Yours,
H. G. B.

---

1. Basil Dean (1888–1978), for four years an actor with Miss Horniman's repertory company at the Gaiety Theatre, Manchester, went to Liverpool in 1910 to help found a similar theater company there. He was the director of the new theater (which eventually became the Liverpool Playhouse) from 1911 to 1913. In the period between the two world wars he became a very influential director, producer, and manager in London. During World War II he was director of ENSA (Entertainments National Service Association, an organization set up to provide plays, concerts, etc., for military camps and munitions factories both at home and overseas, the soldiers' version of which was Every Night Something Atrocious).
2. Frederick Whelen was organizing an anti-Censor petition, with an impressive array of signatures, addressed to King George V.

BOD/TS
To Murray

Kingsway Theatre,
Great Queen Street, W.C.
January 1st, 1914.

My dear G. M.,

I will tell you how you can contribute your twenty-five pounds! Prunella is being something of a success in America and I am at last getting more than a few shillings in fees for it. I have always thought I would like you to take back, if you would, some at any rate of the money with which you helped me to launch it. For the life of me I cannot remember at the moment how much it was, but we can find out. There!

We simply must pull this repertory through; it is now or never. One thing else you could do and, if you please, you really must. Masefield has a brilliant idea that during one week of the repertory (which will last at the Savoy for another three) we shall each of us take a performance, in this sense: after it, come in front of the curtain and make a short but moving appeal to the audience. Really, my speech was a good tip. It affected people in a way that letters to the papers don't, and as we will have our speeches reported verbatim we shall get the double advantage. We want nine people: there is you, Masefield, Shaw (of course!), me. Galsworthy's away. Then, higgledy-piggledy I have in my mind Wells, Bennett, R. J. Campbell, Oliver Lodge, Garvin (who really does like literature and is going to run us hard, he says, in the Observer and the Pall Mall).[1] I want a Bishop; I want a literary politician; I want suggestions from you; I want nine people. I want to know what you think of it but it is now or never and think, oh, think G. M., of being able to do The Trojan Women to a normal evening audience, with clerks in the pit and dock labourers in the gallery. It is well worth fighting for.

Yours,

H. G. B.

---

1. Rev. R. J. Campbell (1867–1956) was a well-known Congregational preacher who occupied the pulpit of the City Temple for twelve years. He later joined the ministry of the Church of England. Sir Oliver Lodge (1851–1940) was a scientist, best known for his pursuit of psychical research; he was the first principal of Birmingham University, appointed in 1900. J. L. Garvin (1868–1947) was the editor of the *Observer* (see letter in Chapter X).

BOD/MS
To Murray

Court Lodge,
Stansted,
Wrotham,
Kent.
Sunday [January, 1914]

Glory be, my dear G. M., but that's great news. We're all very glad— all, being Lillah and I, naturally (plus G. B. S. who is down here and says but Good Lord what age is the man—he founded Toynbee Hall before I was born).[1] And I'm writing now to Rosalind—if she's not with you, get the letter on to her. I'm a week late in writing for I've just been over to Dresden to Hellerau to the Jacques Dalcroze Academy of Eurhythmics, which you know all about. Besides the Eurhythmics there's a Salzmann Man with a system of staging and lighting which is the only modern artificial light staging possible for Greek plays (you know after Bradfield,[2] I swore "never in a stuffy theatre again"). But this—I'll tell you all about it when, if ever, we meet. Will you not be this way at all? Or ask us for an August weekend. But Salzmann—moaning and saying how good his lighting might have been if only he could have spent money on it, but he had nothing: only a wretched 68,000 marks for the experiment. That's Germany. Damn.

Who wants to do the Rhesus? Somebody there must be who'll make a Greek play company—that and nothing else. And the Eurhythmics would be the path to it. It wants that sort of foundation, not on artistic sensibilities (God guard us!). I want to grow a beard. I shall never write plays till I do nothing else. Are you at your H. U. L. Greek book?

But returning to vital matters—that's jolly about Rosalind. Is it six weeks since we saw her—sitting out Nan together and waltzed her back afterwards to some fortress of spinsterhood near Baker Street.

By the way (privately to you) has she taken that flat at Chelsea Gardens? Answer me that. They used not to be very desirable places—but that's years ago and I expect she has her eyes open as to neighborhoods. Still, if you dropped a discreet question then—

Yours,
H. G. B.

---

1. The "great news" is of the marriage of Murray's daughter, Rosalind, to Arnold J. Toynbee (1889–1975), nephew of Arnold Toynbee. Toynbee Hall, in Whitechapel, London, was founded in 1884 by Canon Samuel Barnett and named after the Oxford economist and social philosopher, who died in 1883 at the early age of thirty-one. Shaw was either forgetting the death of the elder Toynbee or deliberately confusing the two for the sake of the joke. Toynbee Hall (with which Arnold J. Toynbee had no particular connection) was and is an institution for making higher education available to the very poor. At first it was staffed on a purely voluntary basis by professors, lecturers, and readers from Oxford; it is now run by the Inner London Education Authority. (For other references to Rosalind Murray, see pp. 256 and 259.)
2. Bradfield is a small but distinguished private school which has a very fine open-air, Greek-style theater.

BOD/TS
To Murray

Kingsway Theatre,
Great Queen Street, W.C.
February 10, 1914.

My dear G. M.,

I am off I think and hope about Saturday or Monday next to Moscow via Berlin. Why don't you come? After all, what is Oxford, even in term time? We could walk across the Hartz Mountains or any other Wald we could find and listen to the birds beginning to sing. If you won't do that (though you are a coward and a cloisteral if you don't)[1] then Lillah and I propose going at the beginning of March to Spain or to Rome and sitting down somewhere there for two or three weeks. What about that?

Yours,
H. Granville Barker
dg[2]

---

1. The phrase refers both to the allegedly cloistered life of the stereotypical academic and to Sir Toby Belch's comment in *Twelfth Night* (Act 1, sc. 3): "He's a coward and a coistrel that will not drink to my niece."
2. An unidentified secretary.

BOD/TS
To Murray

Kingsway Theatre,
Great Queen Street, W.C.
February 14, 1914.

My dear G. M.,

I am off on Sunday night for about a fortnight. Here are these two documents[1] and the Trust Deed is being drawn up for you three to approve and after that we must fire ahead.

How are you? Will you come to Spain or Rome or Algiers in the beginning of March? Say yes.

Yours,
H. G. B.

---

1. See Appendix B for these documents, which present formally his plan for a repertory theater.

BOD/TS
To Murray

Kingsway Theatre,
Great Queen Street, W.C.
March 11th, 1914.

My dear G. M.,

Here are some spoils from Prunella and with luck there may
be some more. It is pleasant to send it you after all this time.* Is
there any chance of getting you for a holiday? Lillah must go away—
she is to be deported as early next week as possible. We thought of
Algiers, and to sit in the desert for a week or ten days with a camel.
I should like to see you on a camel. Is it at all possible? For we
would fit in to anything really restful and sunny that you could propose. We thought of Easter at Seville where they do a sort of Christian version of The Bacchae before the High Altar on Good Friday.

About the Trusteeship, don't be alarmed; I will write to you
further in a day or two.

Yours always,
H. G. B.

*How good it was of you, G. M., to lend that helping hand. Please
God one doesn't forget those things.

BOD/W
To Murray[1]

London   March 16, 1914   9.18 P.M.

To: Professor Gilbert Murray, 8, Woodstock Rd., Oxford.
Dash the repertory. Spend it on coming to the desert with us. We
hope to start Friday. It will make a new professor of you. Do come.

Barker

---

1. Punctuation added to this telegram.

BOD/PC
To Murray

[France]
April 8, 1914

Oh, G. M., G. M., <u>why</u> ain't you here—a-reading of all the
inscriptions and talking Latin to the waiter? And the weather—such
sun! Come along—you'll catch us yet at Biskra Royal Hotel.

H. G. B.

BOD/MS
To Murray

Hotel Metropole,
Monte Carlo.
Wednesday [April, 1914]

Dear G. M.,

<u>Still</u> <u>Time</u>! We are calling on my mother here and don't cross till Friday by the Charles Roux from Marseilles.

Tried to find you after the 2nd part of the Dream[1] but you were surrounded. Hope you did approve—if not wholly. Much wish you were here. We're both tired—we'd holiday you as gently as it were any sucking dove.

Yours,
H. G. B.

---

1. Just before the holiday, Barker directed *A Midsummer Night's Dream* at the Savoy Theatre with Lillah McCarthy as Helena. The production opened on February 6, 1914 (see Chapter II, letter of February 11, 1914, from Archer about the production and Barker's reply of February 14).

BOD/TS
To Murray

Little Franklyn,
Hook Heath,
Woking.
Sunday

Dear G. M.,

Thank you, Sir; that is about what I thought. Shades of Ruskin! But I am not happy, Sir. I see a Tory government juggling with tariffs . . . a quarrel with Germany over some blessed market in Kamschatka or the like and then a row . . . in which you or I or both of us will be shot . . . in the back? And I won't fight, Murray; and I don't want to be shot. I want to live at peace with Hauptmann and Wilamowitz. Do you know what dust is? Please, Sir . . . stuff that you mustn't leave about, because it is full of Germans, which are very dangerous. How is your aidos?
Adoo.

Yours,
H. G. B.

BOD/TS
To Murray

Kingsway Theatre,
Great Queen Street, W.C.
September 12th, 1914

My dear G. M.,

I sign it and would sign it with my blood if anything were to be gained by shedding it, even that much of it. And I can only hope some neutral person has heard of me. My principal admirers are alien enemies. I do not gather whether you want me to procure any other signatures, but if you do send it me back and I will do so.[1]

Yours,
H. G. B.

---

1. I am not sure what Murray had asked Barker to sign, but the letter clearly implies that it was some sort of plea or protest about the war. Murray was a great internationalist and after the war did much work for the League of Nations (and, later, for the United Nations) organizations.

BOD/TS
To Murray

Kingsway Theatre,
Great Queen Street, W.C.
November 6th, 1914

My dear G. M.,

They have asked me (you have asked me) to sign that "To our Colleagues in Russia" letter. I wish I could, if it matters that I should, for there is so much in it that I feel about Russian literature and Russian people too. But the beginning I feel is a little bit too fine for me. However, I could get over that, for if I have not felt it I could at least persuade myself that I ought to have. But the end does seem to me so very deliberately, almost dis-ingenuously, to leave the Russian Government out of the question altogether. I can't even yet feel sure that we are allied to the Russian people as apart from the Russian Government. I hope to God we may be, but I do find certain implications and omissions in those last three paragraphs difficult to get over.

I do wish we could do the Trojan Women, but perhaps it is an end of the War play, not a middle War. I have my eye on it for America, whither we shall have to dispatch all theatre things we have, I fear, sooner or later if they are to be kept alive.

H. G. B.

BOD/MS
To Murray

Connaught Hotel,
Mayfair, W.1
20.2.19

My dear G. M.,

Do you think you could profitably take—or get taken—
some public notice of this?[1]

So much better if educational rather than theatrical people
get interested (wherefore "a Correspondent") and I do think it shows
the right line of new advance. The Times has cut it ruthlessly but the
sense is mainly there.

We go off to U. S. A. for two months on March 1.

Are you all right again?

Our best regards to you and Lady Mary.

Yours,
H. G. B.

---

1. Enclosed was a long article headed "Reconstruction in the Theatre" with a subhead-
   ing "Up from the Soil," written by Barker and published in the *Times* on February
   20, 1919. It suggested encouraging the growth of part-amateur, part-professional
   theaters in the smaller towns and villages of England.

BOD/MS
To Murray

12, Hyde Park Place, W.2
13.10.19

My dear G. M.,

Isn't it a <u>great</u> thing![1] I read it last night to Helen and have
just been—rather too roughly—through it again, but getting hold
nevertheless, as one does, of 50 per cent. more than at the first reading. I hope my scribbles at the margin won't be useless or seem im-
pertinent: they are nearly all from the point of view of speaker or
producer—noting what I could "get over"—or rather could <u>not</u>, I
think, very easily.

The production must be "massive and concrete" like Mr.
W.—'s Hamlet (this sounds like the first sentence of Walkley's notice of it). But—seriously—I have never been more impressed by the
importance of the chorus, not even in the Bacchae, and by the musical importance (in a wide sense). The whole of the first part—almost
up to Agamemnon's entrance—seems to me meant as a gigantic musical prelude to the play—a diminuendo from the triumph song at the

beginning into a minor key of dread—the insistence on the revenges of victory as well as of old ill-doing. And to understand the meaning of this of course you have to be very well up in the family history of the Atrides: it is a double difficulty. But somehow it must be sur- mounted. A strong choric effect of some sort and, I suggest, your programme notes illucidating [*sic!*] this part of the play only, but in as great detail as you can. (Why is the Leader so keen about Menelaus? Is that a stupid question?) I am impressed too with the insistence on the ritual. A producer should mark that very carefully, I am sure.

For the rest—the producer notes the extraordinary good ef- fect of the change from lyric to speech and line by line in the Cassan- dra scene (oh, what a scene! Is the Euripides touch at the end all Aeschylus—or a bit you? Not an insult, but a compliment, in- tended.) Also the striking change of key with the Aegisthus en- trance—the new character—so right to end the <u>first</u> <u>part</u> of a trilogy—and the new note—the new problem.

I could go on writing about it just from this one point of view. Not for me of course to say anything about your work—the translation—but the whole thing does hold and stir one. What more could be said by Greekless me—or anyone. Hackneyed though the phrase is—it is like something hewn out of marble.

Thankyou so much for showing it me.

Yours,
H. G. B.

I think we ought to have started the L of N meeting with prayer. Whenever a Lord Mayor says that "the interest of the City of Lon- don is peace" I think of their Turtle Soup—unjust, I know.

---

1. Murray had sent him for comment before publication the manuscript of his transla- tion of the *Agamemnon* of Aeschylus; it was published in 1920.

BOD/MS
To Murray

Il Castello,
Portofino-mare,
Liguria,
Italy.
9.3.23

My dear G. M.,

I hope you'll feel able to sign this petition for a pension for William Poel. It seems to me a good case, if ever there was one. You

know much of his work. I've known nearly all of it. And Everyman
and the Shakespeare: much done since has rested on his pioneering, I
believe. He has spent his money and himself ungrudgingly, I know.
Our best regards.

Yours,
Harley G-B.

BOD/PC
To Murray

Hotel Beau Site,
Paris.
23.12.25

A shameful confession that the Madras House has kept me till pretty
near now from the House of Atreus![1] How good that with all else
weighing on you, you still can translate them. I'm not the only person
surely who sees, though, how this play fits in with all else and reads
the preface as dated from Geneva.[2] "I praise persuasion gentle
eyed . . . Wise are they and have found the way of peace." But when
you depreciate the trial scene a little, may I remind you, Sir, that a
trial scene is always a "go" on the stage? Yes, from Aeschylus to
Galsworthy—and Shaw—it never failed. This is not only thanks but
a Xmas card with good wishes from us both to you all.

H. G-B.

---

1. Murray had sent him a copy of his newly published translation of the *Eumenides* of
   Aeschylus.
2. A reference to Murray's support of and work for the League of Nations.

BOD/MS
To Murray

Hotel Beau Site
4, Rue de Presbourg,
Paris.
16.10.30

My dear G. M.,
About 27 years ago you told me a story of a certain ? Don,
? The Tutor of St. John's (?) College Oxford listening to an ? essay
by a young ? undergraduate (I must have the technical terms right)
about the Star of Bethlehem; and after 100 lines of learned-sounding
astronomical discourse about parhelion and apogee and perigee, he

interrupted with: I really don't know what you're talking about Mr. Blank. It was just a miracle, nothing else.

Don't say you've forgotten: and if you haven't, be kind and dictate it accurately to your present efficient secretary. For I need this also for a Clark lecture!

I have planned not a bad parallel between Aeschylus' stage craft in the Agamemnon and Ibsen's in Rosmersholm; but I fear it will be crowded out by your loathed Elisabethans [*sic*]. But I'll use it up later.

The other day a respectable elder was staying with us. He also had been at St. John's. I asked if he had known Murray there. He was quite offended. "Murray was much my senior", he said. Nonsense, Sir, said I, leaping the tennis net: he is my contemporary.

I expect people write to you about all sorts of foolish things; so why should not I, about the Star of Bethlehem?

As ever—except for the momentary effect of some French doctoring—

Yours,
H. G-B.

EDD/TS
To Barker

Yatscombe,
Boar's Hill,
Oxford.
May 25, 1931

My dear Barker,

I ought to be doing honest work and your wicked book on Dramatic Method has seduced me and made me not only read it but also want to talk to you about almost all of it. In the Shakespeare part, I think you are a little unjust about the metre. Some of the effects which you specially admire are, to me, metrical effects. Metre to be exact need not be wooden; and verse to be fluid or musical need not be irregular . . . at least that is how I should like to argue. I agree violently about the Restoration Drama. But are you not a little harsh on rhyme? Shakespeare wrote rhyme badly, just as Jonson did. He always jingles it. But take Epipsychidion, or some of Browning—or even me. Is my verse really as bad to speak as the Restoration people? You ought to know, and of course I can't. I should have hoped that, while it did sound strange or foreign—or outside the regular English tradition—it did get certain dramatic effects. Though

I confess I don't know of any satisfactory original English play in rhyme. As to the Cassandra scene, your account is very interesting, but you seem to miss, or not to think worth mentioning, one chief characteristic of the scene. C is under a curse, the curse not to be believed, and she knows it. There is a regular progression. First, the vision, growing steadily in clearness. Then her effort to warn the Chorus, which is first only conveyed through the riddling prophetic language. Then at 1178 she pulls herself together, drops the lyrics, and tries to convince the Chorus by first showing them that she knows the past. She mentions the curse, and they say "Not at all. We believe you all right." She warns them in prophetic language—in a new paroxysm—and they don't understand! 1242: at last she gets the statement quite clear; 1248: they can't help understanding, but they say it is impossible. Then comes her last paroxysm, which leaves them as it were paralysed, not actually disbelieving but just unable to think or act. The dramatic interest is to see the prophetess warning the Elders to stop the murder, and the curse working to prevent her words from having effect. But of course there are other strands woven in, or other vistas behind.

Yours ever,
G. M.

I am rather angry that the pornographers have got the Cambridge Theatre to do the Lysistrata "in a less Bowdlerized version than has ever been seen on any stage". It is a fine play in itself. Given the Phallic festival as an institution, and given a bitter war against which the Comedian is protesting at the risk of his life, it is a magnificent play. But under modern conditions it is merely an exercise in obscenity. Damn them!

BOD/MS
To Murray

Hotel Beau Site,
4, Rue de Presbourg,
Paris.
31.5.31

My dear G. M.,

What is wanted (besides other things, in this wicked world) is that the C. of Intellectual Co-op. should appoint a sub-C. "to determine whether the peace of the world will be better advanced by the development of the static or dynamic drama", consisting of you and me (or I: it could settle that, too). Then I could really thrash out, to <u>my</u> profit at any rate, that business of rhyme and regular metre v. blank verse and rhythm. But oh, the nincompoop I was to overlook (it was just that) the primary scheme of the Cassandra scene, especially as it does not really vitiate the rest of my contention. Thank you for the lesson. I was on the point of sending you the thing before I finally printed it. Then I thought: Geneva and overwork apart, this is not fair. A man must make his own blunders and suffer for them.

I much agree about that Cambridge theatre in its present phase.[1] There is a tall thin man with a soft sleek beard—but that will do when we meet, if we ever do.

Yours,
H. G-B.

---

1. The Festival Theatre, Cambridge, founded in 1926 by Terence Gray, was noted for its seriousness of purpose and its experimental approach to staging. Its productions in 1931 included *Henry VIII*, *The Insect Play*, *The Wild Duck*, *Antigone*, *Hassan*, *Gustavus Vasa*, and *Alcestis*.

BOD/TCC
To Barker

Oxford
December 31, 1934

My dear Harley,

"Come Julia" was a great pleasure.[1] I quite agree about the "quiet beauty" which runs through it. There is a delicacy of touch and observation and a complete abstinence from the obvious effects. I cannot help wondering how Julia got on when she arrived at Leon. I think it must have been rather a shock to her. But the book was a real pleasure to me.

By the way, when you have time look at Agamemnon 1060, p.46 in my translation, where Clytemnestra says to Cassandra:

> "If, dead to sense, thou wilt not understand . . .
> Thou show her, not with speech, but with brute hand."

What do you think the business should be? Does Clytemnestra address the Leader, as I say, or some attendant of her own who has come out? The Leader seems either to stop the attendant or to refuse to act himself, but it is a little puzzling.

Yours ever,
Gilbert Murray

---

1. Helen Granville-Barker's novel, published in London in 1931, evidently had just been given to Murray by the Barkers.

BOD/MS
To Murray

18, Place des Etats-Unis,
Paris XVI[e]
Jan. 4, 1935

My dear G. M.—and revered Professor.

These matters—Agamemnon 1060—are, as the Psalmist says, too high for me.

All the same, I see no point in Clyt. saying that to anyone but the Chorus Leader. And I suppose that the point of her saying it at all lies in the sense she has of the approaching moment when she will strike the blows. She is aching to begin, so to speak, and finds some satisfaction for the moment in telling the Chorus Leader to clout Cass. over the head. We all feel that way at times. As to the Chorus Leader, nothing more natural than that he should say in the Queen's presence: I quite agree, Ma'am, there's no other way of arguing with these furriners; equally, that the minute her back is turned, he (shall we say, G. M., being a man?) should add: what's the use of hitting the poor child! And that effect would be wiped out if Clyt. gave the order to a mere slave.

In my Loeb crib I notice that Clyt. is made to say to Cass.: If you don't understand me then "make sign with thy barbarian hand"—which is rather Irish and I suppose quite wrong*. But the chorus comment is " 'tis an interpreter and a <u>plain</u> one that the stranger seems to need . . ."

And that word "plain" (for which you have "rare") would be an ironic acquiescence in Clyt's command to try the "brute hand".

But there! Greek plays without some[1] guidance are treacherous ground for me.

We're just back from Rapallo—and Laval has gone to Rome. And half my Hamlet M.S. has been lost in the post for 12 days—and I had no copy! But it has turned up—and I feel better.

It is good to be in touch with you again. And I'm very glad you liked Come Julia. Leon is a charming place, all the same!

As ever,
H. G-B.

*Yes. I see your note on the passage.

---

1. Barker's handwriting is unclear here. The word may be "your" not "some."

BOD/TS
To Murray

Mayfair House,
Park Avenue at Sixty-fifth St.,
New York.
January 1, 1941

My dear G. M.,

I take my typewriter in hand—one benefit at least this war has conferred on my friends; I have had to learn the typewriter—to congratulate His Most Gracious Majesty in your person on the repairing of an omission of which I have been conscious for the last thirty years, that of your name from the list of O.M.s so that's that.[1]

If ever you have a minute to spare let us have news of you and yours . . . and may it be of your safety and comparative well-being.

We left France on June 19 and reached Lisbon without much mishap. Letters to England asking what use I might be there produced an unflattering chorus of None, and a recommendation to go and do what I could in the U. S. A. or Canada. It hasn't proved to be much so far—lecturing at Yale; and I go soon to Harvard—but my hope is still for something more appropriate to the moment than William seems to be—our W. S., asset though he doubtless is to us.

I wish I could give you a clear and true view of the situation here. But personal incompetence apart, you know how hard it is to gain one from the standpoint of New York. Every circumstance drives towards intervention and with increasing force. But that again rouses increased and often unexpected resistance and it is difficult to measure the opposing strength. The reaction is violent . . . then suddenly it dies down. The effect comes, I think, from the newspapers showing no sense of proportion. But even the majority of our best friends are still apparently for all help SHORT OF WAR. Any plain threat of imminent catastrophe would push them past that point; of this I've no doubt. But meanwhile they argue, I think, that unity for the sake of smooth and increasing production is of more practical importance. I felt that too when I first came. My doubt is now whether they will ever manage to bring production to "war" pitch unless they find they are themselves "up against it".

The other noticeable—to me—matter is the anti-war movement in the universities . . . even in "conservative" Harvard and Yale. It is the work of a noisy minority and of students only; and it shows in the most ridiculously ignorant "resolutions". So I daresay it is largely the letting off of steam and dissipation of all the anti-Versailles, pro-Soviet (but oh, what IS dear unholy Russia up to now?)

to-hell-with-Europe vapors of the last twenty years. And a professor at Yale said to me: There has been no student OPINION up to now. It is now beginning to form; and it will be pretty sane; faculty opinion, as you'll know, has mostly been strongly with us from the beginning. Seldom a word of the L. of N. That will have its re-birth. I heard in Portugal that the Labour section was coming here from Geneva en bloc. If so, they've not advertised the fact. I should think it would be a very good move . . . to remind the Americans that the League's work was a success—when they took something like their due share in it.

Well, our affection to you and yours. For all my useless-ness—and though I don't really like bombs—I wish I were with you.

As ever,

H. G-B.

---

1. Gilbert Murray was awarded the Order of Merit in the New Year Honours List of 1941.

BOD/TCC
To Barker

[Oxford]
7th February 1941

My dear Harley,

I am so glad to hear from you. I heard some time ago that you had reached Lisbon, but after that all was darkness.

I am not surprised that the Ministry preferred that you should stay in America. They seem to attach great value to having the right kind of people there, not extremists of the Left or Right, who could give some intelligible account of things. They asked me to go, but partly I felt I was a little elderly for so much travel, and partly I did not wish to leave Mary in the blitz. We have exported two grandchildren who are staying with the Frankfurters at Washington, and a number of great-nephews and nieces who are with the Kenneth Websters at Milton, Mass.

Very interesting what you say about the anti-war movement among students. It is like the queer Communist movement in the universities here, not numerous or important, but apparently exercising a fascination on a certain type of clever intellectual with no experience of life. The Master of Balliol referred to them as "an intelligentzia [*sic*] of the worst type". On the whole, the impression here is of the great unanimity of the country as a whole, the enormous popularity of Winston, and a sort of enthusiasm for the King and Queen as they turn up in the bombed areas everywhere and talk in a friendly way to the people.

I am fairly busy. I broadcast to Australia and the Empire and talk about Greece and write. I have also translated the "Antigone" and will send you a copy when it comes out. I wonder what you will think of it as a play. It seems to me splendid for the first two-thirds and then suddenly it goes wrong, perhaps because all the interesting characters disappear. It is rather like the loss of interest in the "Hippolytus" after Phaedra's death, but there the play has time to recover.

Yes, it is a good business that the I. L. O. has gone to McGill[1] and the non-political League work to Princeton. I am greatly hoping that the C. I. P. will find roots in America also. Bonnet is there and the American National Committee has always been very efficient. If I were to go out, it would be for the C. I. P.

It is a queer life we lead. It seems to me that the odds have always been against us and still are, but we have won in spite of the odds so far, and that is a good sign for the future.

Yours ever,
G. M.

---

1. The headquarters of the International Labour Office of the League of Nations was moved from Geneva to McGill University in Montreal, Canada.

BOD/MS
To Murray

Belmont Hotel,
Sidmouth,
Devon.
January 9 [1946]

My dear G. M.,

So you're 80!—and I gather that if you didn't go out of your way to tumble downstairs no-one would suspect it. But I begin to claim quite a long acquaintance with you. Do you remember a one-armed Pathan who did a turn of pretty sound work for you sometime in the last century at Glasgow? Sir, was that not I? And though my memory isn't what it was (I'm more eightyish than you, I suspect) I can look out of window here and be appropriately reminded of

> Bird of the sea rocks, of the bursting spray,
> O, halcyon bird!
> That wheelest crying, crying on thy way . . .

—though there I may stick. A good chorus!

You're really mended, I hope and that the news is even better than that. We were at Oxford the other Sunday and I was nearly looking in on you; but you weren't receiving. We're in refuge here till the English and the French governments between them will let us go back to Paris and our possessions there (5 years in our trunks!). Lady Mary's well, I hope. We both send her, and you too, our very warm regards.

Yours,
H. G-B.

And I send you a long-delayed book.

This, apart from a disconnected fragment of a letter about Coriolanus (which Purdom quotes; see Harley Granville Barker, *p. 275), is the last letter between Barker and Murray which has yet come to light. After some further delay in England, Helen and Harley Granville-Barker returned to their apartment in Paris. Barker, however, was already a sick man, and died in Paris on August 31, 1946. Murray died in 1957, Lady Mary having predeceased him by a year.*

 # Chapter VI

Helen Huntington, 1867–1950

H*elen Huntington, married* to a millionaire husband and living the stuffy, suffocating life of one of the leaders of New York society, was forty-eight years old when she first met Barker. He was more than ten years her junior, had a tremendous reputation in his own field, and, in spite of his self-doubting and introspection, was possessed of a personality both powerful and charming. So far as theater and the arts were concerned, her approach was a purely conventional one for the time in which she lived: to her, the highest art, the profoundest art—and the most respectable—was literature. The theater was "serious" and could be regarded seriously only to the extent to which it embraced serious literature: it was seen as performing the functions—not dishonorable, but certainly secondary—of good illustrations in a novel. In one of her own early novels (*The Sovereign Good*, of 1908), there is a young hero who is a poet. He writes (at the age of twenty and with remarkable ease) a verse play about Ludwig of Barvaria, which he submits to the leading New York actor of the day. The scene in which he goes to see the actor (and his mistress) about the play is very revealing. Helen Huntington treats the young author with admiration and perfect seriousness; the play (being about a "serious" subject) she treats with a ridiculous awe ("It is as good as anything Stephen Phillips ever wrote," she makes one character say about it—though, before becoming too scornful, one must remember Phillips' reputation at the time).[1] The two theater people, however, she mercilessly satirizes, and her satire is of stereotypes rather than of real

---

1. Stephen Phillips (1864–1915) had been extravagantly hailed, on the production of his first two plays–*Herod* in 1901 and *Paolo and Francesca* in 1902—as the writer who would bring poetry back into the English theater. It took the more perceptive critics only a little while to realize the error of this judgment, and Phillips's reputation had already begun to decline by the time Helen Huntington wrote *The Sovereign Good*.

Helen Huntington, in a New York magazine portrait, about 1910.

people. Apparently she had, both by upbringing and natural inclination, an antipathy for actors. Barker was the exception; but Barker
had just finished directing the three most striking Shakespeare productions of the day and was also known as the director of five or six of
Gilbert Murray's translations from the Greek. He had, moreover, written plays himself—serious and important plays—and this last may first
have drawn her attention to him.

It took the combined forces of Barrie, Shaw, and Galsworthy
the whole of 1916 to persuade Lillah McCarthy to agree to a divorce,
Barker fretting and chafing the while and shuttling back and forth
across the submarine-ridden Atlantic. In America, Helen Huntington
was faring little better. Archer Milton Huntington had no special wish
to give up his wife of twenty years' standing to the very man whose
1915 theatrical venture in New York, he, Huntington, had helped to
finance. However, in 1917 both decisions were taken, and the ponderous (and slightly farcical) double-barreled legal machinery was put in
motion. Huntington, presumably to avoid local "talk" in New York
(*his* part of New York City being, in fact, a very small town), chose to
conduct the divorce proceedings in Paris. Both Barker and Lillah were
represented by London lawyers. Early in 1918 Helen crossed from
New York to London. So that they could meet inconspicuously,
Barker arranged for her to live at the Earl's Court Hotel in Tunbridge
Wells, thirty-five miles southeast of London. He chose Tunbridge
Wells, apparently, because he had happy memories of the town from
his childhood and from his early days in the theater. Barker himself,
with the rank of lieutenant, was working in the intelligence section of
the War Office in London. He went down to Tunbridge Wells at the
weekends to see Helen; sometimes they also met mid-week in London.
And from early April until their marriage on July 31, 1918, he wrote to
her almost every day, often two or three times in the same day. He
wrote, immediately upon rising in the mornings, from his room in
Gordon Square; he wrote during his lunch break at the Garrick Club
in Garrick Street (not ten minutes' walk from his office); and after
dining with Barrie (often) or Galsworthy or Archer or Shaw, he wrote
again. The letters are all on the same thin, lined, office stationery,
scribbled at great speed, the thoughts tumbling headlong onto the
paper. The handwriting, never very clear even at the best of times,
becomes almost impenetrable in these letters, none of which is dated.
In two or three of them, the date is mentioned in the text; in two or
three others a rough date can be established by a passing reference
("May is half over"; "June is near"; "Oh dreary-dayed April"; etc.);
in some the mention of war events fixes the date. The order in which
the letters here appear must, nevertheless, be treated as highly conjec-

tural. Helen Huntington's replies appear to be lost, as do some of Barker's letters to her. The ones here reproduced are the ones held by the Humanities Research Center: over the years they must have been shuffled and re-shuffled—whether by Helen herself or by later collectors and archivists it is impossible to say. But the earliest, in date order, rank as numbers 34 to 40 (out of a total of 61) in file order; the first in file order is the 38th in the conjectural date order; and the final ones (in date order), which I conjecture were written between July 1 and July 11, are—so far as their order on file is concerned—numbers 20, 60, 58, 26, 49, and 50.

Apart from their personal content, the Huntington letters have some importance in two other regards: they indicate that Barker regarded his *writing* as his most important work, not his directing of plays (of which—even when he is talking about what he ought to do and what life should be like—there is scarcely a mention); and they give a very vivid sense of what a sensitive (and half-guilty) non-combatant felt about the war and what life in the London of World War I (the "Great War") was like—remarkable as much for the extent of its ordinary, normal proceedings as for its strange and extraordinary ones; and it is the daily juxtaposition of the two that is so poignant. These letters provide one of the best documents I know on the day-to-day life of the city in that strange and terrible time.

The letters are desperate with impatience and frustration and yet are curiously sexless (even allowing for an altered sense of proprieties from 1918 to the 1980s). The almost deliberate counterpointing of private fears and aspirations with the last big German offensive, and the equating of Barker's own volatile nature with the swaying struggle on the Western Front from April to July, lends both a sense of urgency and a sense of design to the letters, as well as giving them depth and dignity. There are, of course, some unintended ironies here and there, partly resulting from the gap of time that separates us from the England of 1918, but partly also from some curious contradictions in Barker's own makeup: "if we are content with household life at its simplest" meant limiting the domestic staff to a butler and a cook. His views on political questions, too, are an interesting mixture of naïveté, perceptions both sensitive and tough-minded, received wisdom, and the instinctive snobbery of his kind and class. And much the same can be said of his patriotism, which is sometimes downright embarrassing in its schoolboy vindictive partisanship but is nevertheless rooted in a genuine and deeply felt sense of place—especially of the *countryside*.

Throughout, he sees his forthcoming marriage to Helen as a communion of souls and a meeting of minds. Whether it really was in the end so we do not know. One could be forgiven a suspicion, in view of the differing styles and levels of their published work in the years after the war, that perhaps that community of the intellect was in the end more imagined than real, more wished for than achieved, but that the ideal was genuine and was genuinely there in both their minds in 1918 can scarcely—in the light of these letters—be doubted. And that they remained devoted to each other at some level of sentience for the rest of their lives is also beyond question. For twenty-eight years, until his death in 1946, they were rarely apart, the frequent journeyings about the continent of Europe and between England and America always being undertaken together. And their daily routine provided, one gathers, a good deal more frequent—and longer—contacts between husband and wife than most work-a-day marriages allow (or than many marriages could stand).

The rare occasions when they were separated provide us with a few more letters, this time from her to him, written in 1940 and 1941 and showing the warmth and affection of their relationship very clearly. Some of these letters are reproduced in the second part of this chapter. It is perhaps worth reminding oneself that Helen Granville-Barker was by then (in spite of the fibs on her visa applications) a woman of seventy-three or seventy-four years of age. And one should also remember that in 1918, when those terribly *committed* letters were written to her, she was, in spite of Barker's inclination to look on her as an untouchable goddess both divine and fragile, a woman of fifty who had been married twice before, had borne (and, in effect, abandoned) a daughter, and had published several novels and several books of verse.

The artificiality of atmosphere and the over-protectiveness which had always surrounded Helen Huntington is reflected in a curious and rather embarrassing letter from her mother, Ellen Maria Gates (1835-1920), to Barker. The letter bears no detailed address and no date, though it could not have been written before mid-1916 or later than mid-1917. It is in an envelope marked "Personal" and directed to "Mr. Granville Barker." Though no address follows Barker's name, the envelope has a postage stamp on it; but the letter has not been through the mail and the stamp is not canceled.

TEX/MS
From Ellen M. Gates to Barker

New York City
[1916]

My dear Harley,

I have been sitting here with my pen suspended above my paper because it is so hard to know just what to say to one who has so suddenly and silently precipitated himself into my life. And yet somehow when I read your letter, I seemed to have known you since the beginning of the years, <u>my</u> years. And now that there is so much to say to you shall I talk a little of myself and more about Helen. Often in my thoughts of her I call her "<u>My</u> <u>dear</u> <u>little</u> <u>girl</u>" and O what a dear sweet little girl she was, you will live to know. A little about her first years: of course she was a wonderful baby, and her father and I were so proud of her.

Well, we left the little western city where she first drew breath and came to the city of Elizabeth, near New York, I think in her 3rd year. She was a little lonesome at first but I did not rest until I found playmates for her and then my whole house became a playground. There were dolls galore and each big medallion figure on the gay parlor carpet was a home for her paper dolls, whom she arranged in "families". One day I asked her why she made such a fuss when I walked through the rooms. She said: "Why Mama, you disturb my families"—the Fitzgeralds and the de Veres and such high-sounding names.

Surely she had a happy childhood. Once when I shut her in a closet, because she had been naughty, and had just closed the door, I opened it to see what made her so very silent. Her face was radiant and she said, "I have had such a beautiful time, I played I was Leonora in the blue tower." She had forgotten why she was in the dark.

Ah! do look out of this window! Central Park is glittering in the sun. If you could come into this smallest of all my rooms which with a sort of pride I call my office, how easy it would be to talk over with you the old times and the new. We are already good friends and between us there is—I hope—both affection and deep understanding. The fact is that I am so "full of days" that there cannot be many years of them left to me now, but dear Harley, there's something beautiful in life's late afternoon. Nothing can disturb me now as it may have done in my younger years. I have suffered much, enjoyed much and I know what living means. I have been in one way particularly blest. My husband, Helen's father, was one of God's dear children, king of himself, proud as a prince, yet with that sweet humility which all great people have and O we were such good friends, he and I. We called each other all sorts of funny names, according to the occasion: I will not tell you all the queer names I answered to when we were alone, but when others were present, I called him Mr. Gates. But Harley, he is dead. Up at beautiful Audubon in one of the Trinity Church yards he lies at peace, dear hands across his heart; and when I go there now, not a leaf stirs on his grave—but someday I shall go and snuggle down in my place close to him and together we will wait the last great trumpet call.

I must not fail to speak of that strange man Milton.[1] He is a perpetual wonder and I am sure that there's no living creature whom he respects, and more than respects, like Helen. He comes here often. Sometimes he arouses my wrath, but it passes in a moment, for he really is so unusual, so many streaks of black beside the golden ones. And he must make a stepping stone of his late, great loss. He does not seem to know just what to do with his time, although he says he is beset by people who want him to do something. I want him to be something, and he knows this and I shall keep on with this plan. I can think of nothing which would please me more than to have him find a big, tactful, beautiful mate for him, someone to make him forget all others. By the way, he says only sweet and generous things of you and he "does hope Helen will be happy". But Happiness! Let me say it again, it has fled from the earth in this war. I fear I have tired you to the bone. Have I? I send this letter to you alone. I shall not read this letter myself—I suppose it is full of repetitions.

Do not forget to write to me and to send me your likeness—the idea of not knowing how you look!

Faithfully,
Your mother, perhaps, someday

I greatly like "Along Fifth Ave".[2] I think of it often, the little wind-driven soul! and yours too.

---

1. Archer Milton Huntington.
2. She means *Souls on Fifth,* a long short story by Barker which was published as a

booklet by Little, Brown in 1916–17. The story is a rather sentimental fantasy, and the "little wind-driven soul" is one of the characters in it.

Barker's 1918 letters to Helen read, in a way, like one very long love letter—too long, perhaps, for anyone to read except the person to whom it was originally sent. The following, therefore, is a sampling only, avoiding to some extent the repetition inherent in the form (a love letter, after all, is not designed to say—at least as its primary function—anything new: its main purpose is to assure the recipient that what was said before is still true). Of the sixty-one letters which have been preserved, some twenty-five are reproduced here, spread out fairly evenly over the period from April to July and chosen partly for the many references to the immediate happenings of the time and partly for the comments on future work and prospects. Before the selection was made, a conjectural order of writing was established for all the sixty-one existing letters: the twenty-five here given have been kept in their correct places, relative to each other, in that conjecturally established order.

April, 1918

TEX/MS
To Helen Huntington

Friday, 7.45 A.M.
My darling love: Such a sense of you all about me. Are you still asleep? Have you slept well? My own, God keep you and send you a good day. I feel you'd like a letter—would you? A week since you came: a week! So long it has seemed—no—so short and yet so long since you came, as if you had always been here. That's how things will be for us always, I think. They'll have that mysterious "double time" (proper to the drama—therefore proper to the right conception of life as "interpreted life"!). And I have a thought for you—which came partly as we talked last night—partly as I walked back—and then more completely this morning as I woke but not completely even now. Something for you to complete—our way of thought, that. It came to you—that now love's task had begun. And so to me, darling, it comes, but not with "task" in the thought—that now begins the time for us when love shall express itself through other things than loving.

      You know, darling, this is different but a part of the same thought—springs from it rather—it is our privilege—perhaps a rare one—to visualise our life, beloved, not our "lives". Most people

perhaps do things bull-at-a-gate by some instinct and never know
what they have done and why till after, long after, if ever. Or some
have mental plans only: they are the "worldly wise"—a very incomplete sort of wisdom. But we, don't you think, going as our spirits
lead yet "visualise"—it seems like a "sensitiveness" to the future—as
if our spirits had long antennae they put out. Yes, I do think that a
privilege; but like all privileges it may be sometimes a burden to the
spirit too. We see but stop and question: will see weaker things in
us—the "unseeing" things—sustain the vision. Darling, some people
only need faith on Sundays and some on quarterdays (when dividends
are paid!)—for quarter days rather. And some only, it seems, about
once a lifetime. But vision calls for faith every day.

No, I can't say "task". (Is it too New England for me? Oh,
but I love your New Englandism as I love all of you, all in you.) I
can only say expression. And I think the reason is that I don't want
to acquire—us to acquire— objective virtues. I don't want the directing power inside me, wherever it lives (where does it live, the everyday commonplace directing power? Not in the head but possibly just
where the top ribs meet in front!) I don't want it to say I love her—
now I will learn to pour out tea really well. Not that I mind tasks—
but my way of doing a task has always to be the forgetting that it is a
task, wanting to do it for its own sake, then losing myself in it. So
now all I want is that into "for its own sake" (the pouring out of tea
really well—I have just poured out mine—hence the simile) should
melt always something of "for Helen's sake".

Sweetheart but we must be patient. I don't mean patient
with "things". For there's the war—which as it is beyond us to settle
except by giving our mites obediently as we are told and as unques-
tioningly as we can—to teach us one great patience with things. But
harder, don't you think, sometimes to be patient with ourselves—to
realise that our natures work more slowly than our desires for them
travel—and always must, but the more surely for that. But not to be
troubled because they, the complex ancestor-made things they are,
must find "their" own path in their own time. Enough if we know
that our spirit rules—as it does—and points the path.

My sweet, my dear, does this sound as if I were sad for
you? No—No—but it may be the other half of something in your
mind, the whole of it belonging to our mind then.

And oh, my Helen must never be impatient with herself.
Our spirits together go the quick way. And when there is a slower
way for the rest of us, oh darling, we must go the pace that I can go
with you—every step of the way.

My own—my dear—till I see you—quite soon. How good!

God keep you. I love you dearly dearly dearly—heart and mind and body and soul.

My Helen.

Later—a little. Beloved, I shall try and come earlier tonight: 6.30: I shall try.

My own.[1]

---

1. The monogram of interlinked Hs above is used throughout his letters to her. It is here reproduced actual size from one of the letters. It varied, of course, from letter to letter, since he obviously dashed it off as a signature. She occasionally, but not invariably, uses it as a signature in her letters to him in the 1940s. A formalized version of it was also used as a badge in all the books which each of them published from 1918 onward.

TEX/MS
To Helen Huntington

Saturday, 7.20 A.M.
My darling: the <u>love</u> of you like a "presence" now—and to wake in the morning and feel you are near, actually near—you. But the care of you too, Helen; for I know—I know even I—relaxing—feel as if I had been beaten all over these last weeks and only "sympathetic" as the doctors say. I think you must lie very straight and still on that sofa and I must hold your hand and not even be allowed to kiss you too much—not yet. And though we'll make plans, we'll make them slowly (what <u>I</u> call slowly, not being the most patient of mortals; though patience might have been learnt these years.) I have the plans. They are like rabbits in a hutch and must only be allowed to pop out one at a time—plans from "Mop"[1] upward.

Darling love, I can't write with an entirely sober "balance" for I'm looking even at pieces of furniture and inkpots with a quite ridiculous pleasure and, I feel (suddenly one "feels" one's face), with a smile. Ridiculous from their point of view; why should I take a sudden pleasure in the ink pot! <u>It</u> doesn't know that it has become quite a wonderful inkpot—now you are here. And I try to promise that you should always have letters sent to you in the middle of the day. But as it is a specially long time to this evening—and oh but I

do want to be sitting by my dear—this till I do, my dear. My dear—
my dear. Beloved.

If you would like to please me you will sample what I send
you—Brand's Essence—and take a spoonful whenever you can't
think of anything else to do. That is how it should be taken. One act
of Deburau[2] I read last night and yes, it is charming. Did this strike
you: it is Sacha's "Cyrano"—obviously suggested by that. And as
moonlight unto sunlight of course, but charming. Oh, beloved, I love
you and you are so beautiful and dear. But I want you to be in such
beautiful places. Still, Brown's is harmless and inoffensive, as hotels
go. I think you must order eggs and grilled sole to eat and you can
still get good oysters if you take oysters. But grilled sole is the thing.
Make them get you a large sole because they grill better—this is wisdom learnt at my club. And then bananas and Cheshire cheese can
still be had and that is good and good for my beloved.

There'll be grey days for a little now and chill but that is
best. Warm weather now would undo us (wisdom culled from Hopher
Wheeler and his garden[3]) but England shall be very beautiful for you,
my own. Don't fear.

Helen—sweetheart—beloved—my Helen: take care of yourself till I come; in, oh, just a few hours' time now. How good; how
better; soon to be best. My darling, I love you.

---

1. Mop, Helen's dog, was with her in Tunbridge Wells: he must have been acquired
   after she arrived in England since, if he had been brought from America, the draco-
   nian quarantine laws would have forbidden his being with Helen for the first six
   months of his stay in the country.
2. *Deburau,* a play by Sacha Guitry about the great French nineteenth-century mime
   Jean Gaspard Deburau, had very recently (1918) been produced in Paris, and Barker
   was beginning to think of translating it and making a version for the English stage.
3. Dr. Charles Edwin Wheeler, Barker's friend of many years' standing, was a homeo-
   pathic surgeon who also translated some plays from the German (e.g., Hauptmann's
   Das Friedensfest); Barker played the part of Robert in this translation in 1900, and it
   was through this production that he first met Wheeler. Though his name was Charles,
   Wheeler was known to his friends as Christopher, and, playing on this name, Barker
   invented the affectionate nickname of "Hopher." See also Chapter V, letter to
   Murray, February, 1911.

TEX/MS
To Helen Huntington

Sunday morning, 7.30.
My own, my darling: Welcome to Tunbridge Wells. Even if I'm not
there to kiss you a welcome, my spirit shall be. And with a clairvoy-
ant eye you could see several phases of your own dear love (is he?)

on the common or in the streets. When he was ten or eleven he used to be brought for Easter or Whitsuntide to the Spa. That was the thing in those days (so queer it seemed, going back there). In the year of grace 1891 my first theatre tour took me there. We played at the Town Hall down by the station—there was no theatre. And at various times since I have been through it—bicycled—walked—motored. Various Harleys are to be found there. But the nett result of all the Harleys, which is about half your Harley (the rest and the best is your love for him), will be there soon, too. My darling.

I hope you'll have your proper rooms in the hotel <u>soon</u>. Very necessary you should take in the sun whenever the sun comes— whenever he is anywhere he'll be there. And be out lots and tell my English country plainly what you think of it and it will only tell you how it loves you—you are its child too.

I wish you could have a car all the time, for the Wells <u>is</u> built round now, of course; and while a car would take you to real woods and fields in ten minutes now you'll have to devise a little. But I think leasings will be possible—a car to a definite place when you want definitely to go there—and drivings of various sorts: a horse, a pony; war hasn't exhausted all the possibilities. And to walk turn to the <u>right</u> when you leave the hotel and that takes you along the top of the common to Rusthall—more common and fields and woods soon.

Beloved, what a new facet of the world, isn't it? For <u>us</u>. The world's only round when it's geographical, but if you add time and humanity to it, then it has facets. And here we are with a new horizon which may take in France and America: <u>will</u>, we almost know. And yet be a new world—God send a good world to you in every single thing. My darling we can make it so, I know; and not by conscious effort but just that our love will make it so—<u>does</u>—does turn all it touches to goodness and graciousness.

I won't boast; for indeed I'm very humble about loving you—humble and proud. I know how little there still would be in me—though giving and being all I can—if you didn't call it forth by loving me—give it me and then call it back. Not boast or promise, but I <u>do</u> <u>know</u>. My dear is to get strong and all herself in simple, ordinary ways. And even that not by an effort: that will come with all the other realities.

At the office: 4.30 P.M.

My darling, in two hours I shall see you but this is for 24 hours hence: and then—a week till I see my Helen. Oh, but time isn't hard on us now is it? Not so hard. For now, though we're kept apart still and it'll be hard—yes darling—yet we've the time between us: it's <u>our</u> time that has begun to be and we'll turn it to use. My Helen; my dear.

Hardly any work to do today. I'm only here like a sentry. My sentry-go is to read and read.

You'll never see my office I expect—I have had three since I came here. This is the best. Such a queer room:—

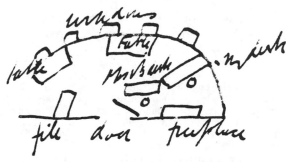

That's not a good plan. I have made the room too small, not enough of a circle, and the furniture is too large.

The door is at the end of a long corridor—100 yards exactly from my chief's room to mine. On the left as you come in the big file for papers. Then a large map of Russia on the wall. Then a table with more papers—also with my tea on it at present. Then the windows come—5 windows with a wonderful view east along the Thames, if only the stone diamonds didn't block it out. Another table with trays on it for putting more papers in—more maps—my desk— another map—the fireplace behind me—another map. All rather grubby and plain; but there are some branches of palm in one corner and some yellow tulips just above my head—I have established a "flower fund". And I wish only that the work were more real and that I had more power to do it. But there it is—I am on sentry-go. "They also serve . . . etc".

I sometimes feel that for my own work I shall be stupid for quite a long time after this is over. But one is experiencing—and you'll be patient with a stupid love, even if he seems a rather lazy love that doesn't even talk. But oh, my own, we can talk or we can sit silent together and say almost as much thinking <u>our</u> thoughts.

Not a letter this at all—I can't write a letter when I'm going to see you. But just for you to find—my hands held out.

Now you're to <u>eat</u> and <u>sleep</u> and take long draughts of air— lung fulls—to put on a pound's weight a week; and darling, think then, when you have put on 20 pounds, about that time. Helen be- loved—so near you are—so sweetly near—a gentle presence with me always and a flame—for remember I always said the spirit of you burnt like a steady flame for me. I do thank God for you—with all I do and all I am; and thank him most that now, from now, I can live for you—be your love.

My darling, my darling, don't be lonely. I'm not far. At any minute you can send—Nellie[1] can ring up—I can be with you at the end of the day. And soon—soon I'll come—week ends won't be long apart.

Helen darling—I love you with mind and body and heart and soul—all—all I am—my Helen—best beloved.

---

1. Helen's companion (and, in effect, servant) was Nellie Dickinson. Her name, given as Helen T. Dickinson, appears on the certificate as one of the witnesses at the marriage of Helen Huntington and Barker on July 31, 1918. She is also mentioned, long before, as an "old friend" in a letter from Helen Huntington to Caroline Densmore Huntington, written from Madrid on March 22, 1896. Evidently she was seconded in 1918 to accompany Helen Huntington from New York to London. (Caroline Densmore Huntington [1861–1954] was Helen's cousin: from girlhood onward these two maintained a lively and friendly correspondence for the whole of their long lives, though in later life they rarely met. Much of what we know of Helen's early life and of her first two marriages comes from her letters to Caroline, the first of which is dated June 8, 1883. These letters are now in the Huntington Library.)

TEX/MS
To Helen Huntington

Monday morning, 7.45.
Darling love: This is a "tomorrow's" letter already—rather a shock to think of the 24 hours between us again. But it has been 48 and more and so much more; we are bringing it down to its proper zero.

This not a proper letter either but just a note which says I'll see you on Sunday, my darling. And two things about that—if you can't get a motor, the man who hires them near Hopher could probably do it all—fetch you—bring you—take us back. But, says Hopher, it would be extravagant—four journeys instead of two and he charges by the mile; running into 50 miles, 1/2[1] a mile, I think—you have come to an economical country you see. But—a motor somehow: far too cold to drive open unless it is very fine and too boring to drive (horse drive) closed and we do want to go and look at Bolebrook. Not much out of the way for a car but too far for a horse. The second thing: the map—Mop and I will walk to meet you along the road I mark—rain or fine—only less far if rain, perhaps, for a thoroughly damp love and damp dog (if you mercifully took them into the car with you for the rest of the way) might give you cold!

And did Hopher win you? I hope; I think. Not a word did

he say about you as we walked back. But then he wouldn't; it is not his nature to. In the first place such a curiously gentle mind—humble not at all the word, but "unegoistic" quite the thing. And he'd feel to say one word of "approval", anything so tame, of someone all the world to me was most out of place. But beyond that this characterises him. He accepts—or not; and down he settled right away into that. One knew (and he had done through me by instinct). Further and deeper things are very inside things with him—things he is and does and you tell them by that which he never speaks of. But he is the real thing in men in all the "human" aspects and I hope he did win my darling. But I thought so, for I thought she looked happily at me for that too.

But I am going to scold. You must not do too much at once: church, a concert, two walks and Hopher to dinner. No: well, yes perhaps; and I won't scold for we'll so soon get your dear body right so that it shan't tire foolishly (our foolish bodies!) And I love—I love to see your spirit (my beloved, my darling, I love you) coming so to life. So now, eat and sleep and breathe lung fulls of air and you shall do all you want to.

At the Club: 2 o'clock.

My own, I shall look out of my window at 6 o'clock and see your train pass close beneath me.[2]

Here is a map and the road marked that you should follow on Sunday to Ashurst. As a matter of fact I shall walk further along the road to the Wells to meet you for the turn up to Hopher's, marked with an x, comes half a mile back: but Ashurst church as a rendezvous in case. And it is not more than 5 miles there from the Wells and not more than another 2 on to Bassetts (Bassetts Farm, Cowden). So, certainly you can get a taxi and if not it is a reasonable "horse" drive and if not (again) the fetching by Hopher's man quite possible. So rest all the week and our Sunday shall be good. God send sunshine.

My darling—my darling—I love you dearly with all—all I am. I love you.

---

1. That is, one shilling and twopence.
2. His room at the War Office overlooked Charing Cross Station.

TEX/MS
To Helen Huntington

Wednesday, 6.45 A.M. [April 10, 1918]
My darling: Well, at least I'm up early. But this is a very dreary
world without you and it seems ages from Sunday and ages <u>to</u> Sunday
and a dreary world for you too I fear, all grey and cold. And this is
April 10, a very deceiving date.

But here's an end to my grumbling for oh, my dear, the
casualty lists of the big battle are coming in: you see them and the
way people are suffering. The enormous number of missing and the
uncertainties of that are worse, in a way, for the people at home.
Mr. Scott's son (Scott of the M. G.,[1] one of the best of men), Mrs.
L. M.[2] tells me last night—I saw her for half an hour when I came
in—was in an observation post when the thing started, right down
at St. Quentin. Nothing more known. That's where I should quite
likely have been had I been sent out observing for guns.[3] But you
know, people in general have got to a sort of callous deadness of
suffering, as if they couldn't feel any more. And I believe that again
makes it worse. How long? Odd how our feelings are "blended"—
personal—national—international—humanity in general (these
aren't the right categories). But I had a flashing vision of your
"blend" just as I first thought of that—too stupid in the head your
dear love is to write it "right". We'll talk it through—for it is interesting—how people vary their blends from time to time and cause
to cause.

Diary for my dear: well, I think that nothing happened
yesterday <u>at all</u>. It was a heavyish day at the office; so as far as that
is concerned it went through quickly. I saw du Maurier at the club
and gave him Deburau. He hasn't enterprise enough to do it, I expect, but he seems the only possible person. At 7 I took a conscientious walk round the Park to get some air, dined at the club, talked a
little to Antony Hawkins and Buckmaster and an unknown. Buckmaster by the way was in Paris during the bombardment and said that
the church hit was "St. Juvais", just behind the Hotel de Ville.
(Darling, it is grey and dark; but what I shall do is to put on a coat
and trousers and take a swift oxygenating walk—less the oxygen, of
which there is little enough in poor London.)

At the Club: 1.10 P.M.
Your dear letter and an English stamp on it (that's a comfort!)—oh, so good to get it this morning. It lightened the skies,
darling. Dreary for you the skies are though, I fear. London is dreary
without you, God knows; dreary in itself too and a grim time it is.

One has to bend one's best and surest thoughts on things and we must—oh, thank God we can—comfort each other.

James Gray[4] a success—that's good. So you'll stick to him now. Much better you should as you like him. Professionally he must be first class.

Helen my own, it seems ages since you went and yet this is only your second day at "The Wells". I caught myself asking then "Why don't I know more of your doings": then I remembered

Leave at 11 on Sunday, please, for I want every minute.

The Earls Court:[5] oh, "hotellish", I know. Perhaps you could find "rooms". First rate rooms would be much pleasanter. But war-time conditions—we must make allowances; and a hotel is "safe" for food service, such as it is.

Oh your picture of the old tramp picking the daffodils from the rubbish heap: what a picture! How pathetic and how meaningful!

I'll have to stop for I must lunch with William Archer and a man who wants advice about a propaganda theatre tour in neutral countries. My advice is not to play the fool. This is no time for telling Holland and Sweden that we can act plays nicely when we want to. Oh, purposeless and frivolous the people we have let get hold of us, some of them. No, not all—not all: God forbid I should say that.

My own,—my dear—my dear: four days more till I see you. No, not quite four days. But how impossible—just how impossible— to be apart. But all of me, all I can send, is with you my darling. And God is good—through all the troubles and amid all the troubles of the world, God is good to us in the real things, the final things. He has given us our love, added that "unto us" and every day a day nearer to not parting. We must be patient then.

Helen darling, I love you with all my soul and mind and heart and body—all of me. My own.

6.45

My darling—just a minute before the train goes.

I forgot to give you the possible cablegram I drafted—this just to be the sense of it—if you think well—it might ease distressing letters.

My own, God keep you and send the week quickly by. I love you. I am so happy in your love.

Take care of my Helen—all my world.

Take care of her.

My Helen.

---

1. C. P. Scott (1846–1932), editor of the *Manchester Guardian*.
2. Mrs. Lee Mathews supervised the music for some of Barker's productions of Greek

plays. She and her husband owned the house in Gordon Square in which Barker had a flat.
3. He had begun training as a gunner before obtaining his commission in Intelligence.
4. Gray was the London lawyer who had been engaged to look after Helen's interests in England.
5. The Earls Court Hotel was where Helen was staying in Tunbridge Wells. The building is still there, on the edge of the Common as Barker describes, though it is used now as the headquarters of an insurance company.

TEX/MS
To Helen Huntington

Thursday, 7.15 A.M.

Darling love: Chill—but nice sky at last and a briskness in the air. And I think—and hope—the worst of the Flanders trial past. A little too soon to say it, perhaps. And then the question—has Foch a blow to strike?[1] I have hopes, because of course I believe in the ultimate stupidity of the Germans. It is on that I would base all <u>my</u> anti-German policy. Taking them, so to speak, as "100" I believe that 1–40 perhaps is stupid, 40–65 very clever (and there they have the better of us), but 65–100 (which is what finally matters: the cream of all achievement) stupid again.

      Your dearest of dear letters arrived for dinner—just after I'd reached the club—the next best thing to having you to dine with. Oh but beloved, I am wanting <u>you</u>—I dined with a stupid book on Russia and the D. N. B.[2] instead.

      I must always do what my instinct tells me with you. Even when I was scribbling in such a great hurry the note to you before I left, I thought: I'll put in "I've left you to add your love, etc. to the cable". Then I thought no, she'll do that of herself. But darling, I wish it had been in—a cable coming from here—though not the first, is it, from here?—without what you usually put in that way, might make your mother feel (might it?) that I was trying to "turn you against her". Can we devise any other short cable that would "bring it in"? Have you anything else to say about addresses or anything? Think.

      I am very glad you sent this. I think it was quite a wise move: since you had to entrust "telling" to third parties and you can't be sure what they said: but you did think it wise yourself didn't you? Oh, I needn't ask; but I never want you to take more of my opinion—not one inch more—than <u>you</u> agree with.

      My whole opinion (about your mother) remains as I said: tell her as much as you feel you can. (Personally I should tell her all—

without detail, but all the facts. But I realise that I don't know her and can't fully judge.) But be very careful that what you leave untold doesn't mislead her about the told part. That's difficult, I know. But mistakes about it—unless she sits quite passive and says little and does nothing!—may lead to trouble of a sort—misunderstandings—

Blue sky gone but the cold wind means that it is blowing up finer, if not fine. What shall we do on Sunday? Hopher's is more or less shut off as he has Penelope's brother—a gunner major on leave—down there. Poor Hopher: Penelope is stuck in France—can't get away yet—and he is very "low".[3] Of course, we'll be slaves of the weather and trains on a Sunday are difficult. I'll look up at lunch time and see what we could do, but I expect it means your commandeering a "cab" again if you can. Then there are places, if the weather isn't utterly vile, we could go: lunch—walk—back! But oh, beloved, we must have our day.

My sweetheart, never think for one minute, for one second that you must try or want to try to drive your mind in harness with mine. (Think how much duller for me if you did! Not, however, that you well could since your mind is much your own mind, producing its own images, not reflecting others.) But I felt you give a little wince almost of fear as I handed you those pamphlets. There was no "afore thought" in bringing them. I happened to find them on my table as I was packing to come away. All my afore-thought was "They're quite interesting, therefore why not give them to her? Why 'fear' to?" No, just this darling I would say: we must never fear ideas because we feel we can't agree with them or ever feel (either) that agreement is necessary. In fact, we can only add to the world's stock by disagreement. But first one must understand what people are trying and wanting to say and do. Heaven knows I don't agree—I'm not now talking of "Labour" policy but of any of the future policies. I don't agree with them en bloc. I still do mightily quarrel with the "spirit" of the Labour people; I think it is too material, too "mob". But if I don't clearly and sympathetically understand, my criticism will be of no value.

And this is true about us, beloved. I think our tendency will always be towards the past, for there completeness lies and in completeness lies beauty. Therefore we must always guard against forgetting the future for it, for if we do we might as well be dead and not alive at all. Breakfast and the paper.

At the Club, 2.15 P.M.

Best beloved, I fear that to get out of T. Wells on a Sunday a motor is the only way. But there are quite good places we could go to—if the weather has lifted at all, and I think pretty surely it will have—and not far. Lamberhurst on one side and Withyam on the other (with Buckhurst Park to walk in) or Penshurst. We could lunch there either at the Inn (very simple!!) or, taking our lunch if it were really fine enough, walk a little (not too much for my beloved) and then drive back.

But as to the cab then will you—if _you_ like this—see what can be done? Trains are hopeless.

My dear one, the week is long again even though the days are busy. Are yours? No, but occupied. And please be ravenous and sleep sound (do you sleep?) and get well and strong. That is your best service to the state at this minute. Work will come and the service of that, don't fear.

My mind isn't quite clear yet as to the furnished house—flat—hotel question so that I won't write confusedly. But we will talk it well out on Saturday. For God knows it is hard enough to be apart and we must have every moment with each other that _is_ possible—we must plan for that.

My darling—my darling—only two more days without you now. (Oh, if that were _really_ so.) God keep you. Take care of my Helen—_my_ Helen.

Helen, darling.

Friday night, 7.15, at the office.

My darling—my Helen: N. D. rang me up[4] and I met her (very peacocky) and got your dearest of letters warm from my darling's heart—oh, warm to mine.

This to find you tomorrow—then comes Sunday. Oh, beloved, the time it has been. But you have had sunshine today. And N D says your appetite is good, that you dispute with her for the last "pertater". I said—in Regent Street—NO Nellie, potato.

Oh sweetheart, sweetheart—and I've only time for this scribble—a longish day—an interrupted afternoon and I must be off to dinner with Norman Wilkinson, once my designer of scenery (the Midsummer Night's Dream), now a Lance-Corporal.

Keep a stout heart over the war news. Yes, it is grave; but it can be a lot worse without being disastrous. And anything short of final absolute smashing conquest is disastrous for Germany. We have just to hold and hold—to stand to our guns, of every sort.

My darling—I hold both your dear hands—I hold you close. Oh, soon I shall again sleep sound and wake with happy eyes. I kiss you for goodnight and good morning and all I am is yours.

My Helen—beloved.

1. Ferdinand Foch (1851–1929) had recently (March, 1918) been appointed Commander-in-Chief of the Allied armies.
2. *Dictionary of National Biography*.
3. Penelope was C. E. ("Hopher") Wheeler's wife. (See also Chapter V, footnote to letter of October 25, 1907, and *passim*.)
4. Nellie Dickinson.

TEX/MS
To Helen Huntington

Wed. morn.: 7.30

My darling: what weather—what times—what everything! You didn't get a chill did you? (I ought not to have walked you so far. That might have been forgiven, but the vile journey back!) And did you stay tucked up warm yesterday? London's depressed—you may guess, what with Flanders and the Service Bill, which, as I've said, were it the wisest bill in creation nobody trusts the government to administer. Oh, the lesson of this war for democracy if democracy will learn it—will survive to learn it, you'll say? Yes I think it will survive—though not by much in France and England. But—must learn it, I say. At any rate I must, for I won't let myself become mentally either Prussian or Bolshevik, the two ends of the scale, the two short-cut methods. No, not either for my mind. But oh, the thinking and understanding and fore-seeing that has to be done. One wonders often enough in these times—times like these Flanders weeks—what one's "destiny" is, or should be (there's always choice in destiny) among all those boys and men who destine themselves to die. I asked my chief yesterday whether he didn't think I ought to try and finish my gunnery training and get a chance to fire a gun! "A hell of a lot of use you'd be", was all he said; which was cheering in one sense for I didn't feel destined to fire guns. But I do wish I were in a lot more danger and discomfort than I am. But that's not the business of war. And I am "under orders". But there's the damnable thing: one feels one could do so much more. That and a certain curious "vanity"—I am not accustomed to being in the background—the front trenches for me, so to speak. But I hardly meet a man at the front or elsewhere who has not the feeling that he is being wasted. And this is marked to be the great tragedy for England when she looks back— "All those riches of men, the only sort of riches there is and she did not know how to use them". And to cap that, one must say "You did not know how to use them in peace—you thought your riches were in other things than they. What else could you expect when war came?"

And the newspapers shouting about "our gallant army and our brave lads", <u>pretending</u> to know—only makes it worse: it comes to the men themselves as a sort of mockery. For stop reading newspapers and talk to a man fresh from fighting about what he knows and you wouldn't think you were speaking of the same war!

Well, if it is my destiny to see and understand and try and <u>say</u> how the wrong has come, how it can be made right, not portentously but so that anyone who wants to feel at all can feel and understand too, if I don't do that as if it were front trench work for the rest of my spared life, I shall be damned indeed.

At the Club, 2.30 P.M.
My darling: No letter from you. I'm a <u>little</u> worried lest you are ill or tired. Oh I must be gentler with you—not drag you for long walks. But your spirit—so "alive", my dear one—we never do think in physical limitations, do we? And the week has begun to be intolerably long again quite suddenly. Yesterday went quickly. Now here it is only Wednesday midday—three more days to run—endless they seem.

I'm disgruntled with office things today—people there behaving more "officially" than usual, which is "badly". Work—real work—isn't done on those lines. However it's the machine and I must be as good a bit of it as I can—ungrumblingly—be. Rain and chill, but the rain is fighting for us in Flanders. <u>But</u> will my dear please take care of herself, of my Helen; and wear the pink thing!

Oh my darling but it is bad being away from you. And I don't seem to have a mind to think with either, so my letters must be dreary wastes of scratches on paper. I want so to be with you. But my spirit <u>is</u> with you, beloved, my own my beautiful
<u>Helen</u>, <u>darling</u>.

TEX/MS
To Helen Huntington

Friday morning, 7.30.
Darling heart: I've been troubled rather since I wrote so hurriedly in the middle of yesterday, lest I said anything about your mother and A. H. and Archibald which will have troubled you[1]—I meant nothing to. I don't believe for a moment that A. H. could or would put any delaying spoke in the wheel of things now. And of course Archibald would tell you at once; but he <u>should</u>, I think, be keeping you well informed that things are going normally on. (But I know what these

lawyers are—all lawyers. They expect you to believe that they make
no allowance for human anxieties. Well how should they?) So I suggested a wire or a letter to him, if you have <u>not</u> heard.

And—as to your mother—I was just thinking of the shortest
way to stop a distressing correspondence, leading nowhere, either a
two-cornered or a three cornered one. But of all this we'll talk. And
indeed I <u>do</u> understand about your mother—what you have felt and
thought these last two years. She, I think, did ruthlessly—with that
"practical selfishness" of the old—what would have done itself or
have needed to be done more gently and gradually later when she
marched off to her independence and her companion. A sign of great
vitality in her of which one should be—one <u>is</u>—glad that she could
see a life for herself and straightway make it. Well, the parallel isn't a
parallel and "pointing morals" is never any good. But confronted
with the fait accompli she must just content herself with <u>your</u> judgment of your future.

Oh darling, what a "dry" beginning of a letter. But we'll
talk. Was there <u>ever</u> a week as long as this!!

Deburau hangs fire: du Maurier is slack about it—Seymour
Hicks now thinks he wants it (that means nothing to you but he
would act it with a <u>bounce</u> and offend every fibre of your taste).[2]

But <u>of</u> <u>course</u> beloved I meant we should do it together—
talking the translation out, such a good way. And good for us—for
you know we are both of us too tired to tackle a wholly creative job
at the moment. Helen too tired—Harley too war-officed.

Music here last night: I came in for most of it—here's the
programme. It was odd. I couldn't listen well and to quartets one
must be able to listen <u>well</u>. But the sound of it took me into another
world. That is so, I think; music does add another "dimension" to us.
But it's the world of "might be". I suppose what we like to call the
"future". But there are "must bes" about the future. It will have to
be a world of bigger views, of a much wider sweep of things. It is
curious—I can't <u>grasp</u> it. If I could grasp it as a whole I'd be what
the world waits for—and that I'm not!! But if only one could get
whole and entire and felt and reasoned-out one little corner of the
vision—well, that is our hope to do. But this is all that is clear to
me: it calls for a thought and an emotion that will cut <u>across</u> and
through many of the old thoughts and emotions about life. Nothing
new: oh, never <u>seek</u> for anything new—since there is nothing new in
Nature—but as Nature does, take the decayed things the "last year's
leaves"—a whole medley of things, as she does—and transmute
them into some one, living, new-born thing. Darling, darling, I love
you—that's the new born thing in our life, our last year's leaves

transmuted and made living and beautiful and that's our sign and our summons that what God has done for our lives, our inner selves, we may do in outer things.

At the Club, 9.45.

Beloved, your dearest of letters—oh dearest <u>you</u>. In 48 hours, yes, I'll be starting out to meet you. Never was such a week.

But, my darling, the E. C. Hotel—you can see me there surely, for I have this precious Monday and Tuesday and I'll get no other days I fear for long to come—except weekends—so if the E. C. <u>is</u> impossible—but don't let us waste them whatever we do.

A little sun coming for you (what a cold damp England you'll think I've given you to—like a sacrifice) and it may work up to fine weather for us, but trust no English April. And two days wet and wasted—My darling!

I shall proceed to search out the Gates family.[3] Indeed, we will possess ourselves of a D. N. B. (do you know what that is?) in 50 volumes—the most fascinating reading. And the London Library, which you had better join soon, will give you the Harleian Society's publications[4] (Yes, he was an ancestor! of a sort!)

And oh, on Sunday I see you. Take care of my Helen till then.

Don't fear about France. It is a horribly anxious time, horribly, and we must look for bad shocks and disappointments yet, but in its essentials I feel sure the line will hold—the armies will hold. Oh, but if these <u>damned</u> newspapers would stop their boasting and howling and abuse when we all do need a steady mind, a firm grip of facts. Don't read them. Read the bulletins and believe nothing else, one feels inclined to say.

My own, God keep you—I love you—oh I love you dearly, dearly, heart and mind, body and soul. My Helen—my darling love.

I incline suddenly to think that it may be better to take Monday only this week and another Monday next or later. What do you say? If I only have two days. I'll prepare for that, anyhow.

---

1. A. H. is Archer Milton Huntington; Archibald is the American lawyer in Paris who was acting for Helen in the divorce proceedings between Archer Milton Huntington and Helen.
2. Seymour Hicks (1871–1949), a popular and versatile actor-manager, also wrote a number of plays and adapted others from the French. He was knighted in 1935.
3. Helen Huntington was born Helen Manchester Gates.
4. The Harleian Society was founded in 1869 for the publication of matters relating to heraldry, family pedigree, etc. It was named after the Harley family, who were the Earls of Oxford. Barker's claim to be descended from that family seems to have no discernible basis in fact.

TEX/MS
To Helen Huntington

Monday morning, 7 A.M.
My dear, my beloved; oh, my darling: Wonderful, so wonderful, to
be near you. To be coming nearer and growing nearer—Helen, to be
giving our lives to each other. Yes, I do love you more and more and
deeper and deeper every day. Consciously I couldn't—for I loved you
with all my conscious self before—but just in surrendering oneself to
love. I do more and more deeply belong to you—my Helen—my
beautiful—my dear.

And now to show the depth of my passion I will write about
drains (not quite, but very near). This I am sure is the practical and
sensible thing for us at the moment: to take a flat if it can be got and
a house if it comes (and that designates the amount of energy you
may spend on the looking). For the flat—if one can find a really nice
one, not too dear—take it and furnish it—for London is the likeliest
place for us to have to "centre" in—for a bit anyhow—for war time.
Not to think to make it more than a pied-à-terre, not too much of a
home (a flat—we shouldn't anyhow; but it can be a refuge). Then it
wouldn't distress me to let it—one's home I should loathe letting.

As to the house, it must be in a backwards and forwards
place—let us say Groombridge[1] is the limit of in-accessibility; and it
must be easy to run and ready to run.

Now darling, if you think that wise, on that basis I'll look.
One must have a basis on which to look.

And you will please be resolute in doing nothing this week.
If any worry crops up, send for me. The office should be slacker this
week; anyhow I always—nearly always—can catch that 6 o'clock.

The German attack—oh! Do you find that the war, after
having been horribly real, now acquires an even more horrible unre-
ality? As if one had been staggered by so many blows and here was
the world going on, so many more blows possible. And if the world
could go on under these they somehow can't be real. When the Roman Empire fell I suppose they didn't notice its falling. Though even
then there must have been backward and forward seeing people who
realized—I think of a little series of plays—the receding of the Empire—the outposts given up (Masefield has done a long thing about
the Legions leaving England); but now things can be crowded into a
lifetime. It is conceivable—quite—that if this war doesn't end soon
the whole East may be ablaze. My hope is better, but it is more than
possible. One's brain staggers under the problem—mine does anyhow. But I think there is this wisdom to be plucked from it: as a

practical problem no man can grasp or solve it, to turn it to his advantage. Napoleon missed it by so much. The Germans, thinking that they in grasping the question so much more firmly and comprehensively, will yet leave out of account enough to undo them, just as Napoleon was undone. I think the only wisdom is to make, to find, your principles and apply them—whether they seem profitable or not. Principles win in the long run and if you have the right ones. . . . If not, of course. . . . But then that is where the thinkers and seers come in. Where are ours and what do they count for in the government today?

   That is my trouble of mind—first and last.

   Breakfast is coming—I shall try and give this to Nellie D at the 2 o'clock.

   My darling—God keep you. Take care of my <u>Helen</u> please. <u>I'll</u> relieve you of the worry of it soon.

   My darling—my own dear love.

At the Club, 1.45.

   Just off to catch N. D. with this—

   The only "lunch" I have this week is Thursday, beloved—that American super-journalist and the Webbs.

   I kiss you and hold you very close.

      <u>My</u> <u>Helen</u>.

---

1. Groombridge is a small village about seven miles south of Tunbridge Wells and some forty miles from the center of London.

TEX/MS
To Helen Huntington

Thursday, 7. A.M.

My darling love: It was just damnable having to leave you yesterday—unnatural. My scribble to you from the office—such a scribble even though I had my room alone—the office so office-y—I'd love you to see it—I thought of that yesterday. The room I have worked in and thought of you in so many hours—if you could see the queer papers that have accompanied thoughts of my dear. But writing to you there never "belongs" except sometimes on a Sunday when it isn't office-y at all. And it was so absurd not seeing you again yesterday—I thought as I walked back here late last night—if I'd been dashing down to dinner—or even to see you a moment on the common when you took Mop his last walk. But we don't want

"snatched" moments—they're unnatural—and the truth is that everything is unnatural for us now darling except being together all the
time—quite simply knowing that "office at 3" still means dinner at
7.30. But I didn't know whether or not to want you to be at King
Lear last night—they did it in one way so badly but they tried so
hard. When they tried innocently hard the play came through all mistakes and shortcomings; and what a play! So—yes I wished you were
there to see those bits at least. The "Blind Gloucester and mad Lear"
scene they missed by sheer bungling and misapprehension. But the
Cordelia-Lear waking scene they couldn't miss and oh, but it does
touch the sky. "But as I am a man I do believe this lady to be my
child Cordelia"; "And so I am—I am?"[1] It does just lift the heart out
of you. But the whole play—such an embodiment of a world trium-
phant under the power of evil, until evil grows megalomaniac and
destroys itself—destroys Cordelia with it, though, "I killed the slave
that was a-hanging thee." "Indeed, my lord, he did." Lear, "fourscore and upwards"—with his naked hands: what a touch!

But Regan and Goneril so reasonable and in the right—until
they've caught hold of power: Lear and Cordelia, so "impossible":
Gloucester the prosperous, respectable person! Kent! Edmund!

Of course he took an impossible story—from one point of
view. It suddenly occurs to me: is this a new observation? Almost
certainly not. Shakespeare was a hopelessly uninventive person.
When you come to think of it, what very bad stories most of them
are—he just took anything. And in Lear, as in Hamlet, the story is
always getting in the way. Edgar as Tom'o'-Bedlam: hopeless—even
Shakespeare can't do anything with it. So always, this is the producer's "tip": you have to find out—Lord, it is easy enough—what
had really interested William and bring that out, suppressing, as
much as you can, what he had found a nuisance. In Lear he got so
sick of the Fool that he dropped him half way through (though it was
an old and successful stunt of his—the fool as the semi-tragic character). Yet everybody—asses!—sees something "effective" in the
Fool and exaggerates him and throws him into relief until the play
reeks with him.

There really is not anything to do with Shakespeare except
to understand him and then to speak him beautifully. The rest is
waste of time. God knows I have wasted too much.

Grey and chill the day, darling, and not till Saturday do I
see you. Helen, darling—Nellie D—yes, I know you'll say "curse the
subject of Nellie D"—And I say so too. But just this: Nellie D must
be mitigated and we must think out quite cool-headly and cold-bloodedly how it is best and most thoroughly to be done! My plan of mix-

ing London with The Wells will do a little, but perhaps not enough,
till you can have done with "the Wells", or at any rate the E. C.
hotel. And by then I can have my other plan perhaps in being. The
"Galsworthy" plan or some equivalent. But what I principally want
you to feel, beloved, is that if Nellie is un-mitigable we can and must
"reform her altogether". We're not helplessly in her hands. There are
other things we could do and can and will, sooner than that you
should go through three months more of torturing irritation. More
than irritation darling, I know, if less than torture. I come to it fresh
once a week and of course it is a pin-prick to me—but the thousand
that it is to you, darling. I cannot have you face it unmitigated. (Oh,
I do curse myself, my Helen, that I haven't made things easier.) I do
quite see: Nellie's manners <u>are</u> getting worse—never mind the
cause—as she gets more "entêtée". Do you think the sternest and
kindest of "talking to" would have any effect (I'd undertake it—I
could find just what to say) or is she "past" that? The only automati-
cally mitigating plan I have at the moment is the flat in London
where you need not be all the time. But if that won't "mitigate"
enough, why then we'll have to do something more drastic, for I cannot and will not have my dear one scratched with briars day after day
(walking through a quickset hedge of life!). And above all you are
not to feel yourself necessarily shut in a cage with her, for that isn't
and need not be so. We are not helpless, darling.

All this not to worry you worse but just because it is in my
mind and my mind is working this way—to work with yours: together. And each day bringing us nearer—<u>altogether</u>. But oh, it is
long my darling and a damnable waiting. And I know how hard
things are beloved—only I want to be so wise for you, loving you <u>that</u>
way as well as all the others.

My darling—Oh, words so poor—But all I am loves you,
you know.

7.45 and the office calling—!

My darling, I am unhappy without you. 30 miles is 30 miles
and more. Too far. Well, we must work through these two days and
so through other twos and threes—happy, happier now God knows
that they are only twos and threes.

I wish Ada[2] would wake up and be friendly again—just for an
hour, say, now and then! But we mustn't hustle her and I want you to
have a room—a real room and more your own—to talk to her in.

Oh beloved—beloved. I send you love, and so much more
than love I want to send, if there is more in the world. Power I want
to send you.

Oh but our love is power—I only need to send love to you. To the best—to the best that is in me—that is me. I do—I do, you know. A better me you want though, darling. I try to make it for you; and loving you—your love does make a better me—all yours to serve you, my darling, <u>my darling</u>.

---

1. Cordelia's reply here ("And so I am—I am?") is in exactly the form in which Barker gives it in his letter, but it is certainly very curious. Even allowing for the fact that he was (presumably) quoting from memory, it is hard to imagine how the question mark got there or what Barker intended it to imply, either about the speaking of the line or about the character of Cordelia. It does not appear in any standard text of the play, and Barker himself makes no comment on the normal reading of the line in his own Preface to the play, published in 1927. It may, of course, be simply a momentary aberration, or even a slip of the pen, but it is worrying, nonetheless.
2. John Galsworthy's wife.

TEX/MS
To Helen Huntington

Friday, 7.30 A.M.

Good morning, my darling: The wind N E again: I don't know what that means for weather except that it is bad for flyers. Oh, well no, perhaps it only brings mist here (from the North Sea) and not in France. Things will be ding-dong there for a good while, but they (the Boches) didn't seem able to get another big swinging attack in. I don't say Amiens is safe—or the coast—the coast less so—but it is safer than it was. And if Foch is going to counter he won't counter yet so one must have patience. "We" must! Those poor devils out there must.

But—if you'd like a little dose of politics—Ireland is a bad business. I can't meet anyone enemy or friend of LG[1] (easier to meet the first now than the second) who can tell me <u>why</u> he landed himself in the mess. The only explanation given by Scott[2] was that he hoped to force Home Rule through the Lords and Ulster with conscription as a bribe, which was inept, to say the least, but Scott didn't think so (apparently—that is according to Hopher and Mr. L. M. [Lee Mathews], who saw him after he'd had a long talk with L. G.—I had seen him before).

No, I suspect Milner[3] who has a perfect genius for doing the right thing in the wrong way—no more devilishly dangerous faculty than that. He nearly brought us to utter grief in South Africa—a similar case: right end to be gained and he almost turned it into a wrong one by the wicked folly of his handling. It puts us hopelessly in the wrong anyhow. How can we say to Austria, "What about Bohemia?" Or even to Germany, "What about Poland?" (though the Poles are biters bit anyhow) with such a report to their hand? And no need—that's the amazing thing—an almost gratuitous blunder. And now the Times—by way of doing something really clever—starts an anti-Popery cry. Oh, my country!

Mudies catalogue: yes, indeed.

Frederic Harrison[4] will be rather dry, I fear—at least, I judge him unfairly maybe by having only known him in his later "What great men we all were" period. He is finally wearying it out in the Fortnightly with mournings over degeneracy—so I'm out of patience with F. H. Buckle![5] That is to take a mean advantage of your dear love, who has never read Buckle—at most dipped in and quickly out. But truly Buckle should be read. And La Mort de Quel'qu'un— yes thank you beloved: I do want to read that, for I think it is a "key" book, by what you say. One ought to read all "Key" books, and before they cease to be key books. Then there are the "basic" books and then the books—can't find a name—the "round the corner" books, unknown bits of one's own subject—must stick to one's own subject or the number is unending—and—oh dear, one never finishes and one never will. We will search Mudies and, later, beloved we will search the London Library catalogue—two unliftable volumes but oh, most attractive.

I lunched with the Shaws yesterday. I had intended truly to have Mrs. Vincent say I was away over the week-end but I answered the telephone (poor Mrs. V: her brother killed. They last had a letter from Italy, then 8 days later, not even knowing he had been moved, a letter from the Chaplain to say he had been killed in France). Massingham, Lion Phillimore[6] and G. B. S. all quarrelling excitedly about the next government! But GBS subdued in these days—he is getting older. However, Lion Phillimore would subdue a brass band—in fact she is such good company that she is bad company. Charlotte very green-eyed and gentle—a great dear with great good sense—real wisdom within her own scope—rather foolish when she slips outside it, as she foolishly feels in duty bound to do now and then. I had to dash away back to the office. And I said I was going away and I might be back next week! But they don't question—one advantage of being attached to the "Intelligence"—you do "go away" at odd moments and never mention why or where.

At the Club, 2.30.

Your letter this morning, my own, and Lolo's. No, indeed what can one say? (Though when you write say something to her from me, if it is only that I knew and felt for her and wanted to say something, wanted her to know—just the sense of community of feeling. That does help a little sometimes.) But oh, the wickedness of it. Of all the wicked things these wicked men have done the Paris bombardment is in its way the worst. Belgium—drunken brutes let loose—they let them loose. Scarborough.[7] Even bombing Paris from 'planes—that they can put up a reason for, a "military" reason (for all they have defiled the word)—the "containing" of French airmen to defend it. But the big gun—nothing to explain or excuse. Just wanton lust.

1. David Lloyd-George (1863–1945) the Prime Minister (he took over from Asquith in December, 1916).
2. The editor of the *Manchester Guardian*. Scott and the *Guardian* were always sympathetic to the Liberal cause, and Lloyd George was now the leader of the Liberal Party (though of a coalition government).
3. Alfred Milner, Viscount Milner (1854–1925), a controversial political figure (though never an elected Member of Parliament), was High Commissioner for South Africa during the Boer War; Lloyd George brought him into the War Cabinet in December, 1916, and appointed him Secretary of State for War on April 19, 1918, a position he held only until December. He had been sent to Russia in 1917 to negotiate on munitions supplies and to France in March, 1918, to try to effect closer liaison and cooperation between the French and British armies on the Western Front. It was, in fact, largely through his influence that Foch (and not either Petain or Haig) was appointed Commander-in-Chief.
4. Frederic Harrison (1831–1923), author, philosopher, and president of the English Positivist Committee, a society formed to support the philosophical views of Auguste Comte.
5. Henry Thomas Buckle (1821–1862), the British constitutional historian.
6. "Lion" Phillimore is Mrs. R. C. Phillimore (*née* Lucy Fitzpatrick), wife of Robert Charles Phillimore (1871–1919), the eldest son of the first Lord Phillimore. R. C. Phillimore was an enthusiastic supporter of the work of Beatrice and Sidney Webb and an early member of the Fabian Society; his wife was also entirely sympathetic to these causes and was herself deeply involved in charitable and social work in and around London. Both husband and wife were long-standing friends of Bernard and Charlotte Shaw.
7. Scarborough, on the Yorkshire coast, had been bombed by German planes, one of the earliest air raids, in fact.

May, 1918

TEX/MS
To Helen Huntington

Wednesday, 7.30 [May 1, 1918]

But darling, if you please, I was up at 6.45! 6.50, to be really accurate; and sitting down to write to you and thinking that perhaps I'd work besides—that at any rate I'd sit and think about some work. Not a bit of use. The letter to you shumbled and tumbled: I told you about my dinner with the JGs[1] and that I'll tell you over again. Then I began to write about your poem and not a sensible or coherent thing could I say as I wanted to say it so I scrumpled it up in a rage. Oh, I am tired in the head, Helen darling, "officed" out of all mental existence. Forgive me and don't think I fuss <u>over</u> much (I do a little, I know). It will pass and I shall have some sense available. But for the minute I am a poor thing. Nothing really about the JGs except that I dined them at Kettners—I had explained before that you couldn't come. They quite understood and we have held next Thursday free—in case my dear feels like dinner then. Afterwards—if you please—we went to the Pavilion Music Hall for half an hour: I had heard that Monsieur Grock, a clown, tumbled about really comically. And I think you <u>would</u> have been pleased for he did fall about over his feet with the utmost neatness and skill and we laughed a lot, though we had to endure a dose of music(!) beforehand and John would stay and see two clickety clackety dancers afterwards. But the 20 minutes of Monsieur Grock was quite nice and inane.

And I wanted—and want—to say things about your poem but it is no use saying them wrong. I wouldn't mind stumbling over it to you in talk—for you'd make the meaning right.

<u>May 1</u>. Oh, a good month to my darling. The wind has shifted a point or two from the N and there is a hint of blue sky. But oh, the chill. I do think we're rather like the trees—our summer faculties waiting to put forth, but all numb still. I know I have a brain!

At the Club, 2.15 P.M.

Oh beloved—a bad day, chill and grey without and within. Your own dear love (is he, please?) is just no use at all!

No news from you yet. Will you be here tomorrow? I'll be better for you if you will—I'll be better for seeing you anyway! But so chill and cold I believe you should stay tucked by a Tunbridge Wells fire. But I am weary for you beloved. Oh never was such an all-to-pieces letter. I'm not ill, please, except that indigestion has gripped me again. Yes, I <u>am</u> taking medicine and it <u>is</u> better. But I'm just a brainless hulk.

My darling—my darling—oh, even the hulk loves you dearly and just one look from you and I'll be all alive again.

Beloved, forgive such a depressing scrawl.

Better tomorrow.

But how is my dear—my <u>dear</u>?

Oh Helen, sweetest—I love you so—and want you.

---

1. John and Ada Galsworthy.

TEX/MS
To Helen Huntington

Garrick Club; Thursday night, 9 o'clock.
My darling, my own darling: Aren't you the dearest and best and
most beautiful being in God's world? Yes—for I say so. That means
your dear letter has come and that love love love for you so outflows
that I must—straight away—tell you that oh, that I love you. That
sounds little, but that I just worship you—that I am all yours, my
darling—my darling, my own.

Mop, lucky Mop, <u>can</u> demonstrate "coram publico" his joy
at seeing you. If I kissed my dear love in the hall at Kettner's I think
she would be both shocked and alarmed! Oh but my darling—my
darling—many kisses in arrear (I love you—I want you).

But you'll not dislike poor London too much for I've settled
Tues. evening for the J. Gs. and somehow we must manage to be just
we four.

And, oh, the day after tomorrow (and it's long to wait) I
see you. Take care of my Helen, of my dear love, my own dear love,
till then. Oh, darling such good life as I will give you—if love can
give it—the minute the minute I can have you all my own. Till then,
forgive me for the hard time—and still a little. So patient you have
been. I daren't say be patient—hold my hand, beloved—best beloved; and oh, not long now till we belong for always.

TEX/MS
To Helen Huntington

Sunday night, 9.15 P.M.
My darling—my darling: London a very purposeless place without
you and I do <u>not</u> look forward to the office tomorrow (sometimes the
office appals me!) and <u>perhaps</u> no you till next Saturday. But otherwise this has been, God knows it has been, a waited-for week.

I feel perhaps I have been a dull dear love for you today—
too like the day itself—but <u>not</u> east-windy. But you love me dull as
well as shining, my darling: my darling, I know you do. I <u>was</u> rather
tired; but oh, such rest and peace as it has been—always the "right-
ness" of things with you, my dear; my dear. Don't be depressed
about your work beloved—not more than is necessary "pour mieux
sauter"—for it is my work too, <u>our</u> work as soon as we can get our
life smooth running day by day; our work in the reallest, simplest
way. I have always seen it so and what I have seen has come true,

hasn't it darling? Not for us to measure achievement but to go ahead and with thankfulness that the test of doing is the wanting to do: the luckiest thing in the world to have work like that (I think of the office and say so). I'm writing quite confusedly beloved, I know—still rather tired. But oh, I hope you are not sitting solitary in the E. C. Hotel, depressed. If depressed times must come I want to be with you—I think I want to be with you most then.

Groombridge: yes darling—I think Groombridge is "meant" even in the most practical way. I think I know roughly the <u>sort</u> of things that can be found and considering how nearness to London and to a station are important in these times and the size of the place and the "sort" of the place, still, the most important matter of all is that we are "drawn" to it. And now for the most practical step: an expert house agent to look over it with you and advise about detail <u>and</u> about the Saintly[1] terms—there is, as James Gray says, a certain amount of bunkum . . . [2]

Darling I am writing the stupidest letter that ever was—full of nothingness, but it is just dunderheaded I am.

Oh, but to tell you I love you; I love you and don't like being from you one little bit.

My beloved—my beloved—my <u>dearest</u> dear.

---

1. Groombridge Place, the fine red brick manor house they were trying to rent, was built in the reign of James I on a site upon which a succession of small mansions had stood from Norman times onward. Its owner in 1918 was Harry Saint, who inherited it from his aunt, Louisa Saint. He never lived in it, however. He sold it in 1919 to Mr. Mountain, whose son, S. Walton Mountain, was still living there in 1980. Saint, who had emigrated to Australia some years before inheriting the estate, returned to England briefly to receive his inheritance and then, after it was sold, returned to Australia. (See also footnote 6 to the following letter.)
2. A quotation—or, to be precise, a near-quotation—from "Cholly," one of the characters in Shaw's *Major Barbara*.

TEX/MS
To Helen Huntington

Thursday morning, 7 A.M.
My beloved: The summer "feel" is in the air at last—and the time <u>is</u> passing. Queer how time goes with drags and leaps according, I suppose, as you look at it—through "hour" spectacles or "week" spectacles—or minute spectacles when you don't <u>want</u> it to go: but then it goes quickest. Time and the sense of time: we make such commonplace, "catch a train", use of it that we've forgotten its <u>great</u> mean-

ings—all of which has slipped out between sitting down, making my
tea and saying good morning to my darling.

Have you slept—please? And has the fever gone?
I had a busy afternoon but it finished early so I got my letter off by
7.30—that's the post which should get it to you in the morning.
Dined at the club with Buckmaster[1] whom I like to talk to because he
does know things, though this talk was mostly by-ends of politics and
the misdoings of Ll-G—that the Maurice letter to the Chronicle
yesterday was censored and an important bit cut out—why Asquith
went to a division on the Parliamentary Enquiry—that it was Balfour
and Henderson "sold the pass" of the last Asquith government (B[2] is
very Asquithian!) and the nemesis that awaited Henderson; that
Ll-G. assented to the turning down of the Austrian offer in 1917 in a
memorandum which said that on the whole he disapproved of turning
it down but. . . ! Which all degenerates into scandal rather soon but
is interesting, well informed scandal at least!

Oh, my beloved, this coming fortnight with the moon growing full and the ground dry there'll be devil's work in France. One
changes one's spectacles about it as one does about time—the ones I
got on when my uncle came in on Tuesday to the ones that say,
"Well, if Amiens does go—or Paris or Calais, 1919 will see a
change". Oh, the burden of it is sometimes too much for one's
mind—though God knows it is the tiniest share of the burden I bear.
(Still, as I'm "told off" to think, I do try and think clearly!) But I
feel if I could be holding your hand (Oh, my dear one), sitting in a
long chair in the Groombridge garden—quite still—and letting the
night fall down, I feel I'd never want to move, do anything, go anywhere, again. Oh, but I have work stored in my head, too. Beloved—beloved: May is half through.

2.15 P.M., at the Club
Darling—my darling: Real sun for you at last. If this
weather lasts we might picnic on Sunday don't you think? Train to
our Groombridge, then a little over the hill towards Ashurst (I have
kept my eye on that bit of country), sit in the sun and shade—tea at
the little Inn again. What do you say?

As to Saturday: I would try and catch the 5.5 if I may come
to dinner at the Earl's Court. But if you'd rather not then I can,
rather more certainly, get the 5.35 to Sevenoaks arriving there 6.44.
If I missed that, my dear one would have to forgive me please and
I'd come on by the 7.15, arriving 8.17 (just in time to take you back
to T. Wells!) Will you say which? I think I can catch the 5.5; I am

almost certain I can catch the 5.35. You mustn't do a Sevenoaks journey if it tires you too badly. I think of course of being able to spend Sunday night with you as well. But picnicing all day may tire you too much and better you should go straight to bed. (I ought to sit by you then and talk and read to you. My beloved, I will.) This is not to make you out a wanklin[3] and easily tireable person instead of my own most robust dear love; but just now you might be extra cared-for in these ways.

My darling; oh, my darling:

This is a hurried lunch-time scrawl but I had to have W. A. (William Archer) to lunch and that kept me. His boy is missing since April 20—but they have hopes. He was very Stoic and Scotch.

Deburau rises over the horizon. Another failure to plan Les Fiançailles.[4] They have taken away my "grant" of £90 a year! I informed them as in duty bound about the windfall of £400 for Prunella, et voilà. A nuisance, but I did feel that it partook rather of State Charity—so I am, perversely, not altogether sorry. We'll talk of Deburau though, Beloved, beloved: today—tomorrow—and then to see you. Take care of my Helen. These wretched letters which tell you nothing of how I love you—not really anything at all. And oh, my dear, so much of everyday love I want to be bringing you and giving you. Forgive me for all that your life lacks now. I won't let it lack it—I won't indeed, my darling. I will bring you—oh, don't let me boast but I know I can—more than you have lost by loving me. Oh, beloved, I never forget. But I know I can bring you good life— apart from our love (if anything good or of "life" could be said to be apart from it). But I want to tell you just of the longing that is in me and the faith, my own, and the power of life and power of love for you.

My Helen—my dear.

I love you, I love you; I love you body and mind and heart and soul.

I love you, beloved. Beloved.

P.S. It was Philip Packer (1620–1683), barrister, Member of the Middle Temple, one of the original Fs R. S.[5] that Evelyn went to see. His father re-built the Chapel in 1625 and endowed it with £30 a year.[6] Richard Waller (1395–1462) was the man who had Charles, Duke of Orleans, in charge (he had captured him at Agincourt); see your Henry V (which you have not got!!) and he found the charge so profitable that it enabled him to rebuild his house. And the Wallers were there before that and remained there till the time that the judge (Packer) bought it. He seems to have been an old ruffian rather. The Saints seem unknown to fame—at any rate to the D. N. B.

1. Stanley Owen Buckmaster (later Viscount Buckmaster), 1861–1934, a Liberal Member of Parliament, was Solicitor-General in Asquith's cabinet. Elevated to the peerage in 1915, he became Lord Chancellor.
2. Buckmaster.
3. This word is explained in the notes to Chapter V. See letters of August, 1905 and February 23, 1912.
4. *Les Fiançailles* (*The Betrothal*) is a play by Maeterlinck, written earlier in 1918 and performed in New York. Charles Cochran was planning to produce it in London and had asked Barker to direct it. Negotiations towards this end were just beginning: the production finally reached the stage on January 8, 1921.
5. Fellows of the Royal Society.
6. Charles Packer, who was Clerk to the Privy Seal, built the chapel of Groombridge Place in 1625 as a thank-offering "Because of the happy return of Charles our Prince from Spain," as the inscription above the door of the chapel says. Charles had visited Spain in that year to sue (unsuccessfully) for the hand of the Infanta in marriage. Charles Packer had built the Jacobean mansion itself in 1618, and this is the house that is still inhabited today. The earlier Groombridge Place was owned, as Barker says, by the Waller family, of which the poet Edmund Waller was a member. Richard Church, in *Kent* (County Books Series, published by Robert Hale Ltd., in 1948), says that in Restoration times the gardens of Packer's Jacobean house were laid out afresh by John Evelyn (1620–1706), who was a great amateur of landscape gardening.

TEX/MS
To Helen Huntington

Monday, 7.15 A.M.

A log and a dog sleep, beloved, and I do think your own dear love is less of a dunderhead this morning. Blue sky—I think even Penshurst will look better today. But we must have grey days and devil woods—oh, poor Helen's ankles; and I wasn't rightly sympathetic—being hauled by Kim on a stick! (And Helen howled when I had my pain! Oh, beloved). But this ought to be our day as well as yesterday; as well as tomorrow. But soon it will be, please God. My darling, don't be scared, not even in the smallest sense. I am awed to be on the threshold. But I know: we know, beloved—beloved.

The two poems were in Helen's pocket for last night. I do like the grown up one the better. But then that is only because I want it more and poems to me are things I either want or don't—perhaps that is true for me of all literature and it is what makes me such a "chancy" critic. But I like the householder poem—I like its form and I like its feel. I'm not sure, though, just what the house is (am I stupid?) that this householder stays in while others go marketward and adventuring. Yes, I think I do want one verse that says what and another verse that says why (and I don't care if I am stupid), but as I want the poem I want the other verses.

I have a brilliant idea—I will get this to Nellie D to bring down and then I can apologise to her for missing her mysterious package, but it did <u>not</u> come by lunchtime. It was something for our picnic. Oh, picnicing is good. It gives us a real <u>stretch</u> of time away from other people. Oh, but to be alone and in <u>our</u> home, with no-body else, we do just need most—the thing we are nearest achieving (and that is a provision of providence!). Darling, about hotels for you—the Hyde Park is likeliest, I feel sure, and <u>you</u>'ll ask about that when next you come up. I'll enquire about the Alexander, but it is probably not so well run (<u>a</u> bit Brown-ish) and will be noisy and dusty in June.[1] June is near.

It is so really wonderful to be arranging things with you—for you.

Oh, often as I have wished you with me I did <u>not</u> last night on the journey up. I had settled comfortably—to <u>sleep</u> if the truth must be told—when at Sevenoaks an onrush of East End Jews! The train was evidently packed[2] and we journeyed to New Cross 5 a side and 5 standing in the middle (the minor horrors of war!) and—well, not to put too fine a point upon it—the atmosphere. . . ! But they were cheerful, pagan, good-natured, young women—all seemed 18 or so and all were married and been down to Sevenoaks to see their husbands. (Munition workers—East End Jews—called up in the latest comb out!) Food was the staple conversation first, then barrack treat-ment. After that, my interest waned, though there was no escaping the conversation. But I did note this: that while their customs were <u>vile</u>—of a vileness indescribable!—their manners were quite good, while two "lower middle-classes" (there you have my abomination: oh, <u>they</u> would make England what please God she shall never be), harmless as to custom, had no manners at all. But it <u>was</u> a journey!

Breakfast and the paper darling—oh—office again.

Nearly 8—you are awake—I give you a good morning kiss. Have you slept well, beloved and best? Temperature? Cheerfulness? My Helen—my darling. I kiss you for a happy day.

At the office 12.15

Oh, darling, such a rush to be writing you even a line in, though <u>for</u> the office it is peaceful today. But I am going to dash up with this to Nellie D so that you may have it, such as it is—a poor scribble—beloved, within an hour or two: as warm with my love as a poor scribble can be.

Twice already have I been interrupted with "Have we circu-lated this?" "Have you seen that?"

Now I must go—my love—my love—oh, all my love and more to fold close round you, my darling—my Helen—my own.

1. Helen was getting restive in Tunbridge Wells and wanted to get into London again. They had, apparently, been unable to find a suitable flat and were now beginning to consider London hotels.
2. A sidelight on local custom and social practice: Barker, as an officer (and gentleman), would naturally be traveling first class; there was an unwritten understanding on British trains that third-class passengers (there was by then no second class) could go into first-class compartments only if the train was so full as to have no further third-class accommodation. So the inundation of *hoi polloi* into the peace and quiet of a first-class compartment would tell Barker that the train was "evidently packed." The fifteen people he mentions ("5 a side and 5 standing") were squeezed into a space designed for six—but six accommodated in some fair degree of comfort.

June, 1918

TEX/MS
To Helen Huntington

Monday, 6.45 A.M.   June 3

    My darling: This time I will write in proper defiance of all lawyers and their delays. This is the day, my dear one.[1] How it has been waited for. And all it means: yet it begins "outsidely", like any other day; even "insidely"—oh, yes, deep inside one, it is different. But I started to say—how hard to fix, when things are done, the real kernel of their doing. This, in that sense, is only a negative—well, only a registering of the actual thing done. Yes, that is it: a milestone. From tomorrow (Please God. I say that, for all my defiance of lawyers!) it will be different, though the few yards this side and a few the other <u>look</u> the same. But we shall take a new breath as it were. In ourselves, where all things happen, and only there, we have been "gathering up", as it were, for a change, for a new stretch of road— nearly <u>our</u> road now, every step of it. Helen darling, words meaning so little now beside even little things I do; but that is wonderful and welcome—easier to <u>do</u> with all one is than to say with only one's brain or rather with one's brain always the final process in saying, and such a ragged brain as it gets to be sometimes. I shall always love to frame thoughts for you darling—to have you, as you do, complete the thought, as I do yours—add the true meaning. But the joy now to be <u>doing</u> and <u>being</u>. Now one can even <u>play</u> with thoughts a bit and put them in their place—a second place often—while the main accent of living is in the doing, sometimes—oh, most often—of such simple things: and the being. Oh darling Helen, I do pray that I shall never disappoint you. But I love you and thank God for you, my dear—oh, with <u>more</u> than heart and soul and body and mind, with some quite unconscious self that <u>is</u> love for you. That <u>is</u>. And it is only in external things—and sometimes quite external—that I must consciously try to do and be always the best I can. Be patient with me, darling, over those things when there is need. But you are, so dear and patient, so understanding, so alert to understand. My dear—my Helen—oh my darling. I love you.

Diary for you: but there's none! I went back to the office and except that I gave Spencer and Knoblock[2] tea in my room, far from the madding office tea room and less poisonous tea—except for that I worked quietly till 7. A few words with my chief—my real chief. He likes a talk with me at times on office matters above my humble station! Whether he talks this indiscreetly to everyone I don't know. I rather suspect it (though he isn't indiscreet!) but if so, it is a part of his charm, for of course it flatters me!

Knoblock has finished a play since he came back from France, sitting up at night to do it. This gives me rather a shock. But I cannot conceive it to be a very good play. However, that is false comfort for the fact that I haven't written really a line these last months. Oh Helen, I <u>hope</u> it isn't that I'm lazy. I don't really think it is. But the faculties I write with are not on the surface, somehow. I have to dig down. But there is always that scarifying dread that I <u>am</u> lazy—not a "sticker". I can and will do Deburau though as soon as it is quite finally settled. I haven't had the confirming letter yet. Then after 7 I went and sat for half an hour in the Green Park, crowded with people—they looked so yellow and "towny" and it was stifling, for London. Parks are the salvation of a city—every city ought to be <u>half</u> parks. Then to dine at the Club and read quite an interesting article of G. M. Trevelyan's on Carlyle (in the Cornhill)—yes, I do think worth your while if a Cornhill is to be found in these days—yes, I think I know how. And so to bed reading a little "Gismonde" as a finish, but my eyes too tired.

How is my beloved? A letter from you today. I am keeping Wednesday free—in <u>case</u>—

The Club, 7.15 P.M.

My Helen—My darling—your dear letter (Sunday's) and the telegram—I think of you at Rye—a happy day, beloved. Mine such a long and full one at the office, but none of that do I want to write. But this—at five o'clock I rang up Medley and—my dear—my very dear—please will you marry me? Perhaps you'd rather not say till we meet. Would you like to think it over? My dear, I will try and make you a true and faithful husband if you will, God helping me.

My darling, I hardly seem to know how wonderful it is that I am asking you—after these years. Helen how patient and good you have been with me. I went on working away for two hours and more after Medley had told me, with just one look out of the window—I had to have that—and now I'm going quite collectedly to dinner with Barrie. But I do know and thank God that I have lived at least to ask you.

Darling, I don't want to write any more. But I do love you—with more and more of me all the time and deeper than I ever knew that any love could ever go and still it goes deeper.

My darling.

---

1. He is referring to the fact that the decree of divorce from Lillah was to become absolute on this day, though he had not yet received official notification of it.
2. Captain Victor A. Spencer served in the same unit as Barker in Intelligence. Edward Knoblock (1874–1945) was a playwright, the author of *Kismet* (1911), *My Lady's Dress* (1914), etc., and, with Arnold Bennett, *Milestones* (1912). He was born in New York; his family name was Knoblaugh, which he changed to Knoblock on becoming a naturalized British subject.

TEX/MS
To Helen Huntington

Friday, 7 A.M.

Good morning, my darling love. Oh, life is very wonderful to have Helen in it.

Grey sky this mŏrning and wind creeping S. W. Oh dear, no rain please till we can shut our doors—and us inside. Then it may deluge and we won't care.

Hopher in a great state of excitement last night that his Penelope really would arrive today—so we had a lively dinner. Hopher also seized with the idea that we four must spend a weekend on the river at Wargrave or Sunning. Some broiling Sunday. A very good rest for my dear one that would be, to lie flat on cushions in a punt under her new shade and draggle one hand in the water for coolth.

Hopher fancies himself in a punt! "Or would you rather be by yourselves?" said he, whereat I assured him NO, feeling very proud the time was coming when we would be by ourselves and then we'd like to be—sometimes!—with people we liked. Oh, my darling, how good God is.

Then I went in and had a long and very "straight" talk to Charlotte S. And she was at her best—very understanding and sound in heart—just a trifle woolly in head (I think that makes one like her more—you will like her I know). They have guessed, of course, that somehow you must be in England ("were we married?" was her first question. She knows nothing of delays of course.) and had been very wondering—why and how and was all well—and had been rather piqued at being "left out" and not quite being sure of why or how long it would continue. (But G. B. S. knows "why"—no need to tell him.) But the best of them is, one talks straight to them: there is never anything to clear up. Full of questions of you, of course: how you were, did you like England, had you felt able to write—not lately, but all this time). You see, except for the first explanations long ago, I have hardly spoken of you at all. Most anxious to see you—so I said yes, when you come to town. So, if you like this, my darling, she will come to see you when you are settled in at the H. P. and G. B. S. shall be relegated to a later date. How long his vanity will stand it I don't know—he'll preen his whiskers like a cat. And very good for him!

However, take his measure, make allowances, and what remains—and that is much—"matters". A strange figure; and if it were only a simple figure so much finer. Refusing to be a combination of weakness and strength, which nobody would mind, insisting on being thought all strength, which nobody believes. Oh, rather typical, I think, of the whole Irish tragedy—a part of it. Well one must try to "understand". But about G. B. S: you know, I view him objectively—split him into watertight compartments, as he has split himself. For part, I've admiration—and affection, too. For the other part: well, I just open my eyes and shut them—and things not to be forgotten keep them open clearer than before.

At the Club. 5 o'clock.

Beloved, I'm rather troubled. No letter from you. Does that mean yesterday was not a good day? Temperature still? Helen, darling, this <u>won't</u> do. We must just take more care and more care till we do conquer it. I won't press a doctor on you against your wish, as long as you don't feel you have to go on taking quinine too much. If you need those things, my dear one (and I dare say you do) then I think we <u>must</u> have them properly prescribed (well, we'll talk of that). But <u>I</u> shall have to prescribe more care and <u>real</u> rest. Sofa and bed and quiet and nothing but hotels till you are really well—no buying furniture or looking at houses or thinking of maids or <u>anything</u> till you are <u>really</u> well. So now!

My own, rather a devil of a day: oh only the usual round and a beastly "theatre-ish" lunch (Les Fiançailles).[1] I've run up from the office to find a letter. None. (Darling, I'm not worried just at not getting a letter; only that yesterday you mayn't have been better.) I shall make a great effort to catch the 5.5 tomorrow—hardly possible to get the 2.30. Let me come straight up and see you—may I? And then if you're not really well, bed and sofa for you on Sunday. Yes indeed.

My darling, my darling <u>little</u> love, oh please take care of yourself—till I can.

I love you beloved—<u>beloved</u>.

---

1. See footnote 4 on p. 335.

TEX/MS
To Helen Huntington

Tuesday morning, 7 A.M.—and past! (Your dear love rather a slug-a-bed.)

But how is my dear love? N. D. came not to town yesterday—that doesn't mean that you're not so well darling does it? Or that you may be coming today or tomorrow—I'll hear this morning, all being well.

I dined with J. M. B. last night as usual and we chatted rather than talked till quite late—late for me: eleven o'clock. The twilight that is so wan at the Wells is wonderful over the Thames. I suppose it is the moisture from the river lends all the colour—but beautiful it was and I did want my dear there to see. By the way, shall we ask J. M. B. to dine next Monday? That would be rather nice, don't you think?

Beyond this only the usual dose of "office". I get to feel a little more, say, like a junior clerk than an office boy. And I got my hair cut (high time): very hard to find time to go to the hair-cutter; almost impossible to find time to go to Mr. Mock who cuts corns! And I went to a house agent and today with luck I'll manage to see some flats.

By the way, too, you remember that little play of Barrie's that I told you of? Forbes Robertson is playing it about the end of the month. We must manage to see it—either at the matinée or at the dress rehearsal. Better the rehearsal: a nice dark empty theatre— I do believe my present loathing for the theatre is loathing for the audience. I have never loved them. I'm reminded because I met

Forbes last night for a minute and he started asking me what I thought. Forbes, when I was first in the theatre, was one of my demi-gods—unapproachable—and to this day I have the old feeling, "What an honour to be spoken to by him!" And when he asks my advice—! Queer to have those childish things linger, but rather pleasant to think they do.

Photographs—darling! This question haunts me. I don't know how to get photographed—the right sort of photograph. I have been only the cause of photographs in others for so long. But there is a man who did some rather good ones—years ago!—of J. M. B. and some people who were always writing, "Would I make an appointment to be added to this 'gallery of public men'?" (That sounds the right sort of photographer—though it depends the sort of public man he made me look like. There are public men—like public houses!) But it shall be done. Which should have priority: flat or photograph?

At the Club, 2.10

Sweetheart—no letter from you yet: but all is well or I'd have heard. I take that to my comfort. A slack office day, but there I have to sit reading many papers. Lunch here with Walpole[1] and talk of Russia; dinner to Penelope and Hopher tonight. And I'm making "flat" attempts but house agents are tiresome and slow.

This turned up this morning, though. For distance it is just possible, because the Lewes trains are good.[2] 18 gns. sounds (and is) a ridiculous rent,[3] but they would want considerably less, I expect, for a six months' or a year's letting.

Darling, this is nothing of a letter for you. But I must be off. Another house agent on my way back to the office.

Oh my dear love—this is only Tuesday and it seems—how many weeks since Sunday night?

Helen—beloved—I love you and I am just not alive away from you.

My dear—my very dear.

I want, please, exact news of how you are and whether you sleep and temperature and all.

And oh—send the days to pass. But life is wonderful—oh, beloved—wonderful because of you.

---

1. Hugh (later, Sir Hugh) Walpole (1884–1941), the British novelist. Among his better known works were *Mr. Perrin and Mr. Traill* (1911), *The Cathedral* (1922), *Rogue Herries* (1930), and *Judith Paris* (1931).
2. Lewes is an ancient town fifty miles from London, almost due south, and eight miles from Brighton.
3. Eighteen guineas, i.e., eighteen pounds and eighteen shillings.

TEX/MS
To Helen Huntington

Sunday morning, 7.30 A.M.
My darling love: I wake with the sense of you so <u>near</u> to me—wonderfully and beautifully near. Were you too tired? No I think not wrongly tired, for tired feet are good for the nerves (I protest my knowledge against all the Swiss doctors, having tried it much myself; but then I must be careful not to try my Helen's feet too much—not too many hot hills to climb).

Having fully digested Mr. Milton V. Snyder's letter (what a name!), I suggest that you should not answer <u>him</u> at all but should write this to Mr. James Gray.

My dear James (if I tell you that it is etiquette to address your solicitor by his Christian name you won't believe me, but I always <u>think</u> of him as "James"):

"This letter, as you will see, may present a little difficulty and I wonder if you'd be so kind as to get me out of it. Could you, do you think, send an answer which would imply that you had received and opened the letter in the first instance as you normally dealt with all business matters for me? Knowing the American reporter and his kind—as I expect you do—I sharply suspect that he wants to question me about personal affairs. In which case, if he must see somebody, I'm sure you'll present him with a stonewall of noncommittal silence more successfully than I shall. If it were by chance about either my book or the work for the blind in France, no reason of course I should not see him when I come to town later. But even then I suspect he would plump in a personal question at the end. I am so sorry to trouble you with this and with such a long letter about it but if I ignore the man he is quite likely either to pursue me to Tunbridge Wells or, if he can't find my whereabouts, to cable back that I am "in hiding" or something of the sort.

But if you think there is any wiser way to deal with the letter you'll tell me of course.

I am—dear James—

Your faithful and obedient client,
H. H.

P.S. Kim is quite well thank you.[1]
P.P.S. The Tunbridge Wells Corporation intend on my departure to present me with an illuminated address in recognition of my efforts to bury all the paper on the Common. It will be an informal ceremony. If you and Mrs. Gray would care to be present the Town Clerk will send you seats (morning dress)."

Darling—no, this is <u>not</u> the letter <u>still</u> continuing—so happy
and well I am after <u>our</u> <u>day</u>. Oh, our wonderful day, and loving you
so that I must write nonsense. But the letter itself is a serious effort!
And more or less what I think you had better write to Gray. You
see, there are various little difficulties if you write to the reporter at
all: the address (though you could head it c/o J. G. and Co); and
then it only puts him off—he'll descend again and, though you can
always say to a reporter, "Go and see my solicitor" he probably
won't while he can keep in direct touch with you. But if J. G. implies
that only he has got the letter and it's quite the normal thing for a
solicitor to have and open all business letters, he may be content with
that.

Beloved, breakfast (waiting this long while—while I write
nonsense and sense and love for you: love, <u>love</u>—in the sense and the
nonsense too—loving you so my dear—<u>my</u> <u>dear</u>) and office. Such a
day it is going to be. My beloved will rest please and a short drive
somewhere, perhaps to the High Rocks for cream. I should approve
of that; and tuck yourself somewhere secluded in Rusthall—less
paper there, rather less—and your book. Oh, but your own dear
love, he would be better company <u>he</u> thinks. My darling but the
beauty and the joy of being with you—of loving you. Thank God for
you, beloved. I do thank God. My Helen—my own.

Oh, <u>I love you</u>.

At the Club, 2.15

Sweetheart: Just finished lunch with Knoblock—lobster and
cheese (I mention it because I think I must bring a lobster to the next
picnic. Does my Helen "favour" lobster?) Now I must finish this and
post it, so that it finds you tomorrow morning for sure.

Beloved, what a perfect day. What is my dear doing and
<u>how</u> is my dear? Darling, you musn't ever go through another "Satur-
day afternoon"—hours of uncertainty and agony of mind. You must
always send to me: for even if anything had happened, together we
could bring it so quickly to its proper level. And I cannot have my
darling suffering.

Quite a busy day at the office, but I feel so well and good
for work—thank <u>you</u> and bless <u>you</u>, beloved. Though I have got 21
bites on my right ankle! Swathed in bandage and Pond's Extract.
And you mocked at your love's complaints! I never mocked at your
stone bruise. How is your poor stone bruise and how are your dear
and best beloved feet?

Oh—I want to be with you—I want to be with you—in <u>our</u>
garden.

I'm very pleased you have taken the Hotel rooms—I am sure it is quite right. And then at our leisure we'll "look round".

See the house "overlooking Ashdown Forest" and between now and your coming to the Hyde Park we'll collect others to see in case Groombridge does not come through—built in the shape of an H though it is (Mr. Saint is built in the shape of an S!).

Better news from France—though the strain is still great. Persistent rumours here that Reims has gone but that the French won't announce it. That can hardly be true though or the Germans would—unless our people are censoring the German communiques, which would be madness!

My darling—my darling. I love you so, love you, <u>love</u> you with all I am and all I ever can be—love you hard—love you with all my life—and you are <u>life</u> to me. Oh, let me be life to you—I can be and I am (and so <u>proud</u> to be), I <u>know</u>. My Helen—my <u>dear</u>.

---

1. Kim was a spaniel living with Helen (as well as Mop). Both Barker and Helen were very fond of animals, and their correspondence over nearly thirty years contains constant mention of a procession of dogs and cats and horses.

TEX/MS
To Helen Huntington

Tuesday morning, 7.15 A.M.
Darling, this is another letter <u>in case</u> Oh, heaven send it doesn't reach you till you no longer want it—but in case.

I'm still in the dark of course about the delay. "All well" means that it is passports or trains failing or possibly some detail of the case.[1] You'll have understood, won't you, just what I meant by the formal phrase in my telegram "You should leave etc.". I'm not alarmed about Paris, though I'll be thankful to have you out of it, but in these times—one forgets <u>how</u> abnormal they are—the first thing that does happen is the holding up of civilian traffic.

My beloved, I can't one bit attune my mind to letters—so ready to see you to begin this next phase for us. (I hate the wordy words as they come.)

But, in <u>case</u> . . .

Oh, my darling I have been <u>with</u> you these last days, ever since Thursay. And now (your letter has come) I know what Thursday was. And little scraps of letters I have written and not sent and I didn't want to send them—my feelings at your coming, things for you to read after I'd seen you and all so needless once you came.

But this if it finds you needing it. Oh, what to say in it, my dear—my dearest, my dear; what to put. Why to—in <u>words</u>.

I have faith, my darling—faith for us both when you need mine too—absolute unswerving faith. Helen, darling, it has never wavered; and its roots deeper down in me, in my life, than anything ever goes. You see what I mean: I have never had to reason or explain, so I call it "absolute". And this too, my dear love, if you wake in the night (oh, my darling), if suddenly I seem unreal. . . . So many words and written words there have had to be. At their best. . . . Though our love has brought us more beautiful thoughts and visions than anything ever in our lives and we'll be grateful for words, for the power of words that has lessened our partings (oh, poor, inarticulate souls), still it is never in these that my faith has wanted—seemed natural to it—to live. But in being things to you, doing things for you; and such simple things, not even loverlike things—but you know. Then know this darling, my darling, too, and <u>anchor</u> to this. As we take each step and it becomes right we should be nearer to each other, my faith which <u>is</u> my love recognises this new phase that has begun comes nearer to its own.

Oh, Helen darling, but I can't write of my love for you. When that was all almost all our chance of expression, then I could; but now, all that is in me turns to living my love. I shall end, I suppose, by being quite tongue-tied, unable to say a word. But then it won't matter if all the words I do say have the meaning of "I love you" in them; and they do now and they will. And there'll be just these three words like a need, all belief brought down to that. I love you.

At the Club, 9.45
Your letter darling, of Sunday. Oh, my <u>brave</u> heart—you—you. And you give me life and strength—the dearness—the fineness of you. I love and worship you, Helen—my own. Yes, I'll keep sane about you, about the moment's troubles. I wish I could advise and help—<u>cursed</u> that Archibald was called away.

But if I can advise by telegraph—the only way—I'll see. I'll think.

But take care my sweet; take care of my Helen.

This is to find you—oh, if it must—still held back from me. But if so, then I'm with you, near you every moment, my heart's blood yours. Our fight and <u>the</u> fight, the great battle, our great battle. Yes, we'll keep steady and brave and no harm can befall.

Helen I love you, my darling and, oh, you teach me what love means, what God is. My darling—my own.

---

1. Helen had gone to Paris for the final stages of the divorce case.

TEX/MS
To Helen Huntington

Wednesday, 7.20 A.M.

Oh, my darling, but these are hard moments. News of you today—
but there's only one news I want: "I have started". The Channel is
open all right; I know of a woman who crossed yesterday. It was only
fog closed it at the weekend (Harker is a fool!) But telegrams are
taking two days to arrive for some reason, so I can't hear quickly
from you and can't advise. But your letter was a comfort of a sort. It
meant that you are "well"—but I know what "well" means at this
moment: the last inch of pluck called on; and I cut off from you by
some damned French official; Archibald gone (a vile bit of luck).
You must make the Embassy talk to them again. But you'll have
thought of that. You really must though, darling—for the French (or
English!) are capable of holding things up for weeks through pure
stupidity. If I don't hear this morning I shall wire Nellie direct to the
hotel—or rather, that you may be obeyed in all things, Christopher[1]
shall wire!

And this letter shall go. Oh, and I thought the last letter
had gone nearly a week ago. But you mustn't be without something,
even this nothingness of a letter (for write about anything I simply
incapably can't). All the front of my mind—your coming: all the back
of it—the battle going on. It is amazing isn't it how Fate does choose
our moments. One keeps steady-minded about the fighting—many
disasters are possible without Disaster—but of course, one's impo-
tence! But thank God England is at her best when a real crisis comes.
At least, I suppose the best and worst are still best and worst; but the
boasters and the cads do shrink to silence and—oh—England knows
her own.

My own—a grey day. Where are you? I welcome grey
weather at full moon times and you travelling. Are you starting today? You might even have started yesterday and the wire only reach
me this morning—but that's too good a hope.

I can write nothing you see, all my meaning being that you
are not to have this letter at all.

But, oh, I love you. And these moments, my darling we try
to turn them to good—do help, perhaps, to purge the selfishness
from my love—though you'll not think hardly—too hardly—of the
selfishness that wants you—wants you here to love.

And you've been really under fire! It is a step higher in
dignity than an air-raid. A queer pride I have in that for you—a
feeling, too, that you have welcomed it (not liked: that would be
foolish), but welcomed it.

The paper is coming with news—oh, what? And then to the Club for news of you. And we must keep steady and sane. <u>We</u>. And soon, darling—please God—always <u>we</u>.

My Helen—my very dear.

At the Club, 9.45

Oh, Helen, beloved—no telegram. I am troubled. I shall wire you to beg Bliss's help—you <u>must</u> get away. My darling I feel so helpless; but I am with you, oh with you, all I can be. Patience, a brave heart, a steady mind and it'll be all right.

Oh courage, my darling. But as if I need to say it to you—<u>you</u>, <u>all</u> courage. <u>My</u> <u>darling</u>, <u>my</u> <u>own</u>.

My mind and soul so loves you, so has faith.

Helen, my dear, my beautiful—I hold your hands. All's well.

---

1. Dr. C. E. Wheeler.

Helen got safely back from Paris to London, with her divorce from Huntington safely arranged. It was now early July, the month in which the German offensive finally collapsed in the face of the dour resistance of the French and British armies. Helen continued to live at the Hyde Park Hotel, and Barker, though he now saw her every evening, continued to write to her almost daily. Two of these letters have survived.

July, 1918

Monday, at the Club, 9.15 [July 8, 1918]
Darling beloved: Are you "all in", too? I suspect so—if you went shopping this afternoon too. But you looked so dear and reposed and sweet at lunch and I loved your dress with the symbolic full moons on it. But tonight, are you very tired? Take care of my Helen, <u>please</u>. Only a little while still and then I can begin to take care—really. Oh but I don't now I know—enough. And I was late for lunch and I'm so sorry. But the W. O.[1] and half a mile to walk for a cab. Forgive me.

Oh, such a day. Mrs. Vincent turned up struggling with influenza so I packed her off promptly and then—you know those days when you are struggling through muddle all the time, doing things but nothing seems done in the end, except that you are pulp. But some things <u>did</u> get done, apart from office things.

I <u>liked</u> Berenson![2] But such an agile mind and my poor mind is not agile at all. His doesn't leap, but it is like an accomplished skater, don't you feel—figures of 8 and inside curves. But such a cultured <u>nature</u> (more than a cultured mind). And if I could re-draw his nose and add six inches to his height he'd be the image of my father! (No—not really!) But a jolly lunch, darling—I hope I didn't talk too much! I felt so stupid; I had to disguise it.

Then, after tussles with Russia, to see Medley at 6 and Medley was really kind and nice. He'll see Gray tomorrow. (Oh, I had a long talk with James through the telephone—he talks at length on the telephone). He'll (Medley) arrange <u>all</u> the formal legal part of the 24th[3] and he has found a Reverand A. Monk-Jones whom I am to see tomorrow, if possible, whom he thinks there will be no difficulty over and who will officiate at the Kings Weigh House Church—my darling.

And I suggest that if a third trustee were needed Medley might act himself, if he would. What do you think? He will talk that over with James too.

And Barrie will fix where we are to dine tomorrow but anyhow (I mean wherever it is) I'll call for my dear love—may I? —at 7.15.

And that's all the news, I think—except that I'll dig up those photo proofs somehow tomorrow. (I daresay you'll hate the Strang.[4] I only remember it was just a "face", but an admirable <u>drawing</u>, I thought—for you see I don't know what I'm like but I can take pleasure in a good drawing—so I took pleasure in that.)

Darling Helen, darling Helen, <u>darling Helen</u>. Now I shall tumble back to bed, my rhyming dictionary (just arrived) under my arm. And tomorrow is Tuesday and the day after Wednesday and then a fortnight. My beloved, I love you and I will be good to you always—always—because I love you so. You know, deep deep down, you know, don't you? But I'll make you know in every little thing. Please God you shall have the best of me—such a better best for loving you—such a much better best, for your loving me, than ever has been, than ever could be—as I thought. But it is to be: to be done: to be proved worthiness of you beloved. So God help me.

Sleep sound and sweet—Helen darling—my own dear love.

---

1. War Office.
2. Bernhard Berenson (1865–1959), the Lithuanian-born American art critic and author.
3. Their proposed marriage date; the ceremony was actually performed, according to the certificate, on July 31.
4. A pencil drawing of Barker done by W. Strang in 1912 (the illustration at the beginning of Chapter I).

TEX/MS
To Helen Huntington

Thursday, 7.15 [July 11, 1918]

My darling: It has been haunting me ever since, and is now, that I left you lonesome by the fire. Not with a broomstick even—I know—but lonesome and "strange". Beloved, I do understand—though do I seem to "overstep" things sometimes? By which I don't mean do I come too close—but step by without taking enough account of the "strange" moments? No, they are not moments—they are "aspects" aren't they? But I do understand and you mustn't feel, my dear one, that I take anything for "granted"—in the wrong sense. But then again I don't want to try and remove such troubles (though again they're not really <u>troubles</u> are they?) by violence even if it is the violence of love. For if they are natural now, then I want them naturally to fade and they will, I know, for I have vision and faith for what is to take their place. Have faith, too, beloved, even in the littlest things. And forgive me if sometimes I'm too tired (never too tired to <u>have</u> faith and vision—never, my dear—but at a moment too tired to express them just as I want to).

And I know too that my "world" must seem strange to you, but not unkindly strange. And, of course, just now—even for what it is—it is "war broken" and out of shape. But you're right: we begin again at the beginning. Strange how the time of world chaos has been our time of chaos. And now I know we shall do our re-building as the world begins to do its own—not ignoring the old altogether but choosing from it and re-shaping. And for that, our faith and vision.

And please God, darling love, you weren't altogether unhappy by the fire. You saw things—oh, I know—but I'm timid now about even little unhappinesses coming to you, little shocks or jars. I can't blame myself for that because I love you that way as well as all the other ways. But yet I do a little because you are so much bigger than all that; and this isn't a world or a time (in the world history) for timidities, is it, beloved? Delicacies, yes: God send I never say anything or am anything to you with a rough touch. But we'll not be timid.

I did walk off with the poem after all, but I was glad, for I can<u>not</u> read things (in that sense) publicly. But my brain was doddery when I read it again last night and this morning I haven't again—yet.

Dear Nellie D with her bang-whang last night—while I was slowly "feeling" my way—rather timidly too—to a mot juste—I do have to "feel" my way over criticism of poetry—for apart from "feeling-prompted" thoughts I have no judgment. (Breakfast and the paper: "In they came these people of importance")

And now I <u>have</u> read the poem again carefully and I take off my hat to it. At first I felt I more wanted it written by the "self"—"self's" point of view of the prison (but that was a foolish thought—feeling I retract on a second reading). But then I give up as a critic for I find that all I do is to yield my mind to be captured and held and to say, "Now you have it" and, "Now the hold is loose", but without really knowing why. No, I fear I am incurably timid as critic except over just my own one subject, and there I know. Now I must dress and "out" and "office".

Till tonight, my darling.

Oh, but that has a good sound—so long it used to be and now just a day's work to do and I see you.

My Helen—keep a brave heart.

My <u>dear</u>.

And today the 11th, my dear one. I know—I know and I understand.[1]

And I pray to God for us both.

Suddenly it comes over me—such a nothingness of a letter to send you when you are needing—are you now this minute?—so much. Forgive me all that I'm not and seem not to be, sometimes, still. But I will bring you such love and strength all I can be—the best, my <u>own</u>.

---

1. I do not know why July 11 had some special significance for Helen Huntington: evidently some entirely private grief with which this date was connected. The mention of it in Barker's letter, however, fixes the date of the letter exactly. There were four months in 1918 in which the 11th fell on a Thursday—April, July, September, and December: April is too early for this letter in view of the reference to seeing her every evening (which he was not doing in April, when she was at Tunbridge Wells); by September they were married. So the only month that fits is July.

They were married on July 31, 1918. Their search for a country house did not end with Groombridge but further afield, at Netherton Hall, in Devon, where they stayed until 1932, when they moved permanently to Paris. No further letters between them have come to light until 1940, probably because they were never apart until then. In April of that year, Barker returned briefly to London to assist with the direction of King Lear *at the Old Vic. Another war is now in progress, and under its shadow Helen writes to him from Paris.*

TEX/MS
To Barker

The Lancaster[1]
7, Rue de Berri
Champs Elysees,
Paris.
Wed., 6.30 P.M.
[April, 1940]

Darling,

      At about 2, when I was finishing lunch with Mme. Le Breton and Anna d'Alens, the concierge came in with a message, from No. 18, that your plane had reached England safely and I thanked God. I hope it was a smooth, and comfortable flight? It's been a lovely day here, but cold. I took Kai for a dull walk, tried to get Loine a <u>colis</u> at a place where they apparently had nothing but chocolate, decided that a colis all chocolate might be a depressing thing and came away. After lunch j'offris le cinema to my guests, and we saw Mason's "Four Feathers" at the Normandie—fighting in the desert, Arabs, and British officers each more noble than the last. Clara de Chambeau came in to have tea with me and now here I am with Elizabeth's (Dashwood's) "Provincial Lady in War Time", which she has just sent me to read. Very amusing—and just the kind of literature that suits the occasion!

      Kai has become very fierce and challenging since your departure—growls when anyone knocks at the door: at <u>any</u> of the doors. Mallet rang up to ask if we would lunch at the Embassy tomorrow but I had to say that you were away and that I had another engagement. The Campbells are going away tomorrow night for a <u>cure</u> <u>de</u> <u>repos</u>. I've just had a letter from Madame de Ganguiron. She has lost the oldest of her two sons and is in great grief. I wish I had known that she was in Cannes when we were there. I could have gone to see her. I've always liked her and found her sympathique, haven't you?

      (Waiter comes with dinner card—most cheerless; Abramsky[2] with letters; maid to close shutters; another waiter with Kai's paté; feminine fondez-germaine to change my shoes—a feverish life!)

      As usual, you see, this is all about myself—but you told me, "once in the golden days", that you would never get tired of hearing me talk about myself. I've certainly put you to the test!

      This letter will probably get to you just as you are about to start for home—if then! So I'll make it short. Somehow, my writing looks like knitting to me. I feel that it ought to be done with a long, thin, blue needle.

How does London look to you—war-time London? You'll
have a great deal to tell me when you get back but <u>no</u> time, I expect,
to put it in a letter. Goodnight, darling, and come back soon to

Helen

Clara de C. is now fighting a "calumnious article" in an American
paper which stated that the American war-dead in France were being
exhumed and burned in lime-kilns as a means of showing French dis-
pleasure that the U.S.A. hadn't come into the war. She is very
heated about it and not without reason, perhaps.

---

1. Helen was staying at a hotel while their apartment in the Place des Etats-Unis was
   being redecorated.
2. Barker's secretary.

TEX/MS
To Barker

The Lancaster,
7, Rue de Berri,
Champs Elysees,
Paris.
Thursday morning
[April, 1940]

Darling,

I've just opened Monday's Times and seen the death of dear
Lady Horner—dear to so many! She was so full of life that it seemed
as if she could just go on to an extreme old age. It was a great shock,
even to me who never knew her intimately, to know that she was
dead. England will never be quite the same, will it?

I'm sorry, darling, that you should have had this shock and
sorrow on your first morning in London. I know what it will mean to
you. (I wish they hadn't printed Lady Oxford's vulgar article!)

The sun is shining a little this morning. I'm going to lunch
with Nellie Mackay and then to see some Oenone[1] she is interested
in. Madame de Margeris has asked me to go to her tea-party but I
am getting to be as shy as a rabbit and think I won't venture. The
Landons are having music dans l'intimité (no tickets) on Tuesday,
and have asked me, 9 P.M. I've accepted.

The night was peaceful: no alerts. Kai and I slept well and
Germaine,[2] in your room, probably dreamed of King Lear—all she
will ever know him! Clara de Chambeau has just called up to ask if I
would dine there tonight. A "family" dinner. I had to accept—though
I hate the idea of going out alone.

Now I must write to Katherine A., who feels, I'm sure, that a wall has gone down behind her. This agonizing feeling of everything crumbling—we all have it now—intensified, terribly, for her. And her son mobilized, perhaps!

Sunday seems still a long way off to

Helen

---

1. Oenone is the nurse in Racine's *Phaèdre*. Helen is saying (rather affectedly) that her friend is interviewing a prospective nursemaid.
2. Helen's personal maid, who eventually accompanied them to America.

TEX/MS
To Barker

18, Place des Etats-Unis
Paris.
Sunday, 7 April [1940]

Darling,

You must have had a bad time going to England! Your letter came when you had forgotten about it, though, mostly—now you will have forgotten it quite! I had the letter on Friday—nothing yesterday.

There is very little to write about: "Journée calme: rien à signaler". Mr. & Mrs. Rushton came to lunch (I asked Mary Churchill Humphrey and Arnavon but they weren't free). We had much talk about the Foyer at Abbeville of course. It promises well and Mrs. R. has deserved success it would seem. I went, at her suggestion, to hear the Contesse de Chaubrieu (Marie, l'Ambassadrice) give a conférence on Desmoulins and his Lucile. (She specializes in love-affairs. Will someone, when she's dead and gone, give a conférence on Charles and his Marie?) However, she speaks well and with grace. After the conférence I walked about cold, grey and mostly silent Paris from the Arc de Triomphe, up the Avenue Foch to the Avenue Bugeaud and so home, laying here and there, as it were, little memorial wreaths: the house where Lurline K. was ill for so long; a glimpse, down a side street, of the place where I spent those bleak and bewildered months with Nellie D.; the house where Laura P. lived with her aunt and cousin; the garden where I had tea with the first-period Roosevelts; glimpse of house where dear Clara had an apartment; house of Ferdinande de L.; street where the 90-years-young Mrs. Crayles lived; house where I was entertained, or rather bored, by a lady—now also dead—whose name I have forgotten; Pavillon, Avenue Bugeaud, where I lived with Harley and where we found "Domino" freezing to death up a tree; street where Anna de Bonard gave parties; pâtisserie where my croissants come from; and so, coldly and drearily, home.

Six long hours for tea, Chopin, King Lear (I'm studying King Lear you'll be glad to know), a little knitting, dinner (wireless out of order), more King Lear, <u>bed</u>.

I have borrowed from your library two fat volumes with flaming red paper dust-covers—Rolli's "History of Shakespearian Criticism" and you'll find me, when you get back, a changed woman, a Shakespearian specialist. Rolli seems a good and worthy jackdaw— but I rather hate his way of referring to "R & J", "The M of V", "M. Ado", "L. L. L.", etc.

Mirza came and mewed at my door at 3.30 this morning. I let him in and he mounted to my bed, the Place dess Etats-Unis, I think, echoing with his purring for some half an hour or so! This morning he had mysteriously vanished—through a closed door, like a wizard.

Forgive a letter all nothingness, full of nothing but "Terre de France", like those horrid little sachets!

Do you ever, like Marcel, feel sorry that you went away and that, "Madame", after all, "etait si gentille"? I wonder!

Today the sun is shining. It's much better than yesterday. I hope it's sunshine in London, too.

Best love,
Helen

TEX/MS
To Barker

18, Place des Etats-Unis,
[Paris]
April 8 [1940]; Monday, 9.30 P.M.

Darling,

This morning the salon was dotted with mysterious small vases—some holding pansies of one colour, some of another, some primulas, some narcissi. Then I found your Valentine and put all the flowers together in a bowl, where they look lovely. (Thank you. I feel as if I were writing to Liverpool instead of Harley and can't let myself go!) Last night I finished King Lear and also re-read part of your preface—with delight.

(An Italian soprano is singing "Caro Nome" in the corner— distracting!)

This has been rather a distracting day with all the new restrictions about heat and hot water. Abramsky, wallowing in gloom, hard at it trying to get various kinds of heating apparatuses. Also the Spanish parlour-maid question is coming to a hopeless head and a Russian haunts the front door trying to get out of us 100 francs to redeem a ring, dear to him because it once belonged to his mother. The carpenter, Decret, has lost one of his children and has sent a faire-part even more magnificent than the last.

I spent this morning—after taking Kai for a walk—doing up things for refugees of various nations (I seem to have as many shoes as a centipede would need if he needed shoes at all), ending up with a non-descript heap of things to be sold to the old-clothes man—in this case, a woman! H. le Breton came to lunch and gave first-aid to my knitting, but it was almost beyond her powers. Then we went to the Salon—not much better than, hardly as good as, the "Independent". After I came home I had a go at my writing-desk, that big chest in my bedroom too—a dreadful job and most depressing. <u>Mountains</u> of typed M.S.—graves of my work, and unmarked graves at that! It's hard to have been a fool all one's life. "Dost thou know the difference, my boy, between a bitter fool and a sweet fool?"

King Lear
(Shakespeare)

It's been a cold day here—colder, I'm afraid, in London?

The radio has—alas!—begun to <u>croon</u>. I feel like putting a blanket over it as one does over the cage of a parrot.

England seems to be sitting more and more under the shadow of Winston Churchill. The shadow of a mighty rock?

"Georges" doing well, but too economical of light. I shall soon have to find my way about the house with an electric light.

My love—but you seem so far, <u>far</u> away!

Helen

The radio, soaring to the heights at last, has wound up the evening with the "Jupiter" and now it is past eleven and I'm off to bed.

TEX/MS
To Barker

18, Place des Etats-Unis,
[Paris]
April 9 [1940]

Darling,

The curse has come nearer. It is like someone dying, someone finally ill, yet whose death shocks and surprises us. This morning

I was trying to write, but with such a weight of fear and strange weakness on me that I could hardly sit up in the bed. Half an hour afterwards Abramsky telephoned to me: "Norway is at war. German troops have invaded Denmark." (Then he asked if he could go to see his dentist—and dashed off!) Sweden has general mobilization. What will come next?

The death of Cardinal Verdin saddens one, too. France needed him.

Yesterday, at Morgan's they seemed pessimistic. How long can England carry on? "Nine million pounds a day!" The Germans can well say that time is working for them, for how can even the British Empire go on indefinitely spending nine million pounds a day?

<u>Later</u>

I've had lunch and Abramsky is back—very gloomy. He thinks that Holland, Belgium and Switzerland will have their turn next and, I suppose, that he will have to go back in the army. I have an engagement with the dentist at 3.30. Afterwards, will go and throw myself into the arms of Clara and Aldehert. I've been telephoning this morning to the former. Even her optimism is shaken but, after all, we knew that War, in the end, must be <u>War</u> and that our seven months of security were only a sort of reprieve. Oh, dearest, I wish you were here.

Your
Helen

TEX/MS
To Barker

18, Place des Etats-Unis,
Paris.
April 11 [1940]

Darling,

Yesterday the breath of Harley was again over the salon, like a south wind, and it blossomed into spring flowers, and I was very thankful for them. Also thankful for your letters of the 8th and 9th which arrived, stamp by stamp, this morning. Tuesday was a very black day here in Paris, as it must have been in London, but yesterday there was a little light in the North and this morning the newspapers are blazing with reassuring headlines. Clara de C. has just rung up to give most optimistic reports of the 700 kilometre fight going on along the Norway coast and that, of course (I mean, her report!), makes one uneasy because of previous experience of her optimism. Of course there is a great deal in the press information now that is terribly confused. By the time you get this everything I can write will probably be as out-of-date as the battle of Waterloo—things go by at such a pace! They say here that Adolf made this move against the strong advice of his generals, etc., so that, if things do turn against him, if there is anything like a débâcle, he will be very badly down, if not "out".

The radio has been cut off this morning—but something may come through at 12.30. If only we could have re-taken Bergen and Trondheim—but there's no confirmation of the rumours that have been flying about, nor of the loss of the Bremen either. Everything that's going on now is of such colossal importance and seriousness. My nervous stomach-ache gets worse and worse and I find myself on Biskama—otherwise I'm quite well.

Yesterday I lunched with Gladys Sewell at the Interallié. It was crowded—many officers, French and British. We saw no one to speak to except Mrs. Colyer. In the evening Madame de Chaubrieu (the Marquise) took me to a concert, coming here, first, for dinner. We heard a piano recital—a very remarkable young Czech pianist called Firkusny. Did you ever hear of him? I never did. He is 27—and only 27, we say now! (I can remember when a man of 27 paid me his addresses and seemed to me as venerable as Moses!) Firkusny is tall, athletic-looking and plays with a vigour, as well as a romanticism, belonging only to youth—at the same time an astounding technique and virtuosity. When he began his C. major Mozart sonata I thought he had too heavy a hand for it, but that was never shown afterwards. He played Chopin's sonata, Op. 58, marvellously; also some Debussy preludes; after that wasted himself—but so brilliantly one was breathless—on Suk, Martinu and a Concert Study by Smetana. I suppose Suk and Martinu were also of his own afflicted race and so had to be honoured.

It's still cold here, but today the sun shines and we can have hot water and central heating until the 15th. It has been a very long time since you went away but I'm so glad that things have gone well and that you've had the joy of doing your King Lear. I wish I could see it.

My love,
Helen

I had already, most grudgingly, sent Knapp-Fisher the £100 he asked for, before your letter came, but I did refer him to the original contract. I would like, please, to have 6 more copies of my book,[1] also

any advertisements or press notices, if he will be good enough to
send them.

---

1. Her *Poems* was published six months earlier by Sidgwick and Jackson in London:
   Knapp-Fisher was the managing editor of Sidgwick and Jackson and a partner in the
   firm.

Barker returned to Paris from London less than a week after the last
of the above letters was written. Six weeks later the German army in-
vaded France, and Harley and Helen Granville-Barker fled to Lisbon
and thence to New York. There, Helen was occasionally left alone for
short periods while Barker fulfilled lecture engagements at various uni-
versities—Harvard, Yale, Toronto, and Princeton.

TEX/MS
To Barker

Mayfair House,
Park Avenue at Sixtyfifth St.,
New York.
Monday [January, 1941]

Dearest,
    This will be a busy and, I fear, a tiring day for you but if
the sun is shining there as gaily as it is here and if your room is
comfortable and you look out on trees and snow, you won't be miserable—and I hope that you will be <u>happy</u>.
    I have taken Pompey to his vet. His temperature is 103° and
Blair doesn't think much of him, but so far there are no symptoms of
St. Vitus, or any other of the horrid things that come after distemper.
Blair said, after some hesitation, that he might go out in the car, if he
was kept quiet and not in a draught.
    I called up Charles Peake, who said that he only came for
36 hours to see Charles Mendl before he left for Hollywood. He will
come again in a fortnight or so, when you will be here. I asked him if
he got my note. He said he did.
    No other news so far this day, except newspaper news,
which you will have. I've been reading "New England Indian Summer", which puts me into your atmosphere—your present atmosphere—and also makes me understand it. Underground things stir
gently for me—Lowell and Norton and Agassiz and Child. I never
read them myself but Father read them and talked about them.

Those serene, distinguished days! Have they been forever lost? I've just been reading this: "For although they" (the New Englanders) "had good hearts and would have rescued a stranger, if they had known how, out of common kindness, they did not know how—and this was the real trouble with Boston". Well, you won't in these days, find this true!

I'm struck by the emphasis Van Wyck Brooks puts on Howells—all through his books. Will people read him when, possibly, they no longer read James?

Love,
Helen

TEX/MS
To Barker

Mayfair House,
Park Avenue at Sixtyfifth Street,
New York.
Monday 1941

Dearest,

Forgive me—and don't be cross—if I don't send my book.[1] I've just read it over and I do feel the thing most to be desired for it—by us both—is oblivion. I do truly now desire it. I did have a poetic impulse—and perhaps some poetic feeling: nothing more. Now it only pains me to have that book given to strangers and have a kindly, polite, personal note from them. Please understand. This is all I want now—I mean the gentleness of being left alone. Don't write me a scolding letter.

Are you having a good day at Cambridge? I think the sun must be shining in your windows there. I've had a day all female friends. I gave lunch to Mrs. B. A. Morton (initials, as the radio says, for "station identification"). Then we went to see the Grecos again. She is very intelligent about pictures—and other things. Then I went to Mrs. Crane's "class" and heard the fervent—but not very well-educated—Holiday hold forth on James Joyce, afterwards reading one of his (Joyce's) short stories and some of his verses. Now I'm back. W.Q.X.R. is doing its bit, Germaine has made me malted milk and the evening papers have come. Isabel Butler is coming to dine with me "tête-a-tête" and I've had a wobbly letter from Anne Corkram. That's all.

My love to you, as always,
Helen

1. I do not know which book she is referring to here. She published nothing in 1940 or
   1941, her last publication being *Poems* in 1939. The ones before that were *The Locked
   Book,* in 1936, and *Traitor Angel,* in 1935, neither of which really fits in with her
   comment ("I did have a poetic impulse"), since the former is an anthology of other
   people's work and the latter a novel. Most probably it is *Poems* that she means; Barker
   must have asked her to send a copy for him to show or present to someone at Harvard.

*In the summer of 1941 she went to stay with some of her Huntington
relatives in Oneonta, New York, in the old family home. Barker had
to stay in New York City for some part of the time because of his work
for the British Information Office.*

TEX/MS
To Barker

Colliscroft[1]
[Oneonta, N.Y.]
June 30 1941

Dearest,

How I wish that you were here and not in that hot and
steaming city! Still, it's hot here, too, very—in spite of the fresh air
and the green leaves. The lawn is thick here with giant robins. The
trees have grown so much since you were here that you would hardly
know the place. Last night we sat out on the verandah till quite late
and there were fire-flies on the lawn and some very high up in the
branches of the trees. I had rather a tiresome journey as my seat, at
first, was right over the wheel of the car and that—needing oiling or
what-not—made such a hellish creaking and groaning, hammering
and squeaking, that, at last, I had to ask the conductor to move me
into another place, which he did most amiably. In another car—there
was no noise, or very little, no bellowing children, no repulsive old
German Jews, and all was well. Mary met me at Albany, gave me a
heavy, but very good, "Sunday dinner" at a nice hotel there and
"George" motored us (in yet another new car, which can accommodate seven—with room left over!) to Oneonta.

Like Amy Corbin's man, "George" does now inside, as well
as outside, work and, as Mother used to say, "is a comfort" to Mary.

I woke up this morning thinking of you—and that beastly
eczema, wondering how you were. I wish that you were here; but
perhaps that would bore you—and it is too hot to walk in the woods.
I had a true inspiration just now and considered proposing to Mary a
large china cabinet to be placed in the upper hall and to hold what I
should refer to delicately as her superfluous, over-crowding orna-

ments. (There are <u>7</u> on my mantelpiece, also 2 clocks, 2 framed pictures and one unframed of the old Fairbanks house at Dedham,
Mass.) And, counting up what the rest of the house can bring forth, I
think the cabinet could be sure of a hundred at least, for a well-
chosen and rather dim corner. However, as the calendar on my table
says (Cordial Greetings from Hartwick College, Oneonta, N.Y.),
"Let more of reverence in us dwell"!

Now I must begin to wash and dress myself and get ready
for what the day may offer.

My love,[2]

---

1. The house was named after Collis Potter Huntington, the founder of the family's
fortunes, who left Oneonta for San Francisco in 1843.
2. The special monogram is reproduced here actual size, in Helen's small, neat, and
careful handwriting.

TEX/MS
To Barker

Colliscroft,
Oneonta.
July 1 [1941]

Dearest One,

It was a joy and a surprise to get your letter last night—hot
and humid though it was! But at any rate you had a pleasant lunch at
the Century and that was something. It has been very hot here, too,
but the air is fresh and sweet-smelling and there are birds singing
themselves to the point of bursting at morning and evening. Also this
place is quite lovely now—all the trees grown tall and even the trees
in the valley shutting out all of Oneonta except the tops of its
chimneys and church towers.

We had a lazy day—a <u>very</u> good hot meal in the middle of
the day and Marion Yager coming to a very good cold one in the
evening. I have found some old music of Edward Pardoe's in the
room sacred to his memory and can play it over on the venerable
Steinway (Mary not hearing very well and "Eva", her retainer, being
stone deaf).

We tried to listen to Raymond Gram last night[1] but the station was too bad. However, the Herald-Tribune came shortly after lunch so we had what news there was in that. (Poor—or, rather, happy—old Paderewski: gone from a world all discord.[2])

So goodbye, darling, till tomorrow night when the traveller returns.

Best love,
Helen

I begin to think there was truth in what that woman said about my being attractive to cows. When M's two Jerseys spied me yesterday they almost <u>dashed</u> across the field. But perhaps it was wrath, not love.

---

1. Raymond Gram Swing, a news broadcaster and commentator.
2. The famous Polish pianist, a refugee to the United States, had died in New York on June 29.

TEX/MS
To Barker

610, Park Avenue,
New York
March 27 [1945]

Thank you so much for your letter with its good news. I read part of the Princeton MS last night but this morning it was wrested from me by someone called Datus Smith, of Princeton, who said, to my distress, that the first MS had been destroyed, presumably in a railway accident. Sad news, but the remaining MS has already sped on its way, properly I think. The weather is lovely here. I hope you're having the same in Cambridge? Today, L. Scott and Mrs. Mc.Grew are coming to lunch with me and later I'm going to some Army-Navy function at Carnegie Hall, for which Kittie H. has a box. I have word from B. B.[1] that she is well and hasn't <u>missed</u> a <u>meal</u>. Also that she has made friends with a delightful young Chinese girl (Pekinese), so has nothing to complain of. The War News is satisfying this morning. A pity Lloyd-George couldn't have heard it, though perhaps it would no longer have seemed important to him! H. Blaine-Beale told me yesterday a sentence from—she said—Deuteronomy (I can't find it there). This is it: "And he saw a sapphire like a very heaven of clearness." It sounds more like Revelation, doesn't it. What a long letter can be written in a small sheet of paper! But now I must stop.

Afftly,
Helen

---

1. Brown Betty, a standard poodle.

TEX/MS
To Barker

610, Park Avenue,
[New York]
Wed. [March 28, 1945]

Dear Harley,

Your letter of yesterday came just after lunch, which Caroline Rasponi took with me here. It's very hot: temperature 82° today. And you say that it's hot too in cold Boston? I gather that the lectures are going well and they'll get better as you warm up (in the spirit) to them.

No news to write you. Yesterday there was a wave of hysteria and optimism over the whole city, wishful thinking of a bad kind. The man at the desk (the one who so admires Brown Betty) told me that peace would be declared, quite certainly, in a few hours, that the stock market had dropped violently, etc., etc. I went to sit in Kittie H's box at a function at Carnegie Hall—the Army & Navy presenting an "E" flag to the blind who have been doing such good war-work and the house was—or seemed to be—seething with excitement over peace. Mrs. Moran has just been in to tell me that the front of the Mayfair is to be "blasted" tomorrow, but that only means that it is to be given a violent cleaning. I hope your MS got safely to Princeton? Did it?

Mildred Gosford's son turned up suddenly, so, quite naturally, she didn't want to take time off for Le Père Ducattillon; and anyhow it's a hot night to go among crowds.

Forgive a dull letter. Goodnight and no dreams!

H—

I had a charming letter from Mrs. Gray (but I think I told you). She is in Boston now and has taken up—as it were—the painting her husband had to lay down. Perhaps you may see her.

TEX/MS
To Barker

610, Park Avenue,
[New York]
Tuesday [1945]

Your letter was given to me as I was starting for lunch this morning at 12.30, though it was received at 11. So this time, instead of ringing to ask what they should do with it, they simply put it in our box! Well, here it is now before me—and good news, except that you're

tired, which obviously you <u>are</u>. To lecture and be the life of lunch
and dinner parties is a double strain, but I expect the lectures are
very good indeed and that you enjoy the dinner-parties and such—
while you're <u>at</u> them.

Poor Hofmeyer has been ordered into hospital—some trouble with his back, he said, and a good deal of pain. I fear he has
been keeping about when he wasn't really fit for it. Too bad.

I've paid Nolan's bill and he's sending a man to take me out
tonight in the car. (Caroline Rasponi is offering me dinner—et moi,
j'offre le Cinema).

The "blasting" of the hotel goes on with fury and a steam-
drill in the street does a sort of obbligato. The giant hooks and their
rope-ladders are now attached to the salon windows, the rug rolled
up and the piano moved just in front of the entrance door. It's all
most exciting.

At the club I saw a lot of women I knew—and infinitely
more I didn't. Dorothea J. was there among the rest.

I have no tickets for the Philharmonic. Are they sending
them? (Nothing could be as beautiful as the Matthew Passion.) Padraic Colum talked yesterday about Humboldt—and now I'm wanting
to read the <u>Cosmos</u>.[1] Have you ever read it? Meanwhile, I'm quite
happy with "Is He Popinjoy". Did I write you that Boyd—your
Boyd—has returned to the Mayfair? He is doing the needful, you'll
be glad to know.

And I think that's all the news.

Afftly,

H—

1. Alexander van Humboldt (1769–1859), the German traveller and scientist, published
his greatest work, *Kosmos,* in 1845.

TEX/MS
To Barker

610, Park Avenue
[New York]
April 4 [1945]

Dear Harley,

Your letter of yesterday has just reached me. I'm glad you
feel that the lectures are going better, but I'm <u>sure</u> they were always
better than you feared. It is very cold here and one window in the
sitting-room has still to be open on account of the "blasting", with its

iron hooks and rope-ladders; also one window in your room. Also, the radiators are cold and stiff as if in death. I keep wailing to the linen-room, to the desk, to the electrician, but nothing happens. However, by the time this gets to you it will be like an open furnace here. The Park is now truly a vision of beauty. This is its "heure exquise". I lunched with kind, nice Mrs. Stuart Duncan and there were four other women, all kind and nice and very, very rich—riches round them almost visibly, like padding! (That word is p_adding, not pudding.)

The man now driving me about is like a rat-catcher to look at, but efficient and amiable. I tried to buy Humboldt's "Cosmos", but nobody had ever heard of the "Cosmos" or of Humboldt and looked in a very nervous, fidgety way at me while I displayed my own—so recently gained—knowledge. Meanwhile I have "Popinjoy" and I'm grateful for it. How very modern it seems, but human relations have little to do with dates and reckonings.

A pleasant and delicious little Italian dinner with Caroline Rasponi and afterwards we spent what seemed all the rest of the night at the Radio Centre, where proceedings of every kind went on. I thought of you—how you would have hated it.

Thank you for the postcards of the old Cleines[?] paintings of flowers. They must have been lovely.

Hurrah, the heat has been turned on! Now I must go and order my dinner and listen to R. Swing.

A very good-night to you.

H—

A month after this last letter was written, they returned to England. Staying once more at the Fortfield Hotel in Sidmouth, Devon, Barker one day hired a car and went over to Netherton Hall and the village of Farway. He spent the day calling on the farmers and village people he had known there fifteen years before. Helen did not accompany him. It is difficult to decide whether one should read anything into this simple fact, or into the change of tone and manner of address which is evident in the last four letters, of 1945, reproduced above.

 Chapter VII

Thomas Hardy, 1840–1928

W*hen Barker first* wrote to Hardy they were, respectively, thirty-six and seventy-four years of age. Barker, with his honors fresh upon him, was established as the leading theater director of London and a young playwright of considerable promise, but he was writing to the greatest and most famous English man of letters of the day. Hardy's reputation, made in competition with Tennyson, Browning, and Arnold, by 1914 stood higher than that of Swinburne (who had died five years before), Shaw, Meredith, Yeats, or any other living writer in English. Writing to Florence Henniker in July, 1921, Hardy said:

> We have had a few pleasant people calling—poets mostly. I am getting to know quite a lot of the young Georgians, and have quite a paternal feeling, or grandparental, towards them. Siegfried Sassoon has been, Walter de la Mare, John Masefield, and next week Mr. and Mrs. Galsworthy are going to call on their way to London. We have also seen the Granville Barkers.

That Barker fully appreciated their relative positions is evident from the tone of the letters reproduced here; indeed, his exaggerated respect sometimes approaches obsequiousness, even after he got to know Hardy quite well and was on terms of particular friendship with him. It is noteworthy that the then almost universal habit of addressing familiars of equal (or would-be equal) standing by their initials—a habit to which Barker was much given— was never applied by him to Hardy. He did get to the point of signing himself "H. G-B.," but he never began a letter with "My dear T. H." Though Hardy would have been the last man on earth to insist upon it, or even to draw attention to it, his position as doyen of English letters was by then both secure and obvious, and Barker was always conscious of it.

As will be seen from the first two letters in this chapter, it

Thomas Hardy, 1915. Drawing by William Rothenstein.

was *The Dynasts* that first brought the two men together. The great epic poem had been published in three parts in 1904, 1906, and 1908; but Hardy's main fame and reputation rested (and, I suspect, still rests) not on his poetry but on his novels, though there were even then some critics (and the number has certainly increased since his death) who would rank his verse as his greater achievement. The last of the novels, *Jude the Obscure*, was published in 1895; four collections of short stories and two of verse interposed in the nine years between this and the publication of the first part of *The Dynasts*, though the latter had been developing in his mind since before the writing of both *Jude* and *Tess of the D'Urbervilles*.

Barker came to *The Dynasts* by a specialist route, partly practical, partly idealistic. He was always a lover of poetry and especially of poetry that could be spoken out loud in public. And when war broke out in 1914 he wanted a play for his theater that would be in tune with the times but would take itself and those times seriously, not seek escape in fluffy nonsense. On both counts *The Dynasts* appealed to him. His awareness of the poem's greatness is a tribute to his critical acumen and sensitivity, since *The Dynasts* was slow to win general approval, and by 1914 its qualities and stature were by no means as widely appreciated as they are today. Barker's production of it, though caviare to the general, was well received by the discriminating. Barker himself was entirely responsible for the selection of scenes from the original work and for the staging and scenic arrangements (which were extremely simple), though Hardy wrote a new Prologue and Epilogue especially for the occasion.

Barker was also peripherally involved with the one play that Hardy wrote with the stage in mind. In a B. B. C. radio talk in 1956, Lady Cynthia Asquith said: "Like so many other writers who have excelled in one branch of literature, Hardy, who had excelled in two, had set his heart on writing a successful play. Confessing this ambition, he complained that the dramatisation of his books had proved a great disappointment." Lady Cynthia, who was secretary to Sir James Barrie, had visited Hardy in Barrie's company in 1921 and on that occasion heard Hardy make this confession. He was evidently in earnest, for by 1923 he had completed the manuscript of *The Famous Tragedy of the Queen of Cornwall* and was sending it to Barker for comment. Barker's detailed replies are included among the letters here reproduced. Marguerite Roberts, in an interesting little book called *Hardy's Poetic Drama and the Theatre* (New York, 1965), gives some further details of the productions of both *The Dynasts* and *The Famous Tragedy*, which are Hardy's only two poetic dramas, or, indeed, his only plays of any kind apart from the dramatization of his novels. It is interesting to note that Granville Barker was involved with both of them.

Hardy lived in a house, Max Gate, which he himself had designed and built on the outskirts of Dorchester. He had been there since 1885, when he moved into the new house with his first wife, Emma. Emma died there in 1912, and two years later Hardy remarried, his second wife being his former secretary, Florence Emily Dugdale. She was thirty-five when they married; he was seventy-four. Max Gate was about thirty miles from Netherton Hall, the country house bought by Helen Granville Barker in 1920, and as the friendship progressed the frequency of visits back and forth increased. On two occasions the Barkers were present when a group of undergraduates from Oxford gave performances of Greek tragedy in the garden of Max Gate especially for Hardy's entertainment (the audience numbered six or seven people on each occasion). In the Houghton Library of Harvard University there is a short description of these occasions, written—and very gracefully—by Helen Granville-Barker. It was Helen Granville-Barker also who described, in a letter to Florence Hardy after Thomas Hardy's death, the last visit he paid to the Barkers at Netherton Hall. It was on his eighty-seventh birthday, in June, 1927. Mrs. Hardy quotes the letter in her book *The Life of Thomas Hardy* (London, 1962): "In the afternoon we left him alone in the library because we thought he wanted to rest a little. It was cold, for June, and a wood fire was lighted. Once we peeped in at him through the garden window. He was not asleep but sitting, walled in with books, staring into the fire with that deep look of his. The cat had established itself on his knees and he was stroking it gently, but half-unconsciously."

The Barkers were out of England on one of their usual winter jaunts to the Continent when Hardy died in January, 1928, so they were unable to attend any one of the three commemorative services held on January 16 at three different churches—Westminster Abbey, St. Peter's Church, Dorchester, and the village church at Stinsford (where Hardy was baptized in 1840). At Westminster Abbey, where Hardy's ashes were buried in Poet's Corner, there were, among the pallbearers, as representatives of literature, J. M. Barrie, John Galsworthy, Sir Edmund Gosse, A. E. Housman, Rudyard Kipling, and Bernard Shaw. Almost all of them were long-time friends of Barker's as well, but he had probably known Hardy better than they had, though in those last years of his life nobody outside his immediate family circle knew Hardy very well or got very close to him.

DOR/TS
To Hardy

The Kingsway Theatre
(Proprietress: Miss Lena Ashwell)
Great Queen Street,
[London] W.C.
Lillah McCarthy
Granville Barker
September 25, 1914

Dear Mr. Thomas Hardy:

Would you care for us to follow the run of The Great Adventure[1] here with a production of the Dynasts? Or, rather, I fear I must say some scenes from the Dynasts. I do not know whether you ever considered an arrangement for the modern stage, but I have spent a little time in working out the possibility as I have been able to see it, and I can extract I find three acts coming, roughly, from the three parts of the complete work and keeping mainly to the scenes that concern England. The first act, Trafalgar, the second the Peninsula, the third Waterloo. If the idea does interest you, may I send for your consideration a copy so marked? I hope to be able to keep some at any rate of the choruses.

Very sincerely yours,
H. Granville Barker

P.S. The Battle of Waterloo nearly stumped me, but I think I can manage even that.

---

1. The play by Arnold Bennett; this was its first production.

DOR/MS
To Hardy

Stansted,
Wrotham,
Kent.
Monday
[September/October, 1914]

Dear Mr. Hardy:

They have wired me from London the substance of your letter. That is good news for us—and thank you too for the confidence you repose in me. I am having a copy of the book with my rough notes of the arrangement sent to you and I should much like to come down for a night if I may and explain the staging. We may or may not be pressed for time with the production—that depends a little on business with The Great Adventure. If I find we shall be, would it suit you to see me on Wednesday? I will wire you tomorrow.

At present we are working out our estimates of cost—rather a serious matter with so big a play in so small a theatre and we may have to arrange for some special finance, but that difficulty can, I hope, be got over.

I read the arrangement through to my wife yesterday (she sends to you and Mrs. Hardy her kindest rememberances; her work prevents her leaving town during the week) and in spite of the great simplification the drama must undergo—from my staging point of view, indeed almost because of it—I am sure one tenders to its dignity best by keeping it simple. I have great hopes that it may move us as much in action as reading it has done.

You must not think me murderous in the cutting. The device of the Reader of Stage Directions (a man) I am confident of; and of the simple strophe and antistrophe (women) is, I think, the best available. They are to be seated in an actual fore-scene—but I'll explain better personally.

I am rejoiced—may I say?—at the prospect of being—I hope—able to do something that I have so much admired.

Very sincerely yours,
H. Granville Barker

DOR/MS
To Hardy

Garrick Club
[London] W.C.
Oct. 25 [1916]

Dear Mr. Hardy,

Thank you very much indeed for the book of poems. I value the gift of it and always shall.

Some old friends I miss—the one about the man riding to Exeter to find his old love, "Valenciennes", one that begins "Is it worth while dear now?" and one called, I think, "A wasted day"— still some must be left out: put them in the next collection, please.

I am tempted to make a very poor exchange with you by sending you my "Red Cross" book that is just out. And indeed I think I will, mainly for the sake of one chapter—that I can hardly be said to have written at all but which contains some of the finest "natural" literature I have ever met.

My very kind regards to Mrs. Hardy and yourself.
Again my thanks.

> Very sincerely yours,
> H. Granville Barker

DOR/MS
To Hardy

> Il Castello,
> Portofino-Mare,
> Liguiria,
> Italy
> 31.3.23

My dear Mr. Hardy,

Did I ever write to you about this that follows? The letter that I meant to write is in my head; whether it ever got on paper I can't be sure.

Some of us are forwarding a petition to the Prime Minister for a Civil List Pension for William Poel. May we have your signature? You know the weight it would carry.

You'll see when the petition reaches you what all the circumstances of the case are. And I think you know Poel's work pretty well—of it anyhow. He has served his cause, I think, bravely and singlemindedly and I think the theatre as a whole has profited much by what he has done and—even better—shown the way to doing.

And he has spent all his substance, quite recklessly.

So if you do think kindly of the matter, will you sign?

We leave here about the 11th: look to be back in Devonshire quite early in May—and look forward very much to seeing you both.

Meanwhile our love and homage.

> Always yours,
> Harley Granville-Barker

DOR/MS
To Hardy

Netherton Hall,
Colyton,
Devon.
4.7.23

My dear Mr. Hardy,

I can't tell you how delighted—and honored—I am that you send me the Famous Tragedy to read and report on.[1]

I shall read it aloud to Helen tonight—the only way, I think, with a play—and then, according to command, I'll say what I usefully can.

We're to see you both soon, we hope. And if Oxford may have you for several, spare us <u>one</u> night, at least, next time.

We're well. But what a winter-in-summer! We send you our love and homage, as ever.

Yours,
H. G-B.

---

1. Hardy has sent him a manuscript copy of *The Famous Tragedy of the Queen of Cornwall,* a verse treatment of the Tristan and Isolde story, written by Hardy for performance in Dorchester by the Hardy Players, an amateur theater company. The play has never been performed professionally; it was published by Macmillan in London in 1923.

DOR/MS
To Hardy

Netherton Hall,
Colyton,
Devon,
6.7.23

My dear Mr. Hardy,

I read—and great pleasure to have your work to read—the Famous Tragedy to Helen the night before last. And now I'll write to you about it.

These are producer's notes only,[1] you'll understand: "the same"—to misquote Vanity Fair—"I shot Mr. William Shake-speare". And if in <u>this</u> preface I seem sometimes to argue with you— well, I would have argued with W. S., if I could have got at him.

Imprimis: the play as I read it stands up square and strong —like the admirable scene you've designed. This is <u>the</u> essential thing and it is partly due to the "Greek" form you've (I think) so wisely chosen. It does bring the story, for once, within compass as a tragedy instead of weaving it out—as usual—to a romance.

As to how the Dorchester Players will do it—such a gift! And I do think that if they'll be careful to do it simply, their sincerity will make up for what they must lack in high buskined style. But I have them particularly in mind in the notes that follow:

p. 6: 1 and 2—it isn't quite clear to me who lands. Not Iseult. Tristram? Nor will it even be quite clear that it isn't the King himself coming up from the ship. Such is the difficulty of making dialogue "without" plain in its intention. And you have adopted, you see, a conventional form which properly allows ships to come in and people to enter the castle in a minute's space. Always a danger in not having the opening quite clear. The fact that I see it has come back from somewhere unknown and that Mark is about to return from hunting, is what as a producer I'd have to emphasise. Even the point that Mark may not hear she has been away— though I see what you gain by it—would distract a little, for me, from the strength of this opening scene.

The chanters generally: Do you mean them to be upon a sort of front stage? I suppose so; and it would be best. They could stand on each side of the main playing stage in front of black—or dark—proscenium wings. The great thing will be to forbid them to move about while they are chanting.

p. 10. Equally it will be safer—if you'd think the effect was not spoiled—to let the Queen sit still. There's nothing so difficult as walking about silently and expressing emotion.

p. 12: 1—Your producer feels you don't need this. The convention allows for arbitrary confidences, though Brangwain is a known confidante anyhow and calling attention to this breaks the illusion, I think.

p. 16: 1—I much wish that Mark could cross the opening at the back, or better still the stage from L to R (unless the opening is very big: and it won't be), as from his council to his revellings and even meet the disguised harper: or have the harper appear in the opening at the back (or would Mark then guess? I think not, according to convention.)

It is really impossible to make a scene "without" effective: hard to make it intelligible. And Brangwain's exit will be very flat (p. 17: 2). Further, you cast a great burden upon the Dorchester players with (3). It seems very simple, but it needs a lot of doing: the entrance, taking off the disguise, the embrace—all in dumb show. It would help them very much if Tristram made the disguised entrance

with Mark there. Then when Mark and his followers had gone, if
Iseult said one line (not more would be needed) to show that she saw
through the disguise. Then, when he was disclosed, if Brangwain
went off to keep watch, that will prevent Tristram and Iseult running
all their "effects" together and nullifying them.

p. 19: 1—Your producer rather wishes he had not to resume
his disguise.

p. 20: 2—Your producer wishes that the direction could be
"she opens the door to the banqueting hall and stands, still visible to
the audience, in the doorway."

p. 21: 1—The repetition of throwing off the disguise is risky.
It is a good technical rule (I don't say it cannot be broken) that one
cannot <u>repeat</u> an effect successfully.

N.B. Iseult of the White Hands must be very simple and
quiet in this scene. If she gets "theatrical" over "no, no: I won't be
any other's wife" it will be dangerous.

p. 24: 1—Important that this "carrying out" should be deliberate and occupy most of the time of the chanting.

Your producer wishes that (p. 25: 2) came at once (before
the chanting) and that Iseult then commanded Brangwain to take her
away. It would help Iseult to "assert" herself again. Then (p. 25: 1)
without the bracketed sentence would come well. 1a could be cut. It
does drop the tension rather and I fancy the most important scene
that is just opening would get a better start then.

p. 26: 1—For much the same reason (<u>i.e.</u> to confirm Iseult
in her queenliness and strength) it would be helpful if Brangwain
could appear silently and, in answer to Iseult's question about I. of
the White-hands, could say "she mends" or something of that sort.
This seems perhaps a detail, but the effect of the interruption as it
stands will be to lower the importance of the two important people.

p. 27: 1—This line of Tristram's is difficult; <u>i.e.</u> I feel I
wouldn't quite know how to say "we shall get over this". As a Tristram, I should wish it had more exact image and meaning. And—
more importantly—the damsel's entrance and interruption, without
any comment from them to indicate how they take the interruption
(which again indicates what <u>sort</u> of an entrance she makes and helps
her to make it)—this is a little difficult for "your producer".

From here indeed to the end of Scene XVIII I feel that
there is, in this particular sense, some under-writing.

If any small speech once existed for Iseult at the end of
Scene XVII (after "exit Damsel") and you cut it out, I could wish
you hadn't. And on p. 29, when "Iseult weeps and he embraces her
for awhile" I'd have been glad of the words. Dumb show is so diffi-

cult. Tristram's dying speech is, of course, beautiful and perhaps the most effective thing in the play.

p. 30: 1—This will all be very effective, I think, if Brangwain does it right: i.e. she must be strong, definite and conventional in her movements. She must, as we say, do a thing and then "hold" it till the effect is made. And she must keep still while the chanters chant.

p. 31: 1—Your producer would very much like these two lines in brackets cut out. The White-handed will find it hard to say them well and <u>then</u> to change her key accurately to "I heard her cry" etc. Whereas she can hit this accurately enough (and it is <u>very</u> important) if she has nothing else to think of.

That is all, I think; and coming to the end I become fairly confident that the life and reality, the true stuff of poetry, in the play—if they can all be brought to feel this—will carry them over the difficulties which their lack of sheer skill will impose on them. If they <u>feel</u> it <u>deeply</u>, <u>speak</u> it <u>truly</u> and don't move except when they've reason for moving, they'll pull it off. And a great achievement for them. A proud thing to have a play from <u>you</u>.

It is Saturday morning when I finish this and in the midst of some grief, for we have just heard that Mr. James Gray, a good and close friend, and Helen's lawyer and counsellor and man of business is suddenly dead. We shall go up to town for his funeral but stay only a day or so.

I do hope these rough notes may be of some use when the Famous Tragedy comes to be done. Again, I'm proud you gave me the chance of making them. Our love and homage to you both, as always.

H. G-B.

---

1. "Producer" meant, at that time in England, director. His notes on the play are written as if he were directing the production.

DOR/MS
To Hardy

Netherton Hall,
Colyton,
Devon.
22.10.23

My dear Mr. Hardy,

I have been much annoyed to find in two booksellers' catalogues some letters advertised that you wrote to me about the production of The Dynasts. They seem to have been in the file of A. E. Drinkwater, who was then my manager. He has recently died and his widow, instead of returning them to me—as she should have done— sold them, together with a few addressed to him. A most outrageous proceeding. Some I have managed, I hope, to recover; two or three appear to be gone beyond recall. There was, I think, nothing private or even very personal in them, nothing that anybody might not have read. But my vexation is not the less on that account. You know, I'm sure, that I would not expose or have exposed any correspondence with you to casual eyes, much less sell it! But the matter must, I fear, vex you and that greatly troubles me, even though the fault—apart from some carelessness—is not mine. This whole modern traffic in letters and signatures is really abominable. Please, though, look over this mishap as far as you can.

We look forward so much to Thursday.

Our homage and affection.

Yours,
Harley Granville-Barker

DOR/MS
To Hardy

Netherton Hall,
Colyton,
Devon.
28.10.23

My dear Mr. Hardy,

Here are some notes for Mr. Tilley.[1] I hope he'll be able to decipher them and they may be of some use.

I think they're all on the right lines. They only need more courage and precision and <u>not</u> do one or two things.

I hope you were pleased. I think you've every reason to be.

I would like to suggest a tiny "cut" or two of lines that are difficult for them to get the true effect from, when a failure to hit the right note may mean hitting the wrong one rather loudly.

Scene XV: I'd take out Tristram's first speech and the Queen's "what Tristram, what?" This is most <u>difficult</u> to make effective; and if he misses the right note may sound bathos.

The possible little cuts at the end I did speak of. The only point of them is to avoid the quadruple "surprise"—two people seeing the corpses that <u>we</u> have been looking at for some minutes. The two actresses won't know how to lend variety to this. And it may lead to untimely giggles—not that it is funny or even that anyone will really think it so. But death on the stage makes the spectators nervous and the slightest jar makes them seek relief in laughter. I have known the end of Hamlet—and with steady professional actors too— made by a slight contretemps into—— But that's another story.

I think it is quite easy to do. Cut a repeated phrase if you can; and if you can't, see that the actresses don't repeat their intonations and gestures. I think on p. 71 Brangwain's speech could quite effectively be:

> "Here's more of this same stuff of death
> The sea's dark noise last night . . . etc."

She need not mention Mark. We see she sees him.

We did so like coming and being with you at the play's making: a real joy and a pride to share something of that sort with you.

As always,

Yours,
H. G-B.

---

1. The director of the amateur theatre company [the Hardy Players] which was producing *The Famous Tragedy of the Queen of Cornwall*. Tilley also played the part of Merlin, which Hardy had added to the original legend especially to provide a part for Tilley, who was an old and valued member of the company.

DOR/MS
To Hardy

Netherton Hall,
Colyton,
Devon.
30.10.23

My dear Mr. Hardy,

Only a line—and not needing any answer—to say that I think B's idea of having the stage pretty dark at the end is excellent. It would much smooth over these difficulties.

The sound of the sea! Ah, no. We must have that in our heads.

I would I were going to see it.

Heavens, what weather. I look out on thick clouds rolling almost to my window.

Yours,
H. G-B.

DOR/MS
To Hardy

Netherton Hall,
Colyton,
Devon.
23.11.23

My dear Mr. Hardy,
The Queen of Cornwall has gone to her most honoured
place among her sister works on our shelves. And thank you very
much indeed. I only wish I could see her all alive and in full fig.
Helen will, and looks forward to it very much. I shall be discoursing
about another Ancient Briton to the Ancient Britons of Bangor.[1] But
I shall be thinking of you and her—and wishing you both a happy
triumph.
It was so good to have you both with us on Sunday. I hope
you weren't benighted returning, nor too cold on the way.
Our love and homage,

Yours,
H. G-B.

---

1. He had been invited to lecture on *King Lear* at Bangor in North Wales.

DOR/MS
To Hardy

37A, Great Cumberland Place,
[London] W.
2.12.24

My dear Mr. Hardy,
I must send you a line of congratulations about Tess.[1] I'm
sure you <u>are</u> pleased that the Wessex folk have done the Wessex
thing so well. Barrie sang praises to us the other day. I wish we could
have seen it. And could have seen you both again before we go to
Paris on the 17th. But a happy winter to you—and may we meet in
the spring: a real spring. Max Gate and Netherton pushing up their
flowers to make it one for us. (Darkness, utter darkness, over London as I write this.)
Helen hears good report of you both. And we're well—at
least <u>I</u> shall be when the doctors have done with me.
Our affection to you both then, as always.

Yours,
H. G-B.

Would you mind sending the enclosed to Lawrence for me?[2] I've left his address at Netherton and I can't trust my memory.

---

1. The first stage version of *Tess of the D'Urbervilles,* prepared by Hardy himself, was presented at the Dorchester Corn Exchange on November 26, 1924, by the Hardy Players. A revised version was seen in a professional production in Barnes, Surrey, with Gwen Ffrangcon-Davies as Tess; it opened on September 7, 1925, and ran for over a hundred performances.
2. See Chapter VIII below for letters from Barker's correspondence with T. E. Lawrence.

DOR/MS
To Hardy

6, Rue de Seine,
[Paris] VI
13.2.25

My dear Mr. Hardy,

I am pretty sure that what Winthrop Ames wants is your play—or nothing. And with good reason.

For long I was almost savagely against the adaptation of books into plays. I contended that the approach to the writing of each must be so different. And I still contend that. But the Moscow Theatre did a version of Dostoievsky's Brothers Karamazov which showed me a way round. They took chapters from the book and the very dialogue as written, not changing a word (culling a few). And they had a reader to read the necessary descriptions of what happened in between. And so they managed to put the book itself—nothing at least that was not a part of it—upon the stage.

And whether your Tess answers to all a playwright's canons or not—though what are they? A play is something that can be made effective in a theatre by human agency. It is your Tess and that is what matters. So, at least, I interpret Ames's desire to see the MS.

Still—! I sometimes feel (though I'll never say so) that the theatre is a sale métier. It ought never to be, but at times it is. Perhaps only a very robustly intellectual people—the Greeks, the Elizabethans, the French of the Grand Siècle—can profit by it and keep it in its place. So if you decide that America and England shall have Tess and Jude and Martin and Bathsheba by the fireside only, I shall sympathise. And after all, that is where we have learned to know and value them.

We send you both our love. Storms have been buffeting you these last few days, I hear. We've had the tail of them and Paris is grey today. News from Netherton is that the primroses are out—with you too, I expect.

Here's to seeing you both in April!

Yours,

H. G-B.

DOR/MS
To Hardy

Netherton Hall,
Colyton,
Devon.
16.8.25

My dear Mr. Hardy,

<u>No</u>, it is by no means customary to part with American rights (I suppose it is these that are in question) or to make any sort of promise about them. Inexperienced dramatists, anxious to have their plays acted, are sometimes cajoled into doing so. But this is the first business thing they should learn <u>not</u> to do. For a "West End" production it would be allowable to give an option upon British provincial rights, upon agreed terms, to be taken up or not in (say) a month's time from the production. At times an option is given besides upon Colonial rights (these should always <u>ex</u>clude Canada, which goes with U.S.A.). But even this is not customary. And in the present case the most you need do—and in all generosity, I should say—is to give an option on provincial rights, to become valid if (and only if) the play is transferred to the West End of London and was at least a month there. I'd further advise you to let any time agreement be contingent upon something of this sort: <u>i.e.</u> if this management cannot make the play a success there is nothing to be gained by their keeping it and everything by your having it back.

But the omens seem good and we wish it all possible fortune. Miss Ffrangcon-Davies is about the best Tess on the market, I should say. Though I don't know her work very well there is what the Americans now call an "otherness" about her which should surely be Tess's hall-mark. Before she was well-known at all she played a small part at Birmingham in a translation from the Spanish that Helen and I did, and we both "picked her out" from the rest of the cast. Ion Swinley too has sensitiveness and intelligence. Yes, the omens are good.

We go off for a week's visiting tomorrow. But we hope to

see you here or at Max Gate when we get back. And our love and homage to you both, please.

> Yours,
> H. G-B.

The note below was written on a postcard but put in an envelope with the enclosure to which Barker refers.

DOR/MS
To Hardy

> 26, Hill Street,
> Mayfair,
> [London]
> 11.11.25

My dear Mr. Hardy,

We are so sorry Florence is ill and cannot come up. But here is something we were going to give her and I had better now send it to <u>you</u> without delay: the information about your desirous but not, I fear, very desirable Spanish translator. Better treat the document, doubtless, as "private and confidential".

Our love to you both.

> Yours,
> H. G-B.

P.S. My informant does not know the man himself. I judge the report to come direct from the police!

What follows is the enclosure, in Helen's handwriting.

Translation of information received from Martinez Sierra
about the Spaniard who wished to translate Mr. Hardy's plays

Alfonso Fernández Burgas: this person lives, together with his mother and a brother called Clemente, at Sicilia Street, number 239, 4^2, 1^a. He is twenty-three, a bachelor, a native of Gerona. He has the qualification of "Perito Mercantil" (one capable of a business career) and devotes himself to business, working as a clerk in an office. He is totally unknown in literary circles, neither has any literary production of his ever been heard of. He is not a member of any association where writers and lovers of literature meet.

His brother Clemente was denounced by the "Juzgado de Guardio" in 1922 for theft of 8,000 pesetas from the "City Bank Club", where he worked as cashier, being arrested in Hamburg three months later. He was in jail in Barcelona until a short time ago but is at the moment provisionally at liberty, with bail. Clemente called himself a Professor of languages and has made some translations of foreign authors—with what success it is not known. As Clemente is under arrest for defalcation, and is known as an adventurer, when he wants to do any business he makes his brother act for him and sign the letters in which he makes proposals for any enterprise. (The name is Burgas, not Bargas.)

DOR/W
To Hardy
Mayfair   25 Nov. 1925   10.20 A.M.
To: Thomas Hardy, Max Gate, Dorchester.
        Congratulations on Tess one hundredth performance and our love to you both.

Helen and Harley

DOR/MS
To Hardy

Hotel Beau-Site,
4, Rue de Presbourg,
Paris.
23.12.25

My dear Mr. Hardy,
        It did so please me—well, I'm sure you know how much—to have your letter and to think of The Madras House meaning something to you, enough for you to write to me so.
        Yes, indeed: the theatre is the curse of the drama—dreadful paradox! But need it be—will it always be? Though I'm tempted, time and again, to seek freedom (and what you say would be—no, not a temptation, but an encouragement to anyone), till I can answer that question with a fatal "Yes", I must stick to my craft, I think. And of course one sticks almost mechanically to a craft one has learnt with the usual pain and grief. And it has its fascination; the discipline of it. And one dreams of a theatre . . . !
        You bring this little burst of egoism on yourself by writing

me such a triad letter: valued for itself and doubly valued as a part of the friendship with you and Florence that Helen and I value—well, there again, I think, I <u>hope</u>, you know how much. But I won't start to tell you. We think and speak of you often.

Here we are, with our salon window looking straight at the Arc de Triomphe, the fire on the Unknown Soldier's grave always burning under our eyes, and at night more brightly. Nearly always a little group of people round it. And the cars whirling round the Place never-ceasingly—a dervish dance.

Till we meet, our love to you both.

Yours,

H. G-B.

DOR/MS
To Hardy

Netherton Hall,
Colyton,
Devon.
1.6.26

My dear Mr. Hardy,

We were thinking of you both this morning—as indeed we so often think and speak of you—and were even jumping to a plan to come and see you when it suddenly struck us, "June 2 is his birthday", so off went our telegram. And it isn't—it's June 1. So this letter brings our love and homage to the right date. But we could send it you any day and every day for that matter.

And tomorrow may you be especially happy in all the love and homage that will be offered you.

As ever,

Yours,

H. G-B.

DOR/MS
To Hardy

Netherton Hall,
Colyton,
Devon.
26.5.27

My dear Mr. Hardy,

    How very good of you to write to me about "Waste"! Need I tell you how I value what you say? Yes, I sometimes wish the theatre "were not"—at any rate that I'd never been concerned with it. And yet, I don't know. . . . Anyhow, for good or ill, it's my job to write plays and write about them. And some day perhaps the theatre of my dreams may be.

    We speak of you often, hope to see you here soon. This <u>is</u> summer, isn't it? Your tree flourishes.[1]

    Our love to you both,

Yours,
H. G-B.

---

1. In 1921 Hardy, on one of his visits to Netherton Hall, planted a *Catalpa syringaefolia* in the garden. It is there still, with a little cast-iron notice set in the ground beside it giving its name, and his, and the year of its planting.

Chapter VIII

T. E. Lawrence, 1888–1935

T*he brief selection* of letters contained in this chapter is different in kind from those of the earlier chapters in that, even though not every one of the letters which passed between the two men is reproduced here (or, for that matter, is still extant), one feels that virtually the whole story of their relationship is contained in the letters themselves. And yet this feeling is not accompanied by a sense that the relationship was casual, trivial, or merely formal. Barker and Lawrence were never close or intimate; in many ways they did not know each other very well; but there was nevertheless an immediate and spontaneous attraction between them which comes out very clearly in these letters. Though the facts are plain and clear and sparse enough, there are some interesting lines here to read between, for anyone who wants to try it. And though the surviving correspondence is so scanty, it adds materially to what we know about both men and serves to illuminate—and not to the disadvantage of either—the characters of both. They had two qualities in common. Both were enormously introspective and had always been so; and when they met in 1923, though their lives had been utterly different up to that time, each had lost his way. In both cases a return to the former mode of life was unthinkable; but in both cases a viable alternative failed to present itself. Both had been brilliantly but rather briefly successful as men of action— sudden, feverish action in circumstances of risk and danger (though of very different kinds); quite suddenly, the world of action had seemed, to both of them, tawdry and inadequate, the ideals shoddy and second-hand. With a mixture of scorn and regret, each had turned his back on the earlier life of activity and by a curious coincidence had chosen retreats within forty miles of each other.

  T. E. Lawrence was born Thomas Edward Chapman in 1888. His father, Thomas Robert Chapman (later, Sir Thomas), left his wife, two daughters, and his family home in Ireland and eloped with the

T. E. Lawrence, 1918. Painting by Augustus John.

children's governess, Sarah Maden. The couple settled in Oxford under the name of Mr. and Mrs. Lawrence. Twice in the future would the son, under societal pressures he felt he could no longer endure, resort to the same defense mechanism or protective coloring previously employed by the father. The image of a person who was in most ways magnificently sane (and in Lawrence's case one has only to read his letters to establish that) retreating into a deliberately constructed personality, so to speak, is a fascinating one and becomes the more so when one realizes that both the instinct for retreat and the method employed may have been hereditary. One can see how such a person would appeal to Barker and how similar, in some senses, Lawrence's underlying attitudes about privacy and the preservation of personal integrity were to the ideas expressed by Barker, both in *The Secret Life* and in, for instance, his distaste for all forms of autobiography and memoir-writing. (Of course, Lawrence, both in *Seven Pillars of Wisdom* and in *The Mint,* did write autobiographically, but these are legitimate exceptions, the former because he was writing about important political events in which he, personally, happened to be involved, the latter because it was written in an attempt to explore—but not to exploit—the very issue of the relationship of an integrated personality to a community.) At the deepest levels, the postures of the two men were very similar on this issue.

Lawrence took a first in history at Oxford in 1910, when he was twenty-two. The following year he was attached to a British Museum archeological expedition to the Hittite city of Carchemish, and this led to further archeological work in Sinai and Egypt under C. L. Woolley and Flinders Petrie. In this way he began to learn Arabic and to develop a great respect and regard for the Arabs. While he was serving in military intelligence in Egypt in 1915, he was appointed liaison officer and advisor to Prince Feisal, younger son of King Hussein of Mecca. The British plan was to encourage and assist an Arab revolt against Turkey, Germany's ally, and Lawrence, more than any other single individual, first brought this about and then carried it to a successful conclusion. At the end of the war he was a member of the British delegation to the Peace Conference in 1919, and from 1921 to 1922 he was an adviser on Arab affairs at the Colonial Office. Feeling, however, that Britain had gone back on wartime promises and had betrayed the Arabs, he resigned this position in disgust and refused many further highly placed positions (including that of High Commissioner for Egypt). Instead, sickened by the crassness of the "Lawrence of Arabia" popular mythology, he changed his name to J. H. Ross and enlisted as an aircraftman (that is, the lowest rank of all) in the Royal Air Force. His identity was discovered after about six months, partly through the prying of newspaper reporters and partly through the curiosity of an inquisitive officer. He was discharged from the Air Force by order of an embarrassed government. In the following year he again changed his name, this time to Shaw, and enlisted as a private in the Royal Tank Corps; in 1925 he transferred once more to the R.A.F.

Seven Pillars of Wisdom, his long and striking account of the events of the Arab revolt and his own responses to those events, was begun in Paris in 1919, during the Peace Conference. The completed first draft was stolen from him in a train at Reading, Berkshire. Urged on by D. G. Hogarth,[1] Lawrence began to rewrite it immediately, an enormous task in view of its length. He completed the second version by the end of 1920 but was dissatisfied with it and destroyed it. During 1921, while working at the Colonial Office (partly in London and partly on various missions to the Middle East), he wrote a third version, of which he had eight copies privately printed by the Oxford Times Press in 1921. This text formed the basis for the Subscription Edition of 1926, to which he refers in some of his letters to Barker. His refusal to publish the book commercially sprang from special scruples he had about money and worldly possessions generally: he felt that his service in Arabia was a kind of crusade and believed it wrong to profit monetarily from the fame that had (accidentally, in his view) accrued to him as a result. He also felt, in a more general way, that a man demeaned both himself and his work when he accepted payment for creative and valuable work, that only menial tasks should be rewarded by payments of money. There is a comment by him in a letter to Bernard Shaw of December 20, 1923 (letter no. 235 in David Garnett's 1938 edition of *The Letters of T. E. Lawrence*), which summarizes his feeling neatly: "It seems I'm to regret the fall of Mr. Baldwin: and to thank you very much for the attempt at a pension. It was exceedingly good of you. Hogarth gave me no idea of it. Why did you think I wouldn't take it? It's earned money which sticks in the throat:—that a man should come down to working for such stuff." Barker, though his solutions to its problems were different in practice from Lawrence's, had something of the same attitude to money: he refused to treat it with respect, let alone reverential awe.

It was Thomas Hardy—or, more precisely, his wife, Florence—who introduced Lawrence to Helen and Harley Granville-Barker. Bovington Camp, where Lawrence was stationed when he

---

1. David George Hogarth (1862–1927), archaeologist and author of a number of books on the Middle East, was keeper of the Ashmolean Museum, Oxford, from 1908 until his death. It was he who recruited Lawrence for archaeological work in Arab countries.

joined the Tank Corps, was only ten miles or so from Max Gate, Hardy's house. Lawrence became a fairly frequent, and valued, visitor at Max Gate. Gillian Avery, in her essay "The Later Years" contributed to *The Genius of Thomas Hardy,* which Margaret Drabble edited in 1976, tells the delightful story of Lawrence's being the only visitor who was allowed to pick up Wessex, Mrs. Hardy's wire-haired terrier. Wessex, apparently, was a dog of some discrimination, who "barked vociferously, tolerated some visitors and attacked others." Lawrence was the one exception that Wessex made. In the series Monographs on the Life of Thomas Hardy, edited and published by J. Stevens Cox, there is a little booklet by Richard Curle called *The Return of Wessex,* ostensibly by "Wessex Redivivus." In this, Wessex is made to say: "There would be a real he-scent that whiffled under the door before Ellen, the maid, could open it, what with bothering about where I had got to. Wow! What a lovely smell it was, a mixed sort of scent with sniffs of sweat and earth, dogs and men, sand and leather and gunpowder. And that would be—as you may have guessed—Lawrence of Arabia. . . . I can tell you, I never pinned him."

The Barkers lived thirty miles from Hardy in the opposite direction from Bovington Camp: visits were exchanged back and forth fairly regularly. So it was natural that Lawrence and Barker should meet, sooner or later, at Max Gate. Natural, too, that it should be a sympathetic meeting: all five people concerned were very private people. Their senses of the world would chime together with a spontaneous harmony.

Lawrence was also, of course, extremely friendly with Bernard and Charlotte Shaw, but there is no evidence, so far as I know, of Shaw's having brought Barker and Lawrence together. As Stanley Weintraub argues in *Private Shaw and Public Shaw,* in a certain sense Lawrence replaced Barker as a kind of surrogate son in the Shaw household. There is some force in this argument. Barker married Helen Huntington in 1918; Lawrence's father died in 1919. There would be a kind of logic in the replacement of one younger man by another in the life of the Shaws at that time (in 1920, Lawrence was thirty-two and Barker was forty-two).

Lawrence was a tremendous letter-writer; the 1938 standard edition of his letters, though by no means exhaustive, contained five hundred and seventy-three letters. In the following year, 1939, Barker privately printed a booklet called "Eight Letters from T. E. L." It is a small gray volume, in stiff board covers, printed on handwoven paper. On its title page there is a printed note which says: "50 copies have been printed and the type has been distributed." Barker's brief preface states:

These eight letters add little enough to one's knowledge of Lawrence, and the second has already been printed in David Garnett's comprehensive collection. Nevertheless future writers about him and his career—and these there assuredly will be—have a prospective claim to every available detail. So, should the originals be lost, it may be worth while to have a few copies made. The omission in letter six is of thirty words of carelessly invidious comment upon a third person, still alive.

These letters are the ones included in this chapter. The letter of February 7, 1924, also appears in the David Garnett volume: the rest have never been published before, apart from Barker's private printing. Barker's two replies, included here, have never before been published. The "carelessly invidious comment," which seems to us now innocuous enough, was about Sir Philip Sassoon. Using the text of the original letter, now in the Houghton Library, Harvard University, I have restored it to its proper place in the letter.

Lawrence's letters all display one peculiarity of punctuation, which I have preserved. In order to represent the process of a thought's gradual completion through a series of unpremeditated stages, he makes frequent use of dots. In no case do they represent omissions. They represent, rather, a cautious (and often ironic) forward groping by the writer. They are as idiosyncratic as the constantly recurring dashes in Barker's letters, but they play less havoc with the sense and the rest of the punctuation and can be retained in print without damaging the reading flow.

HAR/MS
To Barker

[Clouds' Hill,
Moreton,
Dorset.]
2.XII.23

Are you gone yet? I'm reading the play.[1] It's hard, very hard, reading, and interests me enormously. I like close-woven writing, & I'm going to like this, I think.

The reason for a premature letter is to ask whether you would agree to try & read my book.[2] The print is awful (very small, & squalid, & dazing in the eyes) the punctuation nil, the style priggish, the sense hysterical. But it is easy to skip, & after all I don't ask people to read it, only to try.

I had one of the three available copies of it returned to me yesterday, which prompts this letter. You might keep it as long as you liked (Italy, I thought, perhaps . . . . . . you were discussing long books for that . . . . . and this is 340,000 words) and say as much or as little as you wished about it afterwards.

My attack on your retirement was an argument, not a charge. You are happier than me, for at least there is something you want to do, which you think worth doing: and I suppose you don't despise yourself exceedingly. That's one benefit of success.

Yours sincerely,
T. E. Shaw

Address now is:

T. E. S., Clouds' Hill, Moreton, Dorset

---

1. Barker had given him a copy of *The Secret Life*. See other comments on the play in Lawrence's letter of February 7, 1924, and in letters between Barker and Archer in 1923 (Chapter II).
2. *Seven Pillars of Wisdom.*

CAS/MS
To Lawrence

Connaught Hotel,
Mayfair, W.1
[London]
6.12.23

My dear Shaw,

Not gone but on the hop. First to Paris, where we'll be a week at least:

Hotel Lotti,
Rue Castiglione.

(oddly enough i.e. a grim appropriateness if your book
arrives there—as I hope: it was Mark Sykes' ending place[1]). I do—we
both do—badly want to read your book in any form: 350,000–550,000
words if you like. I'm pretty sure it will travel safely to me—book
post, registered or other; not <u>parcel,</u> is my only warning.

Your "argument" on my retirement was a fair retort. And I
welcomed it, partly that I might explain to someone who might care
to know, whom I cared should know, that it wasn't planless. As it
happens, inclination does combine with what I think is wisdom to do
a few years' spade-work. It'll be writing for a while yet.

But even more I welcomed it as it helped towards friendly
speaking with you, which I'd wanted after knowing you for just one
minute.

You have a "Daimon" (we all have, when we've any over-
plus of vitality at all) and he'll call on you again when you have
accumulated enough power. And you need a lot: your "game" takes
a world wider sweep than does mine.

And as for your feelings about what's done: well, I suppose
your religious biologist would say that this whole world has been built
up on a series of well-intentioned mistakes; it being the intention that
persists and survives. For further insight into which consideration see
Act III Sc. 2 of The Secret Life.

Well, we do look forward to the book (Don't forget, either,
to pass our names to your banker friend[2]) and to seeing you again in
the spring.

Yours,
Harley Granville-Barker

---

1. Lieutenant Colonel Sir Mark Sykes (1879–1919), a professional soldier who wrote
   several books about Arabia and Arab affairs, died in Paris. He negotiated the so-
   called Sykes-Picot Agreement with France during the war, which—in Lawrence's
   view, at any rate—betrayed many of the promises made by the British government to
   the Arabs in order to induce them to rise in revolt against Turkey.
2. Lawrence was arranging to get *Seven Pillars of Wisdom* printed privately, on a subscription basis. It was issued in this form in 1926 and published in 1935, the year he
   died (see his letter of April 30, 1924).

HAR/MS
To Barker

Clouds' Hill,
Moreton,
Dorset.
7.2.24

When your letter came, & said "a month" I sighed with
gladness that there was so much time to work out a reply . . . but the
days have dodged me somehow, & I'm all unready still.

You see, while you have been so magnificently persistent
with my literary "builder's yard" I've been reading that polished four-
square play of yours. Is that a comic picture? of an author and a
would-be (would have been?) exchanging books, & tasting each other
meditatively.

Anyhow that's what I've done, with barren results. Your
work is so hard, so intricate, so packed. It is the essence of thought,
a variety of mental Bovril.[1] Shaw (the real one) talked of it with me,
deploring your profusion of material, your introduction of stuff which
would have made eight plays if beaten out thin.

I rather like the pemmican of letters, or rather I used to like
it, when my head was at ease to think over the words I gave it
through my eyes. I thought then that a man could not work himself
too hard, when he opened a new branch to the public. After all the
suffrages worth having are the people who will read your play with
the eager effort you put into it.

And yet, and yet . . . your leisure is so abundant that perhaps
you have been cruel to the larger audience. I don't see you somehow as
only a highbrow for highbrows: but haven't you been forgetful of the
duties of the many? I get up in the morning, & clean boots & make beds
and carry coal & light fires . . . and then all day I work till five
o'clock . . . and when in the evening the choice lies between an easy
thing, like Methuselah, & a hard thing, like yours: why without my will
my hand strays to the left, & I read Shaw. It's not out of sheer laziness:
predigested food is wholesome to a stomach which is weary.

However a bit too much of this. It is a very great thing, that
play of yours. I hate plays, because I'm no theatre-goer, & the un-
practised form is knobby and uncouth to my wits: but the characters
come through the writing with a shout. Your politicians are really
politicians: and though I resent the death which unties a problem I
suppose you felt that it would be unhelpful in you to leave a tangle to
the crowd for their late supper. The thing is clearly meant to be
played, isn't it? Otherwise you would not have sacrificed so much to
the stage-technique.

Strowde is the person who interested me most. Your women passed me by, (revenge perhaps, for I usually pass them, in the flesh): your Serocolds are too usual to be more than ornamental, & I resent a young man's taking rubbish seriously. But why did you make Strowde so weak? There is a luxury in keeping outside, but it is a poor man who will lie asleep in that: and you don't express the fear he must have had of being <u>pulled</u> back . . . the conviction that he'd have to sell the part of himself which he valued, for the privilege of giving rein to the part of himself which others valued, but which he despised or actively disliked.

Also you have missed out the animal. All your characters are intelligences, most of them very witty intelligences (your dialogue is an amazement to me: some ass said Henry James: but <u>he</u> was a porpoise, not a fencing master): but they couldn't be as witty as all that without cracking sometimes, & letting the roar and growling of the beast be heard. Here in camp it's the lesson stamped into me with nailed feet hour after hour: that at bottom we are carnal: that our appetites & tastes & hopes & ideals are beast-qualities, coloured or shaped somewhat fancifully, but material always, things you can cut with a knife: and you have hidden that, out of shame perhaps: out of fear perhaps: or, like Shaw, in revenge.

It seems to me that I have doubly wasted this month, if I've put off the sending you a decent answer, only to write piffle at the end of it.

Per contra I've been very grateful for your letter. I've a despairing wish to believe well of that awful book of mine, though it's a nightmare to me, & I can never agree that it's any good. I wanted to ask you to read with a pencil, & to hack out the rubbish as you went: but it seemed too greedy a request. It's pretty shameless to ask a man to read it at all.

Subscribers to a thirty-guinea limited edition of a hundred copies are coming in, two or three a week. I'm glad to think that you've got it over already.

My regards to Mrs. Granville Barker

T. E. S.

---

1. A popular meat extract.

HAR/MS
To Barker

> Clouds' Hill,
> Moreton,
> Dorset.
> 30.IV.24

This is the letter I should have sent you about my book.

The thing is not to be published: only to be printed privately.

Printers estimates come to £3400 at present. The limit-price people will pay is 30 guineas. Consequently I hope for about 110 subscribers. I want, if possible, just to cover the book's cost.

Type paper & illustrations will be decent: (I hope): & the complete work will not be re-issued in my lifetime.

At the same time the fellows who helped in the campaign want copies, & can't pay 30 guineas for them. So I'm going to give them copies of the text, with perhaps one or two pictures, if these particularly concern them. No such copy to be complete: to be given only to people mentioned in the book: & not to all of them.

So I hope their copies will not compete in rarity-value with the subscribers' copies. But I shall be astonished if the latter appreciate. They start off too dear . . . but it merely happens to be the cost of the book. I don't want any to subscribe unless they are so rich that to waste thirty guineas won't distress them. The printers estimate ten months for the block-making. I can put it in hand only as subscriptions come in: so the book may well drag a year before it is complete. It's under way, well, already.

There are to be no review copies, & I don't want any to get to libraries. American copyright will be secured if possible.

The way to get on the list for a copy is to send word to me: & to send a cheque either for £15.15.0 (the half) or for 30 guineas (the whole) to

> Manager,
> Bank of Liverpool & Martins'
> 68 Lombard St.,
> London E.C. 3

marked "Seven Pillars account, T. E. Lawrence".

Up to date I've got about thirty names. This isn't bad: but is a long way off the sum-total. So if you come across anyone either side of the Atlantic who is, to your knowledge, rich & curious & book-buying . . . will you be so good as to tell him what a chance(?) he may have!

> Yours sincerely,
> T. E. S.

HAR/MS
To Barker

[Clouds' Hill,
Moreton,
Dorset.]
9.V.24

Many thanks for the page. I've decided to make it 14-point, after all, since that reads easier, to my eye, & to the eyes of four out of five of the men in Hut G. 25. Quaint, isn't it, to submit such an affair to such judgement? But it's seldom one can get such an approach to "the man in the street".

Netherton leaves me always with a feeling that camp is a horrible place, & that's a silly feeling, because I've chosen to make my living here, & to fuss about its inessentials is very near self-pity. The perfection of your surface strikes sharper, I expect, on a visitor than it does to the lord & mistress of the place: for one thing, we don't have to deal with a fire or two per week.[1]

Do tell me what your insurance people say. Their faces must be worth a good deal of smiling.

My genuine, birth-day, initials are T. E. C.[2] The C. became L. when I was quite young: & as L. I went to Oxford and through the war. After the war it became a legend: & to dodge its load of legendary inaccuracy I changed it to R.[3] In due course R. became too hot to hold. So now I'm Shaw: but to me there seems no virtue in one name more than another. Any one can be used by anyone, & I'll answer to it: While the postman delivers to my cottage anything with Clouds' Hill on the envelope. He did say, once, quite early on, that my name seemed to be Legion, but that it wasn't his affair. As he's a Salvationist, the New Testament comes naturally to his lips.

Consequently you may tell anyone anything you like about me & my book . . . but please don't put yourself about. I don't want you to start working on my behalf . . . but thought that perhaps you might some day meet a quaint rich person, one who would welcome a new curio for his gallery . . . and who would be grateful to you for the chance of picking up my confessions.

I see that in discussing Netherton, above, I forgot to add that therefore I wouldn't come down again for a while: not till I've ceased to be envious of your state. Many thanks, none the less, for your suggestion of an early return.

Yours sincerely,
T. E. S. (etc.)

1. The Barkers had recently had two small outbreaks of fire at Netherton Hall within a month.
2. Thomas Edward Chapman. He apparently means that his father did not change his name from Chapman to Lawrence immediately on his elopement but delayed until after the birth of two children (T. E. Lawrence was the second son).
3. Ross.

HAR/MS
To Barker

Clouds' Hill,
Moreton,
[Dorset]
18.V.24

It's ungrateful of me not to have written saying that this Sunday was one of my "at home" ones: fortunately, for I've been in bed most of the time with a return of malaria. The rest of a festive day has been spent in issuing coal to cook-houses & guard-rooms. It was very good of you to write as you did . . . but I don't believe you! My company can't be very distracting, since my eyes are always busied in looking at myself: and as for my being in the Army, the reasons for that go back a long way, as far as an unpresentable chapter (87) of my white elephant.

I hope the Hardys were able to attend at Netherton today. Dorsetshire has been laggard in its spring, & the warmness of your place would be a jolly contrast. Please thank Mrs. Granville-Barker for her letter. I'll arrive some time: but not yet a while: when I'm sick of dirt, in fact.

Yours sincerely,
T. E. Shaw

HAR/MS
To Barker

Clouds' Hill,
Moreton,
[Dorset]
5.XII.24

Philip Sassoon—yes, I suppose he can afford an occasional extravagance of the kind.[1] Please tell him I'm delighted. The Bank is

Liverpool & Martins'
68 Lombard Street
E.C.3

Cheques to be payable to T. E. Lawrence, & marked "Seven Pillars Account".

I want about twenty more people to pay up. The bills grow ominously: it is clear that my estimates were too low.

Doctors! What is to do? You should be hearing music in London now: all the best things seem to have been played in the last three weeks. Makes one rather hungry, down here. I hope you are not, have not been, are not about to be, ill.

Mrs. Granville Barker? Bearing up, perhaps, with some difficulty, at the not-having Netherton & Smoke, & Dolf & others within sight.[2] I'd miss the parrot mostly. A slow short-sighted, philosophic mind, it has.

Play-writing? Out of the question. I can't write: and wouldn't if I could, since creation, without conviction, is only a nasty vice. You have to be very eager-spirited to overcome the disgust of reproduction.

Am cutting absolute chunks out of my book, in the revise. Glory be. It's like a bar of soap: lathers the same wherever you cut it off.

Many thanks for getting P. S. to dib up. I like making use of such-likes. Patronage is the best duty of the ultra-rich. P. S. has done his duty.

Yours sincerely,
T. E. Shaw

---

1. Sir Philip Sassoon (1888–1939) was Under-Secretary of State for Air from 1924 to 1929 and 1931 to 1937.
2. "Smoke" was a cat; "Dolf" was an Alsatian wolfhound.

HAR/MS
To Barker

338171 A/C Shaw
R. A. F.
Mount Batten,
Plymouth.
23.XI.32

I have a feeling that this letter has been written to you before: which hurts you more than it hurts me.

Netherton is clearly deserted: but perhaps someone lives near-by who sends letters on. Or perhaps he (or she) lives by reading them. A thin existence if he (or she) depended on me.

My life has been R. A. F., mostly; diversified by eighteen months of supervising the construction and tests of the new R. A. F. fleet of motor-boats—fastish things of a 30 m.p.h. maximum, and very sea-worthy; 40 feet long—and by the translation of the Odyssey in my spare time. The latter activity was very well paid, and that was its raison . . . and the raison that it had.

Your life? I hear rumours of Shakespeare. He is your R. A. F. a twelve-year profession. My time endures till 1935. You can go on till bed-ridden, and afterwards. You win.

Meanwhile Mrs. G-B is really a novelist. One book, two even, are fashionable accomplishments. She has gone on, and peopled a gallery, a class, almost a society, for herself. That seems to me very difficult and remarkable.

I hope you are well—better, that is, than of old—contented, and not broke. That's the golden rule, of wishing others to be as oneself. My regards to her, please.

Yours sincerely,
T. E. Shaw

HAR/MS
To Barker

Plymouth
23.XII.32

Paris is pleasant, you say. My longest experience of it was in 1919, during the Peace Conference. So I shall not ever think of it as pleasant.

And I can't come to your Place and place there,[1] because the Air Force prevents, and the last time (1921) I wanted to cross France they refused me a visa. It is unfortunate to have the name of a spy!

You ask about my Greek. It is rusted and patchy. I can just read enough (that is without a dictionary) to get the meaning and enjoyment out of familiar books—parts of Aristophanes, and the Anthology, the Iliad, Anabasis and Aeschylus. I cannot read a strange Greek book without a crib to help me. There is not a great deal of good Greek to read. I would like to add Herodotus to my repertoire, but am too lazy, or too engrossed with mechanics. During the last two years we have re-equipped the R. A. F. with modern motor-boats—and that has meant a lot of designing, and a lot of intriguing.

Don't read the Odyssey aloud to Mrs. G. B., please. She would die of it, and both of us suffer a sense of loss, as Homer would say. It must have been nice to live in a literary period when even a platitude was a discovery, and clichés were waiting to be made. He was very successful in both these ways, I think.

The Odyssey to me represents—a bath, a hot-water plant and bookshelves in my cottage. So I have no regrets: but it is not one of my collected works. You were unwise to buy it.

I'm glad to hear that Shakespeare approaches vol. iii and finality. What will you do afterwards? After having had a period of acting, one of production, one of play-writing, one of criticism . . . what next?

And me? Oh, I'm going to retire to Dorsetshire, to my cottage, and neglect its garden.

Yours,
T. E. Shaw

---

1. A pun on the Barkers' Paris address, which was in the Place des Etats-Unis.

CAS/MS
To Lawrence

18, Place des Etats Unis,
[Paris] XVI
9.7.33

My dear T. E. S.,
I like to have the little book, and thank you; the little parasitic flea—but why should I also not drop into poetry:

> I like to have this little flea
> Picked from the noble carcase of your Odyssey.
> —not far, not farther!!

Flea or louse—you may have your choice: whether it displays you as morally agile as the one or as coy to searchers as the other. But here is a chastening reflection: I read through those letters with more interest than most works of literary art would cause in me. The bar of soap metaphor does not hold for literary art—try it with a poem or a play! But perhaps that is what is wrong with literary art. See Tolstoy, passim. Too late for me to be saved, however. I must go down to hell, an artist!

When do you get discharged? I then may see you. I begin to think you may have shown a wise prescience when you took refuge in the R. A. F. God knows, I never thought much of the world as it was. Except for sentiment. I don't regret its break up. But to be one of a generation which can only be a drag on the coach to prevent it running down hill too fast. You may live to help tug it up the next hill, having conserved your strength; and that's exhilarating. I shan't. Yes, and you have apprenticed yourself to a <u>machine</u>, also. <u>I</u> fly now—by Imperial Airways; helplessly. But it doesn't seem a bit strange.

Yours,
H. G-B.

What's your address?

Here the traces of correspondence between the two men die out. Lawrence was killed in a motorcycle accident two years later. Barker remained in Paris until 1940 and then fled to Lisbon and thence to New York.

 Chapter IX

Sir John Gielgud, 1904–

Barker's *first meeting* with Sir John Gielgud was in 1928. The young actor was just beginning to make his way in London, and his talents were already recognized. Little more than a year later he would be playing Hamlet at the Old Vic and beginning that career as one of the two greatest actors of his day in the English language, a position which he has now shared with Sir Laurence Olivier for over fifty years. But in 1928 all this was before him, and, though obviously already one of the best of the new, young actors, he was still engaged in fairly humble theatrical pursuits. Barker, on the other hand, was as great and potent and living a legend in the British theater then as Gielgud himself is now.

In his autobiography, *Early Stages* (published in 1939, with a revised edition published in 1974), Sir John tells how nervous he and the other actors were when Barker came to a rehearsal. The occasion was the first production in English of *The Lady from Alfaqueque* and *Fortunato,* both by the Quintero brothers and both translated from the Spanish and arranged for the English stage by Helen and Harley Granville Barker. The two plays were being presented by Anmer Hall as a twin bill at the Court Theatre, London, with Gielgud as Felipe Rivas in *The Lady from Alfaqueque* and as Alberto in *Fortunato*. Breaking his self-imposed exile, Barker came once to a rehearsal of the plays, though only once, according to the account in *Early Stages*. But the impression he made in that one visit was considerable. "We all sat spellbound," says Gielgud: "Everything he said was obviously and irrefutably right."

Barker saw relatively little of the London theater during the 1930s, since he was then living permanently in Paris. Nevertheless, on the occasions of his visits to England, Gielgud sometimes appealed to him for advice and the expression of an expert opinion. By that time, Gielgud was the acknowledged leader of his profession, but his contin-

Sir John Gielgud, 1978.

uing respect and admiration for Barker was both sincere and profound. "He was a master. I feel honoured to have known him," Sir John said to me in a conversation in 1978. It is as a director that Barker is chiefly honored and remembered by theater people, and that was as true in the thirties as it is today; but by 1937, when his correspondence with Gielgud begins, Barker had increased his reputation by publishing three of his five volumes of *Prefaces to Shakespeare.* The first volume appeared in 1927, the second in 1930, and the third in 1937. Since Gielgud's career, by the mid-thirties, had steered him decisively toward the playing of standard works—and especially Shakespeare, for which he was superbly equipped by reason of his magnificently flexible and expressive voice, already recognized as having no equal in the English theatre—the community of interest between the two men was natural and considerable. It was this community of interest, their common passion for the art of the theater, which brought them together and which, over the years, steadily increased the respect and admiration that each of them had for the other. They were not close personal friends, though they were on the friendliest of terms: they were artist-colleagues who each recognized the achievements and the eminence of the other. Gielgud, in fact, found Barker, at the personal level, "a very cold man" who "seemed terrified of familiarity of any kind." "He must have been a bit of a snob, you know," Sir John said in 1978. Helen he thought very dull, a woman who would talk about nothing but her dog and her own poetry. In 1945, when the Barkers returned from New York, Sir John invited them to his house for dinner on the evening of V-E Day, the day that the victory over the Germans and Italians in Europe (there still being the Japanese to deal with in Asia) was celebrated. At the end of the evening the arrival of the Barkers' car was delayed by the crowds in the streets of London, and Sir John, having exhausted all the conversational ploys he could think of, in desperation took his guests down to the kitchen to listen to the peace celebrations on the radio.

    A little over a year later Barker died. The official obituary in the *Times* appeared on September 2, 1946. A few days later, under the heading "Dr. H. Granville-Barker: A Further Tribute," the *Times* published an obituary tribute written by John Gielgud. Even allowing for feelings of *de mortuis nil nisi bonum* and for the fact that Sir John, himself the kindliest of men, has fairly obviously (judging by his autobiography) taken a vow never to give public expression to adverse criticism of *anybody,* the statement he made on that occasion about Barker's approach to theater and his methods of work gives an authentic and freshly felt sense not only of the enormous impression Barker made on the best actors of the day but also of Barker's place as a genuine and serious artist in the theater. The piece is worth quoting in full:

> Granville-Barker at rehearsal—dark business suit, rolled umbrella, red eyebrows shooting out above penetrating blue eyes—working without notes as he sits in an armchair on the stage close to the actors, directing with untiring penetration, speaking quietly, impersonally, only occasionally glancing at the Shakespeare held open in his hand. The actors are spellbound by his authority; they know they will never satisfy him, but, although he is sparing of praise and never flatters, they know that, if anyone can get the best out of them, he can. He stretches their staying power almost to breaking point, but never indulges in personal jibes or destructive sneers. He will say: "You did some fine things in that scene today. I hope you know what they were", and then deliver a formidable volley of adverse criticism. He is incredibly patient, and does not waste a minute. Nobody dares to keep him waiting, to gossip or even to try on wigs and costumes. Everyone watches him, stage manager, understudies, even the charwomen dusting the theatre. Sometimes he seems like a great surgeon, ready to perform the few brilliant strokes that will achieve the perfect operation, and faintly surprised that the patient has not been more perfectly made ready in advance: sometimes like a university professor, brilliantly illuminating every line of text. Sometimes like a great actor, as he rises from his chair to demonstrate a speech. Then he commands the stage, as I have once seen Lucien Guitry do it, with a stillness that is chilling in its authority: his voice still low, full of infinite variation, in spite of a limited range and rather metallic diction, his face alive with thought, emotion, passion, his body relaxed and his gestures few, but dynamic in their breadth and vigour. Away from the theatre he seemed to be shy, distant, rather cold; but this was belied by the warmth of his letters, which were intensely individual, fatherly, kind, and packed with brilliant criticism and advice. I count myself greatly fortunate in being one of the few actors of my generation to meet him, correspond with him over many years, and work with him—though only for a few short weeks—and also to count among my friends some of our finest players—Leon Quartermaine, Laura Cowie, Nicholas Hannen—who shared his early triumphs at the Savoy Theatre and have spoken so vividly to me of all they owe to the inspiration of his genius.

JG/MS
To Gielgud

Ritz Hotel,
London, W.1.
June 16, 1937

My dear John Gielgud,

How pleasant to hear from you!

R. and J. Yes, I liked it much. I could have made reservations, but I'd do that of a performance of archangels. But it was <u>far</u> the best bit of Shakespeare I'd seen in years.

Richard II. I've done no preface to it, nor none am like to do.

My advice! I can't imagine it can be of much use to you. But if a <u>talk</u> might serve any sort of purpose, and if you're within reach between now and Monday night (when we leave London) why it would be jolly to see you again at a less distance; so do fix a time to come in.

Yours,
Harley Granville-Barker

JG/MS
To Gielgud

18 Place des Etats Unis, XVIeme,
Paris.
June 27, 1937

My dear John Gielgud,

I fear I shan't be in England again till—heaven knows when! But—in case you come over—we shall stay in Paris till the end of July; then I hope for the mountains and Salzburg.

It would be very pleasant to see you and to talk. I am only afraid that my counsel—such as it would be—might increase and not lessen your distraction. For distracted—if I guess right—you must be: between two aims; the one, which is really forced on you, a personal career; the other, the establishing of a <u>theatre</u>, without which your career will not be, I think you rightly feel, all that you proudly wish it to be. It was Irving's dilemma; he clung on to one horn of it for a number of glorious years; then he was impaled on the other, and it killed him. It was Tree's; and he would have died bankrupt but for <u>Chu Chin Chow</u>. George Alexander, thrifty Scotsman, replied to me when I congratulated him on the 25th anniversary of his management: well, I've not done much for the drama (though in a carefully limited fashion he had) but I've paid salaries every Friday night without fail, and <u>that's</u> to my credit. And it was. I won't say that there too was my dilemma; because I never had such a career in prospect, I should suppose. But I pinned my faith to the <u>theatre</u> solution; and finding it—with a war and a "peace" on—no go, I got out. It must be your dilemma, I think; for you have rather the Irving than the Alexander conception of your job (by the way I never saw your Hamlet:[1] I wish I had). The question is: have times changed? can you yet hope to establish a theatre? if not the blessed "National" Theatre (but names mean nothing) such a one as Stanislavsky's or even Rheinhardt's of 30 years back? For that you'll gladly sacrifice as much of your personal career as need be—this I see; but naturally you don't want to make the sacrifice in vain. Is a compromise practicable? I don't know. Everyone English will be for compromise, just because they are English. And even the work has to be done in England. Perhaps one must accept there the fruits of the national virtue and failing combined. It makes for good politics but bad art. And so it is, you see, that the question (for me) opens up; no longer for me a practical question, therefore I can still say <u>theatre or nothing</u> and not suffer. For you a devilishly practical one; so, who am I to counsel you? Only I'd say: do not expect to pluck more than a few grapes from thistles, and don't expect them always to be of the best quality!

Yours,
Harley Granville-Barker

But you have given us some fine things and you'll give us more, I don't doubt—by whichever path you go.

---

1. Sir John told me rather ruefully that this was not, in fact, true: Barker had seen the *Hamlet,* but had apparently forgotten it!

JG/MS
To Gielgud

18 Place des Etats-Unis,
[Paris]
October 15, 1937

My dear Gielgud,

I wish we had met for longer yesterday or—I was going to say—not at all. For I must have seemed to you just ungenerously cavilling; and one dislikes to seem that. But I fear I have the old producer's fault—though in him it is not—of talking of what seems wrong, and only thanking heaven silently for what seems right.

But I'll now tumble out my impressions of Richard II for you, and if you pick anything useful out of them for a future time, good. Remember though, that I haven't looked at the player's print for a fairly long time and my memory is a sieve.

I applauded you at first sight for so unselfishly hiding yourself in a corner. But I fear you were wrong to do so. I fancy W. S. thought of the scene as a meeting of the Privy Council—Richard presiding, (The P. C. and the Star Chamber, the King absent*, were the courts of the day for state affairs) probably raised on a dais at the end or centre of the table, formally presiding. And after letting the discussion rip—and actually, I dare say, playing cup-and-ball or reading Froissart or the New-Yorker during the dull parts. But the point is that while W. S. doesn't begin to write Richard till he comes back from Ireland (till he becomes himself, a man and not merely a King) he does keep one guessing and wondering what sort of a man he is up to that point and what the devil he will do next, and the more we see of his cryptic face the better. You got that admirably during the Lists scene—as good a piece of Shakespeare staging as I can remember. But I'd like it done from the beginning. Richard, of course, carries too much sail for his keel and so swings violently from side to side at any puff of wind. But his stillness and silence in between—which W. S. intended, I think, though he had not yet discovered how to make such things positively effective (as Othello's silences are)—show us the poet who is not really living in this practical world at all, but in one of his own imagination.

All the "plastique" of this part of the production and the blending of the scene (but not a word of the D. of Gloucester could I hear. I fancy she was getting her emphasis all wrong) all that scenic invention excellent. Gaunt's death scene particularly, and the colloquy afterwards (though damn all that crossing and genuflection and Dies Irae) first rate.

I like the costumes, except for the fact that they don't always characterise the characters. I understand you not stressing the sexual-pervert part of Bushy-Bagot-Green—though of course the suggestion is there: but very delicately done by Shakespeare, an ex post facto one, only brought in at their dying moment, cf. Gaveston in Edward II. by a man who wasn't a sensitive dramatist—but I think they might be more gorgeously dressed than the others, to show that

*It was, I think, a Committee of the P. C.

they are the caterpillars of the Commonwealth, whereas Bolingbroke and Mowbray and Aumerle should be "rich not gaudy". But why is the poor D. of Y. (who is by the way rather a Polonius—a first study for him?—your man lacks distinction) so shabby?

But my chief grouse is about the verse. It is a lyrical play. W. S. has not yet learned to express anything except in speech. There is nothing much, I mean, in between the lines, as there is in "Macbeth" (for an extreme example). Therefore—I am preaching; forgive me— everything the actor does must be done <u>within the frame</u> of the verse. Whatever impression of action or thought he can get within this frame without disturbance of <u>cadence</u> or <u>flow</u>, he may. But there must be nothing, no trick, no check, beyond an honest pause or so at the end of a sentence or speech. And I believe you'll seldom find that the cadence and emphasis, the mere right scansion of the verse, does not give you the meaning without much of any further effort on the actor's part. The <u>pace</u> you may vary all you like. Clarity there must be, of course. But here, it is really the breaking of the rhythm which destroys it, for as I said, Shakespeare has written one tune and his words are playing that in the treble (I say); if one tries to play another tune with them in the base—naturally we can't understand the thing.

Variety of pace—tone—colour of speech; oh yes, as much as possible, but within the <u>frame</u>. You must not turn W. S.'s quavers into crotchets or semi-breves—or semi-quavers for that matter. And I think each character ought to have his own speech. I thought during the first half of the play they were imitating each other: then I found they were imitating you and your taste for sadder <u>sforzandi</u>: good enough for Richard and clearly indicated for "Down—down I come—" and "No lord of thine, thou haught, insulting man—" appropriate to him but quite wrong for Augustus Caesar-Bolingbroke or Mowbray or the "tenor" gallantry of Aumerle.

The thing got—I began to swear—more and more hung up as it went on, and you began to play more and more astride the verse instead of in it. The scenic invention of the deposition scene was again admirable. B. on the throne, you wandering about below like a lost creature—admirable (but <u>oh</u>, if you'd have let the marvellous and <u>sweet</u> music of that verse just carry you along with it). The <u>tune</u> of that "bucket and well" bit (again the business admirable) and even more of the "No deeper wrinkles yet . . . " It is like an <u>andante</u> of Mozart. Shakespeare has done it <u>for</u> you. Why not let him?

Yes, scenic invention here again admirable, but I fancy that this is meant to be a scenic repetition of the opening with B. taking his place on the very throne on which we saw Richard sitting then.

And your holding up the whole play (progressively so) obliged you to cut the Aumerle conspiracy, the dramatic point of which is merely that it is a swift and excited interlude between the slow (this, good again, I thought) farewell between R. and the Queen and the slow philosophical death scene. "I have been wondering [*sic*] how I may compare . . . etc" the pace of which is changed by the arrival of the groom and goes to the rapidity of the death—but that ought to be a hell of a fight. Note that for all the action suggested in the play there has been no single stroke of violence till then. It has all been done by politics—B. finessing the old D. of G.[1] and taking you without a struggle to when at the end that politician gets his dirty work done for him—it should be very dirty.

Then he comes on—the hypocrite—and condemns Exton. He feels in a sense what he says. But this is why the Bs of this world are successful; they can feel that way.

Forgive this scribble, but I have to write now and thus or not at all!

Yours,
Harley Granville-Barker

---

1. "B" is Bolingbroke; "D of G" is Duchess of Gloucester.

JG/MS
To Gielgud

18 Place des Etats-Unis,
[Paris]
October 19, 1937

My dear Gielgud,

Bless you—for you really are a most satisfactory person to write to, and it pleases me no end that you should have been able to turn all that talk to some practical use. For I repeat, I know how comparatively easy it is to criticize and how hard to do the thing right.

First to clear away that Benson business[1]. B. was good, and God knows he wasn't always, and he did let the thing carry him away—though still and progressively not at the pace it might have. But if he played the "jewels . . . beads" passage slowly it was probably because he could not remember his words. (Never shall I forget the performance from that point of view. I had just been playing Richard, so I happened still to know it, and when B. started off with

> "Old John of Gaunt, time honoured Lancaster
> Hast thou, according to the oath thou swear'st
> Brought hither Henry, thy rebellious son . . . "

and so on. . . !)

And Montague was a good critic, but I doubt if he had much technical knowledge; nor perhaps has Agate—good Shakespeare critic though he is—about the best among the few I read—as much as perhaps he thinks.[2] And his criticism now lapses rather often into the "This sort of thing gives me the pip . . . " method. And after all, for a foundation of criticism technical knowledge is needed. Don't let him worry you. And don't let me worry you either.

I appreciate that difficulty, of avoiding reciting, in giving life to a conventional form, of getting sense and music combined. I be-lieve the solution may lie in doing the things separately at first, sitting round a table—if you have a company accustomed to working with you and to follow—and one day working out the sense, and the next singing the music, and then, when first you go on the stage, doing nothing but the movements (the words merely muttered). Then when all three are so fixed in the mind that you don't have consciously to think of them—but not till then—letting the whole thing rip. Of course it won't come right at the first go off, but you could discuss what is proportionately wrong. Care for which third it is that is harming the other two-thirds and correct this. But it might give the spontaneity—the appearance of it—that is needed. And if you could impress on people: take all the conscious pains possible at rehearsal—i.e. at the partial rehearsals: for sense, for music, for movement: at the full rehearsals, getting these three combined, learn to "let yourself go" and only keep enough self-consciousness to enable you to correct faults (well, you know all about that duplicate consciousness which only an actor, and a real actor, seems to understand). The plan might not work. But for a play like Richard—and for a good deal more of W. S.—it might be worth trying.

I believe Richard plays quickly because in moments of excitement he thinks devilish quickly. He has the "artistic temperament" which we get furious with because so many people sham it. But with him—and with W. S.; it is far more autobiographical than Hamlet—he genuinely either can think or not. This explains those cryptic places in the earlier part.

But when I say think, I mean imagine. He does not think in the scientist's sense. But once his imagination is lit up, the thoughts come at a rush, and he never lacks words—or rather, images for them, cf. Shelley—another of that kidney. And, since he is an artist,

painful feelings are as interesting to him as pleasant ones, in fact
more so, because—a sensitive creature—he can feel them more keenly. But here are pages running away over Richard, of whom you
know a darned sight more than I do.

As to the Merchant, I've never really liked it as a whole. It
hasn't the true thrill in it—except, partly, for Shylock. It is elegant
accomplishment—and how elegant W. S. could make it—and skilled
construction. But his heart was never in the thing. That is why, I
think, both Antonio and Bassanio are really empty—Morocco is as
human as they—and though Portia is a pretty fairy tale, she never
quite comes to life. He does get something into it once he has the
two stories running together in the Trial Scene—and thereafter in the
last bit at Belmont—which gives us the best of Portia, the most lovely
and alive. Of course, there is Shylock. Shylock "got" him—but not
thoroughly until the Tubal scene (in prose: a sign that he was writing
elegant artificial verse for the rest; when he let go, it was into prose);
and not in tune. He meant him to be a contemptible character, the
sordid villain of the play and it was too late to change all the values
without ruining it. You'll do an interesting S. I'm sure—and why not
try it. My fear would be that you'd spoil the balance and the scheme
which I see as Magnificent and Stately Venice: even the young men
stately: and real this side of the story, i.e. real for a fairy tale. Belmont magnificent and quite childishly unreal. The contrast to both
these—Shylock, the sordid little outsider, passionate, resentful,
writhing under his wrongs—which are real—and the contempt of the
Venetians. We dislike him thoroughly and are meant to. But when
you are a Shakespeare how much more you pity people you dislike
(your conscience tells you to) than those you like: you give your love
to them, they don't need your pity. If Antonio and Bassanio had
been made live characters they'd have pitied S. too. As they are
not—our pity goes out to him a bit more. But I think he mustn't
bate one jot of his unpleasantness to gain our pity. He must either
earn it as a most objectionable creature, or not at all. Will you do
this: that's the question—for me.

Have you ever tried Malvolio? You could do something
very good with him. For he had imagination, though, which is
swamped in egotism and so becomes purely ridiculous. You see a lot
of them about—in Chelsea, I expect in velvet coats (they used to
wear) instead of yellow stockings, painting sham pictures and writing
sham poetry and being dreadfully solemn about it. But there is a
tragic side to the man, and again, as with Richard, this comes out
with misfortune, and he acquires dignity.

But your leading lady isn't a Viola—alack—only an Olivia—

the dainty child-princess weighed down with splendour. For Viola you want something really boyish—a Miss Bergner[3] who can speak English <u>and</u> beautifully.

But some day do this: a picture of two great Elizabethan Houses (both alike in dignity, both that W. S. knew something about by this time. In R. and J. he had it all wrong—Capulet is an old Alderman, like papa)—for that is what they are, and <u>all</u> well-bred, down to Fabian. Feste outlawed, Sir Andrew a gallant idiot, even Sir Toby only a drunkard but not spewing drunk.

As to me—oh, no. I have to put it all into books now, and as quick as I can before my time is up. I doubt if I'd <u>be</u> any good as a producer [director] any longer—other reasons apart. I doubt if I've energy and patience left.

But an argument with me—just the two of us—might clear your mind sometimes, and mine. And, you see, you have <u>got</u> it in you.

Yours,

H. G. B.

---

1. Sir Frank Benson (1858–1939), the eminent Shakespeare actor and leader of a famous company of players.
2. C. E. Montague (1867–1928) and James Agate (1877–1947).
3. Elizabeth Bergner (1900–   ), an Austrian-born actress who had some considerable success in British and American theater (and in films) but who never really mastered the language. She played opposite Laurence Olivier in an early film version of *As You Like It*.

JG/MS
To Gielgud

Ritz Hotel,
London, W.1.
Nov. 30, 1937

My dear Gielgud,

I have, thank God, no self-granted moral responsibility towards Sheridan, so I was able to sit back and enjoy myself, which I did, and came away feeling the lighter in heart with the world today a little easier—which, I take it, is how one ought to feel after seeing the S. for S. With the rather fine pleasure too of having seen the best J. S. I remember or am likely to encounter.[1] Forbes-R. was good:[2] but even then, elderly, and the more inexcusable. I liked your dandyism, and shallowness. Just—for me—the right value.

The humanising of the whole thing—even the sentimentalising of it—is justifiable. For after all what S. did was to sentimentalise upon the Congreve tradition. This "man of sentiment" being a man of sham sentiment. Charles and Sir Peter and Sir O. being the genuine sentimentalists. But I'm not sure that so much bon ton need have been sacrificed. Lady S's salon a bit of a bear garden, and the edge taken off Sir Peter. C's softer bits and the fall of the screen, how good, though: one forgot, for a moment, the loss of the rest. And one always knew that Rowley well played and not cut would be not half a bad part.

But I'm beginning to meander into criticism—thank you for a good evening: that's really all I wanted to say.

Yours,
Harley Granville-Barker

---

1. Gielgud played Joseph Surface at the Queen's Theatre in 1937.
2. Sir Johnston Forbes-Robertson (1853–1937).

JG/MS
To Gielgud

Ritz Hotel,
London.
June 26th 1939.

My dear Gielgud,

Your telegram came, and thank you for it. Thank you too for trusting somewhat in my preface. And if, beyond this, I have been of use to you all—it gladdens my heart.[1] Besides which, that rehearsal showed me more than one point I had missed till now. Thanks yet again therefore.

I'm sorry my notes were unusable, but you are sending them, I gather, to Copenhagen—where they may do what they will with them for me. They should, however, acknowledge Sidgwick and Jackson's rights in the matter. And if you want to place any substitute for them in the Lyceum programme, better to collaborate with Frank Sidgwick: telephone to him at Holborn 7927.

We're off again by the Ferry tonight. Good luck on Wednesday. I expect you are, by chalks,[2] the best Hamlet going today. And that is something to say of any man!

Yours,
H. G. B.

---

1. Gielgud had invited Barker to attend a rehearsal of *Hamlet,* which was being prepared in London for presentation at Elsinore, Denmark.
2. A variant, Australian in origin, of "by a long chalk," that is, by a very wide margin.

JG/MS
To Gielgud

Chateau de Gregy,
Brie-Comte-Robert,
S. et M.,
[France]
September 15th, 1939.

My dear Gielgud,

If this war is to go on for long something should be done to save the theatre from falling into the pitiable state (from the point of view of drama itself) into which it fell during the last. And I think you are chief among those who can perhaps do this. Therefore I present you with the following ideas:

1. A company (on the men's side) of soldiers: i.e. of (a) men already in the non-fighting part of the army or (b) called up for this purpose under the new act; (c) men over age being engaged as usual; (d) the staff also to be similarly situated non-commissioned officers and men. Everybody in the theatre, from manager to scene shifter, to have appropriate rank, and the pay and allowances of that rank, and no more. Not too high a range of rank; at most a single colonelcy and so downwards. If more were asked the War Office would veto the affair. But you will see the advantages. This would regularise every man's position, and salve patriotic consciences. And, of course, at any moment the War Office could call men to other duties. From every point of view, however, you would find this to be the linch-pin of any such plan. Recruitment: supplies: organisation: continuity: under this condition, all these would be possible: under any others, impossible.

2. The women should receive strictly equivalent pay.

3. His Majesty's Theatre, which the Government should requisition without delay at a fair rent.

4. Maximum prices 5/-, 2/6, 1/-, and if they could be made 2/6, 1/-, and sixpence, so much the better.

5. Plays of recognized merit only; with Shakespeare the backbone of the list of them.

6. Conventionalized scenery (for Shakespeare the single "Elizabethan" set) to save expense (with this and stock costumes and army pay the finance of the business should not be impossible).

7. A true repertory system; i.e. a variety of plays always in the Bill. The main idea would be to make the theatre a "house of

call" into which anybody on leave or with three hours to spare might drop and be sure to find something of quality being played. Advance booking would be a secondary matter.

8. May I counsel you, if you want to forward this or any other such scheme, to take it in the first instance only to someone of considerable and direct influence in the Government. You can ascertain better than I which of the very few of these are likely to be intelligently sympathetic on the subject. But in default of access to the Prime Minister himself, my mind fixes on Samuel Hoare; it would be wise, I believe, to tell both Robert Vansittart and Lord Esher that you are going to him and ask their advice.

9. You and your dominant position in the acting of Shakespeare (and therefore in the theatre generally) apart, I should have written this letter to Nicholas Hannen, both from an old affection for him and long knowledge of his public spirit and loyalty. I do not know whether you get on well together personally. If you do he might prove a valuable collaborator. So show it to him if you like.

10. But do not publish—and there is no need even to mention—my name in connection with the matter. If something of the sort is to be done, it must be by those who are an active power for good in the theatre today, and among those you are pre-eminent. Therefore if you care to make whatever may be of use in these ideas your own and to improve on them in the light of what you know (and I now do not) to be practical, that will suffice me.

The side of the theatre which we care about suffered during the last war from errors of calculation on the part of those who directed it and from the Government's lack of belief that it could have anything more than a casual entertainment value. As a consequence, the English drama stood humiliated before the world. Those errors should both be repaired this time. The effort at the moment seems to be to provide cheerful entertainment for the soldiers; a very necessary thing, and the projects seem to be in appropriate hands. But someone should already be making plans in the interests of the drama itself, and of the public's interest in that; so that, when the time is ripe, and before it is too late, action may be taken. Don't you agree?

My best regards to you,

Yours,
Harley Granville-Barker

JG/MS
To Gielgud

as from:
Chateau de Gregy,
Brie-Comte-Robert
S. et M., France
September 27th 1939

My dear Gielgud,

I knew that your practically expert eye would spy out the weakness in the scheme. I send you with this a memorandum drafted rather hastily this morning which deals with the points you raise as well as I know how. I am confident that a scheme can be worked out; and it is important to have it ready and to take up a position of "vantage" for putting it into operation when the time is ripe. Important also to have interested the right people (the No. 1s, not the 2, 3, and 4) in it.

Important to get the thing done, if possible, if in any way possible, so that the theatre—that part of it we care about—be not left at the end of this war as it was at the end of the last.

So I do conjure you to go ahead. And whatever I can wisely do to help, I will.

Yrs,
Harley Granville-Barker

The following document was enclosed with this letter.

JG/MS
To Gielgud

Chateau de Gregy.   Brie-Comte-Robert.   S. et M.
September 27, 1939.

Memorandum on J. G.'s letter of September 20.

1. (a) If the Government (? what Department of the Gov't?) have given an understanding to the ENSA[1] which affects the interests of the theatre as a whole, the ENSA should be converted into a body competent to represent those interests in their proper proportions, (b) The simplest plan here would probably be to let the ENSA continue to function in its present form, and form other sections to represent other interests.

2. It is not easy to divide these interests into clear-cut categories. As to their relative dramatic importance: a theatre producing Shakespeare and the other classics, old and modern, is clearly of

greater importance than one doing "revue". But it is considered of-
fensively snobbish to say so, and they have a similar industrial standing. It is wise, therefore, not to take this line of country it if can be
avoided.

3. Recently, however, a clear-cut category has been created, so recognised by the Government, and exempted as such from
the entertainment tax: the theatres which do not operate for profit.
e.g. Stratford, the Old Vic, and there are one or two more. Their
interests and their status differ from those of the others, and consequently they should have special representation on the body proposed
in para. 1, and they may continue to claim from the Government
special treatment.

4. It might be well, under present circumstances, and for
the time being, to unite these interests executively in one. How and
to what extent to do so opens up many problems. But with a common intention to concentrate and limit activities to the point of maximum utility for the minimum expenditure of money and energy, these
should be soluble.

5. (a) To form such a company as we have in mind, it
would be necessary for actors to enlist in it for the duration of the
war under similar self-denying non-profit-making conditions. They
would thus establish their claim on the Government for a treatment
which could not be given to those who remained in the theatrical
market, earning the best salaries they could get. (b) The simplest rule
for this would be the pay and allowances of men serving as officers in
the army, from (say) Major to 2nd Lieutenant, according—roughly—
to their artistic "rank" in the company.

6. As any man between 18 and 40 (?42) may now be called
up, it would be simpler if actors of this age (a) selected by the management for this company and (b) willing to serve in it, should (c) be
called up by the National Service authorities at once. This would (d)
give them a legal status (e) absolve them from any suspicion of shirk-
ing; since it would (f) be in the power of the army authorities (or
N. S. authorities rather) either to leave them there or transfer them
to other work. (g) It is little likely that this would be done. (h) The
only such disturbance would be when the men themselves felt they
would be better in some fighting line.

7. (a) Men over age and (b) women, would receive similar
financial treatment. I suggest that with neither would there be grave
recruiting difficulties. Category (a) is important, but not proportionately a large one. As to Category (b) "names" are not essential; for
the theatre would recruit an audience which would at least not set
overwhelming store by them, and if it did not it would be a failure.

Also there must be women engaged in other war-work who would prefer to play in certain plays only in the repertory.

8. For the Management of the theatre something like a small council might be needed, consisting of

(a) A Chairman-Director, with powers of veto.

(b) A Business-Manager with direct responsibilities towards whatever was the course of the finance.

(c) A Liaison Officer with Government departments; not hard to find some retired General or Admiral.

(d) A representative of the actors.

(e) A representative of the staff.

If (e) were not needed, possibly 2 representatives of the actors.

9. The orchestra and staff Trades Union question. This is delicate. The best thing would be to go first to the right sort of Labour leader for advice. e.g. Greenwood,[2] deputy leader of the Labour Opposition. I should suppose that the Orchestral Union must sooner or later climb down in the matter of pay. The stage hands may not. Both should be as limited as possible.

10. Finance. As ever the chief snag. (a) I doubt if the N. T. people have any right to use their money for such a purpose,[3] or if the Old Vic have any to use. (Lytton is the man, of course, to answer both questions). Stratford has money; as to their powers over it I am not sure. (b) How far the Government would consider that their "non-subsidy" pledge extended is a question for them. But if their help could not be direct—say, even to the extent of providing the army pay of the actors "called up"—it could be indirect and useful. (c) The first War Budget will frighten people. But it will leave certain men willing to give away sums which will only increase their taxes if they keep them. I should not therefore despair of obtaining a sum from private sourses if the prospective donor were asked by the right person. Here if somebody like Samuel Hoare would not function, Lord Baldwin might. He gave his name to the National Theatre project.

11. It would be vital not to have all the bodies like Stratford or the Old Vic directly represented on the management of the theatre. A consultative Council, either with no powers or such drastic ones that they could not use them except catastrophically, would be the only tolerable thing.

H. G. B.
Harley Granville-Barker
Chateau de Gregy,
Brie-Comte-Robert,
S. et M.

1. Entertainments National Service Association, a government-sponsored organization for providing entertainment of many kinds for the armed forces and war workers. (See also Chapter V, letter of February 29, 1912, to Murray, footnote 1).
2. Arthur Greenwood (1880–1954) became deputy leader of the Labour Party in 1935, when C. R. Attlee was elected leader. Greenwood was an early member of the Fabian Society, where Barker got to know him. Shortly after this letter was written (in May, 1940), Greenwood became a member of the War Cabinet under Churchill, who in that month took over the position of Prime Minister from Neville Chamberlain.
3. The National Theatre; he refers to funds held in trust by the Shakespeare Memorial National Theatre Committee.

JG/MS
To Gielgud

> Chateau de Gregy,
> Brie-Comte-Robert,
> Seine et Marne,
> France.
> September 27, 1939

My dear Gielgud,

In my memorandum of this morning, I omitted to deal, I find, with several of your objections. I repair the omission—I hope—now.

If you have a secretary who can master my writing and has the time it would be very kind of you to let her type out my first letter to you and these two memoranda. For I have now neither secretary (mobilised!) nor typewriter, and consequently can keep no accurate record myself of what I say.

> As ever yours,
> Harley Granville-Barker

The following memorandum was enclosed with this foregoing letter.

Addenda to my memorandum of September 27

A. Your point about a possible inability to begin with more than six matinee performances a week: with the projected arrangements for military pay as near as might be all round this should be, as a temporary measure at any rate, financially feasible. It would have one positive advantage moreover, in giving the actors time and chance to "run themselves in". Note that, with strictly conventional scenery for any play which would accommodate it, a rather more conventional style of acting as far as movements and grouping were concerned would be bound to develop. Less rehearsing would (to that extent) be required. I see no great harm in this.

B. I hope I made it clear that actors would, if they were of military age, be taken "for the period of the war". Even if their engagement at the theatre terminated by mutual agreement, they would still be at the disposal of the National Service authorities.

C. Also that no leave for Cinema work nor extra pay for broadcasting would be permissible. But a man's willingness to work under such single-minded conditions would be the necessary test of his fitness for the company. The whole point of the scheme is to provide actors, or a small selection of them, with a more suitable and effective way of serving their country (i.e. by serving their art) than if they were drafted in all sorts of other capacities (incapacities often!) into the army. But this being so, they must expect something—the same discipline that they would be subjected to in the army itself.

D. The actors could not be allowed to earn extra pay by broadcasting. Certain sections of "poetic" plays are to my mind the only things of the kind which broadcast well. Such a company as this would be, of all others, the most fitted for this job.

E. If the Old Vic are brought into this, the first thing they will propose—and urge on the grounds of economy—will, of course, be the use of the Old Vic. This would be unfortunate and might well ruin the scheme. One of the principal problems, I take it, in war-time London is that of getting about. A central theatre is needed. During the last war everything centered round Whitehall. Everybody on leave or doing Government business had to come there at some time. A theatre that can easily be "dropped in" upon is above all needed. No one can "drop in" at the Old Vic. His Majesty's realises all requirements.

There proved to be too many organizational problems and too many factional interests involved for Barker's scheme to be workable. The government decided to approach its responsibility to the arts in a less direct way and the Council for Encouragement of Music and the Arts (CEMA) was set up, with government financing, to take charge of government aid to the arts. This is the body which, after the war, became the Arts Council of Great Britain.

Early the following year, Gielgud played in a production of King Lear *at the Old Vic, directed by Lewis Casson. At Gielgud's invitation, Barker flew from Paris and stayed two weeks in London, attending rehearsals and advising on the production. He refused, however, to be listed as director, and the program read, "The production by Lewis Casson. It is based upon Harley Granville-Barker's Preface to King Lear and his personal advice besides." Before returning to France, Barker wrote the following letter.*

JG/MS
To Gielgud

The Athenaeum,
Pall Mall, S.W.1.
[London]
Sunday morning.
(April 14, 1940)

My dear Gielgud,
     Lear is in your grasp.
     Forget all the things I have bothered you about. Let your own now well self-disciplined instincts carry you along, and up; simply allowing the checks and changes to prevent your being carried away. And I prophesy—happily—great things for you.

Yrs.,
H. G. B.

JG/MS
To Gielgud

18, Place des Etats-Unis,
[Paris]
April 29, 1940

My dear Gielgud,
     Did we ever agree as to the precise moment at which Lear goes off his head?
     I believe that Poor Tom's appearance from the hovel marks it. The "grumbling" inside, the Fool's scream of terror, the wild figure suddenly appearing—that combination would be enough to send him over the border-line. Do you mark the moment by doing something quite new? Difficult, I know, to find anything new to do at that moment. But something queer and significant of madness, followed (it would help) by a dead silence, before you say (again in a voice you have not used before)
               Did'st thou give all . . .
I don't doubt you have devised something. But thinking over the

scene this struck me—ought to have struck me before; perhaps we <u>did</u> agree to it—so I drop you this line.

You're having an interesting, if exhausting, time, I am sure, and I fancy a most successful one. Congratulations.

Yrs.,
H. G. B.
April 30 morning.
I think I have it: see next sheet

What follows is the "next sheet."

. . . . . show the heavens more just.
Lear remain on knees at end of prayer, head buried in hands
Edg: Father . . . poor Tom.

> *make much of this; don't hurry it; give it a "Banshee" effect, lilt and rhythm. At the sound Lear lifts his head. Face seen through his outspread fingers (suggestion of madman looking through bars).*
> *The Fool screams and runs on: business as at present. This gets Lear to his feet. He turns towards the hovel watching intently for what will emerge.*
>
> *Dialogue as at present.*
>
> *Edgar's entrance and speech* Away . . . warm thee. *Much as now. And Lear immensely struck by it. cf. Hamlet-Ghost. Just as it is finishing (Edgar not to hurry it) stalk him to present position for* Did'st thou . . .
>
> *and as he turns for the speech at B.[1] we see that he is now quite off his head.*
>
> *N.B. Once Edgar is on he, Kent and Fool must keep deadly still so that these movements of Lear may have their effect. Translate the Hamlet-Ghost business into terms of Lear and it will about give you the effect.*

I believe this may be right . . . worth trying anyhow.

---

1. He refers to a rough pencil sketch, which he had made in the margin, showing the relative positions of the characters and the direction of Lear's move.

JG/MS
To Gielgud

18, Place des Etats-Unis,
[Paris]
May 6th 1940

My dear Gielgud,

Your letter of the 2nd arrived this morning. I'll take thought and answer it tomorrow.

Meanwhile here's a trifling point:
In the last scene Lear quite ignores (as you now do) the "Tis noble Kent, your friend" and merely gives a general answer "A plague upon you, murderers, traitors all". And later when he looks at him and says "Are you not Kent?" it should clearly be in a highly indignant "How-dare-you-enter-our-presence-after-I-have-banished-you" tone. And when Kent answers "The same, your servant Kent" before he can go on to the rest of the line, the old gentleman should repeat, rather feebly, the magnificent "out of my sight" gesture with which in the first scene he banished him. "He's a good fellow—He'll strike . . . " clearly refers to the Caius impersonation and the tripping up and beating of Oswald. Perhaps we did work this out.

Yrs.,
H. G. B.

JG/MS
To Gielgud

This answers your letter of May 2

18 Place des Etats-Unis,
[Paris]
8th May 1940

My dear Gielgud,

First of all; my advice from the purely business point of view is worthless. I never had much business acumen and my knowledge is now quite out of date.

But to begin with, £60 a week for the Lyceum makes me wonder whether this is not like being lent a theatre for a charity matinee gratis, when the mere expenses are found to amount to £100 or more. However, your men will know all about this.

As to the Lyceum itself, I was only in it once; to see your rehearsal of Hamlet. From where I sat I felt I needed a telescope. But you've acted there. In this too you'll know better than I.

I really don't see that you owe any consideration to the Old Vic governors. In fact the best thing you can do for them is to bring them up against realities. At present, I take it, they are enjoying a quite "unreal" success; i.e. you and the other actors are subsidising them by taking quite "unreal" salaries. If they were paying you at market rates and giving a decent production, they'd have to put up their prices to meet the expense, and if they only get what they think they can financially afford in quality of acting the theatre would be half empty. If they don't already realise this the sooner it is brought home to them the better. And let them inform the British Council and all and sundry of the fact besides. I have no patience with this official and "patriotic" exploitation of art by the methods of the sweat-shop. Your tale of the Elsinore Hamlet was a shocking one.

On the other hand it is a hundred pities to throw away the Old Vic's advantages as a non-commercial enterprise. The saving in entertainment tax must be considerable. And as to a Pilgrim Trust subsidy; that <u>can</u> only be given to an enterprise which does not pay tax—for otherwise the P. T. is simply paying money to the government.

What is really wanted is:

1. Neither the Lyceum nor that dreadful Old Vic but another theatre such as—by my original suggestion—His Majesty's.

2. A combination to which (a) the O. V. governors contribute (so to speak) their exemption from the E. T. and their consequent power of attracting a subsidy; (b) you and the actors contribute your work for basic salaries in return for a 24 weeks guarantee; (c) your Lyceum financiers or others provide the necessary capital; (d) the Treasury agrees to treat it as a non-commercial affair while it remains so, i.e. unless and until there is a profit.

How that should be calculated and divided would be a question, but one not impossible to answer; there are many precedents for this sort of thing. It would have to be calculated upon each production, I expect. First the actors should have some of the balance of their salaries and the capitalists partly recoup themselves. The Treasury might expect a bit then. But in these times it equally might be ready to forgo anything until there was a real profit; i.e. until after the actors had had their full salaries and the capitalists were safe. And that time, of course, comes the sooner if the Treasury does so forgo their claim. As to the Pilgrim Trust—put it on equal terms with the Treasury if you can't do better.

Theatre rent, of course, stares one in the face as usual. Rents ought to be controlled. For all I know the Lyceum may be possible. But cosy it isn't.[1]

Do not think that you are going to get plain exemption for any actors between 20 and 40 after a while. This war is going to be a long and a very unpleasant business. We are only at the beginning of it. "Exemption" will reflect harmfully both upon the actors themselves and the theatre. If they can't be actually called up and put in uniform and then seconded to work in the theatre—which would be by far the best plan—then this precedent of the "official artists" should be cited and some scheme built up on that. But remember that the artists are not in the public eye and the actors literally are, night after night. In about a year's time they may not be able to face their public with equanimity unless they are known to be in the public service.

Othello. I should say that you and Emlyn Williams would make an admirable combination. You'd do an Arab Othello and he a robustly conscienceless Iago very well (from the one thing I've ever seen him do). And if I could be useful to you, a quiet day or so in Paris with you both,[2] going through it as we went through Lear on my first visit—to that you'd be welcome. But to more than that I fear I must say No. To begin with you don't need it. Once you have the flavour of it, the play is dead simple to stage. Lear really is difficult, next door to impossible, and perhaps I did lessen its impossibilities a little; one cannot say more, nor could much more have been done, things being as they were. But with Othello there are no such fundamental difficulties.

Why the deuce don't you do Twelfth Night? A really elegant performance; no clowning allowed. It records William's glimpse of a great household (or let us imagine so). He must have been asked down to Penshurst or Wilton for the week-end. Can't you see him going and buying two new ruffs for the occasion?

You'd make a first rate Malvolio. Hannen as Sir Toby;[3] a gentleman—Olivia's uncle, mind—who disdains to be drunk on anything but vintage burgundy (of which the cellars are naturally full); Haggard for Sir Andrew;[4] an amiably foolish knight, with a real chance, he thinks, of marrying Olivia. Hawkins an excellent Antonio[5] and his wife—if she'd only learn to speak!—quite good for Olivia. Does Edgar (I forget his other name—Robert Harris of course!) sing well enough for Feste? You must have a singer. If not he is a possible Orsino, although Orsino is your middle-aged romantic (Forbes Robertson aged eternally 40 is probably now playing it at the Theatre Divine, Paradise) or he'd be an excellent Sebastian. And of course you want a boyish Viola with a low gently vibrating voice, and a mischievous mite of a Maria.

But a performance with all the elegance that we try to give to the School for Scandal plus romance. A dish, believe me, that you can serve perennially. One no more tires of it than of Mozart's "Jupiter".

I believe that Julius Caesar, played swiftly and ruthlessly and for the sake of its <u>action</u>, always comes fresh too.

Yours,
Harley Granville-Barker

---

1. It is worth noting, in this comment, the echo of Barker's early work in the theater: the Lyceum was Henry Irving's old theater and was eminently suited to the grandeur and sheer size of his histrionic style; Barker's own productions, in the first fifteen years of the century, were predicated upon the assumption that the theater should be small enough to permit quiet, subtle, and detailed (though not necessarily realistic) acting. This was the nature of Barker's revolt against the Irving school and all it represented.
2. In fact, Paris had very few quiet days left. Less than a month after writing this, Barker and his wife left Paris hurriedly in the face of the German invasion. The production of *Othello* did not materialize, and Gielgud did not play Othello until 1961.
3. Nicholas Hannen (1881–1972); see Chapter X, pp. 464–76.
4. Stephen Haggard (1911–1943).
5. Jack Hawkins (1910–1973).

JG/MS
To Gielgud

Mayfair House,
Park Avenue and Sixty-fifth Street,
New York
October 27, 1940

My dear Gielgud,

Your letter of September 29 arrived the day before yesterday. By airmail this <u>may</u> reach you more speedily. About the Hallam Fordham book: no, I'd rather, please, that <u>all</u> mention of my share in the business were omitted.[1] The record of the performance itself (and I cannot, of course, <u>object</u> to a copy of the programme being reprinted) may perhaps be of interest to those who take a technical interest in such things. But as to the rehearsals—that is another matter altogether. We were all doing our best, under the circumstances, and this meant many compromises and much that belonged to the occasion only. I came over merely to give some friendly advice, and, as you know, with many misgivings as to its applicability. I do not want it therefore to "go on record" (as the American phrase goes) nor anything that I do not write and print, and so make myself directly responsible for. I have written the substance of this to Miss Gilder. Thank you for consulting me. I hope my decision may not throw the whole book into the discard. But I do decidedly object to anything, as far as I am concerned, being given to the public, which was not given to the public. (When I'm dead and can't contradict you, do what you like!)

As to Macbeth, I fear I can't be very helpful. I have a five-year old draft for a "Preface" here—a solitary copy which I managed to bring away. But when I shall be able to return to it I don't know. I remember making up my mind that much of the Witch scenes were spurious. But except for Hecate—which is clearly either Middleton or the prompter—we have to accept the stuff as Shakespeare's since it probably replaces what Shakespeare wrote. No—don't cut a line of the Macduff-Malcolm scene. It is meant, I think, to illustrate the demoralisation which the Macbeth-sort of tyranny spreads even among wholly innocent people like Malcolm: you need an interesting Malcolm—in distrust of himself and of everybody else. (Even the Doctor and E. the Confessor—though you may be justified in cutting this piece d'occasion—serve for contrast, i.e. scepticism and faith). This theme of demoralisation and moral cowardice runs all through. Banquo, Ross, Macduff. The murder of the plucky little child, young M. marks the turning point (or rather the news of it when brought to Macduff).

I've never seen one of Rylands' productions.[2] He may only be cut out for the control of amateurs. But discussion with him could only be helpful and illuminating. And I've always heard that his men speak their verse excellently. You'd get admirable ideas from him and I should guess that he'd welcome any sort of collaboration that he could manage. He is a first rate and most "humane" scholar and individual. I'm glad that things are so far comparatively well with you and that work is still possible. I am, for the time being, an Honorary Professor at Yale. I'm told this is of use, and other jobs of the sort and other work is in prospect, as much, I expect, as I can tackle. But I'd be happier digging trenches on the Norfolk coast, although I'd dig them badly.

As ever,

Yrs.,
Harley Granville-Barker

---

1. Hallam Fordham had suggested a collaboration with Rosamund Gilder in a book about the King Lear production similar to her *John Gielgud's Hamlet*, published in 1937. The idea came to nothing, but in 1952 Fordham did publish a "photobiography" of Gielgud.
2. George Rylands was a fellow of King's College, Cambridge, and at that time University Lecturer in English Literature; he was Chairman of the Directors of the Arts Theatre, Cambridge, a governor of the Old Vic, and a member of the Council of the Royal Academy of Dramatic Art. His stage productions at Cambridge were famous;

he later directed the recording, for the British Council, of the entire Shakespeare canon. He never, however, practiced professionally as a theater director.

JG/MS
To Gielgud

Ritz Hotel,
[London]
August 15, 1945

My dear Gielgud,

Here is the V. W. article, and thank you.[1] Very good: though she doesn't add much to the book itself. However, who could? The best of its sort I know.

Interesting: it brings up a subject we broached last night. "I cared more for love and life . . . " But if she had not, she would not have been a great actress. The convinced mummer who is nothing but a mummer does not, I am convinced, give you the best work. The artist "in spite of yourself" he's your man. The mummer the easier to deal with (managerially). You only have to feed him continual popularity. But the rebellious artist whom his art has to conquer—that gives you your E. T.

I am ashamed that I had forgotten the "Lyceum" (yours) performance of Hamlet. I knew that I had seen you at it before, but I could not remember when, and that "extraordinary" occasion escaped my memory. I don't think I told you last night how much and well it seems to me to have matured. All the difficult bits: the Ophelia, Gertrude, R and G ones. These especially which <u>seem</u> so easy: I suppose there's no one at present who can touch you at them. All that it struck me to criticise was the late saner part: from the Gravedigger (how good he is; the simplest and best I've seen!) scene onwards. I'd like the intellectual continuity kept clearer (he is now, past dispute, "sane"). I was troubled now and then by the sudden outbursts of rather (?) forced emotion, passages on the brass: they spoil what a musician would call the melodic line, in this case break into the intellectual continuity. We can be held—at least, you, I am sure, can hold up by quiet, or at any rate <u>controlled</u> tension. And of course I'd like you as detached from the background as possible, you as much among us, so that we share your thoughts. He has thought his problems out, is pretty cold-blooded about them now (the King must die "a man's life . . . to say One") and R and G remorselessly "go to it". And he is ready to die himself. All quite cool and calm. Only that sudden vain heartrending pang for Ophelia and all that is gone. Yes, I'd say: take full advantage of the change from student's age to the stressed "thirty".

You gave us a delightful evening. Good luck in India. You'll find the Indian Shakespeare scholars very nippy.

Yours,
H. G-B.

---

1. Virginia Woolf's review for the *New Statesman* of the new edition of *Ellen Terry's Memoirs,* written some twelve years earlier.

Chapter X

Other Actors and Directors

Whereas *the earlier* chapters of this book have dealt with Barker's correspondence with a single individual, this chapter is a miscellany, as are the following two chapters also. It affords brief glimpses of Barker in his professional relationships with various theater people, extending over his whole career, the earliest letter being written in 1900 and the latest in 1945. None of the correspondence is as sustained, or as important, as that with Sir John Gielgud, but it nevertheless gives some interesting indications of Barker's often trenchant views about plays and about some of the players of his day. Above all, the letters in this chapter reflect a master craftsman discussing the craft which he has learned by practical experience and which he now understands completely. The correspondents are arranged in alphabetical order.

W. Bridges Adams (1889–1965)

After some experience as a small-part actor, Bridges Adams moved, quite early in his career, to directing. He had occasional commissions in London (he directed Masefield's Judith *for the Stage Society in 1916, for example) and became the co-director of Liverpool Playhouse for the 1916–17 season. In 1919, on the recommendation of Barker, Archer, and Shaw, he was appointed director of the Shakespeare Memorial Theatre at Stratford-upon-Avon, a post he occupied with devotion and distinction until 1934. It was under his guidance and as a result of his inspiration that the Stratford theatre developed into a major producing unit, presenting a long summer season of Shakespeare's plays. It was Bridges Adams who first invited Komisarjevsky to direct in England.*

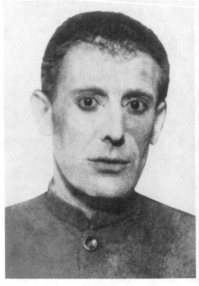

Elizabeth Robins in the New York production
of James Albery's *Forgiven*, 1886.

Dennis Eadie as Falder in John
Galsworthy's *Justice*, 1910.

Joyce Redman as Doll Common and Nicholas Hannen
as Sir Epicure Mammon in Ben Jonson's *The Alchem-
ist* at the Old Vic, 1947.

CALG/MS
To Adams

PRIVATE

Regent Hotel,
Royal Leamington Spa.
20.8.19

My dear Bridges Adams,

I am so glad that you are doing this Stratford job that I want to write you a word about the M. N. D. which I saw last night, even if it is not one of unqualified compliment.

Till the first part was over and the second part well on its way I thought it would be. My spirits were high. There was the whole text and hardly a slip in it. They were speaking it rapidly and enjoying it—and so were we. The whole thing was moving forward swiftly and directly and beautifully—and I blessed you and felt cheered. Any crows I could have picked with you were over differences of opinion only and that made it the more interesting, not less. But—whether as the play went on you had had less time to rehearse it and so lost control, while the actors said "Oh yes, I know an excellent bit of business here" or whether you are overtly guilty (in which case down on your knees before that monument in the chancel) I can't tell, but there came a frightful dégringolade. No change of pace or colour in the verse, no really interpretative relevancy of the scenes, the whole thing smudged over with that accursed romping "business". And what is to be done to a Lysander who spoils his last most beautiful line "And he did bid us follow to the temple" by splitting it in two by a comic yawn? I would shoot him out of hand.

And finally the old obscene clowning of the play.

Here I would shoot you. There is no earthly warrant for it. Shakespeare writing for a cockney audience made greater fun of village players than ever he would have done at Stratford, but even then his conscience revolted and he let Theseus give the artistic snob Philostrate a good dressing down on the subject. But never never would he have admitted this buffoonery.

Now if you are not at Stratford to interpret Shakespeare you have no right there at all. And you have a right there—and the best title, I should think, of any man in England to carry on the work (in view of the real spirit, the real "love in life" which quite patently you bring to it). So, heavily on this sort of thing.

I don't care whether the audience laugh or not at seeing Starveling and Bottom and the rest go on like fifth-rate unskilled music-hall knockabouts. What you do by allowing it is to move them (the audience) suddenly out of the Shakespeare Theatre into the fifth-rate music-hall, that is to say you undo in half an hour all the work you have done during the rest of the play and if there were an instrument which could record soul-states it would record that as debasement. <u>You</u> are such an instrument: go in front and don't watch the play but feel for yourself how the audience has changed.

Besides—consider this. Here is Cecil Sharp teaching on one side of the town the beauties of folk dancing. Here are you contradicting everything he says by making your rustics fall in a heap when they attempt a bergomask. No, no, no.

I write you this diatribe because I really care that you should do something for Stratford that has not yet been done. If you will, I'll fight for you. But if you are not to clean out this rubbish heap then you must be fought against, for your own sake and Stratford's sake—and Shakespeare's sake.

But that must not be when you have 75% of the thing as right as right.

Please understand—I scribble this in great haste—why I write at all, and do not let my swearing seem to drown my praise, which is heartfelt.

Yrs.,
H. Granville-Barker

CALG/MS
To Adams

12, Hyde Park Place,
London
W.2
23.8.19

My dear Bridges Adams,

Good—and again, good! And never mind my grumbling. And I'm so glad you saw it as a mere makeweight to my real appreciation of what you have done. But—you must stick to Stratford if you want to. I am sure much can be done there. And call me as a witness next time if you think I can carry any weight as to the absolute need of their giving you more scope, more <u>money</u> to spend on preliminary work. And if at this go you have slain half the dragons of that deadening "tradition", next time you can dispose of the others. Morris-dancing. Ah no, but we can admit that as <u>dancing</u> it is good and that when William asked for a bergomask he knew what he wanted.

As long as we take our jobs seriously—as the comic does most seriously of all—if you can but knock <u>that</u> into the heads of your young people, be it only by the process of knocking their heads together—all will be well.

And—after the damned artistic desert of the last five years—your work at Stratford has cheered me enormously.

Yours,
H. Granville Barker

CALG/MS
To Adams

Netherton Hall,
Honiton,
S. Devon.
25.4.22

My dear Bridges Adams,

I wish we could have had a talk. However, things seem very well for you at Stratford, to the limit of their immediate possibilities, and of that I'm heartily glad. But my conviction still strongly is that you ought to be permanently established there, able to work and prepare all the year round, with occasional performances during the "close" times of actual preparation. Then the two festivals and such seasons in London, Manchester, Glasgow etc. as can be managed.

To keep that company in being and to train the younger members <u>hard</u>—that's the thing—and the road to better things. Well, my word is for the plan, whenever or if ever it is of any use to you.

I enjoyed All's Well mightily (even at his most 'prentice, what vitality the late W. S. had. And <u>that's</u> what matters). About the acting—I'm all but disabled from speaking, for I disagree with you fundamentally about Helena. To my mind she is one of the "gallant" heroines—a foreshadowing of Viola: "Our remedies oft in ourselves do lie". I think she went ahead with a stiff upper lip and a smile, never shed a tear. And your reading—or your lady's—though I'm sure you could justify it, takes the linch-pin out of <u>my</u> cart.

But it is a joy to see a company working together and working well—and minding what they are doing—and not thinking of their own d—d funniments. And the Lord prosper you and give you good anchorage.

Yrs.
H. Granville-Barker

CALG/W
To Barker[1]

December, 1932

Would you be free consider production here this summer. Othello
indicated but choice possible.[2]

Bridges Adams
Stratford-upon-Avon

---

1. Punctuation added to this telegram.
2. The nineteenth-century theater at Stratford burned down in 1926; the present building, designed by Elizabeth Scott, was opened in April, 1932. One of the new policies,
   warmly advocated by Bridges Adams to go with the new building, was to invite
   distinguished visiting directors for particular plays.

CALG/MS
To Adams

18, Place des Etats-Unis,
Paris XVI[e]
5.12.32

My dear Bridges Adams,

There are half-a-dozen good reasons—touching mainly on
other work—why I can't and another half-dozen as good and (I
think) better why I shouldn't. But I like none the less to have you
still thinking there may be one or two why I should. For among my
reasons is not absolute indifference.

In fact I could write to you at some length upon my "hopes
and fears for Stratford". But, again, those that don't take part should
not interfere—not even with counsel: God knows you'll be over-
loaded with that cheap commodity—unless they are ordained critics.

Forgive the NO, then—and good luck.

Yours,
Harley Granville-Barker

CALG/PC
To Adams

18, Place des Etats-Unis,
Paris
March 7 1937

God send me more reviewers who know what they are writing about
and can write.[1] You betray your secret there, though. You must be—

or mean to be—at some such sort of a job yourself. You cultivate a style.

My only protest: that you should suppose a performance on the lines laid down would be longer than ordinary. You won't, I assure you, find need for one single "pause for business". Every point could be taken in the text's stride.

My only suggestion: that you cannot safely assume the Brudermord[2] to be the bastard brat of the Ur-Hamlet.[3] Safer, I thought, then, to leave it out of the argument. D. W. even leaves out Q1.[4] That I think one can't do. But I wish one could ignore the earlier play, since really we know nothing of it.

Harley Granville-Barker
—and my thanks

---

1. Bridges Adams had reviewed Barker's *Prefaces to Shakespeare; Third Series: Hamlet,* just published by Sidgwick and Jackson, for *Drama.*
2. *Der Bestrafte Brudermord (Fratricide Punished),* a crude and debased version of *Hamlet,* of uncertain date; most critics consider that it derived, perhaps by being pirated by actors, either from the lost, pre-Shakespearean play of *Hamlet* (the "Ur-Hamlet") or from Shakespeare's own play. This would place its origin, most probably, in the late sixteenth or early seventeenth century. The earliest known copy of it is dated 1710.
3. The "Ur-Hamlet" is the lost play which, in all likelihood, provided Shakespeare with one of his principal sources for *Hamlet.* It may have been written by Thomas Kyd. In his review of Barker's *Preface,* Bridges Adams had written: "William Poel shewed us, in "Fratricide Punished"—that curious recollected version of the earlier play—how Ophelia's mad scenes originated in a song-and-dance *divertissement,* stuck in where the plot threatened to flag."
4. He refers to Professor John Dover Wilson. Q1 is the first quarto of *Hamlet,* a notoriously corrupt and unreliable text bearing clear evidence of having been pirated and set down from memory.

Winthrop Ames (1871–1937)

Ames was an American manager and director. When Barker turned down the invitation to become the director of a new repertory theater in New York in 1908, Ames was offered (and accepted) the position. He was a man of independent means who did much to foster serious non-commercial theater in New York.

TEX/MS
To Barker

The Little Theatre,
West 44th Street,
New York.
25 Sept. 1915

Dear Barker,
Herewith D'Annunzio's play.[1]
The translation conveys nothing of the manifest beauty of
the original text, and what remains is, in plot, a cross between "Ham-
let" and "Electra", with an extra case of incest thrown in for full
measure—all done in D'Annunzio's most soul-writhing manner.
Quite impossibly morbid, I think, for any American audience.
Sincerely,
Winthrop Ames

---

1. Gabriele d'Annunzio (1863–1938): the play referred to here is probably *La figlia di
Jorio* (*The Daughter of Jorio*), written in 1904.

Dion Boucicault (1859–1929)

*This is Boucicault the Younger, an actor and dramatist who started his
career in his father's company in New York in 1879. He had a long
and productive career, acting, directing, and writing plays in America,
England, and Australia, though he never achieved the fame or distinction of his father. Among his most famous parts were Sir William
Gower in Pinero's* Trelawney of the "Wells" *(1898) and Carraway
Pim in Milne's* Mr. Pim Passes By *(1920). He was associated for many
years with Charles Frohman at the Duke of York's Theatre in London,
and it is probably in connection with productions at this theater that
the following letter was written.*

TEX/MS
To Boucicault

[no address]
[undated[1]]

Dear Mr. Boucicault,
Thankyou then: I will accept the offer and I understand
that it is in the repertory theatre for 24 weeks from February at £30
per week for any number of performances up to 8, with full salary
for any extra performances. And if I agree to go to any other the-

atre, £30 a week for six performances and full salary for any extra
to that.

[no signature]

---

1. The handwriting is that of Barker as a young man, and the content of the letter
   indicates that it must have been written between about 1896 and 1903.

Sir Lewis Casson (1875–1969)

*Lewis Casson was one of Barker's earliest friends and associates in the
theater and one of his greatest admirers and staunchest champions. He
played ten different parts (reviving some of them several times) in
Barker's repertory seasons at the Court Theatre in 1904–7. When he
became a member of Miss Horniman's Gaiety Theatre company in
Manchester, he adopted many of Barker's directorial and acting methods, as well as following his lead in choice of plays. Casson was one
of those who was most keenly disappointed by Barker's decision to
withdraw from active, practical theater work after the first world war.
During the twenties and thirties they lost touch with each other. In
1945 Casson was knighted for his services to the theater, and Barker
wrote to him.*

DD/MS
To Casson

Ritz Hotel,
London, W.1
June 27, 1945

My dear Lewis,

Long years ago—you'll have forgotten—you came to spend
a Sunday with me in the country; and instead of enjoying yourself,
you spent the time fixing me up an electric bell. And I was grateful
even if (probably) I scolded at you for wasting your time. You've
found wider and better ways of showing your unselfishness and public
spirit since then; and I find myself back—on my way to Paris—just
when the Powers That Be have found at last a more or less suitable
way of acknowledging this. And I'm so glad and I hope you are. God
bless you. Warm remembrances to you both—and the rest. I hope all
is well with them.

As ever,
H. G. B.

Charles Charrington (?–1926)

Charrington was one of the more enterprising of London's actors and directors at the turn of the century. He was especially interested in the production of the more thoughtful, serious, non-commerical kind of play and was responsible, for example, for several of the early productions of Ibsen in London, including the famous A Doll's House *at the Novelty Theatre in 1889, in which he played Torvald Helmer to the Nora of Janet Achurch (1864–1916), his wife. Other Ibsen productions which he directed were* The League of Youth *(Vaudeville Theatre, 1900),* The Lady from the Sea *(Royalty Theatre, 1902), and* The Master Builder *(Court Theatre, 1909). He was active in the Stage Society, sometimes as actor, sometimes as director, sometimes both. It was for this society that the productions of* Candida *and* Captain Brassbound's Conversion, *both of which are mentioned in the following correspondence, were done; also for the Stage Society he played Bohun in the first production of Shaw's* You Never Can Tell *(Royalty Theatre, 1899) and directed Gilbert Murray's* Andromache *(in which he also played Pyrrhus and Janet Achurch played Hermione) at the Strand Theatre in 1901.*

COR/MS
To Charrington

Haymarket Theatre
[London]
May 4, 1897

Dear Sir,
        Although when I saw you yesterday you took my card and kindly said you would consider my name when you were casting "Antony and Cleopatra" I had hardly time to let you know anything either about myself or my work. I am here at the present moment as Cyril Maude's understudy. I am playing, too, a small part.[1]
        As to my Shakespeare work: I do not know "Antony" except just by reading it but during my year's work with Ben Greet I had a good and varied experience of many of the other plays. With him I played Claudio, Don John, Oliver, Orsino, Roderigo, Osric, Starveling, the Clown in "The Winter's Tale", besides other "legitimate" parts.
        You will of course understand that being in a long run at the Haymarket I am most anxious to do all the outside work that I

can, and that therefore I am in hopes that you may see your way to offering me something.[2]

I am, faithfully yours,
H. Granville Barker

---

1. The play was *Under the Red Robe,* an adaptation by Edward Rose of a novel by Stanley Weyman. The production had opened on October 17, 1896, with Herbert Waring and Eva Moore in the leading roles. Cyril Maude, who was a major actor of the day, was playing Captain Larolle. Barker was playing the Major-domo and understudying Maude.
2. However, Charrington did not invite Barker to play in *Antony and Cleopatra.* (Charrington's position in relation to this production is a little puzzling. Although he appears to have been doing the casting, he was neither the director nor the manager and he was not himself in the cast of the play. Janet Achurch played Cleopatra; the Antony was Louis Calvert, who also directed; Ben Greet was the manager. The production was presented at the Olympic Theatre for five matinées and six evening performances in 1897.)

COR/MS
To Charrington

8, York Buildings,
Adelphi.
June 12 [1900]

My dear Charrington,

Thankyou. I should like to play Eugene.[1] I have read through the part carefully today. But we shall rehearse this well, shall we not?

I am glad you think I was successful last night[2] and for my part I want to thank Mrs. Charrington again—and perhaps you will for me—for all her kind work and her tact during rehearsals. I can hardly look back on any such pleasantness.

Will you let me have a copy of Candida. I don't want to thumb my own.

Very faithfully yours,
H. Granville Barker

---

1. Eugene Marchbanks, in Shaw's *Candida,* which Charrington was directing for the Stage Society the following month. It is worth noting that this piece of casting, which later became famous, was Charrington's idea, not Shaw's. Shaw's first choice for Marchbanks was H. V. Esmond, though he bowed to Charrington's judgment after seeing Barker in *Das Friedensfest* (see *Bernard Shaw: Collected Letters,* ed. Dan H. Laurence, 2: 169–71).
2. Barker was playing Robert in the Stage Society production of Hauptmann's *Das Friedensfest.* The play had been translated, under the title *The Coming of Peace,* by Janet Achurch and C. E. Wheeler; Janet Achurch also directed the production. Charrington was the manager or producer.

COR/MS
To Charrington

Prince of Wales's Theatre[1]
[London]
Thursday evening [October, 1900]

Dear Charrington,

You must let me off Charles[2] if you possibly can. The rehearsals will be too long and tedious for me to manage. (I have another reason which I would whisper in your ear.[3]) There is Alfred Kendrick at Wyndham's Theatre but I don't suppose he'd do it: he might for you. But I think E. W. Tarver, Avenue Theatre, would and would be very good.

Please use this messenger boy, who brings this, to send round. If he doesn't find you and leaves the note, write me a line tonight. Of course, understand that not for a moment will I leave you in a hole, but arrange to do without me if you can.

Yours,
H. Granville Barker

---

1. Where Barker was playing the Earl of Rochester in *English Nell,* with Marie Tempest as Nell Gwynn. The play was written by Anthony Hope (Sir Anthony Hope Hawkins) and Edward Rose.
2. The play that Charrington was directing for the Stage Society at this time, and to which Barker must be referring since it was Charrington's only production between July and December, 1900, was *The Three Wayfarers,* a dramatization by Thomas Hardy of his own short story, "The Three Strangers." It has, however, no character called "Charles" in it. There are only two named characters, Timothy Somers and Joseph Somers; the rest are referred to as "Shepherd," "Constable," "Magistrate," etc. One can only assume that, for some reason, a name was changed or added. Charrington's production of the piece was given two matinée performances, one at the Strand Theatre on November 4 and one at the Queen's Theatre on November 11.
3. The secret reason is that he was devoting all the time he could spare to the writing of a new play, "Agnes Colander."

COR/MS
To Charrington

P. O. W. T.
Saturday night [October, 1900]

My dear Charrington,

I have found you two men—Mr. Marvin and Mr. Halkett. They will be down at the Strand at 10.30 on Monday. If the call is altered, or the theatre, will you wire them on Monday morning. They have the same address—57, Charlotte Street, Portland Place.

Yours,
H. G. Barker

<u>P.S.</u> I've found you a third—Mr. Farrar: same address.

COR/MS
To Charrington

P. O. W. T.
Oct. 26 [1900]

Dear Charrington,

I have asked Mr. Pym Williamson about Charles and he's good enough to say that he'll play it, but he wants to read the play, so I have given it him tonight and marked all the business so far arranged.

If you want to see him he'll be here tomorrow of course from 2.30 to 4.30 and 8.30 to 10.30, otherwise his address is 55 High Street, S.W. I'm sure he'll be a most admirable substitute.

Put me to the expense of printing slips if the programme can't be altered.

If there's any further hitch of course let me know and I'll play. Don't think badly of me for this.

Yours,
H. G. Barker

COR/MS
To Charrington

8, York Buildings,
Adelphi
[London]
Nov. 29 [1900]

Dear Charrington,

I very much prefer Captain Kearney, the man in the last act[1] and I don't think that I (or you and Shaw) need be alarmed about the American accent.

I return you the book. Will you let me know about rehearsals?

Thankyou for thinking of me—I shall like very much to be playing in the piece, and that part.

My kind regards to you and Mrs. Charrington.

Yours,

H. G. Barker

---

1. In Act 3 of Shaw's *Captain Brassbound's Conversion,* which Charrington was producing for the Stage Society in December, with Janet Achurch as Lady Cicely Waynflete. This was the play's first production.

COR/MS
To Charrington

8, York Buildings,

Adelphi

[London]

Dec. 4 [1900]

Dear Charrington,

I missed you by five minutes at the Strand today.

Tomorrow (Wednesday) I can rehearse up to 11.45. Thursday I can either rehearse at 11 for an hour—could you begin with my scene?—or I can rehearse at about 12.45 till 1.45. Will you let me have a line about this tonight because I have to arrange another rehearsal to fit in with yours.

Friday the same (about 12–2).

Sorry I missed you today.

Yours,

H. G. Barker

COR/MS
To Charrington

8, York Buildings

Saturday morning [December, 1900]

Dear Charrington,

I'm not in the least annoyed and I think Shaw quite right to speak out.[1]

As I told him, I might under other circumstances have chosen Redbrook[2] and would play it now but I don't see that I can possibly manage to rehearse it—two acts, with complicated business. Remember I have eight performances next week and another long part to rehearse.[3]

Get someone else for Kearney if you can. I shan't be good in it (I don't know any Chicago Americans—the style GBS wants) but of course I shan't be so awfully bad as Shaw makes out either.

If you want me to play[4] tell me the call for Monday and Tuesday and <u>when</u> you'll be doing Act III.

Yours,

H. G. Barker

---

1. Shaw had seen some of the rehearsals of *Captain Brassbound's Conversion* and had written to Barker on December 6 saying (among other equally devastating things): "Unless you can make the acquaintance of a real American & live with him night & day for the next week, the part will ruin you." (See Barker's letter to Shaw of December 8, 1900, in Chapter III above.)
2. Another character in *Captain Brassbound's Conversion*.
3. He had just been invited by J. T. Grein to play Paul Raymond in the Independent Theatre production of a translation by Grein and Martin Leonard of Pailleron's *Le Monde ou l'on s'ennuie* (in English the play was first called *The World of Boredom;* the title was later changed to *The Lion Hunters*).
4. Charrington kept Barker in the role.

COR/MS
To Charrington

8, York Buildings,
W.C.
Dec. 10 [1900]

Dear Charrington,

I have to be at rehearsal at the Avenue at 12 tomorrow. Would you mind again beginning with my scene? Or rather, Act III. Two things I'm making a note here to ask you when I get a chance.

Will Clarkson make me a beard? (There seemed some little difficulty.) Are Nathan's doing costumes? Are the S. S. going to give me exes? I shall be spending money on one thing and another, I may remark.

Yours,

H. G. Barker

COR/MS
To Charrington

8, York Buildings,
Adelphi
[London]
Dec. 15 [1901]

Dear Charrington,

Do you think Paxton would play in "Ann Leete"[1]—Mr. Crowe, about the best of those "wedding scene" parts? I am most anxious to get those half-dozen parts as well done as possible for the scene depends on them. We would only bother him for a week's rehearsal. If you think he won't, can you suggest any other "burly well-to-do farmer"? I'd be very grateful.

Yours,
H. G. Barker

---

1. Barker was preparing for a production, under the auspices of the Stage Society, of his own play, *The Marrying of Ann Leete,* which he himself was directing. The production was presented at the Royalty Theatre on January 26, 1902.

CON/MS
To Charrington

8, York Buildings,
Adelphi
[London]
Dec. 16 [1901]

Dear Charrington,

Many thanks. Certainly: I think every one of the cast should have two guineas.

I have asked Whelan to send you Paxton's address if he has it. If Paxton won't, Rock[1] might as a favour to you or to me. He played in "The Weather-Hen",[2] and for two guineas.

Yours,
H. G. Barker

P.S. Isn't Paxton a member of the Green Room?

---

1. Charles Rock (1866–1919).
2. *The Weather-Hen,* written by Barker in collaboration with Berte Thomas, was produced for a single matinee at the Comedy Theatre in 1899 but proved so successful that it was put into the evening bill for a further fourteen performances.

COR/MS
To Charrington

8, York Buildings,
Adelphi
[London]
April 17 [1902]

My dear Charrington,

I dare not come to your rescue[1] for I am busy writing and it is so seldom that I get a clear time at that, that I dare not desert it. Why don't you try Graham Browne again? He's at the Shaftesbury. (May 5 is a matinée, isn't it?)

I pick these names at random from the front page of the "Era": Grimwood, Trant Fagan, Percyval, Ivan Berlin, A. A., Patrick Evans; these are in the other "cards".[2]

If you want any girl's part (not too important) played I could send you my sister.

Thankyou for MSS.[3] I should have acknowledged them.

George Trollope who is at the Haymarket might like to play. Howard Templeton, who is in the Country Mouse.

Good Lord! Charrington, what energy you have. I feel like "Sir Peter".[4] I never in my life deny you—my advice. But I must not leave writing.

Yours,
H. G. Barker

---

1. Charrington was directing Ibsen's *The Lady from the Sea,* with Janet Achurch as Ellida and Laurence Irving as The Stranger, for two performances (May 4 and 5, 1902) at the Royalty Theatre. Barker was probably beginning work on his play *The Voysey Inheritance.*
2. He is referring to the practice, current among actors at the time, of printing their "cards" in the advertisement columns of newspapers in the hope of obtaining engagements. (Advertisement columns were usually on the front page of a newspaper.) The actors to whom he refers are Herbert Grimwood (1875–1929), H. Trant Fagan, T. Wigney Percyval (1865–?), Ivan Berlin (1874–1934), and Patrick Evans (I have failed to identify "A. A."). Most of these had played under Barker's direction in one or the other (or both) of Barker's own plays, *The Weather-Hen* and *The Marrying of Ann Leete.*
3. I cannot identify these.
4. The reference is to Sir Peter Teazle in *The School for Scandal.*

Dennis Eadie (1869–1928)

"Dennis Eadie, that Protean actor," wrote Max Beerbohm in 1909, in his review of Arsene Lupin, *in which Eadie shared the honors with Gerald du Maurier. And in an earlier review, in 1906, Beerbohm had*

described Eadie as "one of the cleverest and most resourceful of our younger actors."[1] He was also one of the busiest, playing, in his time, with nearly all the best and biggest managements in London. He was the Mephistopheles in William Poel's revolutionary production of Marlowe's Dr. Faustus *at St. George's Hall in 1896; he was one of the regular actors in Barker's repertory seasons at the Court Theatre in 1904–7, playing Menelaus in the Gilbert Murray version of the* Troades, Henry Jackson in The Return of the Prodigal, *Hugh Voysey in* The Voysey Inheritance, *Marlow in* The Silver Box, *and Hector Malone in the 1907 revival of* Man and Superman. *Barker also used him again in the brief repertory season at the Duke of York's in 1910, when he played Falder in Galsworthy's* Justice *and Homeware in Meredith's* The Sentimentalists. *By 1919 Eadie had moved into directing and management, as well as acting, and one of his projects was a production of Sierra's* The Romantic Young Lady, *which had been translated from the Spanish by Helen and Harley Granville Barker. The play was presented at the Royalty Theatre in September, 1920; Eadie himself played the lead, and Barker had some hand in the matter, though it is difficult to determine exactly what.* Who's Who in the Theatre *says, rather enigmatically, "at the Royalty, Sept., 1920, was responsible with his wife for the production of 'The Romantic Young Lady,' for the translation of which play, from the Spanish, they were also jointly responsible." During the months preceding the production Barker wrote to Eadie about it several times. His letters follow.*

---

1. This was in Beerbohm's *Saturday Review* article on the production of *The Heroic Stubbs*, by Henry Arthur Jones, January 27, 1906.

JG/handwritten by a secretary but signed by Barker
To Eadie

12, Hyde Park Place,
[London] W2
17 December 1919

My dear Eadie,

I am so glad that we have pulled "The Romantic Young Lady" through. You won't, I am sure, want to do anything about it till I am back in March[1] and perhaps not for long after, but if by any remote chance you did, my only remark would be that next to your honourable self the play will hang most on the young lady. Here we are up against the perennial difficulty—you want experience and almost above all you want a fresh and fiery childlike enthusiasm in whoever you find to play the part. She must be essentially child-like, trying hard to grow up but not of course in any sense a fool: the ordinary ingenue might let you down seriously.

I feel sure Sierra would like a letter from you. His address is:—

> Senor G. Martinez Sierra,
> Zurbarro 1.1,
> Madrid.

He would be very willing to send us photographs and his prompt book for what use they would be. But I further suggest that he might be asked to find some architect-artist friend of his to do us some coloured drawings for scenery (I believe the colour is a more important thing than anything to get the Spanish touch) but you will do as you feel best about this.

All good luck to you with Crichton;[2] may it delay the appearance of the "Romantic Young Lady" up to the limit that Sierra, my wife and I can endure!

I shall be back early in March.

Yours,
H. Granville Barker

---

1. The Barkers were about to leave on a long-projected visit to America (see Barker's letters to Helen in Chapter VI).
2. Eadie was playing Treherne in a revival of J. M. Barrie's *The Admirable Crichton*.

JG/MS
To Eadie

Connaught Hotel,
Mayfair,
[London] W1
19.3.20

My dear Eadie,

I wired to Sierra. Let me know if you don't hear. Address till further notice: Fortfield Hotel, Sidmouth, Devon.

The only crab about Miss Ward—the old lady's remark that she was a meek and tearful wife. But age works many changes and Miss W's distinction is worth much else.[1]

The ideal cast for Don Juan—Sir Claude Phillips of the D. T.![2]

At your reasonable leisure, read through "The Morris Dance"[3] (will you?) and tell me if it makes you laugh. Winthrop Ames produced it in New York in 1917 and it was a crushing failure.

But at the first performance (the only one I saw) the audience did roll about with mirth, so I have always wondered why. If I didn't dislike blaming actors for what may always be the author's fault (!) I should think maybe it was because the Michael (on whom the whole thing hangs) did his best to wreck it. I don't fancy it was the corpse. But tell me, if you will, what you feel.

Yours,

H. Granville Barker

---

1. A. E. Wilson, in *Edwardian Theatre* (London, 1951), said of Geneviève Ward (1838–1922), "Her very appearance was grand and impressive. She was noble of brow, dark-eyed, deep-voiced and majestic and one can never forget those full organ tones and her measured fineness of diction." American by birth, she was well known in both London and New York and had a long and distinguished career in both countries. She was in the original London production of Ibsen's *John Gabriel Borkman* in 1897 and played Queen Eleanor in Henry Irving's production of Tennyson's *Becket* in 1893.
2. Claude Phillips (1846–1924) was the art critic of the *Daily Telegraph*. He had begun his career as a barrister-at-law whose business took him often to Italy. There he developed an interest in art and became widely known for his scholarship in that field. He was the author of *The Life of Sir Joshua Reynolds* (1894) and was Keeper of the Wallace Collection from 1897 until 1911. He was knighted in 1911.
3. This was a stage version by Barker of *The Wrong Box,* by Robert Louis Stevenson and Lloyd Osbourne.

JG/MS
To Eadie

Connaught Hotel,
Mayfair,
[London], W.1.
Thursday [March, 1920]

My dear Eadie,

What you want for the scenery is—don't you think—an architect who knows Spain. I have enquired after one and will let you know. But failing this Lutyens has been there a good deal and could and I think would turn out two sketches.[1] He works very quickly. Do you know him? I could write him a note if you'd like. But we may hear of an "easier" man.

Yours,

H. Granville Barker

---

1. Sir Edwin Landseer Lutyens (1869–1944) was the architect of (among many other major buildings) the British Pavilion at the Paris Exhibition of 1900, the Viceroy's House, New Delhi (1910), the Cenotaph, in Whitehall, London, and the Roman Catholic Cathedral in Liverpool (1933). He was knighted in 1918.

JG/MS
To Eadie

Fortfield Hotel,
Sidmouth,
S. Devon.
23.3.20

My dear Eadie,

A charming letter from Sierra. I feel inclined to assure him
at once that you realise his ideal and that above all you are not "fashionable nor conceited".

Orange and yellow!! It doesn't sound at all possible. Maybe
they want to flaunt their national colours at us.

Miss Nesbitt. Very clever—very charming.[1] <u>But</u>—is she the
<u>romantic</u> young lady? I'm not sure that—like the movie people—you
won't have to organisc a competition among the "young ladies" who
write for your autograph. Unfortunately, a little acting is needed
too.

Yours,
H. Granville Barker

---

1. Cathleen Nesbitt (1889–1982) played Perdita in Barker's production of *The Winter's
   Tale* at the Savoy Theatre in 1912. At the age of ninety-one, she was still pursuing an
   active career in 1980, both on the stage and on television (see also note 15 on p. 176).

JG/MS
To Eadie

Fortfield Hotel,
Sidmouth,
S. Devon.
28.3.20

My dear Eadie,

I quite agree with you about the scenes—positively and
negatively NO—and my wife testifies that Act I at least is not at all
Spanish—the product of the Spanish scene designer trying to be up
to date, rather.

The scene should certainly be dark (black and gold very
good) and a <u>little</u> threadbare, perhaps, though not dowdy. The only
technical trouble is the position of the window. (Have it made conveniently for your jump. Do you want to jump left handed or right?)
We should show, if possible, its relation to the street so that we don't
have to insist on this too much in the dialogue.

As to Act II—I quite agree. You would have, I daresay, a certain number of up-to-date works of art about.

Mary Rorke?[1] Of course she could <u>do</u> it. But as to being it—she is British and middle-class to the core (and the core used to be rather too comfortably embedded for 80 years of age) I think I'd look further before deciding. It might be possible—faute de mieux—to find someone with that petite aristocratic air—like Carlotta Addison used to have (? Nina Boucicault!)

Sorry I am of so little use now in casting. But how pleasant it is to think that you are doing it!

Regards,

Yours,

H. Granville Barker

---

1. Mary Rorke (1858–1938) was the elder sister of the better-known Kate Rorke. Both actresses had long and distinguished careers on the London stage.

JG/MS
To Eadie

The Fortfield Hotel,
Sidmouth.
8.5.20

My dear Eadie,

It falls out well. We are coming up to town for a week from the 17th—to the Connaught Hotel again and I'll be all at your service.

We must pray to God for a Romantic young lady. <u>Romantic</u>—<u>young</u>—<u>a lady</u>—not to mention an <u>actress</u>—and I grant you that it is asking the Almighty a good deal.

Till we meet.

Yours,

H. Granville Barker

JG/MS
To Eadie

The Fortfield Hotel,
Sidmouth.
27.5.20

My dear Eadie,

I fear I did not make myself clear about the architect. No good consulting Weir himself—but I have asked him to send you if he can the names of any Spanish-wise architects. If he fails I <u>should</u> consult Lutyens (if you approve) and ask him to lend you a Spanish-wise architect. (Mean <u>you</u> should)

I fancy Miss de Solla with all her faults will be better than Miss Rorke with her virtues.[1] She (Miss de S) will have a great pull in her looks. Few—but the Spaniards do look so—she's not ideal. I wish she were really older and had more real character in her (Mary Rorke has not—only more real kindliness) but failing the best she may do—indeed must do.

I know Ada Palmer, I think. She is still the wrong sort. A prehistoric elephant would be better—would be well worth looking and waiting a bit for if you can afford to.

Yours,
H. Granville Barker

---

1. Nevertheless Mary Rorke eventually played the role. Rachel de Solla died suddenly on November 24, 1920, two months after *The Romantic Young Lady* opened.

JG/MS
To Eadie

Fortfield Hotel,
Sidmouth,
S. Devon.
29.6.20

My dear Eadie,

Well, it seems about an even chance whether Miss Jane Cowl weighs in or not.[1] My impression is that Selwyn would like to keep her[2]—but is a little shy of having to keep her in her own plays. However, we'll see.

Meanwhile I am settling <u>not</u> to go to France till August—so that I will be yours to command from July 14th. If Miss J. C. <u>is</u> coming you'll rehearse with an understudy I suppose. If not, you'll experiment if need be with various R. Y. L.'s until you find the best. But I'm sure you're right to break the back of the thing before you go.

Yours,
H. Granville Barker

---

1. Jane Cowl (1890–1950), an American actress, had one of her greatest successes as Kathleen Dungannon in *Smilin' Through,* a sentimental comedy of which she was co-author. It opened at the Broadhurst Theatre, New York, in December, 1919, and ran for nearly three years.
2. Archibald Selwyn, American producer and director of *Smilin' Through,* in which his brother, Edgar Selwyn, played the lead. Barker's guess was correct: Selwyn would

not release Jane Cowl from *Smilin' Through* to join the cast of *The Romantic Young Lady* in London.

JG/MS
To Eadie

The Fortfield Hotel,
Sidmouth.
1.7.20

My dear Eadie,

I hear great things of Miss Edna Best and I notice that she blooms out soon at the Duke of York's as a leading lady—but in a play which has all the preliminary stigmata of failure. Even so, and as something called "Brown Sugar"[1] <u>might</u> be a success, is it worth while putting a stranglehold on her before this event? Unless you know that she is no good.

Yours,
H. Granville Barker

---

1. This was a light comedy by Lady Arthur Lever, which ran for 266 performances. In it Edna Best played a character called Lady Sloane.

JG/MS
To Eadie

The Fortfield Hotel,
Sidmouth.
4.7.20

My dear Eadie,

Will you send me back the MS of "The Morris Dance" (The Wrong Box). I have, as they say, "a use for it".

I see that Edna Best lives and breathes by kind permission of J. E. V.![1]

Yours,
H. Granville Barker

---

1. J. E. Vedrenne, who now had Edna Best under contract.

JG/MS
To Eadie

Fortfield Hotel,
Sidmouth.
7.7.20

My dear Eadie,

<u>Amalia</u>: I don't remember Miss N. W.[1] but she sounds wrong and the casting is important not only intrinsically—because it is the weakest spot in the play—but from your point of view, you as the man. You must show good taste in the matter of mistresses—and not just founded above all on mere physical considerations. I should choose one in fact more like Mrs. Asquith than Mdlle Delysia. Musical Comedy <u>is</u> a good training ground and the part is easy for the right woman, but choose something with chic and an appearance of intelligence—above all nothing <u>fat,</u> as you love the firm of Eadie and Cuzzon.

I suppose you have thought of your Miss Julia James as a possible R. Y. L. I don't know her well enough myself to say.

I am sorry I am so little use over names. Have you thought of Mrs. A. B. Tapping[2] as a possible old servant and of Frances Ivor as a possible grandmother. But if you want any service from me in the matter of seeing people.

And I am concluding that you expect me in London for a fortnight on Monday, July 19th. But if this is altered please give me all the notice possible, for we are still homeless and arranging hotel rooms is not so simple nowadays. Also I am loath to leave my work here a moment before I need.[3]

Yours,
H. Granville Barker

---

1. Norma Whalley, born in Sydney, N.S.W., married Percival Clarke, son of Sir Edward Clarke; her stage career was brief.
2. Alfred B. Tapping and his wife were both on the stage for the whole of their lives. She was always known in the profession (and on theater programs, posters, etc.) as Mrs. A. B. Tapping. She died in 1926 at the age of seventy-three, predeceasing her husband by two years.
3. It is worth noting that Barker now regarded his chief work as his writing: directing plays, even plays which he and Helen had translated, was now a secondary occupation. The work he was busy with was *The Exemplary Theatre* (and the beginnings of the play *The Secret Life*).

JG/MS
To Eadie

> The Fortfield Hotel,
> Sidmouth.
> 10.7.20

My dear Eadie,

  Woe—oh woe in due sense over Jane Cowl's defection—for I would gladly have seen you part your money on the subject. But there is this tinge of relief—I do dread for the part the sophisticated, egotistic leading lady, who will <u>lead</u>—lead her grandmother and you and the typist and all. God bless us, we want someone that can act, but there is nothing very brittle or difficult in the part and it will be worth a lot if, combined with the necessary acting, we can put something fresh and open and confident and on occasion capable of a genuine <u>shyness</u>—rarest of virtues in young ladies on the stage.

  That is why—without attempting finally to turn down Laura Cowie[1]—I recommend you to look elsewhere before you turn to her (I saw her over Deburau and gathered that she is "off" the stage but would "come back" if a real opportunity offered. She made a favour of it. She played Hermia for me in M. N. D.—good but stockish. N.B. I did not see her in "The Freaks")

  That is why too I spoke in my telegram for the openness and confidence of Meggie Albanesi[2] and for a certain charm of shyness of Moyna McGill. I don't know her, I have it from N. P.[3] that she is personally clever. He says she is not "up" to modern comedy yet, but if he means not up to all its usual tricks that might be an advantage (and anyhow N. P.'s comedy is not always of the subtlest, though I respect his judgment of people);

  I threw out the other names in my telegram at a venture. Faith Celli though should perhaps be very seriously considered. I don't doubt G. du M.[4] taught her 70 p.c. of what she did in D. B.[5] but the performance "came off" nevertheless—and it is a method of getting on—if you are driven to it.

  Both she and Moyna McGill are worth serious thought, I believe.

  One name I did not mention—Joyce Carey.[6] I agree with you—born with a flannel petticoat; but I suppose possible. You say Jane Graham is no good? Well—command me. I mean if I can be of real use by coming up earlier and doing searching or interviewing for you, I will with pleasure. I expect you're dead beat, you've had the devil of a season.

> Yours,
> H. G. B.

1. Laura Cowie (1892–1969) in fact did return to a long career in the theater playing many kinds of part, including Gertrude in the Gielgud *Hamlet* at Elsinore in 1939.
2. Meggie (Margharita) Albanesi (1899–1923) was the daughter of "Madame Albanesi" (Effie Henderson), a popular novelist of the day. She died very suddenly of a throat infection at the age of twenty-four. She was a promising young actress who played leading parts in the first productions of Galsworthy's *The Skin Game,* Clemence Dane's *A Bill of Divorcement,* etc.
3. Nigel (later, Sir Nigel) Playfair (1874–1934).
4. Gerald (later Sir Gerald) du Maurier (1873–1934).
5. J. M. Barrie's *Dear Brutus.* Du Maurier played Dearth and Faith Celli played Margaret, the "dream child," in the first production of the play in 1917.
6. Joyce Carey (1898–   ) was the actress to whom Eadie eventually gave the part.

JG/MS
To Eadie

The Fortfield Hotel,
Sidmouth.
13.7.20

My dear Eadie,

All right, I'll be at the Connaught from Sunday night onwards. I think we had better do a few days' work round a table. Could perhaps your S. M. make a <u>very rough</u> and broad model of each scene, 1 <u>inch</u> scale and put a <u>little doll's</u> furniture in it—so that the company may have the thing constantly before their eyes? I have found that a good plan.

All right, I am resigned to the possibility of Miss J. C., ever cheerful. She has many good points—if the petticoats can be induced—or <u>re</u>duced to let her display them.

H. G. B.

JG/MS
To Eadie

Connaught Hotel,
Mayfair, W.1
Saturday, 1.30

My dear Eadie,

If no Amalia has yet been found I am not sure that Providence does not intend Miss Kenham to play it—and for us to have a simpler, softer—more Mary Jerroldish—saucepan-buying young person for the secretary.

Turn this over in your mind while you are changing your

mind while you are changing your make-up this afternoon! It may be a good move. Miss K. is so far very <u>nervy</u>, though I'm sure she is capable.

H. G. B.

JG/MS
To Eadie

Fortfield Hotel,
Sidmouth,
S. Devon.
22.9.20

My dear Eadie,

Bless you—you are a brick and a sportsman to work with and the Lord send us together again over some other job.

As the Scripture has it "Beware when all men speak well of you" and I feared when I saw the advertisement that business was not all it ought to be.[1] But I agree it is worth while on this reception "pushing" the thing a bit and I'm very glad you are doing so—and thank you.

But how the play "goes" is the thing—and that you can tell. How does Act II pan out now? All I can suggest as to the performance is to encourage Miss Carey to do her damndest, and if I suppressed or depressed her—I hope I didn't—bid her forget she ever heard my miniatory voice. Enjoy <u>yourself</u>—that's the only recipe to you. Get Chaun to light a firecracker under Amalia every night just before she goes on. By the way, my wife suggests that she might effectively have been very "made up", pale face, <u>red</u>, <u>red</u> mouth—blackened eyes as all Spanish gypsies do. What do you say?

But do, in anything, feel free to vary and alter. If you feel that, and being in front you can't judge—rely on your instinct—it will carry you right.

As to other Sierras—nothing I've read yet would be much good to you I believe. I did not think much of Madame Afrita which the Senora spoke of. But I'll let you see all that is "Englished" and you shall judge.

One of my own—I wish I could; but my stuff seems to get heavier and heavier in hand. But if I could hit on an idea that amused me, well you shall see if it amuses you, I promise.

Best regards from us both to your wife and yourself,

Yours,
H. Granville Barker

1. The play opened at the Royalty Theatre on September 16. Purdom (*Harley Granville Barker,* p. 197) says it opened in December, 1920, but this is an error. From September 16 it ran for sixty-eight performances.

JG/MS
To Eadie

The Fortfield Hotel,
Sidmouth.
12.10.20

My dear Eadie,

No, our R. Y. L. does <u>not</u> draw the crowd as she should—but she shows some steadiness of demeanour, and I'm glad you feel she is at least tolerable in this respect. The only parallel case in my experience is "FANNY'S FIRST PLAY" which hung on for 8 or 10 weeks in a half-satisfactory way—though one was and could be satisfied with less in those days—hung on to £500–£600, then blazed into the glory of full houses for quite a time and ended, of course, by running to business "fair to good" for—Lord knows how long. Your patience then may be rewarded.

We—my wife and I—want to leave nothing undone so, without recommending it (I, from my own experience, <u>dis</u>-recommend it and her instinct says mildly no), if you'd like any of Sierra's one-acters to add to the bill I'm sure he'd be glad to throw them into it. It is your remark about "not enough for their money" prompts this.

The only one that might suit you—if <u>you</u> cared to play and could get a "Marian Terryish" sort of leading lady to play it with you—would be "The Lover". It is slight and ironic, but very amusing and sympathetic, a 25-minute duologue practically.

As I say we <u>don't</u> recommend—but we don't want to hold back anything that your judgment might approve.

Best regards,

Yours,
H. G. B.

JG/MS
To Eadie

> Fortfield,
> Sidmouth,
> S. Devon.
> 15.10.20

My dear Eadie,

Here is "El Emandado". Read it <u>through</u> rather than <u>in</u> this translation (though you must please forget <u>I said so!</u>) Will you <u>let</u> me have it back soon, for it has to be published.

I sadly agree with you about Miss J. C.—and I much fear there is nothing more to be done than we have done. You might try playing it a different way every night—sticking pins into her—treading on her toes (Has she toes or only feet? The R. Y. L. would have had toes and <u>no</u> feet.)

You might—seriously—remind her of the thing she was told above all others—always to be at boiling point inside and <u>passionate</u>. But she—what is the good of using such words? How to be passionate in Pelham Crescent? And the answer is A Rabbit.

Our best regards to you—and my wife adds a special message to Mrs. Eadie. She hopes she has not forgotten their siestas in the stalls. (My message, really—hers was just of warm regards.)

> Yours,
> H. G. B.

Nicholas Hannen (1881–1972)

*Hannen set out to be an architect but took up acting as a career in 1910. He began in musical comedies (*The Count of Luxembourg, Gipsy Love, The Marriage Market, *etc.). He played Nelson in Barker's version of* The Dynasts *at the Kingsway Theatre in 1914 and was in Barker's New York company at Wallack's Theatre in 1915, playing Dubedat in* The Doctor's Dilemma, *Lysander in* A Midsummer Night's Dream, *etc. Barker and he were firm friends from that time onward. By 1930 Hannen was established as one of the best and most steadily employed actors in London. He was very anxious to get Barker back into the theater as a playwright and his first suggestion was that he (Hannen) should direct* His Majesty, *which Barker published in 1928, and play the leading part of King Henry XIII of Carpathia himself.*

SEY/MS
To Hannen

3, Foro Romano,
Rome, 18.
30.1.31

My dear Hannen,

If I begin to write to you about casting His Majesty the production will thereupon be postponed, I feel, till 1935, by which time I may well be dead and you will be ageing. However, I'll risk it and if I do decease you'll have to give a memorial performance (with the cast dressed in black) so the notes may come in useful anyhow.

And if your present play doesn't make a definite bid to run through the summer[1] you'll have, I suppose, to be ready to jump quick. With regard to which, hadn't you better make some tentative "approach" to one of your two Queens? For a Queen, you know, is as much a <u>sine qua non</u> as you are and you might find yourself stuck.

I put the notes on a separate sheet.

By the way, I saw not your letter in the Times, but Rea's answer to it.[2] Matters cannot be left legally as they are: that is now pretty certain. I believe it will pass the wit of even our legislators to devise an act which will legalise one form of entertainment and leave another illegal. Won't you do better by going for a six day week with contracting-out absolutely barred?

Yours,
Harley Granville-Barker

---

1. In January, 1931, Hannen was appearing in *To See Ourselves,* by E. M. Delafield, which opened in December, 1930; it did not run through the summer.
2. Alec L. Rea (1878–1953) established and directed a repertory company at the Embassy Theatre, Swiss Cottage, from 1930 to 1932.

The notes which Barker sent with the preceding letter have been lost. Barker's premonition about the proposed 1931 production of His Majesty *proved correct, and in 1934 he and Hannen were still writing to each other about it.*

SEY/MS
To Hannen

18, Place des Etats-Unis,
[Paris] XVI[e]
May 10, 1934

My dear N. H.,

About His Majesty:[1] Cochran is off. The friendliest interview in which he said "I feel I shall lose money by it", to which I
replied "Then I don't want you to do it"; and—though he gave signs
of wanting to be coaxed—I would not re-open the subject. For,
though it would have saved us a lot of trouble, I am not altogether
sorry. C and I don't really belong in the same boat. He is out for
"sensation". If a play takes less than £2,000 in its first week and
unless every night club in London is talking about it, he calls that
failure. I sized up my old audience again at Sadler's Wells[2]—not too
many of them, but what did R[illegible] expect? He could have had
double the number at an ordinary theatre, I suspect. However (to
finish with the Voysey), although the thing was a fag and the result
far from perfect, I don't regret doing it. For it has shown me (a) that
my dramatist's-producer's hand has not quite lost its cunning (I
thought it might have) and (b) that there are still people—the
younger generation also—who will sit stolidly through good, solid
drama and go away refreshed and not depressed at the end. They ask
for stimulation, not sensation. Their numbers? I can't tell; but there
should be more for a new play than an old. They are the 5/-, 2/6, 7/6
public.[3] And I always remember, by the way, Harwood telling me
that he could have run The Madras House another hundred nights if
he could have doubled his cheaper seats.[4]

So again I saw Ronald Adam[5] and told him to go ahead
with you if he still wanted to and could. He seems really keen. I
suppose—though he didn't say so—he has still to search for finance.
He'd need much guidance over casting; but there I should trust to
you. I impressed on him—and I impress on you—that as soon as you
return to town you must get together and arrive in a week or two at a
definite Yes or No. The aim and the need (if the play is to have a
chance) is a company with no wrong casting and no really weak
spots. The public must say: "This is real acting." No get-who-you-
can-at-the-last-minute will do.

As to the Queen: if you have thought of nobody other than
Miss Wynyard,[6] I should see what is possible there. She has weight
and authority and brains (and if she were interested might, I suppose,
bring in some extra finance if that were needed). She has not got the

softness of Miss Phyllis N. T.[7] But I fear that she might—especially now—be too much of a stage Queen; and Miss W. is a real human being. I was considerably impressed by her in the Brontë play too.[8] Use your discretion. But my feeling is that she has importance and that this will outweigh defects.

For all the other parts there are alternatives—if you start choosing in time.

Well, go ahead: and I will do what I can to help and make it worth your while.

I imagine—if I may say so to you—that it is about time you did another "full-length" part. Reputation is made by such and it has to be renewed from time to time. The Phoenix—I beg its pardon for confusing it with the Fortune—would be quite a good theatre.

Well, my blessing on you. But get down to tin-tacks as soon as you are back in London, or you'll find yourself drifting off to Elstree or Hollywood or a season in Buenos Ayres [*sic*]. And when the next chance comes, we mayn't be here, one or other of us.

H. G-B.

---

1. The underlining is Barker's. It is unusual. Normally he puts titles in quotation marks. The change may be due to the increase in his scholarly publishing in the 1930s and a consequent modifying of his manuscript practices to fit academic publishing conventions, to which—formerly—he was not accustomed.
2. At the request of Harcourt Williams, Barker had returned to London from Paris to direct a revival of *The Voysey Inheritance,* for which production he again revised the text of the play.
3. Five shillings (£0.25) was at this time about the equivalent of a dollar.
4. H. M. Harwood (1874–1959) was the author of a long list of trivial comedies, now entirely forgotten (even the titles are embarrassing now: *How To Be Healthy though Married, So Far and No Father,* etc.). He was quite a distinguished theater manager, however; he was the lessee of the Ambassador's Theatre for many years. In 1920 he presented there the first production of Lennox Robinson's *The White-Headed Boy* and, in the following year, Barker's version of Sacha Guitry's *Deburau.* In 1925, at the same theater, he presented a revival of Barker's *The Madras House* with Barker himself directing, in which Nicholas Hannen played the part of Philip Madras (the central character of the play) and Claude Rains played Eustace Perrin State.
5. Ronald Adam (1896–   ), actor-manager, lessee of Embassy Theatre, Swiss Cottage (London), from 1932 to 1939.
6. Diana Wynyard (1906–1964).
7. Phyllis Neilson-Terry (1892–   ), daughter of Julia Neilson and Fred Terry.
8. *Wild Decembers,* by Clemence Dane, a play about the Brontë family, in which Diana Wynyard played Charlotte Brontë.

The proposed production of His Majesty *did not materialize, and the next time Barker writes to Hannen it is about a suggested production of* Waste.

SEY/MS
To Hannen

Grand Hotel de l'Europe,
Salzburg
Aug. 13, 1936

My dear N. H.,

Thank you, and again, for seeing MacOwan[1] and for giving
him and sending him and sending me all that very sound advice. You
would not believe how pathetically helpless I feel in such matters
now. You did not acknowledge my letter (a vile habit, 'tis) and I
thought for some days you were ignoring me, and I pay you out by
this long delay in acknowledging yours. But lo, you <u>did</u> what I asked;
and there you have the better of me—for in these days what can <u>I</u> do
for you?

Silence has fallen on MacOwan—which means, I think, that
he cannot manage a Trebell.[2] I <u>dare</u> not let him do the play without
some assurance of something more than competence here. And we
could only find three names to bank upon: Richardson, whom Mac-
Owan swears is good; Massey, whom I would have risked on the
strength of a meeting with him years ago and the sight of his "mug"
(which it is) at the unveiling of the Vimy memorial; and your Donat—
not available immediately, and I gather one of these people who thinks
he can sell <u>half</u> his soul (to the cinema). Is it possible that—fine talk
apart—he'd <u>want</u> to do <u>Waste</u> and face the grind of it?

I suppose that no other available likely man has come into
your mind since. But if one has, send me a wire when this reaches
you (not one of those "Oh-I-really-<u>must</u>-write" letters) and telephone
to MacOwan. The situation might <u>yet</u> be saved.

I was not altogether sorry that some engagement has guard-
ed me from the temptation of asking <u>you</u> to play it and you from the
temptation to do so. Much as I should want you in <u>any</u> play of mine and
would like to be having another "go" at you, Trebell, in his bitterness
and hardness, spiritual egoism and blindness of heart, you would have
to put on like a wig—indeed, you would have to put on a black wig, even
as I did (but it was a good one) in which to play it.[3] You'd understand it
all, of course, and <u>know</u> what to do; but temperamentally it would be so
against the grain with you that you'd never be able to relax for a second
from <u>doing</u> into being—and I shouldn't credit that suicide.[4] Or <u>have</u> you
that <u>much</u> hardened up in these years? No; it's not possible. And you
shall not have to reproach me, if ever we work together again—or I
you—with a "creditable effort". Either we'll make them say, "This is
<u>acting</u>", or we'll leave it alone.

But I continue to regret <u>His Majesty</u>. And if, by the way, you are comfortably "in" with Alderson Horn,[5] and still want to do it, you might broach that subject. I did, to MacOwan as an alternative to the impossible-to-cast <u>Waste</u>, when it appeared that it was— God bless his innocence—a play by me that he wanted to open with, rather than <u>Waste</u> itself. I have recently had a letter from Armstrong at Liverpool[6] asking (for the third time) to do it there to celebrate their 25th year. I've no right to refuse them in a way. But I put to him for the third time the practical difficulty: <u>can</u> he provide a King and a Queen? He says he has a good company. But do <u>you</u> suppose for a moment that he can? And even if you (and some <u>Queen</u>) were available, <u>could</u> he make it worth your while to go and rehearse for 3 weeks and <u>play</u> a fortnight? The thing doesn't seem practical. But then—why write plays? So, as you have noticed, I don't any more.

My best regards to you both,

Yours,

H. G-B.

This address till Aug. 19: a 2½-day post. By the way, you said that Miss (?) Noble could play Amy O'Connell by speaking my lines. Your wits are failing, you are aesthetically debauched and demoralised. I tested the two scenes by reading them through to Mac.O. They are technically just about as difficult as they can be.

---

1. Michael MacOwan (1906–   ) started his career as an actor, but quite early moved to directing. Anmer Hall, who had taken over the newly converted Westminster theater in 1931, appointed MacOwan as the resident director there in 1936. In making his plans for his first season at the Westminster, MacOwan had indicated to Barker that he would be interested in including *Waste*.
2. Henry Trebell, the leading character in *Waste*.
3. In a private performance at the Imperial Theatre on November 24, 1907, presented by the Stage Society.
4. In spite of this judgment Barker eventually accepted Hannen as Trebell and directed the production himself.
5. This was Anmer Hall's real name: Anmer Hall was a stage name.
6. William Armstrong (1882–1952), director of Liverpool Playhouse.

SEY/MS
To Hannen

8, St. Jakob Strasse,
Basel,
Switzerland.
(address till further notice; until mid-October at least, I think)
Aug. 29, 1936

My dear N. H.,

Admirable, the immediate acknowledgment; and it found

me here on Saturday, when I arrived. We have a house here for a month or so. A very pleasant city, Basel; do you know it?

Continued thanks to you. Mac.O. finds none of the three Trebells that I felt I could safely agree to—Richardson, Donat (on your recommendation), what's-his-name (brother of the Canadian Commissioner; name gone; I'm growing old)[1]—immediately available; so Waste is off, or postponed until they are or we can think of other men. Mac.O optimistically declares he knows several; but he rightly won't risk (I warned him not to) my turning them down after rehearsals have started, since I don't know them; and he doesn't present your recommendation with them either.

Armstrong is presumably meditating upon a possible K and Q for His Majesty, I having told him he can—in principle—do the thing if—if—he can find me these.

I gather that Mac.O would not be unwilling to substitute H. M. for Waste if he could get you and had a Queen. And he might be wise to. For, with such simplifying and shortening as I can manage (I have managed a lot in Waste), it might be the better card. But I must, in either case, have a cast.

If nothing more happens I shall try to come to London in Oct.–Nov. and do, after several years, a little theatre-going and see if I can't spy out some likely material.

But meanwhile I suggest that you keep in touch with me and, in particular, let me know the likely or certain fate of this new play you are engaged for.[2] If that should leave you available we might fix up H. M. somehow.

I send you this photograph of Reinhardt's setting for Faust, permanently build into cliff; study in middle, prison unusable, church one side, Gretchen's house the old, real garden (which seemed curiously unnatural): the whole affair interesting but wrong (would have been worse had Faust been a great play), because no focus is possible and your attention is strained or distracted—strained by the effort to concentrate on the immediate action, distracted by the here-and-there-ishness of it all.

Greetings to you both,

Yours,
H. G-B.

---

1. He is referring to Raymond Massey.
2. The play was *Follow Your Saint,* by Lesley Storm. It opened at the Queen's Theatre on September 24, 1936, and closed on October 3.

SEY/MS
To Hannen

Delfter-Hof,
St. Jakobstrasse 8,
Basel,
Switzerland.
Sept. 17, 1936

My dear N. H.,

If you have a moment to spare—but I imagine you for some reason out of London and in the throes of rehearsals—will you once more be kind and note your opinion against the enclosed names. Can any of them safely <u>carry</u> Trebell in <u>Waste</u>?

MacOwan thinks, I gather, that Donat, Massey, Richardson may all three fail him; and he wants alternatives that I will accept. These are his suggestions. Dare I risk any of them? That is the question. I <u>won't</u> risk the play crumbling to bits and Trebell has to carry it on his own shoulders. On the other hand the play more or less <u>must</u> be done. They have gone and (without asking me!) announced it. I can't get to London till October; and then it doesn't follow that I can see any of these fellows act; also it may be too late. I shall then be, once more, most grateful for your counsel. (The rest of the play <u>can</u> be cast: that seems certain.)

Let me know how your new play goes—<u>when</u> it goes.

As ever,
H. G-B.

With the above letter Barker enclosed the following page of notes. The heading was handwritten; the names of the actors were typewritten in capital letters; the parenthetical comments after each name were handwritten. Space had been left under each name for Hannen's comments.

<u>TREBELL</u>: 4 solid acts to carry on his shoulders. And we must be glad to see him when he comes on in the 4th!!

JAMES DALE (I thought him good 20 years ago. Has he really come to anything?)
HENRY OSCAR (don't know him)
MALCOLM KEEN (Have found him goodish. But has he weight and grip enough?)
FRANK VOSPER (? too hollow?)
DONALD WOLFIT (Don't know him. But mayn't this be his legitimate "chance"?)

GEORGE HAYES (Is he enough of a "leading man"?)
FRED O'DONOVAN (successful barrister <u>and</u> Cabinet Minister??)

SEY/MS
To Hannen

> Delfter-Hof,
> St. Jakobstrasse 8,
> Basel,
> Switzerland.
> Oct. 5, 1936

My dear N. H.,

Very pleasant to hear your voice on the telephone telling me that you are free—for some job, I hope, in which I may be concerned—though I'm sorry your latest labours have been wasted.

However, as Trebell is a devil of a temptation (I know how much I get out of you in whatever you do) I wrestled with it when MacOwan came over. I am wrestling with it as I write; and if, after carefully—but <u>carefully</u>—looking at the thing again you say you <u>can</u> do it, I shall have yet another wrestle. But <u>face</u> what is against the grain in it. Trebell has no <u>sunshine</u> in him. That is his tragedy; that is why he kills himself. Can you come on the stage and <u>not</u> impart an extra cheerfulness to the proceedings? I doubt it. But you tell me what you think.

As for the King, though: that, as you know, is built for you and I have never seen anyone else in it. There is, too, more of a success in the play (I must shorten and simplify it a bit) if we get it decently done. But what really sets me writing to you by return is so that I may say that it really vexes me to oppose a curt No to your Athene as the Queen.[1] And please tell her so from me, adding that I have not bated one jot of my admiration for her work. But as you to Trebell, so she to the Queen, with the difficulty added that she would be playing against you and could not play <u>against</u> you. You would both of you speed the thing along with a competence which would leave everyone wondering how you'd ever managed to get into exile.[2] No, the stupid, dull-witted woman who really feels and suffers and the man who lives a happy intellectual life of his own: if you don't get that contrast it is useless performing the play.

See Horne and MacOwan. And don't lose touch.

H.G-B.

---

1. Athene Seyler (1889–   ), Hannen's wife, was one of the most skillful and most

intelligent players of comedy in the London theater; she wrote, with Stephen Haggard, *The Craft of Comedy* (London, 1943).

2. The situation in *His Majesty:* King Henry XIII of Carpathia has been compelled to abdicate and he and Queen Rosamund are, when the play opens, living in exile in Switzerland.

A few days later, probably on October 11, 1936, Barker sent the following notes, without any covering or accompanying letter, to Hannen.

NOTES ON THE CASTING OF WASTE

Horsham:	Harcourt Williams will do because he will understand the man. But he is light weight, and rather too woolly. Horsham is not. He has been and will be Prime Minister, and beneath his easy surface there is iron. He wants playing both easily and broadly, very firmly too. If there were a better man for the part H. W. would be better as Wedgecroft.
Cantilupe:	I have small trust in what you tell me of Alan Napier; 6ft. 4 ins. and gentle; so do not settle him, please, without further argument. Cantilupe is not gentle at all. He has polished manners; that is quite another thing. He is a fanatic—he finds a like spirit in O'Connell—a personality, an ascetic, a "character", a man quite unlike the other men around him. He is thrown into sharp contrast in Act II with the worldly little Mrs. O'Connell: why the devil you don't try Thesiger I cannot imagine. But if there is really anything against this consult me before any other steps are taken. You cannot have a commonplace man for this part.
Farrant:	—is, on the other hand, as commonplace as you like (but not a nice old pantaloon as dear Bromley Davenport is). He is thrown into sharp contrast with O'Connell. He is bluff, good-natured, not a fool, but slow in the up-take. Lloyd is the right type; but (sh!) has not quite the breeding for it. Eric Stanley is about the ideal. Scott Gatty could do it. His keynote is his genial "Come let's be friends and make the best of things" attitude.
Blackborough:	—has far more bite to him. "Bluff good-nature" is the mask he wears, but he is hard and pretty malevolent underneath. A gentleman—from

Leeds! Jeayes has the right weight and appearance for him. But he'll be too soft and too slow in the up-take. Blackborough is neither. He and Horsham—and only they—see at once the <u>realities</u> of the Trebell position in Act III. A man with a sharper nose and a more incisive style would be better.

Wedegcroft:	A "Horatio"—with brains. Not too young. A harmonious voice. A good but not overdone "bedside manner".
O'Connell:	Fisher White (the original) was very good in his way, though a trifle dull. But here, again, is a "character". He must not be an ordinary man (with the ghost of a golf-stick under his arm). He is the Dillon, W. B. Yeats, type of Irishman; the "dark" sort that runs rebellions and pulls them off, too. <u>Cold passion</u> is his keynote. If you get a man who cannot impress these Cabinet Ministers—and the audience—as <u>dangerous</u>, I warn you that you will wreck the third act. He is its centre of gravity. Be very careful, and consult me before making any sort of decision.
Walter Kent:	Any well-behaved young man will do—until you come to the end of the play. He must be able to bring that off—to come on <u>crying</u>, with no shame about it.
Lady Julia:	The most distinguished woman of between 35–50 whom you can get. <u>Real</u> old-fashioned Victorian, Lady de Grey, distinction. Gracious. Perfect speech; she may be a trifle hard: but in the last act she exhibits what she really believes are feelings—and they are, of their kind.
Lady Mortimer:	The most charming and distinguished old lady that you can find. Should speak beautifully. Gentler than Lady Julia.
Frances Trebell:	Miss Scaife is quite right and should be good.
Lucy Davenport:	Honest-eyed. Competent. Fresh. Clean-minded. Wholesome.
Amy O'Connell:	The contrast to Lucy (which is the reason for Lucy being brought into Act II). <u>Now be careful</u>; for if you go wrong you can completely wreck Act II and go far towards wrecking the whole play. She is the <u>femme amoureuse</u>; but she is not

common nor vulgar, (no polite cockney accents, please), not the peroxide blonde. She is pretty and witty besides; very amusing company, or she would not find herself in that society. She dresses very well, and has enough money to entertain in a "chic" way. Lady Julia thinks her "cheap" but that is the worst that can be said of her. What she tells Trebell about herself in Act II is probably quite true. Frances (I think) says that there is "Something of the waif about her". That should help you a little. But what is vitally important to the play—I repeat: you may wreck it if this goes wrong—is the balance of sympathy in her case. We must feel that beside Trebell's future career and the Disestablishment Bill and a fresh start for the Church of England she is a worthless little thing; but we must also feel enough pity for her fate to understand why Trebell—just because he <u>cannot</u> feel it, did not love her and yet begot a child on her, and has seen both die and still can feel no remorse—shoots himself.

So be careful; and in consulting me tell me just the qualities your candidates have and have not.

Rehearsals for Waste *began in November, 1936, with Michael MacOwan directing. He took charge of the early rehearsals, the arrangement being that Barker would come in for the final four weeks, which he did. The following two brief notes were written after the play had opened.*

SEY/MS
To Hannen

Ritz Hotel,
London, W.1.
Dec. 1 [1936]

My dear Beau,[1]

I owe you much, and shall owe you more.

Feel your audience. Keep them with you and carry them forward as swiftly—not hurriedly—as you feel they can understandingly go.

Dare to be a devil.

Never be merely "sad".

And heaven prosper you.

With my affection—which Trebell would not have owned that he valued: but you may, when you're out of his skin.

H. G-B.

---

1. Hannen's long-standing nickname: his wife still refers to him as "Beau."

The following, returning to Barker's custom of thirty years earlier, was written on the backs of three picture postcards and was mailed to Hannen from Paris on December 23, 1936. On this occasion, however, the cards were not mailed separately but were put together into one envelope.

SEY/MS
To Hannen

[Paris]
Dec. 23

(1)

You don't deserve a Xmas card, so you don't: when a man can write to me and say—after, what, 20 performances?—"When Trebell was making love to Amy . . . he . . . swayed on his feet . . . it made me wonder if he . . . was quite sober . . . " Curse you: may you have a miserable Xmas and a blighted

(2)

New Year. Do you expect me to be sitting in front night after night to throw boulders at you? Hopher Wheeler says you are first-rate and have now got the whole thing right. I don't believe him.

But another thing is clear. Repertory and a National Theatre is the only salvation of

(3)

my sort of drama.

I'd have sent you a copy of my Hamlet if I could think you'd read it. But you're like Edward VII—in this only—"Men are your books": for which I don't blame you.

Well, you may have as good a Xmas as you deserve.

H. G-B.

Sir John Martin-Harvey (1863–1944)

An actor of the "old school," an archetypal example of the "actor-manager," Martin-Harvey followed in the footsteps of Henry Irving and was regarded by some—perhaps even by himself—as Irving's appointed artistic heir and natural successor. His work in the theater was, therefore, never very close to Barker's. He was ineradicably associated, in the mind of the popular playgoing public, with the character of Sidney Carton in The Only Way, *a stage adaptation of Dickens'* A Tale of Two Cities; *he played the part for the first time in 1899, when he was thirty-six, and for the last time, at the age of seventy-five, in May, 1939—and countless times in between. Another of his spectacular successes was the title role of Reinhardt's* Oedipus *in 1912, which he revived in 1936. But the staple of his theatrical fare, apart from Shakespeare, was popular melodrama: his big moneymakers (especially on tour) were* The Breed of the Treshams, A Cigarette-Maker's Romance, The Corsican Brothers, *and* The Only Way. *He was knighted in 1921.*

BTM/TS
To Martin-Harvey

Kingsway Theatre,
Great Queen Street,
[London] W.C
Oct. 21st., 1913

My dear Martin Harvey,
I count myself very unlucky that I turn a deaf ear to that persuasive Chairman's letter and more so to the friendly card. But long ago I swore a dreadful oath that while, stamp and rage as one would, one could not get actors and actresses to agitate for the organisation of their work so that destitution would be lessened (as lessened it could be, we all know, if only that were done) I would have no truck with our charitable institutions. I am seriously tempted year by year to salve my conscience on the matter with five pounds or so but I still make a stand and care at this moment to bother you with the explanation. I do so seriously feel that if all the well-meaning people who support the funds could be told: "Help us to organise our work so that we may do it as decent citizens and not as casual labourers, give us non-speculative theatres however you run them—municipally, nationally, or with the aid of disinterested shareholders—and we will reduce our need for charitable help by sixty or seventy per cent." I commend this thought to you among other better ones while you sit in this honourable chair.[1]

Yours very sincerely,
H. Granville Barker

---

1. Martin-Harvey was at that time chairman of an organization called the Actors' Benevolent Fund.

BTM/MS
To Martin-Harvey

Villa Borghèse,
La Bourboule.
12.9.28

My dear Martin Harvey,

Pleasant to hear from you—and queerly à propos, for Nigel Playfair is going to do one of those Spanish translations you speak so kindly of—"A Hundred Years Old"[1]—and he suggested we might try and induce you to play as a tour de force Il Centenario himself. I jumped at the suggestion. But he has to do it this autumn and—bar happy accidents—I suppose you can't look less than a year ahead.

I'll ask my wife if she can think of another of the Quinteros that you might like. She is the Spanish scholar and true translator, not I.

As to other plays: one comes to mind—Le Pauvre sans l'Escalier, by Henri Ghéon, a thing of great beauty, rather like a mediaeval Mystery play and, as he is a devout Catholic, a genuine thing. No great popularity in it, perhaps, but if you could get it put into an English that matched the French—by Walter de la Mare, say—it might give you what you wanted. Ghéon's address in Paris is rue du Vieux Colombier, but I'm not positive of the number: c/o the Societé des Auteurs Dramatiques, 12 rue Henner, would probably find him.

Very kind regards,

Yours,
Harley Granville-Barker

Barry Jackson did Ghéon's "Life of St. Bernard", I think.

---

1. A play by Serafin and Joaquin Alvarez Quintero, translated into English by Helen and Harley Granville-Barker (London, 1927).

BTM/TS
To Martin-Harvey

Netherton Hall,
Colyton,
Devon.
23rd April, 1929.

My dear Martin Harvey,

Thank you for being so forgiving about "A Hundred Years Old". I wish I could do the German thing for you; but I must not try.

I am hung up with work. Shakespeare will weigh on me like a mountain for the next three or four months. Also I think that the Schnitzler affair was—in a literary sense—rather an immoral proceeding. Not ten words of German do I know![1]

Very sincerely yours,
Harley Granville-Barker

---

1. He is referring to his version, in English, of Schnitzler's *Anatol* (London, 1911). C. E. Wheeler helped him with the translation.

BTM/MS
To Martin-Harvey

Hotel Beau Site,
4, Rue de Presbourg,
Paris.
12.11.31

My dear Martin Harvey,

Why, yes, of course you can, and with pleasure.

Terms: will "most favoured nation" suit you? I don't know what these are, but I'll tell my secretary at Netherton to look out the last occasion when a single one was professionally done.[1] But if they don't suit—complain!

I can't remember the title of the thing. I fancy it's "A Christmas Present".[2]

Kind regards,

Yours,
Harley Granville-Barker

You saw the news of Schnitzler's death. He had been "breaking" rather badly towards the end. We never met.

---

1. That is, a single one of the short one-act plays which together make up Schnitzler's *Anatol*. The complete sequence consisted of seven short plays, or scenes. Martin-Harvey had asked Barker for permission to produce one of them.
2. This is the second of the seven sketches, in fact.

William Poel (1852–1934)

Poel was the founder of the Elizabethan Stage Society and the man who revolutionized the production of Shakespeare and the other Elizabethans. Barker owed him much, and it was a debt that the latter freely acknowledged and never forgot. Their work was complementary, and their paths frequently crossed, as several letters in this present col-lection show. The following letter was written after Barker played Richard II and Edward II under Poel's direction (1899 and 1903) and before Poel played Keegan, in John Bull's Other Island, *under Barker's direction (1906).*

TEX/MS
To Poel

High Cross,
Claybrook,
Nr. Rugby.
Monday [January, 1905]

Dear Mr. Poel,

I have not had time before to write and thank you for your kind and suggestive criticism upon Prunella. I would say helpful but alas the play is dead and buried for the moment. I am sending your letter to Housman. I'd like to answer all its points in detail—for as you say expert criticism which is not hopelessly sophisticated is the most useful thing—and the rarest.

I do agree with you that the whole question of a musical accompaniment to the voice wants more serious consideration. We failed occasionally because the orchestration was a little hard to speak through, occasionally because the music itself was doing too much what only the voice ought to do, being definitely tuneful and occa-sionally because we were paying too much attention to the music. But I do believe there is a possibility in a musical background to a voice speaking pronounced metre. I'd like to try it again.

My white face! Yes—I tried it less and more but in getting expression you somehow lost the definite Pierrot quality which was half the character. I feel that someone with cleverer gesture than I could have made you forget the expressionless white face. I was gradually I believe getting into the trick of it.

Won't you have a go at some Peele and Greene soon? By the way, Bernard Shaw is always suggesting Friar Bacon for you.

Suppose they wouldn't allow David and Bethsabe?

Very sincerely yours,
H. Granville Barker

TEX/MS
To J. L. Garvin[1] from Barker

> I1 Castello,
> Portofino-mare,
> Liguria,
> Italy.
> 9.3.23

My dear Garvin,

You are being asked to sign a petition for a civil list pension for Mr. William Poel, founder of the Elizabethan Stage Society.

Much of his work you'll know. I have known most of it and I have never known work done more devotedly, with less self-seeking. And I do think, moreover, that much that is good today in the theatre we owe to him, to the energy and money of his own which he spent recklessly but—for us—profitably.

I hope you'll feel able to sign.

> With kind regards,
> Very sincerely yours,
> Harley Granville-Barker

---

1. James Louis Garvin (1868–1947), journalist, first with papers in northeast England, then with the *Daily Telegraph* in London. He became editor of the *Observer* in 1908 and retained that position for thirty-four years, raising the paper from a near-moribund state to one of the most important newspapers in London.

BERG/MS
To Sir Edward Marsh[1] from Barker

> Hotel de Crillon,
> Place de la Concorde,
> Paris.
> 6.11.29

My dear Eddie,

There is a "please give William Poel an honour" letter going around and it'll come to me for signature in a minute or two and I hope it'll be something I can sign (I rather detest the honour business) for I'd do more than that for Poel.

Look here though, talking of signatures: do you think Winston C. could be got to send a p.c. in response to the same letter you received approving of the National Theatre? I feared that as a past and future C. of E.[2] he'd be shy. But the approval is carefully designed not to commit to the spending of public money. I hardly know him well enough to write to him myself and it is useless sending the formal letter only. I

made a note that you were to be consulted. It really looks now as if
something might be done if the opinion that counts could be mobilised.
And all sorts of unexpected people have approved—Lord Allenby and a
bishop or two and Reginald McKenna!! So put your oar in and row a
stroke or two if you feel well-disposed.

I was kind and good and did <u>not</u> put your name forward for
a paper on the 1880s, which de la Mare is editing.[3] But you shan't
escape the 1890s if I can help it. I will deliver you bound and shriek-
ing—probably to John Drinkwater!

As ever yours,

H.G-B.

---

1. Sir Edward Howard Marsh (1872–1953), a civil servant, scholar, and patron of the
   arts, was, among other things, private secretary to Winston Churchill from 1906 to
   1929.
2. Chancellor of the Exchequer.
3. For the Royal Society of Literature, of which Barker was president that year.

Max Reinhardt (1873–1943)

*An almost exact contemporary of Barker, Reinhardt, the Austrian ac-
tor and director, was—like Barker—one of the moving spirits in European theater in the first twenty years of this century. His style and his
contribution to theater were utterly different from Barker's, but they
had a mutual respect for each other. They met only once or twice.*

BTM/handwritten by a secretary but signed by Barker
To Reinhardt

Kingsway Theatre,
Great Queen Street,
[London] W.C.
Sept. 3, 1913

My dear Reinhardt,

This is to introduce my friend William Poel, though the introduction is probably needless, for I expect you know he is one of
our English Theatre revolutionaries. He founded years ago the Elizabethan Stage Society, and has taught us all (by his great devotion)
more about the staging of Shakespeare and the spirit of playing in it,
I think, than anyone else in Europe.

He goes to Berlin to see all there is to see, and I feel sure
both for his own sake and mine that you will welcome him.

Yours very sincerely,
H. Granville Barker

Elizabeth Robins (1865–1952)

This American actress spent most of her life in England; she was one of the two English-speaking actresses most closely associated with the intro- duction of Ibsen's plays to England (the other being Janet Achurch). Miss Robins was the first actress to play Hedda Gabler in English and the first Rebecca in Rosmersholm, *Hilda in* The Master Builder, *and Agnes in* Brand. *She retired from the stage at a comparatively early age and de- voted her time to literature, publishing several novels and a book of memoirs called* Both Sides of the Curtain *(London, 1940).*

TEX/TS
To Elizabeth Robins

> The William Archer Trust,
> (Drama League Library)
> 8, Adelphi Terrace,
> London, W.C. 2
> 7 July, 1925

Dear Miss Robins,

You may know that William Archer's executors have, under the terms of his will, given his theatrical library to the British Drama League to form part of that now established at 8, Adelphi Terrace. But it is to be handed over to the library of a National Theatre if and when this should be established; and we are the trustees for it.

We want to add to the collection of books a bronze bust; a small tribute to him and to the work he did for the theatre, to stand in the present reference library, where students of the drama will be at work and may be using his books.

Then also, if and when a National Theatre is established, it will not be without a memorial to the man who worked so well to give it being.

But a bust must be made while the records which can help the sculptor are available. Mr. Derwent Wood, R.A. has agreed to do the work and the total cost will be two hundred guineas. Of this one hundred have been provided; and we are sending this letter pri- vately to a dozen of his friends and fellow workers in the belief that they may like to contribute the remainder.

> Faithfully yours,
> Howard de Walden
> Laurence Binyon
> Harley Granville-Barker

Cheques should be made payable to Lord Howard de Walden and sent to this address.

TEX/MS
To Elizabeth Robins

Netherton Hall,
Colyton,
Devon.
20.7.25

My dear Miss Robins,

<u>Of course</u> if Lady Bell[1] will subscribe we'll all be most
happy to have her in the little group. Her name should have been in
the list from the beginning. But this was drawn up in talk with
Charles Archer and he wanted it kept as small as possible.
Hence . . . But I hope she will forgive us. I saw Charles Archer
yesterday and he said, with me, "Of course, etc."

My wife and I also saw last week the clay of the bust. I
hope you'll think it good. Considering that Derwent Wood has had
nothing but photographs to go upon it seems to me a remarkable
likeness and at any rate it gives a distinguished and forceful man.

He is a terrible loss.

We send you our kind regards.

Very sincerely yours,
Harley Granville-Barker

---

1. Lady Florence Bell, wife of Sir Hugh Bell: she was a minor playwright.

TEX/MS
To Elizabeth Robins

Netherton Hall,
Colyton,
Devon.
26.7.25

My dear Miss Robins,

Many thanks for the cheques. I will see them safely
through. And I do hope that you and Lady Bell will see and like the
bust in the D. L. room in the autumn.

Yes, this "crisis" is a bad business.[1] To me though the worst
thing about it is the best. We have at last got down to a position where
stone throwing—in deed or word—is no remedy. And there does seem to
be for the moment a sense of <u>that</u>. But will that moment last?

Kind regards from us both.

Very sincerely yours,
Harley Granville-Barker

1. The reference is to the deadlocked dispute between the coal miners and the mine owners, which was to lead to a lengthy strike by the miners and thence to the General Strike of 1926. Elizabeth Robins was always interested in social movements and in the big political questions of the day. She had, for instance, herself written, in 1907, a play called *Votes for Women!* which Barker directed at the Court Theatre as part of his repertory season there.

Kate Rorke (1866–1945)

Descended from an old theatrical family, Kate Rorke began her own acting career at the age of twelve, her sister Mary being already a professional performer. In 1895 Shaw wrote of her: "All I can remember of the last performance I witnessed of A Midsummer Night's Dream *is that Miss Kate Rorke got on the stage somehow and began to make some music with Helena's lines, with the result that Shakespear, who had up to that moment lain without sense or motion, immediately began to stir uneasily and shew signs of quickening, which lasted until the others took up the word and struck him dead." Early in 1904 Barker was corresponding with Kate Rorke about a production of* Candida, *which was to be presented at the Court Theatre for—in the first instance—six matinees. He wanted her to play the title role, which she eventually agreed to do. This production was one of the chief forces that helped to establish the whole idea of the Court Theatre repertory, and when Barker began the regular series of plays there he included the production of* Candida *in it, presenting it thirty-one times in November–December, 1904, and May–June, 1905. Kate Rorke played Candida in all of these preformances.*

BTM/MS
To Kate Rorke

Vann Cottage,
Fernhurst,
Surrey.
Thursday [Feb./March, 1904]

Dear Miss Rorke,

Many thanks. I would like to come and I ought to come but I fear I can't get away. Never ask you to act for us?—We will!

Yours,
H. G. Barker

Very kind regards.

BTM/MS
To Kate Rorke

8, York Buildings,
Adelphi,
[London.]
March 18 [1904]

Dear Miss Rorke,
Since I wrote to you more things have happened about Candida. I had to put my finances before Mr. Shaw and he strenuously objected to any of the actors having what he called "a speculative interest" in the play and the matinées—though of course he says and wishes you to feel that if all goes well you establish a moral claim to the part. So I had to try for a little more money and I have found it. Now will

The first page of the letter ends at this point and subsequent pages are missing.

BTM/MS
To Kate Rorke

Royal Court Theatre,
Sloane Square,
[London] S. W.
March 23 [1904]

Dear Miss Rorke,
Yes, let us have a talk tomorrow. I fear I can't get out to Hampstead. Will you be in town? I shall be here from 11 to 2.30 rehearsing;[1] after that fairly free. At the worst we can talk through the telephone.
As to money matters: I fear £25 is about my limit. Can you and will you manage it for that?
As G. B. S. would say "Blow the dresses". I know that's a manlike thing to say! When does Terry produce[2] and what about rehearsals? That we must talk of tomorrow.

Very sincerely yours,
H. Granville Barker

---

1. He was directing *Two Gentlemen of Verona* and playing the part of Speed in it. It was part of the bargain that, in return for directing the Shakespeare play, he be allowed to present the six matinees of *Candida*.
2. This is Edward Terry (1844–1912), proprietor and manager of Terry's Theatre in the Strand and no relation to the famous theatrical family. The play at his theater in April, 1904, in which Kate Rorke was appearing, was *The House of Burnside*, by Louis N. Parker. Miss Rorke played the part of Marion Burnside.

Courtenay Thorpe

*Thorpe was an established London actor with a long record of success-
ful performances. When Janet Achurch revived* A Doll's House *in
1897 (she first played it in 1889), Courtenay Thorpe was her Torvald.
Later the same year he played Gregers Werle in* The Wild Duck *to the
Hjalmar of Laurence Irving. Archer wrote of "the remarkable intelligence and originality of Mr. Courtenay Thorpe." He was praised by
both Archer and Shaw for his Ghost in* Hamlet, *Shaw remarking,
"And yet, until Mr. Courtenay Thorpe divined it the other day, nobody seems to have had a glimpse of the reason why Shakespear
would not trust anyone else with it, and played it himself." Thorpe
also attracted very favorable attention in America for his Oswald in*
Ghosts, *and he played Allmers to Mrs. Patrick Campbell's Rita in a
rather poor revival, in 1896, of* Little Eyolf.

BTM/MS
To Thorpe

Adelphi
[London]
July 2 1903

My dear Thorpe,

I must just write you a line to thank you for your note and
the kind things you say about Eugene.[1] Other people have congratulated—but you're different, for you have been <u>through</u> the part and
you know.[2]

I didn't do all I wanted to with him—one never does—but
I'm glad you thought well of what I did do.

Kind regards.

Yours,
H. Granville Barker

---

1. Eugene Marchbanks, in *Candida.* Barker is writing the day after playing the part for
   the first time, in the Stage Society production directed by Janet Achurch at the
   Strand Theatre. This was the first London production of the play.
2. Thorpe played Marchbanks in 1897, when the play was produced for a single performance by Charles Charrington in Aberdeen: the Candida was Janet Achurch, Charrington's wife.

M*uch of the* most important of Granville Barker's corre-
spondence with other playwrights is omitted from this chapter because
it appears in three other places, one of them elsewhere in this volume,
two of them in other collections. I refer, of course, to the letters which
passed between Barker and Shaw and those between Barker and Barrie. The former are contained in part in Chapter III of this book and in
part in C. B. Purdom's *Shaw-Barker Letters.* The latter are quoted
fairly fully (though not in all cases reproduced verbatim) in the same
author's *Harley Granville Barker.* Since Purdom gives a fair impression
of the Barrie letters, it seems superfluous to reprint them here, and
Chapter III makes the Barker-Shaw correspondence as complete as
our information to date allows. The function of the present chapter is,
therefore, to sketch in a few details of Barker's relationships with some
of the other dramatists of the time with whom his work, in various
ways, brought him into contact. As in Chapter X, the letters are arranged alphabetically by correspondent.

Dion Clayton Calthrop (1879–1937)

*Playwright, author, and theatrical designer Dion Calthrop was a
nephew of Dion Boucicault and elder brother of Donald Calthrop, the
actor. He collaborated with Barker in the writing of* The Harlequinade, *a short play which was presented, along with the first production of Shaw's* Androcles and the Lion, *at the St. James' Theatre in
1913. (Donald Calthrop played the part of Harlequin in it.) Barker's
letter below refers to that production.*

John Galsworthy.

John Masefield.

TEX/TS
To Calthrop

Kingsway Theatre,
Great Queen Street,
[London] W.C.
July 14, 1913

My dear Calthrop,
    You are a two-tailed devil. You thought we did not know
you were in town to-day, but we did and have been searching everywhere for you. Half an hour's talk would have saved reams of letter
paper!
    Some details first. Do you think that the cut of the shoulder
is right for those eighteenth century clothes? It seems to me that it
will make them square instead of sloping. But you know I expect,
and I don't. I notice that you have had both the beau's coat and
waistcoat made as trick clothes, but surely he takes off the first lot on
the stage?
    What about the Clown's 15th century dress?
    Your scenery: do you know that all those nice details of
trees to the extreme left of the Styx cloth are lost. Also the same
thing of course applies to the other side. He is holding back that
cloth till the last moment in case you want to amend the design.
    The Italian scene. Trees are half done. They will look very
nice but enormously big. I am a little afraid that the people from the
gallery may not see at all what they are but perhaps it is all right.
    When are we going to have the Wilkinson room and the
cough drop cloth?
    I am seeing Stephenson towards the end of the week I
hope.

<u>Columbine</u>
    Fay Compton is coming tomorrow. I have not much hopes
of her, and really I am in some doubt about those two Alhambra
girls. My mind turns rather to Sheila Hayes. She will have to be
trained by a ballet mistress into the gestures, but on the whole you
have rather a fragile, dark and more or less spiritual looking little
thing, which I really do think is a necessity. She is distinctly pretty
and not altogether of the picture-postcard sort. She may be a fool,
but that we should not discover till we get to work on her. But I
think she is the best thing I have come across so far. What do you
say?
    Here is the proper announcement from The Times. If you
<u>will</u> read disreputable papers—
    But seriously I agree with you: it does not quite work, and I

am sorry. In this irreligious and egotistical world when you and I try either Catholicism or Socialism it always goes wrong. Yes, it is too portentous, but there are difficulties and we must set our wits to work. Stephenson can of course be set down for the music. You can be the writer, and on the programme you can design, but how am I to come in? I would not want to be in at all, except for two reasons. Certainly I cannot appear as writer. On the other hand I have contributed rather more than a producer does[1] and anyhow (this is where the difficulty comes in) we have acknowledged that among ourselves in terms of cash. These are the two reasons: America—I had thought, when we came to negotiate over that, that my name would make it easier to work, though since you startled the Western continent with Damnation Nan or whatever it is called, that is not so important; but the other point is. As manager of course I have to disclose to the people interested exactly what I take, and if I take a share of the royalties while my name only appears as a producer, as it does in Shaw's play, frankly it will look like blackmail, and that you see is a very serious matter. (Can't dictate more or this won't get the post.) It is why we must find some solution. You are good about these things. Don't think I am being captious either.

Yours,

H. G. B.

---

1. He means a director.

St. John Ervine (1883–1971)

This Anglo-Irish dramatist, critic, and novelist was for a time the manager of the Abbey Theatre in Dublin but spent most of his later life in England. His two best plays are probably John Ferguson *(1915) and* Jane Clegg *(1913), though his later comedies, such as* The First Mrs. Fraser *(1923) and* Anthony and Anna *(1926), were well liked in their time. He was the drama critic for the* Observer *from 1919 to 1923 and from 1925 to 1929. He and Barker became near neighbors and—at first—close friends in Devon, as the Barkers were living at Farway and Ervine at Seaton, just outside Sidmouth. They were also both on the Board of Governors of Colyton Grammar School, though not at the same time; Ervine, in fact, replaced Barker as the representative appointed by the County Education Committee when Barker resigned that position in January, 1932 (having held it since the opening of the new school in 1929). In* Bernard Shaw, His Life, Work and Friends *(London, 1956), St. John Ervine wrote: "Once, while staying with*

G. B. S. in Torquay, we took him to lunch with Miss Clemence Dane at Axminster. On the way, we passed the entrance to a road which led to Granville-Barker's superbly appointed house at Farway, a house that was more like a museum than a home, one, too, in which the chief piece was Granville-Barker." It is clear from the passage in the book of which this quotation is a part (pp. 342–45) that Ervine did not really understand either Barker or his work—and did not much care for him personally. But their everyday relations were, with minor exceptions, cordial enough, as these letters show. And it should be borne in mind that when this correspondence began, Barker's reputation in the theater as a leading director was still fresh and stood very high. Ervine would have genuinely valued the critical comments and commendation which Barker gave to the playscripts Ervine sent to him for evaluation.

TEX/MS
To Ervine

> Fortfield Hotel,
> Sidmouth,
> S. Devon.
> 25.9.20

My dear St John Ervine,

Why that is good news—it will be very jolly to meet you. We shall almost certainly be here. No—no more theatre management for me. And not <u>too</u> much criticism for you—though you are a blessing in <u>The Observer</u>—and I'm thankful you bang away at the old Repertory business.

It is the only recipe for long runs—a useful paradox to remember.

I think I saw in Berlin the 275th or 398th—or some such—performance of Shaw's "Doctor's Dilemma" at the Kammerspielhaus. No "long run" system would have done that—but the repertory had—in 3 or 4 years.

But we'll talk—of more interesting things than this!

> H. Granville Barker

TEX/MS
To Ervine

R.M.S. "Aquitania"[1]
26.11.20

My dear St. John Ervine,

What you think of me "in re" the Wonderful Visit[2] I refrain from imagining. But we were called off to America literally at an hour's notice by the sudden illness—and later death—of my wife's mother. I bundled the MS in with my other things but until now on the voyage home I have not had a free mind to read it. My conscience has been fairly clear though knowing that Shaw had your tidy copy more available.

Do you want—still—to know how it strikes me?

I like its beginning—then I get to dislike it very much—then I begin to like it again and end by liking it very much.

If you ask me for whys and wherefores—Act I: introductory all right—its one long scene rather too long. The angel's entrance wants very wonderfully managing—however simply—wonderfully.

And that brings me to my quarrel with Acts II and III. While he is an angel he must be wonderful. While he cannot "develop", he must be striking—like music—dominant (these are my producer's thoughts) and I think you run too many risks with him. To begin with you give him so many entrances and exits—and land your actor every time in the most frightful difficulty. For though he must use the door, as long as he is an angel the effect must be that he appears and disappears. He must be able to make the cheap comedians (this not necessarily a reflection on <u>your</u>, but on <u>their</u>, characters) look small and tawdry, make them sound cacophonous. I'm not sure that you haven't made this too hard for him. I'd have said—as a purely mechanical help—not one unnecessary coming in or going out.

As soon as his "character" begins to develop this difficulty vanishes. He joins the ordinary dramatic game and begins to dominate by inherent interest. And after this humanising—and as a contrast to it—his final "appearance" would be magnificent; so—were I producing—I'd say: Look sharply after Acts II and III.

Who is to do the play? Barrymore seems to be genuinely "hors de théâtre" for a year.

I have to do my last—I hope sincerely!—production—The Betrothal[3]—and that will bring us both to town for the next month. We shall be at the Connaught Hotel, Grosvenor Square, from about Dec. 3 and will hope to see something of you—if <u>you've</u> not flown to

Devonshire—as otherwise I wish you would—to turn out more plays
of your very own.

Best regards,

Yours,

H. Granville Barker

---

1. Returning from America; see letter to Archer of October 23, 1920, in Chapter II.
2. Ervine had sent him the script of the play he had recently completed in collaboration
   with H. G. Wells, a dramatization of Wells' novel of the same title. The play was
   presented the following year at the St. Martin's Theatre, London.
3. This play, by Maurice Maeterlinck, was a sequel to *The Blue Bird*. Barker directed
   the first (and only) London production of the play at the Gaiety Theatre, opening on
   January 8, 1921; C. B. Cochran was the producer.

TEX/MS
To Ervine

Netherton Hall,
Honiton,
S. Devon.
14.9.21

My dear St. John Ervine,

Yes, please do let us see the play.[1] The M.S. would find us
here till Saturday. From Sunday to Thursday we shall be at the Connaught Hotel. Then back here till December—and by all means yes,
we'll look out for the Beresfords—and thanks for telling us.

I have hopes for the S. F. business[2]—but what a useless and
dangerous thing it is to be theoretically right about anything. History
is the one important study and modern history—which, see, is after
all our realistic art—d–d job as it is. The playwriting part of it. Why
does one ever? I write enough for a dictionary to make a wretched
three act play—and so, I bet, do you.

Best regards,

Yours,

H. Granville-Barker

I think the Birmingham date for The Two Shepherds is Oct. 22.[3]
Liverpool is to do it too.

---

1. I cannot identify the play among Ervine's works, and what I take to be references to
   it in the following letter do not help. I assume it to be a play that was never produced
   or published.
2. Sinn Fein, the Irish nationalist party led by De Valera. Irish affairs were approaching
   flashpoint, and the British Prime Minister, David Lloyd-George, was attempting to
   arrange a conference with Sinn Fein.
3. *The Two Shepherds* is one of the plays by Sierra which Barker and his wife had
   recently translated from the Spanish.

TEX/MS
To Ervine

Connaught Hotel
Mayfair, W1
19.9.21

My dear Ervine,

Nonsense—of course it is not unplayable. If I have to criticise—and I <u>have</u> to criticise—

But this <u>sort</u> of play is very hard to criticise. One is trapped in the subject. It is almost too vital and actual for the theatre. That may seem a paradox. <u>Is</u> it? (a paradox) Are there not subjects which will not bear, because of their intensity (but perhaps it isn't intensity!), the added intensity of the dramatic form? Something is to be said against Brieux's Les Avariés on that count. Then there are one's obligations to a subject. Frankly I don't think you've quite fulfilled yours. The lists must be magnificent for such a combat, with such issues, and the champions overmasteringly fine and fully armed. But your professor is no rat of a fellow. You may say he was like that. Ah, but then you must make an atmosphere for him. put him into a three or four act play and by his surroundings bring him to size. But you start with him solitary—make him a piece of sculpture, make him a symbol; and for that he isn't tremendous enough—tremendously satanic or patriotic or virtuous—or even tremendously <u>commonplace</u>. The mother of course is easier to do and she is good. But she wouldn't be so easy if the professor were better!

For sheerly practical purposes you could (and should, I think) cut out repetition after repetition in the early middle of the thing.

But with any of that put right I'd still say: here is a great matter—you must carve it in granite not mould it so—well, sometimes casually—in clay.

Now could you use this as the clay model for a granite achievement? That's—to me—the question.

I have scribbled these opinions very hurriedly—impressionably. I don't pin myself to them. They may be false. But—such as they are—!

All best regards to you both,

H. Granville Barker

TEX/MS
To Ervine

Grand Hotel New Casino,
Casino di Rapallo,
Rapallo,
[Italy]
17.3.22

My dear St John Ervine,

Many thanks—but the E. T. is being put out in America by my usual "Little Brown"[1]—it has only been held up here till now because they take so long to set up and print.

We get to London, I think, for a few days early in April and then—thank God—back to our Devonshire. The one place or the other we shall hope to see you.

If you insult me with flowers I will challenge you—pistols: 20 paces.

We've been well enough, thanks—but the weather—damnable.

Our best regards to you both.

Yours,
H. Granville Barker

---

1. *The Exemplary Theatre* was being published in the United States by the Boston firm of Little, Brown and Co.

TEX/MS
To Ervine

Netherton Hall,
Honiton,
S. Devon.
13.5.22

My dear St. John Ervine,

This is my share of thanks for The Ship.[1] My wife is, I believe, sending you hers separately.

I like it much—and the more in that it demands—commands—a self-respecting theatre for its performance. The old grandmother—admirable, Cornelius excellent (and by the way the two stories of the lark and the sun's going down—nicely done and dramatically right. It always pleases me to find that effect rightly brought off, just because, bungled, it is so inept). I think the father good—the son less good. I wish you could have given him a stronger case—

though I see why you didn't. But it weakens the fabric of the play,
lessens the force of the clash in Act III Sc. 1. And there I regret the
£1000 business. I could have done—and I believe you could have
done better—without it. What a nuisance <u>action</u> is. (So <u>I</u> find. A
character <u>is</u> all right but when he begins to <u>do</u> things—. The lurking
danger, of course, of accommodating them to our requirements instead of their own desires.)

Why I launch out though into all this criticism . . . ? Take it
as a sign that I am interested—and moved beyond polite praises.

And things—minor things—in the play give me joy: notably
the stroke with the grandmother and the revolver—fine and deft, and
a thing for the actors to say "Thank you" for. The grandmother a
magnificent part all through—to say nothing besides of her.

And, again, and finally—Thank God for a play that asks for
a decent theatre.

We'll hope for a glimpse of you in town.

Kind regards to you both,

Yrs,
H. Granville-Barker

P.S. Nay, nay—nobody <u>leant</u> against a Fairy in the M. N. D. or even
<u>touched</u> one.[2] I think I know the bit of business that you mean—but
it just wasn't that.

---

1. Another of Ervine's plays, it was first produced at the Playhouse, Liverpool, on
   November 24, 1922.
2. He is referring to his own production of *A Midsummer Night's Dream* at the Savoy
   Theatre in 1914.

TEX/MS
To Ervine

Il Costello,
Portofino mare,
Liguria, Italy.
4.2.23

My dear St. John Ervine,

Mary Mary arrives,[1] bringing Devonshire into these Eye-
tallian surroundings—and we both thank you. And now I'll read her
properly: I only dipped when the proof sheets were on hand.

When does she appear in N.Y.? Rather amusing in itself it'll
be if she follows the Merchant of Venice with Belasco. I've just
found a review of this in a N.Y. paper. Oh—and we saw a French
version of it in Paris—and would you had been there. For the perpe-

trator must have been reading your Yale Review awhile—and he had
tried to rationalise the plot. You deserve to have seen the results!!

And I—even I—have just finished a "preface" to the thing.
And you—have you finished your sequel?[2] (Belasco ought to follow
up with that.)

We have had three weeks of sunshine but now the skies are
English grey again.

All's well with you both, we hope. We sit here in "fair"
solitude and work. Back late in April I expect—and then we'll hope
to see you.

Our best regards,

Yours,

H. Granville Barker

---

1. Ervine's most recent play was called *Mary, Mary Quite Contrary*. It was produced at
   the Belasco Theatre, New York, in 1923 and in London in the following year.
2. He refers to *The Lady of Belmont*, a play in which Ervine takes up the story of the
   chief characters of *The Merchant of Venice* ten years later. Only Shylock survives
   with any grace at all. The play was written in 1923 and published by Allen and Unwin
   in the same year. It was not produced until 1927, when it appeared at the Arts
   Theatre, London.

TEX/MS
To Ervine

Netherton Hall,
Colyton,
Devon.
2.10.23

PRIVATE
My dear St. John Ervine,

You make me what I know you mean to be a gracious
gesture.[1] But don't be surprised if I find it unconsidered—or ill-considered. Anyhow, if your thoughts turn to the subject again, take this
contribution to them.

I wrote The Voysey Inheritance before I went into management with Vedrenne: it was merely revised for production.

Absenting myself to write Waste, and the general strain of that
affair, were one of the chief causes of the breakup of that management.

The Madras House was written during convalescence from
typhoid and abstention from any management.

As to the producing of plays, I made up my mind sometime
before 1910 that it was futile to plough the sand i.e., in this connection, to make a production and then disperse it, the play to semi-

oblivion, the actors to demoralisation. On the personal count I had made up my mind even earlier to give up acting when I was 30 and producing when I was 40. I made—or contributed to—one attempt after another to create a theatre which should be an institution of some permanence. In 1914 this seemed on the verge of accomplishment (I calculated that by 1919 it might have developed a life of its own, so that I could go free).

Then came the war.

Personal and psychological considerations apart, neither my health nor my aptitude is what it was: and there has been a sharp break of tradition; the new generation is excusably, perhaps, intolerant of the experience of the old—the present establishment of a theatre-institution of scope and importance is not economically feasible; though it will come, doubtless, when there is enough conviction of its need, perhaps in 5 years, 10, or 20.

So in place of ploughing the sands I cast my bread upon the waters; a book on the aesthetics and politics of the theatre, subjects which most practitioners of drama have by temperament or circumstance neither patience nor time to consider; a series of studies of Shakespeare staging which I hope may be of use to some future institution; and—yes—even such plays as The Secret Life, which for all their shortcomings may serve, if only by example, to set actors new problems and to widen the theatre's appeal. It needs widening.

This, then, is my apologia; but not my apology.

As to the S. L. I am mischievously tempted to tell you to read it twice more and to read it as you would read—if you could— an orchestral symphony.

Really it contains no difficulties, except those that are inherent to the subject (and allowing, of course, for my own ineptitudes).

And I imagine yours with it mainly arise from an unconscious tendency to be thinking "How would I have treated this?" Always an interesting speculation, but, I suggest, a critical disability.

Kind regards,

Yours,

Harley Granville-Barker

P.S. I hope, by the bye, you got the copy I sent you.

---

1. The "gesture" was contained in Ervine's weekly column in *The Observer:* on Sunday, September 30, 1923, he reviewed two plays which had recently been published, *Phoenix,* by Lascelles Abercrombie, and Barker's *The Secret Life.* In the course of his comments on the latter he deplored, in rather stringent terms, Barker's decision to give up practical theater work. The review is important both because of these comments (which were in line with the thinking of a good many theater people) and because of its comments on the play itself, which was as widely misunderstood as was Barker's "desertion" of the theater. For this reason, Ervine's review is reprinted as Appendix D to this volume.

TEX/MS
To Ervine

18, Place des Etats-Unis,
Paris.
16.7.33

My dear St. John Ervine,
I see you are to review "Myself and My Friends" by Lillah McCarthy.[1]
I would just like to say this to you, if I may. It is by my own desire that my name is given no prominence in the book. I gather that it does not appear at all; but to this I make no objection. I feel sure that in your review you also will respect both the desire and the lack of objection. That would be friendly.

Harley Granville-Barker

---

1. On July 16, the day Barker wrote this letter, Ervine announced in his column in the *Observer* that he would review three books which dealt with the careers of three actresses: Ellen Terry, Sarah Bernhardt, and Lillah McCarthy. The book about Lillah McCarthy was her autobiographical *Myself and My Friends* (London, 1933). Ervine's comments on it and on Lillah McCarthy's career appeared on July 30. He honored Barker's request and made no mention of either Barker or of the fact that the book rather ostentatiously omitted all mention of his name. (For a full discussion of this matter, see Chapter IV, pp. 171–74.)

John Galsworthy (1867–1933)

Galsworthy was already established as one of the leading novelists of the day when he wrote his first play, The Silver Box, *which Barker directed at the Court Theatre in September, 1906. A careful and compassionate social drama, scrupulously honest and extremely well-observed, it was very well received, and Galsworthy was encouraged to continue in the same vein. He and Barker became great friends in the process, for Barker was responsible for directing the next three Galsworthy plays,* Joy, *at the Savoy Theatre in September, 1907;* Strife, *at the Duke of York's in March, 1909; and* Justice, *at the Duke of York's in February, 1910. They were fairly frequent visitors at each other's houses in the period immediately before World War I, and Galsworthy was one of those whose friendship with Barker weathered the storms of the divorce from Lillah and the marriage to Helen. There were doubtless many letters between Galsworthy and Barker, but I have come upon only two previously unpublished ones.*

TEX/MS
To Barker

Hôpital Benevole,
Martouret,
Die,
Drôme,
France.
Nov. 25, 1916

My dear Harley,

We have just had your letter.

I'm so very sorry you're so hung up. Will it be of any use if I lend you (sans interest of course) half the £2500? If you don't want it at once all the better because the sale of inscribed Stock requires a power of attorney that may be a little difficult out here; but if you do it can be managed. It's very interesting here and I enjoy my massage. I'd like a look at the front well enough in some ways before coming back; but after all if its nothing but sheer curiosity that takes me I think it might be a shame to give Ada an unhappy three or four days. I'm never likely to want to write on that accursed ground. I do hope things will straighten out with you.

Our love to you.

Always yours,
J. G.

TEX/MS
To Barker

Hôpital Benevole,
Martouret,
Die,
Drôme,
France.
Dec. 12, 1916

My dear H. G. B.,

I enclose you a cheque for £1250—my Bank has advanced the money, saving me the delay of Stock-selling.

On second thoughts I'd better keep this back till I get your letter announcing details, for even then you ought to get it within about ten days of your wire to me. We are so glad things are arranged. Let us know whether and when you go to America. I suppose the money will be deposited against the event—it should not be handed over unconditionally of course.

Your letter just came.

My dear fellow, I shall probably repay the Bank the money out of my current account before we're back in England, so don't worry about interest, and I would really much rather you didn't give me a charge on books; I should never make use of it.

Of course, if you can produce "The Fugitive" it'll be splendid.[1] Give it full emotional value. I prefer Estelle Winwood as Clare to risking Jane Cowl which is the other suggestion—it's safer, because Estelle Winwood was really <u>very</u> good in Liverpool and the other is an unknown quantity. The only thing about E. W. is a little lack of class but with your handling she can get over that, and she's really a pathetic figure & has a certain genius. The other I judge is robust. The Malise must be <u>strong</u> & <u>not</u> aesthetic or artistic.[2] Lomas was the ideal—he was just right. The danger of the play is an artistic Malise who at once alienates the sympathy of the audience & irritates them into damning the play.

We both send you our blessing and love and all good speed across the Pond, and back.

Yrs. always,
John Galsworthy

---

1. This play had already been produced: what Barker was proposing was a revival. It was first seen at a matinee at the Court Theatre, London, on September 16, 1913; from there it transferred to the Prince of Wales's Theatre, opening on September 25. It was also presented, in 1914, at the Liverpool Repertory Theatre and by Miss Horniman's Repertory Company at the Gaiety Theatre, Manchester. The new production suggested by Barker did not, in fact, materialize.
2. The part of Kenneth Malise in *The Fugitive* was played in Liverpool by William Armstrong and in Manchester by Herbert Lomas. The original Malise in the London production was Milton Rosmer; the original Clare was Irene Rooke.

Lady Augusta Gregory (1852–1932)

Lady Gregory was the co-founder, with W. B. Yeats, of the Irish Literary Theatre in 1899. When this became the Abbey Theatre, in 1904, she became co-director with Yeats and Synge. She maintained her association with the Abbey almost until her death. Her own plays were not as substantial as those of Yeats, Synge, or O'Casey, but they were nevertheless not without significance and still read well today (and are still quite often produced by the amateur theater). Her work did not impinge directly on Barker's but was a close parallel to it in artistic intent. The really significant thing is that the work at the Abbey Theatre was exactly contemporaneous not only with Barker's work in London but with that of Barry Jackson in Birmingham and Annie Horni-

man in Manchester, as well as with the more widely disseminated con-
tributions of William Poel and Edward Gordon Craig.

BERG/MS
To Lady Gregory

> The Little Theatre,
> John Street,
> Adelphi,
> [London]
> [1911]

Dear Lady Gregory,

We are going to play Act III of John Bull's Other Island on June 30 at Downing Street.[1] I am trying to get the cast that played it at the Court. I may not be able to have the old Patsy Farrell. I wonder—if I can't—whether you could lend us one. In Act III he only speaks a couple of lines at the end, but if it can be a genuine Irish country youth . . . If it can't be, the end of the act may be much spoilt.

The plays comes on about 10 p.m.
You'll forgive my troubling you.

> Very sincerely yours,
> H. Granville Barker

---

1. That is, at the official residence of the Prime Minister, H. H. Asquith. The performance was given at the invitation of the Prime Minister as an entertainment for the
new king and queen, George V and Mary, as part of the coronation celebrations.
Barrie's one-act play *The Twelve-Pound Look* was also presented.

Laurence Housman (1865–1959)

The younger brother of A. E. Housman, the poet and classical
scholar, Laurence Housman first made his name as an illustrator of
books. He then began to write, and in 1900 caused something of a
sensation with his An Englishwoman's Love Letters *(the contents of*
the book were entirely fictional but were at first believed to be tran-
scriptions of actual letters). A most prolific, though not especially dis-
tinguished, author, Housman wrote novels, verse, children's books,
and plays. Perhaps his plays represent his most important work; they
are certainly now best known. The two most familiar titles among
them, Victoria Regina *and* The Little Plays of St. Francis, *both be-*
long to a period after his active association with Barker, Victoria Regina *being produced in 1935 and the St. Francis plays being written in*
the twenties and thirties.

Housman's connection with Barker was, so far as practical matters were concerned, two-fold. They collaborated in the writing of the sweet-and-sour fantasy Prunella, or Love in a Dutch Garden, *which was one of the very early plays in the 1904–7 repertory season at the Court Theatre; Barker supported Housman in his attempts to get the Lord Chamberlain to lift his ban on Housman's* Pains and Penalties, *a play censored in 1911 because it dealt with the monstrous treatment meted out by George IV to Queen Caroline. (Barker encouraged Housman to proceed with a private performance of the play at the Savoy Theatre—which was at that time in Barker's control—and he himself made a speech to the audience after that performance, condemning censorship and moving a vote of censure on the Lord Chamberlain.) The three letters reproduced here all refer to* Prunella.

IOWA/MS
To Barker

1, Pembroke Cottages,
Kensington,
[London], W.
November 4, 1916

Dear H. G.-B.,

Vedrenne asked me to pass the enclosed on to you for comment. He has left out his undertaking to give a certain number of performances every year: you have a note of it, I think, but I forget whether he promised 20 or 30.

I have told him that clause 5 must include Moorat also,[1] and that as regards payment you will probably agree to let me do the mathematics as I alone find them simple and understandable.

Please be <u>under a month</u> in replying. You may bless my doorstep with your cloven hoof any day you like to name—or almost any.

Ever yours,
L. H.

---

1. Joseph Moorat composed the music for several of Housman's plays, including the Nativity play called *Bethlehem* of 1902; Moorat's music for this pre-dated the better-known setting composed by Rutland Boughton, which was written for a revised version of *Bethlehem* in 1923. The music being discussed in this letter is that written by Moorat for *Prunella*.

IOWA/MS
To Barker

1 Pembrook Cottages,
Kensington,
[London] W
Nov. 21st, 1916

Dear H. G. B.

I have seen Vedrenne, and here are the results. The main
points are: he sticks to it that he only offered the percentages here
stated and there is no document showing otherwise. He concedes the
same percentage for the provinces as for London, and promises 30
performances a year as a retainer of the rights. Your verbal emendations to various clauses he accepted in his best tones of nasal contempt—remarking that your brain was deteriorating.

I trust this sees the business through. If so, will you sign and
return to him, and he'll pay us the £100. You are to be asked and are
to answer the following questions:

1. Will you lend him, for costume purposes, the drawings
you possess by Wilhelm, of Pierrot, the Aunts (Maids?), the Gar-
dener and the Boy?

2. Will you send me the name and address of the rather
pleasant lady who trained for the stage at Blackheath. Vedrenne believes it begins with a B.

3. Do you agree to Vedrenne trying to negotiate from Lestocq (relict of Charles Frohman) the score of "Prunella" which he
claims to be his property (as they were Frohman's before him). Or do
you disagree with that statement of facts? (Vedrenne has none of the
music: and was only posing because somebody said he had!)

That's all, I think.

About our right to produce the play between now and Vedrenne's production, Vedrenne says he did not wish to ("couldn't" he
said) bind us legally not to do so. He only asks for "an honourable
understanding" that we will not, by undesirable performances, dam-
age the prospects of the "real production" lying ahead. Which means,
practically, I take it, that we will let him have an objecting word and
some consultative weight, before embarking on any fresh permits
other than amateurs.

He invites suggestions as to "Prunella", for whom he is casting
around and I suppose also for "Pierrot". He suggested Leon Quartermaine as a possible; he would certainly give a clever performance,
rather on the cold macabre lines of H. G. B.'s own, I should suppose.

Vedrenne's wish is to produce when "war tension" is

removed—mainly, I think, when the fear of Zeppelins has quite ceased.

Since I saw you I have almost certainly arranged to leave town between December 6th and 12th, and to be away then for at least two and perhaps three months. So fire at me your emendations if possible between now and then.

Vedrenne is rather bitter with the new act, and might, if Moorat consented, like to include it in his own show. I told him that it <u>did</u> depend on Moorat approving the music—probably on his being able to turn his own hand to it—whether we could let it be done in England.

I am writing another beautiful one-act play.

Ever yours,

L. H.

IOWA/MS
To Barker

Greycot,

New Milton,

Hants.

Dec. 29th, 1918

Dear H. G. B.

The enclosed occurred to me this morning as possible material for that final scene between Prunella and Scaramel which waits your improving touch. Take it and improve on it and reject it as you think well: but let it anyway infect you in the way you should go.

"Bethlehem" was apparently a huge success at Peterborough: they write that they could have filled the theatre for the whole week: as it was, for three nights' running they overflowed and made £250—none of which do I get, as I lent them the show for the sake of proof.

I have sent Moorat his share of the Cardiff pound of flesh. I am told by H. N. Paull that "Prunella" on the "movies" was quite attractive. I wonder, by the way, may it not hereafter be quite usual to keep a record of good productions and great bits of acting by filming them? H. G. B. (as Pierrot) coming down the ladder for ever and ever, and going on his naughty knees as a proof that once upon a time he <u>was</u> an actor of sorts.

Ever yours,

L. H.

John Masefield (1878–1967)

*Masefield wrote about twenty plays in all, and Barker was intimately
associated with several of them, including the very first,* The Campden
Wonder, *which he produced at the Court Theatre in January, 1907. It
was, indeed, Barker's encouragement at the start that kept Masefield
writing plays. Barker valued his work highly (see, for instance, his
letter of January 9, 1907, to Archer). It was Barker who directed the
first production of* The Tragedy of Nan *in 1908 and of* The Witch *in
1911; in November, 1914, he directed an almost Reinhardt-style production of* Philip the King *at Covent Garden, with crowd scenes so
large and complicated that he had a printed booklet of instructions
issued to each supernumary, giving (in a code consisting of letters and
numbers) detailed instructions for every move by every individual (a
copy of this fascinating document is now owned by Robert Eddison,
the distinguished British actor, who was so kind as to lend it to me
while I was working on this present book). Though one or two of his
plays were important in their day, Masefield's standing as a dramatist
is less high and less secure than his standing as a poet; from 1930 until
his death in 1967 he held the position of Poet Laureate.*

TEX/PC
To Masefield

Germany.
August 26, 1909.

I don't think he is Pompey but he is not unlike.[1]
I have told you Wareing cries aloud for Ann P.[2]
Yes I have—coasting up the Tyrrhenian Sea to Genoa now. Thence
home but slowly—while the money lasts.

H. G. B.

---

1. The postcard, though mailed in Germany, is an Italian one (Barker addresses it to
   "Inghilterra"—he obviously intended to mail it while in Italy and forgot to do so),
   bearing a picture of a statue of a Roman soldier-emperor. Masefield was working on
   a play about Pompey at that time; it was produced by the Stage Society in the
   following year as *The Tragedy of Pompey the Great.*
2. "Ann P." is the central character of *Anna Pedersdotter,* a Norwegian play by Wiers-
   Jenssen. At Archer's suggestion and with Barker's active encouragement, Masefield
   was working, though reluctantly, on an English version of the play. Alfred Wareing
   (1876–1942), actor and manager, who had recently started the Glasgow Repertory
   Theatre, wanted to present the first production of the play and was pressing Barker
   to direct it for him. Masefield completed the play in 1910, and in October of that year
   Barker did direct it at Glasgow, repeating the production in London (the Court
   Theatre) in January, 1911, with Lillah McCarthy as Ann. (See also Chapter V, letters
   from Murray to Barker, February 10 and 20, 1911.)

TEX/MS
To Barker

> Rectory Farm,
> Gt. Hampden,
> Gt. Missenden,
> Bucks.
> Sept. 10, 1909

My dear Harley,

It was most kind of you to send me your plays. Thank you very much indeed: it is delightful to have them. I only know Waste: but I have now read most of The Voysey Inheritance & part of Ann Leete. What I admire so much in your work is its fineness and precision; it is like fine metal work, all certain and strong and lithe, all the unnecessary cut away. "How different from us, Miss Beale & Miss Buss."[1]

You know my opinion of Waste. I'll tell you what I specially admire in Ann Leete: your power of suggestion of the dawn. You have made your people talk at the beginning like parts of twilight. Then in the Voysey, Alice & Ethel, especially Ethel, p. 111, where you get a complete character into a speech of seven lines. Clever devil. You are such a subtle devil to think, you get all round your people before you begin, and when you do begin, they just walk out of prison and are thenceforth free. I wish I could do that. I grope around & catch a little bit of a person, & shut it up mighty tight.

But I'll write to you again when I've read both plays. Meanwhile accept my congratulations & my thanks.

> Yours,
> John Masefield

---

1. Miss Beale was the Principal of the Ladies' College, Cheltenham, in the latter part of the nineteenth century; Miss Buss was Headmistress of the North London Collegiate School at the same period. Both were well known for their advanced, but austere, approach to education. An anonymous pupil in one of the two schools wrote a little rhyme that became famous:

> Miss Buss and Miss Beale
> Cupid's darts do not feel.
> How different from us,
> Miss Beale and Miss Buss.

TEX/MS
To Barker

30, Maida Hill West,
[London], W.
March 18, 1910

My Dear Harley,

I want you to know how very much I enjoyed your play yesterday.[1] When I saw you after it, I only gave you that brief criticism of the ruffian in the last Act.[2] He jarred on me; partly because I wasn't prepared for him in that light, & partly, I think, because I felt the need just then, for some direct personal attack upon him, by a woman; his wife, or Miss Yates, or Jessica. A flare-up from any one of these would have made the Act.

For your end, very noble, and very beautiful (it came right home to me, one of the best things you've ever done or said, quite a new piece of thought), all that is wanting is you with a conductor's bâton, or a Knout or something, making your Actors speak up, or shake out stern sails or something. All that bit is music, to be conducted as music.

Now about E. A. B. in the D. N.[3] Harley, if this were Sicily, & my name were Grassi, and the notte were oscura! Dio mio and per Bacco, Harley.

But never mind him. Your play's the finest piece of style & the finest piece of thought & the finest piece of comedy of our time.

With all good wishes to you.

Yours ever,
John Masefield.

---

1. The play is *The Madras House,* first produced at the Duke of York's Theatre on March 9, 1910, with Barker directing. The cast included Sybil Thorndike, Fay Davis, Mary Jerrold, May Whitty, Dennis Eadie, and Lewis Casson.
2. Constantine Madras is the "ruffian."
3. The theater critic for the *Daily News* was Edward Algernon Baughan (1865–1938), who began his connection with that paper as music critic in 1902; he took over the paper's theater criticism column in 1904.

TEX/MS
To Barker

Gt. Hampden,
Gt. Missenden,
Bucks.
Aug. 10, 1910

My dear Harley,

It is always a delight to hear from you. All goes well here, thank you. How are you?

Introductions, sir. The rate varies according to the amount of reading necessary, according to the publisher, and to the market value of the writer.

You are famous, & should use your fame to improve the rates generally given. These are, for ordinary introductions, three guineas for a thousand words. Generally, introductions are sold outright, and the writer receives no royalty on the sales of the book introduced by him. I once got four guineas for a thousand words. I don't think Yeats or Symons ever got more. But I feel that you on Maeterlinck would be such a draw that you might ask for twenty guineas for the whole job, and see what they say.[1] They will probably kick, and pay it. People have come to regard you as a kind of god. Such a request, insolent in me, would in you be counted as part of your largeness of manner. One thinks of you as an Eighteenth Century lord, receiving, for work done, no beggerly sum "per thou", but a purse of guineas, damme.

Another thing, say you won't correct the proofs of the plays, but only your introduction.

I've done my novel. Soli deo gloria. It is about women, egad, the two kinds of them, stap my vitals.

Our love to you both.

Now for my new play!

Good luck to you,

Yours,
John Masefield

---

1. Several of Maeterlinck's plays had already appeared in English translation. Gowan's and Gray were now proposing a volume containing *Alladine and Palomides, Interior,* and *The Death of Tintagiles,* with an introduction by Barker. The volume was published in 1911 under the title *Three Plays.* Archer did the translation of *Interior* and Alfred Sutro translated the other two.

TEX/MS
To Barker

30, Maida Hill West,
[London], W
Dec. 6, 1910

My dear Harley,

It might be said by me as by Theophanes in the play "I was a dirty little boy selling mullet. . . . And through you I have had a play done in Rome". For as you know, you are my father and my grandfather. I have never failed to get from you praise & encouragement & sympathy that have been some of the dearest things life has given me. I am humbled by your great letter of praise, for your work is one of the things that I keep in front of me, to try to attain to. Your fine supple style that has a play and a glitter on it like a sword of the best temper, and the knowledge that the style comes from a mind of that temper instead of from (as with me) a treatment of the trite with extract of literature.

Well, Bless & thank you. And if Pompey is good, know that it is in a great part due to you & Lillah.

Both of you take my warm greetings, & know how glad & proud I was that you were both there to see the results of your encouragement.

Yours,
John Masefield

TEX/TS
To Masefield

Kingsway Theatre,
Great Queen Street, W.C.
July 4th, 1912

My dear John,

Drinkwater handed me your letter a while ago and I ought to have answered it. Apologies, but I have been awfully rushed and worried with other work.

Our position is that of course we want your play[1] and we'll complete the contract as soon as you like and we can agree on it. But of course we should have to put down some sort of a date for completion and delivery and if, you wanting to write and write again over the play, this would be irksome to you, then postpone it until the end is in sight; but it really can be, I think, just as you yourself would like it.

Lillah and I are just off for a month's holiday abroad, getting on a liner to go round Gibraltar and then to some mountains
somewhere. I shall be back to rehearse about August 7th. Where will
you be then? Our love to you all four.

Yours,

H. G. B.

---

1. The play must be either *Philip the King* or *The Faithful,* produced in 1914 and 1915,
respectively. After *Pompey the Great,* Masefield is not known to have written any
other play until these two.

EDD/MS
To Barker

Cholsey,
Berks.
26 Aug. 1914

My dear Harley,

Thank you for what you say of Ronin. Your encouraging
words have been a great pleasure to us in this stormy time.

What work is taking you to Stansted? Is it Charley again?[1] I
hope it is, & that it is really coming now. Do bring it to read to us as
soon as you have a draft of any of it done. We shall be here, I
suppose, till the end of Sept, & there'll practically always be a bed
here for you, & we would love to have you & to talk with you.

Our future, I mean our personal family future, must depend
on the fate of the Allied armies. We may have to give up London, &
live here, on our new potato patch etc. As yet, we do not quite know
how hard the war will hit us, either as a nation or as a family, but
one feels that in either case the old order is dead. I suppose our
individualism will be made less casual than heretofore; & we are still
young enough to give the new thing a shove.

Bless you, & all good wishes to the work.

Yours ever,

John

Pilate: "Crucificatus est". Hope to end draft in 3 weeks.

---

1. Charles is the principal character in the play which Barker was writing in 1914, "The
Wicked Man." He never completed it. Two acts are extant in a typescript now in the
possession of the British Theatre Museum. See also Chapter V, letter of September
2, 1910, from Murray to Barker.

EDD/MS
To Barker

Cholsey,
Berks.
19.IX.1914

My dear Harley,

Thanks for your letter.

We'll be here probably till the 28th or 29th. Do come down
for a night if the spirit moves you, & bring your play & let us hear it,
& then we can talk over this Philip music, & some arrangement can
be made equitable to the composer & to the author.

Pilate is drafted & is now being typed. I'm slogging away
again at this rotten Ronin thing. Please God I may get it at last to go.

I think we must talk about Philip & the music, & it would
be very nice if you would someday get the composer to meet us.

Our love & greetings to you,

Yours ever,
John

Mind you come down & bring Charles. We've a room for you.
All send greetings to Lillah.
Troops training all around us, some squad or so to each of our maids.

BERG/MS
To Sir Edward Marsh[1] from Barker

R. G. A. Cadet School,
Trowbridge,
Wilts.
Sept. 25 [1916]

PRIVATE

My dear Marsh,

Give me—will you?—some advice and possibly some help
about John Masefield. He is at the moment in France writing a book
on the American ambulances and I have—through his wife—rather
bad accounts of his health. He has been over-working and running
himself down for some time. He'll come back soon and proposes
then, I know, to enlist in the Artillery—will have a cadetship later I
suppose on the same terms that I have it. He is only medically passed
for home service. The "hardships" of this training are non-existent to
me during the summer. But to him—during the winter—especially if
he is not fit to start with, I think may amount to something serious
and, again judging by myself, he won't make much of a gunner any-

way. Is there any other sort of job in the army that could be found for him, in which he might be of much more use; and how does one find it?

Of course he won't <u>ask</u> for anything—that I know. And indeed, unless the offer seems to drop from the blue, it is more than likely he'll decline it. Wherefor I mark this private. And see, won't you, that it doesn't get round to him that I have written. But, frankly, to knock up his health to <u>no purpose</u> (as they won't send him abroad anyway) would be waste, wouldn't it?

Very sincerely yours,
H. Granville Barker

---

1. For a brief note on Marsh, see Chapter X, footnote on p. 482.

BERG/MS
To Sir Edward Marsh

Garrick Club,
[London], W.C.
Oct. 15 [1916]

My dear Marsh,

About Masefield—that seems capital. Certainly he must be made to go and see Sir Arthur Leetham and when he comes back to England I'll see—so far as it's possible—that he does. Shall I let you know, so that you may "work" a letter summoning him to the presence? That will be the way of it, I suppose.

I have now been moved to town—so this is my best address.

Many thanks—but you, I know, were almost as interested as I.

Very sincerely yours,
H. Granville Barker

Thomas Sturge Moore (1870–1944)

Like Laurence Housman, Sturge Moore's reputation was made partly as an illustrator of other men's books, partly as a poet. Among his best-known book illustrations are the cover designs for the first editions of two of W. B. Yeats' collections of verse, The Tower *(1928), and* The Winding Stair *(1933). Moore, born at Hastings, was the eldest son of Dr. David Moore; one of his younger brothers was G. E. Moore, the Cambridge philosopher. Sturge Moore's first collection of verse,*

The Vinedresser and Other Poems, *was published in 1899; his first published play was* Aphrodite against Artemis, *in 1901. In 1911 he wrote a one-act verse play on the theme of Judith and Holofernes, which Lillah McCarthy played in 1916. Also in 1911 a full-length play called* Mariamne *was published. Later in life he also wrote critical studies of Correggio and Dürer. His collected poetry, in a four-volume edition, was published in 1931–33. In 1953* W. B. Yeats and T. Sturge Moore: Their Correspondence, 1901–37 *appeared. Barker did not know him well and did not have any close dealings with him, but in the first twenty years of the century both Barker and Moore were reckoned among those in London who were principally responsible for the revival of the serious-minded theater and, especially, the poetic theater. The brief exchange here reproduced comes from a later period and is interesting because it illustrates the instinctive austerity of Barker's view of the artist and the artist's work.*

LON/TS
To Moore

18, Place des Etats-Unis,
[Paris.]
16th January, 1939

My dear Sturge Moore,
Your letter about Gawsworth has just reached me.[1] There can be few people safer to follow in such a question than you. But when I can bring myself to vote for one of these medals—for I normally dislike prizes and competitions exceedingly—I always feel I must try to do so without following anybody—blindly at least.

I thought we had one of Gawsworth's books here, published by the Nonesuch or Hogarth people. But I cannot find it. If however you'd name one or two of them I'd buy and read them, and then vote with pleasure if I felt I could.

It is long since we met; but a great pleasure to hear from you all the same.
As ever,

Yours sincerely,
Harley Granville-Barker

---

1. John Gawsworth was the pen name of Terence Ian Fytton Armstrong (1912–1971), a minor poet who published several volumes of verse in the thirties and forties. He was also the editor, at different times, of several of the "little" magazines, and he prepared new editions of Tennyson and Milton and of some of the prose works of Havelock Ellis. In 1939 he founded *The English Digest*.

LON/MS
To Barker

[no address]
[no date]

My dear Granville Barker,

I also dislike prizes and competitions but perceive that they are sometimes a partial mitigation to the badness of the world.

I would send you my copy of Poems by J. G., etc., only I have unfortunately scribbled in the margins improvements or the reverse, which are thoroughly misleading.

But I do not recommend him on the strength of his absolute poetic achievement which Masefield and Abercrombie have praised more highly than I could, so as to make me feel how likely I am to be wrong. And he has won their praises while under very adverse circumstances and has shown abilities in other lines and a devotion to literature rare indeed.

Yours sincerely,
T. S. Moore

LON/MS
To Moore

18, Place des Etats-Unis
Paris.
Feb. 12 1939

My dear Sturge Moore,

I feel badly about it: and the more so because they do seem to me in my critical inexpertness (I am no judge of this sort) to be real poetry. But I can't vote for that medal. It is most unlikely, however, that I shall vote at all. So if I do him no good I shall at least do him no harm. A Laodicean!—and you will spew me out of your mouth.

But this small favourable thing I can and will do: buy the "Poems" for our British Institute Library here and give the new volume to a sympathetic man to review for our little Bulletin. And since the French student is keen on our stuff of today—keener than is the English, I gather—he will be put upon the small Sorbonne map by these means, if he is not there already. And there may be a harvest, if only of credit. Forgive me.

Yours,
Harley Granville-Barker

Hermon Ould (1886–1951)

Ould was a minor, though not unsuccessful, dramatist whose plays included Between Sunset and Dawn *(1913),* Christmas Eve *(1919),* The Dance of Life *(1925), and* The Light Comedian *(1930). He also published several volumes of verse and a book on playwriting called* The Art of the Play *(1938). His theater work did not bring him into contact with Barker, but his position in the thirties as general secretary of P.E.N., the international organization of authors, did. It is in this capacity that he wrote to Barker, who was a member of P.E.N. The correspondence, though slight, brings out sharply Barker's deep-seated ambivalence about artistic organizations and about the whole matter of contact between artist and public.*

TEX/MS
To Ould

18, Place des Etats-Unis,
[Paris] XVIe
March 3 [1931]

My dear Mr. Hermon Ould,

Buenos Ayres? Good God, no!! No, really I fear it is quite out of the question.[1]

I am sorry that I never turn up to any of the dinners. I never do go to such things. Incidentally—for your address book—I live over here now.

The P.E.N., for me, is a gesture which we should all continue to make. As to its practical efficacy—?

Very sincerely yours,
Harley Granville-Barker

Please formally thank the Executive Committee for the honour they do me.

---

1. Ould had asked Barker to attend a P.E.N. conference as an official representative for England.

TEX/MS
To Ould

Palazzo Ravizza,
Piazza del Carmine 26,
Siena,
[Italy]
22.3.31

My dear Hermon Ould,
    I'm afraid I must say No to the Dutch business:[1] but many thanks to whomever it was had the idea of asking me. My reasons— for I owe them to you: I don't know where I may be in June; I speak neither Dutch nor German; such knowledge as I ever had of their literature is quite out of date and I have no time now to renew it; lastly, I am by no means the man for these affairs. I hate them and too often I show it.
    Again, it is good of you to ask me and thank you. But—no. And you will do better.

Very sincerely yours,
Harley Granville-Barker

Forgive the delay. I have been travelling about.

---

1. Ould had apparently assumed that Barker's objection to visiting a P.E.N. conference in South America was based on geographical considerations and had therefore proceeded to suggest an alternative meeting closer to Paris.

TEX/MS
To Ould

18, Place des Etats-Unis,
[Paris]
June 26 1931

My dear Hermon Ould,
    For your Austrian Writer's Fund, the enclosed £5. A fitting job for the P.E.N. and one is grateful to have it undertaken.

Yours,
Harley Granville-Barker

 **Chapter XII**

Various Correspondents

T*his chapter contains* a few of the more interesting of the letters which have come to light on subjects of particular concern to Barker. Some of them are chosen because they illustrate an aspect of the subject which may be of special significance, others because Barker's correspondent is of special note in the particular context. The letters are arranged by subject.

A National Theater

TEX/MS
To J. L. Garvin[1]

Netherton Hall,
Honiton,
Devon.
1.5.23

My dear Garvin,
Your telegram with its kind suggestions has been telephoned on to me here. I am with you heart and soul about the Shakespeare Theatre—and about Shakespeare, his humanity. The last two Observers have been a joy to read on that account alone.

But I can't do the article, I fear. I'm just back from abroad and dodging about for these next few days. I've other things piled up—and I write so slowly.

Some day of course we <u>must</u> have the theatre—<u>and</u> in London. And then we shall wonder why we never had it before. It is an Imperial necessity: the King, the personal bond of union; and Shake-

Barker, about 1910.

Barker as Edward Voysey in
The Voysey Inheritance, 1906.

speare! And what is £1,000,000? Only a public opinion needs forming. Do form it. You could, as no one else.
>   With kind regards,

Very sincerely yours,
Harley Granville-Barker

---

1. See letter of March 9, 1923, p. 481.

TEX/MS
To R. A. Scott-James[1]

18, Place des Etats-Unis,
Paris, XVI
Feb. 1, 1935

My dear Mr. Scott-James,
>   I ventured to have you sent that book[2] because it was meant
to provide:
>   a) ammunition for advocacy;
>   b) even more important, criticism of inadequate schemes for
the National Theatre.
>   But I really think I'd better hold my tongue for the time.
Everybody knows I'm an advocate. Let the voices of people who
aren't so committed be heard. I may be useful as a critic later on.
>   But I sincerely hope you will be for the <u>comprehensive</u>
scheme in which I believe—and <u>only</u> in which!—the safe economics
of the thing to be. For a hundred people who will gas about Shakespeare and the drama hardly one will study the economics of the
theatre. But it is upon these that the whole business depends.

Very sincerely yours,
Harley Granville-Barker

---

1. Rolfe Arnold Scott-James (1878–1959), journalist, editor, and literary critic, became
   the first editor, in 1914, of *New Weekly* and was later editor of the *Mercury,* succeeding J. C. Squire to that post in 1934. He was one of the earliest advocates of a
   National Theatre and was for many years a member of the Shakespeare Memorial
   National Theatre Committee, to which he was appointed in 1933.
2. He had asked the publishers to send Scott-James a copy of his *A National Theatre.*

TEX/TS
To R. A. Scott-James

Chateau de Gregy,
Bri-Comte-Robert,
Seine et Marne.
30th August, 1938

My dear Scott-James,

Rule me out if only for this reason: I don't know enough about the subject.[1] It would be, moreover, not easy for an Englishman to discover the real truth about it, and very difficult for him, living in France, to write it candidly if he did.

For, of course, the ostensible facts are not the real ones, especially the financial facts, upon which so much of the rest depends. Further the rules do not show, I feel sure, how the machinery really works (I suspect the famous Decree of Moscow of being a fraud[2]). Thirdly, I do not suppose that the story of the influences which have stood in the way of reform is a pretty one. And, finally, I doubt if this present reform will be enduring, for it has been started at the wrong end, by staging attractive "productions" instead of righting the classic repertoire.

But do get a study of the thing done if you can; for the difficulties they are faced with of pay, discipline, a swollen company which they cannot employ all the time for lack of a smaller house besides, by reason of cinema and broadcast temptations, the questions of the propaganda demands made on the company, the advantages of the training, the faults in its conservatism, yet the general impossibility of keeping up any quality under the conditions as a whole—all that would be interesting and instructive.

Brisson, late of the Temps, now dramatic critic (and literary editor) of the Figaro, could do the thing for you if he would. But he'd write more from the aesthetic than the practical point of view, and he might be shy of giving his country away.

Jacques Copeau could write from both points of view. But he is in a peculiar position and might not like to speak out either. Yet, if he could save his face with Bourdet, the present Administrateur General, he might like the chance to.

These two would speak with great personal authority. The most knowledgeable Englishman in Paris—on this subject and a good many others—is Philip Carr; writes well enough though without much bite and is sympathetic to the French. I don't how how frank he would feel he could be. I could put you in touch with either him or Copeau—though I daresay you know both.

But our Nat. Theatre people, as I am tired of telling them,

must work out in detail the practicabilities of their scheme both from the point of view of detailed cost, and from that of what they can give in quantity and get and give in quality for the money. I've challenged them in a book, and thcy ought cithcr to answer the challenge or admit that some such scheme is not merely desirable but necessary. But they go on endowing £100 seats. As if <u>that</u> would save their souls!

As ever,

Yours,
Harley Granville-Barker

---

1. Scott-James had invited him to write an article for the *Mercury* on the Comédie Française, using it for comparative purposes as an example of a national theater.
2. On October 15, 1812, Napoleon, at the head of his invading army, issued from Moscow a decree prescribing and governing the mode of operation of the Comédie Française: to all intents and purposes this decree re-affirmed, in the main, the system appointed in 1680 by Louis XIV (whose prescription was also, incidentally, issued from camp in the middle of a military campaign). Barker, in *A National Theatre* (1930), describes the Decree of Moscow as "an instrument which surely owes more to Napoleon's reputation than to its own wisdom, which is, in any case, as out of date today as the guns behind which it was written" (p. 132).

TEX/TS
To Lord Esher[1]

Ritz Hotel
[London], W.1
July 21, 1945

My dear Oliver,

I take my little typewriter . . . .

I wish you thought you could do with an anonymous as well as with an absentee chairman. This is a warning to you. I am as bad at publicity as I should be at collecting money. But I think, on the other hand, that the more the limelight shines on Director and actors and the less on the Governors the better.

This, though, is where I want to take counsel with you. It will be bad policy, surely, to make an announcement only of the amalgamation[2] (and the appointment of a new chairman). For this will invite the comment that the Old Vic, which has all this time been <u>doing</u> something, has taken on the dead weight of the N. T., which for forty years and more has done nothing at all. Now, I consider that up to very recently, if not now, the O. V. has done very second rate work, which no N. T. worthy of the name should countenance. The N. T. must stand for quality, a quality that private theatres do not attain (comprehensiveness added), or it has no claim on national recognition and support. What has changed the situation and will justify this amalgamation? The O. V. has suddenly attained a standard which puts it at least into the "National Theatre" class. (I could argue that it hasn't given proof yet that it can sustain itself there; but I won't.) Therefore the N. T. holds out a not too condescending hand to it and says: "Come along, and we will do together what you cannot (we argue) do for yourself." We will strengthen the weak places in it, and then we will call this company the NATIONAL THEATRE COMPANY, and there is a lot in a name. (I have been against anything of this sort so far because I feared that with no building in sight the "big idea" would be frittered away in "Old Vic-ishness". Even now I am tempted to say THE N. T. PREPARATORY CO . . . . but it's too long a word, and offers no temptation.) The N. T. Co., awaiting its home, will play wherever it can in London for so many months in the year, and for so many weeks in Edinburgh, Belfast, Manchester, Liverpool, Birmingham, if they choose to invite . . . this to help retain the actors. And we also propose to establish at once a N. T. TRAINING Co., which will travel around everywhere, to all the sort of places that the Arts Council wants evangelised, which will do nothing but the "Classics", which will be filled as far as it suitably can be with young people, who will be admitted on a sort of scholarship-apprenticeship basis (competitive at that), and will compete to pass out into the main N. T. company, and will be expected during their preparatory time to master the preliminary arts of speech and movement, so that . . . God help us . . . they may be an improvement in these on the present people, whom they will succeed. I think the N. T. influence in the Amalgamation can offer that; and the Arts Council will, I take it, be ready with a subsidy; for there'll be no money in this, whatever there may be in the present Old Vic Co., or in the N. T. improvement on it.

      And I suggest to you . . . but here you know the ground, and I don't . . . that the amalgamation should not be announced until it can come bringing these gifts with it. For the mere name of the N. T. committee, with its forty year old projects and promises and sites bought and sold, has become MUD. This involves, I suppose, the fixing upon a Director; upon two, indeed. For the N. T. Co., is Guthrie resourceful enough? For the Training Co. I think a man could be found, of a rather different sort. For this, by the way, would admit nothing but acting based on good speaking and the good play; an Elizabethan stage (convertible to a "Restoration") with no money spent on decorations. By this time, I daresay, the Universities have bred someone.

*The letter breaks off at this point and was left unfinished and unsigned.
Presumably, it was never sent to Lord Esher.*

---

1. Oliver Sylvain Baliol Brett, 3rd Viscount Esher (1881–1963); he was extremely interested in the development of a serious and progressive theater and was a generous patron of the arts. He served, at various times, as chairman of the London Theatre Council, president of the British Drama League, a governor of the Old Vic, and a trustee of the National Theatre.
2. The amalgamation of the Shakespeare Memorial National Theatre Committee and the Old Vic, which had just been agreed to as a step towards the building of the National Theatre.

Shakespeare

Published letter
To the *Daily Mail*

> Savoy Theatre,
> London
> Sept. 26, 1912

Sir,

It is ten years and more since I made that remark to and of Mr. Gordon Craig, that he was an excellent man to steal from. Mr. Craig shortly emigrated, which is the easiest thing for any remarkable English artist to do, and the German-speaking theatres shortly began to give point to my mild epigram. As I am now charged with giving point to it myself, perhaps I may be allowed to elaborate my meaning a little.

Mr. Craig is a bit of a genius (I hope he will agree with me that one must not use that word to the full too rashly) and he is wholly an idealist. He will have no less than the dramatic kingdom of heaven on earth; he will have perfection as he sees it or nothing. I, on the other hand, am but a plodding theatrical shopkeeper, producing plays as best I can, and as well as I know how, for the mere entertainment of the public.

Now, as with all idealists, Mr. Craig's influence has been mainly destructive. Certainly his own production twelve years ago of Mr. Laurence Housman's "Bethlehem" destroyed for me once and for all any illusion I may have had as to the necessity of surrounding every performance of a play with the stuffy, fussy, thick-bedaubed canvas which we are accustomed to call stage scenery, while he opened my eyes to the possibilities of real beauty and dignity in stage decoration. I owe him (we all should) a great debt of gratitude. I gladly acknowledge it.

Then, as far as the production of Shakespeare goes, I am

grateful, too (and again so should we all be), to Mr. William Poel—
that other destructive idealist—who taught me how swift and passionate a thing, how beautiful in its variety, Elizabethan blank verse
might be when tongues were trained to speak and ears acute to hear
it.

So what I am trying to steal—and am proud to be stealing—
from Mr. Craig and Mr. Poel, is a little of the freedom of spirit and
fearlessness of purpose with which they have pioneered. But beyond
that I do protest that all this talk about Craig-ism or Reinhardt-ism,
or Moscow Art Theatre-ism or Russian Balletoxy is futile and—concerning the production of an English classic by three Englishmen—
just a little lacking in national self-respect.

Norman Wilkinson, Albert Rothenstein, and I have set out,
quite simply and sincerely, by the method of trial and error (for he
who makes no mistakes makes nothing), and by the light of our own
wits and imagination to interpret a dramatic masterpiece. All we ask
in return of the critics and the public is to be allowed to make that
trial upon their open minds and natural taste, not upon their artifi-
cially stimulated prejudices. There is no Shakespearean tradition. At
most we can deduce from a few scraps of knowledge what Elizabethan methods were, while as to our modern productions de luxe—
dislike or admire—I am sure Betterton, Garrick, or Kean would be
far too breathless with amazement to take up a part in them at any
short notice. We have the text to guide us, half a dozen stage directions, and that is all. I abide by the text and the demands of the text,
and beyond that I claim freedom. With what result?

See the "Winter's Tale" at the Savoy Theatre. Spend the
evening in a dispute with yourself or your neighbour as to whether
this is right or wrong, ugly or beautiful, whether that is as you last
saw it, or as you never thought it could be—why, you may well go
away worried and confused. But sit there at your ease to listen and
watch, and only ask yourself, when the curtain has finally fallen: was
I stirred and amused, has it been enthralling to hear and beautiful to
see?—and by the answer to that question we will abide, as indeed
we must. I make the challenge with the more confidence, as by the
behaviour of the audience these last two or three performances,
mouselike while the play proceeded, more than generous of their applause at the end, I have no great doubt of the issue.

Contrary to the general (though secret) opinion, I have always maintained that Shakespeare was not—as the phrase is usually
understood—a classic writer, to be buried beneath the dust of a spir-
itless convention and treated to that mouth-homage which so barely
conceals boredom. I hold that he is a still living playwright and a very

good one, thrilling and amusing, full of fine drama and good fun, and of an almost universal appeal to young and old, to the man in the cab and the man on the kerb, if only his plays are played as he wrote them and in the spirit he meant them to be. Now that, within our human limitations, we have done and I challenge anyone, having cleared his mind from a generation of prejudice, to deny it.

H. Granville Barker

Published Letter
To *Play Pictorial*[1]

Savoy Theatre,
[London]
November, 1912

Dear Sir,

Does it come to this, that you enjoyed the performance mightily, but that now you doubt gravely whether you ought to have enjoyed it? Make reasonably sure, one is tempted to reply, that it was Shakespeare's play of "TWELFTH NIGHT"—veritably that—which you enjoyed, and, if so, be dashed to your doubts. But I know where your critical, next-morning conscience pinches; not over the acting, not even the costumes, but over that confoundedly-puzzling scenery. Well, this has an importance, I think, beyond its own merits or demerits.

Something may be gained by discussing the question. For there is a question, a problem, and very glad we should be for a little assistance in solving it. Why does one so often look for that in vain, even from the friendliest critics? Tell me how much you admire, or how utterly you detest Norman Wilkinson's pink pillars, and, as privately and politely as possible, I yawn, and so does Wilkinson. I ask you, when you yourself are trying to set down something important, to have your handwriting admired, or to be tripped up over a mistake in syntax—what are your feelings?

Indeed, as such things go, it is important—this problem of Shakespearean scenery. And, as a new formula, a new convention, has to be found, the audience must learn to see, even as we learn to work in it. And the ideal audience (you, yourself, dramatic critic) might even now begin to cultivate the eye, if not of faith, of prophecy. We need help; I assure you that such experiments aren't easy.

I postulate that a new formula has to be found. Realistic scenery won't do, if only because it swears against everything in the plays; if only because it's never realistic; I can't argue that point now, even if there's need. So we begin again at the beginning.

What are the conditions? We must have a background. What sort? Any sort? But if we have our choice? Well, we want something that will reflect light and suggest space; if it's to be a background permanent for a play (this, for many reasons, it should be), something that will not tie us too rigidly indoors or out. Sky-blue then will be too like sky; patterns suggest walls. Tapestry curtains hung round? Well, tapestry is apt to be stuffy and—archaeological.

We shall not save our souls by being Elizabethan. It is an easy way out, and, strictly followed, an honourable one. But there's the difficulty. To be Elizabethan one must be strictly, logically or quite ineffectively so. And, even then, it is asking much of an audience to come to the theatre so historically-sensed as that.

But a curtained background of some sort? Excellent as a background, if a simple background were all that is wanted. But what about a play's demand for houses, with their doors and balconies, gardens with hedges, a forest with trees? Here is the problem. I state it; its solution does not lie in words but it is an attempt at a solution that we have been making at the Savoy Theatre.

There was much praise, I think, for the palace of Leontes. But—six pillars and curtains to bridge them, granted their proportion and colour needed to be simply right—what could be easier of solution? I see little difficulty where architecture is concerned. The cottage of the shepherd was much blamed. Rightly or wrongly?—I'll offer no opinion. But I doubt if many of the scolders began to know where the rights and wrongs of the matter lay.

The play demanded a cottage, to be put in conventional surroundings, and, therefore, a conventional cottage; to stand against the simplest background and to remain in the nature of a background itself; solve that.

Now Olivia's garden, which needs for the play's purposes at the very least a box hedge to be placed against that same conventional background—that or another. A box hedge truly, when well gardenered, is one of nature's most conventional works. Nevertheless, try the closest-clipped of them in its actuality against curtain or canvas—it will suit about as well as a brier path in a bed of tulips.

To invent a new hieroglyphic language of scenery, that, in a phrase, is the problem. Come to the more difficult aspects of it. What about a forest of Arden? As I hope never to produce the play, my proposal is sufficiently disinterested. Let the Daily———, that organ ever in the vanguard of theatrical progress, offer a prize of £50 for the best design for the Forest Scene in "As You Like It", to set against some conventional background, to be decorative, therefore, not realistic, and to be uncumbrous. Trial and Error is the quickest road forward.

My space is filled. I have not dealt with the minor problems of the traverse-scenes, front-cloths, or front-curtains—call them either of the three—but that is but a shadow of the other.

Faithfully yours,
H. Granville Barker

---

1. A popular weekly magazine: its contents—as its name implies—consisted chiefly of photographs of theater productions, but it also carried some reviews. It ceased publication in the twenties.

TEX/MS
To R. A. Scott-James

18, Place des Etats-Unis,
Paris, XVI
October 27

My dear Scott-James,

You put me to shame. And my hair is burnt to a sizzle. I knew, of course, that "the higher criticism" was your job: but I did not know—and I should have done—this book. For which all my thanks. Your reply to me might well have been: now you've done some criticising of Shakespeare, why don't you try and write a play yourself?

But I don't mind giving myself away to you. I had no proper "critical foundations" (which everyone ought to have) when I started in on Shakespeare (in which one has to specialise): indeed I must—if you ever read the stuff—give myself away to you on every page. And if ever you should want to get back at me, look up my preface to Tolstoy's plays in the collected edition. I had—for conscience' sake—to tackle What is Art? and the old gentleman, denying all the usual premises, is not an easy person to tackle in sheer argument; or so I found, and barked my shins badly.

But sound, severe, impersonal (not the "This book gives me the pip but I really don't know why" sort) is what we even more desperately want. And, incidentally, it is what—back-scratching and venality apart—you can still get over here.

Come and tackle my Waste for me: and I'll bet you a dinner that I can find bigger faults in it than you can—however the many.

Again, thank you. I hope we meet soon.

Yours,
Harley Granville-Barker

TEX/MS
To R. A. Scott-James

Delfter-Hof,
St. Jakobstrasse 8,
Basel,
Switzerland.
Sept. 24, 1936

My dear Scott-James,

There are 2½ slips of comparatively amusing stuff which I have had to cut out of the Hamlet book. You might like them. You may well find them too scrappy. I shall appreciate the point if you do. I'll do my best to tidy them up and send them to you in about 10 days' time—when (as I hope) I'll be free of the rest of the proof. Good of you to remind me.

Yours,
Harley Granville-Barker

I'll have to ask Sidgwick and Jackson; and you'll have to mention—if you don't mind—that the stuff comes from their book.

TEX/MS
To R. A. Scott-James

Delfter-Hof,
St. Jakobstrasse 8,
Basel,
Switzerland.
Octo. 8, 1936

My dear Scott-James,

Here is the Hamlet scrap. If you find it too scrappy I shall be neither vexed nor surprised; for indeed it seems so to me. But it is all I have. If, however, you do want to use it, will you then, please, ring up Frank Sidgwick and arrange with him about any "acknowledgement" or the like. He may want it not to appear till December. But don't ring him up till Monday morning (Sat., I suppose, a dies non) or he won't know what the devil it is all about—till I have been able to send him the rest of the proof and explain.

I slip into the envelope my wife's last book, as S. & J. must be just about to publish it and in the autumn rush it may have escaped your editorial eye.[1] If you don't know the original of the Poilu—the last thing—read the translation of it and tell me if you get through without wanting to cry![2] I have made a dozen attempts to read it aloud and there is one point at which—though I'm a hardened soul—I unashamedly break down. And then tell me in what the peculiar "art" of the thing lies. The original patois is devilishly difficult, impossible, to read in English.

I tell my wife she ought sometimes to send you one or two of her own poems. Squire used to ask for and print them occasionally. But she is shy of editors!

Sorry the <u>Hamlet</u> thing is no better.

Yours,
Harley Granville-Barker

---

1. The book he enclosed was an anthology which Helen Granville-Barker had put together called *The Locked Book,* a collection of verse and prose pieces about angels.
2. The last item in the collection is Helen's translation of part of a poem by Marc Leclerc called "La Passion de Notre Frère le Poilu," about which she says in her introduction, "At Verdun, during the Great War, Marc Leclerc wrote (in the *patois* of Anjou) a poem about a French poilu, difficult, almost impossible, to translate. It was first printed in the columns of the *Echo de Paris* and afterwards published, in book form with a preface by Rene Bazin." Though Helen did not note the fact in her Introduction, it was first translated into English by Arthur Guiterman and published by him in *The Bookman*—New York, not London—in December, 1918.

TEX/MS
To R. A. Scott-James

18, Place des Etats-Unis,
[Paris] XVI
Jan. 1, 1937

My dear Scott-James,

A happy new year!

Again you do me proud—and prompt!—and again I thank you very heartily.

You put your critical finger on a tiresome weakness when you say that I am too apt to find reason for praising mere lapses. It is true. But the confounded fellow (W. S.) has such a knack of pulling out of his errors with credit. He has "had" me once or twice in times past. I become over-careful now. I challenge, however, the instance you pick upon, or rather your own exposure of it. W. S. had no <u>need</u> at all to put the narration (of O's death) into the mouth of the Queen. He had used a "gentleman" to describe her madness: there were 3 or 4 more as obvious ways.

But my main fault—your review lets me see—is that I have not bridged the gulf between your mainly literary standpoint and my dramatic standpoint, from which plays are only <u>incidentally</u> literature; and in this there is no difference between Hamlet and the cheapest

farce—if that is a good play. I must do this somehow or I shall have
written in vain. I'm almost tempted to say sometimes that drama is as
near to music as it is far from literature.

Well, we'll see. But again, thank you for the generous
things—most generous—that you do say. (I don't know, by the way,
what the deuce you mean by "his pacifist speech to Fortinbras".)

Yours,
Harley Granville-Barker

COR/MS
To Alan S. Downer[1]

Mayfair House,
Park Avenue at 65th Street
New York.
March 5, 1944

My dear Alan Downer,

Forgive this delay. I evidently didn't make myself clear
about Othello. My point was that having exercised one's imagination
to create—with WS's help—Venice and Cyprus out of a bare stage
and Desdemona and Emilia—ditto, ditto, plus a Pavy or a Field, out
of the two boys,[2] a Duke of Venice, if you like, out of Mr. Lowin,[3] it
would be jarred by a sudden transportation to the realm of realism: a
real Moor, insistently that, presenting a real Moor. Whisperings
round the theatre: "That's a real Moor, you know." A disadvantage
to him in his performance to be on a different plane.

Well, you couldn't expect The Way of the World to be a
success, could you, if it beat Betterton and his probably quite accomplished company.[4] But what a blessing for you that you don't need it
to be a success as wretched professionals do. So now you all know
something about it, as they never will. Yes, if we can discuss the
author's technique and the actors' and arrive at something near to an
understanding of the vanished audience, we could get lots out of even
the second-rate drama of the past, I do believe. And the W of the W
I find first-rate.

Finally, for that trenchant review of Mr. O. W.[5] I congratulate you. This needed saying and very justly you say it. I must, I
believe, have been taken up to Harlem (by silly people in search of
sillier sensation) to see that Macbeth. As much of an insult to the
negro players (who, left to themselves, would have been simple and
sincere) as to W. S. and us! It really does not pay to treat him[6] as an
Aunt Sally. Yet in the cinema—how admirable his life of Mr.

Hearst![7] But the drama is an old—if not yet wholly respectable—art. And little streetboys must not scribble their fooleries all over it and redden the tip of its nose.

Kind remembrances to your students, and my acquaintances of the faculty, and you. Do look me up if you come to New York.

Yours,
Harley Granville-Barker

---

1. Alan Seymour Downer (1912–1972) was a distinguished American professor of English literature. He graduated from Harvard in 1934, was an assistant professor at Wells College from 1939 to 1946, and was a member of the faculty of Princeton University from 1946 until his death. His 1955 anthology, *The Art of the Play*, is dedicated to the memory of Harley Granville-Barker, and in its Preface he refers to and quotes from this letter of Barker's.
2. Salathiel Pavy (1590–1603) and Nathan Field (1587–1620) were boy actors at the Blackfriars Theatre at the time of the first production of *Othello*.
3. John Lowine or Lowin (1576–1653) was one of the best-known players in Shakespeare's company. His name appears among the "Names of the Principall Actors" in the First Folio of 1623.
4. The first production of Congreve's *The Way of the World*, in 1700, by Thomas Betterton and his company, was not well received.
5. "Mr. O. W." is Orson Welles. Downer had published an unfavorable review of Welles' 1936–37 production, with the People's Negro Theatre, of *Macbeth*.
6. Shakespeare.
7. *Citizen Kane*, the Orson Welles film of 1940.

Censorship

BERG/handwritten by a secretary but signed by Barker
To Sir Edward Marsh[1]

3, Clement's Inn,
[London], W.C.
12 June '08

My dear Marsh,

The position is this: Herbert Gladstone undertook to report the Deputation to the Prime Minister, and presumably to transmit his answer. I suppose he feels that C-B's retirement and death[2] absolved him from doing anything. We don't.

There are, I suppose, two things the Government might do by lifting its finger: (1) Abolish the office of Reader of Plays altogether, leaving the Lord Chamberlain just the shell of his authority; or (2) establish the Court of Appeal which the Deputation suggested. Whether both or either or neither of these is possible without legislation the Law Officers ought to know by this time: I believe they started to find out nearly a year ago. Of course what we want is abolition, but we'd take the Court of Appeal as an interim measure, giving us time to prove that we could behave ourselves. But if it's a question of legislation, I suppose we might as well ask the Government for it directly as ask for the moon, so a Bill is being drafted amending the whole law about licensing places of amusement, which is fearfully chaotic (the music halls are administered partly under an Eighteenth Century Act, partly by a tacit understanding that certain other acts relating to disorderly houses shan't be applied, and of course the litigation about the sketch question is perennial.)

Charles Trevelyan is to introduce it in the Commons and I think Lytton may look after it as far as the Lords are concerned. And it's proposed if possible to get it on the paper (I think that's the correct expression) this Session.

Now I suppose next Session or the Session after the Government might star it, if it seems likely not to take too much time in passing, at least this is presumably the thing to aim for. This is as much as I know, and if there's anything I can or ought to do, you might let me hear, for I'm only in town until Wednesday morning.

Very sincerely yours,
H. Granville Barker

1. For a brief note on Marsh, see Chapter X, footnote on p. 482.
2. Sir Henry Campbell-Bannerman, the Prime Minister, who died in 1908.

Published letter
To *The Times*

Netherton Hall,
Colyton,
Devon.
July 18, 1931

Sir,

Now that the "Sunday performances" Bill is to be reported to the House of Commons with the theatres excluded from its benefit, will it be furnished with a firm definition of what is meant by a "theatre" and a "stage play", and one likely to be effective for, say, the next 10 years or so? Under the new Act is a manager, having performed a play with living actors during the week, to be able to open his theatre on Sundays with a mechanical performance (stereo-scopic screen, life-size figures, perfect vocal reproduction, and all the wonders which the "Talkie" now promises) of the same play by the same actors? And if not, why not? Is he to need the Lord Chamberlain's licence for the one form of the play (as he now does) and not for the other (as he now does not)? And if so, why? How long, in fact, will it be before the theatre managers contrive, if they choose, to make the new state of the law look as ridiculous as the cinema managers made the old?

Is it really worth Parliament's while to replace one legislative anomaly by another? Sooner or later the whole state of the law of the theatre in England will have to be considered, definitions of "public" and "private" performances arrived at, and a number of other vexed questions straightened out. When that happens, one may hope that, at long last, its interests as an art as well as an industry may be taken into account. Meanwhile, with people's minds absorbed by more immediately vital questions, would it not be better (if this is a practical proposal) to pass a short Act temporarily indemnifying the cinemas and the local authorities for their offence against an obsolete law? I imagine that even its promoters are not enthusiastic over a Bill whose outstanding secondary achievement seems to be the giving of the capital invested in the cinema a 14½ per cent. advantage over the capital invested in the theatre: in effect, the protection, under the admired guise of respect for the English Sunday and the recognized need of actors for a day of rest, of a largely foreign industry against a national one.

I am faithfully yours,
Harley Granville-Barker

Publishing

BTM/TS
To Frank Sidgwick[1]

Royal Court Theatre,
Sloane Square,
[London], S.W.
April 20, 1906

Dear Mr. Sidgwick,

I have behaved disgracefully in not writing to you about "The Voysey Inheritance". I went straight to Heinemann after seeing you and he said that he expected to publish it, so there I left the matter and nothing has since happened. The whole thing has gone quite out of my head and hence I forgot even to write you. Please forgive me.

About "Prunella": would you care to come and see it? There is no MS we could send you just for the moment but if you like to come on Tuesday afternoon write to the box office and say you will be there, I have asked them to reserve a seat for you. I spoke to Housman about the publication and he said he would only care to do illustrations to it if they were to be reproduced from wood-cuts done by his sister (he does the drawing and she cuts them). I also think that excerpts from the music should be printed too. This would make, of course, a fairly expensive book but if you care to entertain the matter we should be very glad to discuss it with you. I go abroad on Tuesday but Housman or my partner Vedrenne can arrange my business with you in my absence.

Very faithfully yours,
H. Granville Barker

---

1. Sidgwick was at this time an editor for A. H. Bullen, the publisher. He established the firm of Sidgwick and Jackson in 1908.

BTM/TS
To Sidgwick

Royal Court Theatre,
Sloane Square,
[London], S.W.
Oct. 22nd, 1906.

Dear Sidgwick,

Many thanks for the Shavers Calendar which I like very much to have.

It is exceedingly annoying about Brentanos and I hope Lippincotts will accept it; but if not, clearly Housman and I must have it done. However, can you not give us some idea of cost, for although we hope otherwise I take it neither he and I nor you expect vast profits on the sale of "Prunella" in London.

I have long desired "A Court Theatre Series" but it is almost impossible to get it complete. If you could engineer a combination, then—!

Yours very sincerely,
H. G. Barker

BTM/handwritten by a secretary but signed by Barker
To Sidgwick

Court Theatre,
London
4 June, 1907

My dear Sidgwick,
    You write me the kindest and most charming of letters. Let us know then when you decide about the book and we'll give you any assistance you want.

Always sincerely yours,
H. G. Barker

BTM/handwritten by a secretary but signed by Barker
To Sidgwick

Savoy Theatre,
[London]
23 Sept., 1907

Dear Sidgwick,
    Now the book is out,[1] it suddenly occurs to me that I have never thanked you for it. It is the thing that has pleased me most among the many kind things that have been said & done on our leaving the Court. You know you're the only publisher in London who would have taken the interest to do it, so I needn't inform you of that, but thanks all the same.
    Here is a point. Langdon Coburn has it in his mind to do photographs (you know his photographs, don't you?) of our authors, & of three or four of the actors who have made remarkable successes in parts—in those parts. One object is to hang them in front of our theatre—inside, not out—and Coburn suggested that another & more important might be to include reproductions of them in another edition of MacCarthy's book. Is there anything in this, do you think?

Yours very sincerely,
H. Granville Barker

---

1. Desmond MacCarthy's *The Court Theatre, 1904–1907* (London, 1907).

BTM/handwritten by a secretary but signed by Barker
To Sidgwick

Duke of York's Theatre,
London
May 4, 1910

Dear Sidgwick,

a) If I could get a clear five days from today;

b) if Hampton's Magazine made up its mind to publish The Madras House—a project they're considering;

c) if we could agree without more than four letters on either side that 12 copies are 12 and not 13, and incidentally that you ought to advertise books about twice as much as you do;

then, <u>if you'd like</u>, there might be some chance of whacking The Madras House out at once. But what about a general election (possibly in <u>July</u>, I hear?)

Yours,
H. G. Barker

BTM/hand written by a secretary but signed by Barker
To Sidgwick

Duke of York's Theatre,
[London]
May 9, 1910

Dear Sidgwick,

As to advertisements, right you are. Give me 25% and don't advertise at all.

The King's death gives me breathing space and I'm already at work on the stage directions. Shall I send you the copy act by act?

I'll discover from Hampton's as soon as possible what they mean to do.

Yours,
H. G. Barker

BTM/MS
To Sidgwick

> Court Lodge,
> Stansted,
> Wrotham,
> Kent.
> August 18 [1910]

Dear Sidgwick,

I am the most patient of men but when are my proofs to arrive? It is really necessary, I think, that the play should be out in a month's time.

Would you care to publish Schnitzler's Anatol—translated possibly by Maurice Baring—if I were playing four or five of them[1] and you could sell them on the spot. (I think there'll be a sale otherwise.) You'd have to get it out in a little under 5 years from receiving the copy!

> Yours,
> H. G. Barker

---

1. He means four or five of the short plays which make up the composite piece called *Anatol*. (See also Chapter V, letter of February, 1911, to Murray, and the letter of October, 1910, to Sidgwick, below.)

BTM/MS
To Sidgwick

> Court Lodge,
> Stansted,
> Wrotham,
> Kent
> Monday [1910]

Dear Sidgwick,

Yes, the rights of Anatol would be all right. I think that properly translated or rather rendered it would be all right. Do I gather from you that the version you saw was not good or is it worthwhile your sending me the man's address, in case? But anyhow will you say what is the best publishing proposal you can make on the Baring supposition. It won't be to me you'll really make it, so don't go on the supposition that I shall immediately say "Double".

> Yours,
> H. G. Barker

BTM/MS
To Sidgwick

St. Enoch Hotel,
Glasgow.
Monday [October, 1910]

Dear Sidgwick,

I don't mind sending you a receipt but I can't live on that! You and J. must go out with sandwich boards.

Hurry up with that blessed M. House: it will increase the other sales.

Samuel never answered me. Baring won't do that job: suggests H. Munro ("Saki").[1] Do you know him, or anything of him?

You mustn't go out of your way over "Playgoing in Berlin". If I do it in that form I think it does want somebody with a bookstall habit—Fifield or the like.[2]

Yours,
H. G. Barker

---

1. Munro also declined to do the translation, and finally Barker decided to do an English version of the Schnitzler play himself. As he knew no German, he enlisted the help of his friend C. E. Wheeler. Wheeler made a literal translation of the German text and Barker then wrote idiomatic dialogue from this. (See his reference to the "Barker scenes" in the postscript of his letter of January 24, 1911, below.)
2. It was, in fact, never published in any form and is now, so far as we know, lost.

BTM/MS
To Sidgwick

Court Lodge,
Stansted,
Wrotham,
Kent.
Tues. 1910

Dear Sidgwick,

Does my not hearing mean that the M. H.[1] plates have or have not arrived? Because do let me impress on you again that if you don't get it out a week or more—in fact 3 weeks—clear of Shaw he will wreck all our reviews and our first sales—as you don't advertise.

I shall try to look in to see you tomorrow after 5 about Anatol.

Yours,
H. G. Barker

---

1. *Madras House.*

BTM/MS
To Sidgwick

Court Lodge,
Stansted,
Wrotham,
Kent.
Friday [1910]

Dear S and J,

One further matter.

Of course I have no actual right to complain about your using the design found for my plays for Lady Bell's.[1] But I dislike it, all the same. I have every objection to being, or appearing, one of a series. If the colour also had not been the same it would not matter quite so much. As it is I think you had better consider, if you will, whether not to alter mine for the future.

Yours,
H. G. Barker

---

1. Lady Florence Bell, wife of Hugh Bell, was the author of a number of minor plays, such as *The Dean of St. Patrick's* (1903), *The Way the Money Goes,* 1910, etc.

BTM/MS
To Sidgwick

Court Lodge,
Stansted,
Wrotham,
Kent.
Sunday [1910]

Dear Sidgwick,

Here's the proof with my suggested corrections though ultimately use your judgment about them.

John Street doesn't cancel this address, only Alexandra Court.

My objections on the "series" question remain and are my real ones. I'll take them up again at the next opportune moment. I presume, that is, that your covers for the M. H. are actually done, otherwise the moment could as well be now.

Yours,
H. G. Barker

BTM/part TS, part MS
To Sidgwick

> 17, John Street,
> Adelphi,
> [London]
> Jan. 24, 1911

Dear Sidgwick and Jackson,

Will you please read this letter carefully and ponder it in your hearts? I begin by saying that without doubt I am in some ways an awkward client, what with my American muddle and one thing and another. But that being admitted, please tell me are you as publishers all that I have right to expect?

I came to you, as I think you know, not for the sake of your beautiful eyes, though I admire them very much; but quite cold-bloodedly picking you out as a "small" firm among "big" ones and among small firms for what I hoped you were.

Well now, are you? I hope you are, but please convince me:

1) You are always charming to deal with (if I may say so) and that is a distinct business asset;

2) You make up books very nicely;

3) You are not a banker of a publisher but that is to the good because I object to advances on principle and it teaches me not to run short of cash (see P.S.);

4) You are in perennial difficulties with your binders. Are all publishers like that? I as an ordinary customer have in three weeks only been able to extract a dozen or eighteen copies of the Madras House from you and it seems I can have no more for a week or ten days. If you treat other customers the same, I should think they would proceed to sell and buy other goods;

5) Your publicity department seems ineffective. I read all the papers and rather more than a normal man reads and I have not seen one solitary paragraph about The Madras House nor about Anatol. Nor have I seen a single advertisement. Incidentally, Jackson has the colossal cheek to ask me to start a correspondence in The Morning Leader!! (Apparently to do this part of your job for you).

What is your reply to all this? You are in partnership with me over a certain property of mine. What are you doing off your own bat to exploit that property?

Have you, because you are Sidgwick & Jackson, done anything but what Smith & Jones would have done? Why should I not prefer Smith & Jones to you?

> Yours,
> H. Granville Barker

P.S. As I sign this letter, comes yours of today. Thanks about money but if it really is as inconvenient to you as that—as it is to me to do without it—I will do without it, for I actually can. About Anatol: that is agreed with the rider that after expenses are cleared we start de novo on the Barker scenes—and that the copyright of the book stands in my name. That was part of our conversation (Barker's with Sidgwick) was it not?

H. G. B.

BTM/TS
To Sidgwick

Kingsway Theatre,
Great Queen Street,
[London], W.C.
February 25, 1913

My dear Sidgwick,

As to your publishing house I constantly reserve my opinion. As to you, as the angel who prevents me from appearing all anyhow in print, I am unreservedly grateful, and I marvel at your goodness and patience.

Yours,
H. G. B.

BTM/MS
To Sidgwick

Netherton Hall,
Honiton,
S. Devon.
1.6.20

My dear Sidgwick,

So glad to hear from you! Here I am and to be found more or less always. Whenever you're within reach you'd be most welcome—Devonshire hills restore one's faith in England: yes, every bit as well as the Cotswolds (more than enough be-sung); these wait their singer. Perhaps my wife may qualify; she's more English than I—at a 400 years' jump, so to speak. Anyhow, here we are—have forsworn London for work and quiet. There is a telephone, but no one uses it!

I can't date the Synge correspondence. It must have been

just before I left the Court for the Savoy. Two or three letters passed about the T. W.[1] I never met him. I much wish I had.

Amateur rights of the plays—send to Author's Society: they work for us.

Do let us meet sometime, somehow.

Yours,

H. Granville-Barker

I have now acquired a hyphen—so that for new editions you can annoy the biblio-maniacs a bit more![2]

---

1. *The Tinker's Wedding,* a two-act play by J. M. Synge, was published in 1908 (though Synge had been writing it, intermittently, since 1902). It was first produced in 1909, though not by Barker, who never directed any Synge play. Barker's move from the Court Theatre to the Savoy, to which he refers in this letter, was in the autumn of 1907; Synge died on March 24, 1909, at the age of thirty-eight.
2. See Chapter II above, footnote to letter to William Archer of December 13, 1921, and the comment on Barker's name in the Prefatory Note to this volume.

TEX/TS
To Alfred Knopf[1]

Kingsway Theatre,
Great Queen Street,
[London], W.C.
Oct. 18th, 1913

My dear Mr. Knopf,

Thanks for your letter. It has been mislaid for the moment and there is only one part of it I can write to you about now. That is about publishing Prunella. If all the publishers in America were on the verge of bankruptcy, yet would neither Housman nor I consider taking ten per cent on any book whatever. In the first place it would not save them. I do not know American figures of course but I do know the English ones and though the English publishers' cry is just the same as yours the hard-fisted author can only reply with one word—"nonsense": and books get published just the same, and I personally have 20% for mine from the very first and I intend in future to get 25%. That being said it really is rather foolish that Prunella is not being printed in America as the production is very near at hand. I gave Mitchell Kennerly the chance of it, of which he has not availed himself (no more about that subject for the moment). If Doubleday Page care to do it and will give us 15% up to the time when the book begins to pay them and 20% when it is paying them (on the gross of course, not on the profits) then we will be very pleased to have it done and will leave format and price and that sort of thing entirely to their discretion, only suggesting that to sell in the theatres over here we found it advisable to have shilling copies in paper covers and that some sort of parallel to this in America would probably be a good thing. On that point, however, you might communicate with Winthrop Ames who is bringing out the play and will possibly under-write a certain number of copies.

Very sincerely yours,
H. Granville Barker

1. Knopf at that time was with Doubleday Page and Company, New York. He founded his own publishing house in 1915.

TEX/TS
To Hugh Walpole[1]

Netherton Hall,
Colyton,
Devon.
19th July, 1928

My dear Hugh,

As you see, I am editing this volume on the '70s. Please add to my credit by giving us a paper. We discussed the chance you would at a small meeting; De la Mare who would (will, I hope) be your opposite number with "Women Novelists of the '70s", swearing that you knew more about the subject than anyone, and that your house was full of matter as well as your head! So please let us have a taste of it.

I wish one sometime saw you. You did loom up magnificently to our view for a moment at the Academy, but the moment passed and you with it.

Very sincerely yours,
Harley Granville-Barker

1. See footnote 1, p. 342.

TEX/MS
To Walpole

Netherton Hall,
Colyton,
Devon.
1.8.28

My dear Hugh,

Bully!—as they used occasionally to say in the long, long
(<u>i.e.</u> six years) ago in America. What they now say I know not. You
are less the stranger to G. O. C.[1] now than we are!—<u>and</u> thank you.

I believe we shall be quite a nice little publisher's party.
When the list is complete (I lack 2 subjects still and 3 distinguished
authors) I'll send it you.

Length: anything, I should say, between 7,000 and 10,000
words. I find myself I lecture at about 8,000; and sometimes write it
(after) down to 7,000 or up to 10,000. Quotations help.

When: I'll get Wagstaff to offer you all possible latitude.
And if you lecture late and mean to write first, I'll get it out of you
and into proof first. For I want to get the book out by Easter. He has
explained that they guard you your copyright, etc.

Yet again—Bully! and thank you. "Brackenburn" means
you're at a book.[2] The Lord prosper it, you and more also. Shakespeare is heavy on my chest and will be till the year ends. My wife's
translating bits from a lively Spanish man—though <u>she</u> ought to be at
work of her own, if I'm not, I tell her.

I love Devon: but it slackens one if one doesn't look out.

Yes, let us meet sometime. Kind thoughts meanwhile; and I
like to think I have yours, as you always have mine.

Yours,
H. G-B.

P.S. and N.B. Don't feel yourself tied to a general survey (unless you
prefer that). My notion was to pick one significant work or man who
had been, or were in underserved danger of being, forgotten: to res-
urrect them a bit, not to lay a wreath on their tombs.

---

1. God's Own Country.
2. Brackenburn was the name of Hugh Walpole's country house.

TEX/PC
To Walpole

Tucson,
Arizona.
19.2.29

My dear Hugh,

Your 1870 paper has at last found its way home (with others
for the American edition). What a jolly bit of work—and <u>sane</u>, sane
all through. And I thank you and so will the R. S. L.[1] I'm very glad
H. K.[2] gets your good word—and that Jinx turned up trumps. Proof
correcting: all your editor has to ask is to change any phrasing that
makes it seem a <u>lecture</u> instead of a paper, when you conveniently
can.

Our affectionate regards to you,
H. G-B.

---

1. Royal Society of Literature.
2. Henry Kingsley (1830–1876), novelist, younger brother of Charles Kingsley.

BERG/MS
To Sir Edward Marsh[1]

Netherton Hall,
Colyton,
Devon.
16.7.29

My dear Eddie,

I looked for the familiar "Harley" and set you an example
(after 25 years, about); but, by Jove, no—if you were a child
throughout the 70s, you're my senior and, in memory of the civil 70s
R. I. P., I should show you respect!

I'm tempted to take the credit of sending you the book. But
honesty, my handicap through life, bars the way. You've apparently
forgotten (most of 'em do) that you are a <u>Fellow</u> of the R. S. L. You
have only had your due. But I'll tell you another thing. You were
booked—as a Fellow—for a paper in that series, only most regret-
fully I had to cut your subject out. I give you two guesses about what
it was. You'll have to do one for the pending 80s, though. I shan't be
editor, praise God; but "An Adolescent of the Eighties" is clearly
marked out for <u>you</u>. No excuses. I suspect you now to be leading an
idle, literary life.

I claim your thanks for the book, all the same. After all, I did send it you, in a sense. And the arms on the cover were 2/- extra. When your friends, on your recommendation, buy copies (don't you lend yours) they get <u>no</u> arms. Only <u>Fellows</u> may sport them.

As ever, yours,
Harley G-B

1. See Chapter X, footnote on p. 482.

TEX/MS
To R. A. Scott-James

18, Place des Etats-Unis,
[Paris], XVI
Oct. 7. 1934

My dear Mr. Scott-James,

It is most good of you to ask me; but for the moment I <u>am</u> rather badly tied up with work from which I mustn't turn aside.

If you happened, however, to want something still for the next number, there is just this possibility: the Cambridge University Press is publishing a lecture which I gave at Cambridge in August,[1] and I have added a number of so-called "notes" to it, some of them running to a couple of thousand words. S. C. Roberts definitely didn't want the lecture published in a periodical, but he might feel differently about one of these notes (if you inscribed it as an extract from the coming book). There is one on—and against!—Freudianism in literature which might do: but you could make your choice.

If this is a possibility, perhaps you'd ring up Roberts and ask him. Please only add from me that I don't wish or ask him to do anything which he doesn't think advantageous.

I am sorry only to be able to make such a "left-handed" suggestion in response to a request which it gives me such pleasure to have received. I am an original subscriber to the Mercury and I look forward to seeing the volumes piling up prosperously under your editorship. May I add my good wishes.

Yours,
Harley Granville-Barker

I have duplicate copies of the "notes" here, besides those that the C. U. P. is now setting up from.

1. *The Study of Drama.*

TEX/MS
To R. A. Scott-James

8, St. Jakobstrasse,
Basel,
Switzerland.
Aug. 23, 1936

My dear Scott-James,
    (may we not mutually drop honorifics?)
    It is most good of you to ask me. I am (please God) finishing and pushing a long-delayed book on <u>Hamlet</u> through the press; started today on the proofs. If there were any extractable and sufficiently interesting portion of that which you might fancy—! I rather fear you wouldn't; but if I come across a likely-looking piece, I'll send it to you to see. This will take me all September. After that—? Well, yes; if you could do with something which you have to divide into two, there <u>is</u> a possibility. I'll write to you again about that, if I may and am in a position to.
    Meanwhile I remain, at least, your faithful subscriber and reader.

Yours,
Harley Granville-Barker

TEX/MS
To R. A. Scott-James

Delfter-Hof,
St. Jakobstrasse, 8,
[Basel, Switzerland]
Oct. 16, [1936]

My dear Scott-James,
    The proof of that Hamlet scrap lost 24 hours by being sent to Paris; but I have sent it off to you this morning by air-mail. It is very good of you to print the thing—which is an awful "scrap". I wish I had had something better for you.
    You <u>nearly</u> hit what hits me in the Poilu.[1] The actual point where I give <u>in</u> is:

Behold the tricolour, he said . . .

But I think I <u>can</u> explain how Leclerc does it—though I daresay he can't. He <u>uses</u>, in that:

St. Thomas said: O holy name
Of Jesus, 'tis the very same

the Bible episode which came most home (almost to ours—yours, mine and his—generation of intellectually-conscientiously doubting Thomases (small beer that sort of thing seemed when the war was on)). From this he goes straight to the child's picture-book effect of:

> The Virgin Mother's long blue cloak,
> God's great white beard that saints invoke,
> And Christ, our Saviour's, robe of red . . .

—a daring contrast; your sophisticated poet would think it bad taste. But it <u>gets</u> <u>straight</u> at the child in us, beneath the doubting Thomas. From this he goes as straight to the thought of <u>why</u> he died; the

> Behold the tricolour . . .

with its association of God and Country: the simple poilu, who has taken both for granted, having the reality and all-but-identity of the two brought home to him.

No, I find it an extraordinary piece of art. It gives me just the aesthetic pleasure that an unusual but effective juxtaposition of colours does in a picture. And I don't find that this kills the emotional effect on me. God forbid I should hold that the poet got his effect by thinking it out this way (his secret is, I suppose, something akin to the perfect co-ordination of mind and muscle of the young airman; mind and feeling in the poet's case) or that the critic by finding out how it is done can teach him how to do it. But the reader can be made more sensitive to poetry in general and brought to derive a double enjoyment from it, aesthetic and emotional—well, there we are on a very old track. But I have never had the problem satisfactorily worked out for me. Those fellows at Cambridge are too clever. Undigested Freud is a curse—oh, what a curse! Here's a spare-time task for you!

Yes, do let us meet in London. We shall be there (at the Ritz) towards the end of the month. I'll ring you up.

<u>Here</u> till the 19th. Then, 18, Place des Etats-Unis, Paris, for a few days.

Yours,
Harley Granville-Barker

---

1. See letter to Scott-James of October 8, 1936, p. 532.

TEX/MS
To R. A. Scott-James

18, Place des Etats-Unis,
[Paris], XVI
Dec. 2 [1937]

My dear Scott-James,

These three poems I send you are my wife's, not mine; and
as it is rather odd, you may think, that I send them, not she, let me
explain.

She accumulates a few from time to time and reads them to
me. I comment on them; then she puts them away in her drawer
again. So I occasionally steal two or three I like and send them. I
think, perhaps, I've only ever sent them to Squire, who used to print
them now and then in the Mercury.

A foolish practice, it will seem to you. But, while she rather
likes—is, indeed, pleased—to have them printed, nothing will induce
her to "submit" them in the usual way. Useless arguing. So when I
like them—as I do these three, for I find her very deft at what she
calls her experiments in metre—I occasionally now do.

You may not like them, in which case, no harm is done.
Send them back to me. But if you do, send me a proof for she'd want
to work over them. (If you haven't liked them, she'll not know
they've been sent.)

Forgive me, in any case, the "unusual".

Yours,
Harley Granville-Barker

TEX/MS
To R. A. Scott-James

Gleneagles Hotel,
Scotland.
June 26 [1938]

My dear Scott-James,

I have just seen a—to me, and I believe it might be to
you—most interesting thing upon the origins of Ibsen's "Doll's
House" (1,000 words, I should say) which Charles Archer has translated from the Norwegian. I have recommended him to paraphrase it
instead, since it isn't, strictly speaking, literature and that will take
the unavoidable stiffness out of the translation, and to sent it to you.
But he is backward in such matters, so I recommend you to write to

him. He is, you know, William Archer's younger brother and collaborated in the Peer Gynt translation. His title and address are:

> Colonel Charles Archer, C. F. I.,
> Ramley,
> Worpleston,
> Guildford.
>   —though I daresay you know him quite well.

Kind regards. I hope the Mercury prospers as you wish.
You make it—may one say?—most interesting.

Yours,
Harley Granville-Barker

TEX/MS
To R. A. Scott-James

Park-Hotel Waldhaus,
360, Betten,
Flims-Waldhaus.
Aug. 30 1938

My dear Scott-James,

I would if I could. I'm sure it is a pretty good book. And it is short. And that's—it is I who say it—a virtue. I have the book, in fact. And I started in on it. But for all its promise I just could not go on. This dog could not return to his vomit. <u>Hamlet</u> will be a barred subject to me for years. I had to go through my own book for a second edition. I could not even read <u>that</u>.

Very sorry!

Yours,
Harley Granville-Barker

I'm glad you caught on to that Doll's House thing of Charles Archer's. It is hard to get stuff out of him. Of an appalling modesty. But he knows a lot. He has, too—though they were printed in some odd Norwegian journal—a lot of letters W. A. wrote him about his meetings with Ibsen in Rome about the time <u>Ghosts</u> was on the stocks. Most interesting—to us who <u>are</u> interested in such things.

TEX/MS
To R. A. Scott-James

18, Place des Etats-Unis,
[Paris], XVI
March 3, 1939

My dear Scott-James,

I am deeply vexed—for you, after all your work; for the British public, the righteous few, who will now lose the only thing worth having of its quite important sort.[1] The unrighteous many will now be left with what they deserve.

But you have been deserving so well lately that really I had strong hopes you were pulling through and I am the more deeply vexed for this. Well, it is 5/6 income tax in the £1, I suppose. We cannot have war and preparations for war and literature too—that is all about it. The Dictators strangle their own and we boast that we are left free. But indirectly they strangle ours as well.

You must not feel this is in any sense a personal defeat, nor one for the spirit in which you have kept the Mercury alive. That you have made tell: and, if I may say so, with a fine courage and intention which will not be forgotten.

Yeats' death brings down the curtain too. And my first touch with him was over The Land of Heart's Desire, 1893-5-7? I can't remember. But it is one of those patterns in life which one remarks.

Again—though it is small comfort to say so, and to have no more to say—I am vexed and grieved for you: yes, and angry to see such good and loyal work so ill-rewarded. Yes, angry.

Yours,
Harley Granville-Barker

---

1. He is referring to the demise of the *Mercury,* which ceased publication in February.

Theater Societies and Organizations

WHIT/MS
To Geoffrey Whitworth[1]

Connaught Hotel,
[London], W.
1.7.19

My dear Whitworth,

Here is a very rough memorandum of my present views on the Drama League, which I hope may be of some use to you.

Looking ahead for pitfalls I believe the chief danger is our centralisation. If there is to be any new and <u>healthy</u> growth of drama in this country, it will not be in the West End of London.

An Executive, active in London interests, will tend to depress and not encourage that growth. Not only so, but seven or eight brilliant people, with the weight of the movement on their shoulders, made to feel that initiative must come from them, will—all probably being persons of strongly developed and conflicting opinions—tend to neutralize each other. They will not submit to being "run" by a secretary, even if a secretary could be found to run them. That way, the League may become a mere manifesto-issuing body. To prevent this—and other evils of the same origin—I suggest some such plan as the following:—

1) Foreign Drama (chairman, say, Edith Craig): to be a link with any theatres or similar organizations abroad who want to get in touch with the English movements. I believe there is quite a field for this. Also some of the foreign theatres, especially those of the "new" nations, will be very keen on sending their companies to England and perhaps on doing English plays.

2) Training in Acting and the Professional Status of the actor (chairman, say, Fisher White): link with the A. A.[2] More importantly, to keep in touch with all dramatic schools and methods of training here and abroad.

3) On "Decoration", as N. W.[3] and I used to call it: Look after this "Workshop" and all it may involve.

4) On Repertory Theatres proper (chairman: John Drinkwater).

5) On Village Theatres, "Community" movements, Pageants, etc., a link with the Folk Dance people, etc. Personally I think this is the most important field for the near future.

6) On dramatic teaching in Schools and Universities: there is much to be done over this—and much to be made public that is already being done, especially in America. I am sure it might be possible to establish a Readership in Modern Drama at every university—and the whole question with regard to the schools wants ventilating.

7) On the subject I haven't mentioned, whatever that may be.

These committees to number 5 members each. No executive powers, of course, except by special delegation from the main Executive. I incline to think that two members of the Executive should be on each sub-committee, three appointed from outside. The General Secretary or (and?) Honorary Secretary to run them, of course: this is vital.

My experience in working on these sorts of movements has been that whenever a matter wanting careful attention came up, a sub-committee was always appointed. That was to the good; but it was nominated haphazardly and never had a chance to become an effective body.

Some of these committees would function very little; some would from time to time be hard at work. But I believe a permanent sub-committee plan improves attendance at the main executive, which gets its stuff cut and dried for deciding upon.

If the "outside" members of a sub-committee are appointed by the Council—as I incline to think they should be—they should have the right by a <u>unanimous</u> request (unanimous on any one sub-committee) to have a <u>Council</u> meeting called to consider any report which they hold the Executive has dealt wrongly with. They'd need some protection of this sort to prevent them feeling they were mere cyphers.

We meet on Thursday.

Yours,

H. Granville Barker

---

1. Geoffrey Whitworth (1883–1951) was founder and first director of the British Drama League and for many years honorary secretary of the Shakespeare Memorial National Theatre Committee.
2. The Acting Academy, which became the Royal Academy of Dramatic Art.
3. Norman Wilkinson designed the stage settings for some of Barker's productions (*Anatol, The Winter's Tale, The Trojan Women,* etc.) and provided the frontispiece for Barker's short story *Souls on Fifth* when it was published in the United States in 1917.

SAL/MS
To Whitworth

12, Hyde Park Place,
[London], W.
18.7.19

My dear Whitworth,

Yes, E. T.[1] will be a most satisfactory "draw"—and whatever she says will be the right thing because she says it apart from solider reasons which we can rely on in her.

You, of course, are very much in place.

But to balance us all three, I think you badly need a Labour man like Clynes or an "educator" like Hadow or some such gun.[2]

I am dining with Sidney Webb on Tuesday. If you have found no one by then, let me know and I'll ask him for a suggestion (he wouldn't do——or do it—himself).

I hope you agree that the immediate future of the D. L. stands or falls by the names the Executive will submit for sub-committees. They must be "money-pulling" names too.

Yours,
H. G. Barker

---

1. Ellen Terry.
2. J. R. Clynes (1869–1949), one of the leading Labour politicians in the period between the two World Wars; first elected to Parliament in 1906 for one of the Manchester constituencies, which re-elected him at every subsequent election, except 1931, until his retirement in 1945. Sir Henry Hadow (1859–1937), scholar, educationist, critic and music historian; general editor of the *Oxford History of Music* (1904); dean of Worcester College, Oxford (1889–1909), vice-chancellor of the University of Durham (1916–18), vice-chancellor of the University of Sheffield (1919–1930); he was knighted in 1918.

WHIT/MS
To Whitworth

12, Hyde Park Place,
[London], W.2
10.10.19

My dear Whitworth,

About Manchester—better no hospitality perhaps. My wife and I (she wants to see Manchester and its folk, which shows her still fresh interest in England!) will go up probably on the Sunday and stay at the Midland. The meeting is in the evening, I presume. If you are there and could find someone who would show us over a first rate cotton mill on the Monday evening—<u>that</u> would be welcome. She can't think of any useful person to send her book to. No more can I. W. L. Courtney, perhaps—and J. C. Squire.

Yours,
H. Granville Barker

WHIT/MS
To Phyllis Whitworth[1]

Hotel St. George,
Algiers.
11.2.24

My dear Phyllis,

No, <u>of course</u> I won't be an honorary member. I wish your enterprise well. I'd work for it if I could—but I'm past that. At least, though, I won't seem to damn it by any half-hearted-looking patronage.

There was once a club at Cambridge to which anyone could come, but for a secret list of Honorary Non-members. I recommend you to put on your prospectus: "The hall-porter has strict orders not to admit the following persons. The explanation of this, if needed, is attached to their names hereunder:

Mr. H. G-B:	middle-aged; conservative and stodgy; believes in a National Theatre, Shakespeare without scenery, Educational Drama and Village Plays.
Mr. Somerset Maugham:	has written many successful, yet quite good, plays and continues to offend.
Mr. Bernard Shaw:	will be 70 in a year or two.
Mr. Barry Jackson:	runs repertory at Birmingham; repertory is out of date; and where on earth is Birmingham?"

No, no, believe me, you don't want "names" already made. You must make names—and protest that these candidates of yours are to thrust us from the place we still cumber with our unwelcome presence. Do you suppose that in 1899 the Stage Society went begging for the support of Sidney Grundy, Pinero and Henry Arthur Jones? Smother then your anger and be sure that I advise you for your good—though the advice may come too late. I'll be your 195th member if you'll have me and pay my two guineas like a man, under the name of "Enoch Arden".

Helen and I send greetings, as ever, to you all.

Yours,
Harley Granville-Barker

---

1. Geoffrey Whitworth's wife started an organization called the Three Hundred Club in 1924 "for the production of plays of distinguished merit likely to appeal in the first instance to a small public." It is membership in this club to which Barker refers.

Barker in America

COL/MS
To Eleanor Robson Belmont[1]

11, East 45th Street,
New York
Tues. eve. January, 1915

Dear Mrs. Belmont,

So many thanks—and there is nothing I'd like better. But I hardly dare say yes, for this wretched scenery of ours is still "tossing on the ocean" and we have no news of it. I hope we shall have produced on Sunday–Monday (and we're leaving announcements at that) but I have grave doubts that Tuesday may not find me either in the throes of a first night—or worse, of a scene rehearsal. If all has been well I shall kick myself for my caution. But you'll give me another chance?

Very sincerely yours,
H. Granville Barker

---

1. Eleanor Robson was born in Wigan, England, in 1880. She was taken by her mother to the United States at the age of five and became a professional actress while still in her teens. She made her New York debut at the age of twenty as Bonita Canby in *Arizona* and her London debut four years later, in 1904, as Mary Ann in *Merely Mary Ann* (which was written especially for her by Israel Zangwill). In 1909 Winthrop Ames invited her to divide with Julia Marlowe the leading roles in the opening season of the New Theatre but although the idea interested her she was not able to accept the invitation because of other commitments. Upon her marriage to August Belmont she gave up her acting career but began writing plays, with which she had some modest success: Ames, for example, in 1923 produced a play by her and Harriet Ford called *In The Next Room,* which had a brief run in New York and was subsequently produced and directed by Basil Dean in London. She is mentioned by Barker in his letter of February 19, 1915, to Shaw (see Chapter III).

COL/MS
To Eleanor Robson Belmont

11, East 45th Street,
New York
Sunday night February, 1915

My dear Mrs. Belmont,

I'm so glad you liked it at Wallack's—and how good of you to write and tell us so. Constant watching makes me conscious of defects. Though audiences applaud one knows the expert eye will see them—as you must have done; then the comfort is to know that you still find much to praise so generously.

Very much I'll like to come tomorrow—thank you. The dinner a great pleasure: the opera—my weakness.

Very sincerely yours,
H. Granville Barker

COL/TS
To Eleanor Robson Belmont

Wallack's Theatre
Broadway & 30th Street
New York
February 16, 1915

My dear Mrs. Belmont,

So many thanks for the tickets. And as many thanks for saying that you love the gold fairies.[1] Of course if I can be of any use by opening my mouth for you, and letting whatever comes into it come out of it, for five minutes, I am absolutely and entirely at your service.

I dictate this in rather a hurry, so please pardon my not signing it, as it will be written and sent you by messenger after I leave.

Yours sincerely,
Granville Barker

---

1. As the second play in his repertory season at Wallack's Theatre, Barker presented his production of *A Midsummer Night's Dream,* seen in London the year before. The golden fairies (literally so: they were covered from head to toe with gold leaf) had been a great talking-point in London, and in New York their reputation arrived before they did.

COL/TS
To Eleanor Robson Belmont

Mayfair House,
Park Avenue at 65th Street,
New York
April 19 1941

My dear Mrs. Belmont,

I take my typewriter in hand—I have had no time till now to do so—to make a note or so which may be of some use to your correspondent.

I.

1. When anyone talks about the Treaty of Versailles ask them if they have ever read it. I have. I have a copy of it in my room now. The other thing to read is General Smuts' published explanation of why he signed it. Its faults were not on the whole those of injustice—any judge with the Germans before him as prisoners and something like law to administer would have treated them far more

harshly—but unworkability. Smuts and others of his mind looked to the L. of N. to modify its workings. But that is another story.

2. Attacking Hitler!!! I should have thought that the boot was on the other leg. I had a notion that we were standing up—after letting the Czechs down; but we had no treaty obligations to them—for the small nations that <u>he</u> was attacking. But why should we attack Stalin? We don't want to attack anybody. Some people talk as if we <u>liked</u> this war.

3. <u>Are</u> the Germans happy? Read Dodd's diary—a most illuminating book. Also I should have thought that the value of an idea depended upon its being a good idea. If the Nazi idea is a good one then Christ's—which we have been trying to work towards for nearly two thousand years now—is a bad one.

4. Democracy was not rotten on the Continent. Sweden, Norway, Denmark, Holland, Belgium, not to mention England, Czecho-Slovakia and a few other countries were working it pretty well. Nor was France, except for her "central" politics, working it so badly. There, at any rate, was the most civilised country in the world, and the pleasantest to live in—in a perfectly simple, not a "luxe", fashion. But democracy aims at the happiness of the individual, and envisages peace. Plainly it must be at a disadvantage with a system which ignores the first and organises for war.

II.

1. Why worry so much about the word "democracy"? England is a free country and evidently the Greeks think they have enough freedom for it to be worth fighting and dying for. The freedom of the individual in his daily life: that is the test, not the particular political system under which he enjoys it. What is meant by South Africa being the birthplace of slavery I really don't know.

2. How about Ireland! How about the Civil War? How about the execution of King Charles I. and the Wars of the Roses? Ireland has her freedom, and takes advantage of the protection of the British fleet to proclaim her "neutrality" and enjoy a freedom which would not last a week but for this—while she at the same time jeopardises this very freedom by denying us the use of the harbour bases. That's how about Ireland.

3. India: a big and complicated place with all of its different races and creeds and climates and countries; and as big and complicated a subject. As to England's position there: consider the sub-continent's condition in the 18th century as it really was when we began to take it over—this was <u>not</u> the legendary India of Asoka's day; consider the facts—and as it is now. To hand it over to the Congress, which represents about one third of the population, and that not the

dominant third, which has never learnt to govern even this third, has refused every chance we have given it of learning (the half loaf because it could not have the whole straight away; when it could not for five minutes have by its own authority <u>kept</u> the whole) would be to hand it over to anarchy first and tyranny after. We are the trustees now for India, and we cannot do that.

4. I gather that the Daily Worker[1] was left free to express its opinions—and in what other country in war time would it have been so left?—until it began to try and seduce the "armed forces of the Crown" from their allegiance. Only then was it suppressed. A pity this had to be done by administrative action and not by ordinary process of law. But in war-time you must get things done in a day which in peace time you may let hang on for a year (<u>i.e.</u> such a lawsuit: Rex v. The Daily Worker).

5. Why should we "finish with those Tories"? The question itself shows the sort of tolerance for other people's opinions that the questioner himself would show. And does Labour object to Halifax?[2] This is the first I have heard of it. I think it will be found that he and Mr. Bevin[3] get on capitally together.

6. I have no doubt that air raid shelter conditions differ as widely in London as do living conditions in New York—and London. But it is certainly <u>not</u> true that the poor have nowhere to go. And I challenge anyone to produce an instance of a poor man being refused admission to a rich man's shelter—but, indeed, there are no such things, except in so far as your own house is your own house. Nor do I think you could find an instance of a refusal of admittance, at need, to one of these.

7. and 8. are really too silly and ignorant to answer.

III.

1. There were five Principal Powers to make Versailles, of which England was one, but only one. Why therefore put it all on her? Not to mention twenty-three minor ones, all of whom wanted to have a say, and some of who <u>did</u>—and a very substantial one.

2. Were you cheated? I think we only made these capital errors in this particular matter. Borrowing money from you on France's behalf—and Belgium's and Italy's—once <u>you</u> were in the war. Their credit with you ought under <u>those</u> circumstances to have been good enough. And what we borrowed for ourselves we could have paid back long ago. In fact I should be surprised to hear that we had not. Next: we should not have funded the debt on worse terms than you made for everybody else: look at those you gave to Italy! Next: we should have gone on making token payments until what the Vice-President said the other day in his speech to the F. P. A. was

understood and admitted by everybody. But most important of all, we should not have delivered you moral lectures on the matter. That is what we have never been forgiven—and quite rightly.

3. You should not. But make your own. You won't propose anything that we shan't be ready to agree to—if you are willing to implement it as well. And we'll go one better. If we were to propose "peace aims" now they'd only be called propaganda.

4. Perhaps. But you can't count on it.

5. Democracy won't win unless it is prepared to do whatever is necessary to win. We must go on to the end. One cannot make war on a limited liability basis. A man can't half die for his country. If you come into the war you'll have to do whatever is necessary to help win it. What will be necessary who can say? But this talk of sending troops abroad as being the one impossible thing seems to me beside the point. One might as well object to sending one's Navy abroad. Where one defends one's country is a matter of military strategy. The Germans prefer to fight in other people's countries, it would seem. And from a purely military point of view there is much to be said for it.

6. Yes, you'll be fully armed. But will you be prepared to stay fully armed for an indefinite period? And even if Hitler himself does stop, Hitlerism will have triumphed and will infect—certainly, I should suppose—the whole of South and Central America. Why, there is at this very moment a little native Hitler in every country there, strutting before the glass, and imagining the time when he'll drown all opposition in blood-baths and stifle it in concentration camps; and let the old U.S.A. say what they will, he'll have his great German Exemplar to back him.

7. I think disarmament, and an international police force for at least ten years to keep order in Germany, and then a sort of Educational Occupation for at least twenty—academic freedom restored, with the exiles taking up their old posts again, but given no other authority; a generation of liberal education; a Bill of Rights, and some sort of representative government insisted upon; above all, the liberty of the individual guaranteed—that is the kind of thing I foresee.

8. No, we are not. Nobody is. "We have all sinned, and all come short of the perfect glory of God." But we must just do our best to make this world at least a tolerable place to live in.

This is very rough and ready, and I'm no expert on these matters, God knows. But it may indicate lines that can be followed up. We're off to Washington tomorrow, and will hope to see you when we get back.

As ever,
Yours,
Harley Granville Barker

---

1. The official newspaper of the British Communist Party.
2. Lord Halifax (1881–1959), a Conservative politician, was Foreign Secretary in Churchill's wartime coalition cabinet and in January, 1941, became British Ambassador to the United States.
3. Ernest Bevin (1881–1951), the Labour politician, was Minister of Labour and National Service in Churchill's wartime coalition cabinet.

COR/MS
To Alan S. Downer[1]

Mayfair House,
Park Avenue at 65th Street,
New York.
Sept. 6, 1944

My dear Alan Downer,

Yes, the MS of the Macready journal was destroyed by Nevil Macready after Pollock[2] had used everything they did not consider too personally intimate for publication. So Macready[3] told me. He is still alive—I hope!—a very distinguished soldier: General Sir Nevil . . . Bart., G.C.M.G.,[4] etc. (see Who's Who) was British Adjutant General in the last war, was living in Paris until this one began, used to like to talk of his father, though still a small boy, I suppose, when he died. And _his_ son, also a soldier and a general, was with the British Military Mission in Washington quite lately.

I'm very glad you're going to do something about him.[5] A fine figure: and had he been able to stick to his job and his father not dying bankrupt, would have made a good Lord Chief Justice, I don't doubt.[6] Perhaps you'll be able to decide whether he loved the drama or hated the theatre the more: he never could.[7]

Very kind regards. Look me up if ever you are in New York—and I still am.

Yours,
Harley Granville-Barker

---

1. See note 1 on p. 535 of this chapter.
2. Sir Frederick Pollock (1845–1937), editor of *Macready's Reminiscences and Selections from His Diaries and Letters,* published by Macmillan in 1875.
3. This is Cecil Frederick Nevil Macready (1862–1946), the youngest son of William

Charles Macready, the actor. He published an autobiography in 1924 called *Annals of an Active Life.*
4. Knight Grand Cross of St. Michael and St. George.
5. Downer was preparing to write a book about Macready. It was eventually published by Harvard University Press in 1966 under the title, *The Eminent Tragedian William Charles Macready.*
6. Macready had expressed a wish, while still a schoolboy at Rugby, to make the law his career. He said he disliked the theater and the idea of becoming an actor, though (or perhaps because) his father had been an actor all his life.
7. This was Barker's own position too. His liking for and interest in Macready no doubt owed something to the similarity of their temperaments in this regard.

COR/PC
To Downer

New York
Jan 15 [1945]

Never heard his called anything but Macr<u>ee</u>dy.
Never studied The Tempest but I fancy that if you consider it as a
Mas<u>que</u> and not a <u>play</u>, and recognise the difference of treatment and
tone, it comes out <u>alright.</u>

H. G-B.

Barker as adjudicator at the Dominion Drama Festival, Ottawa, 1936. Photo © Karsh, Ottawa.

Appendixes

Appendix A

Items from *The Times* of Monday, November 27, 1911

New Joint Examiner of Plays: Mr. Charles Brookfield

The Lord Chamberlain has appointed Mr. Charles H. E. Brookfield to be Joint Examiner of Plays with Mr. G. A. Redford.

Mr. Brookfield's duties will commence on January 1 next, and on and after that date an office for the reading of stage plays will be established in St. James's Palace.

All the plays submitted for licence should be addressed as follows:—"The Lord Chamberlain, St. James's Palace, London, S.W." and the envelope marked "Stage Play". Cheques or postal orders for reading fees should be made payable to "The Lord Chamberlain".

Mr. Charles Hallam Elton Brookfield is the second son of Canon W. H. Brookfield, the friend of Thackeray, Tennyson, and many other eminent men, by his wife Jane, daughter of Sir Charles Elton and niece of Henry Hallam. He was born in 1857, was educated at Westminster and Trinity College, Cambridge, and went on the stage under the Bancrofts' management in 1879. He left the stage in 1885. Mr. Brookfield, who is known to his many friends as a most delightful and amusing talker, a gift inherited from his father, published "Random Reminiscences" in 1902, a book full of good stories. He has also written and produced between 40 and 50 plays, including *The Dovecote, The Cuckoo, The Lady Burglar, Dear Old Charlie* and *The Belle of Mayfair* (in collaboration). His wife, who is the daughter of Mr. William Grogan, is the author of "Mrs. Brookfield and Her Circle", "The Cambridge Apostles" and several excellent historical novels.

It is understood that Mr. Redford and Mr. Brookfield will work in conjunction with the Advisory Board nominated to assist the Lord Chamberlain in granting licences to perform plays.

See also Bernard Shaw's letter of this date on p. 123.

Directly underneath the above item, in the same column, appeared the following.

Incident at the Savoy Theatre

It was announced unofficially on Saturday that Mr. Charles H. E. Brookfield had been appointed to act as Joint Examiner of Plays with Mr. G. A. Redford. The rumour gave rise to an interesting occurrence at the Savoy Theatre last night, where the society known as the Pioneer Players had assembled in large numbers to see the play *Pains and Penalties* by Mr. Laurence Housman, to which the Lord Chamberlain recently refused a licence. At the end of the first act there appeared before the curtain Miss Elizabeth Robins[1] and Mr. Granville Barker, and, at Miss Robins's request, Mr. Barker made a speech and proposed a resolution. He said that Mr. Brookfield was best known as the author of a play, *Dear Old Charlie,* which was singled out by several witnesses before the Select Committee on Stage Plays (Censorship) of 1909, including Mr. William Archer and Mr. W. L. Courtney,[2] as a play of which the performance ought never to have been allowed by the Censor. Mr. Brookfield was also the author of an article in the current number of the *National Review,* in which he gave it as his opinion that the palmy days of English drama began to decline with the introduction of the work of Ibsen. Either Mr. Brookfield had written that article as a manifesto on his appointment, or the appointment was given in consequence of that article. In either case the appointment was a scandal and a piece of political indecency. Mr. Barker then proposed the following resolution:—

"That the audience gathered to witness the production of Laurence Housman's forbidden play, *Pains and Penalties,* is of opinion that if the statement is true that Mr. Charles Brookfield has been appointed Reader of Plays, then in view of Mr. Brookfield's recently published opinions on the modern drama the action of the Lord Chamberlain is but further proof, if further proof were needed, that he is hopelessly out of touch with the theatre over which he exercises despotic control, and that the continuance of his legalized tyranny is inimical to the drama's welfare and its good name."

Put to the vote by Miss Robins, the resolution was carried with only two dissentients, one of whom cried, "Too strongly worded!" An hour after the passing of the resolution news reached the theatre confirming the rumour of Mr. Brookfield's appointment.

As to Mr. Housman's play, we find it by no means uninteresting as a drama, and a work of the very highest benefit to the morals and the loyalty of the nation through the glaring contrast it exhibits between the example set by the Monarchy of today and that set by the Monarchy of 90 years ago. It concerns, as our readers may be aware, the fate of Caroline, Queen of King George IV, and shows her surrounded by spies, tried with gross unfairness, and denied her right to be crowned. The play is a careful and able piece of work; and if it wavers too markedly between dramatic truth and the truth of historic fact (the first act, for instance, is a work of imagination founded on fact, the second—the trial scene—was written by Hansard), it is not without movement and cohesion. Miss Gertrude Kingston played her very best as Queen Caroline; Mr. Harcourt Williams gave fine effect to the rhetoric of Brougham; and Mr. Michael Sherbrooke, Miss Auriol Lee and Mr. William Farren were three out of many who did well. One scene represented Georve IV at his toilet between the Coronation and the Banquet, and here Mr. Nigel Playfair and Mr. Ross Shore as the King's valets added much to the gaiety of a play which roused frequent laughter and considerable sympathy.

The attitude of the Censor towards M. Bataille's play *La Vierge Folle* is referred to by our Dramatic Critic[3] in his notice of the production, which appears on p. 10.

---

1. C. B. Purdom, in his *Granville Barker* (1955), mentions this incident (p. 127) but identifies the actress as Gertrude Robins. The contemporary account in the newspaper is more likely to be the correct one (and the incident is more typical of Elizabeth Robins than of Gertrude Robins).
2. Courtney (1850–1928), a dramatic critic and journalist, was for some years the editor of the *Fortnightly Review*.
3. A. B. Walkley (1855–1926), who was dramatic critic for *The Times* from 1900 until his death.

Walkley's notice reads as follows.

Coronet Theatre

"La Vierge Folle"
Pièce en 4 actes de M. Henry Bataille

———

Abbé Roux . . . . M. Louis Tunc
Marcel Armaury . . . . M. Saulieu

Duc de Charance . . . . M. Demorange
Gaston de Charance . . . . . M. Deurtal
Fanny Armaury . . . . Mlle. Eugénie Nau
Diane de Charance . . . . . . Mlle. Jeanne Marcyla
Duchesse de Charance . . . Mlle. Martha Dyermont
Ketty . . . . Mlle. Rachel Berendt

THE CENSOR AND THE PLAY

A door, says the French proverb, must be either open or shut. It would be well if the Court official who, quaintly enough, is in this country appointed door-keeper to the dramatic Muse would remember this maxim. His difficulty in making up his mind over *La Vierge Folle* suggests doubts as to the existence of a mind to make up. Vowing on Monday he would ne'er consent to the performance of the play, by Saturday he consented. The result—apart from inconvenience and loss to the theatre manager, who, we think, has been hardly used—was to turn what would have passed unperceived among the ordinary items of a week of French plays into a "success of scandal". The Censor's striking, if belated, advertisement filled the Coronet twice on Saturday to overflowing.

Some people in the crowd probably wondered what all the fuss had been about and felt that they had been lured to Notting-hill[1] under false pretences. *La Vierge Folle* is no more, and no less, objectionable than scores of other plays exhibiting a "scabrous" situation which have been passed by the Censor without a word. Rigid moralists would prohibit all such plays, and their attitude is at any rate comprehensible and consistent. Not so the attitude of the Censor, who seems to accept some of these plays and to reject others at random, by the toss of a coin. Seeing that the Censor's inconsistency in regard to plays of this class has been more than usually conspicuous when they happen to have been written in French, it has been conjectured that his difficulties have been really linguistic. Some colour is given to this theory by the strange circumstance, announced in another column, that he has now secured the assistance of Mr. Charles Brookfield. *Il ne manquait que ça!* The adapter of *Le Plus Heureux de Trois* and many another Palais Royal farce will certainly be able to do any French translation that may be required. It is not easy to see what other justification there may be for an appointment which the theatrical world in general, we fear, will regard as merely grotesque.

As for M. Bataille's play, it presents the familiar situation of a man between two women, who has, as he conceives, a divided duty—duty to his wife and duty to his mistress. His wife adores him and he is not without a patronizing affection for her. On the other hand, a foolish girl, young enough to be his daughter, has fallen in love with him and he has basely taken advantage of her folly. Now he finds himself compelled to desert either his fond and faithful wife or else the poor silly girl whom he has betrayed and taken from her (aristocratic) parents' home. He finds reasons, a whole chain of reasons, set out in lengthy discourses, for choosing the younger and fresher love. His elaborate logic on the subject, to our thinking, only aggravates his offence. If the man had been a frankly cynical voluptuary intent upon taking his pleasure where he found it, in contempt of social or moral laws, *à la bonne heure!* But we are nauseated by these canting Don Juans, these ratiocinative seducers, who cover their vices in a cloud of syllogisms and argue "about it and about" in long-winded orations on duty, the right to happiness, the spirit of the age, and other tiresome irrelevances. But that is M. Bataille's way, the very odd way of trying to ingratiate his sinners with us by showing that they can be just as terrible bores as though they had never swerved from the path of virtue. If we must be preached at, why, let it be from the pulpit or the bench, but not from the dock! By the way, the pulpit does get its share, if only a minor share, here, a certain Abbé expounding the religious and moral point of view whenever Mr. Talkative-Lovelace will let him get a word in edgeways. But it is not to be expected that a celibate ecclesiastic will be able to out-argue a gentleman who has deserted his wife and seduced the daughter of his friend.

Of course his wife not only adores him as a man but relishes him as a debater, manifestly admiring his arguments even when they are directed to prove that he must leave her for another woman. This is a new kind of Patient Grisel. It may be, she timidly suggests, that he will in time tire of the other woman, and in that case all she asks is that he will come back to her: and the husband magnanimously promises to bear it in mind. Overcome with gratitude for this condescension, the wife then turns upon the family of the man's young victim (who think, poor things, they have a grievance) and calls them names. The next moment the husband rewards her by declaring his love for her young rival to her very face. Yet he is not shot, as he certainly deserves to be, by the young man (indignant brother to the girl), who arrives with a pistol, the weapon being snatched up by the girl to put an end to her own life. The seducer is left weeping over her corpse, but you feel sure that, when he has dried his tears, he will, like John Tanner,[2] "go on talking".

He was played on Saturday by M. Saulieu, who did as well as could be expected in the ungrateful part of a man who is at once odious and ridiculous. M. Louis Tunc was excellent as the Abbé, a grave, aescetic, almost saintly figure, and (in the theatrical as well as the general sense) a wonderfully "good listener". Mlle Bady's part of the wife—it is a genuine "Bady part"—fell to Mlle Nau. This emotional type is familiar in M. Bataille's plays—you will find her in *Maman Colibri* and again in *La Marche Nuptiale*—a woman who, as the vulgar say, is "no chicken",[3] but yet full of passion, and the devoted slave of some (more or less worthless) man. Her love is to her a kind of religious ecstasy, and she invariably suffers martyrdom. Mlle Nau played the part in just the perfervid way demanded, and fully compensated the audience for their boredom in "sitting under" the gentleman who complacently expounded and exhausted the ethical, sociological and philosophical significance of his own profligacy.

---

1. The Coronet Theatre was in High Street, Notting Hill, four miles from the fashionable theater district. It became a cinema in 1923.
2. In Shaw's *Man and Superman*.
3. "No chicken" is a British slang expression meaning "no longer young" or "older than one would suppose."

Appendix B

Documents Issued by Granville Barker in Connection with Repertory Theatre Scheme, 1914

Letter of Appeal[1]

We want to establish in London a Repertory Theatre. By Repertory, we mean that each week there shall be performed at least three, probably four or five, different plays. The Theatre shall be open for not less than forty weeks in the year and during that time from twenty to twelve new productions shall be staged, acted by the permanent company.

The choice of plays shall be catholic, ranging from Shakespeare and Greek tragedy to modern comedy—both English and foreign.

Only by this system of true repertory can a theatre compass the whole range of drama and appeal in the normal course of its work to the good taste of every section of the public, large and small. Let the playgoer consult his experience and judge what other chance he has of seeing many or any of the plays that he most wants to see.

To (help) establish such a theatre we need to find, say, a thousand people who will contribute £25 each and be ready to contribute three further sums of £25 in the three following years, if it is necessary to do so. This money will be placed in the hands of trustees; the first charge upon any net yearly profits of the Theatre will be to pay 5% interest on it: at the trustees' discretion it will be repayable: and it is intended that at the end of three years any further and sufficient accumulation of profits should be used to continue the work.

A Repertory Theatre cannot be expected to make large profits but if its resources are sufficient to provide proper equipment and to make possible a long-sighted policy and economic management there is no reason, I think, why, once well established, it should not always be able to recompense at the market rate the services rendered it and to pay a small interest upon its capital.

The Theatre could be brought into being within six months.

Lord Howard de Walden, Sir James Barrie and Professor Gilbert Murray are willing to be the trustees.

If you are interested enough in the scheme to intend to contribute to it, please allow us to send you a more detailed statement of the matter.

H. Granville Barker

Formal Detailed Statement[2]

The original version of this document had a printed heading, in bold type: "The London Repertory Theatre." This was altered, on the printer's proof, to read "Repertory Theatre." The document read as follows.

Dear Sir,

I send you herewith a cheque for £25 payable to the Bank, Repertory Theatre Account, to be used in establishing a Repertory Theatre in London such as you propose under the following conditions, to which I hereby agree:—

1. All money so contributed is to be held in the names of three trustees, namely:—

   LORD HOWARD DE WALDEN,
   SIR JAMES BARRIE,
   PROFESSOR GILBERT MURRAY.

2. If by the 31st day of July, 1914, the money contributed shall not amount to £10,000, my £25 is to be returned to me.

3. The Repertory Theatre will open on or before the 1st day of January, 1915, or such later date as the Trustees shall approve, and will continue with such vacations as the Trustees may approve for at least three years, subject to the money in the hands of the Trustees being sufficient for the purpose.

4. The Repertory Theatre is to be under your sole management and control, and in respect of such management, you are to be paid five per cent. of the gross weekly re-

ceipts of the performances up to £1,000 a week, and ten
per cent. of all gross weekly receipts in excess of £1,000
per week.

5. The accounts of the Theatre are to be prepared under
the direction of a Chartered Accountant to be nominated
by the Trustees and a Balance Sheet and Profit and Loss
Account certified by such Chartered Accountants are to
be sent to me yearly.

6. The Trustees are to use the money in their hands in financing the Theatre, and I agree to pay to them such further sums as they may call for from time to time during
three years from the first day of January, 1915, within
fourteen days of each call, PROVIDED that such calls shall
not exceed the sum of £25 in any one year and that they
shall only be made if in the opinion of the Trustees further funds are needed to carry on the Theatre. It is clearly
understood that my liability, while it may be less, shall in
no case exceed £100 in all or extend beyond the three
years.

7. If in any of the three years a nett profit (after taking into
account profits or losses brought forward from any previous year) shall have been made sufficient to pay five per
cent. upon the money contributed hereunder, then five
per cent. is to be paid to me on my contributions; and in
this respect, the certificate of the Chartered Accountant
nominated by the Trustees shall be conclusive. If the nett
profit in any year is insufficient to pay five per cent., it is
to be carried forward, and if it is more than sufficient to
pay five per cent. the excess after paying five per cent. is
also to be carried forward.

8. At the expiration of three years the money in the hands
of the Trustees and the assets of the Theatre may, at the
discretion of the Trustees, be used to continue the Theatre upon the terms of this Scheme, or for the endowment
of a Permanent Repertory Theatre, or otherwise in fur-
therance of the Repertory Theatre Movement; but if they
shall not be so used then the affairs of the Theatre shall
be wound up and its assets realized, and so much as shall
remain of the money contributed by me shall be returned
to me. If upon the winding-up of the Theatre there shall
remain any balance after all proper payments hereunder
have been made, such balance shall be your absolute
property.

9. The money which I shall have contributed under these provisions may at any time be returned to me by the Trustees and I shall then cease to have any interest or claim under these provisions.
10. Except as herein provided, I am to have no claim upon the money in the hands of the Trustees, or upon the Theatre or its assets.
11. The power of appointing new Trustees is to be vested in the Trustees.

Name in full _____
Address _____
Signature _____
Date _____

To H. Granville Barker, Esq.

---

1. This is a typewritten document.
2. This is a printed document.

Appendix C

Helen Huntington's Published Works[1]

1900 *Folk Songs from the Spanish* (New York; Putnam): collection of verse

1902 *The Solitary Path* (New York; Doubleday): collection of verse

1906 *The Days that Pass* (New York; Lane): collection of verse

1908 *The Sovereign Good* (New York; Putnam): novel

1909 *From the Cup of Silence* (New York; Putnam): collection of verse

1910 *An Apprentice to Truth* (New York; Putnam): novel

1911 *The Moon Lady* (New York; Scribner): novel

1913 *Marsh Lights* (New York; Putnam): novel

1918 *Eastern Red* (New York; Putnam): novel

1919 *Songs in Cities and Gardens* (London; Putnam): collection of verse

1923 *Ada* (London; Chatto & Windus): novel

1926 *Wives and Celebrities* (London; Collins): short stories

1928 *Living Mirrors* (London; Sidgwick and Jackson): novel

1931 *Come, Julia* (London; Sidgwick and Jackson): novel

1932 *Moon in Scorpio* (London; Sidgwick and Jackson): novel

1935 *Traitor Angel* (London; Sidgwick and Jackson): novel

1936 *The Locked Book* (London; Sidgwick and Jackson): anthology of poems and prose about angels

1939 *Poems* (London; Sidgwick and Jackson): collection of verse

1944 *Nineteen Poems* (London; Sidgwick and Jackson): collection of verse

---

1. This list does not include the various translations of Spanish plays which she published jointly with Harley Granville-Barker between 1922 and 1938. From 1900 to 1918, she published under the name of Helen Huntington, from 1919 to 1944, under the name of Helen Granville-Barker.

Appendix D

St. John Ervine's Column in *The Observer* for September 30, 1923

At the Play: Mr. Granville-Barker and Mr. Lascelles Abercrombie

The dramatist, in England, is no longer content to wait upon the indulgence of managers for the production of his plays, but publishes them immediately they are written, so that he may receive some attention during his lifetime. The cakes and ale will, no doubt, be enjoyed by others after his death, but he can have the satisfaction, slight as it is, of seeing his work in print. A play is not a play until it has been publicly performed, but the alternative to publication for an English dramatist at present seems to be oblivion, and no human being can endure the thought of oblivion, at all events on earth. In time, no doubt, managers will tire of crossing the Channel in search of dirty drivel by mentally-exhausted Frenchmen, and they will be assisted to this desirable state of fatigue by the fact that English audiences have no use for plays, such as "The Elopement", in which girls of eighteen are presumed to be at once pure in mind and infinitely familiar with the language and habits of experienced prostitutes. King Amyntor in Mr. Lascelles Abercrombie's new tragi-comedy, says that—

> Everything in the world fails but dirt.
> The clean things have no power against dirt.
> There is a sort of smearing eagerness
> In dirt; And to find any cleanliness
> To smear is dirt's delight.

Amyntor was in a bitter mood when he expressed himself in that fashion, and the fact that "The Elopement" lasted for less than a fortnight denotes that dirt is not always successful. In the meantime, English authors must be content to write and publish their plays. Perhaps, when they are all decently dead, some manager, forgetting their

582

nationality, will produce one of their plays and make quite an income for himself. It is, of course, something of a crime to be English. There is a rumour that a reporter on the staff of the "Daily Mail" was caught by Lord Rothermere in the very act of taking off his hat to England.

Here are two plays by English dramatists, both of whom are men of distinction. Mr. Harley Granville-Barker does not require any introduction to readers of *The Observer*. What he requires from them is reprobation for his abandonment of the theatre. He has a positive genius for producing plays, but he steadfastly refuses to fulfill his genius. Some say, of course, that he does well to devote himself to writing plays, but I retort to that with the statement that while he was deeply engaged in theatrical production and putting our theatre in a state of eminence which it had not enjoyed for more than a century, he was also writing plays which filled the mind of his contemporaries with high expectations. A man of genius cannot be set down to one job; his activities are as various as his mind. It is only your dull, plodding fellow, your unimaginative expert, who will give the whole of his existence to one piece of work. Shakespeare managed a theatre, and acted parts in plays, and wrote or had a hand in writing thirty-seven plays in a working life of twenty years. Molière managed a theatre and was an actor, and wrote more than thirty plays in a working life of about the same length as Shakespeare's. Ibsen managed a theatre, and carried on a controversial career, and wrote a great many plays that profoundly affected the mind of the civilized world. Mr. Shaw has not confined his energies to writing plays, although he has written one more than Shakespeare wrote, but has engaged in enterprises of all sorts. And what is true of these is true of nearly every man of genius. Twice a year I go to Mr. Granville-Barker and try to bully him into resuming the job he did so finely, and twice a year he tells me that he will never resume it. I think it is a pity; and my sense of its pity is not diminished by this play. "The Secret Life" is almost as long as "Hamlet". It is much harder to understand. I will confess that when I read it for the first time, I had not the slightest idea of what it was about. It has passages of great charm, and the dialogue has a lean strength that is very attractive; but the play, as a whole, is obscure. The form does not help make the meaning clearer. Even in reading, one has difficulty in realizing about whom the characters are speaking, and this difficulty will, I imagine, be increased in performance because a fair amount of the dialogue is uttered by characters who are not visible to the audience. Each of the acts is arbitrarily broken up into scenes. There are three scenes in the first act; five scenes in the second; and three in the third. The second scene of the third act seems to me to be an irrelevance, although I would not take my oath on it; but obviously, if the play were performed, many "cuts" would have to be made in it. I estimate that the whole of the second act would take nearly two hours to perform.

A second reading of the play makes its meaning plainer, and no doubt a third reading would make it plainer still. No one, even after a first reading, can be ignorant of the fact that there is power here, and the author possesses a distinguished mind. But a play ought not to need reading several times before its meaning begins to be plain. If it is hard to understand in the book, where one can turn back and re-read, how much more hard would it be to understand in performance where the mind must be reached immediately or not at all? Evan Strowde, the chief man of the play, asks his sister if she has "never found that the whole world's turmoil is but a reflection of the anarchy in your own heart?" That speech is, perhaps, the key to the play. Strowde and Joan Westbury love each other, but do not marry because each of them is looking for the unattainable, and has at last realized that it cannot be found. That is their secret life. They have been converted to disbelief. They derive no satisfaction from doing the things which they can do, and are embittered by the fact that other things cannot be done at all. They are nerveless and negative. They might marry, but they do not because they are too vague, too gutless to put up their fists to life and give back as many blows as they get. "But why is it," says Strowde to his sister, "that for all your goodness and my cleverness, for all the assembled virtues of this jolly house party, and the goodwill that's going begging throughout the world . . . how is it that we shan't establish the Kingdom of Heaven on earth by Tuesday week?" She does not reply, as she ought to have replied, that the Kingdom of Heaven would not be the Kingdom of Heaven if it were established on earth by Tuesday week, nor does she give him a piece of her mind for refusing to fight for a bit of it because he cannot immediately obtain the whole of it. Because Europe will not at once scrap her armaments, the young League of Nations is to be scrapped instead. Go to, gentlemen, go to! Why did God give us fists if we are not to fight with them for worthy things? I have no use for this Conchy,[1] wishy-washy Tolstoy stuff which would leave good fighting fists entirely in the hands of the blackguards. It is the business of the just man to hammer hell out of the wicked one, and I hope to heaven I shall never live in a world where the just man gives up his job.

I put this book down, after two readings, still bewildered by it. I shall read it again, for it draws me in a singular way. I hate to be baffled, and it baffles me. It bears the dates "1919–22" and I seem to find an explanation in them. Three years is a long time for a man to work on a play. This one did not come to Mr. Granville-Barker furiously demanding to be written; it crept up to him and coaxed him to take notice of it, and, with some reluctance, he seems to have consented. But surely there must be some fury in creation? This gentle, leisurely argument, during which all emotion is carefully refined away, does not go well with the passion to make things. And there is a chaos in the London theatre demanding that Mr. Granville-Barker shall come and make order out of it.

Mr. Lascelles Abercrombie's play is as plain as Mr. Granville-Barker's is obscure. "Phoenix" is austerely-written, without one digression or ornament. It reads more like a one-act play, divided into three scenes, than a three-act play, but that is merely because of the spareness of its style. King Amyntor has purchased a beautiful slave-girl, Rhodope, to give him lascivious comfort after a life spent in austerities. His Queen, in her jealousy, develops great guile. She sets her son, Phoenix, an innocent youth, to wooing Rhodope, and the tragedy consists of the disillusionment of this lad when he discovers that his beloved is his father's drab. The comedy comes from the fact that Rhodope prefers one of the King's soldiers to the King or his son. That is a very bare summary of Mr. Abercrombie's theme, and does not indicate the fineness with which he has treated it. The character of Rhodope is admirably observed. Here, very truly, is displayed the nature of the animal-woman. Rhodope makes no pretences about herself: she is as she is; but also contrives to leave us with some respect for her. The last act of the play is not so effective as the first two. Mr. Abercrombie's hand fumbles a little when the discovery of Rhodope in the tower with the sentinel is made, but the final scene of this act is excellent. Someone should produce "Phoenix". It really is not necessary to wait until Mr. Abercrombie has been dead for ten years. The cast consists of six people, and the play is performed in one "set", so that there is not even the excuse of cost of production to deter anyone from doing it. In the meantime, it should be read.

---

1. Conscientious objector.

Indexes

Note: following the brief subject listing below, this index is comprised of names, divided into four categories. The index of Persons *lists actors and directors; then playwrights; then managers, stage managers, and designers; then critics. The index of* Literary Works *begins with plays and follows with other works. The index of* Newspapers and Magazines *is followed by the index of* Theaters and Other Institutions, *the last category, which includes educational, cultural, professional, and political organizations mentioned in the text and notes.*

Actors and acting, 53, 116, 119, 159, 341, 418–24, 473–75, 480

Censorship: military, 67n; theatrical, 118, 123, 242, 262, 265–66, 277–78, 281, 535–37, 571–76

Conscription, military, 150–51

Films: as records of acting, 507

German theater, 185, 265

Greek plays: interpretation, 208; performance, 139, 141, 224–26, 238, 251–53, 278–79, 280–81, 283, 288–89; translation, 195–298 passim

Japan: earthquake in, 94

National Theatre plan: architects' competition for, 94–95; and Barker, 25, 33, 34, 42, 43, 92–93, 199, 264, 476; committees for, 56, 57, 63, 122; Library, 483; sponsorship of, 422, 481, 521–27

Playwriting: Archer on, 69–70, 75–76, 104–7; Barker on, 68, 74, 77–78, 101–2, 374–77, 496, 497–98, 499–500

Poetics, Aristotelean, 275

Rehearsal techniques, 119–20, 124–25, 232–33

Repertory: playing in, 29, 30, 32, 45–55, 65, 66, 126, 127–31, 134–44, 180n, 228, 249, 250–55, 282, 284, 476, 493, 556, 577–80

Shakespeare: staging of, 59–62, 66, 90, 274, 409-33 passim, 437–38

Theater financing, 135–37, 138, 139–40, 142–43, 145–46, 203–4, 207, 268, 285, 427–28, 486, 492, 506, 577–80

Touring theatrical companies, 44, 117, 118

Verse forms and meter, 291–92

World War I, 65, 66, 68–70, 137, 146, 150–51, 286, 287, 302, 314, 318–20, 322, 323–24, 327, 328, 329, 333, 506–7

World War II, 295–96, 353–54, 356–58, 364, 418–24, 561–65

PERSONS

Actors and Directors

Achurch, Janet, 27, 241, 444, 445nn, 448n, 451n, 487, 487n

Adams, W. Bridges, 28, 30, 108n, 278, 435–41

Addison, Carlotta, 456

Ainley, Henry, 17, 71, 134, 230

Albanesi, Meggie (Margharita), 460

Alexander, George, 29, 50, 51n, 410

Ames, Winthrop, 71, 72, 81, 83, 85, 128, 143, 145, 258, 259, 264, 381, 441–42, 453, 547, 560n

Anson, A. E., 254

Arliss, George, 35, 72n, 73

Armstrong, William, 469, 470, 503n

Ashwell, Lena, 47, 132, 133n, 138, 243n, 253, 371

Askew, Claude, 17

Asquith, Elizabeth, 259
Ayliff, H. K., 121n

Barker, Harley Granville: as actor, 27,
  118; on casting of plays, 46–47, 49, 51,
  130, 177, 230–32, 240, 253, 278–79,
  280, 429, 455–62, 464–76, 491; and dialect words, 155n, 222n, 280n, 334; as
  director, 29, 119–20, 124–25, 258; divorce of, 66, 147–49, 151–53, 191–94,
  301, 339n; and Groombridge Place,
  332n, 333, 335n, 345; on holidays, 178–
  79, 181–87, 210–22, 233–35, 267, 284,
  285–86; handwriting of, 16, 64, 70, 80,
  104; invited to New York, 123, 126n,
  127–41 passim, 260; as lecturer, 66,
  291; marriage to Helen Huntington,
  302–3; marriage to Lillah McCarthy,
  167; monogram, 308, 362; at Netherton
  Hall, 24, 31, 157, 351, 380, 382, 386,
  398, 399, 401, 479; on playwriting, 68,
  74, 77–78, 101–2, 374–77, 496, 497–98,
  499–500; on publishing, 537–55; and
  Red Cross, 24, 66n, 144n, 146, 147,
  188–89, 193, 372; "retirement" from
  theater, 279, 341, 499–500; as theater
  critic, 40, 44; in vaudeville, 269, 270–
  71; as writer, 26, 38, 39, 40, 46, 67, 84,
  86–89, 101–4, 129, 130–31, 146, 149,
  157, 158–59, 272–73, 283, 302, 338,
  386, 394, 395–96, 450–51, 509
Barnes, J. H., 232
Barrett, Wilson, 165, 170
Belmont, Eleanor Robson. *See* Robson,
  Eleanor
Benson, Sir Frank, 207n, 216, 413–14
Bergner, Elizabeth, 416
Berlin, Ivan, 451n
Bernhardt, Sarah, 144n, 501n
Best, Edna, 458
Betterton, Thomas, 78, 528, 534, 535n
Boucicault, Dion (the younger), 124,
  442–43, 489
Boucicault, Nina, 456
Bourchier, Arthur, 122, 202, 270
Braham, Lionel, 130
Brand, Tita, 208n, 224, 241
Brayton, Lily, 207
Brema, Marie, 207, 208, 209
Browne, Graham, 451

Calthrop, Donald, 489
Calvert, Louis, 124, 146, 445
Campbell, Mrs. Patrick, 21, 22, 48n, 52n,
  129n, 132n, 197, 205, 210, 211, 218,
  220, 226, 227, 228, 229, 235, 236, 487

Carey, Joyce, 460, 461, 462, 464
Carter, Hubert, 180n
Casson, Sir Lewis, 24, 160, 173n, 242n,
  242, 245, 252, 253, 272, 276n, 280, 424,
  443, 510n
Celli, Faith, 460
Chapin, Harold, 280
Charrington, Charles, 27, 116n, 444–51,
  487n
Collier, Constance, 235, 237
Compton, Fay, 491
Copeau, Jacques, 524
Corbett, Thalberg, 46, 47n
Courtneidge, Cecily, 70n
Courtney, William, 123
Cowie, Laura, 408, 460
Cowl, Jane, 457, 460, 503
Craig, Edith, 27, 556
Crawford, Alice, 229
Creighton, Walter, 130
Cromwell, Cecil, 231

Dale, James, 471
Daly, Arnold, 120
Davenport, Bromley, 473
Davis, Fay, 510n
De Solla, Rachel, 457
Donat, Robert, 468, 470, 471
Du Maurier, Sir Gerald, 314, 321, 451,
  461n

Eadie, Dennis, 121, 436, 451–64, 510n
Eddison, Robert, 14, 508
Esmond, H. V., 46n, 445n
Evans, Patrick, 451

Fagan, H. Trant, 451
Farren, William, 573
Ffrangcon-Davies, Gwen, 381n, 382
Field, Nathan, 535n
Filippi, Rosina, 203
Forbes-Robertson, Sir Johnston, 22, 253,
  264, 344, 416, 429
France, C. V., 46n

Garrick, David, 528
Gatty, Scott, 473
George, Grace, 146, 147n
Gielgud, Sir John, 10, 14, 24, 32, 176,
  405–33, 435, 461n
Gillette, William, 144n
Graham, Jane, 460
Greet, Sir Ben, 21, 26, 165, 171, 208n,
  445n
Grimwood, Herbert, 451n
Guitry, Lucien, 408

Haggard, Stephen, 429, 473n
Halstan, Margaret, 121
Hamilton, Cecily, 119, 121n
Hannan, Nicholas, 408, 419, 429, 464–76
Harris, Robert, 529
Harris, William, 123, 146
Hawkins, Jack, 429
Hawtrey, Sir Charles, 21, 27
Hayes, George, 472
Hayes, Sheila, 491
Heggie, O. P., 127, 129n, 130, 135, 141
Hicks, Sir Seymour, 321

Irving, H. B., 26, 72n
Irving, Sir Henry, 26, 29, 49, 410, 454n, 476
Irving, Laurence, 451n, 487
Ivor, Frances, 230, 459

James, Julia, 459
Jeayes, Allan, 474
Jerrold, Mary, 81, 510n

Kean, Edmund, 528
Keen, Malcolm, 471
Kendrick, Alfred, 446
Kingston, Gertrude, 128, 184, 208, 209n, 209, 573
Komisarjevsky, Theodore, 435

Lauzette, Raymond, 121n
Lawrence, Margaret, 81
Lawton, Mary, 124
Lee, Auriol, 573
Limerick, Mona, 245
Lomas, Herbert, 503n
Loraine, Robert, 120, 121n
Lowe, Trevor, 46n
Lowine, John, 535n

McCarthy, Lillah, 16, 17, 21, 23, 24, 26, 30, 32, 34, 35, 57, 58, 61n, 111, 119, 125, 126, 130, 132, 134, 135, 136, 143, 144, 145, 146, 147–49, 150, 165–94, 209n, 233, 240, 241, 244, 247, 249, 251, 252, 253, 254, 255, 258, 259, 264, 267, 269, 270, 271n, 271, 276, 278, 282, 284, 285, 286n, 301, 339n, 371, 501, 508n, 512, 513, 514, 516
McGill, Moyna, 460
McIntosh, Madge, 22, 81, 231–32
McKinnel, Norman, 71, 124, 263
McLaren, Ian, 127, 130
MacOwan, Michael, 463, 469, 470, 471, 472, 475
Macready, William Charles, 566n

Marlowe, Julia, 560n
Martin-Harvey, Sir John, 476–79
Massey, Raymond, 72, 468, 471
Matthison, Edith W. *See* Wynne-Matthison, Edith
Maude, Cyril, 444
Measor, Adela, 52n
Minto, Dorothy, 119
Moore, Eva, 46n, 445n

Napier, Alan, 473
Neilson, Harold V., 243n, 243
Neilson, Julia, 467n
Neilson-Terry, Phyllis, 168, 467
Nesbitt, Cathleen, 10, 176, 485

O'Donovan, Fred, 472
Olive, Edyth, 206n, 211, 230, 231n, 231, 235n, 237, 239, 240
Oscar, Henry, 471

Palmer, Ada, 437
Paunceforth, Claire, 26
Pavy, Salathiel, 535n
Payne, B. Iden, 242n, 242, 243, 244, 245, 248, 268, 276n
Percyval, Wigney, 451n
Petrie, Flinders, 389
Playfair, Sir Nigel, 60, 61, 271n, 461n, 478, 573
Poel, William, 22, 27, 34, 108, 119, 170, 180n, 199–200, 201, 202, 203–4, 206, 208n, 247, 289, 373, 452, 479–82, 504, 528

Quartermaine, Leon, 130, 408, 506

Raby, Mary, 52n
Rains, Claude, 467n
Rathbone, Guy, 278, 280
Redman, Joyce, 436
Reinhardt, Max, 184n, 262n, 265, 267, 269, 271, 410, 470, 477, 482, 508, 528
Richardson, Sir Ralph, 468, 470, 471
Robins, Elizabeth, 38, 47, 49, 120, 436, 483–84, 572, 573n
Robins, Gertrude, 573n
Robson, Eleanor (later Eleanor Robson Belmont), 137, 559–65
Rock, Charles, 450
Rodney, Stratton, 232
Rooke, Irene, 210, 503n
Rorke, Kate, 456n, 485–86
Rorke, Mary, 51, 456
Rosmer, Milton, 503n
Roughwood, Owen, 91n

Scaife, Gillian, 474
Scott, Margaretta, 168
Selwyn, Edgar, 457n
Seyler, Athene, 14, 32, 473n
Shaw, Jules, 278
Sherbrooke, Michael, 573
Shore, Ross, 573
Sothern, Edward, 144n
Speaight, Robert, 180n
Stanislavsky, Constantin, 9, 23, 62n, 410
Stanley, Eric, 473
Sullivan, Barry, 159
Swete, E. Lyall, 160n, 232
Swinley, Ion, 382

Tapping, Mrs. A. B., 459
Tapping, Alfred B., 119, 199, 459n
Tarver, E. W., 446
Tearle, Sir Godfrey, 278, 280
Tempest, Dame Marie, 22
Templeton, Howard, 451
Terry, Ellen, 27, 432, 501n, 557, 558n
Terry, Fred, 467n
Terry, Marion, 231
Thesiger, Ernest, 160, 473
Thorndike, Dame Sybil, 32, 160, 168, 510n
Thorne, Courtney, 487
Thorne, Sarah, 17
Tree, Sir Herbert Beerbohm, 29, 49, 53, 55, 65n, 67, 121–22, 122n, 144n, 170, 207n, 249, 262, 266, 267, 268, 269, 272, 273
Trollope, George, 451

Vanburgh, Violet, 253
Vosper, Frank, 471

Wade, Alan, 247n, 248n, 253
Ward, Genevieve, 203, 237, 453, 454n
Waring, Herbert, 445n
Weeden, Evelyn, 52n
Welles, Orson, 534–35
Whalley, Norma, 459
Wheeler, Penelope, 125n, 145, 149n, 241, 253, 255, 316, 339, 342
Whitby, Arthur, 232
White, Fisher, 474, 556
Whitty, Dame May, 510n
Williams, Emlyn, 429
Williams, Harcourt, 119, 230, 276, 467n, 473, 573
Williamson, Pym, 447
Winwood, Estelle, 503
Wise, Thomas, 139
Woffington, Peg, 26
Wolfit, Sir Donald, 471

Wontner, Arthur, 71, 278, 280
Wynne-Matthison, Edith, 230, 231, 240, 245, 246n
Wynyard, Diana, 466, 467

Yurka, Blanche, 81

Playwrights

Abercrombie, Lascelles, 500n, 517, 582–85
Aeschylus, 288–89, 290, 291, 292, 293–94
Albery, James, 26

Barrie, Sir James M., 179, 180nn, 242, 250, 259, 301, 341, 342, 349, 369, 370, 380, 453n, 489, 504n, 578
Bataille, Henri, 573
Bell, Lady Florence, 484, 543
Bennett, Arnold, 282, 339n
Bjørnson, Bjørnstjerne, 81
Brieux, Eugène, 41, 275, 496
Brookfield, Charles H. E., 21, 123n, 277, 571, 572

Calthrop, Dion Clayton, 489–92
Carr, Comyns, 56
Chesterton, G. K., 83

Dane, Clemence, 82n, 111, 461n, 467n, 493
D'Annunzio, Gabriele, 442
Drinkwater, John, 74, 133n, 482, 556

Ervine, St. John, 91, 111, 172, 492–501, 582–85
Euripides, 114, 135n, 141, 197, 198, 208, 228, 255, 258, 259, 263, 265, 268, 273, 289

Ford, Harriet, 560n
Fox, S. M., 23
France, Anatole, 126, 129n, 136

Galsworthy, John, 32, 107, 123, 126, 152, 194, 239n, 246n, 248, 249n, 250, 251n, 259, 282, 290, 301, 326, 330, 367, 370, 452, 461n, 490, 501–3
Ghéon, Henri, 478
Gilbert, Sir W. S., 197
Goethe, Johann Wolfgang von, 64
Greenwood, Walter, 176n
Gregory, Lady Augusta, 503–4
Grundy, Sidney, 559
Guitry, Sacha, 24, 40n, 309, 467n

Hankin, St. John, 44, 180, 181n, 239n
Harcourt, Cyril, 52n
Hauptmann, Gerhardt, 27, 41, 123n, 286, 309n, 445n
Hichens, Robert Smythe, 129n
Hofmannsthal, Hugo von, 266, 272
Hope, Anthony (Sir Anthony Hope Hawkins), 446n
Housman, Laurence, 173n, 504–7, 515, 524, 538, 546, 572, 573

Ibsen, Henrik, 9, 10, 22, 27, 35, 38, 41, 45, 48, 49, 51, 52n, 72n, 81, 82n, 84, 88, 100, 114, 123, 158, 159, 228n, 243n, 273, 291, 444, 451n, 454n, 553, 554, 572

Jones, Henry Arthur, 146, 273, 452n, 559
Jonson, Ben, 78

Knoblock, Edward (formerly Knoblaugh), 17, 338, 339n, 344
Kyd, Thomas, 108

Lacy, John, 82n
Lessing, Gotthold Ephraim, 123n
Lever, Lady Arthur, 458n

McAllister, Allister (pseud., Anthony P. Wharton), 243n
Maeterlinck, Maurice, 22, 24, 41, 70n, 135n, 153, 155n, 206n, 243n, 335n, 495n, 511
Marlowe, Christopher, 22, 452
Masefield, John, 23, 52n, 59n, 135n, 167, 262n, 264n, 270, 276n, 282, 323, 367, 490, 508–15, 517
Maugham, W. Somerset, 22, 559
Milne, A. A., 442
Molière (Jean Baptiste Poquelin), 134, 135n, 273
Moore, T. Sturge, 176, 190, 515–17

O'Casey, Sean, 503
Ould, Hermon, 518–19

Pailleron, Edward, 449n
Parker, Louis N., 486n
Phillips, Stephen, 299
Philpotts, Eden, 23
Pinero, Sir Arthur W., 21, 56, 70, 146, 205n, 277, 442, 559

Quintero, Joaquin Alvarez, 478
Quintero, Serafin, 478

Robinson, Lennox, 467n
Rose, Edward, 445n, 446n

Sardou, Victorien, 263
Schnitzler, Arthur, 23, 41, 125n, 270n, 271n, 479, 541
Shakespeare, William, 10, 22, 81, 90, 100, 159, 174, 216, 274n, 279, 290, 291, 295, 325, 374, 401, 402, 437–41, 444, 477, 479, 485, 500, 521, 527–34, 548, 583
Shaw, George Bernard, 13, 15, 16, 17, 22, 23, 29, 31, 35, 41, 50, 51, 54n, 56, 108, 111–63, 167, 168, 169, 170, 174, 177, 192, 194, 195, 208n, 208, 209n, 214, 222, 223, 238, 243n, 246n, 250, 259, 266n, 282, 301, 328, 332n, 340, 370, 390, 391, 395, 396, 435, 444, 445n, 447, 448n, 449, 485, 486, 487, 489, 492, 493, 559, 572, 583
Sheridan, Richard Brinsley, 416
Sierra, Martinez, 383, 452, 453, 455, 462, 463, 495n
Sophocles, 272
Stace, Henry, 60
Storm, Lesley, 470n
Strindberg, August, 123n
Sudermann, Herman, 22, 41
Sutro, Alfred, 45n, 50n, 56, 511n
Synge, J. M., 503, 545

Taylor, Tom, 26n
Thomas, Berte, 21, 38, 450n
Tolstoy, Leo, 531, 584

Van Druten, John, 168
Wharton, Anthony P. *See* McAllister, Allister
Wiers-Jenssen, J., 59n, 508n
Wilde, Oscar, 44

Yeats, W. B., 202n, 474, 503, 511, 515, 555

Managers, Stage Managers, and Designers

Adam, Ronald, 466, 467n

Belasco, David, 498
Brady, William A., 147n
Burton, Percy, 143, 144n, 145

Cochran, Charles B., 335n, 466, 495n
Courtneidge, Robert, 70
Craig, Edmund Gordon, 9, 504n, 527, 528
Curzon, Frank, 125

Daly, Augustin, 60
Daubeny, Sir Peter, 34
Dean, Basil, 280, 281n, 560n
Drinkwater, A. E., 133, 135, 139, 141,
  270, 378, 512

Frohman, Charles, 23, 146, 179, 180nn,
  227, 229, 250, 251, 254, 255, 256, 257,
  258, 259, 260, 267, 268, 269, 442, 506

Gilder, Rosamund, 430
Gray, Terence, 293n
Grein, J. T., 22, 39n, 449n

Hall, Anmer (pseud. of Alderson Horn),
  405, 469, 472
Harrison, Frederick, 65n
Harwood, H. M., 466, 467n
Horn, Alderson. *See* Hall, Anmer
Horniman, Annie, 242n, 443, 503n,
  503–4

Jackson, Sir Barry, 167, 478, 503, 559
Jones, Robert Edmund, 82, 129n

Leigh, J. H., 165, 197, 200
Lestocq, William, 256n, 268, 506

Rea, Alec L., 465n
Ricketts, Charles, 119, 176n
Rutherston, Albert (formerly Rothen-
  stein), 91, 528

Selwyn, Archibald, 457n
Shubert, Jacob, Lee, and Sam, 128

Terry, Edward, 486n
Trench, Herbert, 179, 184, 249, 263, 266,
  267, 268

Vedrenne, J. E., 23, 45n, 50, 53, 56n,
  117, 118, 121, 207, 222n, 228n, 232,
  234, 235, 236, 237, 241n, 243, 244, 458,
  505, 506, 507, 538

Wareing, Alfred, 280, 508
Whelan, Frederick, 65n, 121, 271, 281n,
  450
Wilkinson, Norman, 60, 218, 528, 557n
Williams, John B., 143

Critics

Agate, James, 414
Archer, William, 15, 22, 23, 25, 26, 29,
  32, 35–110, 69–70, 75–76, 80–81, 82n,
  104–7, 114, 117, 118, 158, 201, 213,
  219, 228n, 239n, 242, 246n, 246, 264n,
  268, 269, 272, 301, 315, 334, 393n, 435,
  487, 495n, 508, 508n, 511n, 546n, 554,
  572

Baughan, Edward Algernon, 62, 510
Beerbohm, Max, 82n, 85, 158, 159, 451
Boyd, Frank M., 63n

MacCarthy, Desmond, 27, 28, 109, 169,
  170–71, 214, 539n
Matthews, Brander, 274
Montague, C. E., 414

Nathan, George Jean, 123n

Palmer, John, 33

Scott, Clement, 37

Trewin, J. C., 6, 63n, 172, 174

Walkley, A. B., 27, 288, 573n

Others

Archer, Charles, 43n, 96n, 110n, 484,
  553, 554
Aristotle, 275
Armstrong, Terence Ian Fytton (pseud.,
  John Gawsworth), 516n
Asquith, Lady Cynthia, 369
Asquith, Herbert H., 149n, 156n, 258,
  333, 504n
Asquith, Margot, 149n, 459
Atlee, Clement R., 423n
Aubrey, John, 78n

Baldwin, Stanley, 390, 422
Balfour, Arthur James (later Earl Bal-
  four), 333
Bantock, Granville, 256n, 257, 258, 260,
  276
Baring, Maurice, 541
Barker, Albert James, 16
Barker, Mary Elizabeth, 16
Berenson, Bernard, 348
Bestermann, Theodore, 82n
Bevin, Ernest, 563, 565n
Binyon, Laurence, 483
Blake, William, 175
Boughton, Rutland, 505n
Bowes-Lyon, Angus Patrick, 92n
Bradley, A. C., 211
Brailsford, H. N., 213n

Brett, Oliver Sylvain Baliol, 3rd Viscount
  Esher, 58, 419, 525, 527n
Briggs, Frances, 34
Buckingham, Duke of, 82n
Buckle, Henry Thomas, 328, 329n
Buckmaster, Stanley Owen, Viscount
  Buckmaster, 314, 333, 335n
Bullen, A. H., 538n
Bulwer-Lytton, Sir Edward, 26
Burne-Jones, Sir Edward, 218
Burns, Robert, 96n
Butterworth, Thornton, 170, 175

Campbell, R. J., 282
Campbell-Bannerman, Sir Henry, 535,
  536n
Cannan, Gilbert, 56, 250n
Carr, Philip, 524
Cave, George, Viscount Cave of Rich-
  mond, 151n
Chamberlain, Neville, 423n
Chapman, Sir Thomas R., 387
Churchill, Sir Winston, 153, 297, 423n,
  481, 482n, 565n
Clynes, J. R., 557, 558n
Coburn, Langdon, 539
Collins, John Churton, 117, 246
Colum, Padraic, 365
Courtney, W. L., 558, 572
Crippen, Hawley Harvey, 275n
Criss, Thomas Ball, 31n

Dalcroze, Jacques, 283
Dashwood, Elizabeth, 352
Davies, Walford, 234
De La Mare, Walter, 367, 478, 482, 547
Delvin, Diana, 14
De Valera, Eamon, 495n
De Walden, Lord Howard, 483, 578
Dickinson, Helen T. ("Nellie"), 213, 318,
  324, 325, 335, 336, 341, 347, 350, 354
Dostoievsky, Fedor, 381
Downer, Alan S., 534–35, 565–66

Ellis, Havelock, 516n
Evelyn, John, 335n

Farr, Florence, 209, 222, 223, 224, 225,
  232
Field, Roscoe & Co., 153n
Fisher, H. A. L., 273n
Foch, Ferdinand, 316, 327, 329n
Fordham, Hallam, 430

Galsworthy, Ada, 326, 330, 367, 502
Garnett, David, 390, 392
Garnett, Edward, 56

Garvin, J. L., 232, 481, 521
Gates, Ellen M., 304–5, 316, 320
Gladstone, Herbert, 535
Gosse, Sir Edmund, 45, 54, 370
Gray, James, 315, 332, 343, 349, 377
Greenwood, Arthur, 422, 423n
Grock, Monsieur, 330

Hadow, Sir Henry, 557, 558n
Haigh, Arthur Elam, 222n
Halifax, Lord, 563, 565n
Hardy, Florence, 160, 370, 372, 383, 390
  399
Hardy, Thomas, 23, 66n, 160, 367–86,
  390, 399, 446n
Harrison, Frederic, 328, 329n
Hawksley, Bourchier F., 227
Hazlitt, William, 35
Heinemann, William, 48–49, 537
Henderson, Effie ("Madame Albanesi"),
  461n
Henderson, M. I., 197
Hoare, Sir Samuel, 419, 422
Hogarth, David George, 390n
Housman, A. E., 370, 504
Howard, Lady Mary, 197, 202, 205, 207,
  209, 222, 249, 250, 288, 296, 298
Hueffer, F. M., 259
Humboldt, Alexander van, 365n, 366
Hunt, Leigh, 35
Huntington, Archer Milton, 31n, 153n,
  191, 301, 320, 322n, 348
Huntington, Caroline Densmore, 321n
Huntington, Collis Potter, 30, 31n, 362n
Huntington, Helen, 16, 17, 24, 30, 35,
  67n, 72, 73, 78, 82, 83, 93, 111, 149n,
  150n, 158, 160, 174, 177, 191, 193, 288,
  293n, 299–366, 370, 377, 380, 382, 383,
  384, 391, 401, 405, 407, 452, 453n, 478,
  495n, 501, 533, 545, 553
Huxley, Julian, 273n

Ibsen, Lillebil, 81
Ibsen, Tancred, 81

James, Henry, 396
Jebb, Sir Richard, 197
Joffre, Joseph Jacques Césaire, 133n
Joyce, James, 360

Kahn, Otto, 54
Keeble, Sir Frederick W., 167, 168n
Kingsley, Henry, 549
Kipling, Rudyard, 173n, 259, 370
Knight, G. Wilson, 31
Knopf, Alfred, 546

Laurence, Dan H., 14, 113, 234n, 445n
Lawrence, T. E., 90n, 381, 387–403
Leclerc, Marc, 533n, 551–52
Leetham, Sir Arthur, 515
Leslie, Shane, 160
Lever, William Hesketh, Viscount Lever-
    hulme, 104n
Lewis, Sir George, 151–53, 194
Lewis, Sinclair, 83
Lloyd-George, David, 156n, 327, 329n,
    333, 363, 495n
Lodge, Sir Oliver, 282
Low, Sir Sidney, 181n
Lutyens, Sir Edwin Landseer, 454n, 457
Lytton, Lord, 56n, 234

Macready, Cecil Frederick Nevil, 565n
Maden, Sarah, 389
Marbury, Elizabeth, 81, 82n, 123n, 128
Margoliouth, David, 275
Marsh, Sir Edward, 481–82, 514, 515,
    535, 549
Maskelyne and Cook, 225n
Mason, A. E. W., 352
Massingham, H. W., 123, 180, 181n, 328
Mathews, Lee, 327
Mathews, Mrs. Lee, 234, 238, 247, 255,
    314
Mathews, Myles, 141, 148
May, Frederick, 31n, 40n
Medley, C. D., 153n, 171, 194, 338, 349
Medley, J. C., 19
Meredith, George, 45, 452
Milner, Alfred, Viscount Milner, 327,
    329n
Moorat, Joseph, 505, 507
Moore, G. E., 515
Morgan, Margery M., 31n, 40n
Morley, John, 234n
Munro, H. H. (pseud., Saki), 542
Murray, Gilbert, 21, 29, 45n, 58, 73, 114,
    135n, 144n, 184, 195–298, 299, 309n,
    444, 452, 578
Murray, Rosalind, 256, 275, 283
Murray, Sir Terence, 197

Packer, Charles, 335n
Packer, Philip, 334
Paderewski, Ignace, 363
Page, Curtis Hidden, 129n
Pankhurst, Christabel, 259
Paull, H. N., 507
Pease, Edward R., 32n
Phillimore, Mrs. R. C. ("Lion"), 328,
    329n
Phillimore, Robert Charles, 329n
Phillips, Sir Claude, 453, 454n

Pitt, Percy, 226, 230
Pollock, Sir Frederick, 565n
Purdom, C. B., 14, 31n, 40n, 113, 113n,
    122n, 162, 171, 172, 173, 174, 190, 195,
    239n, 298, 463n, 489, 573n

Reade, Charles, 26
Redford, George A., 54, 118, 123n, 250n,
    262, 263, 277n, 571
Reich, Emil, 259
Roberts, Marguerite, 369
Roberts, S. C., 550
Rylands, George, 431n

Sassoon, Sir Philip, 392, 399–400
Sassoon, Siegfried, 367
Scott, C. P., 314, 327, 329n
Scott, Elizabeth, 440n
Scott, Walter, 45
Scott-James, Rolfe Arnold, 523, 524,
    531–34, 550–55
Shaw, Charlotte, 328, 339, 391
Shelley, Percy B., 414
Sidgwick, Frank, 417, 532, 537–46
Smith, F. E., Lord Birkenhead, 151n
Spencer, Victor A., 338, 339n
Spurgeon, Charles Hadden, 157n
Squire, J. C., 523n, 533, 553, 558
Stevenson, R. L., 250n
Swinburne, Algernon Charles, 78
Swing, Raymond Gram, 363n, 366
Sykes, Sir Mark, 394
Symons, Arthur, 511

Tennyson, Alfred, 454n
Toynbee, Arnold, 283n
Toynbee, Arnold J., 283n
Trevelyan, G. M., 338
Trevelyan, Sir Charles, 536

Vansittart, Robert, 419
Verdin, Cardinal, 357

Waddington, S. P., 276, 278
Wagner, Richard, 118, 120
Walpole, Sir Hugh, 342, 547–49
Webb, Beatrice, 126, 324, 329n
Webb, Sidney, 126, 324, 329n, 557
Weintraub, Stanley, 190, 391
Wells, H. G., 259, 282
West, Mrs. George Cornwallis, 122n
Weyman, Stanley, 445n
Wheeler, Charles Edwin ("Christopher"
    or "Hopher"), 125n, 145, 148, 149n,
    245n, 261, 271n, 309, 312–13, 316, 327,
    339, 342, 347, 445n, 476, 479, 452n
Whitworth, Geoffrey, 31, 555–58

Whitworth, Phyllis, 558–59
Whitworth, Robin, 14
Willoughby de Broke, Lord, 93n
Wilson, A. E., 454n
Wilson, John Dover, 441n
Woolf, Virginia, 432, 433n
Woolley, C. L., 389
Wordsworth, William, 28
Worsham, Arabella, 31n

Yates, Edmund, 37
Young, Sir John, 79n

Zorn, Anders, 145n

LITERARY WORKS

Plays

Admirable Bashville, The (Shaw), 23
Admirable Crichton, The (Barrie), 453
Agamemnon (Aeschylus), 288–89, 292,
  293–94
Aglavaine and Selysette (Maeterlinck),
  206n
"Agnes Colander" (Barker), 22, 40n,
  41n, 446n
Alcestis (Euripides), 293n
Alladine and Palomides (Maeterlinck),
  511n
All's Well that Ends Well (Shakespeare),
  78, 439
Anatol (Schnitzler), 23, 269, 270, 479,
  541, 544, 545, 557n
Androcles and the Lion (Shaw), 23, 126,
  127, 129n, 130, 131, 132, 134, 135, 136,
  138, 139, 140, 144n, 145, 167, 168, 489
Andromache (Gilbert Murray), 197, 444
Anna Pendersdotter (Wiers-Jenssen). *See*
  Witch, The (Masefield)
Anthony and Anna (St. John Ervine), 492
Antigone (Sophocles), 293n, 297
Antony and Cleopatra (Shakespeare),
  54n, 211, 444
Aphrodite against Artemis (T. Sturge
  Moore), 516
Arizona (Augustus Thomas), 560n
Arms and the Man (Shaw), 243, 246n,
  247n
As You Like It (Shakespeare), 416
Avariés, Les (Damaged Goods) (Brieux),
  496

Bacchae, The (Euripides), 199n, 203, 222,
  223, 225, 229, 241, 247, 285, 288
Back to Methuselah (Shaw), 153–57, 159
Beatrice Joanna (Archer), 81
Becket (Tennyson), 454n
Belle, The (Leopold Lewis), 119
Belle of Mayfair, The (Brookfield), 571
Bethlehem (Laurence Housman), 505n,
  507, 527
Betrothal, The (Maeterlinck), 24, 126n,
  334, 494
Between Sunset and Dawn (Ould), 518
Beyond the Horizon (O'Neill), 91
Bill of Divorcement, A (Clemence Dane),
  461n
Blue Bird, The (Maeterlinck), 495n
Brand (Ibsen), 483
Breed of the Treshams, The (Rutherford),
  477
Brown Sugar (Lady Arthur Lever), 458
Burgomaster of Stilemonde, The (Maeter-
  linck), 70n
Campden Wonder, The (Masefield), 52,
  508
Candida (Shaw), 22, 27, 124, 160, 197,
  216, 444, 445, 485, 486, 486n, 487
Captain Brassbound's Conversion (Shaw),
  22, 116n, 147n, 444, 448n, 449n
Carlyon Sahib (Gilbert Murray), 21, 197
Case of Rebellious Susan, The (Jones), 22
Charity that Began at Home, The (St.
  John Hankin), 239n
Christmas Eve (Ould), 518
Cigarette-Maker's Romance, A (Hannan),
  477
Collected Plays with Their Prefaces, The
  (Shaw, ed. Laurence), 150n
Coriolanus (Shakespeare), 101, 298
Corsican Brothers, The (Boucicault), 477
Cuckoo, The (Brookfield), 571
Cyrano de Bergerac (Rostand), 309

Damnation Nan (Calthrop), 492
Dance of Life, The (Ould), 518
Dark Lady of the Sonnets, The (Shaw),
  266
Daughter of Jorio, The (D'Annunzio), 442
Dean of St. Patrick's (Florence Bell),
  543n
Dear Brutus (Barrie), 461n
Dear Old Charlie (Brookfield), 571, 572
Death of Tintagiles, The (Maeterlinck),
  22, 134, 511n
Deburau (Guitry), 24, 40n, 309, 314, 321,
  334, 338, 460, 467n
Devil's Disciple, The (Shaw), 123, 241n

Distaff Side, The (van Druten), 168
Doctor Faustus (Marlowe), 452
Doctor's Dilemma, The (Shaw), 51, 123, 124, 125n, 126, 127, 129n, 130, 132, 134, 138, 139, 140, 239n, 464, 493
Doll's House, A (Ibsen), 45, 49, 444, 487, 553, 554
Dovecote, The (Brookfield), 571
Duchess of Malfi, The (Webster), 176n

Edward II (Marlowe), 22, 480
Electra (Euripides), 204, 210, 211, 218, 222, 223, 224, 225, 226, 227, 228, 232, 233, 245, 251, 252, 260, 272, 442
Eliza Comes to Stay (H. V. Esmond), 46n
English Nell (Hope and Rose), 22, 446n
Eumenides (Aeschylus), 290n
Everyman (Anon.), 199–200, 208n, 235n, 290

Faithful, The (Masefield), 513n
Famous Tragedy of the Queen of Cornwall, The (Hardy), 369, 374n
Fanny's First Play (Shaw), 121n, 132, 133, 133n, 136, 138, 273, 463
Farewell to the Theatre (Barker), 24
Fascinating Mr. Vanderveldt, The (Sutro), 49, 50
Faust (Goethe), 470
First Mrs. Fraser, The (St. John Ervine), 492
Follow Your Saint (Lesley Storm), 470n
Fortunato (Quintero), 405
Fratricide Punished (Anon.), 108, 441n
Friedensfest, Das (Hauptmann), 27, 309n, 445n
Fugitive, The (Galsworthy), 503

Getting Married (Shaw), 122, 126, 134, 145
Ghosts (Ibsen), 118, 487, 554
Goetz von Berlichingen (Goethe), 90
Great Adventure, The (Bennett), 371, 372
Great Catherine (Shaw), 128
Green Goddess, The (Archer), 35, 72n, 83, 91n, 93n, 109
Gustavus Vasa (Strindberg), 293n

Hamlet (Shakespeare), 22, 79, 100, 228, 405, 410, 417, 427, 428, 442, 461n, 476, 487, 532, 533–34, 551, 554, 583
Harlequinade (Barker and Calthrop), 489
Hassan (James Elroy Flecker), 293n
Heartbreak House (Shaw), 87, 150n, 159
Hedda Gabler (Ibsen), 45, 47, 48, 49, 52n, 483

Heimat (Sudermann). See Magda (Sudermann)
Henry VIII (Shakespeare), 293n
Herod (Stephen Phillips), 299n
Heroic Stubbs, The (Jones), 452n
Hippolytus (Euripides), 195, 197, 199n, 200, 201, 202, 203, 208n, 209n, 210, 224, 225, 227, 242n, 244, 245, 251, 252, 253, 261, 279, 297
His Majesty (Barker), 16, 24, 31, 160n, 198, 464, 465, 466, 468, 470, 473n
House of Burnside, The (Louis N. Parker), 486n
How to be Healthy though Married (H. M. Harwood), 467n
Hundred Years Old, A (Quintero), 478

Insect Play, The (Kapek Brothers), 293n
Interior (Maeterlinck), 511n
In the Next Room (Eleanor Robson and Harriet Ford), 560n
Iphegenia in Tauris (Euripides), 134, 135n, 141, 251n, 251, 252, 253, 256nn, 259, 260, 261, 268, 269, 276, 279, 280
Irene Wycherly (Anthony P. Wharton), 243n

Jane Clegg (St. John Ervine), 492
John Bull's Other Island (Shaw), 121, 124, 214, 216, 480, 504
John Ferguson (St. John Ervine), 92, 492
John Gabriel Borkman (Ibsen), 454n
Joy (Galsworthy), 501
Judith (T. Sturge Moore), 190, 435, 516
Julius Caesar (Shakespeare), 430
Justice (Galsworthy), 251n, 452, 501

King Lear (Shakespeare), 10, 24, 77, 100, 325, 351, 353, 355, 356, 358, 380, 424–27, 429
Kismet (Knoblock), 339n

Lady Burglar, The (Brookfield), 571
Lady from Alfaqueque, The (Quintero), 405
Lady from the Sea, The (Ibsen), 444, 451n
Lady of Belmont, The (St. John Ervine), 499n
Land of Heart's Desire, The (Yeats), 555
Law of the Sands, The (Hichens), 129n
League of Youth, The (Ibsen), 22, 27, 45n, 444
Life of St. Bernard, The (Ghéon), 478
Light Comedian, The (Ould), 518
Lion Hunters, The (Pailleron). See World of Boredom, The (Pailleron)

Little Eyolf (Ibsen), 47, 487
Little Plays of St. Francis, The (Laurence Housman), 504
Love on the Dole (Greenwood), 176n
Lover, The (Sierra), 463
Love's Comedy (Ibsen), 35
Lysistrata (Aristophanes), 262, 292

Macbeth (Shakespeare), 90, 100, 180n, 412, 431, 535n
Madras House, The (Barker), 16, 23, 28, 100, 126, 127, 129n, 130, 131, 134, 138, 176n, 180n, 250n, 251n, 254, 256, 262, 270, 271, 290, 384, 466, 467n, 510n, 540, 542, 543, 544
Magda (Sudermann), 22
Magic (Chesterton), 83
Magician, The (Archer), 74
Major Barbara (Shaw), 114, 123, 126, 128, 139, 146, 222n, 223n, 226n, 238, 332n
Maman Colibri (Henri Bataille), 576
Man and Superman (Shaw), 17, 49, 167, 173n, 239n, 263, 452, 576n
Man of Destiny, The (Shaw), 22
Man of Honour, A (Maugham), 22
Man Who Married a Dumb Wife, The (Anatole France), 126n, 127, 129n, 130, 136, 140
Marché Nuptiale, La (Henri Bataille), 576
Mariage Forcé, Le (Molière), 134
Marianne (T. Sturge Moore), 516
Marrying of Ann Leete, The (Barker), 22, 28, 84, 158, 159, 198, 450, 451n
Martha Washington (Archer), 81, 82
Mary, Mary, Quite Contrary (St. John Ervine), 498, 499n
Masks and Faces (Tom Taylor and Charles Reade), 26
Master Builder, The (Ibsen), 45, 72n, 120, 273, 444, 483
Medea (Euripides), 211, 233, 234, 235, 236, 237, 238, 239, 242, 245, 251, 255
Member for Turrington, The (Stace), 61n
Merchant of Venice, The (Shakespeare), 415, 498, 499n
Merely Mary Ann (Israel Zangwill), 560n
Midsummer Night's Dream, A (Shakespeare), 23, 59–62, 126, 130, 131, 133, 136, 138, 140, 286, 318, 437–38, 464, 485, 498, 561n
Milestones (Knoblock and Bennett), 339n
"Miracle, A" (Barker), 22, 40n, 41n
Misalliance (Shaw), 132, 134, 139, 251n
Money (Lytton), 26
Morris Dance, The (Barker), 453, 458
Mr. Pim Passes By (Milne), 442

Mrs. Warren's Profession (Shaw), 22, 118
My Lady's Dress (Knoblock), 339n

Nathan the Wise (Lessing), 123n
Notorious Mrs. Ebbsmith, The (Pinero), 21

Oedipus Rex (Sophocles), 118, 121, 184, 256, 258, 259, 260, 261, 262, 263, 265, 266, 268, 269, 271n, 271, 272, 276, 477
Oliver Cromwell (Drinkwater), 74
Only Way, The (Langbridge and Wills), 477
On the Rocks (Shaw), 168
Othello (Shakespeare), 100, 185, 429, 440, 534, 535n
"Our Visitor to Work-a-Day" (Barker and Thomas), 21

Pains and Penalties (Laurence Housman), 505, 572
Paolo and Francesca (Stephen Phillips), 299n
Pauvre sans L'Escalier, Le (Ghéon), 478
Peer Gynt (Ibsen), 44, 50, 54, 54n, 55, 82, 83, 239, 554
Phèdre (Racine), 354n
Philanderer, The (Shaw), 124, 125n
Philip the King (Masefield), 134, 508, 513n, 514
Phoenix (Lascelles Abercrombie), 500n, 585
Poet and the Puppets, The (Brookfield), 21
Pretenders, The (Ibsen), 9
Prisoner of Zenda, The (Anthony Hope), 27
Prunella; or Love in a Dutch Garden (Barker and Housman), 173, 203–4, 205, 206, 207, 209, 281, 285, 334, 480, 505, 506, 537, 546
Pygmalion (Shaw), 128, 132, 138, 146

Reformer, The (Cyril Harcourt), 52n
Rehearsal, The (Buckingham), 82n
Return of the Prodigal, The (St. John Hankin), 181n, 452
Rhesus (Euripides), 283
Richard II (Shakespeare), 22, 27, 200, 409, 411–13, 480
Rococo (Barker), 23
Romantic Young Lady, The (Sierra), 452, 457n, 463, 464
Romeo and Juliet (Shakespeare), 409
Rosmersholm (Ibsen), 45, 291, 483

St. Joan (Shaw), 159, 160n
School for Scandal, The (Sheridan), 416, 451n
Second Mrs. Tanqueray, The (Pinero), 21, 129, 205n
Secret Life, The (Barker), 24, 28, 31, 85n, 85–89, 91n, 92, 95–104, 106, 159n, 198, 389, 393n, 394, 459, 500, 583–85
Secret Woman, The (Philpotts), 23
Sentimentalists, The (Meredith), 45n, 452
Ship, The (St. John Ervine), 497–98
Shulamite, The (Knoblock and Askew), 17
Silver Box, The (Galsworthy), 32, 239n, 248, 452, 501
Six of Calais, The (Shaw), 168
Skin Game, The (Galsworthy), 461n
Smilin' Through (Jane Cowl), 457n
So Far and No Father (H. M. Harwood), 467n
Strife (Galsworthy), 248, 501
Sweet Lavender (Pinero), 70

Tempest, The (Shakespeare), 566
Tess of the D'Urbervilles (Hardy), 369, 381n, 384
Three Plays (Archer), 82n
Three Wayfarers, The (Hardy), 446n
Tinker's Wedding, The (Synge), 546
To See Ourselves (E. M. Delafield), 465n
Tragedy of Nan, The (Masefield), 167, 254n, 283, 503
Tragedy of Pompey the Great, The (Masefield), 276n, 508n, 512
Trelawney of the "Wells" (Pinero), 442
Troilus and Cressida (Shakespeare), 100
Trojan Women, The (Euripides), 141, 203, 204, 206, 207, 209n, 209, 210, 224, 237, 241, 251, 252, 254, 263, 272, 282, 287, 452, 557n
Twelfth Night (Shakespeare), 23, 60, 126, 207n, 284, 415–16, 429, 529
Twelve-Pound Look, The (Barrie), 504n
Two Gentlemen of Verona (Shakespeare), 486n
Two Roses (James Albery), 26
Two Shepherds, The (Sierra), 495

Under the Red Robe (Edward Rose), 21, 27, 445n

Vice Versa (Anstey), 21
Victoria Regina (Laurence Housman), 504
Vierge Folle, La (Henri Bataille), 573
"Village Carpenter, The" (Barker). *See* "Wicked Man, The" (Barker)
Vote by Ballot (Barker), 23

Votes for Women! (Robins), 485n
Voysey Inheritance, The (Barker), 23, 28, 47n, 74n, 86, 87, 100, 120, 222n, 223, 225n, 229n, 240, 248, 451n, 452, 466, 467n, 499, 522, 537

Waste (Barker), 23, 54n, 77, 86, 87, 118, 233n, 234n, 238n, 239n, 241, 244, 245, 386, 468, 469, 470, 471, 473–76, 499, 531
Waters of Bitterness, The (S. M. Fox), 23
Way of the World, The (Congreve), 534
Way the Money Goes, The (Florence Bell), 543
Weather-Hen; or Invertebrata, The (Barker and Thomas), 21, 38, 39, 40n, 450, 451n
What Every Woman Knows (Barrie), 180n
Where There Is Nothing (Yeats), 202n
White-Headed Boy, The (Lennox Robinson), 467n
"Wicked Man, The" (Barker), 23, 262n, 513n
Widowers' Houses (Shaw), 114
Wild Decembers (Clemence Dane), 467n
Wild Duck, The (Ibsen), 45, 46, 49, 88, 228n, 293n, 487
Will Shakespeare (Clemence Dane), 81
Winter's Tale, The (Shakespeare), 23, 176, 176n, 444, 455n, 528, 557n
Witch, The (Masefield), 23, 59n, 138, 263, 269, 270, 271, 280, 508
Within the Law (Anon.), 63n
Wonderful Visit, The (St. John Ervine), 494
World of Boredom, The (Pailleron), 449n

You Never Can Tell (Shaw), 54n, 207, 208n, 444

Other Works

Ada (Helen Granville-Barker), 581
Annals of an Active Life (Nevil Macready), 566n
Apprentice to Truth, An (Helen Huntington), 581
Art of the Play, The (ed. Downer), 535n
Art of the Play, The (Ould), 518
Attic Theatre, The (Haigh), 222n

Babbitt (Sinclair Lewis), 83
Bernard Shaw: His Life, Work and Friends (St. John Ervine), 111, 492
Bernard Shaw: The Collected Letters (ed. Laurence), 113, 234n, 445n

Both Sides of the Curtain (Robins), 483
Brief Lives (Aubrey), 78n
Brothers Karamazov, The (Dostoievsky), 381

Cathedral, The (Walpole), 342n
Come, Julia (Helen Granville-Barker), 293, 294, 581
Common Sense about the War (Shaw), 129, 137
Court Theatre; 1904–1907, The (MacCarthy), 27, 539n
Craft of Comedy, The (Seyler and Haggard), 473n

Dictionary of National Biography, The, 172, 197, 316, 322, 334
Doomsland (Shane Leslie), 160
Drama of Political Man, A (Margery M. Morgan), 31n
Drawings for the Theatre (Robert Edmond Jones), 129n
Dynasts, The (Hardy), 23, 65, 369, 464

Early Stages (Gielgud), 405
Eastern Red (Helen Huntington), 150n, 581
Ellen Terry's Memoirs, 433n
Eminent Tragedian William Charles Macready, The (Downer), 566n
English Dramatists of Today (Archer), 35
Englishman's Love Letters, An (Laurence Housman), 504
Exemplary Theatre, The (Barker), 24, 33, 156n, 158, 459n, 497n

Folk Songs from the Spanish (Helen Huntington), 581
Four Feathers (A. E. W. Mason), 352
Four Stages of Greek Religion (Murray), 262n
From the Cup of Silence (Helen Huntington), 581

Genius of Thomas Hardy, The (ed. Margaret Drabble), 391
Governance of England, The (Low), 181n
"Great Stupidity, The" (Archer), 73n

Hardy's Poetic Drama and the Theatre (Marguerite Roberts), 369
Harley Granville Barker; Man of the Theatre, Dramatist and Scholar (Purdom), 31n, 40n, 172n, 298n, 463n, 489, 573n
"Heritage of the Actor, The" (Barker), 85n
History of the Fabian Society, The (Pease), 32n

John Gielgud's Hamlet (Rosamond Gilder), 431n
Journey to Heartbreak (Weintraub), 190
Jude the Obscure (Hardy), 369
Judith Paris (Walpole), 342n

Kosmos (Humboldt), 365, 366

Letters of T. E. Lawrence, The (ed. Garnett), 390
Life of Gladstone (Morley), 234
Life of Sir Joshua Reynolds, The (Claude Phillips), 454n
Life of Thomas Hardy, The (Florence Hardy), 370
Living Mirrors (Helen Granville-Barker), 581
Locked Book, The (Helen Granville-Barker), 361n, 533n, 581
Lost Leader, The (Bridges Adams), 28n

Macready's Reminiscences and Selections from His Diaries and Letters (ed. Pollock), 565n
Marsh Lights (Helen Huntington), 581
Milton (Blake), 175
Mint, The (Lawrence), 389
Mr. Perrin and Mr. Traill (Walpole), 342n
Moon in Scorpio (Helen Granville-Barker), 581
Moon Lady, The (Helen Huntington), 581
Moonseed (Rosalind Murray), 275
Myself and My Friends (Lillah McCarthy), 169–75, 501

National Theatre, A (Barker), 523n, 525n
National Theatre; Scheme and Estimates, A (Barker and Archer), 23, 25, 32, 54n, 57–58, 63n, 66, 70n, 93n, 240
Nineteen Poems (Helen Granville-Barker), 581
Old Drama and the New, The (Archer), 84
On Dramatic Method (Barker), 82n, 291–92
On Dreams (Archer), 82n
Oxford History of Music, The (ed. Hadow), 558n

"Passion de Notre Frère le Poilu, La" (Leclerc), 533n, 551–52
Player's Shakespeare, The (ed. Barker), 24, 91n
Poems (Helen Granville-Barker), 359n, 361n, 581

Prefaces to Shakespeare (Barker), 24, 31, 407, 441
Private Shaw and Public Shaw (Weintraub), 391
Provincial Lady in War Time, The (Elizabeth Dashwood), 352

"Reconstruction in the Theatre" (Barker), 288
Rise of the Greek Epic, The (Gilbert Murray), 241n, 276
Rogue Herries (Walpole), 342n

Samson Agonistes (Milton), 200
Second Jungle Book, The (Kipling), 173n
Seven Pillars of Wisdom (Lawrence), 389, 390, 393n, 394n, 397
Shakespeare's Dramatic Challenge (Wilson Knight), 7n
Shaw-Barker Letters, The (Purdom), 14, 113, 113n, 114n, 162n, 489
Solitary Path, The (Helen Huntington), 581
Souls on Fifth (Barker), 146, 304n, 557n
Sovereign Good, The (Helen Huntington), 299, 581
Studies in Shakespeare (Churton Collins), 246n
Study of Drama, The (Barker), 550

Tower, The (Yeats), 515
Traitor Angel (Helen Granville-Barker), 361n, 581

Vinedresser and Other Poems, The (T. Sturge Moore), 516
Virginibus Puerisque (Stevenson), 250n
Voltaire, Montesquieu and Rousseau in England (Churton Collins), 246n

William Archer: Life, Work and Friendships (Charles Archer), 43n, 110n
William Poel and the Elizabethan Revival (Speaight), 180n
Winding Stair, The (Yeats), 515
Wives and Celebrities (Helen Granville-Barker), 581
Wrong Box, The (R. L. Stevenson and Lloyd Osbourne), 454n

NEWSPAPERS AND MAGAZINES

Alloa Advertiser, 37
Atlantic Monthy (magazine), 46n, 73n

Bookman, The (London), 108
Bookman, The (New York), 533n

Cornhill Magazine, 338

Daily Chronicle, The, 333
Daily Mail, 141, 527, 583
Daily Mirror, 167
Daily News, 62, 510
Daily Telegraph, The, 37, 165, 454n, 481n
Daily Worker, The, 563
Drama (magazine), 27, 31n

Edinburgh Evening News, 37
English Digest, The, 516n
Everybody's Magazine (New York), 129n

Figaro, Le, 524
Fortnightly Review, The, 147n, 573n

Hampton's Magazine, 540

London Figaro, The, 35

Manchester Guardian, The, 314, 329n
Mercury, The, 523n, 553, 554, 555

Nation, The, 35, 181n
National Review, The, 572
New Statesman, The, 109, 433n
New Weekly, The, 523n
New York Herald-Tribune, 123n, 363

Observer, The, 78, 282, 481n, 492, 493, 500n, 521, 582, 583

Pall Mall Gazette, 282
Play Pictorial, 529

Quarterly Review, The, 85n, 91, 92

Saturday Review (London), 113, 452n
Strand Magazine, 169

Temps, Le, 524
Times, The (London), 27, 93, 123, 138, 233, 268, 288, 328, 353, 407, 465, 491, 571, 573n
Times Literary Supplement, The, 38n, 109, 110n, 111, 134, 163
Tribune, The, 35, 51, 52

Western Morning News, 34
Westminster Gazette, The, 138
World, The, 16n, 35, 37, 38

Yorkshire Evening Post, 33

THEATERS AND OTHER INSTITUTIONS

Abbey Theatre, Dublin, 492, 503
Acting Academy, The. *See* Royal Academy of Dramatic Art, The
Actors' Benevolent Fund, 477
Aldwych Theatre, London, 34
Ambassador's Theatre, London, 467n
Arts Council of Great Britain, The, 424, 526
Arts Theatre, London, 499n
Avenue Theatre, London, 21, 446

Bayreuth Opera House, 91
Belasco Theatre, New York, 499n
Berg Collection, New York Public Library, 14
Birmingham Repertory Theatre, 167
Bodleian Library, 14
Booth Theatre, New York, 35, 145
Bradfield College, 283
British Drama League, 24, 483, 527n, 555–58
British Institute, Paris, 24
British Library, 14, 38n, 126n
British Theatre Museum, 14, 262n
Butler Library (Columbia University), 14

Calgary, University of (Library), 14
Cambridge Festival Theatre, 292, 293n
CEMA (Council for the Encouragement of Music and the Arts), 424
Century Theatre, New York (previously called the "New Theatre"), 54n
Chicago, Art Institute of, 145n
Columbia University, 54
Comedy Theatre, London, 21, 450n
Cornell University Library, 14
Coronet Theatre, London, 263, 573, 576n
Court Theatre, London. *See* Royal Court Theatre

Dorset County Museum, 14
Dramatists' Club, The (London), 147n, 277
Duke of York's Theatre, London, 23, 29, 45n, 180n, 249n, 251n, 252, 256n, 264, 442, 452, 458, 501, 510n, 540

Edinburgh International Festival, 34
Elizabethan Stage Society, 34, 479, 481, 482
Embassy Theatre, Swiss Cottage, London, 465n, 467n
Empire Theatre, New York, 146
English Positivist Committee, The, 329n

ENSA (Entertainments National Service Association), 281, 420, 423n
Eurhythmics, Academy of, 283

Fabian Society, The, 22, 32, 43n, 137, 169, 170, 178n, 180, 242, 271, 423n
Fortune Theatre, London, 467

Gaiety Theatre, London, 24, 126n, 495n
Gaiety Theatre, Manchester, 242n, 243, 443, 503n
Garrick Theatre, London, 50

Hardy Players, The, 374n, 381n
Harleian Society, The, 322n
Harvard University, 24, 54, 295
Haymarket Theatre, London, 21, 27, 63, 65n, 444, 451
Her Majesty's Theatre, London (later known as His Majesty's Theatre), 65n, 129n, 138, 207n, 424
His Majesty's Theatre, London. *See* Her Majesty's Theatre
Home University Library, 272, 275, 283
Houghton Library, Harvard University, 14, 270
Humanities Research Center (University of Texas), 14, 25, 167n, 168n, 169n, 170, 170n, 172n, 176n, 302
Huntington Library, 14, 312n

Imperial Theatre, London, 22, 23
Independent Theatre, The, 39n, 42, 449n
Iowa, University of, 14
Irish Literary Theatre (later the Abbey Theatre), 503

Kingsway Theatre, London, 23, 58, 59n, 66n, 121n, 125, 132n, 133, 133n, 135, 139, 140, 152, 243n, 279, 280, 281, 284, 287, 371, 464, 477, 482, 491, 512, 545, 546

League of Nations, The, 198, 287, 289, 290n, 296, 297n, 584
Little Theatre, London, 59n, 121n, 125, 184n, 186n, 262, 276, 277, 504
Little Theatre, New York, 145–46
Liverpool Playhouse (formerly Liverpool Repertory Theatre), 281, 435, 469n, 498n, 503n
Lyceum Theatre, London, 427, 428
Lyric Theatre, London, 22, 197, 199

Moscow Art Theatre, 62n, 528

National Liberal Club, 51, 206n, 219
National Theatre, New York, 82n

New Century Theatre (Society), 38, 41, 42, 56n
New Theatre, Cardiff, 56
New Theatre, London, 160n
New Theatre, New York, 32, 54n, 138, 140, 258, 259, 264, 560n
Novelty Theatre, London, 444

Old Vic Theatre, London, 83, 351, 405, 421, 422, 424, 428, 525–26, 527n
Olympic Theatre, London, 445n
Opera House, Bayreuth, 119

Palace Theatre, London, 23, 270
Phoenix Theatre, London, 467
Pilgrim Trust, The, 428
Players Theatre, London, 61n
Prince of Wales Theatre, Birmingham, 57, 247
Princess Theatre, New York, 128
Princeton University, 24

Queen's Theatre, London, 470n

Regent's Park Open Air Theatre, London, 168
Royal Academy of Dramatic Art, The, 557n
Royal Court Theatre, London (also known as Court Theatre), 23, 27, 28, 41, 43, 45-55 passim, 111, 113, 114, 173n, 181n, 195, 200n, 202n, 202, 206n, 207n, 214, 218, 224, 269, 270, 405, 443, 444, 452, 485n, 501, 503n, 505, 508, 508n, 546n
Royal Shakespeare Company, 33
Royal Society of Literature, 24, 31, 482n, 549
Royalty Theatre, Glasgow, 262, 452
Royalty Theatre, London, 22, 444, 463n

Sadler's Wells Theatre, London, 466
St. James's Theatre, London, 23, 29, 32, 33, 35, 51n, 93n, 125n, 129n, 489

St. Martin's Theatre, London, 495n
Savoy Theatre, London, 10, 17, 23, 29, 54n, 56n, 123, 174, 235n, 239n, 241n, 242, 244, 282, 286n, 455n, 501, 505, 528, 529, 530, 546, 572
Schauspielhaus, Coin, Germany, 185
Schumann Theatre, Berlin, 265
Shaftesbury Theatre, London, 82n
Shakespeare and Old English Comedy Company, 26
Shakespeare Memorial Theatre, Stratford-upon-Avon, 28, 78, 421, 422, 435, 437, 438, 439, 440
Shakespeare Stage Society, 172
Sinn Fein, 495n
Stage Society, The, 22, 27, 39n, 42, 45, 116, 121, 202, 435, 444, 445n, 446n, 448n, 449, 450, 469n, 487n, 508n, 559
Strand Theatre, London, 27, 444, 487n

Terry's Theatre, London, 22, 486n
Théâtre du Porte Saint-Martin, Paris, 129n
Theatre Guild, The, 82, 83
Theatre Royal, Manchester, 56, 57
Theatre Royal, Margate, 21
Three Hundred Club, The, 559n
Toronto, University of, 24
Toynbee Hall, London, 282, 283n

United Nations Association, The, 198, 287
University of London Library, 14

Vaudeville Theatre, London, 27, 444

Wallack's Theatre, New York, 23, 30, 61n, 127, 130, 131, 135, 138, 139, 464, 560, 561
Walnut Street Theatre, Philadelphia, 35
Wyndham's Theatre, London, 446

Eric Salmon is visiting professor of theatre at Reed College; he has held similar appointments at various other universities in the United States and Canada. He has published widely on aspects of the theater and drama in journals and magazines on both sides of the Atlantic. His biography *Granville Barker: A Secret Life,* was published in London in 1983 and in North America in 1984; other books include *The Dark Journey,* a study of John Whiting as dramatist (1979), and *Bernhardt and the Theatre of Her Time* (1984).

The manuscript was prepared for publication by Jean Owen. The book was designed by Richard Kinney. The typeface for the text is Times Roman, designed under the supervision of Stanley Morison about 1932. The display face is Cheltenham bold condensed. The text is printed on 55-lb. Glatfelter text paper. The book is bound in Holliston Mills' Kingston cloth over binder's boards.

Manufactured in the United States of America.